Erich Ludendorff

Perry Pierik

Erich Ludendorff

- Biography -

Aspekt Publishers

Erich Ludendorff

© 2023 ASPEKT Publishers
© Perry Pierik

Amersfoortsestraat 27, 3769 AD Soesterberg, Netherlands
info@uitgeverijaspekt.nl - www.uitgeverijaspekt.nl

Cover design: Mark Heuveling
Inside: Sjoerd van 't Slot
Translation: Isabel Oomen

ISBN: 9789463380218
NUR: 680

All rights reserved. No part of this publication may be reproduced, stored in a retrieval system or transmitted in any form or by any means, electronic, mechanical, photocopying, recording or otherwise, without the prior permission of the publisher.

For my parents

Table of contents

	Introduction Ludendorff and the short twentieth century	9
1	'Bring discipline to this man'	15
2	Tannenberg: an impending disaster on the Eastern Front	37
3	Warsaw	77
4	Winter in Masuria and crisis in the German leadership	103
5	Viceroy in Kaunas	119
6	At the height of his fame	135
7	Ludendorff's dictatorship	147
8	The Russian Revolution and the disappearance of the Eastern Front	159
9	The Bloody spring of 1918, Ludendorff's last chance	171
10	The Black Day	187
11	Exil in Sweden by 'Nacht und Nebel'	203
12	The Counter-Revolution	219
13	The aftermath of the Kapp-Putsch	239
14	The Völkisch movement	253
15	The murder of Walther Rathenau and a rehabilitation at Wannsee	271
16	On the eve of the Feldherrnhalle-Putsch	289
17	'We are marching!' The Bürgerbräukeller Putsch	323
18	'There are few Germans behind me anymore'	335
19	No Man's land	351
20	The paper front: the publications of the Ludendorff House	371
21	Ludwig Beck and Ludendorff's last chance at a return to the political arena	407
22	A grave in Tutzing	432
23	House no. 2 on Mühlfeldstrasse	433
Notes		437
Literature		479

Introduction:

Ludendorff and the short twentieth century

A historian is a retrospective prophet
The voice of a buried time
- Heine

There are several biographies about Erich Ludendorff. What most of them have in common is that they stop at 1918, the end of the First World War. This is unjustified. Ludendorff developed into the strongest man on the 'right' in Germany's political and military spectrum, both in the war and in the interwar period, at the peak of his long career, between 1915 and roughly 1925. Thus the years after the war were also of great importance. He was not only an important general who, together with Paul von Hindenburg, formed the OHL (Oberste Heeresleitung), which led Germany de facto militarily after the resignation of General von Falkenhayn, but he was also the main conspirator against the Weimar Republic after World War I. He collaborated with the assassins of Karl Liebknecht and Rosa Luxemburg, and was also close with the assassins of Walter Rathenau. Furthermore, he was the foreman in two coup attempts, the Kapp-Putsch and the Feldherrnhalle-Putsch, which should really have been called Ludendorff-Putsch - I and II, and came close again in 1935, this time against Hitler. He was also a publisher and distributor of defamatory writings of unprecedented vehemence, such as *The Protocols of the Sages of Zion*, which created grounds for the Holocaust, and an unprecedented conspiracy theorist. Moreover, Ludendorff was already negotiating with the German government in the infamous Wannsee villa, 17 years before the 'Final Solution' was decided there, and in his house the most fatal friendship of the 20th century was struck: between Heinrich Himmler and Auschwitz commander Rudolf Höss. If we add to this his role in the communist revolution and the blinded train that Lenin used to travel from Switzerland to St. Petersburg, then the picture of this man turns out to be more multifaceted than just the general known to history. Ludendorff's name even turned up in an alchemical swindle, in which he, in collaboration with Freikorps assassins, created so-called gold to finance his own newspaper.

There is a clear dividing line in his life between the First World War and the period after it. In the first part, everything was about winning the war for Germany. Here, we see Ludendorff as a disciple of Moltke and Schlieffen, his military examples. His whole working life, which spanned almost his entire existence, was dominated by the military-strategic challenges. However, his attitude to this was so rigid that it initially brought him into conflict with the German General Staff. 'Teach this man discipline', was the message when he was dismissed from the staff, but, the developments in the August days of 1914 changed everything. The capture of Liège, in which Ludendorff played an important part, brought him back into the sights of the General Staff, and at Tannenberg, together with Von Hindenburg, who had been hastily brought out of retirement because of the Russian attack on East Prussia, he cashed in on his soldierly glory. After Von Falkenhayn's dismissal following his failure at Verdun, the heydays of the Von Hindenburg and Ludendorff duo began, the latter often being both the executor and the mastermind. His influence would continue to be felt until his dismissal in 1918.

That Ludendorff was committed to wage a war had become clear by then. His role in the unrestricted submarine war, as well as in the Russian Revolution, was major. In particular, his role in the Russian revolution has not been recognised until now. With regard to the submarine war, we will see that the maritime arguments were snowed under by Ludendorff's military continental desires. And so, submarines were used to break open the stagnant western front. All this would be disastrous. Ludendorff's role in war economy, in which he had gained experience as a commander in 'Oberost' (northern part of the Eastern Front), and his role in other aspects of warfare, such as employment and propaganda, have also been underexposed.

After the war, the break came. The once-feared military leader became a refugee as a result of the Council Republics. From Sweden, he looked back on the dramatic course of the war and the Treaty of Versailles, which was considered a deep humiliation. The Emperor was gone and Germany was looking for a new way. Ludendorff was an icon from the past but with a name that had a historical ring to it. The reactionaries saw their chance and Ludendorff became the central figure of an ongoing revolt against the Weimar Republic. The driving force was his belief in the 'daggerhead' legend; Germany had not been defeated at the front but by treachery in the hinterland. This idea made Ludendorff, often from behind the scenes, the driving force behind coups, ('Ruf') assassinations and propaganda. This second part of his life was dedicated to explaining why Germany had lost the war and by whose treachery, since they needed to be sure the blame would not be placed in their own backyard. Over the years, Ludendorff's ruthless persecution of his enemies would lead to increasingly sectarian behaviour. From 1925 onwards, his power and influence went downhill.

The "Freikorps" and "Great Germans" grouped around Ludendorff and were the driving forces behind the careers of Hitler and the NSDAP. Hitler, discovered as an orator, was catapulted into politics by the military, and the two men worked side by side for some years. During the disastrous elections (1925) and since his acquaintance with his sectarian second wife Dr. Mathilde von Kemnitz, the change took place. Ludendorff increasingly withdrew from practical politics and focused on his own world.

With the 'Tannenbergerbund' and a new interpretation of religion, the 'Bund Deutscher Gotterkenntnis (Ludendorff) e.V.'. He fought everyone he considered guilty of German misfortune: Jews, communists, freemasons, Catholics, occultists ect. This action took on increasingly strange traits, causing his following to dwindle rapidly. Nevertheless, Tannenberg's fame was never completely lost and Hitler, who was displeased with the very principled Ludendorff, could never completely free himself from Ludendorff's fascination. They fought each other, but in the end they reached out again. Only a short time before that, General Beck and other high-ranking military officers had begged Ludendorff to take the lead in a coup against Hitler. Ludendorff, who felt his strength diminishing, and already had two revolutions to his name - not counting the Russian one - decided against it after long hesitation. Instead, he opted for the safety of his second wife and his *Ludendorffers* who had remained loyal to him until then. He died in December 1937, and Hitler honoured this trench-era commander with a state funeral. In Tutzing, at the Starnbergersee, Ludendorff was given a final resting place, against Hitler's wishes.

History is always written in retrospect. Due to Hitler's prominent role from 1933 onwards, Ludendorff's driving role soon disappeared from view. His increasing unworldly sectarianism from 1925 onwards was also to blame. Yet Hitler's rise cannot be explained without the historical figure of Ludendorff, and his 'missing years' were in fact the years of Ludendorff. May this book correct this.

How does a historian arrive at a subject? A few years ago, when a collection of my most important pieces on the Second World War was published, it seemed as if there had been a premeditated plan, in retrospect. Subconsciously, the subjects meshed together. Of great importance was a study by Eberhard Jäckel that I read back in my student days: *Hitlers Weltanschauung*. Jäckel dismissed Hitler as an 'enigma' and placed his political operations in line with his convictions. Jäckel took evil seriously. The ideology of National

Socialism focused on two central points: the war against the Jews and the conquest of 'Lebensraum'.

One of my very first books was about Hungary 1944-1945 and was in fact a synthesis of Jäckel's thesis. Hungary was where the last Jews of Hitler's 'Festung Europa' were hiding. Given that Horthy's Hungary was an ally of Nazi Germany, they pursued their own policy towards Jews, which, although anti-Semitic, did not involve the destruction of the Jewish community. Only after the military occupation of Hungary in March 1944 did the Holocaust begin. The Hungarian Jews were among the last to go to the extermination camps. In addition, the German military effort in 1944-1945 was dominated by raw materials. Oil was always capitalised by Hitler in his 'Lebensraum' concept, and attempts were made to both preserve the Hungarian oil fields south of Lake Balaton and recapture those in Romania near Ploesti. This plan was far too ambitious, and the Red Army's Vienna operation on 16 March 1945 was launched before the Danube River could be reached.

Hungary was a practical example of Jäckel's thesis because of these two elements. It was therefore important to follow these spearheads of Hitler's ideology and policy, because Hitler consistently adhered to them. This eventually led me, through the book *Hitlers Lebensraum*, later republished under the title *The Geopolitics of the Third Reich*, to concern myself with the thoughts and 'legitimacy' behind the German conquest plans of mainly Eastern Europe, which were to help form the 'Kontinental Empire' of Nazi Germany. To this day, it is remarkable how little has been written about this pillar of Nazism, while there are libraries full of the Holocaust.

In my dissertation on Karl Haushofer, under the supervision of Prof. Henri Beunders, I elaborated on the most prominent influential geopolitician of those days. While working on the book *Hitlers Lebensraum*, I already came across the figure of Erich Ludendorff, whom, like his other biographers, I of course knew mainly from his position in the First World War. However, my interest and astonishment grew as I became increasingly aware that his great influence continued after 1918, mainly in the 'Grundlage Arbeit', which he actually carried out for the anti-Semitism of Nazism. His involvement in the distribution of *The Protocols of the Sages of Zion,* the linking of his historical name to this cause and, above all, the link between the 'dagger shot legend' and anti-Semitism, were of fundamental importance for the later introduction of Nazism's politics of the Jews. The fact that Ludendorff was subsequently involved in the revolutionisation of Russia, the passage of Lenin's blinded train to St. Petersburg, and in the planning and financing of the revolution through support for Israel Helphand ('Parvus'), made Ludendorff a pivotal figure in history.

If one were to characterise Ludendorff's role with seven-mile boots, one could say: without Ludendorff no Lenin and without Ludendorff no Hitler. Both the revolutionary of communism and the revolutionary of National Socialism were catapulted into active politics. Of course, there are many comments to be made about this, but the pattern is undeniably there. It is a well-known political phenomenon: sometimes people create their own monsters. Lenin was brought into play to subdue the Eastern Front, but produced a new enemy of stature, one that would hold Europe in its grip for more than 70 years and exert its influence globally through the Cold War. The launch of the 'big mouth Austrian', as Hitler was called right from the start of his political career, ultimately also unleashed a force that turned against the world and Germany itself. When the downfall of Nazi Germany was imminent, Hitler issued the famous Nero order, in which he de facto demanded Germany's self-destruction. Only through sabotage and chaos of his own shriveled institutions was this prevented.

So Ludendorff's shadow did not end in 1918. I see in this the most important addition to the sometimes very readable and good biographies that exist about Ludendorff, such as those by Nebelin and Goodspeed, to name but a few. The memoirs of many eyewitnesses, such as Breucker, a renegade, are also a grateful source. However, the bridge that Ludendorff formed between the two wars, and his revolutionary dynamism of which he was a decisive part, have never been mentioned or neglected. In fact, it is inconceivable that the name Lenin simply does not appear in the most authoritative biography of Von Hindenburg, Ludendorff's superior, and it is a sign of great naivety that Ludendorff's biographer Nebelin completely downplays his role in Lenin's journey to Switzerland. In short, the historical dimension of the figure of Ludendorff is well known in facets (Tannenberg, Hindenburg Line) but his role behind and in front of the scenes after 1918 is much less known and, partly due to the enormous influence of Hitler, simply forgotten later on. Moreover, the role that Ludendorff played during the First World War was also considerably larger than is often thought. Behind the calm and self-confidence of Von Hindenburg stood the boundless energy of Ludendorff.

After studying Hungary, geopolitics and Karl Haushofer, Ludendorff formed a synthesis within his own work. He linked geopolitics to anti-Semitism, and moreover, he linked the two world wars together. Just as the twentieth century could best be explained by the 'short 20ste century' (1914-1945), and the Cold War until 1989 was a consequence of this, the years 1915-1925 were of great importance for Ludendorff's role in this. Strategist and tactician from 1914-1918, and ideologist and 'politician' from 1918-1925. In the following years, as we have already seen, sectarianism pushed him more and more into the background, ending up in the sleepy cemetery of the picturesque town of Tutzing, where even the residents have forgotten him.

Dr. Perry Pierik
Soesterberg

Chapter 1

'Bring discipline to this man'.

In the night of 5 to 6 August 1914, the men of the 14th infantry brigade from Halberstadt, commanded by Gene-ralmajor Von Wussow, assembled for the advance to the West. While the units were regrouping, the local commander, General von Emmich of the X. Army corps arrived. The general was on the move so late for a reason: a historic military undertaking was about to take place. The X. Army corps had brought five brigades into the field which had been delegated from the area around Aachen to the front at Liège. As a leading group they had to take the strategically situated city of Liège in the Meuse valley by storm. There was great pressure on Von Emmich and Von Wussow, because no less than two of the five armies that executed the Schlieffenplan were dependent on a breakthrough in the sector around this city.

The Schlieffenplan was the German military response to the danger of a two-front war. This strategy was based on the idea that economically underdeveloped Russia, with its poor infrastructure, was mobilising more slowly than the other powers, which would give Germany the time to deal with France militarily first and then turn eastwards. All this was only possible under the tremendous pressure of an iron-clad schedule of long day marches, train transports, mobilisations and the capture of strategic targets. A dangerous hold-up in the timetable was the city of Liège.

The Belgian defenders were well aware of the strategic importance of their city. In 1914, Liège had grown into a considerable industrial city, but given its location as an access road and junction to the flat North of France, the city was of great strategic importance. In order to be able to defend the city on the Meuse, Brussels had already decided in 1890 to erect a series of fortifications around the city. North of Liège lay the fort Pontisse, east of it the fort de Barchon, under Salve the fort de Evegnée, just west of Micheroux the fort de Fléron and south of the city the fort de Chaudfontaine. Right at the edge of the city there was also Fort La Chartreu-se and in Liège itself the citadel high up on the hill. These magnificent and partly very modern forts had a peaceful occupation of 6,000 men, but in a war situation they would be reinforced to 19,000 soldiers. Floodlights ensured that the defenders could fight on even at night and a dozen artillery pieces per fort would assault an attacker. The commander of Liège was General Gerard Mathieu Léman, who could, if time allowed, also have infantry units nestle between the forts to create an almost impenetrable line. He was also promised 20,000 construction dollars for this purpose. In total, the defence plan provided for a force of up to 30,000 men.[1]

Time was the crucial element in the Schlieffen Plan, and time was of the essence in the attack on Liege, for the location of the forts and the watercourse had all the elements to slow down, with all the consequences this had for the large manoeuvres required. Von Emmich had to prevent Léman from bringing his additional troops into the field and holding on by all means. In order to prevent this, his superior, General Von Bülow of the 2de army - of which the X corps was a part - released three cavalry divisions to try to cut off the Belgian defenders of Liège from their hinterland so that reinforcements could not reach the fortresses and the citadel. Furthermore, the five brigades that reported in the night of 5 to 6 August would have to sneak between the forts to take the city and citadel by surprise. In total, Von Emmich had about 25,000 infantry and 8,000 cavalry, as well as 124 artillery pieces at his disposal.

Von Wussow's 14de brigade seemed somewhat disoriented as they gathered around Micheroux. The soldiers were 27 kilometres from the safe city of Aachen and seemed to have to get used to the idea of war. Von Wussow's troops were very vulnerable at that moment. While they were gathering, the German officers kept looking to the west, to Fort de Fléron, from where fire could be opened at any moment. The fast-growing German force was now an easy prey. But miraculously nothing happened and at 1 a.m. Von Wussow gave the order to advance. The tension was palpable as they passed the fortress, but nothing happened. It would not be the only miracle around Liege. The war had begun.

The X. Army corps now rapidly advanced to Rentinne. The brigade found itself right in the middle of the German attack. North of them the 34ste and 27ste brigade were operating, while south of them the 11de, 43ste and 38ste brigade were covering Liege.

Von Emmich's command post was somewhere at the rear of the column of Von Wussow's men. In his company was Erich Ludendorff, who was appointed as 'Oberquartiermeister' between the X. Army corps and Von Bülow's 2de army. Thus Ludendorff was a "Schlachtenbummler", as he put it, an officer without troops, a traveller between two headquarters. But he was at the centre of the Schlieffen Plan, and he knew it. The 'Denkschrift' (memoir) that was written between 1909 and 1912 about the storming of the fortress of Liège was his work. The fortress was known to be so strong that only a surprise attack could be successful.[2] Between Rentinne, La Chartreuse and the hills in front of the city, the German advance went wrong. The column stalled and Von Emmich was trapped in the convoy. The reason why the advance had stopped was unclear. Ludendorff immediately offered to go and see what was the matter, something Von Bülow would also like to know. He left Von Emmich and went to the front. It turned out that the soldiers had lost contact with the front groups and had thus stopped just before Rentinne for no apparent reason.

Ludendorff, although not a direct commander, immediately understood the danger and decided to take the lead. The soldiers now entered Rentinne in complete darkness. But once in the village, the troops became disoriented and Ludendorff and his soldiers left the place by a different route than planned and ran straight into a shower of bullets. 'I will never forget the sound of bullets hitting bodies', Ludendorff wrote in his memoirs.[3] Ludendorff had to withdraw his troops and take cover in Rentinne at once, which he actually felt was against his soldierly honour - 'they must think I was a coward',[4] but it was for a higher purpose. When Ludendorff finally arrived on the right road, he found Friedrich von Wussow's adjutant there, with the brigade commander's horse. Here Ludendorff was again confronted with a setback, as the young man informed him that Von Wussow had been killed.

This report proved to be correct. Von Wussow was the first general to lose his life in the First World War, and thus a dangerous vacuum had been created in the power structure. With the few soldiers that Ludendorff had around him, he now took the road towards Queue du Bois, encountering the lifeless bodies of his own troops along the way. Ludendorff realised that he had to give direction to the operation. At that moment the Belgian artillery opened fire. Ludendorff narrowly escaped death. The night became more and more chaotic. By now units of the 4de and 27ste brigade were mixed up. It was of great importance to regain the initiative. Some officers managed to sneak up on the Belgian artillery through the gardens of the village and eliminate it. When it was light, Ludendorff directed his own artillery forward and the houses where the Belgian defenders had nested were set on fire. Shortly afterwards, the German troops were on the Chartreuse hills, and Liege, the great grey city with its citadel, lay below them.

Ludendorff was very worried. The soldiers had had a tiring night, field kitchens were left behind and morale was not good after the chaotic night fighting and the general's death. Ludendorff rustled up food from civilian houses and tried to encourage his soldiers. He also gave Liège a foretaste of what was to come by firing grenades into the city to make the Belgians ready to negotiate. It was bluff poker. Ludendorff had few troops at his disposal and the artillery ammunition was not yet at the front. There was nothing to be seen of the other brigades that should have broken through.

Ludendorff hesitated between regrouping and action. The Schlieffen plan was clear: speed, drive out the enemy with a bayonet if necessary. But that was easier said than done. An additional problem was the growing number of Belgian prisoners of war, which by now amounted to about a thousand men. Suddenly, a white flag was hoisted above the citadel of Liège. Ludendorff consulted Von Emmich feverishly. 'Wait until they send a sub-commander', was Ludendorff's advice, but Von Emmich decided to send Hauptmann Von Harbou. It turned out that the flag had been hoisted without permission of the Belgian commander. 'A difficult night lay ahead of us', Ludendorff wrote in his war memories.[5]

Meanwhile, Ludendorff had sent scouts and orderlies to the rear to orient himself on his own position. Nobody came back, new orders were not forthcoming. It looked as if his small unit was pushed forwards alone on the banks of the Meuse. If the Belgians were to attack, Ludendorff's small force would simply be crushed. Ludendorff 'parked' his Belgian prisoners in the fortress La Chartreuse, which the Belgians had not manned. He had the relatively large Belgian force guarded by only one company of soldiers, whose commander looked at Ludendorff as if he had lost his mind. But these were emergency situations and Ludendorff had to take risks. That same evening, he ordered Hauptmann Ott to capture the Meuse Bridge so that the storming of Liège could begin the next morning.

Ott was successful. The bridge was taken. On the way, Belgian troops surrendered. The next morning Ludendorff followed with the bulk of the troops. Oberst Von Oven had received the order to take the citadel. This was the last strategic stronghold in the city. A too enthusiastic defence of it could bring down the - already weak - building, and have enormous consequences for the German plan of action. So of course something went wrong at this critical moment. Von Oven's troops did not storm the citadel but turned, for reasons that have never been explained, towards Fort Loncin. Later, when Ludendorff arrived in Liege by car and heard no more shots near the citadel, he thought it was already taken by Von Oven. He drove to the entrance gate and was amazed that not a single German was to be seen. This did not stop him from banging on the gate with his staff, upon which a surprised Belgian soldier opened the gate. Ludendorff was not taken aback by this, but stepped inside and loudly demanded their surrender. Meanwhile, units of the brigade approached the citadel and the defenders lost courage. The unbelievable happened: the citadel capitulated and hundreds of Belgian soldiers gave themselves up as prisoners of war to Ludendorff. A liaison officer without soldiers became the hero of Liège.

There were hundreds of German prisoners in the citadel, from the other brigades. The different numbers of the German units had convinced Léman that a huge German force was at the gates of the city, after which a considerable part of the defenders of Liège had fallen back to the west, to avoid destruction. Léman had hoped for a tough defence from those who stayed behind, but they apparently thought otherwise. The garrison, according to a Belgian historian, consisted partly of reservists and was badly organised.[6] The ever stern-looking Ludendorff was enough to bring down morale. Immediately afterwards, German units took over the citadel and set it up for defence. The crossing of the Meuse was successful, the passage through Liege secured. The other forts around Liege were now blown up by the incoming (heavy) artillery. These were sometimes fierce battles, but we were no longer on thin iceF. 'Der weitere Weg war frei', Ludendorff noted after the war.

For Ludendorff, the *Pour le Mérite*, the *Blue Max*, the coveted military distinction, which also fell to Von Emmich, awaited. Though, more important was the fact that on the night of 5 to 6 August, history was written. A military success had been achieved, which would not be repeated until May 1940 at Eben Emael, and a career was born. Against all odds: the career of Erich Ludendorff.

The officer began his long journey, which would take him from the battlefields of the First World War to the Feldherrnhalle in Munich, where he linked his name and fame to one of the most powerful and feared men of the 20th[ste] century: Adolf Hitler. Ludendorff's historic mission had begun. The fact that this mission arose from a mixture of chaos, luck and blunders, as so often in (military) history, was soon forgotten. What if the Belgians had blown up their Meuseburg, what if Léman had rallied his men and driven the Germans back to Retinne at the point of the bayonet? What if only one Belgian had used his weapon after Ludendorff had given his jaunty knock on the door? Recently, the historian Sophie de Schaepdrijver pointed out that a pro-German betrayal in the Liège case was also of great importance. A Belgian who worked for the Germans had given the order to evacuate some fortifications around Liege, exactly in the sector where Ludendorff was operating. The spy was later caught and executed, but the damage had already been done. This anecdote belongs to the secret history of the war, because it is not to be found in Ludendorff's book about his war memories, nor in the bulk of the literature.[7]

Anyone walking into the study of Erich Ludendorff's parents in 1886 would have come across the following image. Above a leather couch hung busts of the various Prussian princes, Frederick the Great neatly in the middle, depicted just slightly larger than the rest. Next door, on a shelf in the corner between two walls, stood a beautiful box containing shrapnel from the war 1870-1871. Hanging to the right were three sabres, which father Ludendorff had carried in 1866, 1870 and 1871. Between the triangle of these weapons hung a small frame, in which a piece of the tapestry of the Castle Bellevue near Sedan was wedged, where on 2 September 1870 Napoleon III had handed over his sabre to the German Prince Wilhelm.[8] Erich Ludendorff called this study characteristic of the situation in his parental home.

Ludendorff was born on 9 April 1865 on an estate in Kruszewnia (Krufzewina) near the town of Schwersenz (population 3000) in the province of Posen (Poznan) in East Prussia (present-day Poland). Ludendorff, like many famous people in autobiographical work, was rather modest about it, possibly also to show off his own feathers, but it was a decent estate of 221 hectares, purchased in the 1950s of the 19de century. The house itself was rather plain. His father, Wilhelm Ludendorff, was personally in charge of the farm business, and the staff started working in the stables at 4am. Initially, Ludendorff's father opted for a military career. He proudly served in the 12de Berlin Gardekavallerieregiment. However, the early death of his father, August Ludendorff, and his sick mother, made him return to Stettin. The trace of the Ludendorff family leads back to Pommern (Rheinland-Pfalz) in the 17de century. The family included ship owners and merchants and they had achieved considerable prosperity. August Ludendorff had already set up a small factory at a relatively young age: the *Ludendorff's Rum und Destillationsfabrik*. After his father died and he inherited, Wilhelm Ludendorff decided to turn to agriculture and bought Kruszewnia. The people in the homonymous hamlet, about sixty in number, worked mostly on the farm.

Kruszewnia lay in the disputed German-Polish borderland. From 1830 onwards, the area had increasingly fallen into Prussian hands and had been 'eclipsed' by assimilation policies. Nevertheless, the area was considered an 'outlying area' and his future in-laws, the prestigious family of 'Justizrat' Friedrich August Napoleon von Tempelhoff, who lived in Berlin on the posh Gendarmenmarkt, regarded Wilhelm Ludendorff as a provincial who was not only after the hand of one of his seven daughters, Klara, but also after the family fortune. This was partly due to the fact that Wilhelm Ludendorff did not outsource the hard work in the fields to a landlord, but went into the fields himself, which was not common at the time. Of course, Wilhelm's lack of blue blood also played a role, although there was a family saga with connections to Swedish nobility (Gustav I). At a family meeting, Ludendorff biographer Manfred Nebelin writes, the frustrated Wilhelm once let slip "that he was sorry he could not offer his wife a palace".[9] But after future father-in-law Von Tempelhoff squandered a large part of his fortune on the stock market, he gave Klara his blessing, and she moved with him to Kruszewnia. Several children were born to the marriage and Erich Ludendorff was the second son after Richard. His full name was Friedrich Wilhelm Erich Ludendorff, the first two names being anchored in the Hohenzollern family. Where the name Erich came from is not entirely clear. Nebelin speculates whether it is the 'Swedish Erik'[10] or that the name was inspired by *Der fliegende Hollander* by Richard Wagner, a popular play in those days. [11]

Erich Ludendorff later described this period as growing up in rural solitude.[12] But it was a happy time, together with his brothers Richard (1861), Eugen (1868), Hans (1873) and his sisters Elsbeth and Gertrud. Contact with the parental home was maintained even after his father's death in 1906, until his mother's death in 1914.

From an early age, he seemed to have been cut out for the military. Father Wilhelm Ludendorff was proud of his contribution to the wars of 1866 and 1870-71 in which he had served as Rittmeister. He derived a certain authority from this and could be addressed as 'herr Rittmeister'.[13] When his father left for the front, his mother cried bitter tears. Ludendorff explicitly mentions this in his book *Mein mi-litärischer Werdegang*. They convinced him at a very young age that the war was something very serious. Within the walls of the house, not a bad word could be spoken about the monarchy, because father Ludendorff cultivated a "filial love" for the royal family. [14]

It was the time father Ludendorff spent with the hussars, an army unit, that fascinated the young Erich. It was therefore no great surprise when, at the age of twelve, Ludendorff joined the cadet corps in Plön, Holstein. Here, the children were trained to be officers. It was a harsh training, which put a rough end to youth. Plön was a well-known cadet school, but the children of higher rank served at the cadet school in Berlin.

Ludendorff's difficulty in relating to others was already evident in his early years. Perhaps it was because of his lonely childhood in desolate East Prussia that he withdrew strongly into himself. Nevertheless, the teachers recognised Ludendorff's seriousness and reliability, for already at the age of thirteen he became headmaster and saw to it that fourteen boys had their cupboards, beds and uniforms neatly arranged.

In his spare time he visited Berlin. During a walk, the young Ludendorff one day met Field Marshal Graf von Moltke, who had just left the army headquarters where he lived and worked, accompanied by his adjutant. Ludendorff would later spend years of his life in the same building. Ludendorff immediately jumped to his feet and saluted, while the tall, slender figure of Moltke passed him by, and the old man slowly answered the greeting with a friendly smile. Ludendorff stood face to face with that history of Germany which hung on the wall in his parental home in his father's study; Königgratz, Gravelotte and Sedan. It took some time, Ludendorff later wrote, for him to come to his senses. Would I ever be capable of such a great thing?[15] Ludendorff would not see Moltke again until 1891, when he passed away and his body was laid out, and Ludendorff served at the *Kriegsa-Kademie*.

At seventeen, Ludendorff was transferred to Wesel in the Westfälischen Infanterieregiment 57. Ludendorff was glad about that; the regiment had an illustrious history because of its strong performance in the Loireveld march of 1870. These were relatively carefree years for Ludendorff. It is hard to imagine now, but in those days Ludendorff was known as an enthusiastic dancer, who liked to show off his skills in public. In his memoirs, he even mentions that he once performed in the local lodge of Freemasonry, in ignorance of course, because later he would fight this order as the core power of the 'überstaatliche powers' with fire and sword. Bismarck's 'Kultur-kampf' against Rome and Catholicism also passed him by in those years.

There were small excursions in summer, there was singing and laughing, the *Westphalian song* and songs about the Rhine resounded from the exercise sites when they had their day off, there were concerts and carnivals with plenty of drink.[16]

In April 1881, these carefree years were over for good. The German military leadership had recognised Ludendorff's qualities and decided to promote him more quickly. Ludendorff was immediately transferred to Wilhelmshaven. This was a special event, because Ludendorff was appointed battalion commander of a *Seebataillon* (marine infantry). With this, Ludendorff held a special position, because his daily environment had become the navy, but he remained an officer of the army. This was not an easy position, because in every army, including the German army, there was a certain competition between the different army units. It gave him an insight into international relations. Ludendorff made his first sea voyage on the *Rione*, a sailing ship, where he had to make do with a modest place next to the pantry, the cook's quarters, but between 1889 and 1900 he also travelled on the increasingly modern German warships. He visited the cities of Bergen and Trondheim in Norway, went to the Scottish Highlands, the Isle of Wight, the ports of southern England and Sweden.

His experiences with the navy also brought him into contact with the colonial issue. In Germany, there was a great deal of concern that they had missed the boat on this issue internationally. Even a small country like the Netherlands had a formidably larger colonial empire than Germany. Ludendorff realised the disadvantage that Germany had, at a time when colonies were seen as essential to the status of a superpower. Everything became even clearer when the young Kaiser Wilhelm II visited his grandmother, the Queen of England, near the Isle of Wight in August 1889. Ludendorff was on board the German flagship making the voyage to England. The British fleet had set out on parade on either side of the waterway. It took forever to sail past the huge fleet. It was clear that London wanted to show Germany her maritime muscle. And she succeeded; it was extremely impressive, but had the opposite effect. From that moment on, the young Kaiser Wilhelm II strove for parity. On board the *Baden*, the Prince of Wales - later King Edward VII - and Kaiser Wilhelm II met. Ludendorff found Edward VII to be a remarkably friendly man, but later he would see him quite differently, namely as a free mason master who was deliberately working on Germany's downfall. [17]

It was at this time that Ludendorff's gaze 'sharpened', as he put it. In 1890, he became acquainted with the Danish hatred of the Germans that was alive at the time when the Kaiser added Helgo Land to the Empire, following a controversial swap deal with England regarding East Africa. The Emperor made jolly jokes during the meal, but Ludendorff realised that Germany did not only have friends, though the general climate was quite friendly, also when Ludendorff, after a long preparation, went to the 'Kriegakademie' in the winter of 1889-1890, where he stayed until 1893.

At the time, he made trips to St. Petersburg, Moscow, the Crimea and Warsaw. The idea prevailed that Russia and Germany were traditional allies. But Ludendorff noticed some other things when he was at a gala evening organised by the German ambassador Von Werder. Although the Russian nobility danced much livelier than the German nobility and the local beauties had decked themselves out in glittering jewels, there was something frantic about it all. His interpreter, who was refining Ludendorff's Russian - he had obtained a diploma in interpreting as a minor in Germany - also gave him a taste of the hatred that existed in poor Russia towards the rich upper class. There was already something of the new era in the air.

In mid-April 1894, Ludendorff was assigned to the Grand General Staff. The head of this department was Alfred Graf von Schlieffen. Ludendorff was now in the military heart of Germany. However, for the time being he had to be content with a modest position. Due to his fluency in Russian, Ludendorff was assigned to the Russia section. However, the section in which he was placed was mainly concerned with Russia's neighbours, so that the Balkans,

Scandinavia, China and Japan became his new field of work. Zealous as ever, Ludendorff set to work immediately. He saw this as a new opportunity and quickly got to grips with the details. Shortly afterwards, Ludendorff was able to hand over his first 'Denkschrift' to his immediate superior, General Von Sick. This dealt with the Sino-Japanese tensions, in which Ludendorff drew attention to the determined way in which Japan was working on its strength. Here, Ludendorff referred to the fact that a large British naval mission had left for Japan and that London apparently saw merit in the Japanese capacities in international power politics. Von Sick was shocked by the far-reaching conclusions which Ludendorff drew, but after some hesitation he passed the 'Denkschrift' on to Von Schlieffen. The latter was surprised by the zeal and insight of the new man in the genealogical staff and by the serious tone of his 'Denkschrift'. Schlieffen decided to pass the "Denkschrift" on to the court, where it eventually ended up with Prince Heinrich, the Emperor's brother, who looked down on the Japanese; a mentality that the Emperor was also guilty of. [18]

Ludendorff's "Denkschrift" brought him success and disappointment. Success because the war between China and Japan actually broke out in 1894 and Ludendorff was subsequently appointed Hauptmann in the General Staff. His analyses had found appreciation among the officers, but the disappointment lay in the political field. When in April 1895, the peace between China and Japan was signed in Shimonoseki (also called Peace of Maguan), Russia, France and Germany chose the Chinese side. Ludendorff considered this an unwise decision. Japan had locked itself around Port Arthur and Manchuria and it seemed important to Ludendorff for Germany to have a power at the back of Russia, so that Moscow would always have to keep an eye on two fronts.

With this position, Ludendorff was already concerned with the essence of German 'security thinking' at a very young age. This thinking was anchored in the reality that Germany was a Central European country with more neighbouring countries than any other. Germany's geographical positioning, the young Ludendorff observed, brought with it all kinds of consequences. It was not a geographically defined entity, it was a typical transition zone, a transit area. The rivers cut through the country in an awkward vertical way, there was no solid core. This was also reinforced by the strong historical and regional differences in the empire. The empire was young, had little tradition and therefore relatively little cohesion. The Germans had lived, as Z.R. Dittrich put it, 'for centuries as a loose people's substance'[19] from which, mainly through external pressure (French Revolution, Napoleon), a more individual character had emerged. The search for this German 'Staatswesen' and its mission and tasks in this world remained a nagging point of concern in Ludendorff's development, and with him in an entire generation.

But soon Ludendorff did not have to occupy himself with the greatest strategic questions of Germany. He was transferred to Magdeburg, where he would serve for two years as Ib. of the IV. army corps of General Von Haenisch in march 1896. On the one hand, Ludendorff left for Magdeburg in good spirits. He was relatively close to his parents' home. On the other hand, he was frightened by this city which was still unknown to him and which he only knew from the terrible stories of the Thirty Years' War, when the city was largely reduced to rubble. However, by the end of the nineteenth century, Magdeburg had grown into an industrial town squatting on the Elbe. The surroundings of the city were fertile, but without striking beauty. Ludendorff led a regular, somewhat boring life. He got up at 7 a.m. or even earlier to ride his horse for an hour and a half. He often complained about the uninspiring landscape and the paved streets and bridges he had to ride over. For Ludendorff, being a countryman, Magdeburg represented a new era that made him look back on bygone times with nostalgia. Ludendorff was 'völkisch' at heart.

His task as a staff officer (Ib) was not spectacular, but not unimportant either. It was the usual field work that a professional soldier had to be trained in. Twice a week he presented his activities to Haenisch, which consisted of exercises, arranging holidays, map distribution and the like. In this way, he got to grips with the military. The training grounds that the German army had developed were new. The modern tactics had become too large-scale for the former exercise grounds. Ludendorff could often be found on the Loburgt training ground. Thus, two years passed.[20]

After Magdeburg came Thorn. 'I had no uncles or aunts', he wrote in his *Mein militärischer Werdegang (My military career)*.[21] This made it impossible for him to escape from his latest station: a real field position this time, in the garrison of Thorn on the Weichsel (Vistula) River, i.e. on the Russian border, for Poland did not exist as an independent nation in those days. The red of the staff on his trouser legs was replaced by the red of the regular infantry. Ludendorff became commander of the 7de company of the 61ste Pomeranian regiment (7/61). 'God, king and fatherland' was the banner of the troops, but where were the people, Ludendorff wondered. Prussia was above all a "Gottesstaat", as the Hohenzollerns saw it, and Bismarck too spoke more of state than people. Ludendorff's experiences during the First World War would call this state-minded view into question.

Ludendorff's company was at an outpost, a good forty-five minutes' journey from Thorn, at Fort York on the Weichsel. His accommodation was small and his gloomy foreboding was reinforced by the low morale of the soldiers in this forgotten corner of the world, on a frontier that Ludendorff, not least in view of his own experiences in Russia, saw as very important and dangerous. 'I would not have thought this possible in the Prussian army', he said looking back. To make matters worse, shortly afterwards the casemates were flooded by excessive rainfall and the Ludendorff unit had to be moved to emergency accommodation. Everything went wrong. [22]

Ludendorff was billeted in Thorn and travelled to his company every day. 'My predecessor must have been an enormous failure',[23] he concluded when he saw the state of discipline. Ludendorff set to work and by means of severe punishments, drill, exercise, meticulous uniform care, marches and songs, as well as history lessons, he managed to restore the spirit of the old army. Slowly, he won back the esteem of his soldiers. Ludendorff learned that it was of great importance that his soldiers knew what they stood for. This also included his history lessons. To his horror, there were soldiers in his company who did not know who Bismarck really was. Ludendorff shook his head. How could one expect anything from such soldiers if they did not know which 'great people' they came from?[24] 'People', Ludendorff once again thought, stood above state and sovereign.

Ludendorff drove his soldiers through constant practice, imitating conflicts with the Russians. 'Here, I already took a breath of war', he thought, during the long dark days at the Weichsel; the border that was already hermetically sealed by Moscow. Only occasionally did one see Russian soldiers in the distance. It had something threatening about it.

In 1889 and 1899 the regiment went on manoeuvre exercises around Lautenburg and Marienwerder, in the area that would later form the Polish corridor. For Ludendorff, however, it was all German territory, 'new German earth'[25] that he got to know. Ludendorff detested the later loss of Poland, in which he saw the hand of radical Catholic forces,[26] and attributed it to the fact that the Germans 'did not know geography'.[27] Ludendorff was already teaching his company 7/61 history; his teacher's mentality would develop over the years.

During these years, Ludendorff had little time to develop his theoretical skills. From early in the morning, 05.00 a.m., until the evening, he was busy getting his unit in order. In the evening, after his meal in the officers' casino, he went to bed early and tired. In his spare time he studied the courts and beautiful castle in Thorn. The legacy of the Teutonic knights strengthened Ludendorff's historical connection to the area. According to Ludendorff, the Polish population was 'not unfriendly' to the Germans, but since Albrecht von Hohenzollern had converted to Protestantism in the past, tensions in the region had risen. Furthermore, he followed the international developments, which were dominated by violent conflicts; war in South Africa, between Boers and the British, war between Spain and the United States over Cuba and the Boxer Rebellion in China.

After two years, the day came when Ludendorff could leave the hard days in Thorn behind him. Looking back, however, he was not negative about it; he had learned to love the area and had found the time very instructive. Ludendorff was transferred to Glogau, the province of Posen (Poznan), his home province. He soon enjoyed the typical flat land, and the people. Older now, he also had more of an eye for human relations, and he actually wondered why the Polish question was not on the agenda of military training. During the mobilisation of 1870, Polish recruits had failed miserably and had ducked out of the fight.[28] Although the province of Posen had belonged to Prussia again since the Congress of Vienna in 1814, in everyday practice the matter was much more complex.

Ludendorff was assigned to the 9^e infantry division, which together with the 10^e division formed a part of the V. army corps. Ludendorff was staff officer (Ia), *Generalstabsoffizir*, and spent most of his time in Posen preparing for large-scale field exercises and focusing on organisational matters rather than on field command. Ludendorff had turned from a tactician into a strategist. The troops went into the field very regularly, with the staff making sure that they trained somewhere else each time, so that the troops would get to know the different types of terrain and their characteristics. The 9de division trained at Goldberg, Jauer, Schweidnitz, Jarotschin, Meseritz, Görlitz and Hirschberg. It also took part, as a corps component, in the so-called Kaisermanöver, the very large-scale exercises, at which Kaiser Wilhelm II himself was conspicuously present. The officers also went on regular tours of duty to get to know the terrain on the eastern border of the *Deutschtum*.[29]

Ludendorff felt like a fish in the water. Especially since the commander of the 9^e division, Hahn, gave Ludendorff plenty of room. As staff officer, he allowed Ludendorff to prepare the 1901 field exercises independently, which Ludendorff did with great dedication. When Hahn left the division in the summer of that year, Ludendorff was momentarily anxious whether the new commander, Eichhorn, would allow him to work as independently as he did. In the end, he had to give way a little, but was able to prepare the field exercise of 1902, in which mainly units from Glogau and Liegnitz participated, relatively independently. The exercises were complicated and included infantry, supply and drain troops, pioneers, artillery and cavalry. There were referees who calculated which of the two sides - because the units fought "against each other" - had won. The referees made the 'Massenwirkung' count for a lot.[30] It was a lesson Ludendorff did not forget. It was important that at the place where the battle would be decided, a maximum number of his own troops were on the battlefield. In the early days of 1914, he would take this lesson to heart and achieve remarkable results.

Another "highlight" for Ludendorff was the Emperor's Parade in Posen in 1902. Kaiser Wilhelm II and his wife Auguste Viktoria came to Posen for two days for the parade and slept in the military headquarters of the V. Army corps, which had been specially rebuilt for the occasion. Ludendorff, always a bit rebellious, could not refrain from noting in his *Meine militarischer Werdegang* that he thought this was a bit much. However, the parade itself he saw as very important. It gave soldiers and leaders the opportunity to 'look each other straight in the eye' while marching by. According to Ludendorff, it was a good measure of the troops' strength and discipline. [31]

His residence was a temporary house in a suburb of Posen. Posen was a typical Polish town, but according to Ludendorff, the soldiers did not 'actually ever go there'. Only the part between the railway station and the military headquarters was "German". Ludendorff's 'outside' was 'a cold house', but he had decorated it as cosily as possible. With his savings he had bought his first pieces of furniture, so that his house also started to become a real home. The happy time was overshadowed by what Ludendorff saw as dark omens. The Balkans stirred again, when in 1903, King Alexander and his wife Draga were murdered. Serbia turned away from Vienna and headed towards Russia. Ludendorff also suspected that the British-French side was showing signs of cooperation, which did not bode well either. This was mainly due to the British sovereign Edward VII, who had ascended to the throne on 22 January 1901 and who, in Ludendorff opinion, was pursuing an anti-German policy. But his unrest was still unclearly defined.

Ludendorff spent more and more time on the great Prussian strategic problems. He was especially concerned with mobilisation, the issue of stages, time planning, mobilisation, provisioning and material provisioning. Germany had 25 years of military personnel at its disposal. This calculation could be obtained in the following way:

A soldier was:
-2 years in active service
-5 years in reserve
-5 years with the *Landwehr* I
-7 years in *Landwehr* II
-6 years in the *Landsturm*

It was a great military machine, which Ludendorff saw as an opportunity. The task of providing the empire with a sublime military structure was universally embraced with great self-evidence. However, it would not be accurate enough for Ludendorff.

He got the opportunity to work on this himself when he became section chief of the Grand General Staff in Berlin in March 1904. His official function was chief of the '2-Deutschen-Abteilung des Grossen Generalstabes'. Here, Ludendorff could deal with grand strategy. The responsibilities that fell to Ludendorff were enormous: his department consisted of several sections, which occupied themselves with mobilisation and border defence. There was a section dealing with German border fortifications, as well as a technical section. The department had all kinds of specialised sections that monitored countries and territories, issued press releases and conducted espionage. There were separate sections that monitored countries: Section 1 was concerned with Russia, Section 3 with France and Great Britain (remarkably in one section!), Section 4 studied enemy fortifications - and convinced Ludendorff of the importance of Liège, Section 5 focused on Italy and Austria-Hungary (the allies, one hoped), there were topographical and cartographical Sections. Ludendorff was the spider in the web. He was to hold this heavy position until January 1913, interrupted only by a short period between the autumn of 1906 and April 1908, when he taught at the military academy.[32]

The position of the Grand General Staff almost had something mythical to it in Germany. This had everything to do with the fact that the existence of the German nation was linked to the military. It was wars that had brought Germany out of the lethargy in which it had been sinking since the Thirty Years' War. It was the subsequent crushing defeat of the Prussians at Jena-Auerstadt against Napoleon that confronted the German nation with itself and its impotence. Under Gerhard Johann Scharnhorst, the German officers had been brooding over how to implement social and military reforms that would shake off French domination. Large parts of southern and western Germany were under direct French control, other parts of Germany supplied soldiers for the little Corsican's campaigns. How important the Scharnhorst think tank was becomes clear when we see how many thinkers of the period, Gneisenau, Boyen, Grolman, Von Clausewitz, became famous, and could measure up to the famous home-grown field men: Blücher, Bülow, Kleist, Thielmann. Since then, people had been working on the reunification of Germany, on the 'Innerdeutsche-Geschichte'; a national awakening, which was cashed in on the battlefield at Köningratz under the inspiring political leadership of Bismarck and the military leadership of old Moltke.[33] Exactly sixty years after the blunder at Jena-Auerstadt, the Prussian army showed overwhelming superiority against its opponent, in this case the Austro-Hungarian army, after Denmark had already been defeated in 1864.

Before the famous battle against the dual monarchy, a German divisional commander had said, 'All well and good, but who is this Moltke?[34] After the battle, the question was never asked again. What had been dreamed of since Scharnhorst was suddenly part of German history again: in the eyes of one Clausewitz, whose *Vom Kriege* became one of the most important works of military philosophy, Moltke was the ideal image of the military leader that the 'endangered' German nation needed.

The German military leadership was revered again, just as Ludendorff regarded the commander of the large general staff almost as a saint: Von Schlieffen, who held his position until 31 December 1905, to be succeeded thereafter by the young Moltke, nephew of the old one. Even in 1935, Ludendorff had trouble finding words to describe Von Schlieffen. He limited himself to a few remarks: Schlieffen was the teacher and the strategist, 'a better one could not be imagined'. He had a 'distinguished character', and a 'wonderful sarcasm'.[35] But, Von Schlieffen had a very difficult task ahead of him. Under Scharnhorst and Moltke, the empire had been established, and now Von Schlieffen had to preserve it. Under Moltke, the ideas of preventive war had been developed and Von Schlieffen had to build upon this. Bismarck had at an early stage already warned about the consequences of this policy. Pre-emptive war was at odds with his alliance policy. Therefore, it was very important that there was competent political leadership, which could curb the preventive thoughts within the German General Staff. Here, Bismarck had Clausewitz on his side, who already believed that in every military decision the 'wondrous Trinity' should not be lost sight of.

The Trinity meant that both sovereign and politicians, as well as people and military, had to be involved in political considerations with possible military consequences. Only this way could a fiasco be avoided. It was a wise lesson, which was soon forgotten in the August days of 1914.

Von Schlieffen's famous plan - named after him - concentrated on the western front. There, the German army would have to deal with the French threat in a preventive war, in order to wage the war in the east afterwards. After all, the French army threatened the most important German industrial areas, and Von Schlieffen estimated that a war against Russia would take much longer than one against France. Ludendorff noted in his memoirs that Von Schlieffen had no clear plans about what the battle in the east should look like. It was, in Schlieffen's opinion too, 'too unpredictable', which would also come out in 1914. So, the centre of gravity of German actions had to be in the west. This was no easy task, as the French army was scarcely weaker in number than the Germans, even though the population of France was 40 million, compared to 60 million Germans. The French forts around Belfort, Epinal, Toul and

Verdun were also feared. Von Schlieffen knew these fortifications from his own experience. As *Rittmeister,* Von Schlieffen had experienced Könninggratz, and during the Franco-German war of 1870, Von Schlieffen had led the siege of Toul and the siege of Mont Marion. Both fortresses had fallen only after heavy German artillery bombardments, which is why the German units in the Schlieffen plan, which had to turn most right (Liège), had heavy supporting artillery. The German plan of attack was a revolving door, so to speak, which allowed large German units to get behind the French lines. All this at the cost of the Belgian neutrality, a plan that Von Schlieffen had put forward for the first time in 1904.[36] Von Schlieffen was never able to wage 'his war'; he remained a bureau strategist and was suddenly - surprisingly - replaced in 1905 by the young Moltke, who had been the Emperor's adjutant-general until then. Moltke had to be inducted by General von Stein, who gained considerable influence within the General Staff. Ludendorff had reservations about Von Stein, who was very diligent, but also pedantic and annoyed by advice from subordinates. Since Ludendorff was not the kind of man to keep his mouth shut, all this was not without tension.

It seemed as if the natural relationship between politics and the military no longer existed. At that time, the old Moltke had unhindered access to the Minister of Defence, Von Heeringen, and he could also approach Kaiser Wilhelm I without any problems. This had created a distance between politics and the army. Bismarck's warning began to crystallise, and the wondrous Trinity came into play.

The most important exponent of Ludendorff's military career before World War I was his constant study and re-examination of the Schlieffen Plan. He saw his actions in Thorn, in the fortress on the Weichsel and in Glogau, on the borders of the Deutschtum, entirely in the light of the larger strategy. In addition to all these reflections, the Ludendorff family was struck by the death of father Wilhelm Ludendorff. 'He was the example of German man', Erich Ludendorff thought back. For the rest of his life, a portrait of his father would stand in his study.[37] He decided to temporarily join the Kriegsakademie, as this gave him more opportunities to be with his mother and sisters. His lectures began on 1 October 1906 and Ludendorff, like all the others, took his task very seriously. He taught not only military history but also tactics and had his pupils solve up to fifty tactical problems at a time. A hard lesson was the best. In 1907, he took the students to Silesia for fieldwork. In the lecture theatres he dealt with Metz (August 1870) and Sedan (September 1870) as well as Könninggratz. In 1906, he visited the battlefield and was shocked by the epitaphs, on which Czech predominated. Again he thought he saw a threatened Deutschtum. In his eyes, these were again unfavourable omens of approaching disaster. Other Germans were not alert enough in his opinion.

He also saw shifts within the norms and values of 'das Militär'. *Seine Majestät* was suddenly abbreviated to S.M., unimaginable for Ludendorff, who was not without criticism of his emperor. Major politics also worried him. Austria-Hungary annexed Bosnia-Herzegovina, which was already under their control, to the dual monarchy. It intensified the antagonism in the Balkans and drove Serbia towards Russia. Increasingly, Germany had to take into account that the Russians would fight on the French (British) side. He also foresaw that there was a big chance that war would break out in the east. The Schlieffenplan was then inevitable.

The Schlieffen Plan was more topical than ever and Ludendorff was concerned about how the plan stood. Ludendorff had, as soon as he arrived in Berlin, calculated the plan according to the latest state of affairs. He arrived at about 62 divisions for the western front, plus some smaller units, and about 10 divisions for the eastern front.[38] In his opinion, these were too few units to execute the Schlieffenplan as the master had intended.

This gave Ludendorff endless headaches. Just before his departure, Schlieffen went through the attack plan one more time. A major problem on the Western Front was the strong French lines between Epinal and Namour (Namur). Since Germany stuck to the offensive strategy, the advance had to go through (neutral) Belgium. On the twelfth day of mobilisation, he calculated, the fortress of Liège had to fall in order to be able to advance via Liège-Namour to the rear of the French (British) units. Conversely, the Germans feared that the *Entente* (collective name for the states that stood against Germany and Austria) would attack German territory from Alsace with strong forces. To prevent this, troops had to be freed up increasingly to strengthen the German southern flank, which had to defend itself above all else. In 1905, it was calculated that 54 German divisions would be deployed north of Metz, eight to the south and ten to the east. In 1914, when it came down to it, 54 divisions were deployed north of Metz, just as in 1905, 16 (!) to the south of it - which were thus missed by the offensive - and 9 to the east. The reserve was only 6.5 divisions.[39]

In almost ten years, despite Ludendorff's insistence, the Germans had not succeeded in further strengthening the right wing (north of Metz), and especially its flank near Liège. To make matters worse, the eastern front had been further weakened, by one division, in the same period. To Ludendorff's horror, the reserve troops had insufficient material at their disposal. For example, these units had no field kitchens and no artillery. Without food and fire cover, Ludendorff had little faith in these troops, even though they had been counted as full units in the plans. In Ludendorff's view, there were too few soldiers for the plans that had been drawn up. This was true in 1904, and again in 1905, when Von Schlieffen made a big trip along the western borders with his officers - Ludendorff was at that time, to his regret, stationed in the navy in Kiel for a month - and it was true in 1914. In Ludendorff's eyes, therefore, there was no other conclusion possible than that the Schlieffen Plan was too ambitious for the means. There was too little money, and there were too few men. Most importantly though: there was no alternative plan. Schlieffen had been declared 'sacred', but had in the meantime also been undermined. This combination of factors made it difficult to form new plans. Ludendorff was principled to the extent that he was a constant reminder to Moltke and Von Stein of the weaknesses in the Schlieffen plan. He pointed out to them that generals and politicians should not reason that 'when the time came', additional troops would be built up. America and Great Britain, separated from their enemies by the sea, could afford such a luxurious wait-and-see attitude. Germany, however, surrounded by its enemies, could not. Unfortunately, Moltke and Von Stein could not control the ministers Gossler and Von Einem either and they kept muddling along. 'They counted divisions which were not there at all', Ludendorff insisted. To his frustration, Ludendorff also discovered that 600,000 men, who had been trained, were not to be found in the reserve units. Due to lack of money, they had been left out of consideration. To solve this, Ludendorff developed the idea of 'überplannmässige' troops, which were only mobilised at the outbreak of the conflict, and which were to serve as garrison troops, so that the fighting units could actually continue to fight and were not lost to occupation politics. Old Moltke had already pointed out the importance of this in the war of 1870, when he lost many front troops to guarding prisoners of war.[40] Nothing came of this either. The only improvement that Ludendorff managed to implement was that within the reserve units, the troops were divided by year of birth, in order to prevent that mid-twenties and soldiers of forty years old were put together in the unit. 'That cost nothing,' Ludendorff remarked sourly.[41]

Historians have always, when reporting on the August days of 1914, talked about the Schlieffen Plan. Actually, this is not quite correct. As we saw, between 1904 and 1914, with the change from Von Schlieffen to Moltke jr., the rightmost army group (which had to make the 'revolving door') was not strengthened, while the more southern front was strengthened. These were Moltke's adjustments to the Schlieffen plan, so the 1914 campaign actually started with plan Moltke (II). Von Schlieffen was almost mythological and infallible in name, but in practice German strategic policy, struggling with the problems of the two front war, had been changed several times; Moltke I, for instance, thought that

Germany should first focus on the east, Russia, and then deal with France. His successor, Von Waldersee, who served between 1888 and 1891, adapted this plan. In view of the military winter experience, it was best in a two-front war to defeat France first in winter time, but to wage the war against Russia first in summer time. In the Schlieffen era, it was felt that the Russian threat had diminished somewhat in comparison to the French threat, and the scenario of first France, the 'revolving door', returned, followed by Russia. Moltke II, appointed in 1905, began tinkering with this Schlieffenplan again and came up with an unfortunate interim solution, which we have already referred to above as Moltkeplan II. Where Von Schlieffen was prepared to give up temporary ground if the French were allowed to attack, Moltke II decided to hold out and go into battle. This cost units, which were now no longer available for the Schlieffen turn. In 1915, Moltke II confessed that his plan had been a failure. He believed that it would have been better to stick to the plan of his famous uncle, and that the Russians should have been defeated first. He was less certain about the weakening of the right flank in the west.

Ludendorff's attitude in this matter was ambivalent. Ludendorff was, in the spirit of Von Schlieffen, a convinced opponent of a first move against Russia. He stuck to the concept that France had to be defeated first. In doing so, he went along with the Moltke II concept, believing that both objectives, reinforcement on the left and right wing, were necessary. The left wing was also important because he thought a French offensive in that area was very possible and that the German connections behind the front were at risk. On the other hand, Ludendorff was convinced of the enormous importance of the one-armed encirclement of the French army on the right flank, which had to have sufficient troops at its disposal. In practice, however, German policy proved that these units could not be mustered and so they were left with a far too ambitious battle plan. It was to Ludendorff's credit that, knowing the scarcity problems in the west, he indicated during his campaign in the east at Tannenberg and the Masurian Lakes that he did not need reinforcements from the west when they were urgently needed on the western front. The German leadership eventually provided them anyway, and from the right flank no less. This indicated that not only did the German political leadership fail to recognise the consequences of the Schlieffen Plan, but Moltke II apparently did not believe much in his own 'double concept' (taking action on the left and right) either. As a result, the operations were half-hearted and therefore fatal. There was no alternative to the Schlieffen/Moltke plan; politics and 'das Militär' had failed in this.

This lack of alternatives was blamed on Ludendorff in post-war historiography. The historian Hans Delbruck believed that by implementing the Moltke II plan, a 'watering down' of the Schlieffen plan had in fact taken place. As a result, the operation had become 'soulless' and doomed to failure. Given his important position, Ludendorff also had to take this criticism to heart.[42] Of course, Delbruck was right, the Moltke II plan was simply inseparable from Ludendorff. However, on the other hand, Ludendorff had constantly argued for additional measures to make Moltke II possible. Hartmuth Mahlberg has pointed out that in successive years, such as 1909, 1910 and 1911, Ludendorff sent long letters and speeches to his superiors and the Ministry of Defence in which he pointed out the seriousness of the situation. In 1909, he spoke about the necessary reinforcement of the armed forces, which he continued to emphasise in the following years. In 1910, he even talked about the 'being or not being' of Germany and in 1911, he referred to the German nationalistic outbursts from the Napoleonic Era, 1813-1815. *Wir mussen wieder ein Volk in Waffen werden' (We must become one people in arms again)*, he wrote. [43]

It is important to note here that a 'narrowing' of the question of guilt to 'das Militär' also does not do justice to Clausewitz's wondrous Trinity. After all, what about politics? In his *Das deutsche Jahrhundert*, Eberhard Jäckel, looking back, embraced George F.W. Hallgarten's thesis, which goes back to the question of how it could come to pass that Germany had to fall back on military scenarios for a war on two fronts simultaneously. Was it not precisely the function of politics to prevent this? However, the relationship with the West was sacrificed by the occupation of Alsace-Lorraine after the War of 1870-1871 and the British were put at risk by the German fleet buildup. The prevention of a conflict with Russia was therefore extremely necessary, but did not succeed. The German-Russian contradictions proved greater than the diplomatic initiatives, while the French in particular proved themselves a master of the diplomatic game. Hallgarten pointed out that the two-front war was mainly the result of the 'double elite' in Germany. By these two camps, Hallgarten meant, on the one hand, the old agrarian elite, who were particularly influential in the eastern part of Germany, and on the other, the newly industrial bourgeoisie, who advocated free trade and fleet-building. The 'innerpolitical' compromise that this produced, namely that of conservative and nationalliberal forces, ensured Germany's isolation. This laid the foundations for what the American diplomat George F. Kennan called the 'primal catastrophe'; the First World War. [44]

Bismarck had pointed out that strong German leadership was needed to steer Germany's 'innerpolitical' problems in the right direction. But since Kaiser Wilhelm II took office through the death of his father, the 100-day Kaiser Friedrich III, history had a different scenario in store. Much has been written about Kaiser Wilhelm II and his unfortunate contribution to history. Some historians, such as Emil Ludwig, have largely attributed this to the Kaiser's physical handicap, his immature left arm, which, according to Dr Paul Tesorf, led to a 'spiritual Entartung'. But we can be much more objective in demonstrating the difficult character of the emperor. In truly all facets of 'Grosse Politik', Wilhelm II preferred the conflict model. He was Prussian-ostelbic towards the Russians, Protestant towards the (Catholic) South, imperialist towards the British, nationalist towards the French, belligerent towards the Far East (China) and incendiary towards the Islamic world (against the British and French). Graf Ernst zu Reventlow, who was not lacking in conservatism, believed that Wilhelm II suffered from *Cäsarengefühl*, which put Germany on a dangerous path. When taking part in parades the Kaiser tilted his head to look like Frederick the Great. [45]

Following on from this, Ludendorff biographer Tschuppik rightly believed that the Emperor had also personally contributed to the implementation of the Moltke II plan. The reason for this would be the obsessive way in which the Emperor held on to the possession of Alsace-Lorraine. A reversion of that territory to France was intolerable to him. That is why he was very keen on Moltke II's plan, rather than the original Schlieffen plan. From this point of view, it was understandable that Moltke took the Emperor's wishes into account in his adjustments. Because of this, Tschuppik thought an 'unmilitärische Natur' had come into play. [46]

Ludendorff, as an obedient officer, did not spit his poison at the Emperor, but at Moltke. However, it is interesting to read in his memoirs that he also regarded other hobbyhorses of the Kaiser with growing concern. In the days that Von Schlieffen made his last journey along the western borders, Ludendorff was - as we saw - back in Kiel, where he had been stationed at the beginning of his military career. He was astonished by the new developments in the fleet and the construction of new warships. He understood immediately that this was a very expensive business for which the Ministry of Defence spent a large part of its budget. All that money was not available for the land forces, and the funds for a proper handling of the Schlieffen Plan/Improvement Moltke II plan were lacking.[47] The navy was a prestige business of the German emperor. Even a notorious truth-teller like Ludendorff did not dare to touch it.

Nevertheless, Ludendorff's constant zeal for the preservation of Von Schlieffen's ideas had become a stumbling block. In 1912, he had been bade farewell in the main headquarters and Ludendorff had been transferred to West Germany, where he became commander of a Fusilier Regiment, later to take up the staff position he held during the battle of Liège. 'Bring discipline to this man', was the comment Berlin had included in his assessment. [48]

Chapter 2

Tannenberg: an impending disaster on the Eastern Front

'Luik was a special favour of fate',[49] commented Erich Ludendorff when looking back on his adventurous and fortunate start of the First World War. Thanks to Ludendorff's resolute action, the citadel had fallen easily into German hands. The right wing of Von Schlieffen and Moltke could start the 'revolving door'. While units marched, the heavy artillery (which Von Schlieffen had prescribed after his siege of Tours) was rolled forward. These were super-heavy mortars, partly borrowed from the Austro-Hungarian army and partly produced by Krupp's own factories,[50] which were to knock out the strong Belgian fortifications around Liege. Ludendorff witnessed the shelling of Fort de Pontiffe and Fort Loncin, commanded by Colonel Victor Naessens, who was also hosting the Belgian commander Leman. Fort Barchon had been taken earlier, and fort Chaudfontaine partially exploded.

The huge shells went off in such a slow trajectory that they could be followed by the eye. The effect was as spectacular as it was horrific. The third shell at Fort Loncin hit the ammunition magazine. The concrete positions literally flew apart. The Belgian soldiers of the 530-man garrison crawled out of the rubble blackened and shouted 'don't kill us', which surprised Ludendorff ('We are not barbarians'). Soon, the fortifications were no longer an obstacle. 'A stone fell from my heart', Ludendorff noted in *his Kriegserinnerungen.*[51]

The German press proudly reported the result. One even spoke about the *Secret of Lüttich*, so easy had the heavy settlements fallen. 'Hooray in Liege', Emmich had telegraphed home, and Kaiser Wilhelm II had kissed Moltke on both cheeks. The hurrah-patriotism burst out in full force. It was proudly mentioned that even a zeppelin had been used in the attack on Liège. This sounded more exciting than it was; the first bomb dropped from an zeppelin[52] on an enemy target (Liège) was a dud. The next bombs exploded, but it could not be called a precision bombardment. In addition, the zeppelin was under such heavy fire that it was leaking more and more gas. The *Luftkreuzer* had to return to its base in Cologne at an accelerated rate, but finally ran aground near Bonn and had to be scrapped.[53]

In total, about 4500 Belgian soldiers had been taken prisoner. Among them was the 64-year-old commander of Liège, the proud General Leman, with his impressive broad moustache. He was found half suffocated under the ruins of the fort Loncin, destroyed by a 42 cm canon, and made prisoner of war. The German officers received the poor general, gave him something to drink and praised his brave defence. General von Emmich even handed him his sabre again, as gentlemen amongst themselves and as a sign of 'German chivalry'[54]. Leman had not expected this and was visibly moved. After a medical examination, Leman was taken to Magdeburg, where he was taken prisoner of war. From there, he wrote an emotional letter to the Belgian king, in which he wrote that he had fought to the hilt and had only been captured, instead of killed, because he had lost consciousness. He asked the king for forgiveness.[55]

German losses were limited, although among the dead were Prince Friedrich Wilhelm zu Lippe, a scion of the ruling House of Lippe, and Generalmajor Karl von Bülow, the Chancellor's youngest brother.[56] The French press reports of 20,000 German losses were exaggerated[57]. Von Stein, Moltke's right-hand man, praised the results achieved. 'Every expert can understand the greatness of this achievement', he said.[58] Meanwhile Liege had been placed under German military administration. The commander of the city was Generalmajor Bayer, who in collaboration with mayor Kleyer tried to get normal life in the city going again.

In the euphoria, the downsides of the battle around Liège were overlooked. The initial chaos and setbacks were unleashed on the civilian population. John Horne and Alan Kramer investigated German war crimes in 1914. The Entente propaganda circulated stories of the 'Huns' who would 'cut off the hands' of women. This was an exaggeration, but the German troops tended to blame the misfortunes on the civilian population. They spoke of the Franc Tireurs Krieg, in which Belgian civilian troops would attack the German troops from behind. In retaliation, executions were frequent, and houses were set on fire. Often, the German losses were not the work of 'Franktireurs' (civilian fighters), but of their own fire, which caused accidental casualties. Between 5 and 8 August 1914, 21 executions were carried out around Liège.[59]

For Ludendorff, there was little time to enjoy this first spectacular success. There was marching to be done; the iron script of military logic had begun. On 21 August, Ludendorff stood on the banks of the Sambre and watched the soldiers of the 2ᵉ Garde division cross the river at Namour. The next day he was already on his way back to Germany; he had been summoned. A new assignment in the east awaited him. He said goodbye to General von Emmich and his Chief of Staff, Graf von Lambsdorff, whom he had both learned to like in the short time he had worked with them. Via Hotel Union in Aachen, he then had to go on to Koblenz, to the headquarters of the General Staff of the Army, the OHL. On his return journey, he saw burning houses in the night. Modern war had already shown the first facet of its horrific face.

Meanwhile, Von Emmich had been nominated for the high distinction *Pour le Merite*. A few days later, it was Ludendorff's turn. For Ludendorff it was obvious that Von Emmich, as the highest commander, should receive the decoration first, (although he generally thought that nobility was favoured) but the fact that he only received his decoration in Koblenz from Kaiser Wilhelm II made it clear to him that he still had enemies in the headquarters. On the other hand, the medal was still an important recognition, and, as the historian Wien noted, a sign that things were wrong in the East.[60]

In his war memoirs, Ludendorff modestly noted that the success at Liege was not the work of one man alone, but that several men had to share in the glory.[61] Liege, with Tannenberg, would later be Ludendorff's most acclaimed success. One of the men who praised him without restraint was the always critical (later) 'General der Panzertruppe' Hermann Balck, seen by many as one of the best German generals of the Second World War. In his memoirs he wrote after the fall of Liège: 'In the afternoon I came to my battalion. Seven officers and 150 fighters were killed, wounded or missing. Most of them by their own fire. Liege has always stayed with me. It was a clear victory for the soldiers. The middle corps and the officers were not up for the situation. At the same time as the Belgians, our retreat was ordered. Nobody except Ludendorff had the guts to face this crisis. Generals who were later given major commands failed here. Ludendorff [...] by his great strength of will and the ruthlessness of his own person brought the victory. The success was exclusively his work'.[62]

The promoted Ludendorff was in the centre of attention. In Koblenz, too, people had apparently become convinced that the 'troublemaker' Ludendorff could also be a 'problem' for the enemy, and thus a weapon for the Reich, which was unexpectedly threatened. Despite the positive news around Liège, there were serious developments in the east.

The tsarist troops in the east had taken action much earlier than expected and were now threatening large parts of Prussia. There was even panic. After all, the Schlieffen Plan and the Moltke II Plan based on it had not planned for such a rapid reaction from Moscow. Ludendorff had received a cry for help from his headquarters in Koblenz: 'We know of no other man whom we can trust, perhaps you can still save the situation in the east'. It sounded rather hopeless. The letter, signed by Moltke's right-hand man, Von Stein, went on to say that they realised that by removing Ludendorff from the Western Front, they were taking him out of the decisive phase of the Schlieffen Plan. 'You must make this sacrifice for the fatherland', said von Stein, who hoped that Ludendorff 'would not be angry. It is a difficult task, but you will succeed', von Stein concluded encouragingly. This letter, confirmed by Oberstleutnant a.D. Theobald von Schaefer, historian at the Reichsarchiv in 1927, is to be considered authentic and a deep bow of the OHL to Ludendorff, the man who had to be 'disciplined'. [63]

At 06.00 hours in the evening Ludendorff arrived at the OHL in Koblenz. From one of his subordinates, Captain Von Rockow, Ludendorff had already learned that he had to take command in the east under Von Hindenburg, where the German 8^e army near Gumbinnen had run into trouble against the Russian Memel (Njemen) army, commanded by Von Rennenkampf. Although Ludendorff regretted that he could no longer be with the decisive days in the west, his thoughts were now fully in the east, Thorn, Kulm, Graudenz, Posen. His footsteps were everywhere; it was his native soil. He was proud of the words of recognition in Von Stein's letter. He was also deeply moved when the Emperor pinned the *Pour le Merite* on him and complimented him: 'Those were my proudest and most touching memories from the war'. [64]

Immediately afterwards, duty called again. At 9 o'clock in the evening, a special train left for the east with Ludendorff on board. Koblenz, the city where Moselle and Rhine meet, was left behind for the new adventure. The survival of the Deutschtum was at stake for Ludendorff. At 04.00 in the morning of August 23rd, he met General der Infanterie, Paul von Beneckendorff Von Hindenburg on the platform of Hannover. Von Hindenburg was an impressive sight, although he - taken out of retirement and sent to the front - looked a bit odd in his peace uniform, which no longer fitted him very well due to the extra kilos of pension fat. But Von Hindenburg, born in 1847 in West Prussia, was a happy man. He felt ashamed to sit at home in wartime as an old soldier and had eagerly accepted his appointment. Hindenburg was a very experienced soldier. As an adjutant, he had experienced the Battle of Königgratz in 1866. He had retired in 1911 and now, at the age of 66, was embarking on his second career. He had insisted on this himself. After his military service he and his wife had retreated to Hanover, dreaming of a future peaceful life on the estate at Neudeck. But von Hindenburg was alive every time his son, Oskar, came home with his army comrades. Oskar von Hindenburg served in the 3.*Garde Regiment zu Fuss*, a unit in which Von Hindenburg himself had served and he enjoyed the stories as well as the service of his son-in-law, who was in the dragoons. So when war broke out, he wrote to the General Staff: 'If you need anyone, do not forget me, I am mentally and physically fit'. When the OHL finally questioned him, Hindenburg's answer was short but firm: 'Bin bereit!' [65]

At the time of his appointment, Von Hindenburg was still known within the military apparatus as simply Von Beneckendorff, and the administration entered the general under the B. It was only after his enormous fame from the battle of Tannenberg, in which the press constantly spoke of Von Hindenburg, that he went down in history under this name. [66]

In Hannover, it was the first time that Ludendorff and Von Hindenburg saw each other. According to Von Hindenburg's biographer, Wolf J. Bütow, both men liked each other immediately. They spoke in the same measured military style, were both infantrymen and Prussians. The age difference, Ludendorff being seventeen years younger, was not a problem. [67]

After a short discussion of half an hour, Hindenburg proposed to sleep. Ludendorff agreed, but with his restless character hidden behind his formal, somewhat stern exterior, sleep must have failed to come while Von Hindenburg gladly placed earthly concerns in God's hand. It was this ever-quiet figure in the background that would help the sensitive Ludendorff to achieve his soldierly glory, but could not prevent his eventual failure because of this same characteristic. Hindenburg biographer John W. Wheeler-Bennet, who spoke to many eye witnesses at the time, stated in his book *Hindenburg: the wooden Titan* that it was clear to the German General Staff right from the start that Ludendorff would take the real lead, even though Von Hindenburg was his superior on paper. Hindenburg was the 'Dickschädel', with nerves of steel, who would 'reflect the genial light of Ludendorff'. [68]

This is a bit much, but the letter from the General Staff to Ludendorff did have a tone of hope and expectation. Perhaps the memory of Ludendorff's tremendous drive during his years on the general staff as well as a slight feeling of guilt played a role, and of course his remarkable performance at Liege. Ludendorff was not only a high-calibre officer, but apparently also had the luck of war on his side. Moltke, who was sensitive to 'special gifts' - he was related to the mystic Rudolf Steiner - possibly recognised something in the ever-serious Ludendorff, who hardly seemed to care about personal ambition, but devoted himself to the greater cause, daring to offend those people who were better kept happy in order to have a smooth career. The determination that this entailed was also shown by the fact that Ludendorff already gave the first orders to the east from Koblenz, even before being introduced or even having exchanged a word with his chief Hindenburg.

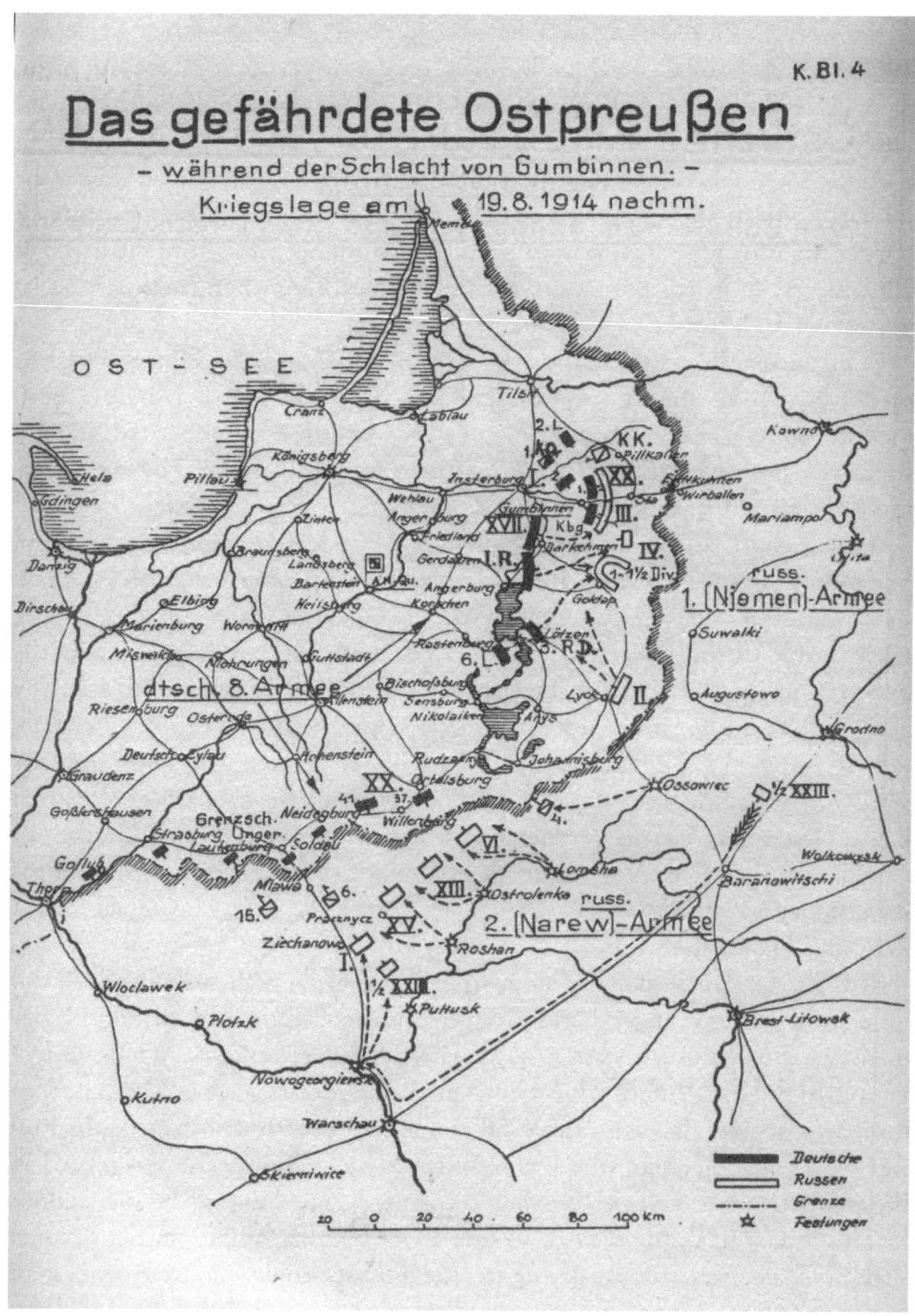

Front situation at the start of the Russian offensive August 1914

With the appointment of the Hindenburg-Ludendorff duo in the East, history had taken a strange turn with Ludendorff's career; he was caught between power and opposition. Power in his time with the General Staff, where he had worked to perfect the Schlieffen Plan within Moltke's wishes. Opposition because he did not choose the comfort of his officer's life, but was so involved that he had to leave the field as a troublemaker. Due to the miraculous events near Liège, he now had a second chance. He was also caught between strategy and tactics. He had given the lion's share of his military days to strategy, in Von Schlieffen's and Moltke's headquarters. but he had achieved his success with tactics, by pushing through at Liege with few men in the right place. These elements, the hovering between power and opposition, and between strategy and tactics, were to become a thread running through his life.

In the east, the German army was initially under the command of Generaloberst Von Prittwitz und Gaffron and his Chief of Staff, Waldersee. The 66-year-old Von Prittwitz, nicknamed 'Der Dicke', was notorious for his vanity and, according to the historian Barbara W. Tuchman, owed his career more to his flair and the way he presented himself to the Emperor than to his military capabilities. Moltke had reservations about 'his man' in the East from the start. In order to keep an eye on him, Moltke had sent his confidant Von Waldersee to Von Prittwitz's staff. But Von Waldersee had just been operated on and was not fit. Within the staff Moltke had to fall back on the 1. staff officer, colonel Max Hoffmann. [69]

For the defence of Prussia, Von Prittwitz had the 8ste army at his disposal, which consisted of the I. army corps (Von François), XVII. army corps (Von Mackensen), the XX. army corps (Von Scholz) the I. Reserve corps (Von Below), and a number of loose units, such as the 3de reserve division (Von Morgen), three Landwehrbrigades and the garrisons of the Weichselfestungen Thorn, Graudenz and the Baltic fortress Königsberg and some other small fortified towns. They defended an area which was divided into two halves by the Masurian Lakes. Von Schlieffen had already pointed out the strategic opportunities that this geographical feature offered. It split the Russian army in two in the event of an attack. To reinforce this, the fortress of Lötzen was stationed in the middle of the wetlands, like a breakwater sticking far out to sea. Aerial reconnaissance units and Jewish-Polish spies tried to provide the German army with information. [70]

Shortly after the outbreak of hostilities, Von Prittwitz was in trouble. Despite all justified criticism on Von Prittwitz, his very first actions in East Prussia have often been misrepresented. In the literature, it is often presented as if Von Prittwitz, immediately after the arrival of Rennenkampf's army in East Prussia, stormed the Russian army like a chicken without a head. This is not correct. Von

Prittwitz, who moved his headquarters to Bartenstein on 16 August, was indeed preparing for the 'border battle'. To this end, he wanted to nestle his troops behind the little river Angerapp, but overlooked the obstinacy of Von François of the I. Army corps.

Von François came originally from a military family in Normandy. His grandfather was a Freikorps fighter ('Schill') and his father, Bruno François, had been killed on 6 August 1870 during the Franco-Prussian War.[71] This very capable officer did not hesitate to wait for the Russians, safely tucked away behind the Angerapp and, immediately on the 16th, passed Gumbinnen and pushed on eastwards towards the Russian border. Von Pritwittz ordered him to stop his loney advance - without flanking cover - that same day, but the 58-year old hothead of Huguenot origin said that he wanted to stop the Russians as close to the border as possible, as to not have to give up territory. To Von Prittwitz's painful surprise, it turned out that Von François was serious. On 17th, his corps was at Stallupönen, near the border with Russia. On that day, after the Russian border in the east was secured by a Japanese declaration on 15th, Von Rennenkampf's army went into action. Over the full width of the front an enormous army force rolled towards Von François. However, for the time being, he had the luck of the draw on his side. In his sector, where the Russian III. corps was located, consisting of the 25th and the 27th Russian infantry division under command of General Jepantschin, the Russians had arrived a bit earlier due to coordination errors. Therefore, Von François had a limited force to deal with and smelled his chance. From the church tower of Stallupönen, he immediately led his troops, the 1st infantry division (Von Conta), the 2nd infantry brigade (Paschen) and the 2nd infantry division (Von Falk) into battle. The attack struck above all the 27th Russian infantry division by surprise, just east of Stallupönen. The Russians were beaten back and Von Falk proudly reported 3,000 Russian prisoners of war.[72]

The battle for East Prussia had thus begun with a tactical victory for Von François' I. corps right in the border area. Even so, Von François was in great danger because now the corps of Paul von Rennenkampf was moving along the whole front. Von Prittwitz had told Von François by telephone that he had to withdraw immediately in the direction of Gumbinnen. Von François answered: 'Inform General von Prittwitz that General von François will withdraw as soon as he has defeated the Russians'.[73] Prittwitz then sent his staff officer Grünert to see if Von François would follow his orders.[74] Although Von François eventually fell back in the direction of Gumbinnen, the situation had now changed dramatically. The Germans had smelled blood and Von Prittwitz was now considering an earlier counterattack. In view of the overall situation, Staff Officer Hoffmann considered Von François' action, however understandable, to be a mistake.[75]

Indeed, the wayward action led to German overconfidence. The Russian advance on 19 and 20 August was hesitant, partly because of problems with the supply and withdrawal troops, but also because Von Rennenkampf saw that Samsonov, south of the lakes, was developing slowly and wanted to keep pace. However, the most decisive argument for Von Prittwitz to be tempted into a counter-attack at an earlier stage was the fact that due to Von François' actions, the closed front at the Angerapp did not exist, thus rendering his original plan meaningless. A dangerous and for Von Prittwitz fatal scenario was now unfolding.

Von Prittwitz decided to take his chances. Initially, the operation seemed to be going well. On 20 August, the gratifying news arrived in Koblenz that the 8th army had gone into the attack at Gumbinnen. From the western front also came good news: in Alsace-Lorraine the German troops made good progress and the German right wing moved into Brussels. But in the night of 20 to 21 August, Von Prittwitz revoked the positive news. Russian reinforcements had arrived from Warsaw and he took his troops back to the west. The failed attack at Gumbinnen had been carried out, among others, by August von Mackensen's troops. Von Mackensen was a driven soldier who was very keen not to let the Russians into Prussia. But he also realised the limitations of the German army, which was relatively weak in the east. 'I foresee a long war', he wrote to his wife, 'it is all or nothing'.[76] The attack was far from favourable. The Russian artillery, traditionally much feared, welcomed the bravely attacking German troops, who suffered heavy losses. Another cause of Von Mackensen's problems, according to Max Hoffmann, was the fact that the German troops had entered the battle too hastily after having chased Russian reconnaissance units ahead of them. Without thorough artillery preparation, Von Mackensen had now come up against well-developed positions.[77] The exact losses are not known, but are somewhere between 8 and 9,000 men, divided over approximately 7,000 men at Von Mackensen and 2,000 men at Von François.[78]

Von Mackensen let out a sigh of relief when the order to retreat came from the commander of the 8th army, Von Prittwitz. Unfortunately, the retreat immediately threatened to turn into a flight: soldiers of the 35th division of the Von Mackensen corps had fled and even thrown away their weapons.[79] The situation developed much more dramatically than at Stallupönen. This time, the Russians achieved a tactical victory. 'The fallen are a shining example of German soldierly courage', Von Mackensen noted consolingly in his diary.[80]

As the situation near Gumbinnen worsened, so did the pressure on the XX. corps south of the Mazurian lakes. Von Prittwitz informed the supreme command in Koblenz that he did not think a simple retreat was sufficient and that he wanted to retreat behind the Weichsel River.

On 21 August, there was direct contact between the OHL and Von Prittwitz and in the evening Moltke managed to speak - via primitive connecting lines - with Von Prittwitz himself. It became clear to the OHL that after his bloody experience at Gumbinnen, Von Pritwittz no longer believed in a battle east of the Weichsel. In fact, Von Prittwitz told Moltke that he even doubted that the Weichsellinie could be held with the weak units. [81]

It was now immediately clear to the OHL that Von Prittwitz was mentally broken by the setback. Max Hoffmann rightly noted in his memoirs, *Der Krieg der versäumten Gelegenheiten*, that the option of retreating behind the Weichsel River posed a great psychological danger to 'weak characters', by which he obviously had Von Prittwitz in mind.[82] It was von Prittwitz's first real front experience, whereas both his Russian counterparts were veterans of the Russo-Japanese War. New leaders were needed, and von Hindenburg and Ludendorff came to the helm.

But were there still opportunities east of the Weichsel? Max Hoffmann thought so. In fact, in his book, published in 1923, he was not so negative about Gumbinnen. Gumbinnen had mainly been a setback for Von Mackensen, the other units were not in such bad shape at that time. In fact, according to Hoffmann, victory was in the air, until the message came through the artillery general, Von Scholz, that Samsonov had become active south of the lakes. At that moment, Max Hoffmann was at the headquarters in Ortelsburg together with staff officer Grünert. 'I fear that the nerves of the Commander-in-Chief cannot cope with this,' Hoffmann told Grünert. 'Ideally I would not pass on the message, then we would (successfully) end the battle tomorrow and then turn against the Warsaw Army (Samsonov)'.[83] Grünert pointed out to Hoffmann that one could not withhold such an important message from Von Prittwitz and Hoffmann realised this as well. Revenge for the temporary setback at Gumbinnen thus eluded the Germans, Hoffmann believed, but at the same time he claimed that Von Prittwitz's detachment, which indeed followed this message, was already the prelude to Tannenberg's victory. [84]

Left or right, for Hoffmann the victory seemed clear from the very first moment, but that was in 1923, when he put his memories to paper, and hindsight is wise. Of course, for the sake of historiography, he did not want to have failed during his service under Von Prittwitz, and he counted himself as the spiritual father of Tannenberg under both commanders.

The changing of the guard was not very elegant. The staff officers knew that Von Prittwitz had been replaced even before the general did. The latter kept his disappointment to himself and bid a dignified farewell. [85]

Ludendorff and Von Hindenburg arrived on 24 August in Rastenburg - where Hitler would later have his headquarters Wolfsschanze - for a meeting with the officers. At that time, Von Hindenburg was still a relatively unknown officer. Hoffmann met him for the first time in his life. Ludendorff, on the other hand, had been the talk of the town since 'Liege'. His efforts to make the army more effective before the war were also well known. Moreover, Ludendorff and Hoffmann had lived in the same building in Berlin for four years and had been stationed together in Posen. Therefore, it was Hoffmann who informed the newly arrived officers about the situation at the front. [86]

Von Scholtz was nervous and hesitated whether his troops could hold out if Samsonov threw the full weight of his forces into the fray. It was clear that Von Scholz, following Von Prittwitz, also felt the need to move westwards. Ludendorff immediately put an end to this. To stand to the last man was his command for the XX. army corps. He pointed out that the I. Army corps of Von François, after an emergency transport by train from the northern sector via Königsberg - Mariënburg - would join the southern edge of the XX. Army corps and that the lines of Below would be reinforced by troops which Ludendorff took from the Weichsel garrisons.

Intuitively, Ludendorff had sensed the situation well. Knowing how weak the right wing of the Moltke II plan was in the west, he realised that Von Prittwitz's vision, holding out on the Weichsel until help came from the west, might be too optimistic. For the time being, the Eastern Front had to rely on its own strength and maintain operational leeway. Ludendorff opted for a renewed effort east of the Weichsel. From Koblenz, 1000 kilometres from the front, he already ordered the hasty retreat of the units north of the lakes to the Weichsel to be halted. He ordered the units to hold their ground for a while and then to turn south, which made it clear which way Ludendorff was heading. He decided, making full use of the geography of the country, to first deal with Samsonov's 2nd Russian Army, south of the Masurian Lakes.

Samsonov was known as one of the most talented Russian officers. He was new to the Western Front, but had gained war experience as commander of a cavalry division in the 1904-1905 Japanese war. At 43, Samsonov had been appointed general. In 1909, he had ruled Turkestan as a governor until he had to report for mobilisation in Warsaw. Here, he was given the command of the 2nd army. [87] Ludendorff opted for the *Entscheidungsschlacht* (decisive battle), a victory which should give the Germans in the east a reprieve for a while. They would be able to sit out any setbacks on the western front. A very ambitious plan.

The *Entscheidungsschlacht* did not begin offensively, but with defensive battles and complex regroupings. Ludendorff's long experience in calculating stages came in very handy now. The southern flank, the XX.- and I. corps had to stop Samsonov's advance, while the most important units of the troubled northern front, Mackensen and Below, had to march south in forced marches, and Von François' troops were transported by train. Ludendorff, supported by his superior Von Hindenburg, who approved all his plans, took an enormous risk in doing so. Not only were the garrisons of the Weichselestungen already 'used up', but the northern flank of the Mazurian Lakes was also left dangerously exposed. Ludendorff tried to hide this exposure of his northern front behind the 1th cavalry division, which was trying to give Von Rennenkampf's troops the impression that there was still a closed German front facing them.

The balance of forces along the entire front was strongly in favour of the Russian north-western front, under whose command Von Rennenkampf's and Samsonov's troops fell. This front was commanded by the cavalry general Shilinski, assisted by his chief of staff Dranowski. In total the Russians had 540,000 men and 1600 pieces of artillery at their disposal; in units 21 infantry divisions and 10 cavalry divisions, or 354 battalions, 331 squadrons. The German army could counter this with 180,000 men and 600 pieces of artillery. [88]

So on paper, the German chances were not very favourable. Nevertheless, Ludendorff's measures turned out to have a positive effect on the military. The - mostly Prussian - soldiers in the east were very keen not to give up their homeland to the Russian invaders. This had also been the reason for the impetuous deployment at Gumbinnen. But after the loss of this battle, morale was affected. The feeling of defeat was reinforced by the subsequent retreat to the west. Ludendorff had hardly arrived, or a new order came in on the staff of the XVII. corps: 'Break off the retreat to the west, march south.'

Major Graf von Schwerin of the staff of the XX. corps immediately brought the message to Von Mackensen. A feeling of relief came over the troops, apparently there was still a chance, maybe Gumbinnen was just a setback. 'I remember the cheerful mood that suddenly arose', Von Schwerin recalled. *Die Neue Parole: heran an den Feind!*, noted Major von Winning of the 36th infantry division in his memoirs.[89]

Under cover of the 1th cavalry division, the regrouping of the German forces from the north wing began. The I. Reserve corps reached, after a 35-kilometre march in heat and over roads full of refugees, the Seeburg area on 25 August. Von Mackensen's troops, who had lost as many as 200 officers at Gumbinnen, had an even longer march to make, but managed to turn south for 50 kilometres. For the time being, it seemed to go well on the Northern Front.

The real problems came with Von Scholz. While Von Rennenkampf was gasping for air after Gumbinnen, Samsonov's troops were rolling freshly westwards. Ludendorff had to stop this advance if he wanted Samsonov's troops to be caught south of the Mazurian Lakes, in a corner between the advancing units of

Von Below and Mackensen and the troops of Scholz and Von François. So, hold on, hold on, was the watchword, while every man, every gun was brought to the starting positions of the *Entscheidungsschlacht*. Even the Landwehrbrigade, which stood near the lonely fortress of Lötzen, was added to the northern force.

Meanwhile, the XX. army corps had to pull out all the stops. On 23 and 24 August, the battle dangerously concentrated on Frankenau, Lahna and Orlau in the area of the small river Alle. The heaviest pressure was on the 37th infantry division, in command of Generalleutnant Von Staabs, which was sandwiched between Landwehrbrigade 70 and Generalleutnant Von Morgen's 3rd reserve division. Furthermore, the 41th infantry division (Generalmajor Sonntag) and the Unger division - which consisted of assembled garrison troops - under Generalmajor Fritz Unger, belonged to Von Scholz's troops that had to slow down Samsonov. The 37th division was in the thick of the battle. The division had to defend an area with a twelve kilometre front line, which was simply too much for one division. In Frankenau, it came to heavy fighting between the 75th infantry brigade under command of Generalmajor Von Boeckmann and the Russian troops of the XV. corps under command of General Martos, consisting of the 6th and 8th infantry division. Supporting Landwehr units fled due to the heavy Russian artillery fire. A crisis situation threatened to break out. Russian infantry used the panic on the German side to advance with their infantry to the southern edge of Frankenau. German artillery arrived at full gallop and stopped the attack in the nick of time.[90] Then the Russians launched an infantry attack on both sides of the Rontzken - Frankenau road. The brigade managed to fend off the attacks and Boeckmann reported that the two sides were in position within 400 to 600 metres of each other.

Even more serious was the situation with the 73rd infantry brigade near Lahna. Firstly, the Russian corps had done reconaissance of the road by sending three squadrons Cossacks in the direction of Lahna. As soon as the German artillery had their eyes on them, they opened fire and the Russian units fell apart. Then followed a large-scale infantry attack from Dietrichsdorf towards Lahna - Allendorf. When a hill west of the town also threatened to fall into Russian hands, an encirclement of this part of the 37th division began to take shape. At Orlau, the Germans had to go back over the Aller and set fire to the bridge. The Russians followed close behind, despite heavy German counter-fire, with large but 'necessary' losses. When the full weight of the attack then turned back on the 73rd brigade, Staabs had to send reinforcements quickly, including the 151st infantry regiment. A total of four and a half German battalions rushed at the Russians. It resulted in terrible battles. Major Schelle, commander of the second battalion of regiment 151 (II./151) was killed at the head of the attack, sword in hand. Major Hupfeld, commander of I./151 was seriously wounded. Jaeger commander Weigelt was killed in the attack near the bridge of Orlau. Brigade commander Wilhelmi of the 73rd brigade, had to intervene personally. On his white mould, as if on the parade ground, he appeared among the troops. Members of the staff followed with rifle in hand. By noon the swampy area around the Aller was back in German hands, though many soldiers were knee-deep in mud. Staabs now threw in one last battalion, III./46, which was preceded by regimental commander von Heydebreck, also on horseback, who pushed the Russians even further back along the Allendorf - Orlau road. A Russian banner with the St. Andrew's Cross on it was captured from the lifeless body of a Russian officer. [91]

For Von Scholz, the first danger seemed to have passed. But a similar danger to Gumbinnen appeared immediately. The German soldiers, as well as the Russians, were too eager for success. Von Scholz of the XX. corps had given orders not to follow the Russians on the other bank. Yet, this happened here and there. In the darkness, this resulted in confusing fights. Generalmajor Wilhelmi inspected the lines and had to conclude that the units were mixed up. He tried to restore order and authority and above all to set limited targets, not least because extremely hard fighting was going on around Lahna, and it was not yet clear which side was the strongest. Many of the German officers in the town were killed. [92]

During the night Von Scholz had contact with Staabs. The latter confirmed to Von Scholz that his unit would hold out on 24 August, if necessary. This was a great relief to Von Scholz, who after all had received the explicit order from Ludendorff and Hindenburg to stop Samsonov. However, the defenders tried to make the best use of the night to bring the units back together and return them to their starting positions. The situation was not disastrous, but not great either. Wounded men had to be left behind and whole units were lost. II./147 could only bring two companies into the field, and one company, the 6th, had lost no less than 150 men, including its commander, twice. By morning it appeared that the Russians had temporarily given up Lahna and Orlau. The front was taken back in some places, in a practical way. Not every unit was informed in time. The next day II./150 was still on post. The Russians quickly slipped left and right around the unit. It became a bloodbath, yet without further consequences for the outcome of the battle. The German artillery of the unit was overrun. The gunners resisted with shovels and sticks to the last soldier in bitter hand-to-hand combat.[93]

The next day, 24 August, Von Hindenburg and Ludendorff were at Von Scholz's headquarters in Muehlen (later it was moved to Tannenberg). They had made it through the night, but bad news came in morning. The Russian

XIII. corps emerged near Schwedrich, the XV. corps remained active near Orlau-Lahna-Frankenau, while south of the German 37th division, near Gilgenburg, the 41st division and the Unger division felt the increasing pressure of the Russian I. army corps. In addition, Samsonov put forward another corps, the XXIII. which had to operate between the XV. corps and the I. corps. Ludendorff and Hindenburg understood that the XX corps was still in danger. It was of the utmost importance that it would not come to a full showdown because, given the balance of power, this would only lead to the destruction of Von Scholz's troops. Therefore, Scholz was given permission to retreat the front in the centre, near the 37th and 41st infantry division, to the line Damerau - Muehlen. This retreat went well. A Russian cavalry division tried to intervene quickly, but was successfully punished for this attempt. Dazed horses without riders ran in front of the German positions.

Thus Ludendorff's first objective had been achieved: Stabilisation of the front directly opposite the XX. corps. This phase of the battle of Tannenberg has been forgotten by almost everyone, but still thousands lost their lives here. One brigade of the 6th Russian infantry division alone had lost 2900 men. In total, the Russian losses on these two days were estimated at approximately 4000 men. More than a hundred men had been taken prisoner by the Germans, a small foreshadowing of what was to come. General Martos informed Samsonov that his units were exhausted and asked for a day of rest before 25 August. The German front could take breath for a moment, although during this prelude to Tannenberg 1500 on the German side were killed. [94]

In the night of 24 to 25 August, Ludendorff and Hindenburg sat around the cards again in their headquarters in Riesenburg. *So far so good*, was the summary of the battle so far, but a series of difficult problems presented themselves:

- Was Von Scholz's front strong enough to withstand Samsonov's attack the next day?
- Could additional reinforcements from the Weichsel front be brought in to reinforce Von Scholz? There had been reports of Russian cavalry units causing unrest between Thorn and Mlawa
- Were the units marching south from the north on schedule and would they be able to begin their much-needed attack on 26 August; not only as part of the *Entscheidungsschlacht*, but also as a much-needed relief for Von Scholz's XX. corps. When could Von François' units become active?
- To what extent were the Russians aware of the exposure of the front for Rennenkampf's Memel army?

Ludendorff and Hindenburg could rid themselves of some of their worries. The von Scholz corps was not up for discussion; they had to continue to hold out against Samsonov. 'Every further retreat means defeat', said Ludendorff.[95] In a telephone conversation, Ludendorff informed Von Scholz that he would 'hold out to the last man'.[96] It was clear that they were playing with fire. Samsonov had 96 battalions at his disposal against 63 German battalions, which partly still consisted of weak Landwehrtroepen. In addition, Ludendorff and Von Hindenburg had only the Russian I., XV. and XIII. corps at their disposal, while new units were already emerging. But there was no choice.

The situation was more favourable for the units rushing towards Allenstein. Here, everything went according to plan and there was even an opportunity: one of Samsonov's units, the XXIII. corps, had fanned out in the direction of Von Below's and Von Mackensen's approaching units. However, there was disturbing news from the area of Von Rennenkampf's army, which had begun to move again. The question arose whether Ludendorff and Von Hindenburg would actually have Von Below's and Von Mackensen's troops at their disposal for their *Entscheidungsschlacht* or whether they were needed north of the Mazurian Lakes.

Finally, there was Von François' force, whereby Von Hindenburg urged Von François to start the attack on the 26ste from the south-west, as part of the *Entscheidungsschlacht* and to relieve Von Scholz.

It was clear that the cards had not yet been played and that the outcome of the battle of Tannenberg was still undecided.

But in the hours that followed, there was an important twist. In quick succession, the German High Command received two Russian orders that had been sent carelessly and unencoded. The first concerned Von Rennenkmapf's Memel Army. It defined the objectives of the advance: Gerdauen - Allenburg - Wehlau. Ludendorff heaved a sigh of relief. This was not very deep into Prussian territory. It was clear that the Russians - partly due to supply problems - were not operating very fast. The corps of Von Below, Von Mackensen and Von François were rightly released for the *Entscheidungsschlacht*. Shortly afterwards, the second order, sent by radio and received by the radio station of Thorn among others, fell into German hands. It gave valuable information about Samsonov's Narew army.[97] Again, the objectives were so limited that Ludendorff understood that it would not come to decisive fighting with Von Scholz's XX. corps. This would allow his front to be maintained and the pincer to slowly close in from the south and north from 26 August onwards. Indeed, the most important conclusion that could be drawn from the radio messages was that both Von Rennenkampf and Samsonov had no idea about the German regroupings and the impending operation against the Narew army.

In the course of 25 August the situation slowly eased for Ludendorff. The signs were favourable, although they were not out of the woods yet. A military reconnaissance plane had spotted many Russian trains bringing reinforcements from Warsaw to the front.[98] This was, of course, disturbing news, but Ludendorff correctly calculated that they would not arrive in time for the decisive battle he had planned for 26 August. He calculated it would take a few more days for the reserves to get there.

On the 25ste the XVII. corps and the I. reserve corps of Von Mackensen and Von Below roughly reached the area between, from north to south, Gross Schwansfeld and Seeburg. The 6th Landwehrbrigade from Lötzen joined just southwest of Roessel. The XX. corps of Von Scholz kept its positions and lay roughly around Hohenstein - Muehlen - Tannenberg, and now received support south of its position from the units of the combative Von François and his I. corps, around Gilgenberg and Lautenburg. Due to this good news, Ludendorff and Von Hindenburg let their last 'but' slip. Von Mackensen had, until then, only directed two units slowly southwards, in order to be able to turn up at the last minute and, in the event of a tempo increase by Von Rennenkampf, to punch into the southern flank of that army. As the hours of 25 August slowly ticked away, Ludendorff and Hindenburg decided the time was right. 'Everything to the south', was the order given to Von Mackensen. Not a soldier, outside the 1st cavalry division, stood between the Masurian lakes and the fortress of Königsberg. A meagre division defended a front 50 kilometres long, but Von Rennenkampf operated with the greatest possible circumspection. 'On 26 August we attack', was Ludendorff's verdict. In order to be of immediate use to the battered XX. corps, Von François had to open an attack in the direction of Usdau, situated along the road Marienburg - Warsaw. For this purpose Von François' corps, with its 1st and 2nd infantry division, would be supported on the southern flank near Zielun just across the Russian border by the 5th Landwehrbrigade, a six battalion strong unit, supported by a squadron and 22 artillery pieces under the command of Generalleutnant Von Muelmann.[99]

It was this plan that Ludendorff fought his biggest battle over on 25 August, namely with the notorious obstructionist Von François. Von François, whose troops were slowly arriving, saw Ludendorff in the afternoon and he told him determinedly that a large encirclement attack seemed much better to him than the breakthrough which Ludendorff had in mind. Von François wanted to go with his corps around the 1st Russian army corps of the Narew army,[100] roughly via Zielun, where the Landwehr was located, via Lopowjez to Mlawa and from there hit Samsonov in the southern flank. But Ludendorff was no Von Prittwitz and strongly opposed this plan. An encirclement of the 1st corps would take a lot of time and Ludendorff did not want to loose any more time. He wanted to support the XX. corps. Besides, Von François' attack had been coordinated with the XVII. corps and the I.resvere corps, and he wanted to keep his stage agreement. Moreover, Von François' plan meant a frontal extension, and for that the 8st army had too few units. Limitation shows the master, and in this case Ludendorff was right. Von François' 1st corps and the Landwehr assigned to it had to attack towards Usdau and roll up the Russian 1st corps under command of General Artamanow and his chief of staff Blagowjeschtschenski (22nd and 24th infantry divisions), and thereby separate it from the rest of Samsonov's army. In this way, Von François would also become an effective threat to the southern flank of the Narew army. It was a tough conversation. The historian Wolfgang Venohr characterised Von François as a 'Prussian from head toe, a steely fellow, without a shred of respect for his superiors when he thought he was right'.[101] Unfortunately for Von François, Ludendorff was cut from the same cloth and did not budge an inch in this first conflict of command since his arrival in Prussia. 'I'm not used to getting orders from younger officers,' Von François snapped at Ludendorff. 'You'll have to get used to that then,' Ludendorff replied with angrily pursed lips. '*Die Unterredung wurde laut*', noted H. Rewaldt in his book *Tannenberg*. It was von Hindenburg who finally intervened, after first listening in silence. '*Die Wucht seiner Dienstjahre zwangeren François zum Nachgeben*'. Convinced that they had got their way, Ludendorff and Von Hindenburg left François' headquarters.[102]

Wolfgang Venohr has called this decision on 25 August, for a limited breakthrough at Usdau, decisive for the battle of Tannenberg.[103] However, this gives too much of an impression that a sudden decision was taken by Ludendorff on the afternoon of August 25st, or that something unique and exceptional happened. This was not the case. Although it was a typical Ludendorff decision to advance the operation here by a relatively small tactical step. Ludendorff had only outlined the strategy and left it to the late hour of 25 August; thus dependant on the movements of Von Rennenkampf, whose last units he released very late. Thereafter, he filled out the operation step by step, always ready to make adjustments if necessary. Here, Ludendorff made the right decision, but in the spring of 1918 this tactic meant his downfall, as we shall see.

After long days of tense perseverance, August 26 arrived. At last, Ludendorff could counterattack. The orders were sent. Von François' 1st corps was to attack towards Usdau and was to be supported by the right wing (southern wing) of the XX. corps. The rest of Von Scholz's front was to remain defensive, only the 3rd reserve division near Hohenstein was to be brought to the front on the northern flank. On 26 August, the XX. and I. corps had the following frontal picture from north to south: 3ʳᵈ reserve division at Reichenau, the Unger division at Poeltzdorf, the 37ᵗʰ division at Tannenberg, the 41ˢᵗ division at Gilgenburg, the 1ˢᵗ division at Tautschken, the 2ⁿᵈ division at Kielpinj and the 5ᵗʰ Landwehr at Lautenburg. Opposite them, also from north to south, were the Russian XIII. corps, the XV. corps and the XXIII. corps, in total about nine divisions, plus two divisions through Mlawa in supply, the 3ʳᵈ garded division and the 1ˢᵗ division.

The first stage of Ludendorff's counter-offensive became a disappointment. Once again, Von François was at the centre of the matter. Von François had observed, with concern, in the night of 25 to 26 August that a large part of the corps artillery still had not arrived. Nevertheless, an attack was to be made the following day. Indeed, Von François' two divisions and the supporting Landwehr went into action. The troops crossed the river Welle, while pioneers of the corps tried to build another bridge. Von François' first objective was the town of Seeben, where the terrain conditions were in favour of the defending Russians. The crossing of the river by General von Conta's 1ˢᵗ division went well, but on the east bank at Seeben, the German units, Infantry Regiment 41 and Generalmajor von Paschen's 2ⁿᵈ Infantry Brigade, came under Russian (artillery) fire. Von François moved his own headquarters on the east bank of the Welle early on and took a personal look at the situation at Tautschken. With Gumbinnen still 'in the legs', the commander of the I. corps decided that it was irresponsible to continue the attack on Seeben without sufficient artillery support. Although new batteries were constantly arriving, it took time for them to be fully deployed. Von François decided to stop the attack of the 1ˢᵗ division.

The situation with the 2ⁿᵈ division was little better. Under Generalleutnant Von Falk, the unit succeeded in capturing the village of Gross Koschlau, after the Russian army had evacuated it. The attack started slowly because of the swampy terrain, while the Russians bombarded the German troops with their artillery from the surroundings of Usdau, Von François' actual target of the march. The 5ᵗʰ Landwehrbrigade under command of Generalleutnant Von Muelmann hardly had time to fire on the 26ᵗʰ of August. The Russians gave way to serious confrontation and effectively disrupted the German advance with snipers and artillery. [104]

Ludendorff and Hindenburg were at their wits' end. 'I was deeply disappointed', Ludendorff confessed,[105] when the fall of Usdau failed to materialise. The stalling of Von François' attack had consequences, since the attack of the XX. corps depended on the advance of the 1ˢᵗ corps. The long awaited day thus began with a setback. However, Von François maintained that the real breakthrough could only take place after the arrival of his 112 guns.[106] Von François met his commanders half-way, in that the troops at least exerted pressure and gained some ground. The German railways, meanwhile, did what they could. It came to unusual images of modern war. A German train with a battalion of infantry on board even advanced to the railway bridge at Tautschken, while Russian artillery shells struck around the train. The battalion was unloaded under fire and sent directly to the front. There was no time for a meal from the field kitchens. 'The troops walked with grumbling stomachs towards the artillery fire', wrote the Reichsarchiv. [107]

Due to this setback to Von François' corps, the front of the XX. corps was also partly doomed to passivity. Von Scholz could always have carried out a supporting attack, but without a real offensive from Von François, there was not much to support. However, the artillery duel between the two sides continued. This led to the curious situation that the German artillery officer Hell had to take his own Gutshof under fire because it was occupied by the Russians, a painful situation.[108] When it became clear around 13.00 hours that Von François had started his attack after all, and Ludendorff sent the Oberquartiermeister Gruenert to Von Scholz to urge him to take action, and the corps finally started the attack at 14.45 hours.

Within the XX. corps this was still a very relative concept. Proportionally, the Russians were the strongest in front of the German positions here, and there was a problem with the 37st infantry division around Muehlen, as the Russians were well entrenched in the hills and the Russian artillery was very effective there. A captured Russian artillery general remarked that even in his campaigns in Manchuria he had never seen such effective Russian artillery fire as he had at Muehlen. Indeed, the place was largely burnt down and the German troops had to partially evacuate it. Here and there, however, counter-attacks gained ground. The German infantry still had a very good morale, with a loud 'Hurrah!' they went forward. [109]

Better results were achieved by the 41st division, the only unit which had not yet had any front-line experience. The troops had been in retreat for days and all their energy was now unleashed. 'Our boys are unstoppable', reported the Reichsarchiv.[110] Near Gilgenburg, across vast potato fields, the infantry advanced. The Russian artillery was effectively fought by the Germans and the Russians fell back. At 5.45 p.m. regiment 152 entered the town of Ganshorn, along with 200 Russian soldiers that had been taken prisoner. The German losses were 9 NCOs and 63 men.[111] Other units were less fortunate; regiment 148 lost 600 men and the 72nd infantry brigade counted 550 killed, wounded or missing men.

The 27st, one day later than planned, was finally brought the breakthrough. Von Hindenburg and Ludendorff left early to take over the coordination of the I. and XX. corps. The headquarters of the 8th army had been moved from

Riesenburg to Loebau for this purpose. The day began like a dream. Very early on the message came that Usdau had been conquered by Von François' troops. 'The battle is won',[112] the incredibly stressed Ludendorff immediately exclaimed. However, the joy was short-lived. It turned out to be a false report. When Ludendorff and Hindenburg arrived in Gross Damerau, they heard that the place was under German artillery fire but not yet taken.

Both in town and in the surrounding hills the Russian units held firm. It was of the utmost importance that Von François now broke through, to form the ring of encirclement from the south and to relieve Von Scholz. Parts of Von Conta's 1st division now moved frontally against Usdau, while other units, regiment 'Kronprinz', made a circuitous movement from the north. By noon, German units were entering the town from three sides. Two hundred Russians of the 85th infantry regiment, who had defended the town to the last, were taken prisoner.[113] Usdau had fallen!

The ironmaster Von François had kept his word. After the arrival of his cannons he had struck, and successfully. He personally drove past the positions and saw the hills, which were strewn with dead Russians. 'It was one of the most gruesome pictures I ever saw'.[114] Then, he drove on to Usdau, where Von Conta had already arrived at 11.30 am. Von François now smelt blood and immediately set off in pursuit and pushed on to Niostoy. The Russians fell back towards Soldau - Mlawa. The estimated losses were about 2,000 men for the Russian I. Corps of General Artamanow and about 430 on the German side.[115]

The tasks of the XX. corps were also limited on 27 August. The main thing was to hold out and exert pressure. Of greater importance was the success of Von François and what happened on the northern flank, with Von Below and Von Mackensen. Here, the *Entscheidungsschlacht* was very promising. Some units had already marched 200 kilometres. The biggest enemy had been the pace, and many units had *Fusskranke* soldiers, which had thinned out some units considerably. Some equestrian units had ridden so much that the horses had to be led by hand.[116] On the 26th, the Von Mackensen corps arrived east of the Grosslautersee with the 35th and 36th divisions. The I. reserve corps attacked the Russian positions south of this lake, just west of Gr.Boessauersee, near Klein Boessau and Sauerbaum. A breakthrough followed on both fronts, so that Von Below and Von Mackensen met around Gross Boessau and Kleinsack, north of Bischofsburg. From there, the units advanced on the 27ste to Passenheim. Near Mensguth, a Russian providential column was overtaken, and a pay wagon containing 200,000 roubles fell into German hands.[117]

It was clear that the Russian VI Corps had been taken completely by surprise by the attack from the north. Samsonov's advance had suddenly turned into a retreat, with more and more units, including artillery, being overrun in the retreat. Ludendorff ordered the troops to get as close as possible to Allenstein that day, which several units succeeded in doing.

On the 28th, Ludendorff and Von Hindenburg went to Von Scholz's headquarters, just south of Gilgenburg. Ludendorff always chose to visit the front sector where the most problems were. Now that the attack from the south (Von François) and the north (Von Below, Von Mackensen) was going so well, it was important to disengage the front of the XX. corps. Unfortunately, this proved considerably more difficult than expected. The front was still under great pressure of the Russian XV. and XXIII. corps, whereby especially the XV. corps between Reichenau and Muehlen was causing great problems. Dureing the meeting, it became clear that an offensive manoeuvre was out of the question and, more over, regroupings had to take place to prevent a breakthrough. The 37ste division was moved from the front at Tannenberg to the north flank of the XX. corps, and a new Landwehreenheid, 'Goltz', was rushed in. 'We returned dissatisfied', Ludendorff thought, looking back on his visit to Von Scholz. [118]

However disappointing it was that Von Scholz could not go on the offensive and had to use all his might to take the weight of Samsonov, there was a positive side to it. Samsonov was still marching westwards, and it was clear that the Russians still did not understand what was happening: the encirclement of the Russian centre, while the VI. corps on the north flank and the I. corps on the south flank were being pushed to the periphery. In the middle remained the XXIII., XV. and XIII. corps: the units which were to be crushed in the *Entscheidungsschlacht*.

Ludendorff's first target was the XIII. and XV. Russian corps. Von Below's 1st corps was ordered to come in behind these corps, while Von Mackensen had to cover the eastern flank through an advance towards Ortelsburg, Jedwabno. Yet, even here Ludendorff had to be on top to make adjustments. Major Drechsel of the I. corps reported that Allenstein was much stronger defended than expected. Ludendorff therefore decided to deploy the Goltz division entirely on the northernmost flank of the XX. corps. The unit was led to Biessellen by train, and from there the unit pushed on to just north of Hohenstein. Here, the Russian XII. corps was separated from the XV. corps, if only by Landwehr.

Immediately afterwards, a disturbing message followed: the Russian corps on the northern flank, the XIII., was falling back from the Allenstein area to Hohenstein, thus right in the back of the Landwehrbrigade that had just arrived. The tactical gains could slip away from Ludendorff. There was no way back, the XX. corps had to, despite all problems, go for it. The regrouping of the 37th infantry division to the north flank was done remarkably quickly and almost

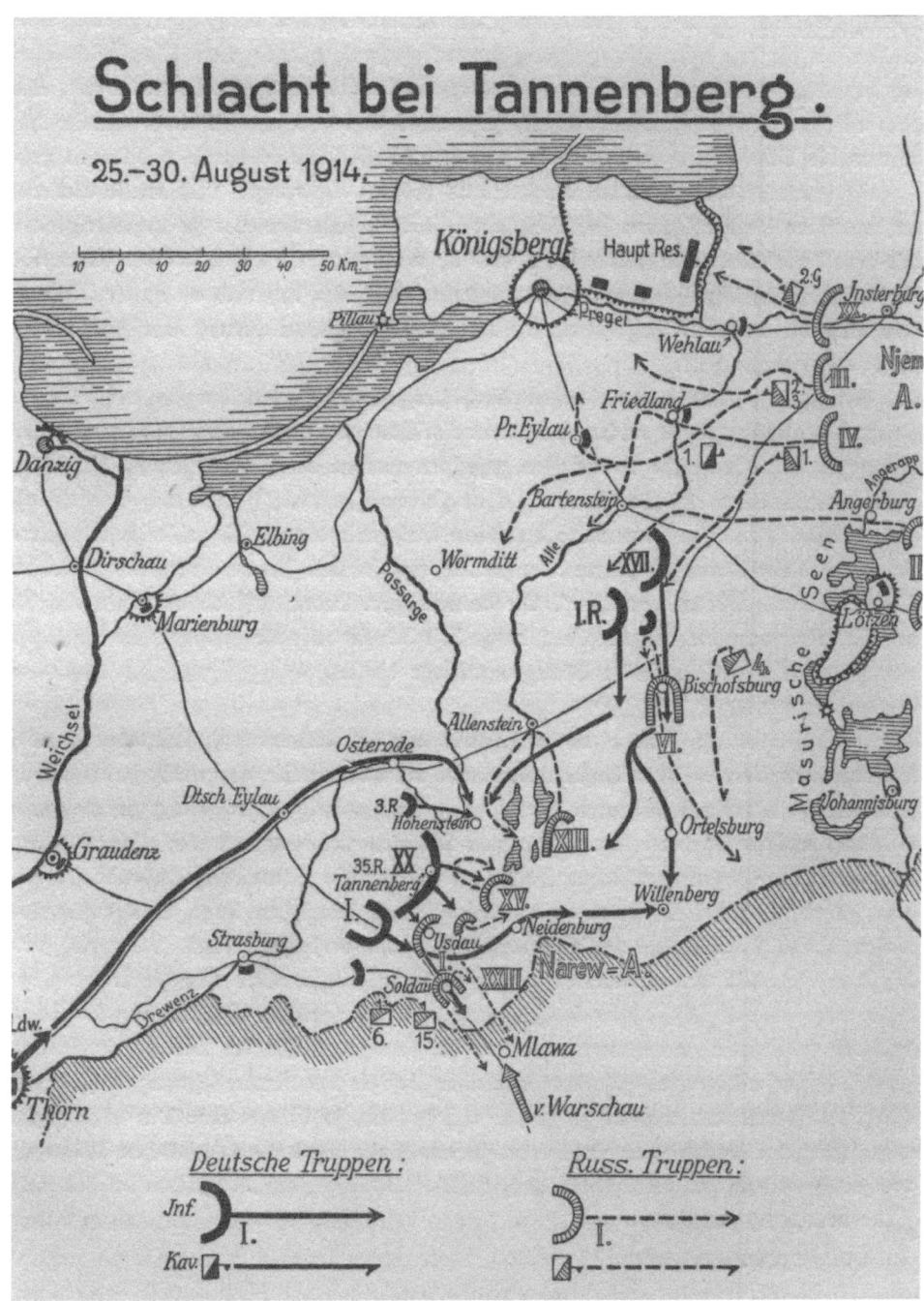
Battle of Tannenberg

immediately the unit was deployed at Reichenau. The 3rd reserve division also moved to the east. Furthermore, the 41st division, on the south flank of the XX. corps now had to deflect to the north in order to, at least, fully burden the Russian XV. corps.

This was a difficult operation; an advance via Waplitz to Paulsgut, a coup de grace. Generalmajor Sonntag's division paid a high price for it. Despite support from cavalry of Lewinski, and King Albert of Saxony - brave dragoons from Allenstein - the units came under fire from the 8th and 2nd Russian infantry. These Russian infantry units were also attacked, but the forced nature of the offensive made the German attack particularly costly. The developments with the 41st division were described in detail by Oberstleutnant a.D. Albert Benary in 1933. Sonntag had ordered the attack in the earliest hours. Before that, the Freiherr Hiller von Gaertringen 4th Posener regiment No. 59 had assembled. The morning mist was 'thick as potato soup' wrote Benary; the soldiers could not see their hands in front of their eyes. Without a compass, they were helplessly lost. The Russian troops, according to Benary especially the 2nd Russian infantry division, were ready in an ambush. The regiment was soon in big trouble, so General Sonntag gave the order to the other troops of the 41st division to relieve the regiment 59. However, this attack too quickly failed in the Russian machine gun fire. The units fell back to the starting positions near Seythen. The advance via the Adamheide to Waplitz had become a costly adventure. According to Benary, regiment 59 was largely destroyed.[119] This was a slight exaggeration, but the losses were considerable. On the 28th the division lost about 1300 men, and 28 officers. The Russian losses are not known. At Waplitz, 159 were later buried.[120]

Among the German losses were over 300 men, commanded by Major Zickhardt, who had become prisoners at Waplitz. They were cut off from the rest of the division and had run out of ammunition. An attempted breakout, according to Benary in the name of Germany: *'Deutschland über alles' (Germany over all)*, was caught in the Russian fire after only a few metres. Major Zickhardt then broke his sword, had his soldiers destroy their guns and surrendered. The Russians treated the prisoners well. Not many days later, the men of the 41st infantry division were relieved by their own troops.[121]

The attack by the 41st division was not in vain. The 37ste division under command of Von Morgen quickly arrived, with under its command the Unger division, and was immediately thrown into battle against Hohenstein, and with success. Russian losses began to mount slowly: in Lichteinen 500 Russians were taken prisoner of war, in Droebnitz hundreds of Russians died in their trenches and near Sauden, a Russian column was attacked by surprise by the advancing German troops, killing 600 tsarist troops. At the end of the day, Unger's

The memorial of the battle of Tannenberg, which was destroyed by the German 'Wehrmacht' in the Second World War at the retreat

unit of the 75th brigade entered the burning Hohenstein. A milestone had been reached, even if the price was high on that 28 August. [122]

The fall of Hohenstein was not the only great victory. Von François also achieved very good results. The 1st corps pushed that day from the surroundings of Neidenburg to Schmettau and even to Willenberg. At the same time, Von Mackensen's units advanced from the north towards Von François' troops via Ortelsburg to Willenberg. Which means that while there was heavy fighting at Hohenstein with the XIII. and XV. corps, all Russian corps, including the XV. and parts of the XXIII. were now largely cut off from the hinterland.

Now Samsonov realised the danger. Suddenly it had become clear that the centre of Russian power was in a threatening north-south pincer, while to the west of the Russians the determined front of Von Below and Von Scholz threatened. There was only one way: back, while there was still time.

Around the fiercely contested Hohenstein were extensive sections of the Russian XIII. and XV. corps, which were now suddenly trying to retreat. Von Below rushed forward on the 29th and personally led the attack of the 1st reserve division from hill 191 near Grieslienen, just north of Hohenstein. The units were positioned favourably to lay siege to the retreat route Hohenstein-Morken and further eastwards. Artillery targets were transmitted from a balloon, while taking great care to distinguish their own units from the Russians. The Reichsarchiv reported that it was a prize-giving exercise, the like of which would hardly be seen again in the First World War. Infantry, artillery, horse and carriages, everything seemed to move at once and offered grateful targets for the German artillery. [123]

In other places, two battalions of Von Below's reserve troops captured the approach and withdrawal troops of two complete Russian divisions. A problem arose as to how to cash in on this result. It was necessary to secure the spoils, but that would take time and the men of the I. reserve corps were very tired after the gruelling fighting of the last days. The German commander decided to take care of the situation and eliminated the Russian grenades and ammunition supply by throwing everything into a local lake.[124] In a divisional order that day it was said: 'The enemy is completely defeated, it is now a question of exploiting our success'. [125]

The slaughter continued between Waplitz and Kurken. Von Scholz' and Von Below's units reached out to each other. In several places, larger groups of Russian soldiers had fallen into German hands. Everything was still unclear, 500 men here, 1500 men there. In some forest areas, it still came to a losing rearguard action. Ludendorff appeared in the front sector. In the meantime messages from Samsonov had been received. It was clear that the Russians were aware of Ludendorff's deadly stranglehold. Rennenkampf promised help and would urgently send cavalry divisions southwards. It was necessary to strengthen the northern flank of the encirclement and the 37th infantry division was ordered to do so. This took away from the destruction of Samsonov's core group, but by the evening it had become clear that this core group was already largely defeated. Around Hohenstein alone, losses on 29 August were estimated at 8000 men.[126] Hohenstein had become a burning town. 486 German soldiers were killed.[127] On the hill west of the city, the Tannenberg memorial would rise.

Von François' advance had almost taken on the character of a 'Blitzkrieg'. Russian pilots took off in their rickety little planes, while the German artillery was already firing at the runways. Retreating supply and drain troops were overtaken by German ulans (lightly armed horsemen) and successfully fired upon. Near Muschaken, a cash box containing 32,000 roubles fell into German hands, along with a large consignment of coffee and bread, and 600 prisoners. At Willenberg another 800 men were captured. The loot was collected and taken westwards in a column of almost 1,000 vehicles.[128]

Von Mackensen's corps also kept up the pace. The Reichsarchiv even reported that soldiers fell asleep during the march, bumped into their leaders and woke up again. The march continued into the night, even though it was remarkably cold. Ortelsburg was on fire when Von Mackensen entered it. It had been evacuated by the Russian VI. corps, which was largely out of the encirclement, and with two divisions, the 4th and the 16th, continued to make relief attempts for the surrounded units. Ortelsburg made a desolate impression. The streets were full of abandoned equipment. The population came out of the shelters in surprise when they heard that the German troops were back in the city. Von Mackensen had, like Von François, advanced so fast that the food could not keep up. With empty stomachs they had to fight. Von Mackensen ordered the officers to dismount from their horses and thus set an example for the men.

At Jedwabno a strange incident occurred. While Von Mackensens artillery gave one salvo after another, suddenly a Cossack horse with a white flag came riding straight towards the German positions. The unit ceased firing and was surprised to see that it was Major Zickhardt of the German Infantry Regiment 148 who had fallen into Russian hands a short time before. Due to the sudden change in the odds, he and more than 400 other soldiers were released and could now rejoin their own troops.[129]

On 30 and 31 August, the bloody conclusion of the Battle of Tannenberg took place. In practice, it consisted of the prevention of breakout and disengagement attempts by the tsarist army. The breakout attempts involved the Russian XIII., XV. and XXIII. corps, which were located roughly between Burdungen and Omulefofen and tried to escape southwards towards Wallendorf and Rettkowen. But Samsonov's breakout attempt was too late. To the west were the 3rd reserve division and the 41st German infantry division, and to the south the 2nd infantry division and parts of the 1st corps, which together with Von Mackensen's units, the 36th and 35th infantry divisions, also cut off the road to the east. A smaller Russian force, which was already east of the 35th German infantry division, tried to break out near Willenberg. The escape attempts took place in the east at Ortelosburg, and in the south at Neidenburg. These were units of the Russian VI corps under General Blagowjeschtschenski and units of the 1st corps under General Artamanow. In addition, there was the threat of Von Rennenkampf in the north.

Ludendorff and Von Hindenburg followed the developments closely. On the evening of 29th, Ludendorff already estimated the Russian losses at 10,000 prisoners of war[130] and the on 30th, there was cause for even greater euphoria. On the battlefield between Allenstein - Hohenstein - Neidenburg and Ortelsburg, between 20,000 and 30,000 Russians are estimated to have been taken prisoner. Large numbers of artillery pieces were also counted, which were abandoned in the country.[131] Von Hindenburg sent out a message that the enemy had been completely defeated and that the Kaiser and the Supreme Command expressed their appreciation for the efforts of their own troops. However, there was more good news: it became clear that von Rennenkampf's army had little to fear. Again, Russian radio messages fell into German hands. The attempt at liberation had been stopped; indeed, Rennenkampf was on the retreat.

The advance of Rennenkampf's Memel army had been unconvincing all those days. Generalleutnant Brecht's 1st cavalry division had successfully slowed the Russian advance. In order to cover the units south of the Masurian lakes as much as possible, the northern flank had increasingly been handed over to the garrison of the city of Königsberg, commanded by Von Pappritz. The garrison was overloaded and had to fall back to the Deim line of defence from the River Aller. At Königsberg, it came to fierce artillery duels. This led to tense moments on the northern flank of the 8th army, but Ludendorff and Hindenburg took this for granted in order to have extra strength south of the lakes. Rennenkampf had made an attempt to force the fortress Lötzen, on the road Königsberg - Bialystok, to surrender, but the proud commander Busse called the Russian negotiator's call for surrender on 27 August an 'insult' to the occupying force of Lötzen, which consisted of four and a half battalions Landwehr and Landsturm, as well as a small amount of artillery. Although the unit had been behind the Russian lines since 25 August, Busse proclaimed to the negotiator that Lötzen would not surrender 'until the garrison was in ruins'. The Russians, units of General Scheidemann's II. Army corps, preferred not to storm the fortress. The fortress, safely encamped behind a water barricade, would not be easy to take. The siege units and material had to concentrate on the big loot: Königsberg.[132] But none of that came to pass. The looming demise of Samsonov was the signal for a retreat. In the radio message that brought Ludendorff the good news about the retreat, it was reported that the Russian troops had to destroy as many railway and telegraph lines as possible. [133]

This threat was gone for good. The most dangerous news now came from the south: Artamanow's attempt at disengagement. When the reports about this came through the Flieger-Abteilung 6 of the fortress Graudenz, Von François' units were scattered over a wide front. The only unit that could be placed directly at right angles to the Russian army's advance was a battalion, Major Schlimm's I./45, which was located at Neidenburg. Just south of the town, near Berghopf, a position was quickly set up. Meanwhile, Von François began to scrape together troops from all directions. On Sunday, 30 August, many units of the division were at war near Willenberg. There was nothing to do but to free small units where possible and let them make their way back to Neidenbrug. Von François had stored his own headquarters in Modlken and from there the flank of the troops of the I. Russian corps were attacked from the east. But it would still be exciting. Not much later, the report that Schlimm could no longer hold the front near Berghof came in. Von François now galloped forward in person and threw everything he had at the battle. The encirclement of the bulk of the Samsonov forces was not to be undone by this disengagement attack by Artamanow. Units of the 2nd and 1st infantry divisions were thrown into the fray, artillery units were rushed in and Landwehr troops and even units of the 41st infantry division of Generalmajor Sonntag, which had experienced such hard days before, came to bear, and successfully so. The Russian advance began to falter due to increasing resistance, right on their direction of advance and also in the flank. Artamanow hesitated and then gave up. About 500 Russian soldiers fell into German hands near Berghof, 350 Russians were left behind on the battlefield. The Flieger-Abteilung of Lieutenant Winckler confirmed the Russian retreat. [134]

With this retreat, the Russians again missed an important opportunity to save Samsonov. Max Hoffmann was rightly surprised by the relative ease with which they managed to repel Artamanow. It was probably a combination of Von François' energetic performance, Mühlmann's successful artillery intervention, the earlier Russian losses at Usdau, and Artamanow's overestimation of the German forces. The latter explanation was certainly an option, given that Russian intelligence, as well as liaison services, were hopelessly weak. It seemed that the Russians were operating largely in the dark and that there was little coordination. Hoffmann rightly called the Russians' constant uncoded radio messages an 'incomprehensible levity'. [135]

Another dangerous moment occurred at Von Mackensen. There, Ortelsburg had already fallen into German hands on the 29th, but General Von Hennig had ordered his men of the 35th infantry division under the command of Generalmajor Von Hahn to march directly on Wellenberg, more to the south. The small unit which had remained at Ortelsburg was suddenly cut off from the surrounding area by Russian cavalry units of the VI. corps. Von Hahn was in doubt as to what to do. On the one hand, it was very important for the encirclement to advance towards Willenberg, however, on the other hand, no gap should be created at Ortelsburg. The problem solved itself here, when his units suddenly encountered Von François' troops, who had already come towards Von Mackensen from Willenberg itself. Now, Von Hahn could safely turn his troops around and successfully relieve Ortelsburg. There it had come to heavy fighting with Russian units. The town's church tower had collapsed under artillery fire. [136]

In the sweltering heat of late summer, 31 August, the last Russian breakout attempt near Puchalowen was squashed. In one of these last battles, the commanding general of the 1st infantry division, General von Trotha, was killed. Heavy fighting had taken place near Janowo with Russian troops from many different units all trying to escape. At close range, German artillery fired into the enemy lines. Russian clergymen tried to keep up the courage. Prayers and church songs could be heard amid the violence of war.[137] Von Trotha believed that a general should be at the front of his troops and personally led the soldiers. It came to hand-to-hand combat. The Russians, according to Von François, showed once again their excellent military attitude by storming towards their downfall singing. Thousands of Russians were left dead. [138]

The Russians now began to surrender en masse. Rittmeister Von Puttkamer witnessed a local capitulation of 210 Russian officers and 11,000 men, together with 2,000 horses and 41 artillery pieces. This happened in the vicinity of Willenberg. The capitulation was preceded by a short negotiation with a Russian clergyman who had reported to the Germans armed with a white flag. More and more generals were now also captured, such as General Klujew of the Russian XIII. corps and General Martos of the XV. corps, who was taken prisoner by Hauptmann Grun's I./43. Von François walked along the long rows of prisoners of war, looking for the lifeless body of Von Trotha. He saw the terrible spectacle of the blood-soaked battlefield. Here and there the wounded lay groaning among the dead. A Russian battery, with crew and horses, had fallen. Just in front of them lay the fallen German soldiers of 12th company of Regiment 3.

Their hands still clasped the rifle with the bayonet planted. Captain Schoene lay there as the front body. Not much further away lay the large disembodied body of the commander of the Russian 24th infantry regiment. General von Trotha was found near a forest near Pucholowen. A bullet had pierced his neck. His body was recovered and laid to rest in the church of Neidenburg. Of the battalion of regiment 3, all officers were killed. The units were led by the non-commissioned officers. In the middle of the battle, when the troops passed the lifeless body of one of their commanders, the Feldwebel would let go a long stride and the eyes would turn to the right, thus honouring the fallen commander. [139]

On 30 August, a relieved Ludendorff was already able to report to Koblenz that 25,000 prisoners of war had already been removed from the battlefield, and that this number would rapidly increase. This was indeed the case, until 3 September - according to the estimates of the Reichsarchiv - about 92,000 Russians were taken as prisoners of war. Furthermore, thirteen Russian generals had fallen into German hands, 350 artillery pieces and enormous quantities of equipment and horses. The number of Russian dead will never be known. In the official graves rest 6739 fallen Russians. The 'Reichsarchiv' calculated the total Russian losses at 120,000 men. Sixty trains brought the prisoners of war to the hinterland. [140]

The German losses were estimated at 1891 killed, 6579 wounded and 4588 missing, which was a total loss of 13,058 men. The largest number of casualties was suffered by Von Scholz's XX. corps, with 631 men. In addition, of the 6579 wounded, the XX. corps had to mourn more than 3000. It was the price the corps had paid to prevent Samsonov's breakthrough to the west. Von Mackensen's corps, which had suffered such heavy losses at Gumbinnen, had now mercifully emerged from the battle with only 93 killed, 275 wounded and 103 missing (a total of 481 men). After the XX. corps, Von François had suffered the greatest losses: 360 killed, 1376 wounded and 597 missing (2333 total), but on the other hand had achieved spectacular successes. In addition, in the days that followed, the number of German missing men was considerably reduced and the wounded returned to their units, so that the total German loss was considerably less than the 13,000-plus men counted immediately after the battle.[141] The Reichsarchiv eventually determined the actual losses to be approximately 4000 men, of which the XX. corps with 1417 men and the 1st corps with 516 men had suffered the heaviest losses. [142]

This huge victory was immediately followed by tremendous cheering. The victory, which was called the Battle of Tannenberg, named as revenge for the defeat of the *Ordenritter* on 15 July 1410, who were defeated there by the slaves, had come unexpectedly. What should have been a mere gain of time was turned into a resounding victory by Ludendorff and von Hindenburg. The *Entscheidungsschlacht*, fought entirely over the inner lines, had become an overwhelming success. Historical comparisons were being bandied about at every opportunity. Some compared the victory to the battle of Sedan[143] from the Franco-Prussian War of 1870-1871, others compared the battle to Cannae, from 216 BC, when Hannibal and his troops from Carthage defeated 86,000 Roman infantry soldiers and riders with only 40,000 of their own troops. The battle plan of Cannae had become Hannibal's military testament, an eternal blueprint for the encirclement battle. The weapons had changed, said Von François in his memories of the battle, but the tactics and strategy were still the same.[144] Max Hoffmann called the battle 'one of the greatest victories in history' [145].

Even if we stick to the facts, Tannenberg was an extraordinary military event. 153,000 German troops had defeated 191,000 Russian troops, while a second large Russian army (Von Rennenkampf) was still around. The situation had changed from a threatened East Prussia to a German counter-offensive. The concept of the *Entscheidungsschlacht* had worked, Samsonov's army had been largely defeated and the balance of forces on the northern part of the Eastern Front was now considerably better, although East Prussia would only be safe once Von Rennenkampf's army was also defeated. Thus, the scenario for the second battle, the Battle of the Masurian Lakes, was born.

While Ludendorff and Von Hindenburg were looking at the cards, the Tannenberg myth was already beginning to play a role. This myth consisted not only of skewed historical comparisons, but also of the forgetting - at least for the general public - of the first lessons at Gumbinnen, in which the tsarist army had shown itself to be a tough opponent. In short, the war in the East was far from won. Moreover, the Eastern Front was much bigger than the front against Prussia. The k.u.k.-army (double monarchy of Austria-Hungary; k.u.k.= *kaiserlich und königlich;* k.u.k.= *Emperor and Kingly)* was not developing very well and it would not be long before the German troops would have to play as a rush goalie behind this front line, in order to avoid collapse. Tannenberg was not an *Entscheidungsschlacht* out of luxury, but out of necessity. Ludendorff had chosen this concept precisely because he saw the situation, especially in the west, as worrying. He rightly distrusted the stage problems and weakened northern flank of the Schlieffenplan and in the middle of this operation Moltke had also released troops for the eastern front. To make matters worse, these came from the extreme flank which had to make the greatest turn. Although Ludendorff had indicated that these troops were not needed, they had been sent anyway. They came too late for Tannenberg and were missing in the west at a crucial place, although it is hardly conceivable that Schlieffen (Molkte-II) could have succeeded with these units there, for that the adjustment of the original Schlieffen plan would have been too great. The *Entscheidungsschlacht* Tannenberg was therefore primarily an answer to Ludendorff's general doubts that there would be an imminent collapse of France, as well as an immediate protection for East Prussia and even Berlin.

One of the consequences of Tannenberg was that the borders of the Hindenburg-Ludendorff duo were hardly questioned any more. From one day to the next they had become the heroes of Germany. To the outside world it was above all Hindenburg's victory, as can also be seen from the title of the book in which Von François wrote his memoirs: *Hindenburgs Sieg bei Tannenberg*, in which he also immediately mentioned the second myth: *Das Cannae des Weltkriegs*, as if the comparison with Hannibal was valid (only the balance of power was very different) and as if the race in the east was already over.[146] The Russian army had suffered a defeat, but still had millions of soldiers and much, much space at its disposal. But the average German believed that Hochmeister Ulrich von Jungingen, who had died at Tannenberg in 1410, had been avenged here. Historical awareness, and especially its mystifications, was very common in this part of Europe. It is interesting to note that the time documents of Tannenberg, and the interwar period pointed out that the battle of 1410 was lost by the Germans to the Lithuanians and Poles through treachery, thus a kind of early variant of the 'dagger' legend, which formed shortly after the collapse in 1918.[147]

Naming the battle after Tannenberg was a politically clumsy decision, as it was offensive to the Poles. Ludendorff had already pointed out in the past that Berlin did not succeed in mobilising Poles sufficiently for the German Empire. In Polish national consciousness, the battle of 1410 stood for an achievement and was known as the Battle of Grunwald. Now Tannenberg 1914 was shown as the 'germanic sword' that 'hit the slaves on the head' as the historian Karl-Heinz Janssen put it.[148] Later historians, from the Ludendorff camp, such as H. Rewaldt, considered 'that Tannenberg was not only a battle against the Russians and a revenge on earlier Great Slavic expansion, but that it was also a battle against Rome, Judah and Freemasons'. The poison of the dagger legend had by then already penetrated the the history books.[149]

Ludendorff, von Hindenburg and Hoffmann all claimed to have coined the name Tannenberg for the battle.[150] In any case, it was von Hindenburg, as commander, who requested permission from the Kaiser, who, with his lack of political 'Fingerspitzengefühl', immediately gave it. Ludendorff had initially been reluctant to draw comparisons. Somewhat superstitious as he was, the name Tannenberg frightened him, reminded him of a painful historical defeat. According to Karl-Heinz Janssen, Ludendorff refused to set up his headquarters at Tannenberg during the battle. Within the General Staff, the battle of Allenstein had been discussed for a long time, but in the end, this turn was taken. Tannenberg came to stand for German military success. It had become a 'sign of loyalty' of Germany to the Deutschtum in the east. It was estimated that no fewer than 34,000 Prussian houses had gone up in flames,[151] but the Russian 'steamroller' had been stopped by 'self-sacrificing German soldiers'. 'God gave us a great general,' time documents read. A new word was even invented to honour Hindenburg: *Grossfaz*, which stood for *grosster Feldherr aller Zeiten*, conveniently forgetting that Ludendorff was also the man behind Tannenberg. Besides Hindenburg's large signature, the orders also bore a fan-like 'L', for Ludendorff.

Hindenburg soon realised that he should not get in the way of the gifted Ludendorff, but should accompany him as far as possible. *'Ich weiss auch nichts Besseres, Gott geb's'*, was often his comment on Ludendorff's proposals, for Ludendorff was always concrete and always came up with clear plans, although often ideas of the short term, but at Tannenberg they had worked great.

The shadow of Tannenberg would prove to be a long one. On 18 September 1927, a grand monument was unveiled at Tannenberg in the presence of Chancellor Marx. The designers, two Berlin architects, the Krueger brothers, were modestly inspired by Stonehenge.[152] So they went for imperishability. One year later, a communist Reichstag delegate expressed his 'highest esteem' for the battle of Tannenberg.[153] Barracks were named after the battle. Tannenberg had fallen into the grip of war romanticism, of field-men on hills, waving banners and horse-drawn artillery, as in the best Napoleonic days. Tannenberg would also become the 'Lehrmodel' of German strategy, whereas it had much more to do with tactics. Tannenberg, therefore, as 'Sandkastspiele', as a wrong lesson for the future, as part of a dangerous all-or-nothing scenario, the scenario that had so dominated Germany since the Schlieffenplan.

'Had I lost the battle, I would have lost it alone', Von Hindenburg later remarked. There was much truth in this, for as Tannenberg became more of a historical fact, more spiritual fathers of the battle came to be. Both the vain lieutenant-adjutant of the 8th army, Max Hoffmann, and Von François, later claimed a large part of the victory, and Von François pointed out that he had made 60,000 prisoners of war.[154] The latter was supported in this by none other than Winston Churchill, who in his position as Secretary of the Navy gave Von François the credit for Tannenberg. Although Von François had fought bravely and taken a major part in the battle, the entire concept of Tannenberg could not, of course, be attributed to someone who had only operated at corps level. Churchill's statement was heavily exaggerated.[155]

Hoffmann later gave a tour of the battlefield and showed Von Hindenburg's headquarters with the remark 'this is where the Commander-in-Chief slept during the battle of Tannenberg'.[156] For the general public, it made little difference. Tannenberg was mentioned in the same breath as von Hindenburg and to a lesser extent Ludendorff, who would claim credit for the battle after the war, and rightly so. 'Your old man will become a famous man', joked Von Hindenburg in a letter to his wife.[157] And he was right. Of course, as Graf von Kielmansegg and the historian Walter Görlitz also pointed out, Tannenberg had been the work of superiors, but in terms of style and drive, as well as justification in collaboration with von Hindenburg, it was Ludendorff's work. This credit has also been given to Ludendorff in more recent studies, among others by Wolfgang Venohr, who incidentally compared the battle of Tannenberg with two other tactical German victories of the Second World War: Kharkov, March 1943, and Shitomir, November-December 1943, where respectively Paul Hausser's II. SS corps and Hermann Balck's XXXXVIII.pz.-corps achieved similar victories. This comparison is interesting because these were indeed tactical victories. Tannenberg was an *Entscheidung* only in so far as it concerned the fate of Samsonov's army, the war was not decided by it.[158]

The greatest recognition of Ludendorff, however, came from Von Hindenburg himself. 'It was my main task to give free rein to and support Ludendorff's thoughts and superhuman labour'.[159]

Samsonov did not live to see the end of his army. He was a broken man when the demise of his troops occurred. He realised the extent of his defeat, for numbers alone told only part of history. The troops that Moscow had put into the field were first-class units, while the German opponent had had to use mainly Landwehr and Landsturm soldiers. All this made the Russian defeat even more bitter. 'The tsar trusted me, how can I face him after such a disaster', Samsonov confided to his subordinates. During his attempts to break out, Samsonov had increasingly suffered from asthma. With map and compass in hand, he fell behind. After giving some soldiers a letter for the tsar he withdrew among the trees. A shot was heard. His staff immediately understood what it meant. Samsonov had taken his own life. The staff officers tried to find the body in the forest, without success.[160] The search did not last long, as German flares were everywhere, illuminating the landscape for a short time. The troops of the German 8th army were close on the heels of the Russians. They fled further, south-eastwards, and most of the staff came through. German troops found the lifeless body of Samsonov, with his striking grey beard and a bullet wound in the head, and buried the general at Willenburg. In 1916, with the help of the Red Cross, his widow managed to bring his body back to Russia, where Samsonov

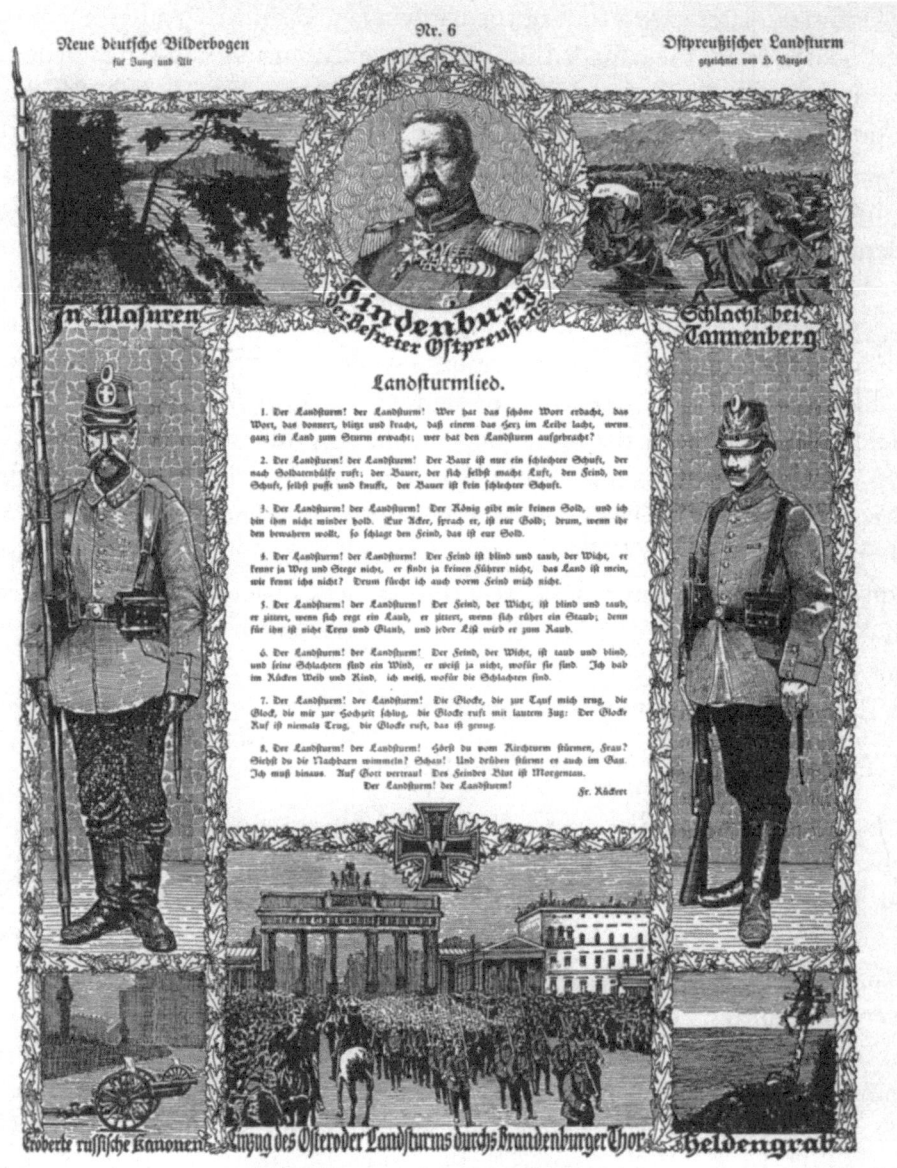

Large-scale Von Hindenburg devotion after the Battle of Tannenberg

was reburied. 'With Samsonov we also buried our hopes', said the Russian officer Danilow.[161]

Despite this dramatic turn of events, Tannenberg's defeat did not reach Russia so quickly.[162] The Russian media also had good news to report: great successes against the Austro-Hungarian army in the battle of Lemberg. In contrast to the relative public calm around Tannenberg in Russia, a debate arose in Germany about how the Russian defeat could be explained. What had gone wrong with this army which was so strong on paper? There were rumours of an old feud between the two Russian corps commanders: Von Rennenkampf and Samsonov. This feud would go back to the battle of Liauyang, where Samsonov had had to defend the Yantai (Yentai) coal mines. Samsonov's Siberian Cossacks had not been able to stand up to the Japanese troops there and he had appealed to Von Rennenkampf to help him in vain. The generals had met each other later on at Mukden station and, according to legend, their adjutants had had to jump in to prevent a brawl. According to the historian Wheeler-Bennet, it almost came to a duel.[163] Unfortunately, since the Tsar wanted to deploy only his best officers in East Prussia, they had been ordered to 'bear with each other'.[164] Before leaving for the front, the Grand Prince had arranged a meeting between the two men to take the tension out of the air. Von Rennenkampf and Samsonov met in Snamenka and shook hands in the presence of the Grand Duke Sergei Mikhailovich and officer Shilinsky. Von Rennenkampf reportedly was 'visibly moved' by this gesture. In a broken voice he said: 'In this hour there are no personal enmities. We may only think of the victory over our armies and for Russia'.[165] At the farewell, Shilinski is said to have shaken hands with both generals and stated that 'Liauyung' had been erased from memory.[166]

Although there is evidence that there were indeed tensions between the two commanders - Tuchman speaks of von Rennenkampf's 'strange behaviour'[167] - the conclusion that these were at the root of the German successes was exaggerated. Both commanders obeyed their superiors, so if there was poor communication between them, it was mainly due to that. The *Reichsarchiv assumed* that there might have been irritations between the two commanders, but that it was unproven that these had had a negative effect on the battle.[168]

More recent studies, such as those by the British historian John Keegan, make no mention at all of the tensions. This is strange, because according to Max Hoffmann, the animosity between the Russian commanders was known in the days of Tannenberg. The British historian Wheeler-Bennet reported that Hoffmann had heard about the quarrel as late as July 1914. After the war, when the cognac was flowing, he told that Tannenberg had been lost to the Russians on the platform of Mukden. The matter intrigued him since he had been a military observer with the Japanese army in Asia, where he had heard the rumours first hand.[169] In his memoirs, Hoffmann wrote that he had already discussed the matter with Ludendorff. [170]

Ludendorff was also curious about the Russian operation. He had summoned the Russian General Martos, commander of the Russian XV corps (6th and 9th infantry division). During his attempt to break out, Martos had run into two Polish peasants who agreed to show him the way. However, these Poles had lured him directly into a German ambush, during which his Chief of Staff, General Maczugowski had been killed by German machine gun fire. Von François, however, treated Martos as a gentleman, invited him into his car and offered him chocolate and wine, as befits a good host. Ludendorff asked what the Russian plans had been, to which Martos replied that he had only been informed about tactical matters. At that moment, writes the Canadian historian Goodspeed, Von Hindenburg walked in. Martos was startled by his tall figure. Hindenburg grabbed Martos' right hand with both hands and addressed him calmly in trailing Russian. He said that Martos would get his sword back and that he had fought bravely. Then both Ludendorff and Von Hindenburg left the room, realising that they would probably never fully understand what had happened on the Russian side. [171]

What was clear was that the Russians had had major problems of a technical nature. This is what Norman Stone expressed in his influencial work *The Eastern Front 1914-1917*.[172] The struggle between Von Rennenkampf and Samsonov was due to more general tensions within the Russian army, which had been undergoing reforms since Moscow's defeat in the Russo-Japanese War. Some of the General Staff belonged to the traditionalists, who wanted little reform, while others were keen on it. The commanders of both Samsonov and Rennenkampf belonged to different parties, which resulted in poor communication. In practice, Von Rennenkampf simply carried out orders as he turned towards Königsberg instead of coming to Samsonov's aid en masse, as the Germans overheard radio messages. This fact makes the existence or non-existence of a quarrel between Samsonov and Von Rennenkampf of secondary importance.

Another myth surrounding the Russian defeat would be that the Russians had rushed to help their French allies. France owed its victory on the Marne to Russia's 'self-sacrifice,' as the tsarist foreign minister S.D. Samsonov noted in his memoirs, adding that Samsonov would not have been ready to invade Prussia.[173] In reality, the tsarist army had been substantially rebuilt since 1906 and Moscow spent no less than a third of its budget on defence. Admittedly, much money was lost on prestige projects, such as the Russian fleet, which was largely crushed against Japan, but this was also a 'luxury' afforded to the vain Kaiser Wilhelm II. In 1914, Moscow again had more than 114 divisions at its disposal, compared to 96 German divisions. The Russians had 6720 artillery pieces at their disposal, compared to 6004 on the German side. In eighteen days, the Russian railways were able to mobilise 100 divisions against the Centrals, which indicated that Russia's special and social backwardness to the West was much greater than its military backwardness. This social backwardness was evidenced by the fact that over a third of Russia's officers had not even finished secondary school, and that most of her generals were not ethnic Russians, indeed many bore a German name. The dependence on 'foreign' commanders did not always lead to gentle treatment of the soldiers. Stone gives the example of an officer who 'drew lessons' from the Russo-Japanese war, attributing the failure of the Russians to cowardice. To punish this, he deprived the Russian cavalry of their rifles. In this way, they had to get close to the enemy. In reality, the Russian shortcomings lay in the material, which by 1914 had caught up with them. In fact, Russia had spent more money on defence in recent years than Germany. [174]

The main cause of the Russian failure was the poor communication with the Russian Supreme Command and between the corps themselves. The contact was partly by letter. Only a handful of telephone lines were available and telegraph equipment was scarce and slow. In addition, Von Rennenkampf had gained the impression that he had won an important victory at Gumbinnen and that the Germans were in retreat. His reconnaissance had failed hopelessly in the following days. Samsonov had understood from the orders he received from his superiors that the German army was in retreat and had not seen the pincer operation coming. It has been rightly pointed out that the Russian army apparently relied too much on its superiority and underestimated the German troops. The Russian effort was fragmented, whereas Ludendorff concentrated his troops. In addition, the Germans had, as Hoffmann later put it, another important ally, namely the Russians themselves. The fact that the Germans had been able to eavesdrop on their orders had allowed them to take great risks, which resulted in battlefield successes.[175] Finally, Ludendorff himself also dispelled a myth about the Russian army. Several studies claimed that thousands of Russians had drowned in swamps. This was not true, there were no swamps at all, Ludendorff noted in his memoirs. [176]

While the soldiers were bivouacked for the moment and the song of thanksgiving *The Battle of Leuthen* sounded in the evening, Von Hindenburg and Ludendorff entered the church of Allenstein.[177] They attended mass in this old German town of knights. God had been merciful to Germany. Allenstein itself had also been merciful. During the occupation of the town by the tsarist armies, there was hardly any looting or burning, because the mayor had informed the Russians that the town was undefended. Other towns and villages fared much worse, especially in the area where Von Rennenkampf operated.[178]

Chapter 3

Warsaw

The echo of the artillery salvoes from Tannenberg had scarcely died down, when at the headquarters of Ludendorff and Von Hindenburg new orders came in from Koblenz. Among other things, it read that reinforcements were coming towards the Eastern Front: The XI. army corps, the garde reserve corps and the 8th cavalry division. Furthermore, Koblenz ordered the expulsion of Von Rennenkampf's army in the direction of Warsaw,[179] which also determined the new direction of advance. The troops were to turn southeast, which had everything to do with the rapidly deteriorating situation of the Austro-Hungarian troops.

'I did not get a moments rest', Ludendorff wrote in his memoirs. 'I had to prepare the regrouping for the next campaign, and that was an extremely difficult task'.[180] However, as after the capture of Liège, there was a sign of appreciation from the supreme command. Ludendorff received the *Eiserne Kreuz II. Class* for his part in the victory of Tannenberg. 'When I think of Liege and Tannenberg, my heart fills with a feeling of satisfaction,' he noted. 'Anyone who honestly earned it should wear it with pride'.[181]

The newly announced troops were themselves released by the OHL for the Eastern Front. This happened by telegraph at the beginning of the battle of Tannenberg. Initially, three corpses were involved, later the OHL asked if it could also be two. Ludendorff immediately agreed, for he had asked for no reinforcements given the course on the western front. The reports on the western front were relatively favourable for the moment and Ludendorff had his hands full in the east and simply had no time to study the developments elsewhere.[182]

South of the German 8th army, in Galicia, the situation with the Austro-Hungarian army was anything but rosy. The Chief of Staff of the Army of the Dual Monarchy, Conrad von Hoetzendorf, urged the 8th Army to cross the Narew

River as soon as possible in order to create some breathing room for the Austro-Hungarian Army. Von François' I. corps and Von Mackensen's troops were in the most favourable position for this purpose. But such a manoeuvre was unthinkable for the time being, since the threat of Von Rennenkampf remained on the northern flank. There was nothing to do but to put all their weight in stopping Von Rennenkampf first, and then come to the aid of the allies as quickly as possible.

Again, Ludendorff faced a complicated scenario. There was an enormous time pressure and after a possible success - Von Rennenkampf's army was a first-class force and thus not a 'walk over' - the troops had to be immediately deployed in a new hotbed.

An advantage for Ludendorff was that he could fight over his inner lines. As a master of stage warfare, he was the right man for this new battle. Within a short time he managed to position the troops of the 8th army well. He had a number of advantages. The brave fortress of Lötzen now stood, far to the east, like an annoying thorn in the Russian flesh, and Königsberg formed a solid fortress in the hinterland. Between Wormditt and the Russian border he now positioned the Guard Reserve corps, I. Reserve corps (east of Guttstadt), XI. corps (west of Lautern), XX. corps (Gross Boessau/Bischofsburg), XVII. corps (Passenheim) and I. corps (east of Ortelsburg) from north to south. Furthermore, he kept the southern flank, over which he wanted to advance later via Mlawa, protected by the units of Goltz and General Von Muelmann who had gathered around Neidenburg and Soldau. As early as 4 September, the German units were ready for battle.

Ludendorff rightly pointed out in his memoirs that the Germans had been lucky that the Elbing-Königsberg railway line was still intact, which would have allowed a rapid shift of troops from the 'Samsonov Front' to the 'Rennenkampf Front'. Other railway lines were damaged after the setback at Gumbinnen, but here too, German pioneers and engineers were able to restore things quickly. Of particular importance was the line Thorn - Allenstein - Korschen, the last place being the most eastern. The railway line and station could be restored within 48 hours,[183] so that there was now again a direct line from the Prussian hinterland to the front. This gave the German counterattack the opportunity to gather its own forces with speed and form the sledgehammer blow which Von Rennenkampf had to throw back to the east.

The balance of power was more favourable to the Germans than it had been at Tannenberg. Due to the reinforcements in the west by the 1st (XI. army corps), 2nd (garde reserve corps) and 3rd (8th cavalry division) army, Ludendorff had now 8 infantry divisions, 5 reserve divisions, 1 Landwehr division and 2 cavalry divisions at his disposal. Von Rennenkampf had 15 infantry divisions and 5 cavalry divisions at his disposal. However, it should be noted that a Russian infantry division had 16 battalions, compared to 12 in a German division. The ratio of soldiers was therefore 2 : 3 in Russia's favour. As for the artillery, the situation was more favourable for Ludendorff, here the ratio was 5 : 3 in the German advantage.[184]

By now, Von Rennenkampf was aware of the impending danger. The commander of the north-western front, Jilinsky, had informed him on 30 August that the German 8th army would now focus entirely on its Memel army. Not unjustly, Jilinsky pointed out the enormous importance of interrupting the German railway lines as much as possible. He also pointed out the danger emanating from Lötzen, from where the German troops could launch an attack in the back or flank of the Russian lines. The report of Samsonov's demise had struck like a bomb. The news was brought by courier to Von Rennenkampf, who was billeted in the *Gesellschaftshaus* in Insterburg's municipal park. Colonel Sawitsch passed on the message.

'How many men were taken prisoner,' Rennenkampf asked, 'twenty thousand?'

'Sixty thousand', was Sawitsch's answer.

Some officers of Rennenkampf's staff jumped up in fright. Rennenkampf remained seated.

'And Samsonov?'

'Samsonov is dead'.

'Killed?'

'No, he shot himself'.

'Impossible', a startled Von Rennenkampf exclaimed.[185]

Von Rennenkampf decided to dig his units in between the Baltic Sea and the Masurian Lakes. In itself, this was not an unwise tactic. The Russians were traditionally good at building positions and the general rule was that in a frontal attack on an extended line, the attacker should have a force superiority of 3 : 1. Von Rennenkampf knew that the 8th army had no such superiority at its disposal and hoped to let the German counterattack in front of the Memel army bleed out this way.[186]

But Ludendorff had no intention whatsoever of allowing his troops to break down in a full frontal attack against Von Rennenkampf's 80 kilometres of well-developed front line. He decided on a unilateral encirclement, combined with a frontal attack.

Ludendorff wanted to start the encirclement from the south and would be largely carried out by the ironmaster Von François and his I. corps. They could

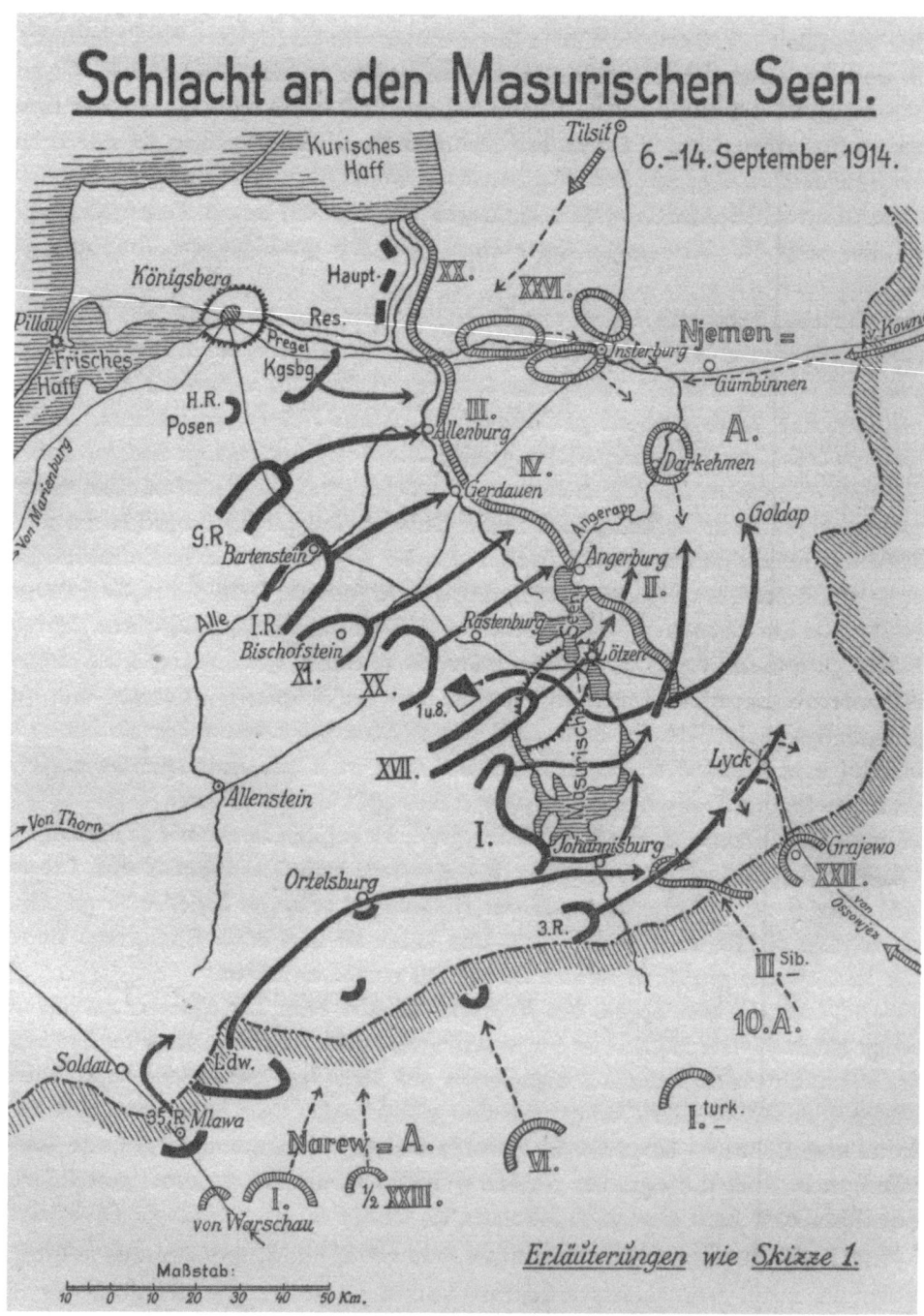

Battle of the Masurian Lakes

flank Von Rennenkampf's troops partly south of the Masurian Lakes and above and below Spridinger via Johannisburg from the south-west, while Von Mackensen's XVII. corps would bet on Lötzen and the other units would attack frontally.

This tactic provoked criticism from his professional brethren. The impetuous Von François was the most uncompromising in his criticism. He believed that a double encirclement should be launched from both the northern part and the southern part at the expense of the centre, which would have to be weakened for this purpose. On paper, Von François' plan was not bad, and such a weak centre could be very attractive even to the slow Von Rennenkampf, but the northernmost terrain was a disaster in terms of infrastructure, and did not lend itself to the rapid stage operation that Ludendorff had in mind. Also, the water connections there were a difficulty that could be exploited by Rennenkampf.

Max Hoffmann shared the opinion that a double encirclement was not possible.[187] He also had his own vision of the whole operation and believed that the southern flank should be stronger than it was currently formed by Ludendorff. This criticism was taken up by Ludendorff in his memoirs. Indeed, a 1 : 1 situation there would have been more favourable than the attack Ludendorff had now foreseen. It is possible that Hoffmann's criticism also reminded Ludendorff of the criticism on the Schlieffenplan, adapted by Moltke, where precisely those units on which it depended were too weak and the centre (near Lorraine, here between Guttstadt and Bischofsburg) too strong. In fact, Ludendorff's tactics were contrary to the Schlieffen idea. Ludendorff worked with a compromise formation, probably mainly due to practical considerations. He deployed the troops in a specific order, adherring strictly to his stage programme, and so they could be formed as quickly as possible. Time had always been the central point in Ludendorff's plans. He wanted to leave Von Rennenkampf little time to dig in, and the troops were already needed elsewhere. The battle of the Masurian Lakes was not to be a beauty contest, but rather a tactical victory that would free the Eastern Front.

But the battle soon developed much more unfavourably than hoped for. Von Rennenkampf's plan seemed to work. The Russian troops were deeply dug in and the German troops suffered considerable losses in the storming of the Russian positions. The little artillery the Russians had at their disposal intervened successfully in the battle and inflicted heavy losses on the Germans. It was especially Von Scholz's XX. corps that fared badly. This was, of course, no coincidence. From Bisschofsburg, this unit was again in the centre of the battle, while the corps at Tannenberg had suffered relatively heavy losses. But Von Rennenkampf was also uncomfortable with the situation. His intelligence service had picked up radio reports of a German flanking attack from the vicinity of the Königsberg fortress. These were false reports, spread by German intelligence. Von Rennenkampf was therefore surprised when Von François' southern flank started to move. The historian Asprey stated that Ludendorff's plan of attack had 'almost worked'.[188]

Indeed, Von François succeeded in pushing through Nikoliaken and Arys, then Lötzen and Kruglanken to the Rominter Heide in a few days. South of the 1st corps followed the 3rd reserve division and Landwehr van Goltz who had followed via Bialla and settled near Grajewo on the Russian border. German cavalry units pushed through on both sides of Lake Wystiter to Wirballen and Kalwarije. The other corps followed up to the line Gross Audowoehnen, Insterburg, Gumbinnen, and Goldap.

It is interesting to note how the battle of the Masurian Lakes eventually developed into an ordinary frontal showdown, in which Von François' I. corps was deployed more frontally than swiftly. Ludendorff remained above all the tactician in this battle, constantly adapting his basic plan to the circumstances. Several historians, such as Venohr, have pointed out that Ludendorff was very nervous and that von Hindenburg, as was suspected at Tannenberg, helped Ludendorff keep his cool.[189] The great fortune for the battle against Rennenkampf was that he himself could not keep his cool and, despite initial defensive successes, became increasingly afraid of meeting a fate like Samsonovs. Thus, he began to hesitate and finally withdrew his troops.

This created an extremely dangerous situation for the Russians. A retreat in the middle of a battle could easily turn into flight. These messages reached Ludendorff and Von Hindenburg in the night of 9 to 10 September. 'One can imagine the joy in the headquarters', Ludendorff reported.[190] 'I would be lying if I did not say that this is very pleasant for us,' Hoffmann noted.[191]

While the unilateral encirclement was still far from complete and the battle was developing more and more frontally, the battle's chances suddenly turned. Ludendorff admitted that the battle was far from decided at that point. The right flank, Ludendorff noted in his memoirs, consisting of the 3rd reserve division under the command of General von Morgen, had come up against too strong a Russian force at Bialle Luck and Ludendorff feared that the advance there would come to a standstill[192] Then came the report from the front around Gerdauen, more north, that the Russians had left the positions. Ludendorff understood at once that the task now was to pursue the Russian units as fast as possible.[193]

Rennenkampf had been seized by the same feeling that had struck Von Prittwitz at the beginning of the war. Although his own troops were well dug in, the most natural line of defence for Rennenkampf was the Memel, as the Weichsel was for Von Prittwitz. The result was an extremely chaotic situation. Ludendorff mentioned in his memoirs that the pursuit operations did not go as hoped. The troops had little room on the few roads, their own columns accidentally shot at each other. The encirclement manoeuvre of the southern corps was out of the question; everything simply had to move forward, hoping to overrun as many of Von Rennenkampf's units as possible.

'The result was less conspicuous than at Tannenberg', Ludendorff thought, looking back. 'An operation at the back of the Russian armies proved impossible'.[194] Nevertheless, the battle had delivered what the Germans needed. Von Rennenkampf had been pushed back from Prussia into Russia and the Memel army had suffered considerable losses in these operations.

'Once again we have an important and positive phase of the campaign behind us,' Von Mackensen noted from his headquarters in Budweitschen on 13 September. 'God's mercy is with us'. On Russian soil, at Wirballen, Von Mackensen ordered twelve gun salutes.[195] Von Hindenburg wrote in his memoirs that the Russians rushed back to their homeland three rows at a time.[196]

Ludendorff mentioned 45,000 Russian prisoners of war in his memoirs, the same figure was also used by D.J. Goodspeed. Others, like Baer and Norman Stone, spoke of 40,000 and 30,000 POWs respectively. In the twenty-eight days, Goodspeed thought, the Russian 1st army had lost 145.000 men in total, besides the 45.000 prisoners of war, 100.000 dead and wounded. In total, according to Goodspeed, Von Rennenkampf would have lost 200 artillery pieces.[197] The total loss for Samsonov and Von Rennenkampf together amounted to 310,000 men and 650 artillery pieces.[198]

As for the German losses during the battle of the Masurian Lakes, there is less clarity. Norman Stone reckoned that German troops had lost 100,000 men out of 250,000 deployed. Stone pointed out that this bloody pattern was a preview into the future of the First World War, where such monster losses would prove to be 'normal'.[199] If Stone's figure is correct, it is important to realise that these were most probably deaths, injuries and missing persons combined, and that the total losses for Germany were considerably lower. Von Mackensen, in his notes of 14 September 1914, has recorded the figure of about 9000 German losses, of which 1500 belonged to his own XVII. corps.[200] These losses would also be more proportionate to the battle around Tannenberg. The figure of 9000 is also used by Ludendorff-biographer Franz Uhle-Wettler, who estimated the Russian losses at 45,000 prisoners, 70,000 killed and wounded and 150 cannons.[201]

After the war, Ludendorff looked back with some satisfaction on the way the battle was qualified by the historians, as a kind of by-product of Tannenberg. It was an 'Entscheidungskampf' he thought, which had succeeded partly because the Russians had not been aware of their own strength. [202] In the latter, Ludendorff was certainly right. Von Rennenkampf was still reeling from the fate of Samsonov when he withdrew. His motto was: better to come home with half an army than to be destroyed in the Prussian land he had hoped to conquer for his Tsar. The British historian John Keegan, in his *The First World War,* believed that the Germans won the battle of the Masurian Lakes because of their superiority. This claim is completely false. As we saw, Von Rennenkampf still had a small superiority and reserves were still on their way to the front. Keegan's remark that Von Rennenkampf, after the defeat of Samsonov, 'refused to acknowledge defeat', is completely misrepresentative. When the battle of the Masurian Lakes began in early September 1914, the outcome was by no means certain. [203]

With a feeling of triumph, Ludendorff and Von Hindenburg moved into their new headquarters in the Dessauer Hof in Insterburg, where Von Rennenkampf had also been quartered for some time. The innkeeper had some interesting stories to tell after he had been with the Russians for nineteen days. During the capture of Insterburg, two German soldiers had been billeted in the hotel and the innkeeper quickly had them put on waiter's suits to save them from captivity. Russian troops then searched the entire building for bombs. In the cellar they found carbonated bottles which were immediately taken outside. Only when they understood that the innkeeper needed them for the beer could they return to the boarding house.

According to the innkeeper, the Russian officers had taken to it and the cider was flowing excessively. The adjutant of Grand Duke Nikolai Nikolayevich, colonel Von Graewen, who was also billeted for some time, had the male waiters replaced by women. When Von Rennenkampf heard about this, he immediately put an end to it. The Russian officers had spent so much money that the cash had run out at some point. The adjutant of the grand prince had it written on an account and promised to pay with 'colonial goods'. When the goods were near Istenburg, the town fell back into German hands. The innkeeper of Dessauerhof was perhaps one of the few Germans for whom liberation could have come a little later. [204]

A biographer of Von Hindenburg sketched another tragicomic story about the German commander. Exactly one year after the liberation of Istenburg, on 11 September 1915, Von Hindenburg arrived in the town by car. At that moment, a commemoration of the liberation one year earlier was taking place in the centre of Istenburg. A policeman who was supposed to keep order stopped Von Hindenburg's car in a rude way and made it clear to the driver that he was not allowed to continue but had to take a diversion around the town centre. For years to come, this particular form of thanksgiving from the city was the subject of amusing stories in German headquarters about the transience of fame. [205]

In Insterburg, Ludendorff inspected the Russian positions outside the town and breathed a sigh of relief that the units of the 8th army had not had to storm them, as they were well-developed. Insterburg had been neatly preserved. Von Rennenkampf had the town's wine cellars guarded by armed sentries to prevent excesses. However, discipline was not maintained everywhere. Cossacks in particular had been rioting terribly in some places in Prussia. Ludendorff was in a victory mood when on 14 September, the order came in to transfer the troops. Ludendorff was immediately summoned to Breslau, to serve as chief under General von Schubert, who was in the process of establishing the Army Süd there. The fatherland called for new duty. [206]

This new duty lay in supporting the Austro-Hungarian troops. Conrad von Hoetzendorf had raised a cry for help for the Austro-Hungarian divisions that had run into serious problems against the Russian army. It soon became clear to Ludendorff that the Austro-Hungarian ally was of a different calibre than his own troops. This had everything to do with the complexity of the Vielvölker State. The authorities in Vienna had to issue the mobilisation call in eleven different languages[207] in order to actually reach all subjects. The burgeoning nationalism within the ethnic patchwork caused increasing tensions between the different ethnic groups. There were even lynchings here and there, including against Czechs, whom the Grand-Austrians thought had shouted 'long live Serbia',[208] the country that had lit the fuse, according to most patriots. The mood changed in the empire. People reacted differently to the war in Vienna, Budapest or Prague. The Austrian historian Rauchensteiner mentioned both apathy and enthusiasm. And the enthusiasm would also be short-lived. Stock exchanges in the dual monarchy had plummeted, people held their breath and sought comfort: 'Gott erhalte' could be heard in the streets…[209]

What exactly had happened? Between 23 August and 12 September, along the almost 300 kilometre long front between the Vistula and Dniester rivers, the troops of the Dual Monarchy and the Tsar clashed. At first it seemed that the troops of the Habsburg Empire would be successful, but both sides of the front strengthened their troops and the Russians got more and more grip on the situation. After the 3rd Austrian army in particular was defeated, Conrad had to declare a general retreat on 11 September. Conrad had hopes to stabilise the front behind the San River, but soon Ludendorff was told that this was too optimistic an estimate and the area of Dunajec, 250 kilometres west of Lemberg, was called. [210]

This disastrous development had everything to do with the *grand strategy* of the dual monarchy. This was also strongly dependent on the success of the Schlieffenplan. For Vienna had to operate on several fronts at the same time: in the Balkans, and in Galicia, which meant great pressure rested on the armed forces. From the outset, the Austro-Hungarian Supreme Command therefore hoped for support from the German forces in their fight against the Russians in Galicia. There were two difficult conditions: the Schlieffen Plan had to succeed and, before any troops would be released from the Western Front (if any), the Germans had only the 8th Army, which, as we saw, was already a very limited force compared to the supremacy of Samsonov and Von Rennenkampf. Only through successful action at Tannenberg and the Mazurian Lakes could Ludendorff help the Austro-Hungarian troops with German Eastern Front troops.

Now, it had not actually been Vienna's intention to seek a major confrontation with the Russian army in Galicia. However, the overconfidence of the August days brought a tenor which we had also seen in Von François, which resulted in the fact that it was better to fight the war in the neighbour's garden than on ones own territory. From this point of view, the k.u.k. troops had come into action north of the River San on 23 August. Initially, as treacherous as Von François' success in reckoning with Gumbinnen, the advance went smoothly. Psychological motives also began to play a role. The Balkan operation against the recalcitrant Serbs had become more difficult than expected and the advance through Galicia, *'frisch und fröhlich'* - 'we only see Jews', reported one Tyrolean unit -[211] was good news for the home front. But it would not stay that way for long.

Over Brody and Tarnopol, strong Russian armies advanced. Among them was the first mobilised reserve division, which, according to Austrian historian Manfried Rauchensteiner, indicated that the Russians had already started mobilising in July and were thus well prepared for war.[212] Materially speaking, they were also well prepared compared to the k.u.k. troops. The Russians had better artillery, more machine guns and, above all, more men. East of Lemberg (Lwow/Lviv), a city that more than any other symbolised the fault line between east and west, things went wrong. General Brudermann's 3rd army was defeated by the tsarist units and on 2 September Lemberg fell into Russian hands. The fall of Lemberg, the capital of eastern Galicia, was primarily a psychological blow. The euphoria of victory was replaced by a defeat that was rapidly becoming apparent. The supreme command looked for scapegoats, Brudermann was dismissed, and with him a long series of other officers. There were also complaints about the soldiers, 'they were bitches', and about the Germans, 'we bear the burden alone'.[213] But the truth was that the Russians were simply stronger in the frontal showdown that took place. There was only one solution: back. A dangerous slide had begun.

After this information was given to Ludendorff by telephone, he was immediately confronted with a huge problem. There was a certain comparison with the Von Prittwitz and Von Rennenkampf case. Once an army was running, it was very difficult to bring it back under control. It was high time that Ludendorff shared these new insights with headquarters. The telephone conversation that followed brought more bad news. On this warm September day, Ludendorff heard that the Schlieffen plan had failed in the west. The French government had left Paris in a hurry on 2 September, but the French army had held its ground in a twelve-day battle along the River Marne. The far right wing had proved too weak to make its 'revolving door' complete. Von Kluck had marched southeast of the French capital, instead of encircling Paris from the west. Between his 1st army and Von Bülow's 2nd army, a gap had opened and there were no reserves to fill it. A hastily assembled French corps, commanded by General Gallieni had thrust fresh troops into the flank of Kluck's army. As a result, the German withdrawal had begun on 9 September. On 12 September, German troops were back at the river Aisne. The other armies, which were in the field west of Verdun, also had to give up ground. Ludendorff heard by telephone that Moltke had been badly hit. 'Traurige Julius' was a broken man. He felt he had failed. [214]

When the Eastern Front was discussed and the big problems for the dual monarchy were taken into account, Moltke authorised the creation of a new army, the 9th, which was to come to the aid of the dual monarchy. Ludendorff was to be the Chief of Staff under General Schubert, who was to deploy this army in Breslau. [215]

Ludendorff protested. *Never change a winning team*, he must have thought, when he pleaded to simply bring the whole 8th army to the south to let it exist as a 'unit' and to repeat the scenario of Tannenberg. The northern flank, after defeating Von Rennenkampf near the Masurian Lakes, would be relatively quiet, so that one could end up with relatively small units on the northern flank. The 8th army could then come to the aid of the Austro-Hungarian troops. Moltke asked for time to consider and the telephone conversation was broken off.

Ludendorff was left in uncertainty. What was certain was that this was the last conversation Ludendorff had with Moltke as his superior. The beaten man was replaced the very next day by General Erich von Falkenhayn, the Prussian Minister of Defence.[216]

The next morning Ludendorff was already on his way south. The frontal situation was uncertain, as were the German plans for regrouping. It had rained heavily and the ground was soaked. On the way, Ludendorff saw large streams of refugees and burnt houses. The rain began to come down harder and harder. By nightfall he reached Posen, his old fortified town, where he had been quartered ten years earlier. He realised that if he failed, his homeland would also be reduced to ashes. On the morning of 16 September, Ludendorff finally reached Breslau by car. Here, too, a gloomy report awaited him. His eldest stepson, Franz Pernet, who served with the 39th fuseliers, had been wounded in the head by a shrapnel during the fighting for Bouconville in France.

We will speak about Ludendorff's marriage later, but for now it is enough that this was a serious injury. Margarethe Ludendorff, Ludendorff's wife, did not leave his bed for the next few weeks, but the strong young man recovered and Margarethe was able to place the *Iron Cross on the* pillow next to his head. He healed well and Ludendorff gave him permission to report for pilot training.[217] Then, there was finally some good news. The supreme command had decided not to split up the winning team and to send Von Hindenburg and Hoffmann along to the south. The 8th army would defend the front in Prussia. The lion's share of the forces of the new 9th army was provided by the 8th.

Thus, Ludendorff's wishes were met. When Von Hindenburg and Hoffmann arrived, Ludendorff was already visiting the staff of the Austro-Hungarian army. He spoke with the Austrian commander, Archduke Friedrich and Chief of Staff Conrad. It was clear that in their three-week battle the Austrians had suffered a greater defeat than the Russians at Tannenberg. As many as 250,000 men had been killed, wounded and missing, while another 100,000 soldiers of the dual monarchy had been taken prisoner. Manfried Rauchensteiner even puts the loss at 400,000 men, of whom 100,000 were prisoners of war of the total of 800,000 men that Vienna had taken into the field. The Russians would have lost 250,000 men, of whom 40,000 were prisoners of war. In his memoirs, Hoffmann spoke of 'unheard-of losses'.[218] Many German-speaking officers were killed, a loss that could hardly be replaced.[219] There was an almost panicky retreat of the army of Germany's ally, which tried to save its skin in the pouring rain through muddy roads. On the west bank of the Wisloka as many as 40 divisions were crammed between the Weichsel and the Carpathians. Yet Conrad was still reasonably optimistic and believed that, with German help, he would be able to return to action in October. Crude as Ludendorff could be, he did not refrain from criticising Vienna's war preparations. A large part of the pre-war army had been destroyed in a few weeks, and now Berlin could come to the rescue.[220]

But there was no time for squabbling amongst themselves. The focus had to be on the current front situation and what Germany could do to stabilise the front again. Back in Breslau, Ludendorff consulted with Hindenburg and Hoffmann. Ludendorff proposed to repeat the Tannenberg scenario. He assumed that by defeating Samsonov, there would always be a weak connection between the Russian troops north and the attacking force that was close on the heels of the Austro-Hungarian army. In this vacuum the newly formed 9th army could push through. Ludendorff, in turn, could carry out his stage tactics by rapidly attacking large parts of the new army in the Weichselboog and capture the strategic stage city and railway junction of Warsaw. The troops of the dual monarchy could use this pressure to recapture lost territory. [221]

Another comparison with Tannenberg came to mind. At that time the fortress of Lötzen stood as an annoying sting in the front (the back) of the Russian army. Now the Austro-Hungarian troops passed through Przemyśl to the west and left thousands of wounded in the garrison town. These could, as long as they recovered quickly, take up arms again, because under the command of Field Marshal Hermann Kusmanek von Burgneustädten Przemyśl was developed into a formidable fortress, much larger than Lötzen, and also much stronger.

Przemyśl, the fortress whose name 'no German could spell or pronounce' (C.H. Baer *Zweiter band*, 223) was named after the Polish prince of the same name who founded the town in 750. Przemyśl had been a fortress since the 11th century, and had withstood sieges from Swedes, Cossacks and Zevenburgers. For centuries, the town maintained political and religious ties with the German-speaking territories. Under Field Marshal Hess, the town's defences had been modernised at the end of the 19th century.[222] The fortress was defended with 1,000 kilometres of barbed wire, 48 kilometres of ramparts and 200 artillery positions. Some of them still dated from 1861 and were of little value, but others were very modern and in any case stronger than those of the Russian force under Borislov that was besieging the fortress. Kusmanek von Burgneustädten rejected a request for capitulation on 2 October because, according to the Russian general Radko Dimitriew, 'military luck had left the Austro-Hungarian troops'. [223]

That was the calibre of men Ludendorff liked to work with. There were opportunities on the Eastern Front, still, despite all the dangers and the fact that Germany had already crawled through the eye of the needle twice. Ludendorff would get his trains rolling again on the internal lines, launch an attack and give the allies some air, after which they too could move forward.

While General Von Schubert, who was initially to take charge of the 9th army, was now given command of the 8th army, Ludendorff began to assemble his troops. The 8th army would continue to have the I. army corps, the I. reserve corps, the 3rd reserve division, the Landwehrdivision Goltz, the 1st cavalry division, some Landwehr units and the garrison of Königsberg. The new 9th army would consist of the I. garde reserve corps, the II. army corps, the XVII. corps and the XX. corps. The troops were assembled north of Cracow, while Von Hindenburg and Ludendorff moved their headquarters to Beuthen.[224]

Ludendorff's direct opponent was now Grand Duke Nikolai, a tall and military man. Nikolai had a formidable army at his disposal and his strategic options were far from exhausted despite the loss of Tannenberg and the setbacks of Von Rennenkampf. Now that the Austro-Hungarian troops were defeated, Nikolai was particularly keen on dealing with Ludendorff's troops. The Grand Duke realised that the German units were the greatest danger to Russia. The advance via the seam Samsonov-Warsaw was a logical one and on 22 September, during a consultation in Cholm with General Iwanow, Nikolai decided that the Russians should concentrate large amounts of troops between the Weichsel and the San, so that the German units would be caught in a trap. This would give the Russian units the opportunity to destroy their opponent and continue the advance against the German territory. Von Rennenkampf's army was also instructed to do this and by the end of September it resumed its attacks against East Prussia and the German 8th army.

For the plans between the rivers San and Weichsel Nikolai gathered a huge force. In the southernmost part was the 9th army, in the centre around Iwangorod (Deblin) the 4th army and north of that the 5th and 2nd army. In total there were about 60 divisions (against Ludendorff's 18 divisions), together about 1,250,000 men. The balance of forces was roughly 1:4 in favour of Russia.[225] To this were added new units in Von Rennenkampf's hinterland, the 1st and the 10th army. To make matters worse for the Germans, the German attack plans had fallen into the hands of the Russian army, so Nikolai was well aware of the balance of power. This advantage was shortly offset by the fact that the Russian plans in turn fell into German hands, after Von Mackensen's units ran into a Siberian division near the Polish town of Grojetz on 9 October.[226]

None of this prevented Ludendorff from sticking to his plans. This is typical of the war risk the Germans constantly took in these first months - due to the lack of a real *Grand strategy* in the east as a result of the Moltke legacy. In addition, the 18 German divisions were not at full strength due to the battle of Tannenberg and the Masurian Lakes. But Ludendorff was caught up in the coercive scenario that had unfolded on the Eastern Front. The Austro-Hungarian troops could only be set in motion again through German success and sustained pressure.

At least there was good news from Przemyśl, where the Russians had begun their bombardment of the fortified town on 3 October. On 5 October the Russians had started their assault, but they were beaten off and suffered heavy losses. The Russians had used 15, 18, 21 and even 24 cm. guns, but the forts held firm.

When the Russians moved into a castle at firing distance from the fortress with a staff, the Austro-Hungarian troops even used their secret weapon: their 30.5 cm cannon. Before the cannon could fire, the windows were removed from the surrounding streets. In three shots, the castle and its staff were pulverised. According to time documents, such as the *Wiener Reichspost*, this only made the Russians more furious and 'with whips the Russian officers drove their troops to the walls of the fortress'. Only in the south did they manage to penetrate to a fortress, when they attacked the garrison with eleven battalions. But there was no breakthrough here either. On 11 October, the siege was abandoned with 50,000 men lost, according to the *Wiener Reichspost*, which may have exaggerated a little here, but which reflected the grim atmosphere of those days very well. [227]

Even the first battle at Grojetz, which Von Mackensen won, was a support for the double-monarchy army, which was creaking at the seams and which desperately resumed its march eastwards. The roads on which the German-Austrian-Hungarian advance took place were sunk in mud. Even on the main road of the German attack route, Krakow-Warsaw, the mud came up to the knee. By night it was so cold that the ground froze. Wind blew across the land, and from their dilapidated houses, stoic Polish peasants and black-clad Jews with ringlets silently watched the German soldier, the *Landser*. But Ludendorff ruled with a firm hand, always keeping an eye on the daily tempo. Despite the extremely bad road conditions, the German troops managed to march 30 kilometres a day, so a week after the start of the attack on 28 September, German units were at the Weichsel.

Following this, the advance of the double-monarchy had started on 4 October, and the next day they crossed the Wisloka River and reached the San on 9 October. The attack by the German allies was 'well under way', Max Hoffmann noted in his memoirs.[228]

This new success of the Austro-Hungarian units had everything to do with Grand Duke Nikolai's plan. Units were withdrawn from the southern front in order to make the Russian attack force for the German 9th army as strong as possible. Ludendorff had in any case succeeded in relieving the double monarchy. Now the question remained: how would the new German-Russian showdown end?

Some of the Russian troops were deployed frontally against the German units, others gathered to make a pincer manoeuvre. It was a grand plan, a 'good plan' as Hoffmann believed. [229]

The German troops had now advanced from their starting line between Kalisch and Tarnow to just in front of the Weichsel River and, moving with the Weichsel Bank, were now turning northwards towards Warsaw. From north to south, Ludendorff had the 18. Landwehr, 8th cavalry division, 35th reserve, XVII. corps, XX. corps, garde reserve, XI. corps at Cracow and then the 1st Austro-Hungarian corps. Especially the units from XX. corps turned in (from Random) in northern direction. Yet, the advance was not without setbacks. Soon, the numerical strength of the tsarist troops made itself felt. The Russian units succeeded in establishing large bridgeheads on the western bank of the Vistula, and repeated German attempts to push them back in an easterly direction failed. It was mainly hardened Caucasian units that held on with great determination near Koshenice, even though their artillery barrages were literally in the waters of the Vistula. [230]

The German attack on Warsaw was hampered by the difficult bridgeheads on the eastern flank. In addition, Russian units around Warsaw were rapidly reinforced. Not only did units gather to the west and south of the city, but strong troops also gathered at Nowogeoriewsk to the north of the city to apply Nikolai's pincer manoeuvre. A dangerous situation began to emerge. The Caucasian units tried to enlarge their bridgehead in continuous attacks. With difficulty the German troops were able to repel these attacks, which resulted in terrible losses for the Russian army. The other Russian bridgeheads proved unviable, so the front along the Vistula became a reasonably stable front after all. But the Germans had lost time and the matter turned to Von Mackensen. The question now arose again of what exactly the German strategy should be. What were Von Mackensen's real chances. Hoffmann wrote in his memoirs that one had to persevere now, gain time to give the Austro-Hungarian units on the San room to thrust eastwards. This might force the Russian Grand Prince to free up units for the southern front again, after which the German chances could be reconsidered. The chances of a tactical victory at Warsaw now seemed slim; rather they would have to be careful not to be caught in the crosshairs themselves.

But the Germans were not the only ones in a difficult position. The Russians, too, were close to despair. Nikolayevich had increasing difficulties in keeping the Poles for the Slavic cause. Every day the words *Still Poland is not lost* echoed through the streets of Warsaw, to keep up the courage, but there was hunger in the city. There were 60,000 unemployed and hunger riots were feared. In addition, the windows of the city were shaking from the artillery fire in Warsaw's front yard. For the Poles, it was clear that the Germans might show up at any moment, even though the Russians tried to keep their nerve. Huge streams of wounded passed through the city streets, and the staff of the Reichstag had already been evacuated to St. Petersburg. Polish despair of the Russian regime was also evident when the pro-Slavic poet Tadhäus Micinski was deported to

Russia.[231] Even within the pan-Slavist camp, belief in the tsarist potential had apparently been shaken.

Francis McCallagh of the *Daily News* from Chicago was in Warsaw during these days and noted that zeppelins and even several German planes appeared simultaneously - 'one could speak of a squadron' - over the 'Polish' capital as omens of Von Mackensen's troops. According to the reports, the Germans were twelve kilometres from the city and the Russians were bringing everyone who could carry a gun into the field. 'The fighting is more serious and intense than at Tannenberg', McCallagh thought.[232]

Stumbling between strategy and tactics, Ludendorff was above the cards every day. In any case, the first plan, air for Vienna, had succeeded. Now, it was time to fight for the sequel. Anxiously, he inquired constantly about Von Conrad's progress. It seemed that the advance east of the San would not go smoothly. So Von Mackensen, who had stopped just south of Warsaw on 12 October, had to stand his ground. It was raining incessantly, and the German pioneers were working hard to improve the roads and railways. The telegraph poles had been destroyed by the Russians, so that all orders from Von Hindenburg and Ludendorff had to be transmitted to the front by orderlies.

Meanwhile, 14 divisions had gathered against Von Mackensen's five divisions. Coupled with the exciting hours around the Weichsel bridgeheads, this created a situation in which Ludendorff 'didn't sleep a wink'.[233] From 15 October on Von Mackensen was in heavy combat with the Russian army. Since the advance across the San did not go smoothly, Ludendorff had to gain time. A request to the Austro-Hungarian General Staff for reinforcements was unsuccessful, and since the German army could not free up any troops due to the situation on the Western Front, Ludendorff even tried to use a direct line to the Emperor Franz Joseph in order to free up troops from the dual monarchy. However, the Kaiser refused to intervene in the military. Ludendorff had no other option than to regroup his own limited resources in the Weichselboog in an extremely complicated and not without risk. The aim was to bring as many units as possible northwards, so that Von Mackensen could withstand the increasing pressure from the (south) east and north.

'We must perform the impossible', said Von Mackensen in a letter home, 'but let no one know',[234] he added. Like Ludendorff, Von Mackensen feared the verdict at home. 'What must they think at home'[235], Ludendorff wrote in his memoirs about the retreat before Warsaw. For it had become clear that Von Mackensen was in an extremely dangerous situation and that a retreat had become inevitable. But since the troops were in combat, it was very important to go back 'not too early and not too late'[236].

Ludendorff consulted with Von Hindenburg, who approved the retreat plans. On the night of 17 October, Von Mackensen fell back. The Warsaw dream was over and the time gained by the Austro-Hungarian troops at the San had not been sufficiently used. And yet, on paper, things had looked reasonable. The dual monarchy had almost half a million men here and during the last three weeks considerable reinforcements had arrived on the k.u.k. front. Only the cavalry had lost some of its strength due to a lack of horses. But the recruitment system was functioning. As a result, 477,000 troops and more than 26,000 horsemen were available[237]. Under General Svetozar Boroevic, the army of the dual monarchy had relieved Przemyśl, but the progress was only short-lived.

The German troops fell back to the line just south of Lowitsch to Nowo Miassto, where the XX. corps joined in. Ludendorff had succeeded in placing a Landwehreen unit between Von Mackensen and the XX. corps so that there were some fresh units in the front line. The whole manoeuvre was skilfully executed and the great crisis was over for the moment, but the retreat was not. The Hungarian 1st Army, which formed the southern flank in the Weichselboog, now began to recede strongly. Manfried Rauchensteiner estimated that the 1st army lost between 40,000 and 50,000 men in the so-called 'Battle of Iwangorod'. In the night of 17 to 18 October, the Russians had crossed the San further south themselves, now that the Austro-Hungarian troops were so hesitant. The 9th army was in danger of being airlifted.

On 27 October, Ludendorff gave the order for the general retreat. The Russian army remained close behind the Germans, but the retreat was orderly. During the advance, Ludendorff had already placed explosives everywhere in order to destroy the (newly built up) infrastructure again, which now happened. A burned-out Poland remained behind.

The Austro-Hungarian officers scolded the Germans whose 'adventure on the Weichsel' had brought these problems with it. The Germans, on the other hand, saw themselves as victims of Viennese incompetence. The latter was also evident from the fact that the supply of the Austro-Hungarian army was so poorly organised that the liberators of Przemyśl immediately began to plunder the town. Normally, the fortress held provisions for 90 days, but the hungry liberators immediately made a hole in it. 'Przemyśl' is firmly in our hands', the press chanted, but they did not mention that the town had been 'eaten out'.

When the army of the dual monarchy had to fall back to the west, and Przemyśl was once again surrounded, the situation did not look as rosy as it did at the first encirclement. Instead of 85,000 soldiers, there were 130,000 in the city, and instead of 3,000 horses, there were 21,000, while food for these faithful quadrupeds was in short supply. The population had also increased by 30,000 due to the return of refugees, all of whom had to be fed.[238] A dark scenario was unfolding.

In the meantime, the commanders had come to new insights. 'Modern' warfare also had its limitations. The German advance, with or without resistance, came to a halt at about 100 kilometres (at least for a few days) from her railway lines. The Russians, relying heavily on their horses, could push for 120 kilometres, but even then they were out of air.[239] The maps thus showed that the Russian army, even with its current successful advance, would still come to a halt before the German Reich borders, which it did around 2 November.[240] The Germans would have to use this moment again to seize the initiative.

In view of the unfavourable balance of power for Germany, it was clear to Ludendorff that the Germans had to retain the initiative as far as possible and try to defeat the enormous Russian steamroller blow by blow. It was time for new important strategic consultations. Ludendorff was summoned to Berlin to meet Von Falkenhayn. This conversation came at an important moment, 'our better leadership cannot withstand the continuous superiority in the long run', said Von Mackensen rightly.[241] The eastern front was in great danger. The genius behind the conversation was Ludendorff's Austrian colleague Conrad, who tried to convince Berlin to release more troops for the Eastern Front.

Ludendorff's journey to Erich von Falkenhayn took place at an important moment in the developments on the Western Front. On 17 October, the day of Von Mackensen's retreat near Warsaw, the offensive near Ieperen had begun in the west. Ludendorff's thoughts were already turning to new German offensives; offensives which would actually mask the relative weakness of the central powers. The Germans wanted to enforce something that history had already rejected after the catastrophic August and September days. Especially in the West. The Ypres offensive was already an alternative to the failed Schlieffen plan. On 14 September, Von Falkenhayn had been appointed to the position of Moltke, who officially went on 'sick leave'. This had everything to do with the fact that the German armies were stranded at the Marne and eventually even had to accept the retreat. Paris had remained French. By mid-September, the Western Front had come to a standstill, but it was far from stable. The German front between the Oise and Reims was struggling to hold and in Champagne the situation was also worrying. The Franco-British troops smelled a victory, but both sides still had to learn their limits.

The new strongman at the top of the German army, Erich von Falkenhayn, was above all focused on the Western Front and relations between the Von Hindenburg-Ludendorff and Falkenhayn duo would soon become very tense. The reason for this can be easily found in Falkenhayn's memoir[242] which he - like Caesar - wrote in the third person. Von Falkenhayn largely blamed the Eastern Front for the setbacks in the West. They had 'suffered a lot' from the delivery of the three (eventually two) army corps to the east, whereby Von Falkenhayn conveniently forgot that Ludendorff had not asked for these reinforcements. Von Falkenhayn pointed out, and rightly so, that these units came from the extreme right flank, which was missed at the Marne.[243] Furthermore, he believed that 'all reserves had gone east', referring to the reinforcements that Von Hindenburg and Ludendorff had received during their operations in Galicia.[244]

Here, Von Falkenhayn showed no understanding whatsoever of the context in which these measures had been taken. Firstly, they were not particularly large reinforcements, secondly, the 8th army had been split into two armies (the 8th and the 9th) and, most importantly, the new 9th army had faced the task of giving air to the demoralised and particularly hard-hit army of the dual monarchy, allowing them to recover.

Studying Von Falkenhayn's notes from the first months of the war, it seems that the Eastern Front interested him more politically than militarily. The most important thing was that the Austro-Hungarian units were not defeated in such a way that the political balance of power changed to the disadvantage of the Centrals, whereby he especially paid attention to the position of the Balkan states and Turkey.[245] The fate of the poorest people at the San played a subordinate role.

Von Falkenhayn's thoughts were, as with Von Schlieffen, on the Western Front. That was where victory was to be sought. He started with the in itself correct conclusion that the German military headquarters had to be moved closer to the front, which was done. The generals packed their bags and went from Luxembourg to Charville-Mézieres. He also looked at the Channel coast as a place where Germany could seize the initiative again and separate the British allies from the French. For Falkenhayn stated that the course of the battle of the Marne was a serious setback, but not the final defeat of Germany. Like Von Schlieffen, Falkenhayn now largely left the East for what it was and went in search of that one capital victory. A truly fatal and brutal period of the First World War had thus begun, which would rage on until the end of 1916 and would bear witness to a stupor the world had not yet known, eventually centring around the name of Verdun.

The relationship between the Supreme Command and the Ludendorff-Hindenburg duo was to become very difficult. But for the moment, Falkenhayn got his way. Ludendorff would have to make do with what he had. Possibly Ludendorff also agreed with this, based on his thoughts with Von Schlieffen. Ypres

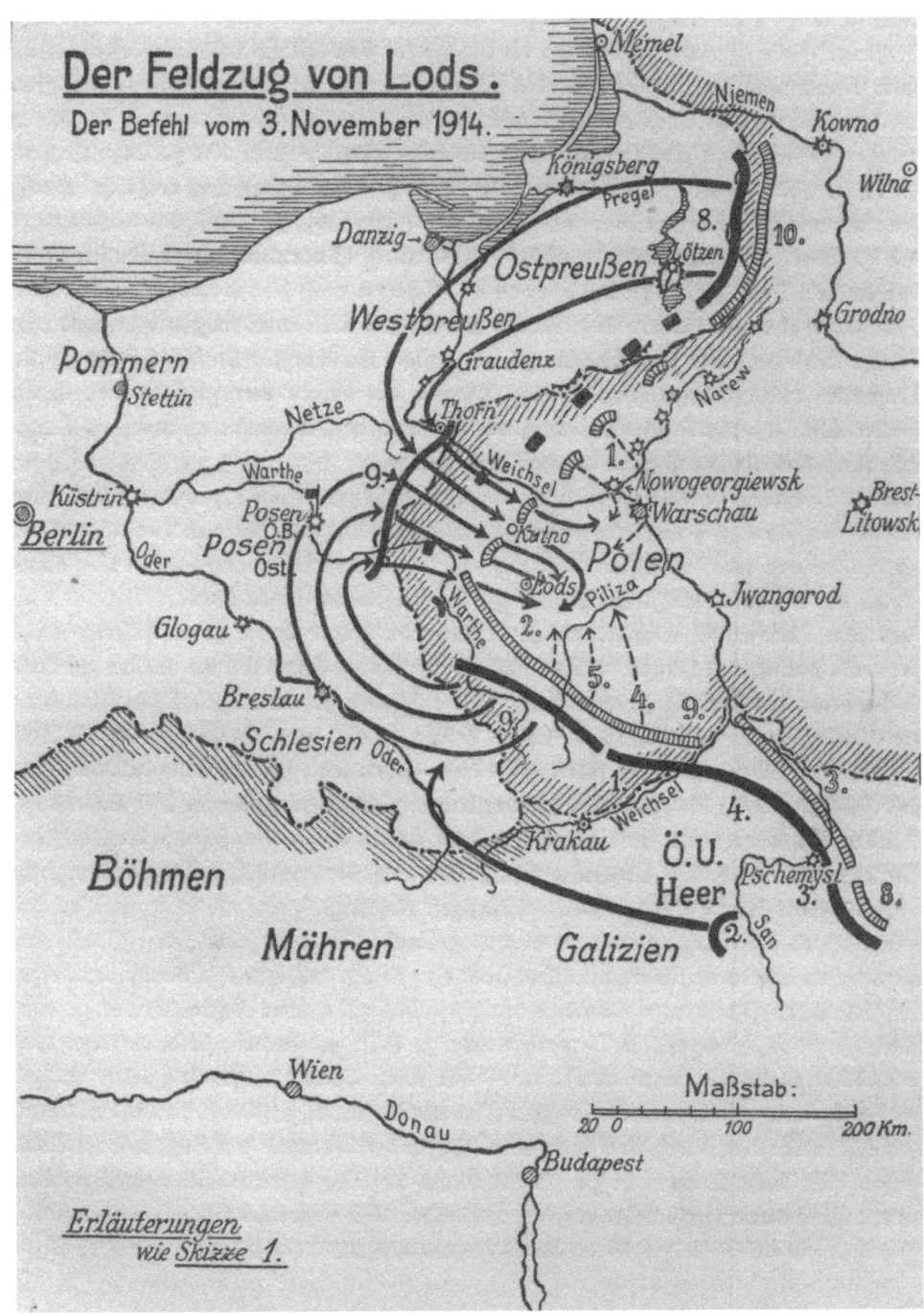

Battle of Warsaw

promised, at least in the eyes of Von Falkenhayn, still a possibility to seal the war by a big battle, and after that there were plenty of troops for the East front. The situation in the east was also quite different. Ludendorff could not make a concrete proposal that would have a decisive effect on the war. [246]

Ludendorff was glad when he left for the East again. The peaceful situation in Berlin had disappointed him. The people were not serious enough for him, and seriousness would not leave Ludendorff, once the cheerful dancer of old, until his death. [247]

Back in the East, the chain of command had in any case become clearer, on orders from on high. Von Hindenburg, assisted by Ludendorff, now commanded the Supreme Command Ost which extended to the 8th and 9th armies - the latter now under command of Von Mackensen. The situation was very serious, but Ludendorff's prediction that the Russian offensive would come to a standstill proved true. Thus, a moment of reflection was possible.

Ludendorff had led the retreat with an iron fist. He was constantly approached with requests to spare roads, bridges, railways and important economic targets (coal mines), but Ludendorff categorically refused. He had everything of war value - except for food - destroyed, so that the tsarist army would be in a 'barren' area and would slow down the advance, which it did.

Meanwhile, new units trickled in, mostly Landwehreen units of relatively low value. The reserve divisions were also not yet sharp enough for Ludendorff. 'The people have heart, but they are not yet soldiers', [248] he wrote.

In order to maintain the situation on the slowly stabilising front, the Supreme Command Ost had at its disposal the I., XX., XVII., II., V., and VI. army corps, stationed in East and West Prussia, Pomerania, Posen, and Silesia. The headquarters of Von Hindenburg and Ludendorff had been moved to the royal castle in Posen, where it would remain until February 1915. Here you could feel 'the pulse of the German nation', [249] Ludendorff thought.

In his mind, a new great plan was already maturing. Possibly under the impression of Falkenhayn's great ambitions in the west, Ludendorff's thoughts were once again conjuring up a *Gesamtplan*, a total battle, which would suddenly change the course and allow the German-Austrian-Hungarian army, which had just been driven back, to head east again, in a blessed march which would determine the outcome of the war. Where could such a result be achieved? Again Ludendorff's eye went to the dividing lines between the armies, that ever so vague in-between area, where opportunities might lie. What if the German army now gathered its forces in Silesia and from there between Thorn and Wreschen in the area of the 9th army and the southern flank of the Masurian area? The Russian 1st Army lying west of the Weichsel could be punched in the flank, then perhaps a great victory over the Germans was waiting there.

The maps were rolled out again. To the north units from the Graudenz area could give support, while from north to south the XXV. corps, I. reserve corps, XX. corps, XVII. corps (near Wreschen) the XI. corps and the II. corps could destroy the gathering units of the I. army on the west bank of the Weichsel in a crescent located between Neidenburg and Kreuzburg (where the 2nd k.u.k. army joined up). There were uncertainties in the story. For example, there were strong units around Nowo Georgiewsk, just north of Warsaw, which could throw a spanner in the works, and other armies further south. But the always serious Ludendorff also had an optimistic side, maybe in a surprise action it would be possible to defeat the 8 to 10 Russian divisions - which were suspected to be in the direct front field - and possibly causing the whole front to shift. This would give air and space to the large but cumbersome Viennese army and of course to the 8th army, which now remained weighed down by Von Rennenkampf's relentless punching actions, which had finally caused the 8th army to fall back into the Angerapp-Stellung.

The main burden of the attack was to be borne by Mackensens 9th army, which for this purpose moved its headquarters to Hohensalza.[250] Here, the troops began to gather in the Silesian terrain. It was an undertaking typical of Ludendorff, who again made extensive use of stage technology and interior lines. The logistical operation went like clockwork and was described by one historian as a 'masterpiece'.[251] The risks were also similar. Troops were deployed that could not be missed elsewhere. Nervous days would begin, only one small mistake and the consequences would be disastrous. This, too, was typical of all German operations, both at the highest strategic level and often in the immediate field. But Ludendorff felt he had no choice, in view of the overall situation.

On 11 November, while in the west the battle of Langemarck made its appearance in the history books, the German attack began.

'We were facing a new beginning', Hoffmann thought, looking back. The Russians celebrated their 'victory' before Warsaw and drew energy from this for renewed offensives.[252] Time was running out. The city of Lódz was seen as the focal point of the new action. There, the concentrically attacking German units could meet and hopefully crush large parts of the I. Army. Von Mackensen had a total of 11.5 infantry divisions and five cavalry divisions at his disposal. The units were reinforced with additional artillery, which had been made available by the various fortifications. The XXV. reserve corps had been assigned additional officers as well as some machine gun units from the Thorn fortress.

The attack was to be carried out 'quickly and energetically', Grünert reported to Von Mackensen just before the attack.[253] However, developments were not very hopeful from the start. The Russian units, hardy troops of the V. Siberian corps, were surprised by the sudden German attack, but put up strong resistance. Eventually, they soaked up the entire front. A certain optimism arose; had it not been the same way with the Masurian Lakes? The positions near Wlozlawek were first stormed by the 41st infantry division, which tried to carry out a concentric attack. Finally, during the night, the 49th reserve division managed to take Wlozlawek. The division commander was not with the troops and was killed. On 13 November, the retreat of the Siberian units was noticeable, but on the 14th heavy hand-to-hand combat took place again near Dombe.[254]

It was clear that the Russian army commander Scheidemann did not want to cooperate with Ludendorff's total solution. The XVII., XI, and XX. corps carried the main burden of the attack. Heavy fighting raged around Kutno for three days, which in some sources has gone down in history as 'The Battle of Kutno'.[255] Around 17 November, the German units were close to Lódz. But here the attack stopped. At first there were radio messages suggesting that the Russians wanted to retreat but at Lódz, Russian units, including those from other Russian armies than the 1st, quickly piled up. The XX. corps was even slowly pushed back under this heavy pressure. 'Nothing could stop them',[256] Ludendorff later noted.

At Skiernjewitz and Brsheshiny the situation became tense. There was even a threat of German units being trapped, partly due to the fact that the German north wing, although achieving good defensive successes, had advanced only slowly. An exciting moment then arrived. Hoffmann called from headquarters to see if Von Mackensen could hold out. Von Mackensen withdrew for a few minutes, then reported back to his fellow officers and said, 'We are staying'.[257] Quartermaster Sauberzweig, who was present, called this his most emotional moment of the war. It was, in his opinion, the moment when the decision was made to defend Germany east of the borders, and Von Mackensen decided to do so, no matter how difficult and risky the situation was. He also noted that Hoffmann had asked this question without Ludendorff's knowledge, because Ludendorff, Sauberzweig believed, would have taken Von Mackensen's stand for granted.[258]

This indicates that the situation for Von Mackensen was more dire than Ludendorff revealed at the time and during the writing of his memoirs. After the war, Hoffmann, too, dismissed the matter somewhat timidly and spoke of a 'major setback'.[259] After the war, Von Mackensen recalled that the operation had been little discussed beforehand and he felt that he had been on his own. In his notes, he retrospectively portrayed the battle of Wlozlawek and Kutno as a victory, which they were at best tactically, and even then laboriously. Wlozlawek and Kutno were only stations on the way to Ludendorff's great goal. [260]

In the night of 23-24 November, the plight of the Germans ended and the German breakthrough to the north succeeded, lifting some divisions out of the near position of the Russian counterattacks. The situation calmed down somewhat, but this was by no means the result hoped for. However, the 3rd gardivision of the XXV. reserve corps, among others, had taken about 10.000 Russian soldiers prisoner, whom they managed to carry with them during the retreat. Despite this success of division commander Litzmann, it was not the intended destruction of the 1st Russian army.

What the supreme command achieved in the end was that the Russians, who suffered very heavy losses during their attacks on the retreating German units, also revised their front line. As a result, Lódz fell into German hands on 6 December 1914 and the front line stabilised between Sochatschew - Rawna - Chentziny.

The year 1914 had brought no decision in the East. Not in the field and not in politics. On the day Lódz fell, Chancellor Von Bethmann-Hollweg visited the German staff in Posen, where he met Max Hoffmann. The latter asked him why, as Chancellor, he did not make it clear to foreign countries that Berlin had no intention of continuing to occupy Belgian territory after the war. Von Bethmann-Hollweg agreed that this was also Germany's policy, but that he could not say this openly because then his position would be jeopardised. Hoffmann was astonished that a politician did not dare to say what was good for his country for fear of his job. For men of the Prussian code of honour, to which Ludendorff also belonged, such political handiwork was incomprehensible, and for Ludendorff, in the long run downright despicable. The suspicion and antipathy for Weimar, with its 'party chaos' and small particularist sectional interests, would result from this. Hoffmann understood that the image of a permanent German occupation of Belgium would be unpalatable on the continent, especially to the British, who traditionally pursued the *balance of power*. A political solution to the military scenario that had got out of hand was not on the horizon.

Winter fell along the eastern front. At Gumbinnen, German and Russian officers came out of their trenches and handed out rum, cigars and cigarettes. A harmonica provided some music. There was dancing in the snowy fields. 'The war was still chivalrous', said Von der Falk, commander of the 2nd Insterburger infantry division. [261]

Chapter 4

Winter in Masuria and crisis in the German leadership

The year 1915 began for Ludendorff and von Hindenburg again in the Masurian region. Here, the 8th army of Fritz von Below with 100,000 troops had been holding out along a 170 km long front against the Russian 10th army of General Siewers (220,000 men). Von Below had limited himself to the defence along Gumbinnen, Darkhemen and the Angerapp.[262] After the failure of the ambitions in the Weichselboog, the focus was on the old front sector. Reinforcements had arrived; four new corps, the XXXVIII., XXXIX. and XXXX. reserve corps and the Saarbrück XXI. army corps. For the most part, these were new, inexperienced troops from the reserve, which resulted in a rather strange age structure within the units of the Oberost. However, Von Hindenburg and Ludendorff were happy to receive reinforcements, despite the fact that the supreme command concentrated its efforts on the western front.

Von Hindenburg and Ludendorff saw opportunities. There were similarities with previous operations. The new enterprise began, as always, with large-scale troop movements. The new units were to be stationed on the northern flank of the 8th army, and to this end were to be transformed into yet another new German army, the 10th, commanded by Generaloberst Von Eichhorn. This would cause a shift of power in favour of the Germans. Ludendorff had calculated that they would have about 250.000 men at their disposal against the 220.000 Russians. The aim was to turn the new army from the north to the east and southeast into the flank of Siewer's troops, while the 8th army would have to break through in a frontal attack after thorough artillery shelling around Johannisburg. The whole thing therefore most resembled the first battle of the Masurian Lakes.

The goals were, as always, ambitious: the destruction of the Russian 10th army. Ludendorff followed a very practical concept. He wanted to break the Russian armies one by one. In doing so, he had to make sure that the Austro-Hungarian army would remain intact and the war would be concentrated outside of German territory.

As always, there were snags. Ludendorff had heard that a new Russian army was being prepared in the surroundings of Nowogeorgiewsk, north of the Weichsel River, which would bear the number 12. The winter battle in the Mazurs against the 10th Russian army was therefore under time pressure. The bulk of Ludendorff's tactics relied on temporary superiority.

From north to south, the German army - in early February 1915 - looked as follows. South of the Memel between Tilsit and Darkhemen was the 10th army under Von Eichhorn's command. This army consisted of the 5th infantry brigade, the XXI. army corps, the XXXVIII. reserve corps, the XXXIX. reserve corps the Landwehrdivision Königsberg, the 1st cavalry division and some units around Tilsit. The lion's share of the load would be six infantry units, from north to south the 31st, 41st, 78st, 77st, 76st and 75st infantry division. These units would push from the front between Lasdeken and Schorellen to the southeast on the extreme north flank, followed by the 1st cavalry division, which had done such excellent defensive work during the Tannenberg battle. To the south, the main force of Von Eichhorn's 10th army would be supported by some Landwehr units operating between Insterburg and Darkhem. The focal point of Von Below's 8th army was all the way south at Johannisburg, where the majority of the XX. and XXXX. corps was encamped on the Johannisburg heath. At Lötzen, further north, was a second spearhead of the 1st corps, supported by Landwehreen units. At Darkhmen, the 3rd reserve division joined up with the 10th Landwehrdivision of the 10th army. The objective here was to break open the front near Johannisburg with artillery and then advance with the infantry.

On 7 February the starting signal was given. In order to confuse the Russians, the actions in the south near Johannisburg started a day earlier than those of the 10th army. On 7 February, the battle in the swampy, boggy area of Johannisburg began. It was anything but easy terrain. It was snowing incessantly and the Russian defenders had well-developed positions. There was no direct attack on Johannisburg on the first day, but a number of important preliminary combat operations were carried out successfully.

The 2nd infantry division managed to reach the west bank of the Pisseck and capture a bridgehead at Snopken. The 79th and 80th reserve division also advanced and took up favourable positions. In some places the Germans had penetrated 40 kilometres into Russian territory.[263]

Nowhere along the front, however, were there any signs of Russian encirclement or retreat. It seemed as if the Russians were completely unaware of the pincer operation Ludendorff had in store for them. Siewers did react to the actions near Johannisburg; reinforcements arrived from the south at breakneck speed. The local commander Liztman of the German XL. reserve corps immediately threw units of the XL. reserve corps from Kolno in a southern direction, towards the marching Russians. They were surprised and beaten back, leaving hundreds of prisoners of war and some artillery pieces behind.

Now the way was clear for a frontal attack on Johannisburg, which was launched by Von der Falk's 2nd division. These units, soon supported by flanking attacks from the 80th reserve division, closed in on the town from several sides. Siewers had reinforced Johannisburg - as it was an important traffic junction - with two infantry regiments, whom initially put up considerable resistance, which resulted in house-to-house fights. But the fear of being surrounded set in and the Russians fell back while more than 3,000 men were taken as prisoners of war by the German troops. Johannisburg was in German hands. [264]

That was a good start, but nothing more. By now the Russians had realised that this was a major operation, not only from the front around Johannisburg, but also further north, near Lötzen and - more importantly - near the German 10th army on its extreme northern flank. Siewers tried desperately to strengthen the front in the south opposite the 8th army, because here he would have the best hope for reinforcements, which were coming from the south. The weather came to the aid of the Russians. While Below was pushing his troops to the limit and the 3rd cavalry brigade was deployed where the 2nd division had been successful, it started snowing heavily. There was a blizzard, which made the roads more and more difficult to traverse. There was also a lack of oats for the horses and the sled-mounted guns often had to be pushed by soldiers. Provisions too started to fall behind. The winter battle therefore had to be fought on partly empty stomachs. Despite this, the 80th reserve division conquered Drygallen,[265] during the night of 9 to 10 February, but after that the advance towards Augustow slowly came to a halt due to renewed Russian resistance. The terrain also favoured the Russians, consisting of a chain of lakes.

Further north, the German attack also went according to plan. At Lötzen, the troops of the 1st Army corps made good progress and at Darkhem and the 3rd German reserve division managed to take several hundred prisoners of war. More important here was how Von Eichhorn's 10th army fared. Here too, the bad weather played a role. There were snowstorms, which meant that the field artillery often could not be deployed and had to drag along behind the German infantry, which was marching with great difficulty. But Von Eichhorn had imposed an iron discipline on his troops and they marched on, driving the Cossacks from their forward positions, who fell back into the woods, and from there continued to frustrate the German advance. In the end, however, the Russians were not able to stop the German troops that were turning in south-eastern direction. Burning villages marked the retreat route of the Russians, who did not want to leave any shelter.

At Wladyslawowo, the Russians tried to stop the Germans again, but as if on cue, the German troops attacked. The men had been marching for 29 hours incessantly and were chilled to the bone. Quarters were available here and nothing seemed to stop them. The Russians had to retreat and left 1,000 men as prisoners of war.[266]

Even more martial misfortune awaited the 10th army. At Eydtkuhnen and Wirballen, the 56th Russian reserve division was taken completely by surprise. The unit was apparently not yet aware of the German advance and thought itself safe behind the Russian lines. As many as 10,000 soldiers fell into German hands, as well as 6 artillery pieces, 80 field kitchens, three field hospitals and enormous supplies. The XXXIX. reserve corps was immediately relieved of its supply problem.[267]

The 8th army now focused on Lyck. Ludendorff urged his soldiers to make haste. There were indications that the Russians were starting to fall back to the east and the Lyck road junction was of great strategic importance. But the place was defended by the III. Siberian corps, which bravely held its ground. Even the experienced 2nd infantry division and the 5th infantry brigade were initially unable to break the resistance. New snowstorms presented themselves; the barrels of the rifles and cannons became clogged with snow and the water in the water-cooled machine guns froze. Near Baitkowen, on 12 February, the 5th brigade was even temporarily beaten back. Only when the 80th reserve division attacked the Siberians from the south did the front start moving again. On 14 February, Neunenbyrg, south of Lyck was captured and shortly afterwards the town and 5000 Russian soldiers fell into German hands. In the burning centre of the town, the various German units met, having had to keep in touch by primitive means. On the burning market square, the prisoners of war and the 14 captured artillery pieces were gathered. In total, the XL Reserve corps had now taken 34 officers and 8,000 men prisoner since the start of the winter battle. The bridge two kilometres east of the city had been blown up by the Russians during the retreat in order to gain time. German pioneers immediately set to work.

Kaiser Wilhelm II visited Lyck on 14 February. His visit was later transformed into a drawing by Felix Schwormstädt and shows a triumphant Kaiser being celebrated by the troops amidst grimacing Russian prisoners.[268]

The soliders could not rest yet. After Lyck, Augustow was on the programme. Due to the frontal attack to the east and the southward turning attack of the 10th army, more and more Russian units were trapped. It was of the utmost

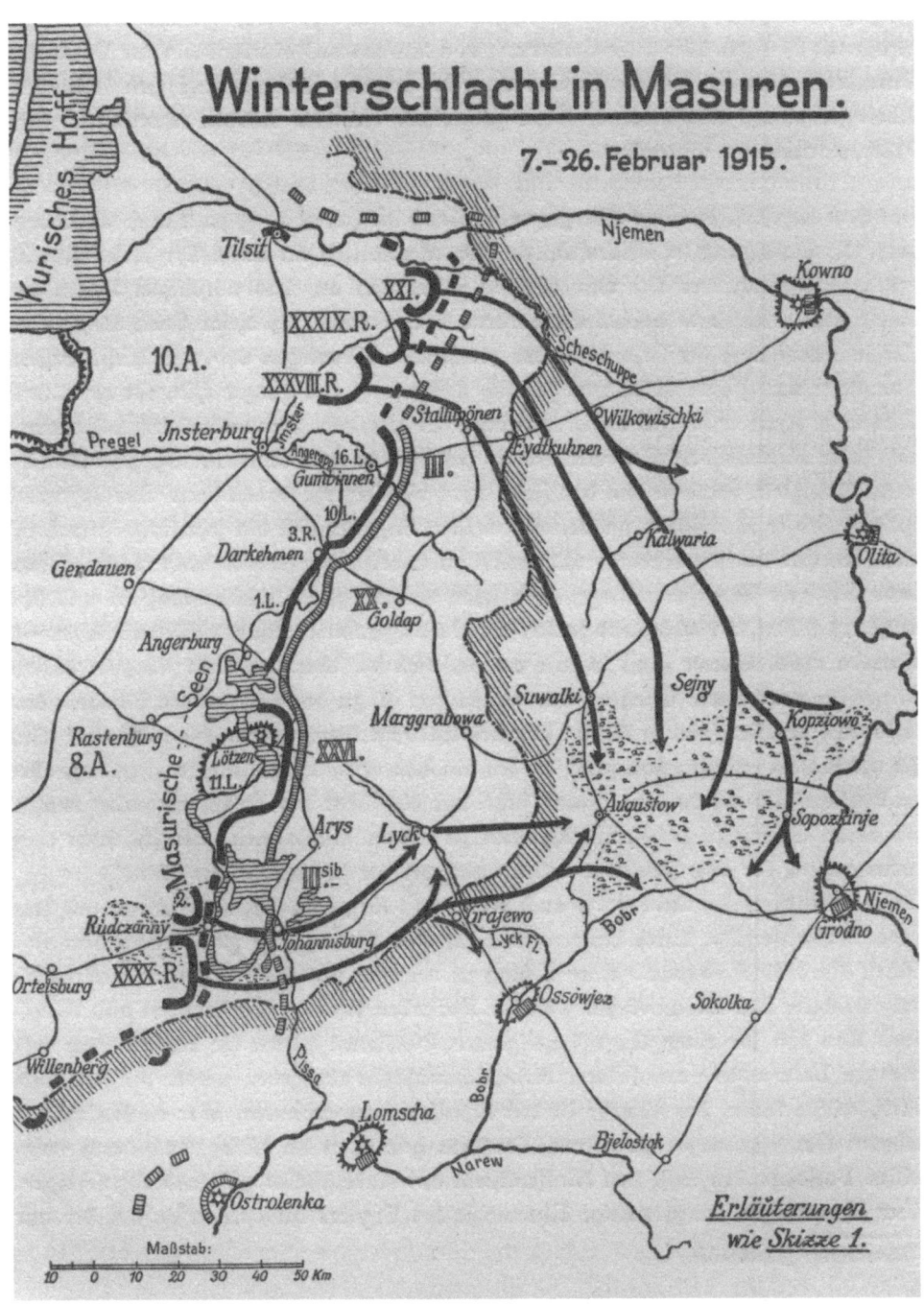

Battle of Masuria

importance to Ludendorff that the Russians would have no time to restore the front and bring in reinforcements, or to escape. As in all of Ludendorff's operations, great risks were taken. The units deployed to defend the southern flank of the XL Reserve corps were now brought in at breakneck speed to be directed towards the city via a breakthrough of the 79th Reserve division near Rajgrod, south-west of Augustow. Further north, the 3rd cavalry brigade had achieved great success by crossing the Augustowski Canal as early as 15 February. The 2nd infantry division, the 5th infantry brigade and the 3rd reserve division were now all thrown forward. On 16th, the battle seemed to be pinned down, but shortly afterwards the front began to move again and the Russian troops began to give way. On 17 February, the 8th army scored a major victory by entering Augustow. Again, 5000 Russian soldiers and twelve pieces of artillery were captured. [269]

Equally successful were the days of the 10th army. After the initial heavy fighting, the Russian army was now on the run. In some places, the German troops were ankle deep in sugar, oats, bread and tea, which the Russians dropped from their moving wagons into the snow. Many wagons were overtaken and thousands of boots and other equipment - including all possible stolen items from Prussia, even women's clothing - were captured. The troops of the 10th army sometimes marched up to 40 kilometres a day and on 16 February, they were just north of Augustow. On 17th, it came to very heavy fighting there. Ironically, the 17th German regiment lost its flag for some time until it was found, literally buried under a pile of corpses.[270]

Ludendorff and Von Hindenburg followed the war effort closely. On the map, the results looked spectacular. The movements had been made, but were they successful? In the night of 17 to 18 February, the first reports came in from the 8th and 10th armies, which painted a picture of about 60,000 Russian prisoners of war.[271] However, it was clear that there were still many troops in the forest areas who were trying to escape to the south or east. Bitter fighting took place in the following days, with both sides suffering heavy losses. The German commander Von Estorff of the 65th infantry brigade was killed. Near Krasnybor, the Russian troops were literally driven into the ice-cold Memel. Again and again, the Russians fought bravely, even in hopeless situations, and tried to break through the encirclement. Still, the troops of the 8th and 10th German armies were very eager to do well. Ludendorff even issued the first directives to extend the front to the Memel River. On 21st, another 30,000 prisoners of war were reported. The final balance showed a resounding German victory - even greater than Tannenberg. 110,000 Russian soldiers had been taken prisoner, 11 generals had surrendered and about 300 artillery pieces[272] had fallen into German hands. Four Russian divisions, the 27th, 28th, 29th and the 53rd reserve division, had been completely destroyed. About 100,000 Russian soldiers had died. The 10th Russian army had been wiped off the map. [273]

Surprisingly enough, the Winter Battle of Masuria has remained a relatively unknown battle of World War I. This is probably due to the fact that from its inception, it never had any strategic importance and had the 'limited' objective of destroying the 10th Russian Army. The relations on the Eastern Front, let alone the complete power constellation, did not change because of it. Ludendorff was well aware of this: 'we are one step further in our decision against Russia',[274] he believed. Nevertheless, the battle was described by some historians as a second Cannae[275] and the French historian Cartier called the battle 'more perfect than Tannenberg'.[276] Ludendorff had pushed back the front to the Narew-Bobr-Memel line and thus put a whole new situation on the map.

After the war, the historian Karl Tschuppik pointed out that Ludendorff's operation had another special feature. Ludendorff had made the entire southeastern turn while strong Russian fortifications stood at his back; at the Memel, Kaunas, Olita and Grodno, the Bobr Ossovietz and Lomsha, and at the Narew. It was all part of Ludendorff's tactics, taking risks to be locally strong, and exploiting this opportunity to achieve maximum results, which was what happened here.[277]

The battle was also interesting from another point of view. As a diversion to the operations of the 8th and 10th armies, the 9th German army had made a diversionary attack near Bolimow, using gas grenades to carry out an artillery bombardment, which Max Hoffmann had observed from the church tower. The effort was disappointing as the cold weather meant the gas had little effect. [278]

Here again, the war showed its dark side. The Russian retreat had also been indicative of the harshness of this war. The country had been burned, and dozens of Polish Jews had been hung from tree branches by the Russians on suspicion of espionage. [279]

With the winter defeat in Masuria, an era ended. It was a time when the Eastern Front had been subordinate to the Western Front and when Oberost had had to fend for itself. Due to the limited means available to Ludendorff and Von Hindenburg, it had mainly been a continuous rocade of units: from Mazuria to Tannenberg, from Tannenberg to Mazuria, to Warsaw and the Weichselboog to Lódz, from Lódz to the Mazurian Winter Battle. All of this relied heavily on Ludendorff's stage technique and the logistical skills of the German army, coupled with the discipline of the German soldier.[280] Meanwhile, things had changed and the Eastern Front was no longer a grey spot on the German map. Von Falkenhayn, after major failures in the West, turned to the East, albeit temporarily.

A long struggle for power preceded this. The crux of the matter was that since he had replaced Moltke, Von Falkenhayn had had good contact with the Emperor, who had been holding his hand over his eyes for a long time. This was nothing new, it had also happened to Moltke. Only when the setbacks (Marne) became too great, the Emperor had to drop his favourite.

Von Falkenhayn, tall and charming, was a man who succeeded in winning over the Kaiser. Many studies have been written about Wilhelm II. The picture that emerges from them is one of a very complex man, living in a complex time. He himself has said that the early death of his father, Friedrich III - the '99 Day Emperor' - meant that he had to skip a generation, as it were, when he ascended the throne. He had to deal mainly with the 'old men' from his grandfather's generation, whom he admired, such as Bismarck, but who also 'stood in the way' of his own politics and the new era. However, that new era was a very problematic one. There were great social, economic and political changes. Germany was transforming from a regional power to a superpower, from an agrarian state to an industrial state, from a colony-poor country to a country that wanted a place in the sun. Wilhelm II gladly personified this new era, which earned him the nickname 'Volldampf'. Germany's new position of power brought with it a dangerous mixture of uncertainty and hubris. Behind the emperor's proud 'es ist erreicht' facade was a great deal of uncertainty, which was well reflected in his attitude towards England. Queen Victoria was his grandmother and his own mother was British as well. Wilhelm could not harmonise these two loves, London and Berlin. The basis of a discord with England was thus in place. The Kaiser also saw a major role for Germany in the world. He warned against the 'yellow danger' and called for a united Christian action. In this, too, he knew little about how to keep up: his ideas were unrealistic and within his own country he alienated the Catholics. In addition, the emperor was plagued throughout his life by physical inconveniences, such as his immature left arm, for which he was ruthlessly treated in his youth. According to some historians, the inferiority complex that resulted from this was instrumental in the emperor's erratic character. Others believe that the Emperor was able to overcome the disadvantages of his handicap and that his capriciousness was more due to a lack of oxygen at birth. Whatever the case, the fact was that Germany had a complicated man on the throne, who did not interfere too directly in the day-to-day affairs of the front, but who did interfere in personnel matters.

The Oberost did not lie well. This had everything to do with the characters of both Von Hindenburg and Ludendorff. We have already seen that Ludendorff was not afraid to speak his mind and that this could make him appear rude. This was a major drawback for the mild-mannered Emperor. Von Hindenburg and the Kaiser had had a difference of opinion in the past on a 'Kaiser' manoeuvre and Wilhelm II had not forgotten that either. In this respect, Moltke and Von Falkenhayn did better. They were able to strike the right chord with the Kaiser and thus leave their mark on the war.

For the Von Hindenburg-Ludendorff duo, this was sometimes difficult work. When they indicated in January 1915 that the southern Carpathian front needed German help, Falkenhayn reacted negatively at first. When Oberost then took measures himself, a German army under the command of General Linsingen was finally made available. Von Falkenhayn probably felt that he was presented with a fait accompli and 'punished' the duo by appointing Ludendorff as Linsingen's right-hand man, thus pulling the successful duo apart. Von Hindenburg had to obey, but on 11 January, Ludendorff, Conrad and Linsingen met for consultation with Von Hindenburg. It was not the first time that Falkenhayn tried to play off Hindenburg and Ludendorff. This time Oberost struck back in a letter from Von Hindenburg to the Emperor, in which he not only pleaded for the 'recovery' of Ludendorff but also suggested to reinstate Moltke in his function. This was of course a direct attack on Falkenhayn. Von Hindenburg also let it be known that he would be available for the position himself if necessary, of course with Ludendorff as his right hand man. The Oberost had thus made a bid for the highest possible position in the field.[281] Similar noises were heard from the political arena. At the beginning of January 1915, Chancellor Von Bethmann-Hollweg asked himself if Von Falkenhayn should not be replaced by Ludendorff.[282]

The Emperor did not go so far as to dismiss his favourite Falkenhayn, but he did admit that a transfer of Ludendorff to the southern front was very unfortunate - especially just before the start of the Winter Battle in Masuria - and reversed the decision. When the Winter Battle resulted in a major victory, Falkenhayn must have gritted his teeth. From Maas to Memel, wrote Hindenburg biographer Bütow, the name of Von Hindenburg sounded at the *Stammtisch*. He was again, as with Tannenberg, the hero of the day. The name Ludendorff also became more and more famous. Falkenhayn, on the other hand, with his horrific trench warfare in the west, where at Ypres they fought for every metre, appealed less to the imagination. Here, no ground was gained and no spectacular numbers of prisoners were made. The enormous attention for von Hindenburg was not entirely justified, Max Hoffmann wrote in a letter to his wife: 'With the victory in Mazuria, von Hindenburg has no more to do than our daughter Ilse'. Hoffmann saw Ludendorff (and himself) as the men of the *Winter Battle*. This is also acknowledged by Hindenburg experts such as Bütow who, in his biography, admitted that Ludendorff was the 'pearl' of Oberost.[283] Yet von Hindenburg did play his eternal role, that of a rock-solid, nerveless commander-in-chief, who spoke encouraging words and, at the right moment, kept his back straight. When the Russians near Mazuria threatened to escape from the encirclement and Ludendorff and Hoffmann almost panicked, Hindenburg said: *'Mein Lieber Ludendorff,* God has given us much more luck than we deserve, it is not to be expected that it would suddenly stop now. Those who run always run faster than their pursuers. But the snow will also stop the Russians; 80,000 men are surrounded, a great success. Everything else can wait until tomorrow'. Hindenburg laid down to rest and Ludendorff expressed his surprise: 'do you know what the most wonderful thing about this story is? This man actually sleeps through the night. He has nerves' [284]

These iron nerves were not just for show. On the evening before his election as Reich President in 1925, Von Hindenburg went to bed at the appointed time. When his son woke him up early in the morning, very excited, to tell him of his election, Hindenburg asked if he could not have told him an hour later. [285]

The tensions between Oberost and Falkenhayn would continue and soon reach a new climax.

In the meantime, new developments had taken place, causing Falkenhayn to intervene in the east. Using the grand strategy as an argument, Von Falkenhayn believed that the British action at the Dardanelles (actions against Turkey) meant that Germany had to strengthen its position in the east to guard the 'land-bridge' with Turkey. Von Falkenhayn now wanted to take revenge through success, and he had found the way to put the Oberost out of action for this purpose. He put the new operation to relieve the Austro-Hungarian army in the hands of Von Mackensen, and his right-hand man Von Seeckt, who were old friends from their days in the XVII. army corps in Danzig. [286]

Falkenhayn was able to keep Von Mackensen out of Oberost's clutches by placing the command of the new operations in Galicia in the hands of the allies. Conrad von Hötzendorf was to be the leader of the forthcoming operations and for this purpose brought the 4th army into the field. Von Mackensen's force became a new army (the 11th), consisting of four army corps. Oberost's territory was reduced to the area from the Baltic Sea to the city of Lódz. The area south of that was the area where Von Mackensen was allowed to try his luck at war; a battle that would go down in history as the Gorlice-Tarnow battle.

Von Mackensen himself was, by the way, completely surprised by his appointment. He had suddenly been ordered to report to Von Falkenhayn in Charleville, where he arrived on 18 April after a 26-hour train journey. There, Von Falkenhayn informed him of the plans. The very next day, Von Mackensen left for the east, but not without a quick visit to Moltke during a stopover in Berlin.

He met the loyal man in the study on the Königsplatz, in the same room where Von Mackensen had stood with old Moltke and Von Schlieffen. Moltke was a broken man. He saw little in the *Durchbruchschlacht,* which hung over Von Mackensen's head. With the modern firepower, such an attack was doomed to failure, he orated. With a heavy heart, Von Mackensen left Berlin. He realised that - if the fortunes of war turned - the fate of Moltke would befall him. It was the last time he saw 'Julius' Moltke; the man died barely a year later. [287]

The new operation started on 2 May 1915. This was preceded by an inevitable showdown between Oberost and Falkenhayn. The reason for this was that both camps saw a different solution for the dilemma in which Germany found itself. Both agreed that the two-front war was debilitating for the German Empire, but Von Falkenhayn continued to see the west as the decisive part of the war and thus wanted to put things back in order with a limited operation - Gorlice-Tarnow - and then concentrate on the western front again. Von Hindenburg and Ludendorff agreed that the western front was the most important front, but believed that the war could only be won there if there first was a victory in the east. The destruction of the tsarist army had to come first. After that, they could focus on the west.

Due to the difference in opinion on the two sides, two think-tanks about the forthcoming operations on the Eastern Front were created. This has gone down in history as the Memel - Narew debate. The Narew solution was the most limited, and the plan Von Falkenhayn chose. It involved the German and Austro-Hungarian forces conducting a limited pincer operation from the north (Narew) and from the south, roughly the Iwangorod-Cholm line, cutting off Russian forces between Warsaw and Brest-Litowsk on the Bow River. Von Mackensen's new troops, the 11th Army and the Austro-Hungarian 4th Army, would operate from the south, supported on the right (west) flank by the 1st Army of the Dual Monarchy, while Oberost would deploy the 9th, the 12th and parts of the 8th Army.

Oberost felt that this was too limited a goal. It was feared that the entire operation would become a frontal showdown too soon and that it would therefore not be possible to deal a devastating blow to the Russian army. Oberost had developed an alternative, a push from East Prussia north of Kaunas along the Memel, passing Wilna and then turning towards the Pripjat marshes, with Baranowitschi and Minsk as final objectives. This was much more ambitious, but also involved more risks.

Von Falkenhayn, however, wanted a limited operation, also in terms of time, in order to be able to quickly move the beacons back to the west. He got his way. Ludendorff was furious and wrote a very bitter letter to Moltke.[288] There was also an intermediate option, which was not realised. Staff Officer Major von Bockelberg, Ludendorff's Landsturmbrigadier since July 1915, argued for an alternative operation across the Bobr River, past Osowiec, towards Brest-Litowsk. He was inspired by an 1897 plan of General Von den Goltz. In his *Denkschrift* of that time, he thought there were several choices: Narew (Falkenhayn), Memel (Ludendorff) and Bobr (Von Bockelberg). The latter he preferred. Initially, Ludendorff seemed to be in favour of this 'intermediate solution', but in the meantime the interesting alternative fell through. [289]

Von Falkenhayn may have set limited targets, but he left nothing to chance. In total, the front line of the 11th army covered 45 kilometres, where Von Mackensen deployed five corps under the command of Freiherr von Plettenburg, Von François, Von Emmich, Von Behr and Ritter von Kneussl[290] Opposite Gorlice lay the XXXXI. reserve corps. The Russian positions first had to be weakened. In style with the operations on the western front, strong artillery units were assembled. Under the supervision of artillery specialist Generalmajor Zoethen, two heavy Austro-Hungarian batteries (15 and 12.5 cm) were assembled, and a number of German artillery units of lighter calibre under the command of Oberleutnant Meiler and Major Bracht. In addition, the corps itself had 108 artillery pieces at its disposal. Commanding the corps was the energetic Von François, who also had at his disposal 18 battalions (21 officers and 953 men each), 4 squadrons, 43 machine guns, serving in the 81st and 82nd reserve divisions. His right hand man in the operation was Oberstleutnant Von Müller.

On 2 May 1915, the offensive began - at 6 a.m. - on what was to become a warm spring Sunday. There was still a slight haze over the fields when the violence erupted. The artillery was well supplied with information by wire reconnaissance. Soon the western part of Gorlice was on fire. 'Only Jews and Catholics live there', a Prussian officer remarked rather insensitively.[291] The oil refinery east of the city also went up in flames, as did farms and straw roofs.

Some of the Russian soldiers in the positions under fire fled to the east, but were largely destroyed by the massed and scattered German shells. After three hours, the Von François corps arrived. An important role was played by the 82nd reserve division under the command of Generalmajor Fabarius. He had put together a special shock troop of five battalions under the command of Oberst Kaupert. He had to prevent difficult street battles in Gorlice and capture the city from the surrounding hills, hill 357 and the cemetery hill - the Jewish cemetery. Thanks to the 'rain of steel', as one Russian prisoner called the bombardment that lasted until 09.00,[292] the attack was a success and the first two important targets were taken as early as 10.00. Russian reinforcements were blown apart by the German artillery, so the Russian officers were unable to build up a well-organised resistance. [293]

The *Durchbruchschlacht* Gorlice-Tarnow succeeded miraculously. The Russian army was soon in retreat across the entire front. In only fourteen days, the German army and its allies managed to advance 150 kilometres. As Ludendorff suspected, the battle of annihilation was not fought. It became a battle of pursuit, in which the Russians lost ground and suffered losses, but did not fall.

Gorlice-Tarnow thus became yet another tactical German victory, which Ludendorff felt was too meagre, especially since this time it had been the centre of gravity of German military operations. The total number of losses for both sides was, as usual, difficult to indicate. In any case, the Russian 3rd and 8th armies were badly hit. On 16 May, the Russians estimated a loss of 100,000 troops, although a British observer, retreating with them to the River San, believed the losses to be 'colossal', and considerably greater than estimated. He guessed that of the 250,000 Russian troops, about 40,000 reached the San River unscathed.[294] Goodspeed estimated that the Russians lost about 140,000 men as prisoners of war.[295] The *Reichsarchiv* presented the German losses in the opening days as relatively small, with losses mainly in Generalmajor Von Stocken's 81th reserve division, which, as part of Von François' XXXXI. reserve corps, stood in the focal points of the front. But the losses for the initial days were barely 500 killed and nearly 1600 wounded, to which were added similar losses for the 82nd division.[296] In the days that followed, which turned out to be bloody pursuit battles, during which the Russians fought for every metre, the Centrals' losses had risen considerably. Robert Asprey mentions the number of 90.000 men lost.

Oberost looked on this success with dismay, although some criticism was not out of place. His own losses were high and the loss of terrain was insurmountable for Russia. Had this operation brought the Russians back to the negotiating table? The answer was no.

Of course, we never know how Ludendorff's Memel alternative would have turned out. However, Ludendorff's criticism that the Narew plan would lead to a frontal showdown was entirely valid. Another point of criticism was the fact that with this frontal attack, Von Schlieff's tactical and strategic thinking was pushed aside. He had always warned against such manoeuvres. However, under the influence of the stationary western front, where Von Seeckt in particular had had experience, this tactic had been applied to Görlice-Tarnow. The whole plan, by the way, had come from Conrad, although Von Falkenhayn later drew it somewhat to himself. Conrad again proved to be a clever military man, but with a weak army, although the Austrians, according to Von Mackensen, had 'behaved bravely'.[297] Nevertheless, the Austrian government was in bad shape when shortly afterwards, Przemyśl was recaptured by the German 11th army, and not by his own troops. Von Mackensen apologised by saying that if he had had to wait for the Austrians, he would still be standing in front of the town. [298]

After Przemyśl, Lemberg was added to Von Mackensen's victories on 22 June and from then onwards, he would fly the flag at his residence on Gorlice day. Max Hoffmann, who belonged to Oberost's troika, could understand the operation at Gorlice. He thought that there were great opportunities in the Ludendorff concept, but that, given the time pressure, Gorlice was the right alternative.[299] For that matter, Oberost was also part of Gorlice's success on a modest scale. In the weeks before Gorlice, Oberost had to divert attention from that front section through its own operations. This entailed manoeuvres around Suwalki, in the Memel area and in Lithuania, where they gained considerable ground and the Russians even briefly feared for Riga. Furthermore, in the area of the 9th army it was decided to launch a new gas attack. Max Hoffmann had his reservations about this weapon. The construction of the gas pipes took a long time and the weapon had a structural problem: the wind direction. In the east, the Germans needed western wind, in the west eastern wind. Most of the time, it was the other way round.

If the Entente also started using gas, Germany would be at a disadvantage. Later on, Hoffmann spoke to the designer of the gas attacks, *Geheimrat* Haber, who told him that he had warned the Supreme Command about this and had insisted on firing the gas by grenade, which they had failed to do. On 2 May, however, the 9th Army launched a gas attack anyway. When the German infantry followed later, and there was still shooting from the Russian lines, it was assumed that the gas attack had failed. Later, Hoffmann heard that the opposite was the case, the Russians had suffered heavy losses. During the second attack, the wind changed and the Germans themselves suffered considerable losses. [300]

Now that the Russians were driven against the River Bug, it was time to determine the new course for the east. The Emperor personally came to the east for it. Oberost already had plans for the continuation of the campaign. The front moved in July-August to the line Warsaw, Nowogeorgiewsk - Rozan - west of Bialystok - Augustow to the Memel area. There was still the possibility to go deep over Kaunas - Wilna, into the hinterland, to win a decisive battle. Ludendorff ordered Max Hoffmann to be ready when he passed on the first orders.

With this order, Ludendorff left on 1 July for talks with the Emperor and Von Falkenhayn. However, things turned out differently. There remained a constant difference of opinion between Von Falkenhayn, who wanted short limited operations and wanted to concentrate again on the west, and Conrad and Ludendorff, who wanted to continue in the east. Conrad, of course, paid attention to what was beneficial for the dual monarchy, Ludendorff, to what he considered to be strategically correct for Germany. Again, the decision was negative for Ludendorff. Falkenhayn was afraid to sink into the Russian land, he was also suspicious towards Conrad, he feared the 'Balkan adventure'. [301]

It was decided to improvise on the Gorlice plan, to cut off the existing new frontal arc, with Warsaw at its centre, again. It was a glorified continuation of the existing situation, required no difficult stage manoeuvres. Hoffmann waited in vain for Ludendorff's telephone call, which finally came the next day, 2 July. He heard the news, which was negative for Oberost. In his memoirs, Hoffmann noted that with this missed opportunity the possibility of a German victory in the east was over. He did not call his memoirs *Der Krieg der versäumte Gelegenheiten* for nothing. [302]

Opinions on this are and remain divided. The British historian Lidell Hart indeed believes that the German leadership missed the victory there. The German historian Ritter, however, believes that all of this merely showed Ludendorff's lack of realism and exaggerated expectations. [303]

Despite the protests of Ludendorff and Oberost, the new offensive began on 13 July. It was successful. By 17 July, German troops were at the Narew. The Russians soon realised that Poland was lost and withdrew further back over the entire line. This was exactly what Ludendorff had feared. Once again he urged a change of direction. It was not too late yet, he thought. But Von Falkenhayn got his way and the advance continued. The Russians retreated in 1812-like fashion. Whole areas went up in flames, including large towns such as Brest-Litowsk. Max Hoffmann cynically remarked that this was to the German advantage. They did not have to take care of the 80,000 inhabitants[304] At the end of July, Cholm and Lublin fell into German hands, and on 5 August Warsaw fell. Oberost also took advantage of the war opportunities and pushed the Russians further back into the Courland and Memel area. In the headquarters there was joy, but Ludendorff stood by with 'a bleeding heart', as he wrote Moltke on 15 August. 'Time and again I have said that the Russians would go back in front, and that is exactly what has happened'.[305]

During the 'festivities' at the conclusion of Gorlice, Ludendorff and Von Falkenhayn met each other once more. This was during a visit to the captured fortress of Nowo-Georgiewsk, where no less than 90,000[306] had been made prisoners of war, including many generals.[307] A train had been specially arranged for them, after which Von Hindenburg and Ludendorff, accompanied by Major von Bockelberg, left. Hoffmann meanwhile continued to look after the shop.[308]

The reception was cool. Von Falkenhayn at one point turned to Ludendorff and asked if he was finally prepared to admit that he - Von Falkenhayn - had been right. 'On the contrary', Ludendorff snapped at him, after which the Emperor tried to save the atmosphere with some light-hearted topics. [309]

While this showdown was taking place, Nowo-Georgiewsk was still smouldering. The Weichsel Fortress was one of the last fortifications on the river banks to fall into German hands. For mysterious reasons, the Grand Duke had decided to hold this fortress. German time documents state that the Russians had planned to evacuate the fortress earlier, but that there had been French intervention in the fortress shortly before the hostilities.[310] In any case, as Ludendorff found out during his visit, the fortress was no match for the enormous shells of the Austrian artillery that had been brought to it by rail. The encirclement of the fortress had begun on 9 August and ten days later it had already fallen, even though the German infantry consisted solely of Landsturm and Landwehr. The heavy artillery had done the job.

Between all the festivities, Ludendorff made sure that the heavy guns were returned to the 10th army, where the Grodno fortress still had to be conquered. Perhaps the tougher defence of this fortress had to do with new international developments, from which hope was drawn. Italy had chosen the Entente and this meant 900,000 new soldiers against the Centrals. Romania, as a result of the current German-Austrian-Hungarian success, was still neutral for the time being. However, it was a waiting, watching power, keeping its eyes fixed on the 'game'. 'The Italians are unfaithful bandits',[311] said Von Mackensen, and that was one of the few things agreed upon within the ruins of the still smouldering Nowo-Georgiewsk.

Chapter 5

Viceroy in Kaunas

In the summer of 1915, Oberost's headquarters were moved to the city of Kaunas, the second largest city in present-day Lithuania, better known to the Germans and Poles as Kowno. The front had become stationary by now and, due to the interference from on high, there was little operating space for Ludendorff and Von Hindenburg. 'Ludendorff is bored', Max Hoffmann thought. [312]

In Kaunas, Ludendorff had taken up residence in two villas owned by the Tillmann family, a well-known 'Russlanddeutsche' family. Together with Max Hoffmann he shared a house, while the military meetings were held in the building of the military government. In this building, photos and paintings of the tsarist family still hung on the wall, but it was easy to heat up and Ludendorff did not need any embellishments. On the walls soon hung large numbers of maps on which Ludendorff followed the front events in detail. Ludendorff found himself on historic ground. Exactly 103 years ago, Napoleon Bonaparte had been here and had impatiently watched the 'Grande Armee' crossing the Memel. The house in which the French emperor had stayed still stood, as did the Russian monument from 1812 in the market square, which consisted of an obelisk, one of the supporting chains of which had been hit by a German shell. The Memel River flowed stately and wide through Kaunas, taking in the fast-flowing Wilja just north of the city. The river immediately caused Ludendorff headaches due to enormous amounts of drift ice, which destroyed the wooden bridge and cut off the connection to the east bank. This was not without danger. Kaunas itself had fallen into German hands without too much difficulty under the fire of 42cm shells (the forts were of poor quality, as there was brick under the 'concrete'), but to the east lay the Russian lines and a counter-offensive was always to be feared. The bridge was soon repaired. [313]

The area was characterised, as Frentz put it, by a 'melancholy wildness', from which emanated an almost 'cosmic influence'. It was an area where the 'Slavic character' thrived. On the other hand, there were also many traces of Deutschtum in the country. It was therefore a typical transition region, with a multi-ethnic population, in which Latvians, Lithuanians, Russians, Belarusians, Poles, Jews and ethnic Germans (Volksdeutschen) lived. Ludendorff saw it as his task to prevent the area from falling into the 'Polentum'. Yet, he wanted to do this with an eye to Polish interests. Already during his years in Posen (Poznan), he had shown an understanding for the specific wishes of the different population groups. Ludendorff served the German interest, but was prepared to follow a sensible policy, which was more than could be said of most 'nur-Soldiers' of the Prussian Corps.

In Kaunas, his enormous work ethic once again showed itself, which was also his best weapon against the disappointments that Oberost had recently had to endure. It seems that even the German emperor was troubled by this. In this period, he tried more than once to persuade Ludendorff to be elevated to the peerage. However, Ludendorff rejected this.[314] Ludendorff was more stubborn than vain. For Ludendorff, the whole was more important than his own role and he expected the same attitude from others. Reserve officer Von Gagl, who had an administrative function in Oberost's staff, thought that Ludendorff's working strength 'knew no bounds'. His strenght and performance were 'far beyond human requirements'.[315] Compliments were not to be expected from his subordinates. He did reward good workers by placing more and more trust in them, which in turn increased the demands. Counterarguments were tolerated, but they had to be presented quickly and objectively. In some cases, he would then give in. Von Gagl was scolded one day for not returning a report that Ludendorff had marked as urgent. Before the astonished officer, who knew nothing about it, could say anything, the connection was broken again. A short time later, the telephone rang again, and again it sounded in a short one-way conversation that Von Gagl had not yet received the documents because another Ludendorff employee had forgotten to pass it on. The man had been replaced. End of message. This was a typical performance by Ludendorff. Another officer waited politely for some time in the room next to Ludendorff's study until the general discovered him. 'Why are you waiting so long, that is precious time', Ludendorff told him. Rules of politeness were subordinate to his aim of operating as efficiently as possible. 'He knew how to bind and inspire people', said General Von Eisenhart Rothe, who served as Oberost's quartermaster.[316] Von Einem, the former Minister of Defence, wrote in his memoirs that he had a very energetic colleague during the First World War. To illustrate this work ethic, he wrote

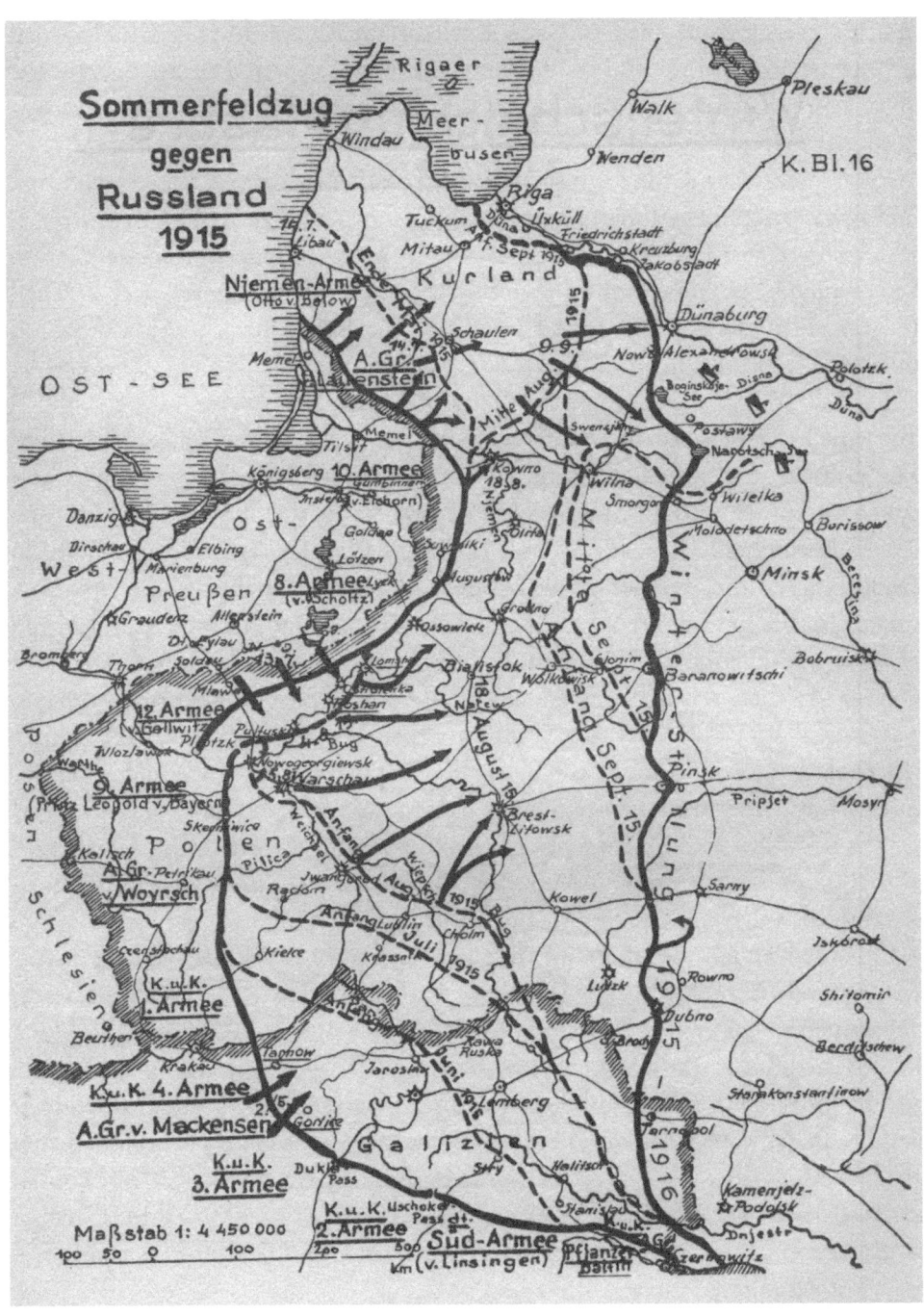

Front course 1915

that his energy came close to Ludendorff's. Von Einem described Ludendorff as 'businesslike, strong, full of ideas and completely open'. But he was also the 'most hated and loved general in the German army'. 'Everything about Ludendorff was masculine', said Von Einem. [317]

Even 'medics' underlined this, such as Gerhard Venzmer in *Körpergestalt und Seelenanlage*, a publication of Kosmos, *Gesellschaft der Naturfreunde* in Stuttgart, who believed that Ludendorff owed his energy to an 'athletic-muskuläre Körperbau', which he had in common with other 'great historical figures' such as Cecil Rhodes, Ernst Moritz Arndt and Friedrich Nietzsche. According to Venzmer, this build stood for the 'Tatmensch'. [318]

The time in Kaunas became an important phase in Ludendorff's life, as he would gain political power for the first time. More and more, his task would be to govern the occupied territory. Kaunas itself showed that this was no easy task. The city had been hard hit by the events. The population had fallen from 75,000 to 18,000 due to the violence of war. Ludendorff appointed Ernst Sikorski as organiser for the restoration of order in the city. The Russians had taken everything of value with them on their retreat. Even the horses of the fire brigade were not spared, and there was no more flat land. Therefore, a provisional map of the city was immediately made, dividing it into five districts. A trustee from each district was then employed to advise the German administration as a so-called 'Beirat'. In this way, trust and knowledge were gained. Support and work was arranged for the poor, the streets were repaired and the Memel was dredged. Sikorski said of this time: 'Ludendorff could not possibly have taken care of everything himself, but his spirit was running through the city'.[319]

Outside Kaunas, too, there was much to do in the Lithuanian land. For this purpose, the area, equal to the surface of France, was divided into a number of departments: Courland, Lithuania, Suwalki, Wilna, Grodno and Bialystok.[320] In this area, Ludendorff managed to restore order in a remarkably short time and to introduce a successful German administration. To this end, Ludendorff had roads, railways and libaries built, and courts established. He even had theatrical performances and film evenings organised. Horses and wood were confiscated, barbed wire produced, captured Russian weapons converted for German ammunition. The Canadian Goodspeed thought that Ludendorff was as good an administrator as he was a strategist. [321]

At Oberost, Ernst Sikorski recalled that in 1937, there was a 'discussion' whether Ludendorff was a better general or a better official. Among his greatest successes, Sikorski counted the fact that he had built a railway between Kaunas and Ponjemon, and the fact that he had managed to bring the 58 vacant estates

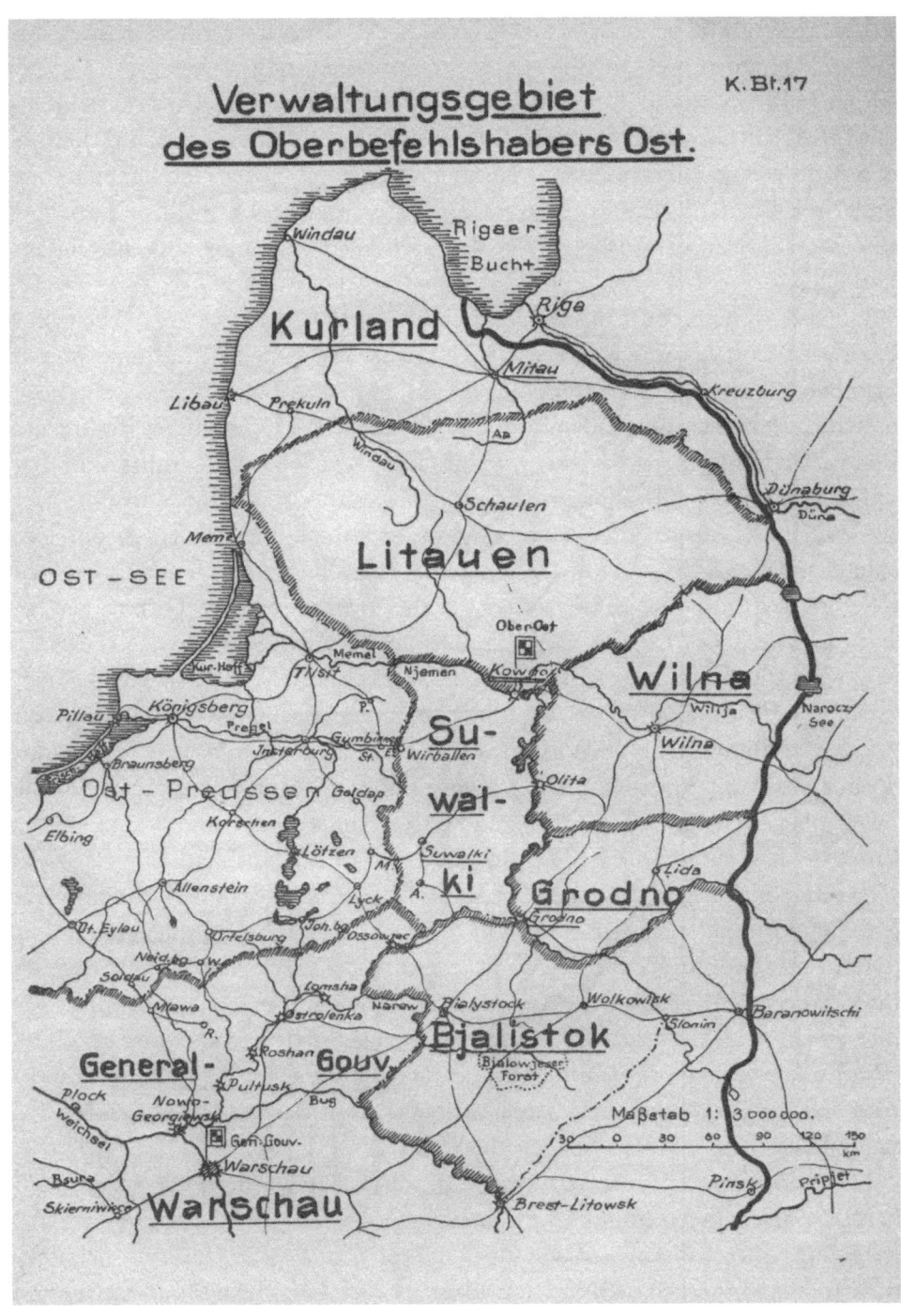

Oberost

in the area (16,800 hectares of arable land) back into cultivation.[322] 'I am dividing up kingdoms here', an amuzed Hoffmann noted in his diary.

Oberost's success did not go unnoticed. One newspaper reported that Ludendorff used the horses of two cavalry regiments to assist the farmers and that the population, especially the Jews, were much better off under German rule than under the Russians. The State Secretary of the Interior, Dr. Helffrich, made a trip through the area and noted with satisfaction that the harvest was abundant in the fields.[323]

Ludendorff held court in the east. Due to the stationary nature of the front, Oberost almost became a viceroyalty. High guests, such as the Emperor and members of the great German noble families, visited regularly. Photos have been preserved showing Von Hindenburg, Ludendorff and Hoffmann pacing around Kaunas station, waiting for the Emperor. The pictures give the impression that the gentlemen actually thought they had more important things to do. After all, Wilhelm II was mainly seen as a patron of Von Moltke and later Von Falkenhayn. The well-known pro-German world traveller Sven Hedin also visited Oberost. Hedin's visit, among others to the fortress town of Lötzen, had an amusing anecdote in that Hedin himself made two Russians prisoners of war, who were apparently war-weary. A remarkable result for a neutral Swede.[324]

There were also many foreign military observers on the staff, including Von Adlercreuz for Sweden, Julien for Brazil, Mirescu for Romania, Von Baldivia for Spain and Kuang Djie for China. A long-standing guest of Oberost was also the writer/poet Richard Demel. This 'graubärtige Landsknecht' and 'kerndeutsche Patriot'[325] had earned the EK-I in his 52nd year of life, and had composed the song *Hoch am Gewehr den Blumenstrauss*, which recalled 'happier' war days.

Ludendorff had a special interest in the press, which he considered very important as a mouthpiece for German interests. This involved political tact, as the various ethnic groups tried to consolidate their influence. For example, the Lithuanians quickly moved their press agency *Dabartis* from Kaunas to Wilna in order to emphasise the 'Lithuanian character' of this city. In the press, Belarusians suddenly endorsed their letters with 'Wilna in Belarus'. They did this, for example, in their 'daily newspaper' the *Howon*.

Ludendorff had to intervene several times to stay at the helm. In order to keep a grip on the contents of the newspapers, which often appeared in languages other than German, Ludendorff appealed to a local Zionist association, which, due to the geographical spread of its members, had the infrastructure and the language skills at its disposal. In total, nineteen periodicals were involved, five of which were 'foreign-language', including a Jewish newspaper. The press spectrum included the: *Kriegszeitung, Grodnoer Zeitung, Die Woche im*

Osten, Mitausche Zeitung, Ostgalizische Zeitung, Bilderschau, Dzienik Wilenski, Bialystoker Zeitung, Zeitung der 10. Armee and others. It was typical for Ludendorff that he personally visited several printing houses and shook hands with everyone. Ludendorff always invested in his people and expected hard work in return. One of the printers picked up a newspaper from the press and showed the name Ludendorff which had just appeared in printing ink. Ludendorff burst out laughing.

It is interesting to note that Kaunas was a typical 'Jewish city'. Kaunas had four Protestant churches, 19 Catholic churches and no less than 44 synagogues (and one mosque). There was also a Jewish gymnasium in the city, as well as four Jewish schools with Talmud and Torah sections.[326] There are no indications that Ludendorff acquired his later anti-Semitic ideas here. Many Jews had suffered under the Tsarist regime. 'Glaubensstark und voller Weihe ist des Juden Kaisertreue', said Jonas Kreppel in his 1915 book *Der Weltkrieg und die Judenfrage*. Although this was a Jew living within the Austro-Hungarian administration and thus loyal to Emperor Franz Joseph, this feeling was widespread. Kreppel even called the war against Russia a 'holy war', because of Russia's 'medieval character', in which he particularly referred to anti-Semitism. Despite the fact that 300,000 Jews fought in the tsarist army, pogroms occurred regularly.[327] Anti-Semitism was also often used politically by the tsarist regime, as in the infamous Kiev trial of Mendel Beilis on the eve of World War I. Beilis was accused of ritualistic murder and was sentenced to death by hanging. The murder - of a young man, Andre Luschinsky - was in reality the work of a criminal family, the Cheberiaks. Even long after it was clear that Beilis had nothing to do with the murder, the authorities continued to harp on about his guilt, and highlighted other similar 'ritual crimes'. [328]

Ludendorff had entered new territory but gained important experience in the political game. In his 'Verwaltungsgebiet', for example, he had declared a trade monopoly for the authorities on salt, sugar, matches, alcohol and cigarettes.[329] Ludendorff thus did good business which benefited the home front. His goal was an orderly administration, no lack for the occupied territory, and what was extra to the fatherland. In his memoirs we can read that he had pleasant memories of this special time although he took it, like everything else, very serious. He spoke of a "Kulturtat". [330]

The Viceroyalty in Kaunas also had a dark page. Research by Abba Strazhas for the Eastern Europe Institute in Munich shows that there were many problems too. From the beginning, for example, there was considerable partisan activity in the area. This struggle was - partly due to the enormous territory, as well as the terrain, with many woods and swamps - relatively successful for the partisans and difficult to suppress for the German administration. That the problems in the Oberost area were only recently 'historically (re)discovered' has to do with Ludendorff's successful press policy at the time. The historians started to believe what Ludendorff wanted them to believe, namely that the area was only an inexhaustible source of wealth for the fatherland. A partisan war was of course not part of this. In the reports to Germany, the occupation authorities did not speak of partisans, but of gangs and bands of robbers. Here is a parallel with World War II, where the Reichsführer SS Heinrich Himmler decreed that the word 'partisan', which had a certain romantic connotation, was banned.

The historian Strazhas, who also researched Lithuanian and Russian archives, reports considerable partisan activity. The 'Feldgendarmerie', for example, was only one of the units the Germans used to maintain peace and order, and by 31 January 1917, they had taken no less than 4050 partisan prisoners. The actual number - given that garrison troops and regular units were also deployed - must have been much higher. [331]

Ludendorff's problems in the area were actually complex. There were all sorts of groups of Russians in the German hinterland who had until then escaped captivity, and they were supported by passive and active resistance from the population of Courland and Lithuania. The terrain allowed these soldiers to hide and operate against the Germans. This number of Russians increased rather than decreased because Russians often escaped from German captivity. It must be remembered that (up to January 1918) there were no less than 1,300,000 Russians in German captivity, including 11,000 officers (in contrast to the 100,000 Germans in Russian captivity, including 1,800 officers), and that their treatment was not always good. A Russian report quoted by Strazhas described the particularly cruel Guestrow and Hammerstein POW camps, where 40 people a day died from malnutrition alone. Thus, there were plenty of Russians who wanted to escape and fill the ranks of the partisans. Soldiers also trickled in from 'Austrian' territory (another 1,000,000 Russian prisoners of war). The Russian authorities also saw military opportunities in the partisans and actively supported them. The command lay with no one less than Grand Duke Mikhailovich and later even with the Tsar. For example, a separate partisan unit was created in the 3rd don Cossack division, in which ethnic Lithuanians also served. The units snuck through the German lines, such as in winter over the frozen Naroc Lake, in order to get behind the German lines. Some units gained notoriety in those days, such as the groups "Orlov" (15th cavalry division) and "Klimov" (Cossacks). Other initiatives, such as the partisan detachment "Durov", which even came to discuss its mission with the tsar in person, failed before the start. Shortly after the unit was set up, the commander, drunk and arguing with the wrong man in Moscow, ended up in the tsarist dungeons instead of behind the German lines.

Not all Russian commanders were happy with the freebooters on their side. Especially of General A.A. Brusilov, it is known that he found the self-willed operation of the partisans an abomination. His criticism was partly justified. There are cases known where the Cossacks indulged in anti-Jewish atrocities in the German hinterland, instead of fighting the Germans. This happened among others in the places Sabacius, Vabalininkas, Viesintos, Anyksciai and Rokiskis, already in 1915.[332] Still, there were also military successes, such as the blowing up of the bridges at Gozhi, Druskininkai and Svencionys, which caused problems for the German supply and transport troops. This in turn forced the Germans to take countermeasures, which sometimes took place on a large scale, such as an anti-partisan action along the Rietava-Laukuva country road, which hardly achieved anything.

Such partisan activities, which also involved the killing of German supply troops in ambushes, led to atrocities on both sides, which sometimes also caused warning from the homeland. Eduard Bernstein, for example, a leading Social Democrat, believed that people should never have voted for war credits when they knew 'all that was happening in the East'. He was referring to the atrocities and executions committed by the Germans.

The harsh German reactions were partly due to the traumatic experiences the Germans themselves had had in East Prussia at the beginning of the war, where the population had been terrorised by the Cossacks, who were again at the centre of many partisan activities. Some soldiers applied the 'eye for an eye, a tooth for a tooth' concept. The Lithuanian writer Gabriele Petkevicaite-Bite recalled these abuses, but also mentioned that fortunately there were also German soldiers who calmed down their colleagues, which also shows that not all abuses took place on orders from above. But there were indeed mass executions, which also belonged to Oberost. In Kalvarija, 170 people were executed and 70 more in Vilkaviskis.[333]

Furthermore, frustration surrounded the problem of the emerging national consciousness - of the Lithuanians in particular - which posed growing problems for the Germans. The Russian administration had learnt their lesson from the political unrest of 1905, and had subsequently given various ethnic groups more space. For example, the Lithuanian language was recognised and they had their own representatives in the Duma, the tsarist advisory body. Thus, a certain national 'Erhebung' was taking place in Lithuania and the arrival of the Germans was viewed with suspicion. Strazhas speaks of the emergence of a 'spontaneous resistance movement'.[334] The partisan activities were based on a certain tradition, going back to 1812 and the Napoleonic invasion.

Oberost was therefore by no means a mere laurel and its problems were controlled and covered up as best it could. Ludendorff did not get the partisans under his thumb, but neither could they prevent the German exploitation of the area. Ludendorff acted with a combination of understanding and ruthlessness. The fatherland had to be served.

That homeland was under increasing pressure. A freezing winter had passed over Germany. Russia was still a dangerous opponent, despite the series of German successes in 1914 and 1915. The French held out, as did the British, who were mobilising more and more forces and resources in their inexhaustible empire. Germany was a besieged fortress. Ludendorff and Von Hindenburg studied Germany's chances in the east. A logical goal would be the elimination of the Russian troops in the front arc near Riga. It would be a limited attack, but one where a good result could be expected. It enabled the Oberost to eliminate another Russian army and thus further weaken and discourage Tsarist Russia. However, for this action some extra divisions were temporarily needed and so Ludendorff presented himself to Von Falkenhayn in Lida in January 1916. Knowing that troops were scarce, he also deployed his viceroyalty, using administrative arguments. The German harvest of 1915 had been the worst in 44 years and Germany could make good use of the extra Russian prisoners of war on the land. On 29 January, Ludendorff returned, disappointed. Von Falkenhayn again concentrated on the Western Front, with the British as his main enemy. By his own logic, he could hit them the hardest by collapsing the French front.

Under the cover name of 'Gericht', the plan had arisen to bleed out the French at Verdun. According to a message to the Kaiser, Von Falkenhayn believed that the French were on the verge of collapse and that the self-inflicted showdown against the strong positions at Verdun would force the French to bleed their army dry.

Ludendorff rightly wondered whether it was wise to attack the enemy precisely where he was strongest. 'Does this man know Von Schlieffen at all', wondered a somber Ludendorff. Even the German crown prince, who was to help lead the attacks, shrank from it and preferred to operate in the east. Unfortunately, Von Falkenhayn still controlled the situation and had the Emperor in his grip. He could also be very convincing. Max Hoffmann initially backed down after a speech by Von Falkenhayn, only to recover later. 'Falkenhayn is the evil spirit of Germany,' he said at the time, referring in connection with Verdun to the senseless 'Kindermord' at Ypres.[335]

Although the burgeoning battles at Verdun upset the Entente's plans for 1916, they still had plenty of initiative left. The Italians were preparing for their fifth battle of Isonzo, the British were gathering troops at the Somme and the Russians were also preparing an attack. For this purpose, the Oberost received messages from defectors. They told that the Russians would go on the offensive near Narotschsee.

Ludendorff and his staff were suspicious of these reports. The mud season was approaching and there were poor logistical conditions in the area. Therefore, on 11 March, Ludendorff left for Berlin to attend the wedding of Prince Joachim von Preussen, where he heard that on 16th, the Russian offensive had begun after all. Ludendorff immediately travelled back. Between Narotsch and Wieschniesee, the tsarist troops had arrived. They had been resupplied with ammunition and men, after five relatively quiet months. Oberost would have to endure this test of strength entirely on its own, as there were no operative reserves available due to Verdun.

The Russian offensive began in new style. The Tsar's troops had assembled an unprecedented amount of artillery, which was more reminiscent of the Western Front than the Eastern Front. The bombardment lasted no less than two days in full force and was then followed by three days of very heavy infantry attacks. Kaunas was the deeper target of the Russian attacks, which were launched in three locations, as well as on secondary fronts as a diversionary tactic. The main results were achieved by the Russians between Narotsch and Wischnjew lakes, where the situation became 'critical' according to Ludendorff.[336]

Oberost's reinforcements almost had to 'wade' to the front, so bad had the mud become. Exhausted, the infantrymen reached their positions. Luckily for Ludendorff, the terrain on the Russian side was even worse, so that here too the steam soon died down under the attack. Ludendorff's assessment, which had brought him to Berlin, proved itself correct; the terrain and season did not lend themselves to an offensive. Logic apparently played a less prominent role in St. Petersburg. The Tsar himself had assumed command of the troops and was determined to support the offensives of the western allies with the necessary drumming in the east. The attack ultimately ran aground in 'Sumpf und Blut' and the Russian losses were 'ausserordentlich'. The German front held, although some positions between the lakes were lost and here and there German units were overrun by the numerically much stronger Russians. On 28 April, thanks in part to good artillery support, the lost terrain would be recaptured from the tsarist troops.

After the dust had settled, the emperor visited in May. The atmosphere was somewhat charged. Von Hindenburg and Ludendorff followed the developments on the other fronts very tense. There was good news, apart from their own defence success. There was joy when the report of the victory at Skagerak came in. Ludendorff was relieved, because he had always had his doubts about the fleet aspirations of the Imperial army. Now, it appeared that this fleet was a significant force after all. His joy was dampened when, not much later, he learned of his own losses, which were considerable. Tirpitz' fleet proved too big to be ignored, but too small to force a decision. The result was that after Skagerak, the Germans switched more and more to the submarine weapon. According to Ludendorff's employee Hoffmann, this choice was justified. The submarine weapon was the answer to the British hunger blockade. Germany had its 'back against the wall'. On the other hand, Germany had too few submarines when the war started. Hoffmann thought that this was a typical German problem. They had great plans, good successes, but just too little for victory. He believed that this also applied to the gas weapon.

This feeling of powerlessness and frustration also applied to Ludendorff's Oberost. The March offensive of the Russians, now forgotten by historians, showed that the war in the east, due to the German fixation on the west, was far from over, despite all the stage successes of Oberost at Tannenberg, the Masurian lakes, Lódz, Warsaw and the March winter battle. The Russian army had recovered reasonably well during the quiet months and had the necessary supplies at its disposal. By January, the Russians had 1.693.000 soldiers on their feet with 1.243.000 rifles at their disposal. A few weeks later this had risen to 2 million men with as many guns. In terms of artillery, the tsarist army had 1,000 shells per barrel, the amount needed for offensive operations. This made the Russian armed forces an enormous army, but its strength should not be exaggerated. The Russian possibilities in the east were mainly due to the fact that Oberost had so few units at its disposal and to the fact that the Austro-Hungarian army performed even worse than the Russian troops. The relative strength of the Russian army was also reflected in the fact that in the First World War, Germany mobilised more troops than Russia, and Russia slightly more than France.[337] This was due to the fact that Russia had many young men of conscript age, but did not have the training capacity, nor the equipment and officers, to actually deploy them. In view of these facts, it is clear that during all this time there were unique opportunities for the Germans in the East. Sadly, Von Falkenhayn's course remained directed westward; after Ieperen it was Verdun to which his eye was fixed, and where a terrible slaughter was going on. In the end, however, it were new developments in the east that gave Von Falkenhayn's regime its death blow.

This had everything to do with Aleksey Brusilov. The battles between the lakes were 'only' the introduction to a series of offensives, for example near Riga, but above all on the central front, roughly from the area south of the Pripjat marshes to Bucharest, in eastern Galicia.

The origin of all these activities was to be found in the agreements the Tsar had made with the French General Joffre on 6 December 1915 at Chantilly. The difference with the previous battles, however, was that these did not take place in the thawing mud but on passable roads, and that they were mainly aimed at the weaker Austro-Hungarian army. In addition, Brusilov's troops were well equipped and prepared, and a considerable amount of artillery had been assembled, as in the March fighting.

Brusilov was an experienced officer. He had fought at Przemyśl and had defeated the Third Austro-Hungarian Army earlier in the war. The objective of the new offensive was none other than Lucik and Lemberg. The attack was to be carried out from north to south across a broad front by five armies: the 3rd (Lesh), 8th (Kaledin), 11th (Sakharov) and 7th army (Schhevbacher). The Centrals had to face the 4th k.u.k. Army (Ferdinand), the 2nd k.u.k. Army (Böhm-Ermolli), the German South Army (Bothmer), and the 7th k.u.k. Army under command of Pfanzer-Baltin.

Although the Austro-Hungarian and German air forces warned that the Russian forces were gathering, the troops of the dual monarchy were convinced of a coming defence success. The troops were in their positions and would give the Russians a 'warm welcome'. This optimism was diametrically opposed to those who distrusted the Czech units of the k.u.k. army because of their 'Slavic sympathies'. Von Falkenhayn, trapped in his ambitious plans on the Western Front, had no extra troops available. People clung to the fact that the Russians had their problems too, and they did. A document has been preserved stating that between May 15 and July, the Russian 7th army lost 10,432 men to desertion, for the 8th, 9th and 11th army it was 24,621, 9855 and 13,108 men respectively. In other words, whole divisions.[338] In the process, Brusilov noted in a report to the tsar and the supreme command, the Stavka, all sorts of fraternisation arose between central troops and the Russian army, and the soldiers, even officers, visited each other in the trenches, such as Lieutenant Zavadski, of the 8th squadron of mortars, who was mentioned by name in the report.[339]

If Brusilov wanted to keep an army, it was not necessary to remain stationary for too long. On 4 June, the offensive was launched which would go down in history as the Brusilov Offensive. Despite the fact that the offensive was conducted over a very long front, it was a great success. The attack was well prepared and the Russian artillery performed it skilfully. The Austro-Hungarian troops, unlike the German units, proved not to be tough enough to withstand the attacks. The Russians had shelled the enemy positions for a long time with their artillery before attacking with the infantry. The Czechs lived up to their unreliable reputation by defecting en masse here and there. Commander-in-Chief Conrad swallowed his pride after only a day and called on the Germans for help. Von Falkenhayn immediately responded that he had no troops available.

On 6 June, it was clear that in some places the front had been torn open over a depth of 75 kilometres. 'Those terrible Ruthenians have gone over to the Russians again', the Germans thought desperately. The 'Mährischen Regiment nr.8' went on the run en masse. The German General Linsingen demanded the resignation of the Archduke Joseph Ferdinand, who was clearly incapable of leading his army capably. It was highly unusual for this far-reaching demand to be granted immediately. There was no time for long toes as the Emperor Franz Joseph was reported as a 'new Königgrätz' at the court in Vienna. The Austro-Hungarian officers, some with wives and even entire families, hurried in their cars to the hinterland, while the wounded remained in the field.

Franz Joseph banged his fist on the table and demanded reliable news from the front, because he read more in the foreign media than he heard from his soldiers. Emergency sessions were organised at the court, during which the very elderly Franz Joseph regularly dozed off, but nevertheless got enough information to understand that an enormous disaster was looming.[340] The 4th k.u.k. army was now led by General Tersztyanszky, an officer known as 'rücksichtslos', but more talented than Ferdinand. However, a retreat could not be avoided. On 10 June, the 7th army collapsed after fighting near Okna, thirty kilometres from Czernowitz. The Germans travelled back and forth to the k.u.k. headquarters to save the day. 'We are completely in German hands', Conrad thought bitterly, but understood that he could do little against it. The army of the dual monarchy had lost its credibility with the success of the Brusilov offensive.

The German general Von Seeckt was deprived of the Balkan front and transferred to Conrad's Austro-Hungarian staff, where he replaced colonel Zeynek, who was sent on leave. Ludendorff went to see Von Seeckt, and both found that the situation was very dangerous. Units were dragged from everywhere to save the cause, even from the western front. Von Falkenhayn had to bow to reality and was left no choice. Even Turkish units were used which, according to Ludendorff, functioned well, even if they had to get used to the way of war. The Oberost extended its influence to the Pripjat area, in order to create order in the chaos. In the end, Brusilov did not achieve an operational breakthrough, but his armies had gained a lot of ground and killed or captured astronomical numbers of soldiers of the k.u.k. army. Most sources put the losses at 226,000 men, out of a total of 475,000 troops that the k.u.k. army had in the field between Pripiat and Bukovina. [341]

In the meantime, the front line had moved eerily close to the Hungarian border, especially in the south. Brusilov could have been even more successful if there had not been disagreements within the Russian camp. The Russian generals Evert and Kuropatkin believed that there were also good Russian opportunities north of the Pripjat marshes, in Oberost's territory. Yet, other generals, including Brusilov, pointed out that the recent setbacks during the thaw had indicated that it was better to operate against the k.u.k. army than against the tough German divisions. Nevertheless, Stavka held on to over 700,000 troops north of Pripjat, even when Brusilov, who had 60,000 troops tied up in casualties, needed reinforcements very urgently to make a real strategic breakthrough. Instead, Evert undertook an offensive in a small front sector, heavily supported by artillery, in which, although two k.u.k. divisions were thrown back, two German infantry divisions of Oberost restored the peace. Evert lost 80,000 soldiers, compared to 16,000 losses on the German side. These battles, which took place near Baranovichi, showed that Brusilov was right and that the real operative possibilities lay against the troops of the dual monarchy. Precious time had been lost.[342]

On 27 July, urgent consultations were held in Pless with the German Emperor and the field commanders. It was decided to put increasing pressure on Vienna to convince 'Grosspapa' that the general supreme command should be a German affair and that this was also to the advantage of the k.u.k. troops. Ludendorff was present at these negotiations and fully agreed. A common supreme command became 'unavoidable'. As well as other changes in the supreme command. The position of Von Falkenhayn, who after the failures on the Western Front also initially misjudged the situation on the Eastern Front, became weaker and weaker. Within the political circles voices were raised to push Von Hindenburg and Ludendorff to the front. A new drama gave a final push. On 14 August 1916, radio messages were received from which it became clear that the Romanians were making contact with the Entente and that cooperation was in the air. This would bring yet another enemy.

Romanian politics had been overwhelmed by the Brusilov offensive and the concomitant heavy losses to the k.u.k. army. The decision to assist the Entente was at odds with the country's military planning. The reasonably modern army had aimed its fortifications to the east, to Russia, in the so-called Sereth Line. Now, suddenly, the enemy was in the west.[343] But in Bucharest, hidden behind eighteen modern forts, this 'detail' was pushed aside. It was time for a revision of the borders, especially with the Hungarians.

Ludendorff and Von Hindenburg observed all these developments with increasing disquiet from their new headquarters in Brest-Litowsk, where they had moved into the old fortress. The quiet days of Kaunas were now definitely behind them. The Brusilov offensive had brought Ludendorff from the sidelines back into the focus of the war. Brest-Litowsk was a reminder of the horrors of war. The city had been largely burnt down. The citadel in which Ludendorff took up residence looked like a small prison, and 'it smelt musty and damp', he wrote in his memoirs.[344] He had trees cut down to create light and was once again at work in his small room when, on 27 August, news arrived that Romania had indeed declared war on the Central Powers. One day later, Ludendorff and Von Hindenburg were ordered to report to the Kaiser.

Chapter 6

At the height of his fame

The war was two years old when Ludendorff left Brest-Litowsk for the Kaiser in Pless. The German press did its best to portray the situation for Germany as rosy as possible. On paper, there were results to report; 2.658283 prisoners of war for example, and the fact that Germany occupied 431.000 km² land, most of it in Russia (280.000 km²), but also large parts of Belgium (29.000 km²), France (21.000 km²) and Serbia (87.000 km²). These occupied territories, according to the *Frankfurter Zeitung*, were a fistful for Germany if peace talks were to begin.[345] The setbacks, such as the loss of the town of Brody during the Brusilov offensive, were dismissed as minorities. This was only a 'provincial town' with eighteen thousand, mostly Jewish, inhabitants, which otherwise 'had no strategic significance whatsoever'. People also tried to minimise the losses of the k.u.k. army. The Russians would have deported many inhabitants from the conquered areas and counted them as losses of the k.u.k. army. The increasing animosity against the Centrals, like the declaration of war by Portugal, was brushed aside as unimportant. This 'vassal state' of Britain was of no importance. Zeppelin attacks on London, which were of no military significance, were celebrated as a success. But that did not alter the fact that there was growing unease about the friction with the United States, which was watching developments in Europe with suspicion.[346]

Ludendorff and von Hindenburg knew better when they went to Pless. The offensive in the west was hopelessly bogged down, they counted on major counter-actions from the British and the French. On the sea, they were faced with the difficult choice of the unrestricted submarine war, in the east, the k.u.k. army was badly beaten and the tsarist army since the Brusilov offensive again a party of importance. To top it all off came the betrayal of Romania. These developments on the Eastern Front had paralysed the central offensives against

Italy. The balance of forces, despite all the fancy numbers, favoured the Entente, which had a 3:2 advantage in the west.

Ludendorff knew that a great task might await him in Pless, as he had done after the fall of Liège. The hopeless attacks in the west and the problems in the east had seriously undermined Von Falkenhayn's position. Even Kaiser Wilhelm II, who had a personal aversion to the intransigent Ludendorff, distanced himself from his favourite, who had visibly aged due to the developments and walked around with a drawn face and a set mouth. The signs of this could be seen in the last few meetings in Pless. At the discussion on 27 July, when Von Falkenhayn again tried to marginalise Oberost's influence, the Kaiser had even become angry and had shouted that he 'would not leave the room until the matter was settled'. Von Hindenburg and Ludendorff had then got their way, at least in so far as their position of power on the Eastern Front had been extended in a southern (k.u.k.) direction to the area around the town of Brody. From there to the south, Von Seeckt watched over the front. On 30 July, Von Falkenhayn had not turned up at the Imperial banquet, an omen of his crumbling power and the fact that he found it hard to face. In fact, Oberost's camp already saw their chance on that date. Together with Hoffmann, Ludendorff tried to get Von Hindenburg to give Von Falkenhayn's shaky position a final push. But as usual, Von Hindenburg hesitated for a long time. The old general considered such a request rather unmilitary. These discussions always had the same course. Ludendorff turned red and Hoffmann, for whom the world had no secrets, turned his eyes to heaven.

'The situation is serious', General von Lyncker had said over the phone, and this became apparent immediately upon arrival. Ludendorff, who travelled together with Major von Bockelberg and Von Hindenburg, was awaited at the station by Von Lyncker. Here, they were told that Von Falkenhayn would be replaced. Ludendorff knew what that meant, for von Hindenburg would not relinquish his brilliant shadow. The choice for Von Hindenburg was an automatic choice for Ludendorff. Ludendorff was appointed 'Zweiter Generalstabchef', which was reformulated into 'Erster Generalquartiermeister' on Ludendorff's request. This was a test of vanity, power and small-mindedness, although the influence of hierarchical thinking within 'das Militär' can hardly be overestimated. Max Weber spoke of Ludendorff with a mixture of realism and derision: 'Deutschlands Nummer eins'.[347] But perhaps it was more than vanity. Ludendorff also wanted to emphasise that he too was emphatically responsible for policy, and not just Von Hindenburg, even though Kaiser Wilhelm II mockingly called him 'Der Feldwebel' behind his back.[348] 'The appointment is like a dream', Von Hindenburg wrote to his wife, 'what a turning point, by the hand of God'.[349]

The emperor tried to make the transfer of power go smoothly. Even the Empress was employed for this purpose. In front of Pless Castle, Kaiser Wilhelm II, Von Falkenhayn and Bethmann-Hollweg were already waiting for Oberost's men. After a short ceremony, Von Falkenhayn shook hands with Von Hindenburg and bowed slightly. He wished him God's blessing. Then he turned and left the palace without giving Ludendorff the time of day.[350] The Emperor remained behind with his new team, men who were much less like him, his old dissidents: Von Hindenburg, whom he found unimaginative and wooden, and Ludendorff, whose lack of humour and honour he feared. 'The Emperor has a hangover, because of Von Falkenhayn's resignation,' wrote Admiral Von Muller. When the Chancellor tried to console the Kaiser that the people would welcome Von Hindenburg's appointment, the Kaiser grumbled that 'he could not care less about the opinion of the people'. [351]

However, the change of power was a 'necessity', as the historian Karl Tschuppik put it[35]; Wilhelm II had no choice. With the fall of Von Falkenhayn and the earlier debacle with Von Moltke, also a confidant of the Kaiser, Wilhelm II had lost power. Although he was officially the supreme commander of the German army, his position would become more and more symbolic. Now was the time for what Von Hindenburg called the 'happy marriage',[353] the Von Hindenburg-Ludendorff duo. Von Hindenburg resolved to give Ludendorff's 'superhuman labour power' free rein and, if necessary, to provide it. That was Von Hindenburg's task. [354]

The next few months were the most glorious of Ludendorff's career, although they were only partly due to resounding victories in the field. It was precisely the mastering and restructuring of the almost impossible situation in which Germany found itself that elevated Ludendorff to the pinnacle. The package of measures with which he set to work immediately after being appointed to his new position was reminiscent of his first appearance after the fall of Liège. While the army in the east was falling back after the unfortunate battle at Gumbinnen, it was Ludendorff who intervened in the situation from a thousand kilometres away. He did so again and made three crucial decisions:
1) He stopped the madness at Verdun
2) He decided on drastic front reduction on the Western Front
3) He dealt with Romania

Of course, Ludendorff had to have a strong power base to push through these measures. Therefore, during the first days, Ludendorff immediately appointed some confidants to important positions. They were all very diligent and loyal men, such as Major Wetzell, who replaced Oberst Tappen in the staff, and Major von Bockelberg, who took charge of organising the 'Ersatz', the replenishments.[355]

One of Ludendorff's first visits was on 5 September to the army headquarters of Crown Prince Rupprecht von Bayern in Cambrai. Ludendorff shuttled back and forth between Charleville and local headquarters for his command. The OHL's supreme command, with an eye to the Eastern Front, remained in Pless. Upon arrival in Cambrai, Ludendorff was received with a guard of honour from the Von Rohr storm battalion. Here, Ludendorff saw for the first time the new German 'Stahlhelm', which was still unknown in the east.[356]

From 21 February 1916 onwards, the exhaustive battle of Verdun had been raging. All in all, the Germans had thrown in some 50 divisions, but had only gained a small amount of ground against the French, who were stubbornly defending themselves under the command of General Pétain, appointed on 31 March. Fort Douaumont had fallen, but there was no decisive breakthrough. In the end, the German losses amounted to approximately 362,000 men against 336,831 French.[357] Moreover, in counterattacks the ground gained was lost again. Ludendorff thought the massacres at Verdun were not in the tradition of Von Schlieffen and ended them immediately. 'Verdun has cost us a lot of blood', Ludendorff stated in his memoirs. In addition, the longer they fought, the worse the situation had become for Germany. The soldiers were stuck in the 'Trichterfeld', and the leadership was fed up.[358]

In addition, the British had begun their great offensive at the Somme on 1 July. This great battle continued until 13 November and was a slaughter unparalleled in history. The rainy soil coloured blood red on the Western Front as 55 British divisions, far larger than the average German and French division, bayoneted the rifle and tried to break through the front. But the German positions held firm, even though they were in crisis and ran out of ammunition. Germany lost 650,000 men, British losses amounted to about 420,000 and French losses to almost 200,000.[359] Ludendorff noted with concern the increasing physical and psychological strain on the German soldiers. Since the German army hardly had any reserve troops left, the units had to stay at the front for a long time, in an almost permanent drumbeat. Only in the rear trenches could they get some rest, but that rest was relative. The material and physical superiority of the Entente began to take its toll. One could also see it in the air armoury, which became more and more important. Ludendorff scraped everything together and passed the test at the Somme, albeit with difficulty. He personally saw to the distribution of the ammunition supplies, which were brought in from the hinterland. In this way, the few shells were at least delivered to where the Entente was most dangerous.[360]

It was in these days that Ludendorff drew up his plan that would lead to a brilliant solution to the German problems: the front reduction. This was a revolutionary idea in those days, where people fought for every metre. 'Great mistakes have been made and it is high time to put things in order', Ludendorff stated.[361] Ludendorff understood that the weak Germany, which in terms of material also had to keep its allies, Vienna, Istanbul and Sofia, on their feet, had to prepare itself for the long lasting 'Abwehrschlacht'. For this purpose, Ludendorff, inspired by Oberst Fritz von Lossberg and his experiences at the Somme, advocated in-depth defence.[362] The infantrymen were now too stuck on the battlefield. They had to become agile infantry again, shock troops, who could move in a depth field, in which the German artillery and newly established machine gun and machine gun units also had to play a role.

In practice, one German infantry division was needed for every five kilometres of front. A shortening of the front could in this way free up much-needed divisions to serve as strategic reserves. This not only had advantages in defence, but they could be deployed in threatened frontal sectors. This would also give the German army opportunities for future offensive operations.

On 8 September, Ludendorff had an important meeting with the commanders of the Western Front in Cambrai. The facts spoke volumes, 3,900,000 Entente soldiers stood against 2,500,000 German soldiers.[363] As was typical for Ludendorff, he immediately dictated a large number of measures which he considered necessary. Given the political cover Ludendorff enjoyed and the appointment of his own people to key positions, it was mainly a matter of organising to get, at least the material part, done. And organizing Ludendorff could do well, trained as he was in the stage discipline of Von Schlieffen. The troops, Ludendorff thought, were mainly exhausted because they were constantly at the front. They were mainly concerned with survival; confidence had to be regained and the German soldiers had to know that fresh units and optimal artillery were behind them, and they themselves had to react flexibly in the depths of defence. All this, said the historian Wolfgang Venohr, made an 'overwhelming impression' on the officers present. The uncompromising attitude and persuasiveness of the deadly serious Ludendorff brought a 'new spirit' to the German camp.[364]

Not Ludendorff the strategist, but Ludendorff the organiser was at work here. When the officers met again on 17 January 1917, only four and a half months later, Ludendorff had kept his word. On the Western Front, the soldier from Ernst Jünger's novels had emerged. The self-confident soldier, whom Ludendorff also had re-trained during their stay in the hinterland. The positions were equipped with artillery officers who used their signal pistols to call for artillery support in case of enemy attacks. The artillery had gone from one gun every

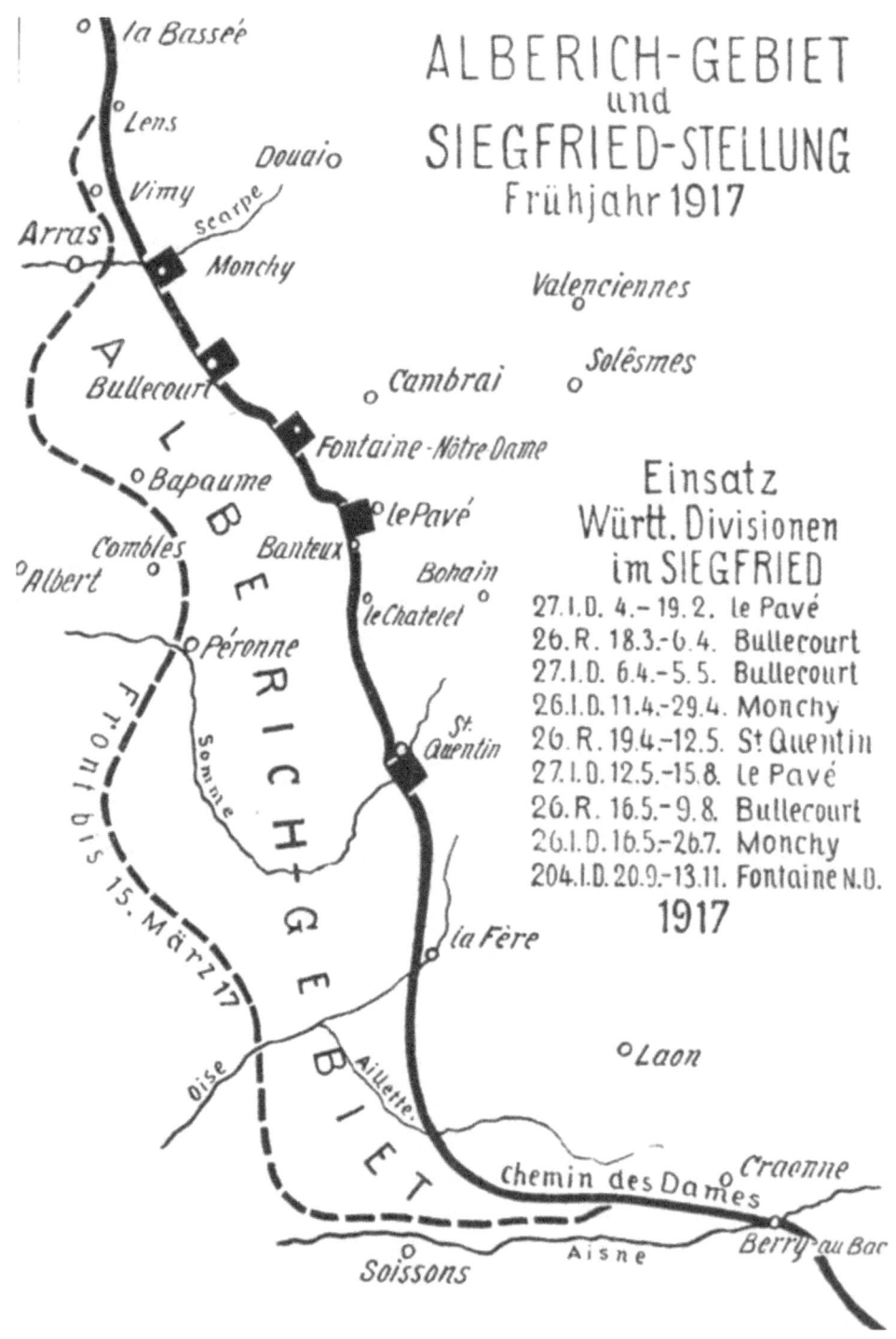

Alberich retreat and Siegfried Line

hundred metres to one gun every fifty metres. This involved an annual production of 5,000 barrels. Warfare was rationalised. [365]

Through all these measures, Ludendorff succeeded in stabilising the western front. The former NATO officer and Ludendorff biographer Franz Uhle-Wettler spoke of an 'innere Konsolidierung'.[366] In addition to technical improvements in production and training, the self-imposed retreat, the so-called 'Alberich-Rückzug' was the core of the stabilisation. Alberich was the magic dwarf from the Germanic legends, and indeed there was something magical about Ludendorff's decision. Behind the existing lines, Ludendorff had the so-called 'Siegfriedstellung' built, which ran from Cobourg -Arras -St.Quentin to Soissons. On 19 March 1917, the Germans succeeded in taking back 29 divisions from the winding front line to the new 'Siegfriedstellung'. The Entente was stunned and it was not until 5 April 1917 that 'contact' with the German units was restored.

This was not only because of the surprise element of the 'Alberich retreat', but also because of the fact that a front, encrypted in a trench system, could not be shifted just like that. In total, a terrain with a depth of thirty kilometres had been given up just like that. But Ludendorff was concerned with the rationalisation of the front. The shortening of the front provided him with fourteen divisions immediately, so that Germany could build up an operative reserve again to resist enemy attacks and possibly also to take up arms itself again.[367] Apart from the flawless 'Alberich Movement', the construction of the 'Siegfriedstelling' was also a top achievement. No less than 70,000 workers had worked on it and 50,000 railway wagons and 450 boats had been used. Ludendorff removed a total of 37,000 wagons of material from the evacuated areas; nothing of any value was to be left behind. [368]

Finally, there was Romania. That country was one of the main oil producers for Germany and its allies. German oil production was about 80% of pre-war needs. Considering that the British blockade successfully cut off oil supplies from overseas, that 80% was still quite an achievement. However, compared to the Entente, which now used and had at its disposal twice as much oil than before 1914, Germany was in a vulnerable position. Lord Curzon did not say that 'the Entente swam to victory on a wave of oil' for nothing.[369]

It was none other than General Von Falkenhayn who was allowed victory here. As commander-in-chief of the 9th army, he was deployed against the Romanian troops. Under command of General Vasile Zottu, 23 infantry divisions and two cavalry divisions of the Romanians were mobilised. The expectations in Bucharest were high. They had only declared war on Austria-Hungary in order

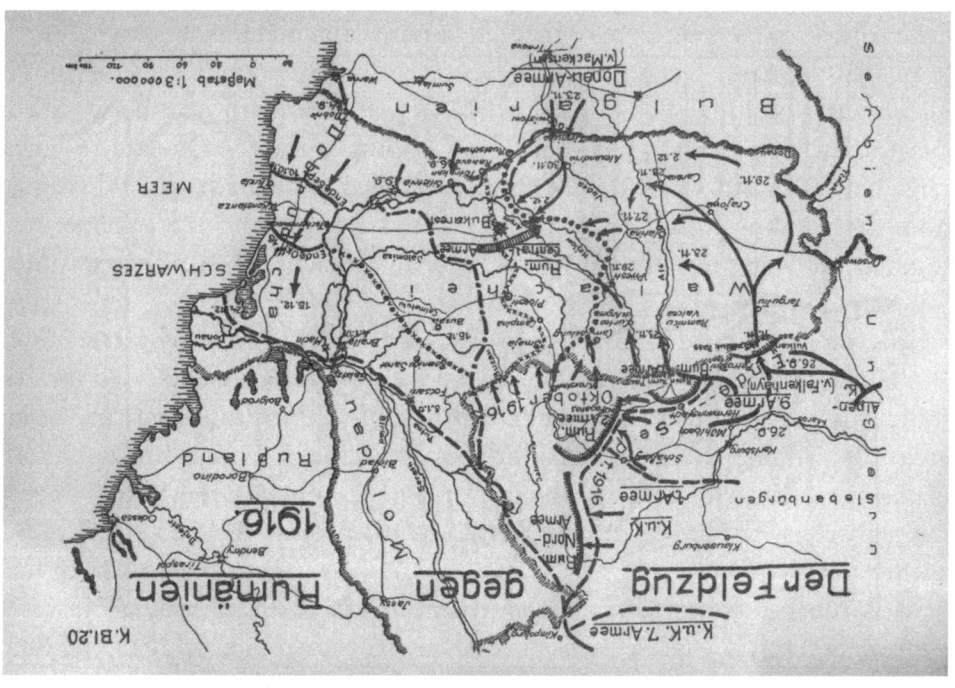

Campaign against Romania

to keep the Germans, who the Romanians thought would be too busy with the Brusilov offensive and the Somme, out of the war. In this way, Siebenbürgen and parts of Bulgaria could be conquered. Zottu dreamed even further. He suggested that the Romanians should be at Debrecen in eastern Hungary on their 39th mobilisation day.

Zottu's 370,000 men were initially met only by a hastily assembled army of 34,000 - mostly Hungarian - soldiers under command of General Arz von Straussenburg (the so-called 1st army), but troops of Von Falkenhayn's 9th army and German-Bulgarian-Turkish units under Von Mackensen from Dobrudscha in the south soon joined them. This energetic concentric approach against the very slow and fragmented Romanian army proved extremely successful. 'Herrliche Siege' followed, as the later famous Africa corps general Erwin Rommel put it.[370] The Romanians advanced as if they had never looked at a map before. Railways and railway stations, essential for foraging, seemed unheard of and supplying their troops quickly became a huge problem. In addition, the central ammunition depot in Bucharest was accidentally blown up, resulting in the loss of millions of cartridges. 'The Romanians are bad soldiers', Ludendorff thought before the campaign, and he was right.[371]

To the shock of the Entente, the relatively small central armies (eventually about 200,000 men), which had been partly formed by further skimming from the western front, quickly managed to take over the initiative. The only delays were caused by the slow Hungarian railways and the rugged terrain.[372] Especially the attack from the south was unexpected. Only in the mountain passes did the Romanians hold out temporarily, but then it was all over. 'This is an enemy we can defeat in the field,' thought Von Falkenhayn.[373] On 23 November, the central troops crossed the Danube and Von Mackensen advanced via Sistor to Bucharest. All this did not go without problems. For a moment, in the morning haze, Von Mackensen's Bulgarian soldiers threatened mutiny. They feared the wide river and the rickety boats. Von Mackensen managed to get hold of better boats and under the cheerful accompaniment of the regimental band, the soldiers were finally prepared to risk the dangerous crossing.[374] On 6 December, the Romanian capital already fell. The modern fortifications were blown up by the fleeing Romanians themselves. A French military delegation under General Henri Berthelot, who came to the rescue, could not turn the tide. The Russians, too, had their hands full after the Brusilov offensive stalled. It was above all the fighting near Kowel and in Galicia that tied the Russians' hands. There was a large Russian army north of the Pripjat marshes, but it could not move forward during the Brusilov offensive and thus stood idly by. Where the Russians did cooperate with the Romanians, the cooperation was traumatic. It soon became clear to the Russians that the newfound allies had little fighting spirit. In some encounters between Russians and Romanians, the latter surrendered immediately because they thought they were facing Bulgarian units. In the end, the Stavka did not have many soldiers left to save Bucharest. A cavalry corps was sent, but it had to cover a distance of 600 kilometres. On the way, the horses' hooves had to be re-shod, which could take a week in Romania. By that time, Bucharest had fallen. The Stavka's main concern was to preserve Moldova as a shield against the Centrals.[375]

In Bucharest, according to the astonished Von Mackensen, who had rushed ahead of his troops in a car like a "Blücher", there was hardly any sign of the war. The cafés and terraces were full and the shops were open. 'What a light-hearted, superficial people', Von Mackensen noted of his experiences. As thanks for his role, Kaiser Wilhelm named a cruiser after the general.[376] Erwin Rommel, looking back on the Romanians, said that they were 'skilful mountaineers' but that Romanians, with their curiously pointed field hats, 'were not very good soldiers'.[377]

The Romanians had miscalculated. The Germans had stood firm for their allies, and Turkey and Bulgaria had also declared war. In barely twenty-five days, the Romanian danger had been averted. At the end of 1916, the Centrals stood at the river Sereth. The Romanian army then numbered only 70,000 soldiers[378] and was supported by the Russians on all sides. 'It was not smart of the Russians to let the Romanians enter Siebenbürgen on their own', said Von Hindenburg in his memoirs. The fall of Bucharest, however, was not the fault of Romania's allies but of the Romanians themselves. An example of the poor discipline in the Romanian army was the flight of divisional general Socec, who simply abandoned his troops. Later, this case came before a military court, but the Socec file 'disappeared' and the general went free.[379] The Sereth had not become the Marne, despite the efforts of the Russians and the Frenchman Henri Berthelot, who had served on the Marne under Joffre. The Entente forces destroyed the Romanian oil fields and harvest as thoroughly as they could. The suffocating smoke covered the humiliated Romania. The conqueror of Liège was at the height of his power.

After the fall of Romania, Ludendorff threatened to get into a diplomatic row. The Bulgarians also made their appearance at the distribution of the booty. The envoys of the Bulgarian king Ferdinand, who had remained loyal to the German emperor, wanted to cash in on their contribution. The ancient Macedonian-Bulgarian bond was to be strengthened territorially and the Black Sea coast of Dobrudja was on the list. Kaiser Wilhelm awarded the port city of Konstanza, which had also been conquered by the Bulgarians, to Sofia. But Ludendorff did not give in so easily. When the Bulgarian military envoy General Gantchew visited Ludendorff, he told the astonished Bulgarians that Germany claimed a strip of land on the Black Sea. A part of Dobrudja was to become a German Black Sea port, he announced. Gantchew pointed out to Ludendorff that such a narrow corridor was not a realistic policy. The German troops would be isolated. 'If you are difficult, I will show no more interest in Bulgaria's wishes,' Ludendorff snapped at Gantchew. The Bulgarian did not allow himself to be swayed and replied: 'It would be extremely beneficial if your 'Exzellenz' would stop taking an interest in us, and leave it to Foreign Affairs'. Ludendorff rose from his chair with a red head. He pointed to the door and said: 'Adieu!' [380]

Chapter 7

Ludendorff's dictatorship

The stabilisation of the western front and the successes in the east almost concealed the fact that the glory days of the German army were waning. There were all sorts of new dangers on the horizon. Ludendorff reacted as he always did: he worked harder, pressed his chin further and further against his chest and radiated intransigence. Von Hindenburg stood behind his brilliant apprentice as always, juggling with divisions, corps, armies, and, at this time, also with production figures and social issues. Ludendorff, who slept only a few hours a day, seemed to have the 'philosopher's stone' in his possession for the time being, given the drastic changes for the better since Oberost had been given total command. But appearances were deceiving, and a series of compiled issues demanded attention: there were new military-technical developments that caused concern. For example, the gas war had broken out in full force; the tank weapon was making its appearance; the submarine war was becoming a full-scale reality; Germany was suffering under the British hunger blockade, which was causing scarcity; in the east, the Russian revolution was taking place; and there were signs of war weariness in the dual monarchy.

France was the first country to use chemical weapons. In August, the French army already used tear gas. The Germans followed suit in October 1914 at Neuve Chapelle.[381] After several gas exercises in the Oberost area, which are described in Max Hoffmann's memoirs, the Germans used gas massively near Ypres in April 1915. This was also where the first large number of casualties occurred, with an estimated 5,000 killed and some 10,000 wounded.

On 25 September 1915, the British retaliated at Artois-Loos with gas attacks of their own. After this, it was impossible to imagine trench warfare in the West without gas. One of the low points was the German gas attack during the solstice, 22 June 1916, near Verdun (Fort Souville). Here, the Germans tried to fire more than 100,000 gas grenades at the French positions in a short time. Although this number was not entirely achieved, more than 1600 ammunition barrels of grenades were fired at the French. The Germans had equipped the shells with the new phosphorus gas, which the French gas masks did not yet have protection against. To prevent the gas from evaporating quickly in sunlight, the attacks were partly carried out after sunset. This was a very macabre war. The French artillery reacted alertly and managed to hit some of the stores of the German chemical shells, causing losses on the German side as well. [382]

In the summer of 1917, a very deadly variant was added: mustard gas, which forced the soldiers to protect themselves in very impractical clothing in the already uncomfortable trench 'Alltag'.[383] According to Hoffmann, Germany had missed a great opportunity with regard to the gas weapon; it was too little and too late for the Germans to come up with it, and he drew a comparison with the submarine war.[384]

The first initiative regarding the tank weapon also came from the Allied side. It was the British who, as early as in October 1914, came up with the first plans to break through the difficult terrain and stellar warfare. Initially, a tractor-like construction was considered, but gradually the tank (initially a pseudonym) came into the picture. This had everything to do with the fact that the existing military resources were insufficient to get the stagnant front going again.

In February 1915, the British conducted the first experiments to this end. The makers and designers had to contend with sceptical executives, including Lord Kitchener, the man made famous by his victory over Omdurman in 1898. In January 1916, the first live-fire exercises were conducted. Counterfeit German 50mm guns were used against the first armoured vehicles and the next month the results were proudly shown to Kitchener, Lloyd George and Balfour. This was the deciding factor, and in April the first 150 tanks were ordered for the British forces.

The tank became part of the Entente's strategic thinking. Sir Douglas Haig even urged the use of tanks at the Somme. It took until August 1916 before the first tanks were available for the front. At Cambrai, opposite the Gruppe Arras and Gruppe Caudry at the Canal de la Escaut, the first larger deployment of tanks took place, although it was modest with 32 tanks. Entente pilots then reported a breakthrough thanks the new weapon - an advance to the town of Flers. The infantry, so the reports then said, went after it jubilantly. At Verdun, no less than 14 million shells had been fired, without a breakthrough; here, a handful of tanks brought about a shift in the front.

On the French side, the tank fire test was held on 16 April 1917 at Berry-au Bac, within the framework of the French 5th army. Here, 128 tanks of the Schneider type were used. Again they were successful, although the losses were high. A quarter of the French tank crews were killed, 81 tanks were lost. However, the Entente command was convinced of the possibilities of this weapon and thousands of tanks were ordered, and would reinforce the battlefields on the western front at the end of 1917 and in the course of 1918. [385]

Like Kitchener, Ludendorff initially underestimated the new tank weapon. In December 1917, the German army had only three companies of their own tanks, the unwieldy A7V, a hastily assembled juggernaut that hardly resembled a tank, but rather resembled a moving fortress. Typically, the Germans had seven tank companies at their disposal, the other four being captured Entente tanks. These were collected and refurbished in Charleroi and made ready for use by their own troops. The lion's share were Mark IV tanks, the most important British tank of the war, of which 1015 were produced in various versions.[386]

Due to the parity with regard to the gas war - the fact that on the western front there were more westerly winds than easterly winds (thus favourable to the Entente), and also because they had missed the boat with the tank development, another weapon came to the foreground more strongly than ever: the submarine.

There had already been international tensions because of the generous torpedoing policy of the German submarines, in which sailors and passengers from neutral countries - and especially important: from the United States - also lost their lives. The most notorious affair was the torpedoing of the *Lusitania*. This 6,000-tonne crown jewel of the Cunard Line was one of the fastest ships in the world and its torpedoing in May 1915 caused great international outrage. The *Lusitania* was not the only incident in which American citizens lost their lives. In April 1915, two American steamships were torpedoed, as well as the British ship *Falaba*, which also had Americans on board. [387]

At the end of 1916, beginning of 1917, the submarine war came back to the top of the agenda. Considering the enormous consequence of restarting the unrestricted submarine war, namely the entry of the US into the war, it is almost inconceivable today that the German supreme command, within which Ludendorff had a heavy voice, dared to take this step. It seems like political and military suicide. And yet there were many reasons why the German supreme command ultimately chose this extreme weapon.

- The US threatened war against Germany but had actually been involved in the conflict for a long time. The North Americans were already supplying the Entente with war material.
- The US could threaten war but did not (yet) have a real army that could be

sent out as an expeditionary force.
- Should this expeditionary army be formed, then according to German estimates it would take about a year before American troops were on the European continent. During that time, Germany could try to bring the Entente powers to their knees with its unrestricted submarine warfare.
- For the German High Command, and certainly for Ludendorff, the submarine war was the ultimate weapon that could tip the balance in favour of German victory. Ludendorff had stabilised the other fronts, despite the numerical superiority of the Entente and the problems with gas and tanks. But a victory in the field was not achievable. Victory required an additional weapon; the Entente had tanks, the Germans their submarines.
- The German admirals supported Ludendorff's opinion. They foresaw a large-scale operation which could starve Great Britain to death in a very short time. This would turn public opinion in Great Britain against the British 'Warlords' and put the BEF, the British expeditionary army, in a difficult position. On 22 December 1916, the Navy had sent a 'Denkschrift' with this meaning to Von Hindenburg. The document was called 'Ueber die Notwendigkeit des uneingeschraenkten U-Boot-Krieges' that reached the OHL office via Admiral Henning von Holtzendorff, the Chief of the Admiral Staff. This report carried weight.
- A successful German submarine war could further end the British hunger blockade of Germany.

Finally, if fully successful, the submarine war would also be able to prevent the arrival of American troops on the European continent.

The equally historic and fateful decision to restart the unrestricted submarine war was taken on 1 February 1917, after earlier consultations on 9 January at Pless, in the presence of the Kaiser, Von Hindenburg and Ludendorff. Ludendorff, whose main concerns now, as with Von Falkenhayn, lay on the Western Front, was motivated by his unceasing concern to hold out against the numerical superiority of the Entente. He hoped that the submarine war would already weaken the Entente front in the short term. Von Hindenburg, as usual, supported Ludendorff and reported to the Kaiser, and his argument carried much weight, that without the unrestricted submarine war he could no longer take responsibility for the operations. In fact, Von Hindenburg threatened to resign, although it was not expressed so loudly. The Kaiser's hands were tied. The pressure on the politicians who were watching, such as Bethmann-Hollweg, was enormous. He was no match for the 'pair of Titans' who pushed through this terribly far-reaching decision in just half an hour. Bethmann-Hollweg, in turn, now consulted with the Head of the War Cabinet, Hauptmann Valentini, and toyed with the thought of whether he should resign now. In the end, everyone remained seated, but the German's fate was sealed.

Ludendorff, who in addition to the strategic plans was never averse to an internal coup, tried to further jeopardise Bethmann-Hollweg's shaky position with the Kaiser by proposing his resignation. In the passing shadow of the U-boat debate, an internal power struggle had begun. Still, the Kaiser was not the kind of person who would easily dismiss his confidants. Wilhelm II had lingered over Moltke, and over Von Falkenhayn. Now he was covering Bethmann-Hollweg, just as he would leave the duo Hindeburg and Ludendorff at their posts for a long time to come.

On 31 January, the German envoy in Washington delivered the fatal news to the American authorities. The Jewish magnate Albert Ballin, owner of the Hamburg-America Line, had stormed into Ludendorff's office. This 'verdammte Jude', as Ludendorff called him, had told him the truth in no uncertain terms: 'I may not have long to live', he thought, 'but you, you will be put to death during the war'. [388]

A dark prophecy hung over Ludendorff. Ballin's concern was justified, also from a military point of view. A total of 105 submarines were available, but at the time of launch, the actual number of immediately deployable ships was much smaller. In addition, all parties suffered terrible losses as a result of the new course. Germany would lose the astronomical number of 178 submarines in the Great War.[389] The German submarine fleet had been strongly forced into existence. When the war broke out in 1914, there were 400 submarines worldwide, but Germany had only twenty at its disposal. The French and British navies together had 200 submarines available in 1914. It was an emergency programme for the German Navy, although they were able to deploy them with astonishing effectiveness. Yet, here too, it was too little and too late.

Ludendorff's decision to allow unrestricted submarine warfare to take place - February 1917 - initially brought about a crisis in British naval policy. Losses rose dramatically, but the introduction of convoy warfare turned the tide. In total, more than 2600 Entente ships, mostly of British origin, were lost. Once again the Germans fought a magnificent battle, but without it being decisive, and with all the consequences that this entailed. [390]

The passing of political criticism of the unrestricted submarine war exposed another problem of the military dictatorship that was emerging in Germany. The military seemed to interpret any doubt expressed by Bethmann-Hollweg as defeatism. The historian Czech-Jochberg believed that Bethmann-Hollweg had understood nothing of the German geopolitical situation. He illustrated this by pointing out that in the August days of 1914, he had spoken of a 'peaceful mobilisation'.[391] The Schlieffenplan was wasted on Bethmann-Hollweg. When the submarine war did not yield the desired result, 'das Militär' did not hesitate to blame the critic of the unrestricted submarine war. Bethmann-Hollweg's 'resistance' had delayed the submarine war and thus caused it to fail, which was a blatant lie.[392] The former Minister of Defence, Von Einem, put it somewhat more tactfully, but also attacked Bethmann-Hollweg for his critical attitude towards the developments of the war. He believed that Bethmann-Hollweg was 'a pleasant and humorous man', a 'good civil servant with the gift of the word', but that he was not cut out for war. Bethmann-Hollweg was, from the outset, after 'Verständigung' and lacked the specific warlike qualities of a Poincaré, Clemenceau or Lloyd George, who wanted to win the war without compromise. Bethmann-Hollweg's 'Verständigungspolitik' led to 'Unentschlossenheit'. [393]

Theobald von Bethmann-Hollweg had found himself in a difficult position, allowing the 'Diktatur Ludendorff' to grow in power. The left side of politics had strong expectations of reform from the politician, who himself had also indicated that he wanted to break the power of the 'ostelbian Junkers', but between word and deed lay reality. The historian Fritz Fischer believed that Bethmann-Hollweg was actually much more conservative than he was willing to admit. In practice, Bethmann-Hollweg was a supporter of a kind of Wilhelmine polder model, in which he wanted to keep the various extremes in check. The result in the long run was that everyone became disappointed. In the eyes of the left, he did not offer enough counterweight to the 'Alldeutschen', conservatives and national liberals. In the eyes of the conservative bloc, Bethmann-Hollweg was a 'Flaumacher', a 'bundle of nerves' and 'stickler for power', who wanted to saddle Germany with a false peace. In the matter of the unrestricted submarine war, Bethmann-Hollweg simply had to deal with too many parties at once. A political troika of conservatives, national liberals and centre - in the form of Kuno Graf Westarp, Ernst Bassermann and Peter Spahn - had made it clear to the Chancellor that they supported the unrestricted submarine war; indicating that there were also strong pro-forces in parliament. Ludendorff lost the submarine war but won the political debate. [394]

The political struggle led to a long debate among historians about the position of Bethmann-Hollweg versus 'das Militär'. Hans Herzfeld believed that the Chancellor had so skimped on the defence budget even before 1914 that Germany was bound to lose the war. However the left-wing historian Willibald Gutsche protected him and blamed Germany's downfall on the overzealous military ambitions of the Hindenburg-Ludendorff duo, with the latter in particular getting a thrashing as a militarist and the reincarnation of evil.[395] Conrad Bornhak took a middle position and characterised the Chancellor as 'a pessimistic philosopher without national panache'.

The latter with some justification. Indeed, over the course of time, Bethmann-Hollweg had worked his fingers to the bone. He had worked sincerely and diligently to save Germany from the two-front war, and had served the same purpose as Ludendorff. However, he had made a pig of himself trying to take on Tirpitz and the Emperor's fleet policy. Due to these ambitions, peace attempts with Great Britain had come to nothing, and because of the Emperor's 'Mittelafrika-Politik' and the Moroccan crisis of 1911, relations had already gone sour before the war. 'Germany had taken too many risks', Bethmann-Hollweg rightly said to Bülow.[396] 'Grossreeder' Albert Ballin supported this. He had fully supported the Kaiser's maritime ambitions, but also had a fancy of merging with Great Britain, rather than the collision course chosen by Wilhelm II. Unfortunately, his warnings came too late. Even Bethmann-Hollweg had not succeeded in convincing his political supporters of his concerns. He had scrupulously concealed the disappointing performance of the German 'Militär'. Theobald Bethmann-Hollweg was not the revolutionary that the progressives and conservatives thought he was. He was a manoeuvring man, who, for a long time, maintained the myth of order and calm, whereas in reality Germany was facing huge problems. An illusion had been created, as Fischer rightly believed, about the war situation[397], and this phantom was in reality a house of cards that was tottering. In this foggy political shadow play, Bethmann-Hollweg earned the nickname the 'rätselhafte Kanzler'. [398]

Carl von Clausewitz's wonderful triumvirate, a good command structure between politics, sovereign and general, was seriously disturbed by the disrupted relations between the 'Diktatur Ludendorff', the chancellor and the doubtful emperor. Ludendorff's dictatorship felt strong and developed a stubborn 'Alleingang'. John Lee, biographer of the *Warlords' Von Hindenburg and Ludendorff*, called their actions 'bonapartist'.[399] On the other hand, the decision did not leave him cold either. These days, Prince Max von Baden was in Berlin and reported that the 'mood was very mixed'. One hovered between 'hope and fear', and among the military 'there was no overconfidence'. This last resort was 'taken with great care'. [400]

The new power of Von Hindenburg and Ludendorff was reflected in the domestic political and economic changes that resulted from the war's increasingly heavy burden on German society. The Centrals produced about 19% of the world's industrial goods, against 28% in the Entente. Demographically too, the Centrals were at a considerable disadvantage, with 144 million inhabitants against 656 million. As a result, the Entente had more people, more industry, more space (colonies) and more money to make the war a success. As the years went by, war inflation worsened the already uncomfortable position of the Centrals. Indexed, the British lost 10% of their wealth, and the Germans 25%. Even initial German successes, especially against the French economy in Northern France, were reasonably restored by Paris in the course of the war. German imports in 1915, however, were only 55% of what they had been before the war. In addition, Germany lost its overseas territories and the Entente was reinforced by the US during the course of the war. [401]

As a result of the already existing economic demographic - and therefore industrial - backlog, Germany had already started to organise the shortage early in the war. Walther Rathenau, the AEG leader, played an important role, and under his influence the 'Kriegsrohstoffabteilung' was formed in 1914. The longer the war lasted - and the hunger blockade by the Entente became more and more pronounced - the more far-reaching measures were necessary. Thus, in January 1915, bread was on the bill, in April the potatoes, and from autumn on almost the entire food package was on the bill. In May 1916, the 'Kriegsernährungsamt' was set up to streamline the problems of food supply.

Ludendorff, who as a soldier in Kaunas had also been extensively involved in civilian issues, in addition to the military assumption of power within the OHL, also put his full weight behind increasing the OHL's participation and influence in these issues. For Ludendorff, the home front was just another facet of the front, where the leadership, in his view, had to proceed with military logic, and also with military toughness, where necessary. Ludendorff spoke of 'total war', as Nazi propaganda minister Joseph Goebbels would later do. 'Whoever deploys the strongest and most ruthless population, wins the war', Ludendorff stated in a letter to Johannes Kaempf, the Reichstag president, on 23 November 1916. [402]

Indeed, he conducted this internal struggle ruthlessly. After Von Falkenhayn's departure, a great deal changed at the top of the German war administration. Under the leadership of Ludendorff, confidant Max Bauer, a liaison between the OHL, heavy industry and politics, the so-called 'Hindenburgprogramm' was established. This organisation ensured a synchronisation of the interests of the OHL (Ludendorff/Von Hindenburg) with those of industry and society. This programme started in September 1916 and on 1 November of that year, the 'Kriegsamt' was established, under the command of yet another Ludendorff confidant, railway specialist Groener - also a member of the 'Kriegsernährungsamt' - who had to see to the implementation of the ideas which originated from the think tank of the 'Hindenburgprogramm'.

With this, Ludendorff held important keys to omnipotence in Germany. The Kriegsamt had included in its ranks a number of important leaders of German industry, such as Kurt Sorge of Krupp-Gruson, Prof. Klingenberg of the AEG factories, and Paul Reusch of the Gutehoffnungshütte[403]. All people from the business world, with great knowledge and access to the industrial top. In addition, the top echelons of the Ministry of Defence, Von Hohenborn and Von Wandel, had been pushed aside and replaced by Von Stein, with none other than Groener as his replacement, so that through the 'Hindenburgprogramm' and the 'Kriegsamt' Ludendorff's long arm now reached into the Ministry. This was not the only political power Ludendorff secured. Two other important Ludendorff confidants, Oberst von Winterfeld and Oberst von Haeften were appointed as advisor to the Chancellor and advisor to Foreign Affairs. Finally, there was the supreme leadership, the Kaiser, who had clearly lost strength, confidence and, as a result, influence, partly due to his two failures with Moltke and Von Falkenhayn. Therefore, on 31 August, a letter - almost a diktat - was sent from Ludendorff to the Ministry of Economic Affairs, in which he said that he expected the entire economy to slow down in order to give priority to the German arms industry. Thanks to his contacts with Bauer and Groener, he was assured of support from industry to push through these ideas. Bauer also had good contact with the more moderate left-wing forces in German politics, such as Matthias Erzberger, which meant that they also turned a blind eye to the Ludendorff dictatorship. [404]

Already in October, a memo was issued by Gustav Stresemann, who praised the efforts of Hindenburg and Ludendorff to mobilise the home front.[405] Drastic measures were indeed taken. Among other things, a new law was pushed through, the 'law on patriotic assistance', through which more could be demanded from citizens and workers. The press was also kept under strict censorship. Stresemann praised the achievements of the new OHL, but did the measures really work?

The answer is yes, if you look at it in the relatively short term. Indeed, by tightening its belt, the German empire managed another remarkable feat. The historian Nial Ferguson believed that Germany, even given its much more limited economic resources, was actually more effective in its war mobilisation than the Entente powers.[406] This went against the grain of many, who believed that Berlin's 'state socialism' must have been fundamentally less effective than the capitalism and 'laisser faire' of the Entente - Jay Winter, among others. When we look at the numbers, we must conclude that there is much to be said for Ferguson's thesis. For example, the Germans produced 47,000 aircrafts in the First World War compared to 45,000 for the French and 32,000 for the British.

In terms of artillery, the most important weapon in World War I, Germany also kept pace with 39,000 guns produced, compared to 34,112 by the French and 20,914 by the British. More serious was the arrears of the dual monarchy, which produced only 7,200 aircraft and 11,560 artillery pieces in the same period. Mobilisation was also similar; Berlin put 2.9 million into the production process, compared to 3.1 million for the French and 2.8 million for the British. The Germans' war debt of 39 billion US dollars was also comparable to that of the French (27 billion) and the British (34 billion).[407] The financing on the German side was mostly thanks to Rudolf Emil Albert Havenstein, affectionately called 'Mein Geldmarschall' by the Kaiser.[408]

German industry had not failed during the war years. A total of 222 million German shells were produced, 160 million of which were used on the Western Front. Therefore, there was no real structural shortage of artillery shells during the entire war. Where industrial production was behind schedule, this was due to choices (tanks, for example) made by the OHL.

The 'keeping up' with the German war economy through the 'Hindenburg Programme' (which would have been better called the 'Ludendorff Programme') did not come without a price for Germany. The focus on heavy industry was ruthless and came at the expense of the prosperity and well-being of the German people, especially the poor. In the long run, the 'Hindenburg Programme', with its one-sided focus on war industry, contributed to the erosion of the German people. The real dagger in Germany's back was the slow depletion of reserves; the hunger that softened the bones, the hunger that eroded the legitimacy of the regime.

The mortality rate in 1917 was a frightening 21%.[409] The winter of 1916-1917 was not called the 'Kohlrübenwinter' (turnip winter) for nothing. There was hunger, the people lived more and more on surrogates, there was black-market trade, inflation and growing discontent, but the production belts were rolling and shells were going to the front. There were voices of warning, such as that of Ulrich Graf von Marschal, head of the Military Cabinet, who believed that Ludendorff's war, wich had become extreme, would lead to damage to monarchy. These were prophetic words, but von Marschal was still a voice in the wilderness.[410]

An interesting question remains how Ludendorff had been able to push through the 'Hindenburgprogramm' in such a ruthless way and thus establish the Ludendorff dictatorship. First of all, of course, there were his own merits; his victories in the field, his good performance as Viceroy of Kaunas -although that may have carried little weight-, the name he had with Von Hindenburg as 'saviour' of the fatherland, as well as the failure of his competitors, Moltke and Von

Falkenhayn. Besides, it was also a personal merit of Ludendorff that, despite his frankly difficult and angular character, he could gather good people around him and could work well together with them. Besides von Hindenburg, of course, Max Bauer and Groener were important here. Yet, what also played an important role, and what Marxists have always mistaken for a 'conspiracy' between big business and the imperialists (the OHL and the Kaiser), were contacts between Ludendorff and the German elites. A well-known organisation, for example, was Carl Vollmöller's 'Deutsche Gesellschaft 1914', but of more importance was the so-called 'Mittwochsgesellschaft', founded by Reichstag member Bassermann and professor Ludwig Stein. This club, founded in 1863 and with 79 members, mostly important industrialists, politicians and journalists, had influence behind the scenes. The group met confidentially at the Hotel Continental and its members included such notable people as Walther Rathenau, Moltke, General Alexander von Kluck and Prince Guido Henckel. The former envoy Von Stumm, the banker Hugo Mankiewicz, industrialist Hugo Stinnes, journalist Hugenbergen, professor Otto Hoetzsch. The founders Stein and Bassermann had chosen a special composition of the 'Mittwochsgesellschaft'. They had appointed twelve members, who in turn each appointed four members. Besides the permanent members, the Mittwochsgesellschaft also regularly had 'guests', such as the counts Apponyio and Andrassy, so that we can speak of an exquisite and powerful company.

Via Harry Graf Kessler, son of a wealthy banker and also a not unimpressive writer, we know more about this 'club', to which Walther Rathenau invited him at the time. According to Kessler, Rathenau was very fond of Ludendorff from the very beginning. Initially Rathenau, who visited the von Hindenburg-Ludendorff duo in Kaunas, had been particularly charmed by von Hindenburg, but in practice he was disappointed. He soon realised, like many others, that Ludendorff was Oberost's man, and due to Von Falkenhayn's disappointing results, the man of the new OHL command. Ludendorff, according to Rathenau, was open to new ideas, and was to a certain extent childlike, but in such a manner that it did not take away from his genius. [411]

The 'Mittwochsgesellschaft' strongly represented the interests of German big industry. These were the gentlemen with whom Max Bauer and Groener maintained contacts for the 'Hindenburg Programme' and the 'Kriegsamt'. Kessler thought that the influential Rathenau, who considered himself one of the most influential men in Europe[412], wanted to be German without 'restrictions', partly because of his struggle with his dual Jewish-German identity.[413] This identity struggle contributed to the fact that, at least initially, he also took the hard line that paved the way for the Ludendorff dictatorship. In other words, the Ludendorff dictatorship was not the work of one man, the OHL or the Kaiser, it was the product of a common interest.

The policy of Bethmann-Hollweg, the policy of the diagonals - thus encompassing the entire political spectrum - was therefore no longer possible in the long run. This gave Ludendorff air for the moment to implement his far-reaching plans for both the home front and the real front, but undermined his position and the existing structure in Germany over the course of time. We know with certainty that a meeting took place between Ludendorff and Duisberg, the foreman of the Krupp factories, on 8 and 9 September 1916.[414] Shortly afterwards, on 13 September, Ludendorff rained down his steely fist on German war politics. At a provisional low point in his life, he wrote to the German governors of Belgium and Poland, saying that he needed workers for the 'Heimatfront', in order to keep the war production running at full speed. Initially, recruitment had been voluntary, but only 26,000 people had come forward[415] So there was no enthusiasm, for Belgium was plagued by high unemployment. Ludendorff therefore believed that the workers had to be forced to come and work in Germany, even if, as he wrote, there were social and international objections against it.[416] Unfortunately, his work plan - which ultimately had to include 700,000 Belgians and 300,000 Polish Jews [417] - was ultimately not carried out to its ultimate conclusion, partly because the means of housing and raw materials were lacking in order to actually employ the workers.

But the steel pact of hyper-nationalism was closed. One more time, Ludendorff wanted to take the big plunge. The front lines had been shortened, weapons were once again available, Romania was sabotaged and hopes placed in U-boats. Ludendorff, the man who had been removed from the General Staff, had Germany at his feet. But it was a chained and hungry Germany, loyal at heart, but hollowed out.

Chapter 8

The Russian Revolution and the disappearance of the Eastern Front

'I am more afraid of the revolution than of defeat' - Erich Ludendorff

With the unrestricted submarine warfare, Ludendorff stepped outsidehis comfort zone. That was the fate of his position in the OHL; he was no longer standing with his boots in the swampy grass of the Mazuren. He was increasingly waging a paper war, and the concept the Navy had presented to him was in fact a second Schlieffen Plan. Again, everything was at stake, and the timetable hung over Germany like a sword of Damocles. The starvation of Britain had to outrun any reaction from the Entente and the US.

Initially, the German submarines had been very successful, sinking almost a million gross tonnage. Winston Churchill said that the shipping lane south of Ireland was beginning to look like a ship graveyard. At one point, there was only six weeks of food left in England. The turnaround came when the Entente successfully implemented both offensive (laying mines) and defensive (escort sailing) measures. The starvation of England was stopped, and the losses of German submarines began to increase dangerously.[418]

To make matters worse for Germany, the American reaction was not long in coming. On 3 February 1917, the USA broke off diplomatic relations with Germany and in April of that year, they joined the war. What many had warned the OHL about had happened. Even before joining the war, the US had a great affinity with Great Britain and with France, and moreover, the US had invested a lot of money in London and Paris. In addition, US President Thomas Woodrow Wilson was an Anglophile, who considered the submarine an 'inhuman weapon'.[419] A reinforcement of the western front for the Entente began to take place as a result, which was cumbersome for Ludendorff. The miscalculation concerning the successful seamine policy and convoy sailing worked its way into a second Marne drama.

Despite his delayed right, Bethmann-Hollweg had to resign. On 13 July 1917, he stepped down. Ludendorff thought that this change of power had taken far too long, and he thought that Germany's political leadership was 'living from hand to mouth'. It also bothered him that there were not more men of action, in contrast to the officer corps, which had been 'brought up to decide'. 'Politics is poor in men', he said in his memoirs. That Bethmann-Hollweg's warnings were, in retrospect, prophetic, escaped Ludendorff's notice.[420] George Michaelis became the new chancellor.

The American reinforcements were of great importance, for the year 1917 had also become a great war of attrition. We can conclude that the tactics of Von Hindenburg and Ludendorff to shorten the western front by means of the 'Alberich-Movement', mentioned above, whereby one fell back on the Siegfriedstellung (March 1917) along a 100 kilometre front between Vimy and Crouy, paid off.[421] Also, new tactical regulations had been worked on that Oberst Bauer, Hauptmann Geyer and General Fritz von Below had collaborated on and which had been laid down in the manual 'Die Abwehrschlacht'. In addition, Ludendorff used a variety of other tactical prescriptions in his own immediate area of operations, thus optimally utilising the defensive power of the German infantry.[422] The Entente achieved some successes here and there, but nowhere was there a strategic breakthrough, no matter how large-scale and well-prepared one was. The French losses under General Nivelle in April 1917, between Reims and Soissons, were so bloody that the French army mutinied. Leave-takers in particular showed little inclination to return to the front. They sang the *Internationale* and waved red flags. A new spirit of the times presented itself. Philippe Pétain, the hero of Verdun, was rushed into action to save morale. The flying tribunals were also set up and 432 death sentences were pronounced, 55 of which were carried out to turn the tide. At Arras (March-April 1917), Messines (end of May 1917) and Ypres (July-November 1917), the British went on the offensive. Every time there were smaller partial successes, such as the conquest of the Vimy hills, followed by a limited success at Cambrai in November of that year, which we have already discussed. No strategic breakthrough - for example to the important ports of Zeebrugge and Ostend - was made despite new methods of attack, underground passages near Messines and tanks near Soissons and Cambrai.[423]

At Cambrai, things had been tense. It was at 8 a.m. that Ludendorff was informed of the tank breach. Reinforcements were gathered in a frenzy. From the hinterland, more or less equipped infantry divisions were rushed to the front. It was a race against time. The troops arrived by train and the whole thing took three days. There was a lack of trucks to provide further logistical support. Support was requested from the units of Kronprinz Rupprecht, who were operating on the northern flank of Cambrai. By 23 November, everything that could be done was done. 'I could do no more,' Ludendorff noted, 'fate has decided'. Looking back, Ludendorff was frank about the British chances at Cambrai. Had the enemy exploited the situation and the momentum, his troops would not have been able to close the front.[424] The attack finally stalled around the town of Bourlon, after five days of heavy fighting. The British lost 45,000 men, the Germans 41,000 and 9000 prisoners of war. In addition, 165 German artillery pieces had fallen into British hands. The German Western Front ultimately held.[425]

The developments on the Italian front were also very bloody. Here, the balance shifted somewhat for the Centrals, thanks to a successful Austro-Hungarian offensive with German help of the 14th army around Tolmein, in which large Italian units were trapped near Caponette in October and November 1917 because the supreme command withdrew too late. The operations had started under difficult conditions. The mountain roads were so narrow that, contrary to normal procedures, the artillery had to advance first and begin the battle, with the infantry to follow. This was against all the rules, and if the Italians acted swiftly, it would have been a great risk. However, things turned out differently. The Italian positions were bombarded with brisant and gas grenades, after which the infantry moved in and quickly gained ground. The entire Italian front between - from north to south - Flitsch, Karfeity, Tolmein, Canale (Isonzo front), was shaken. The commanding Italian General Cardona was an old school man, and lived more in Napoleonic times than in the 20th century. The short, fierce bombardment and the rapid advance afterwards caught him off guard. The Italian army was also suffering from a lack of ammunition and its fighting morale had declined over the years.[426] When the signal for the retreat was finally given, Italian losses had already risen to more than 300,000 men in killed, wounded and prisoners. However, here it also proved difficult to definitively cash in on the results of the war. Under the hastily appointed new commander Armando Diaz, the Italians clung to their defensive line around the Piave River and repulsed the successive attacks. Ludendorff felt that with more vigorous pursuit the results could have been even more successful, but concluded that these were the 'luckier days'. The Italian army had been 'thoroughly defeated', he believed, and the operations had achieved what could be 'reasonably expected'. Rome announced a parliamentary enquiry into the defeat. Despite all these successes, even this Isonzo battle (there were twelve of them) did not represent a definitive breakthrough.[427]

The latter operations happened after major revolutionary upheavals had taken place in Russia. Even with all the enormous battles in the West and on other fronts, the real news of 1917 lay in the East, which would also have a great impact on the war effort in the spring of 1918. After the Brusilov Offensive of 1916 and the collapse of Romania, the front had more or less stabilised in 1917, apart from Kerensky's desperate offensive of July 1917, running from the Baltic areas along the River Düna, past Riga, Friedrichstadt, Jakobstadt, Dünaburg along the Naroc Lake, via Baranowitschi along Pinks (Pripjat marshes), via Kowel and the surroundings of Tarnopol and the Sereth River towards the Carpathians, to flow into the Black Sea at Galatz.

Despite relative calm on the Eastern Front, the Russian Revolution came. This brought about an enormous upheaval. The reaction of Ludendorff was very interesting. In his war recollections, he said: 'How often had I hoped for the revolution [...] but it had always turned out to be a pipe dream. Now that it was here, it came as a surprise'. He went on to say that this development was 'a burden off his mind' and then emphasised the shadow side that was to come: 'That it would later undermine our strength, I could not yet foresee'.[428] Ludendorff thus expressed his surprise, but also hinted that there had apparently been hope. It was also striking that Ludendorff immediately dealt with the question of guilt: he blamed the Entente without further ado. His argument was not very convincing: 'What reasons they had for this were not clear to me'.[429]

Ludendorff's hopes for the revolution and his reproaches to the Entente came from a 'bad conscience'. Lenin's name appears only once in Ludendorff's war memoirs. This is at odds with Germany's revolutionary efforts against Russia, plans that have been characterised by one historian as being as malicious as they are genius, and with enormous consequences.[430] Ludendorff's 'hope' of revolution was in fact backed up by deeds and was thus much more than a 'pipe dream'. As Germany faced enormous superiority in the First World War, it opted for highly unorthodox approaches on several occasions. The most striking were of course the unlimited submarine war and the gas war. But they also did not shy away from the better 'heating' work in uncongenial regimes. Just as France tried to wrest the Rheinland from Germany after 1918, lost colonies and even tried to separate Bavaria from the Empire, Imperial Germany followed similar geopolitical shortcuts.

The long arm of Berlin also appeared outside Russia in the Caucasus, Ireland, in Mexico (Zimmermann telegram), the Middle East, and later in the Crimea. Warfare and irredentism through revolution would be worthy of a study in itself, but here we must confine ourselves to Russia.

A key role in the German connection to the Russian Revolution was played by the mysterious Israil Lasarewitsch Helphand (Gelfand), better known as Alexander Parvus, a Jew from the Minsk Ghetto, born in 1867.

Parvus had revolutionary ideals and understood that Germany and the revolutionaries had a common interest in overthrowing the Tsarist Empire. In

Turkey, Helphand reported to the German ambassador Konrad 'Freiherr' von Wangenheim, who took Parvus so seriously that he advised Gottlieb von Jagow at the German Foreign Office to receive Parvus. On 9 March 1915, two years before the revolution, the plan was already on the desk of the German ministry.

Through Parvus, the circle around Lenin, who stayed in Switzerland, had come into view. Leon Trotsky, at that time Lenin's fellow combatant, said about Parvus: 'A great figure [...] he completely mastered the Marxist jargon [...] he had a wide view'. According to Trotsky, the 'astronomical final goal of the proletariat had come considerably closer'. Parvus himself had seen the Russo-Japanese war, which had turned out unhappily for Russia, as the glorious dawn of the coming revolution. After this war, Parvus believed, the Russian proletariat would become the 'avant-garde' of the revolution. The year 1905 brought great unrest, but the Tsarist regime remained in power. With the First World War, the time seemed ripe. [431]

The preparations for revolution were led from Denmark, Copenhagen, from where Parvus - under the cover of economic activities - started to build up a revolutionary network in Russia. Through neutral Denmark, contacts were maintained with Germany, which provided him with money and goods through its diplomatic post to achieve his goal. According to Gerhard Schiesser and Jochen Trauptmann, who investigated the German financing of the October Revolution, Parvus had an insatiable appetite for money. [432]

Via Scandinavia, money and goods found their way to Russia by smuggling. In effect, Germany was circumventing the export ban to Russia, but the secret operations justified the means. The smuggling route yielded money because of the increasing scarcity in Russia, and enabled Parvus to get not only weapons and explosives into the country, but also people. A fishing business and a shipping company also gave him access to Russia. He satisfied the Danish authorities by using his commercial and political contacts to secure additional coal supplies, which was welcome, since Denmark also suffered from the British hunger blockade.[433] Parvus combined his diplomatic talents with commercial spirit and revolutionary drive.

The extent of German involvement in the revolution in Russia has remained somewhat obscured. The fact is that German documents prove beyond doubt that German money was flowing via Parvus to Russia to bring about the revolution. In a letter of 23 January 1916 from the German ambassador to Denmark, Graf Ulrich von Brockdorff-Rantzau, to Chancellor Von Bethmann-Hollweg, the donation of one million roubles was mentioned. Literally it read:

'Copenhagen, 23 January 1916 - secret!
[...]
Dr Helphand has returned to Copenhagen after a three-week stay in Sweden, where he was in contact with Russian revolutionaries in Stockholm, and informs me of the following. The sum of one million roubles made available to him has been forwarded immediately and has already arrived in St. Petersburg'.[434]

Such a course was in line with the range on which Von Hindenburg and Ludendorff established their 'dictatorship'.[435] In his war memoirs, Ludendorff dwells extensively on the 'spiritual weapons' of war, which is quite remarkable for a military man.

His analysis of Germany evoked the image of a somewhat naive nation which - since Bismarck - had limited its foreign policy mainly to maintaining peace. Germany's enemies would have taken advantage of this and would have amply won the propaganda battle with Germany. Germany underestimated the 'forces working against them', and in response the concept of 'power' had to be put back at the centre of politics. There had to be an end to what he called Germany's 'uncertain and vacillating policy'. In military terms, he stated that even a defensive war could only be won 'by attack'. The development of a 'national consciousness' was therefore of great importance. By introducing and mobilising political terms like 'right of self-determination', the Entente had, according to Ludendorff, succeeded in causing great problems, which the Habsburg Empire in particular suffered from. And just as the British had 'infected' China with opium, Germany was 'slandered' with notions such as war guilt, the legends about the Belgian 'franc tireurs' (freebooters), an alleged lack of morality and other matters which Ludendorff dismissed as a 'Lügenfeldzug'.[436]

To win the war of ideas, the OHL went far. In 1916, the OHL tried to bring the press under central control. Ludendorff considered the media to be an important support for popular morality. In his opinion, the German press, as well as politics, had been too naive, aiming at peace instead of peace through victory. The real 'masters of propaganda' were, in his opinion, the British, and he especially praised Lord Beaverbrook.[437] Bethmann-Hollweg initially curbed the efforts towards restriction and censorship, but after his departure, military dominance shifted in that direction as well.

Whereas the Centrals 'suffered' under the political force of 'self-determination', in Russia the concept of Bolshevism worked. Lenin and his followers had worked their way up in power between March 1917 and November 1917. After the great riots of 8 March 1917, a provisional Duma government was established and on 16 March, czar Nicolas II abdicated. Exactly one month later,

Lenin arrived in Russia from Switzerland and the Councils tried to seize power. In July, the situation worsened and Lenin had to leave for Finland for a short period time. On the night of 6-7 November, they finally struck and on 9 November, they proclaimed the armistice. The revolutionisation of Russia was immediately rewarded with the silencing of the cannons.

There is an interesting telegram from this period, dated 29 September 1917. It stated that the latest events in Russia had been successful only because 'the Bolshevik government enjoyed our constant support'. Here, Ludendorff certainly referred to the conquest of the city of Riga. Staff Officer Otto Schmidt, attached to the 8th German army, was there when the conquest took place. 'A bright autumn day, and cheers of liberated Germans (Volksdeutschen). The soldier's life was worth living just for this moment'.[438] In October 1917, Ludendorff wrote a telegram thanking the Foreign Office for their help with Oberost's front propaganda and especially for their 'subversive activities'. In this telegram, Ludendorff also praised the funds that had been made available to the revolutionaries, and stated that he had always supported the revolutionary forces in Finland.[439] The Foreign Office had certainly played a leading role in the passing of Lenin and his comrades to Russia by train, but it had been OHL and Ludendorff personally who had given permission. Politics, through Parvus' contacts with Friedrich Ebert, also played a role. Parvus had used his influence for this purpose, after failed attempts by Swiss socialists to arrange a 'transit' for Lenin. These attempts had failed because many politicians in Bern considered the matter too brisk in view of Swiss neutrality. Via the secretary of the Socialist Party, Fritz Platten, the help of Parvus was eventually sought. 'Comrade elephant', as Karl Kautsky jokingly called the corpulent giant, did not flinch at anything. With the self-confidence that everything could be arranged and bought - which brought him a lot of enmity in leftist circles (Boecharin did not like him, calling him 'devil') - he found his way. Via the German East-Europe experts Wilhelm von Mirbach-Harff and Maltzan, Parvus managed to get through to the offices of politicians (Matthias Erzberger), and subsequently made contact with the OHL. According to the historian Wheeler-Bennett, 'the veto lay with Von Hindenburg and Ludendorff', but Parvus managed to convince them that Lenin was the man to get Russia out of the war. He would make short work of idealists like Kerensky, who 'had rose-coloured glasses on'.[440]

How aware Ludendorff was of the 'explosive charge' of 'his' revolutionaries was shown by the fact that he personally gave the order stating that they were only allowed to travel through Germany in a blinded and guarded train, without stopping. Ludendorff was terrified that the Bolshevik virus would escape. To be on the safe side, he added that the occupants of the train 'must not be distinctly anti-German'.[441]

Journalist Maximilian Harden later referred to the train history as a 'great joke of history', based on the mutual misunderstanding of two parties who believed they could use the other. In the words of Trotsky: 'Ludendorff thought: through Lenin I will bring down the Patriots, and then I can deal with the Bolsheviks. Whereas Lenin thought: I will ride in Ludendorff's train through Germany and make him pay later'.[442]

Ludendorff's biographer Manfred Nebelin believes that Ludendorff is absolved of historical consequences because he did not know Lenin personally and simply could not have foreseen the outcome.[443] This facile conclusion, presented almost as a careless statement by a respected biographer like Nebelin, shows that the historical interconnectedness and responsibility of the OHL with regard to the Russian Revolution still has not penetrated the DNA of history and historiography. Nebelin allows himself to be taken in by Ludendorff and should have taken Ludendorff's emphatic, but poorly substantiated, attribution of guilt to the Entente in his memoirs as a pointer. In practice, it was the Entente powers that tried to prevent Lenin's transit. This was done by the Secret Intelligence Service of the British Embassy in Stockholm (the journey went via Sweden), in this case Major Stephen Alley. When they could not stop Lenin in Sweden, Alley used his influence to stop Lenin at the Russian border at Tornea.[444]

The smoke screen that one cannot seem to see through has its origins in the communist mystification of the train journey. Afterwards, Lenin and the communist propaganda marginalised the role of the supporters - the OHL and Parvus. They were terrified of having to share the honour of the revolution with imperial-bourgeois Germany and the parvenu Parvus. That would also be difficult to sell ideologically. Lenin himself was afraid for his image and did not want Germany to pay for the trip. The money went through Parvus, and the Polish communist and foreign minister Radek Sikorski bought the tickets. The fact that Parvus took money from Germany disturbed Lenin to the extent that he already distanced himself from his generous donor during the trip. Yet, that the relationship existed was also proven by a message from the Berlin offices, dated 17 April: 'Lenin's arrival in Russia has succeeded. He is working fully as desired'. The question whether Ludendorff knew Lenin personally or not is in fact irrelevant; Parvus was known and so was the purpose of the mission: the revolutionisation of Russia. Furthermore, Ludendorff's direct involvement was confirmed by the Russian historian A. Ivanov, who stated that the first German officers to receive the train at Gottmadingen station - Lieutenant Von Buhring and Captain Von Planetz - had both been personally instructed by Ludendorff. Von Buhring spoke fluent Russian. Moreover, the OHL would have negotiated extensively with Lenin about the train trip, partly due to the many conditions that both parties set. These negotiations were conducted on the German side by Georges Sklarz who, according to the historian Goodspeed, again served under Ludendorff. [445]

Dealing with Lenin's infamous train journey to Russia remains complicated. It is typical that in Wolfram Pyta's recent biography of Ludendorff's colleague Von Hindenburg, the name Lenin does not appear at all.[446] The name Parvus is missing in Nebelin as well as in Pyta. Ludendorff-biographer Franz Uhle-Wettler limited himself to the statement that 'Germany's support for Lenin was fruitful'.[447] Wolfgang Venohr, who was engaged in unravelling legends around Ludendorff, like Pyta, does not mention Lenin, nor do other historians of both more recent and older work, such as Wolfgang Ruge, William J. Astore and Dennis E. Showalter, Schultze-Pfaelzer, Martin Lüders and others, hardly mention Lenin's train journey and the OHL's involvement, if at all. In reference works such as the *Enzyklopädie Erster Weltkrieg* edited by Gerhard Hirschfeld, Gerd Krumeich and Irina Renz, Parvus is not mentioned and the German involvement in the revolution is dealt with in one sentence. Not for nothing did the historian Werner Hahlweg characterise the history of German influence on the revolution in Russia as the 'conspiracy of silence'. [448]

Misunderstood or not, the shadow play of the OHL and the secret services, running through department IIIb of the German General Staff in cooperation with Foreign Affairs, was part of the Russian Revolution. This policy went beyond mere support for Lenin and the Bolsheviks. Also directly along the front line, the interference in Russian politics was actively supported by psychological warfare. There were special Russian-speaking agents at the front, who, by means of pamphlets, newspapers written in Russian and word-of-mouth reports, aroused the growing doubts of the Russian soldiers about the politics in the hinterland. This was successful. German units reported to the Supreme Command that the Tsarist troops were disintegrating and were not unwilling to receive information from the German side. In the no-man's-land between the fronts, the situation visibly relaxed. Other left-wing revolutionaries were also supported and there was no hesitation to support nationalists in Ukraine, where there had always been a great deal of animosity towards Russia. This policy of divide and rule was not at odds with Parvus' Bolshevik revolutionary plans. In his battle plan for the revolution of Russia, sent to the Ministry of Foreign Affairs in 1915, he had already pointed out the usefulness of the 'nationalist card'.[449] For the Bolsheviks, any means was sanctified anyway, as the world would soon learn through the *Holodomor* (Ukrainian Famine) and through the *gulags* (political prisoners).

The long-term German intervention in Russian politics could not hide the fact that there was also a deeper cause behind the Russian revolution. In fact, it was based on a social revolution. The old authoritarian order of tsar and nobility, based on autocracy, orthodoxy and patriotism, had long since passed its peak. In fact, there were four parties, each dissatisfied in its own way. There was the nobility, whose image had been dented by the 1905 revolution and the lost war against Japan (1904-1905). Besides the tsar and the nobility, there was bourgeois-capitalist Russia, which, although small in percentage (about 0.5%), was growing in influence. Until then, people had obediently supported the nobility, but now that the latter was degenerating more and more, and the economy had been booming since 1908, this 'second echelon' was becoming more impatient and demanding. The economic boom had also created a proletariat in the cities, the revolutionary constituency that Lenin hoped for. These workers lived in poverty and were receptive to reforms. The peasants, too, were less and less satisfied with the czarist regime. The peasant, despite his miserable circumstances, had always been convinced of 'the just tsar'. Still, the passionately desired land reforms did not materialise. Surrounded by discontented people, the Tsar clung too long to his most trusted power base: the nobility who owned the agricultural land. Besides all these problems, rapid urbanisation also played a role. In addition, many thousands of soldiers were on the move in and around the cities, which always resulted in an internal security risk. Finally, of course, there was the general malaise of the war, into which the Tsar personally had fallen deeper and deeper. A revolution was the result. [450]

The revolution was followed by negotiations with Germany. Lenin's decree for peace resulted in consultations at Brest-Litovsk between Berlin and the council communists. From November 1917 onwards, negotiations were intense, with Lenin, Trotsky and Bukharin hesitating about the course to be followed. It was clear that Germany had territorial wishes, and that the new Soviet Union could do little against this. On the other hand, they tried to stall, because they expected the communist revolution in Europe at any moment. Karl Liebknecht, leading figure of the Sozialdemokratische Partei Deutschlands, had once spoken of a 'class war against war'. [451]

When was the moment? This created a twilight zone between war and peace, which eventually led to the independence of Ukraine and German influence in the Baltic region. Poland was also lost to Russia. It would become the prelude to the Russian Civil War and the Polish-Russian War. On 3 March 1918, the Treaty of Brest-Litowsk was concluded. The Soviets signed reluctantly. The peace had almost caused a split among the Bolsheviks - between the doctrinaire hotheads Bukharin and Trotsky on the one hand and the more cautious Stalin and Zinoviev on the other, who supported Lenin. [452]

The dramatic changes on the Eastern Front - the end of the two-front war - created a new situation in which the OHL saw new opportunities. To the press chief of the Austro-Hungarian Army, Glaise von Horstenau, Ludendorff confessed that if he had known that Russia would collapse as a result of the revolution, he would have postponed the unrestricted submarine war.[453] This remark shows that the influence of the revolution in Russia could have been even greater than it already was. How great was the influence of the removal of the Eastern Front? Answering this question is easier said than done. At first glance, of course, there were huge gains: the enemy in the east of Germany had been eliminated and one could now focus on the western front. This would provide Ludendorff with new offensive opportunities. Being able to operate offensively also provided a great psychological advantage for the German soldier, who finally felt the German superiority again. Ludendorff himself was full of new possibilities. Would salvation still come to the front at five minutes to midnight?

It is indisputable that the release of forces from the east gave the German military leadership new offensive possibilities. However, in spite of this, there were continuing major structural problems, which could not be overcome by the freed divisions of the Eastern Front.

Germany, despite the removal of the Eastern Front, remained a landlocked power. The new chaos that had arisen in the East continued to create instability and economic aid from the East was inconceivable for Germany. In short, the geopolitical reality of the Empire changed remarkably little, despite the earth-shattering events of the Russian Revolution.

In the process, Germany was confronted with the arrival of the Americans in the West. The result was that Germany was, once again, caught in a military coercion scenario. The new decision had to be taken soon, before the bulk of the American troops were ready for combat at the front. This meant operating again with the Sword of Damocles above them, which seemed to be Germany's constant fate in the war. There were simply too many enemies and too few resources.

Finally, the military-technical problems were enormous. The OHL would have to bring the lion's share of the German East Army westwards and this was an enormous logistical operation, almost comparable to the August 1914 days. In addition, a new attack plan had to be drawn up, under great time pressure, which was not easy after a long period of defence. This had to be done not only on the drawing board, but also in the field, which meant that Ludendorff soon travelled from one army group to another to discuss the situation with the generals on the spot. An additional complicating factor was that not all German generals agreed that the battle on the Western Front deserved priority. Some believed that there was an important strategic victory to be gained against the Italians. Ludendorff also saw these opportunities, but tended more towards the Western Front, which was definitely the main front. It was here that the Americans would become active.

Within the Western Front option, there were also various camps. Some believed that the exhausted French troops had to be tackled first, while others focused on the British. Yet another view was to attack the troops precisely on the dividing line between British and French. Some argued for a limited operation, for example again at Verdun, other generals believed that an attack should be made over a broad front, where the question arose whether it should be an attack or a series of 'hammer blows' that would exhaust the enemy.

Ludendorff also had to deal with politics, despite the 'Diktatur', and was not entirely satisfied with the new 74-year-old compromise chancellor, Graf Georg von Hertling, whom he did not describe as a 'war chancellor'.[454]

With this characterisation, Ludendorff made it clear that, as far as he was concerned, the war was not yet being waged 'comprehensively enough'. He experienced his actions as a 'shunt between Scylla and Charibis'.

In his biography, the historian Venohr raised the question of whether Ludendorff might have thought of taking the political helm himself.[455] There were certainly circles that supported this view. Ludendorff probably realised that his political experience was too limited, that his hands and feet were already tied to developments in the field and at the military operating tables, and that this was too far a leap. His political actions would wait until after the collapse of the German empire, when he seized power during the Kapp-Putsch and later with Hitler in Munich, 1923.

Chapter 9

The Bloody spring of 1918, Ludendorff's last chance

At the meeting in Kreuznach on 19 December 1917, in the presence of the Kaiser, von Hindenburg, the Foreign Minister Kühlmann and the Chancellor von Hertling, Ludendorff was not focused. On the agenda were above all the 'Ost' problems. Ludendorff's thoughts were on the Western Front, the last chance now offered in the spring of 1918, before the Entente would have become an unbeatable force with the arrival of American troops. The efforts of the Kerensky Offensive and the Haig Offensive still clung to the troops, but new important tasks lay ahead. Ludendorff had begun planning the coming operations at Mons on 11 November. He did this with the men who in his eyes were really at the helm, the Chiefs of Staff, not the Supreme Commanders themselves, who he had not even invited. With General Kuhl, Chief of Staff to Crown Prince Rupprecht and Colonel Wetzell he had sat down to think out the 'Kaiserschlacht', the spring offensives for 1918 that had been codenamed 'Michael'. With divisions released from the east, they returned to the concept of the all-decisive 'Entscheidungsschlacht'.

With these men, Ludendorff had assembled an excellent team and showed once again that he did not care much for protocol. Ludendorff only looked at people's talent and shrugged off rank and reputation, a characteristic that the Emperor in particular found difficult to accept. Through Ludendorff's influence it happened that people like Hoffmann and Brückmüller, with the rank of Oberstleutnant, were held in very high esteem and that Lossberg, the man behind the defensive doctrine, who was only Oberst, saw his ideas introduced to the entire German army. At Mons, the forthcoming action of the infantry was entrusted to a captain, Hauptmann Geyer. Artillery tactics were determined by another captain, Hauptmann Pulkowski. [456]

This young team certainly had its advantages. It was diligent, resourceful and driven. But the result was that they were, in part, still 'untrained' men, who could not compensate for Ludendorff's 'nur-Soldat' status. In addition to the major strategic problems, there were many minor inconveniences. The German divisions were by no means all in good shape. Some troops were even malnourished, or one-sidedly fed. There was a lack of horses and weapons. Many divisions were considered to be so-called 'Stellungsdivisionen', similar to the Second World War concept of 'bodenständige' divisions, which were like the former garrison units, i.e. units which were actually not mobile and of second rank. These units were often more suited to the defensive than the offensive. The immobility of the units could not be compensated for by lorries, which were in short supply. In total, the German Empire had 23,000 trucks at its disposal, compared to 100,000 on the Entente side.[457]

Ludendorff believed that the German attack in the west should be directed at the British army. There were good reasons for this. It was the British who were the backbone of the western front. The French army had been weakened further and further after the terrible battles of attrition, and Paris was finding it increasingly difficult to keep its divisions at full strength. In the spring of 1918, five divisions even had to be disbanded because there simply were not enough soldiers left. The first American divisions that arrived, the 1st, 2nd, 26th, 41st, 42nd and 93rd, were immediately directed to the French part of the front, that ran via Reims, Verdun, Nancy to the Swiss border. The British had been able to keep the French in the saddle because of the ironmaster Sir Douglas Haig, who, like a Von Falkenhayn, in an unceasing optimism had constantly put his troops on the offensive against the German positions.

Ludendorff believed there was a chance to break through the British front, which ran from the coast to Laon. It is important to realise that Haig was far from being thrown off balance by the dreadful results at the Somme and Passchendaele (third Ypres battle), or by the failure to make a real breakthrough at Cambrai. He wanted to stick to the offensive idea and pleaded in London for reinforcements. The infantry divisions in particular were beginning to be understaffed. The British historian Martin Middlebrook calculated that an average of about 2000 men per division was missing.[458] However, there were still a number of strong overseas divisions, the so-called British Empire Divisions, of which the Australian and Canadian divisions were particularly feared because they consisted of war volunteers, in contrast to the (otherwise also good) New Zealand division. The weakest link in the British sector was formed by two Portuguese divisions; Middlebrook spoke of the 'unhappy contigent', operating at only half strength.[459]

The British divisions were not undermanned due to exhaustion, like the French. Here, there was a political agenda. David Lloyd George and his allies ensured that a large part of the replenishment simply stayed in Britain, so that Haig could not get his divisions to full strength (read: attacking strength). Lloyd George did not do this because of pacifist ideals. He believed that Britain should take its chances against Turkey and therefore thwarted Haig. This internal sabotage was, of course, not a textbook example of Von Clausewitz's miraculous trinity either. The collusion, the Prussian war philosopher pointed out, was in practice more of a power struggle, and Haig, to his frustration, was 'kept short'.

However, the enormous plans that emerged on the German staff maps would have quickly put an end to British offensive possibilities. Ludendorff intended to do what no one had succeeded in doing before: force a breakthrough on the western front. The best divisions were brought from the east to the west, with especially many cavalry units remaining in the east to continue occupying the vast country. In total, Ludendorff assembled around 70 German infantry divisions in the front sector around St. Quentin, as well as a formidable amount of artillery. Altogether, around one million German soldiers were involved in the preparations for the German spring offensive.

Ludendorff's intention was to hit the British from the line of demarcation with the French, especially in the area around St Quentin, and then, after the breakthrough, to advance northwards towards Arras and thus to roll up the British lines from the south. This was not the only plan of attack devised by the Germans. There were others, with code names and all, north and south of St Quentin, but Ludendorff had come to the conclusion that this was the best front sector for an attack. It was here that the retreat from the Hindenburg Line had begun, and where the German front was very stable.

For the attack he had two armies at his disposal, the army of Prince Rupprecht and the army of the German Crown Prince Wilhelm. Of these, three armies were deployed, two of which were Rupprecht's, commanded by Tannenberg veteran Otto von Below and Cambrai veteran George von der Marwitz. The Crown Prince's army, commanded by Oskar von Hutier, also a former comrade of Ludendorff from the east, fought on the southern flank and had mainly a supporting function, to prevent the French from coming to the aid of the British from the south when the roll-up towards Arras started.

As many as 32 divisions were to participate in the first wave. A number of older soldiers had been replaced by younger ones and Ludendorff continuously trained the men. Much attention was paid to the new storm troops, which would be deployed against the strongest defensive positions of the British. The units would advance behind a 'Feuerwalz', which would shift 200 metres every four minutes. The hope was to pulverise the Entente positions with grenades and gas (using a new mixture to penetrate British gas masks). No fewer than

6,473 pieces of artillery had been collected for this purpose, of which 2,435 were heavy and 73 super-heavy. Some of this, and this was another huge logistical operation, had been brought in from the Eastern Front, and the artillerymen had to take part in very realistic terrain exercises, which were not without losses. It was the usual Ludendorff concept that took place: stage politics, logistical feats, thorough preparation and training of the men. The troops were in all respects ravaged by the 'maladies' of war, yet they were the ones on whom Ludendorff - and thus the German Empire - had set the cards.

Ludendorff's plan was not uncontroversial. In January 1918, the Kaiser had asked OHL staff member Max von Hoffmann for his opinion regarding the upcoming spring operations. Hoffmann was reluctant to give his opinion. He had recently been promoted, and clearly did not want to degrade his superiors. However, the Emperor pressured him, stating that it was his duty to inform the Emperor fully and honestly, without any reservation. He confessed to the Emperor that he was in favour of a compromise peace. Shortly thereafter, on 2 January 1918 in Schloss Bellevue in Berlin, the Kaiser loudly proclaimed Hoffmann's views towards the OHL, directing his verbal arrows mainly at Ludendorff. He even had a map made in which he had drawn Hoffmann's recommendations. In vain, Hoffmann, who knew the angular character of Ludendorff all too well, tried to speak to Ludendorff alone for a moment.[460] This, however, did not succeed and damage could not be prevented.

Ludendorff reacted as Hoffmann had feared and expected. Ludendorff's face turned a deep purple and his voice rang as if his uniform was too tight around his neck. He felt that the Kaiser had no right to pass him by and ask his subordinates for their opinion. Von Hindenburg, always more diplomatic, sided with Ludendorff but resolved the embarrassing situation by saying that the matter would be looked into again. The Emperor, who often allowed himself to be intimidated by Ludendorff, quickly dismissed the matter. 'I will wait for your report'.

Of course, it did not come to that, as Ludendorff's plans were mainly determined by the OHL, but the damage was done, as Hoffmann feared. The relationship between the two men was broken. Von Hindenburg later wrote a letter to the Kaiser in which he emphasised that it grieved him that the Kaiser apparently attached more value to the opinion of others than to Ludendorff and himself. The letter was written in Ludendorff's tone of voice, and he undoubtedly had access to the text and had a say in it.[461]

This quarrel was typical and showed the impotence of the emperor. The very next day, Ludendorff tried to have Hoffmann dismissed, which the Kaiser prevented. As compensation, the head of the civil cabinet, Rudolf von Valentini, fell, a man who was considered by the OHL to be 'too leftist' and therefore not sufficiently patriotic. Ludendorff's favourite, Friedrich von Berg, became the new man. Thus the emperor compromised. [462]

The greatest damage of all was the fact that Hoffmann's strategic insights were now 'put to rest' for the OHL. And this while Ludendorff could use many critical and sharp minds around him, now that the largest offensives were about to begin. Precisely from his position as a confidant, as well as from his knowledge of the complicated character of Ludendorff and his knowledge of how the marvellous pair Ludendorff-Hindenburg worked together, he had been able, more than anyone else, to exert a moderating influence.

In the east, Hoffmann was still involved for some time in negotiating the peace treaty with the Bolsheviks and, at the end of March 1918, saw the last units of the eastern front leave for the western front. According to Hoffmann, this was actually the moment to hold out on the defensive and take advantage of the peace in the east in terms of raw materials and food.[463] In *Kriegsführung und Politik*, a book that appeared in 1922, Erich Ludendorff reacted to Hoffmann's thesis without explicitly mentioning it. He concluded just the opposite. Ludendorff ignored the possibilities that might exist in Bolshevik Russia, but noted that the harvest in Romania, another supplier, had failed in 1918, making the already precarious food situation even worse. Time was therefore not in Germany's favour and Ludendorff felt that 'nothing spoke in favour of a policy of wait and see'. Besides, he noted, the army was ready. [464]

On 21 March 1918, the inferno broke loose. The morning before, Ludendorff had sat down to breakfast and referred to a Bible text from the prayer book of the 'Böhmischen Brüder', Herrnhüter. This Christian group believed that man was totally depraved and held on to the Holy Scriptures. This book contained a Bible proverb for each day, and the proverb for March 21st was: 'This is the day of the chosen people'. 'Should we not then have confidence in tomorrow's offensive?', Ludendorff asked. [465]

The enemy lines had been bombarded with pamphlets as part of the psychological warfare that had worked so well in Russia. It played on the emotions of the 'Tommy's'; 'the Russians, Romanians and Montenegrins had already given up the war, and the British were spilling their blood for territory that would bring them no profit'. [466]

That day, 21 March, the wind was favourable for the gas attacks and preparations were sufficiently completed. A five-hour artillery bombardment began. Not only the British positions were targeted, but also depots and traffic junctions. It was a surreal sight, the artillerymen with their gas masks on, putting shell after shell into the guns until the barrels were red hot. After five hours, the mortars took over from the artillery, the 'creeping fire' towards the British lines began, and the well-trained German storm troopers came out of the trenches and crept behind the slowly westward shifting conflagration towards the British positions. Over their heads flew the planes of the German 'Luftwaffe' who were firing at the enemy positions from the air.

From Avesnes, Ludendorff and Von Hindenburg followed the battle. As always, Hindenburg was calm, while Ludendorff was nervous and waited for the first reports from the front. These were encouraging for Ludendorff. Hutier and Marwitz reported that the storm troopers had successfully overrun the first line of the British troops behind the fire roll. Von Below's troops, 17 divisions in all, had some difficulty in keeping up with the roll of fire, but later in the day they came back on schedule.

The first signs were therefore favourable. Ludendorff's choice of attacking the British 5th army, which was to provide the lion's share of the defence, seemed a fortunate one, for this was one of the weaker British armies. It was led by a commander who, according to British military specialist John Keegan, owed his position more to his loyalty to his immediate boss, Douglas Haig, than to the confidence of London.[467] The British 5th army was led by cavalry officer Hubert Gough, a Passchendaele veteran, who faced a difficult task. His troops had to move into former French trenches in the front sector and these were notoriously poorly maintained. Gough had tried to reinforce the positions quickly, but the 5th army had relatively few workers. This was a major shortcoming, for the First World War was fought not only with rifle and bayonet, but also with the spade. In February 1918, the number of workers in the area of the British 5th army was 18,000. That was not many and they had to be employed largely to improve and maintain the road network so that at least foraging could continue. There was hardly any time for building up the positions. Measures had been taken to improve the situation and by March, thanks to Chinese and Italian labour, the number of workers had been increased to around 40,000, but this was too late to actually strengthen the front sector before the start of Ludendorff's 'Michael' offensive. [468]

The next day, this positive news continued. The second line of the British was also penetrated. The best news came from the centre from where Hutier's German 18th Army was operating. Gough's British 5th was retreating under immense pressure from German artillery and infantry and this was taking such form that the British 3rd army under General Byng, further north, was increasingly caught in the attack and forced to fall back as well. In Asvernes, these reports were followed with growing excitement by Ludendorff. A general retreat of the Entente seemed to be taking place. Now, all they could do was wait for a real breakthrough. Were the ragged clad attackers capable of this? The euphoria of the early days was enhanced by another aspect, which, although not of any tactical value, did have a moral one. A new 22cm railway gun from the Krupp works had been worked on in secret and this huge monster, the 'Kaiser Wilhelm Geschütz', opened fire on Paris and would fire almost 300 shells at the French capital until August. The German Kaiser, always lacking in tact, applauded this 'success' and personally broke the news. At the station, he shouted to the astonished soldiers that the war had been won and the British defeated. He had champagne bottles opened at lunchtime. [469]

Ludendorff had no time for theatre. He was concentrated on the developments at the front, the bridgehead which his troops had managed to fight across the Somme near Péronne. In several places the British had been pushed back tens of kilometres, in others, especially near Von Below, the advance had come to a halt after about ten kilometres. At this point in the battle, Ludendorff's - always problematic - grey area between strategy and tactics was already becoming apparent. Apart from the facts, reports and strategy, he was also caught up in the delusion of the battle, something that was also difficult to escape from. Ludendorff received the various commanders and expressed his concern about Von Below's tentative successes, and he decided to hand over three fresh divisions to his army immediately, but he also made a strategic adjustment. He ordered that the 6th army under command of General Von Quast, who was not originally part of 'Michael', should help to smoothen the attack of Von Below's 17th army by carrying out an attack towards Arras-Saint Pol. Arras was one of Ludendorff's objectives, but was intended for the second phase of the battle, where the rolling up of the British positions from south to north was planned. Now, there was talk of a frontal assault by Von Quast's 6th army on the British positions - which would be a much more loss-making operation - following a yet unsuccessful breakthrough by Von Below. A setback was 'solved' with a risk.

During the discussion at Asvernes, Ludendorff suggested a second adjustment, which came from the situation in the field. Marwitz's and Hutier's positions on both sides of the Somme River were to be exploited, with Marwitz focusing on the centre while the successful Hutier would turn south towards Noyon against the French. Hutier's covering role thus became more and more offensive. The lure of success southwards was hard to resist but it was the British who Ludendorff had chosen as his target. A field of tension was growing.

The problems increased when successful attacks also suffered delays. By no means had everything to do with the strength of the Entente. The German troops had fallen into a kind of funnel-no-man's-land, and the supplies had the greatest possible difficulty in reaching the troops. In addition, the pressure on Von Below had increased so much that tactical insight was also beginning to fade. Ludendorff had intervened hard on 26 March and telephoned, in a high tone, to demand the resignation of Von Below's chief of staff, who would later become the military historian Krafft von Dellmensingen. This had made an impression. Von Below attacked the next day with nine divisions 'a la Russe'. This meant storming forward shoulder to shoulder, a 'Napoleonic technique' in the age of the machine gun. The Germans were mowed down and the breakthrough failed. The losses were terrible. Ludendorff immediately halted the attack at Von Below, and again transported units to the centre. His knowledge of the stage now seemed to become a handicap; he had too many options, too many directions of attack, but it was questionable whether more troops in the funnel chaos at the centre was the solution. The madness carousel of the First World War showed its face here in no uncertain terms. Ludendorff was caught in it.

The momentum escaped the OHL. On the Entente side, Foch was appointed commander-in-chief and no fewer than 28 French divisions were rushed out to stop the German attack and the imminent breakthrough at the British. After the war, Ludendorff was blamed for not having broken through to the centre when the opportunities were there; the question is whether this would have saved the operation. Could Ludendorff have resisted the urge to take his chances in the centre as well as in the south, or could he have been content with a centre penetration and then a joint roll-up of the British positions with the Marwitz army and Von Below? When the final order came to break through to Amiens, the chance was gone. There were reports of German units getting drunk and looting Entente supplies. Contrary to propaganda claims, the Entente units were far better equipped than the ragged soldiers of the OHL.[470]

While these job tidings came to Ludendorff, he also received the news that his second stepson had fallen. All three of his stepsons were pilots. The first had been killed in a dogfight over the Flemish coast in September 1917 and had disappeared into the waves, only to be washed ashore later. His second stepson went missing on 23 March 1918. Later, the wreck of his plane was found by a German-Jewish officer, Oberleutnant Sulzbach, who identified it. The man, who went into exile in 1937, was thanked by Ludendorff with a personal letter and photo with signature. He wrote a difficult letter to his wife: 'My sweet, sweet wife! I am standing at Pieckchen's grave. There is no doubt, there is'. The grave had been made by the English, 'with love', Ludendorff reassured his wife, and informed her that he had had a photograph made. 'He had your scarf on,' he wrote, 'and his hands were folded. Poor dear wife, how great is your suffering? I cannot find words of comfort. But I can tell you one thing, I loved this boy. The last time we were together he said to me, "Father, what a wonderful childhood I had in Düsseldorf." He was full of his profession and did everything with great seriousness. Everyone liked him... I would immediately sacrifice my so-called fame if I could get both boys back. God protects you, my wife! Your old sweetheart'. Later he returned to Pieckchen's death in several letters, writing that his death had 'taken away' his 'spirit of life'.

Ludendorff sent flowers from Pieckchen's grave folded in a cardboard box to his wife. Eventually Pieckchen was buried near Ludendorff's headquarters. Ludendorff confessed to his wife that he had done this 'out of selfishness'. He wanted to keep him with him, so that he could visit the grave, and he wanted to be there when Pieckchen was reburied in Germany. 'I have just come from Pieckchen's grave', a wistful walk with a sad heart'. Rudolf (Ludendorff's adjutant) regularly sprinkled the flowers with water.

This personal drama overshadowed the smouldering country around St. Quentin, where Ludendorff had rallied his troops against the British 5th army and the units that had come to Gough's aid. Ludendorff and von Hindenburg struggled with the interpretation of the battle. It was clear that 'Michael' had started very successfully. A British historian called the first day of the operation the first defeat of the BEF since the outbreak of trench warfare.[471] On that first day 7,000 British soldiers had been killed and about 21,000 made prisoners of war. Ludendorff had lost 10,000 men, which was more than the British, but considering that the German troops had had to cross no-man's-land, the losses were mild. Well-known British divisions such as the 36th (Ulster), the 14th, 18th and 58th divisions had been pushed back across the full breadth of the front, and only small isolated contingents of troops, such as South African troops and the Leicestershire Regiment, had managed to hold positions on the first day. As we have seen, however, success could not be sustained decisively, and the final tally, after the fall of Amiens, was that the Germans had lost some 250,000 men, some as many as 303,450, between 21 March and 10 April 1918. The latter figure included total German losses along the entire front. The Entente lost 320,000 men and 1,300 pieces of artillery.[472]

There had been a great crisis, not least on the Entente side, where the French general Petain angrily compared the British commander Gough to the Italians at Caporetto, and that was not a compliment. The 'British crisis' had allowed the French General Foch to strengthen his authority in the Entente hierarchy.[473] The bottom line was that the British defeat at St Quentin was ultimately no strategic result for the Germans.

The causes of the failure of the 'Michael' offensive are still being debated. The then colonel Wilhelm von Leeb, later army group commander during operation

'Barbarossa' in 1941, believed that the main cause was the shifting of the direction of attack, i.e. the abandonment of the strategic plan. Indeed, we have seen that Ludendorff again allowed tactics to take precedence over strategy, resulting in a policy of drifting. Von Hindenburg was again unable to correct Ludendorff in this matter. There were also a number of practical reasons that we should perhaps emphasise. The British troops fought bravely, the German troops were already tarnished by a long war and had all kinds of flaws. The battle took place in a ruined infrastructure, partly caused by the earlier Somme battles. Also, not all plans turned out as one would have hoped. In particular, the large-scale artillery bombardments had not always brought about what was hoped for. As Verdun had already shown, even the largest-scale artillery bombardments were no guarantee of decisive success.

Operation 'Michael' had been launched with the aim of becoming a decisive success. The goals had not been achieved. The British front had not been broken up, and a decision on the western front - before the intervention of large American units - had not been achieved. Germany had had to wait more than a year for this opportunity. In his memoirs, Ludendorff spoke honestly about his disappointment. The breakthrough was indeed a 'glänzende Waffentat' (brilliant victory), but 'strategically one had not won what one had hoped for'.[474] The failure of the fall of Amiens was also seen as a great disappointment. 'The great battle for France is over', said Von Hindenburg.[475] The almost 90,000 prisoners of war[476] that the Germans had made could not make up for that.

The lack of decisive success should have set off alarm bells in the political arena, since even this exceptionally well prepared and large-scale attack had not brought about the turnaround. Clausewitz's 'war is politics by other means' should now have been put into practice. But there were no new orders for von Hindenburg and Ludendorff, nor did they sound the alarm to the Kaiser or the War Cabinet. The result was that the general duo were soon caught up in the enormous pressure that the war 'alltag' put on them. There were many problems to be faced. After 4 April, there had been all kinds of 'additional battles', sometimes of considerable magnitude. In addition, a new front had come into being, which had to be expanded urgently. After all, they had left their own 'safe' lines and moved into the no-man's-land of the Entente. Now, a stable front had to be established with great speed. In addition, Ludendorff searched feverishly for possibilities to find the lost momentum somewhere.

The rival and successor operations of 'Michael' were suddenly very topical again. Again Ludendorff chose to attack the British and Flanders, and the area around the Kemmel and Scherpenberg south of Ypres became the new battleground. However, here the British were in a better position than Gough's troops. The 1st and 2nd British armies were in the oldest positions on the Western Front, which were well developed. Ludendorff had sent his artillery specialist, Bruchmueller, to the front sector in question but, as we saw with operation 'Michael', the use of artillery also had limitations. Moreover, the Entente troops had no intention of giving up even an inch of front. Douglas Haig's infamous 'back to the wall' order went out to the troops. To stand firm was the motto. Foch refused to send French troops for reinforcement when the battle broke out in early April, but together with Belgian support, the BEF stood firm. The first news of the battle reached Ludendorff on 9 April.

Shortly after 'Michael', another huge offensive was underway. The reports were initially favourable, Bruchmueller said. Hope revived. Would it still be possible to throw the British against the Channel coast and drive them into the sea? Could this separate the British units from the French? Kaiser Wilhelm II had come especially to the headquarters of Ludendorff and Von Hindenburg in Avesnes and stayed the night of the 9-10 April 1918. The Kaiser spoke a number of kind words to Ludendorff, who had celebrated his birthday on 9 April and had turned 53, not forgetting the personal loss of Ludendorff's son. Ludendorff mentioned it in his memoirs and also emphasised the heavy responsibility that rested on the Emperor, someone with a completely different "nature" than himself. The Kaiser had an aversion to war, Ludendorff thought, and it was just such a man who had to lead Germany in the post-Bismarck era. This expressed Ludendorff's sweet memory of the 'iron chancellor', who was almost as sacred to him as Von Schlieffen. Besides, he wrote, Kaiser Wilhelm II did not have the right men around him, who were prepared to demand everything necessary from the country in times of war. Herein lay our fate, Ludendorff wrote with a sense of drama in his *Kriegserinnerungen*. [477]

The heavy burden he attributed to his emperor also weighed on Ludendorff himself. The new battles in Flanders were therefore, once again, of vital importance.

The first reports of success in Flanders brought a moment of hope, but how realistic was it to expect much from this plan 'Georg' (also called St. Georg and Georgette) given that the larger-scale 'Michael' had failed. Not for nothing did the well-known military historian B.H. Liddell Hart call this new plan of attack 'more desperate than reflective'.[478] Ludendorff had indeed succeeded in moving artillery to the northern front, but due to the severity of 'Michael's' battles he had fewer infantry divisions than desired. Still, there were successes, especially around Neuve Chapelle, not least with Portuguese Entente units, which were not known for their great military tenacity. These were the 2nd Portuguese division, which had just been about to be replaced by British troops. The breakthrough was, of course, good for the Germans, but it did not actually reach the front sector where Ludendorff needed success the most. The Portuguese defeat was actually fortunate for the British, Liddell Hart thought.[479] Most of the ground was gained along the southern part of the front, which stretched roughly between Comines and La Bassee. Ludendorff had deployed tanks in addition to the artillery preparation during this offensive. It was one of the rare occasions when the Germans were able to do so. Their influence was limited, but the German troops still managed to capture Armentières and Merville. Mount Kemmel, part of the ridge on the Ypres front, also fell into German hands.

The newly appointed Commander-in-Chief, Foch, ordered the recapture of Kemmel, without success. Moreover, the further German breakthrough also failed. The units of the German 4th and 6th army - the Kronprinz Rupprecht army group - did not consist of "Angriffsdivisionen", as Ludendorff stated.[480] A new balance sheet could therefore be drawn up after 25 April, when the climax of the battle of Kemmel slowly faded away. The rapid change of front had not brought Ludendorff what he hoped for. There were, however, a number of positive points to note. First of all, the British had been hit. Of the 59 British divisions, no less than 53 were at least once or more deployed. To compensate for the losses, new troops had to be brought to the European continent. Half of the French divisions had also come into action to repel 'Michael' and 'Georg' as well as support attacks. But this was offset by large German losses - after the relatively favourable 'defensive battles' of 1917. In the process, Ludendorff observed, the 'Angriffsfreudigkeit' of several divisions had diminished and 'that gave food for thought'.[481]

Also of concern was the battle between St. Mihiel and the Moselle, where the first major fighting took place with American units, foreshadowing the growing American presence at the front. What was also a bad sign for the care of the German units was the fact that captured supplies in Entente hinterland had been looted. The German soldier was hungry, and this affected morale. NCOs and officers had difficulty, Ludendorff noted with growing concern, in asserting their authority. In addition, the - according to Ludendorff always weak - home front had taken the legal weapons out of the hands of the army command by dealing too softly with deserters. Trials often took place too late and far from the front, so that the 'Blut und Eisen'-context was no longer in sight of the judicial authorities. This led to 'too lenient' judgements and court rulings. The U-boat war was also developing less and less favourably, and was a growing concern for Ludendorff, who had after all been partly responsible for the deployment of this controversial weapon. The German envoy to Austria-Hungary, General von Cramon, told Ludendorff in no uncertain terms that the Austro-Hungarian public now finally expected results against the American troopships. Ludendorff announced that he could not possibly shield the thousands of sea miles, but the reality was even more serious: there was hardly an American who did not cross the ocean unscathed. The German U-boat weapon, after initial spectacular successes, was increasingly lagging behind. The British also carried out attacks on the German U-boat ports of Zeebrugge and Ostend. [482]

It was at this stage of the war that Ludendorff first looked defeat in the face. He had also found an initial explanation for this. Whereas he had initially pointed at the stronger Entente troops, now the increasingly louder voices of protest from German society began to explain the crumbling German chances of victory. Ludendorff was irritated by the negative mood on the home front, while the soldiers in the field were doing their duty and had 'a much harder time' than the civilists.[483] It was also dangerous, because soldiers who had been at home brought the negative mood with them to the front. Another factor was that the German army had lost many good officers and non-commissioned officers in the recent battles, which could have caused the negative spirit to resurface. Army and people, Ludendorff believed, had to form 'one body and one soul'. With this, Ludendorff clearly showed that he had a different way of thinking than Von Clausewitz in *Vom Kriege*. 'Das Militär' was clearly not a derivative of the people and politics, but more or less became the conscience of the nation. The fact that decision-making in wartime had to be influenced by the interaction of sovereign, general, people, was ignored by Ludendorff. 'An army cannot remain healthy if its people are not healthy either', he noted in his *Kriegserinnerungen* on the occasion of the Kemmel Battle of Ieperen.[484]

What had started as 'the great battle for France' now grew into a series of hammer-blows along the front, of which 'George' was also a stage. This would have been the moment where Von Hindenburg would have had to intervene, but Ludendorff could continue to do so. Day and night, almost without rest, he was imprisoned by only one thought: how the Entente front could be torn open and rolled up and how, against all odds, victory for Imperial Germany could still be secured. Was it his sense of honour for Tannenberg that drove him forward, suggested Ludendorff biographer Wolfgang Venohr. Ludendorff's interest in the matter was not so private; he identified his own fate with that of the German nation, and his ideas about what would be good for Germany as the only way out of the deadly dilemma in which the Empire had found itself in '14-'18. He felt responsible, and wanted to return Germany through a military victory to a Bismarckian order of stability and respect.

The third spring offensive, which followed on 27 May 1918, on both sides of the town of Soissons, had all the typical Ludendorff elements. It opened with a diversionary attack on the French. The intention was to lure the British southwards and then, by means of a fourth offensive, to move against them. Whereas in 1917, the Entente had failed in its attacks, the Germans now broke through the front again over 55 kilometres in length and penetrated into French territory, partly to a depth of 45 kilometres. They even reached the Marne, the 'Schicksalfluss' of 1914. The sweet temptation of success did its work again. Ludendorff realised that the diversionary attack - note: an operation involving 41 German divisions - was a success, and decided to exploit it. The troops were thereby, as one historian put it, sent 'ins Blaue', without clear direction and purpose, until the attack was watered down. [485]

At the beginning of June, the attack was over. Ludendorff remained as combative as ever. The action of the Germans on the Marne had suddenly brought up the name of Paris several times; old memories of the 1914 campaign had resurfaced. Were there still miracles in the world? But the battles of attrition were increasingly eroding the already weakened German army. It began to look as if Ludendorff's hammer blows were mainly taps on his own fingers. The average strength of a German battalion on 1 July 1918 was only 650 men (152 fewer than on 21 March 1918), and was soon to fall dramatically still further. The 200 divisions Ludendorff had in the field constituted in reality only 160 divisions, the 195 Entente divisions - including twenty American divisions - constituting a force of 215 divisions at German strength. The American divisions had double the strength of the German units. The 65,000 men prisoners of war that the Entente had suffered in this last battle did not alter this. [486]

Inevitably, new German offensives (the so-called Blücheroffensives) followed; 9 June and 15 July went forward again. The attack of 9th, like the one before it, was a diversionary attack. It lasted only two days, by which time it was already clear that the German troops could not achieve success. The offensive of 15 July, plan 'Marneschutz', also failed. This was an offensive along the Marne, east of Chateau Thiery, while attacks were also made east of Reims. Here also, partly due to the artillery support of Bruechmueller, there was initial success. But from the lines behind, the German attack was finally repulsed in a bloody fashion. Meanwhile, Ludendorff was again directing reserves towards Flanders, while he himself also moved to the front more northwards, towards Tournai, in order to be closer to events.[487]

Ludendorff's problems were piling up fast. There was Spanish flu among the soldiers, Bolshevik ideas penetrated the troops, there was hunger and lack, German soldiers who had been prisoners of war in Russia brought a 'negative spirit' with them, there were deserters - a conspiracy was even discovered of a few hundred Alsatians who wanted to escape to the Netherlands - and small particularistic Bavarian ideas resurfaced, hand in hand with angry noises about the Emperor and the Crown Prince. The 'Umsturtzel elements' spread.[488] Ludendorff's collaborators had also noticed something new. Ludendorff had always been the most emotional man of the Von Hindenburg-Ludendorff duo, but during the last few weeks, the severely over-tired Ludendorff had become more and more irritable and it seemed as if he had less and less control of himself. His relatives tried to shield his nervous attacks from the outside world, while the tormented Ludendorff, perhaps the greatest tactician and stage specialist of the war, bent deeper and deeper over his front maps and ran his fingers over the blood-stained map of the Western Front. There was only one thought in his mind, where, where could Germany once more seize the initiative and show the world that the 'Landser' of 1918 was still able to realise Von Schlieffen's dream at the last minute, despite all the setbacks. Von Hindenburg looked on, and kept silent... as always.

Chapter 10

The Black Day

Ludendorff was in the headquarters of the Rupprecht army group when the dreaded news arrived that the Entente had embarked on a major counter-offensive. This message came out of the blue. After all the effort, and partly also remarkable successes in this umpteenth year of war, the OHL had to endure this too. Ludendorff had just been studying the maps of the Flanders front in Tournai, hoping that after the battle of the Marne around Chateau Thierry and Reims, he would be able to deal another sledgehammer blow to the British front (plan 'Hagen'). But of course the Entente had no intention of leaving the entire initiative for the spring and summer of 1918 to the Germans. The message that reached Ludendorff on 18 July reported a large-scale Entente offensive near Villers-Cotterets, which would involve heavy tank support and a breakthrough of the German lines. It all sounded worrying. The plans at Tournai disappeared from the table and Ludendorff hurried southwards.

The always fearless von Hindenburg was already waiting for Ludendorff on the platform, which was not a good sign.

The French had gone into the attack with no fewer than eighteen divisions and American divisions - 28,000 men strong each - and had put the six German divisions on the west bank of the Marne in enormous difficulty. The troops of the French 10th and 6th army were supported by 580 aircraft and 345 tanks, of which 135 were Renault M17/M18 tanks, 123 were Char Schneider M16 and 87 were St. Chamond M16 tanks.[489] Tank production was now in full swing and began to have an increasingly strong influence on the battlefield. The Entente, unlike the Germans, saw in the tanks the answer to trench warfare. The British focused on the real heavy tanks, whereby the production of the Mark-V tank was the main activity (there was a 'male' and 'female' type, and one could easily roll over a trench of 4,5 meter width), while the French (in cooperation with the US) focused on the light and medium tank, whereby the Renault tank M17/M18 was popular. From mid-April 1918, the Renault factories produced 24 tanks a day. In total, by mid-1919, the Entente had planned to field 20,000 tanks and 15,000 armoured vehicles. Over the course of the war these numbers were not realised, but it was a fact - also during the offensive of 18 July - that the influence of the tank weapon was growing rapidly. The French were more successful than the British in this, mostly because they pooled their tanks, a wise practise that they unfortunately abandoned in 1940. [490]

Ludendorff immediately set to work on countermeasures. The stakes were high. This front sector was known as 'the second Marne' and referred to the push through to Paris. Von Lossberg, Ludendorff's confidant, was sent forward, but had to conclude that the German positions were hopeless. There was no other way: the battle had to be stopped with a direct retreat. The German units suffered heavy losses, 29,000 German soldiers were taken prisoner and about 168,000 were killed or wounded.[491] When the smoke cleared, the OHL could draw up the bleak balance sheet that the German army had shrunk from 5.1 million to 4.2 million men in just six months.[492]

That the situation was now more than serious, was shown by the fact that even Von Hindenburg wrote a sombre letter to his wife. He let it be known that Germany might lose the war, but, he added, there was nothing he could do about it; Germany lacked inner strength.[493] Apparently, it did not occur to Von Hindenburg that the German people might have a more realistic view on the outcome of the war than the OHL and the War Cabinet. Oberst Mertz von Quirnheim, operations officer at the OHL, also noticed that the OHL always used strange arguments for its 'explanations'. Ludendorff showed Von Quirnheim his Herrnhuetter prayer book and the motto it contained for 15 July. 'I am not superstitious,' Ludendorff said, 'but still'. Von Quirnheim was astonished. [494]

With the 'Second Marneslag', the last German offensive of World War I had come to an end. Ludendorff realised this, perhaps unconsciously. In any case, he grasped at straws and argued with his subordinates. Especially the staff of the 7th army, and Oberst Wetzell in particular, got it. Generaladjutant von Plessen was at the headquarters on 29 July and noted: 'The mood is at its lowest and Ludendorff must be comforted by Von Hindenburg'.[495]

Indeed, Von Hindenburg was the reason why Ludendorff was still in office at all. As a result of the surprise attack by the French and the cancellation of the psychologically important Marne offensive, Ludendorff had offered his resignation to Von Hindenburg. Wolfgang Venohr rightly remarks that von Hindenburg should have let Ludendorff go already after the failed March offensive, but the men had a deadly stranglehold on each other. Von Hindenburg's presence at the station after Ludendorff's hasty return trip to the south had already shown that the old officer could not manage without his apprentice. His tactical master's eye usually succeeded in quickly restoring the front, and in his indomitable energy went out the door, order after order, moving the unwieldy trench army where it was needed.

However, the machinery was definitely grinding to a halt. The number of soldiers in the battalions was still falling and in October 1918 it would only amount to 420 men per battalion.[496] Von Hindenburg did not let Ludendorff go. Three more months of suffering followed. The total number of German divisions on the Western Front was still 186, but the actual occupation provided troops for only 95 divisions. The Entente brought 205 divisions into the field, 30 of which were American, which together, counting by full German divisions, made up a force of 235 divisions. The balance of power was thus 2:5 in favour of the Entente. As far as tanks were concerned, the situation was even more serious. There were hardly any German tanks and the balance of power was 5:1 in favour of the Entente. By the autumn of 1918, the war had been lost - in everyone's eyes - both in terms of production and in terms of manpower. [497]

Even in this hour of need, the possibility of an 'Entscheidungsschlacht' was sought. Major Niemann stumbled upon the rich fantasy that Ludendorff was playing with. Niemann was sent by the Emperor to Ludendorff to ask how the front reduction would work. Due to the series of Blücher offensives and the Entente countermeasures, the front was no longer of an advantageous straight line as it had been with the Hindenburg Line. Ludendorff himself had always been the man who emphasised and implemented this very rational warfare. Now, however, he brushed off this request as a kind of bitter criticism. 'Shortening the front', Ludendorff immediately made it clear that this was 'out of the question'.[498] After all, the German divisions would soon be moving towards Amiens, towards the west. Ludendorff only wanted time to reorganise and then move forward again. Indeed, new plans were already being made, such as an adapted smaller plan 'Hagen', further attack 'Kurfürst' on both sides of the river Oise around Montdidier and Soissons, and other plans. Further hope was drawn from technical imperfections on the Entente side in the tank actions. For example, in some places 40-50% of the Entente tanks failed in the first days. These were very high losses indeed. As far as the battle of 18 July and the following days are concerned, the tank deployment and loss figures have been precisely preserved:[499]

German retreat

Day:	tanks deployed:	tank losses
18 July	223	102
19 July	105	50
20 July	32	17
21 July	100	36
22 July	82	48

This was due to the technical imperfections of the tanks and therefore their vulnerability, as well as the fact that the different arms' tasks did not yet sufficiently support each other. Yet, thanks in part to the deployment of the French tanks, there had been a remarkable success, which the Entente had not been able to achieve in 1917 when there were fewer tanks. Ludendorff's one-sided attention to the imperfections of the tank weapon did not change this.

The Germans also noticed that the Americans were appearing more and more often at the front. In the operations of 18 July 1918, a total of 9 American divisions were counted in action. This caused concern and again put pressure on all (unrealistic) plans of the OHL.[500] The developments at the front and at home would soon bring Ludendorff back to reality. The 'black day' for the German army, 8 August 1918, was approaching at a fast pace. It was to be the beginning of a series of 'Zermürbungsangriffe', as the Germans called it, with which the Entente sought to bring Germany to its knees. After a long series of German offensives, it was now Foch's troops' turn.

The first attack should improve the starting position for future operations. For this purpose it was important to fight the important supply road Paris-Amiens free of German artillery fire at last. This could only be done by throwing back the German lines over a wide front. The line Morlancomt - Mericomt - Harbonnieres - Hangest-en-Santerre was chosen as a guideline, with some support attacks. It was a combined British-French operation with the British of 4th supported by Canadian and Australian troops. In total the British had over 500 tanks and 2068 artillery pieces at their disposal. The French XXXI. corps of the 1st French army supported the operation with 616 artillery pieces and 90 tanks. A thousand aircrafts were also brought into the field.

Opposite these units, which were well rested, were heavily weary divisions of the German 2nd army. Some divisional commanders had repeatedly urged Ludendorff to shorten the front. For some stretches of front only sixty rifles were available for half a kilometre of line, which was very little. Normally one division had to occupy 5 kilometres of front. Of the 2nd German army in the sector in question, the divisions 27 and 117 were fully deployable, but the 54th, 198th, 41st, 225th and 14th were only reliable as 'position divisions', i.e. in defence.

The 13th, 243rd and 192nd divisions needed rest and were at the end of their strength, and the 43rd, 107th and 109th divisions simply had to be relieved.[501] The strength of the 'position division' was also relative, if we look at the 41st division. In March 1918, the division had lost 1500 men in the fighting around Arras. Shortly afterwards, 1,000 men had been lost to Spanish flu and through the fighting on 15 July, the unit had lost almost another 500 men, 15 of them officers. 'If we do not have to fight, maybe we can recover,' the division commander told the OHL, but they could not afford that luxury.[502]

The offensive of 8 August started as a classic World War I operation with a heavy artillery bombardment. The artillery was followed by waves of attacks. The first wave consisted of 8 divisions of infantry, supported by 192 tanks, mostly Mark-V tanks. Three hours later, three more infantry divisions plus three cavalry divisions would follow, again with tank support of 228 tanks. This force was supported on the flank by the French, operating slightly differently with their lighter tanks, using them mainly in village and town battles. The commander of the British 4th army, General Henry Seymour Rawlinson, who had replaced the unfortunate Gough, and his Chief of Staff, General Montgomery, were making history. Rawlinson was the son of a noted Assyriologist and had had front-line experience in India and Burma. They broke through the positions of the German 2nd army over a width of 30 kilometres. The three army corps, the British 3rd under General Butler, the Australian corps under General Montah, the Canadian corps (four divisions, each over 20.000 strong) under General Currie, as well as General Kavanagh's 'mixed' cavalry corps (consisting of the 1st cavalry division (Mullins), the 2nd cavalry division (Pitman) and the 3rd cavalry division (Harman) which was largely British but included Canadian units within the ranks of the 3rd cavalry division, embarked on an offensive that would have the world in its grip both militarily and morally.[503]

The German front was roughly divided into two parts. The Somme ran east-west through the front at Mericoert, so that there were units north and south of the river. In the north, the 43rd and 27th divisions (and the 108th division rushed in later by Ludendorff) were badly hit by this, while south of the Somme, from north to south, the 13th, 41st, 117th, 225th, 14th (Bavarian) and 192nd divisions received the full weight of the attack. Somewhat in the shadows were the 233rd division - all the way to the north, already practically leaning against the front of the 3rd British army - as well as the 24th division at Contoire, which was in the periphery of the attack of the 1st French army.[504]

At the northernmost part of the area of operation, the 43rd and 13th divisions were hit by the attack of British (3rd division) and Australian (58th and 3rd division) troops. The resistance they encountered was remarkably small. 'The resistance was generally weak', noted General Montgomery, Chief of Staff of Rawlinson's 4th Army. Only here and there did the British-Australian units encounter organised German resistance. At Warfusée, for the first time, it came to a bigger fight. Here, German units had taken hold, and in a concentric attack, supported on the flanks by tanks, the 4th British Army managed to defeat the Germans, defeating a battery of 15 centimetre artillery and its crew.[505] By the end of the day the 43rd division had been beaten back and practically all the divisional artillery was in the hands of the Entente.

The reports received by the OHL were very disturbing for Germany. The front was ripped open over a length of thirty kilometres and the Entente troops penetrated up to eleven kilometres into the German hinterland. Almost all the objectives set by the Entente were achieved on the first day. The Reichsarchiv called this day 'Die Katastrophe des 8. August 1918'.[506] The total loss of the German 2nd army was 26 to 27,000 men, including 650 to 700 officers. About 400 German artillery pieces had fallen into the hands of the Entente.[507]

It was not so much the losses that made 8 August go down in history as the black day for the German army. The losses of Johannes Georg von der Marwitz's 2nd army were considerable, but other things mattered: the battle had once again taken the Germans completely by surprise and showed that from now on the initiative lay with the Entente. This battle also made it clear that, unlike in 1917, the Entente was now able to achieve breakthroughs. It became clear to the OHL that Foch was serious. In fact, Foch was now following the same strategy as Ludendorff with his Blücher attacks. The difference was that Foch had the units and the material for it, the Germans did not. Reserves which Ludendorff had rushed to the front, and which eventually also succeeded in rebuilding a more or less coherent front line, were called 'war extenders' by the retreating units. Kaiser Wilhelm II took the news with striking resignation. 'We can only draw one conclusion', he said, 'we have reached the end of our possibilities. The war must end'. [508]

In Avesnes, Ludendorff received one bad report after another. The breakthrough was wide and relatively deep, especially in the Canadian sector. Artillery positions had been overrun, divisional headquarters taken, and in Proyart the headquarters of an army corps had been blown to bits by Entente tanks. Several divisions had completely disintegrated and effectively ceased to exist. Although things eventually stabilised within 48 hours, this battle of Amiens felt like a very heavy defeat. 'August 8th', Ludendorff wrote, 'is the black day of the army in the history of this war'.[509] More than a de facto military defeat, it was the day of truth, when the own limitations and the possibilities of the opponent were suddenly demonstrated. The truth hurt the eyes and was unbearable for a man like

Ludendorff, who in the end thought he could win the war almost on willpower.

The symbolic meaning of Amiens also got through to Vienna. From the Donaumonarchy, Spa headquarters was told that Emperor Karl would be coming for consultations in the middle of August. Von Hindenburg clearly outlined the situation that had now arisen: 'It is quite different to be unsuccessful in an attack operation than to fail in a defence operation'.[510] Indeed, von Hindenburg and Ludendorff had been defeated on the terrain they understood best, but it was also a concept they had neglected because of their offensive ambitions. The price for this was now being paid.

On 12 September, it became clear that the American units under General John Pershing were no paper tigers. On that day, the first full-scale American attack took place in the marshlands south of Verdun. They hit the German units that had not yet fully regrouped in the Hindenburg Line. The attack by Pershing's two army corps was a complete success. After a heavy artillery bombardment of 2900 guns, the Americans succeeded in driving the Germans back and taking more than 13,000 men prisoner. The success of the newcomers was so great that it made the French - who had waited years for their offensive success - a little jealous.[511] Lossberg advised Ludendorff to fall back on the Hindenburg Line across the entire front. There was hesitation, which was understandable. In fact, it meant that the German army would be back in the same position as in 1914. The pointlessness of the war gnawed at the 'Landser' in the field who, like the home front, had suffered hardship for years.

There was also unrest in the Austro-Hungarian double monarchy. There, the old emperor, who had experienced so much suffering on his way of life, had finally died in November 1916, well into his eighties. Since heir apparent Franz Ferdinand had been assassinated in Sarajevo in 1914, the throne and the onerous task of keeping the creaking 'Church of Nations' together fell to Emperor Karl. Throughout his life, Karl had been neatly kept out of the equation. For Franz Joseph, Franz Ferdinand was the new strongman, and the latter made sure that Karl had no part in anything. The young man had a somewhat meaningless existence as a result, which he took very much to heart. But he was of good will and did what was asked of him. When an aunt and his grandmother sent him to a suitable bride, Zita von Bourbon-Parma, he married her without grumbling and it grew into true love. They settled down in Castle Hertzenberg, and until the infamous assassination attempt in Sarajevo, Karl seemed to be destined for oblivion. Now he had to carry the torch of St Stephen's crown, and hold together the patchwork of peoples as Franz Jozeph had done. This was actually an impossible task. The 'magic wizardry', as the historian Andics described it,[512] had disappeared. Franz Ferdinand had grown so old that there was hardly anyone in the dual monarchy who could imagine an emperor other than him.

Karl had to 'fight his way into' the system. The civil service, which had been an important power base for the previous emperor, reacted with suspicion and wait-and-see. Karl did not have a fighting nature and he also lacked the rebellious energy of Crown Prince Rudolf, who polemicised against his own father in the Viennese press at a very young age before choosing death at the Mayerling hunting lodge. Since Karl's accession to the throne, the situation for Austria-Hungary in the First World War had seriously deteriorated. He faced a crisis of legitimacy because of his 'ignorance', he lacked experience and he struggled with the nationality question which arose under the pressure of Wilsonian self-determination. He underestimated the 'Hungarian card' in the political poker game and feared the revolutionary upheavals like in Russia, where the tsarist throne had suddenly disappeared. Militarily, things were not going well either. On the Isonzo front with Italy, battles dragged on endlessly. The relationship with Germany was also under pressure because of the disappointing results and Karl's wife Zita was very anti-German. Karl ventured into the slippery terrain of secret diplomacy, believing that peace was the precondition for being able to cope with the growing nationality problem in his country. It soon became clear to him that he was facing a difficult task. Through a descendant of the Bourbon-Parma family, Karl tried to make contact with the Entente powers in Liechtenstein, which resulted in the 'Sixtus affair'. No results were achieved and the matter became more and more pressing. The Emperor's Chief of Cabinet, Arthur Graf Polzer-Hoditz, pointed out to the Emperor that action had to be taken on the nationality issue, otherwise the Habsburg Empire was expected to be revolutionised.

Under these circumstances, Emperor Karl arrived in Germany to negotiate the future of Europe with the OHL and his Imperial colleague Wilhelm II. Just before that, the last emergency measures had been taken by Vienna. Massive amounts of food had been brought in from Ukraine to alleviate the initial emergency, and on 15 June the last major Austro-Hungarian offensives had taken place against the Italians. Four days of bitter fighting had taken place. 50,000 Italians had been taken prisoner, but there had been no breakthrough. Vienna, too, had its operation 'Michael'. A 'Siegfriede' was no longer possible. Karl understood that the Germans still hoped for at least a 'Vergleichsfriede', but Karl himself was more pessimistic and more hasty. He feared major problems internally; peace was the key to retaining the throne, with or without his allies.

The meeting turned into a strangely dressed-up ball. Out of politeness, Karl had put on the uniform of a Prussian general, including a "Pickelhaube" on his head. Kaiser Wilhelm, who was fond of uniforms and owned about 500, was dressed as an Austrian general. However, this mutual protocol could not hide the fact that the Sixtus affair had not yet been forgotten. The Germans were also confronted with a new foreign minister, Stephan Burian von Rajecz, as a substitute for Ottokar Czernin, who was old and well-known in Germany. A new indicator of the growing distance between Vienna and Berlin.[513] The two emperors, who sat opposite each other, thought that the fate of Central Europe was still in their hands, the reality was that developments were indomitable.

The meeting in Spa was chaotic. Karl believed that a call for peace should be addressed to the world, 'To All' would be an appropriate title. The Germans wanted to take a more cautious course. The OHL believed that the German army was not yet defeated, and that acting too eagerly could send the wrong signal. The Kaiser and the OHL were more inclined to make cautious contact with the Entente via the neutral Netherlands. However, events overtook the negotiations. In the middle of the dispute, Burian was told by his ministry that Great Britain had declared Czechoslovakia an ally of the Entente. Czechoslovakia? The central powers looked at each other in the negotiating room in Spa with open mouths: did that country exist at all?

In the meantime, there was already a considerable force in turbulent Russia of about 50,000 Czech soldiers calling themselves the Czech Legion, who had Czech-Slavic aspirations, and who were now being supported from London. Parts of this so-called Czech Legion had also been on the front line in Italy for some time to fight against the dual monarchy, which was obstructing the national cause of Czechoslovakia. Karl could not stay another day in Spa. He said goodbye to Kaiser Wilhelm and again urged direct peace talks. Von Hindenburg kept his calm as ever and believed that Vienna was acting too hastily. Kaiser Wilhelm expressed his fear that the alliance was in danger, which was an understatement.[514]

Back in Vienna, Emperor Karl accelerated his work on an 'Verständigung' with the forces that were destroying the Empire. Burian appealed for peace on 14 September, but the Entente responded with offensives. These were directed, among other things, against Bulgaria, which was forced to withdraw from the war. The first indications of this came on 25 September and a few days later it was done. 'The bottom is out of the barrel', Burian now thought gloomily.[515] The Bulgarian front had been wobbling for some time and there were food shortages in the country. The Bulgarian ambassador in Berlin, Rizow, had already opted for peace initiatives and, via Stockholm, the Entente was sounded out.[516] In mid-October, Karl tried to save what could be saved from Schönbrunn and the Hungarian hunting lodge Gödöllő near Budapest. The new concept for the future of the dual monarchy was presented: the federal state. A good plan perhaps, but it was too late to reverse the process. The separation of the constituent peoples was in full swing, even the Hungarians no longer remained loyal. Kaiser Wilhelm had turned out to be an 'expensive friend' and the dual monarchy did not survive the First World War. On 30 October 1918, the words 'Hoch die Republik! Wir brauchen keinen Kaiser' were heard.[517]

Ludendorff was struck by these new developments. He had tried to reinforce the French-threatened front in Bulgaria with German divisions via Macedonia. However, the German military envoy in Sofia informed him that nothing would help. The Bulgarian Tsar Ferdinand had abdicated and the Bulgarian troops, which were reasonably well supplied with provisions and weapons, simply had no desire to fight any more. Through the German experience in Romania, the OHL knew that this region of Europe sometimes had its own peculiar laws, which did not fit into the thinking of soldiers who had been trained in the spirit of Von Schlieffen. The fall of Bulgaria, however, affected Vienna in particular.

In the west, disastrous news also continued unabated. On 27 September, the Entente opened a new attack in the already blood-soaked country of St. Quentin and Cambrai. The next day, Belgian troops joined in an attack towards Ghent. Foch brought the German 'Stellungsdivisionen' out of balance, who were slowly fading away and could not catch their breath anymore. Ludendorff literally got on his nerves. In Hotel Britannique, where he had his quarters, he lost his self-control under these new reports. He cursed the Reichstag, the Kaiser, the fleet and even the fatherland. His staff anxiously closed the doors when his tirades broke out. These became more frequent, and kept pace with the bad reports that rushed towards Britannique from all sides. At 6 o'clock in the evening of September 28, Ludendorff descended into the room below him where Von Hindenburg was keeping quarter. Ludendorff looked very pale and was trembling all over. The Field Marshal and the 'Erster Generalquartiermeister' looked at each other without words for a long time. Then Ludendorff began, jerkily, to list the arguments why Germany should ask for an armistice. While Von Hindenburg listened, his eyes filled with tears, but when Ludendorff finished, he nodded in agreement. He stood up and took Ludendorff's right hand in both of his. Then they both turned around without saying another word. [518]

Ludendorff may have become a difficult man to work with because of the extreme stress, but his supporters from the very beginning did not distance themselves from him. It was in fact Max Bauer who, at the beginning of September, took an important step to help restore Ludendorff's mental health. First, he turned to Von Hindenburg's private physician, Dr Muenter, who established that Ludendorff was severely overworked. 'A less healthy body would have col-

Western Front offensive 1918

lapsed long ago', he commented.[519] Bauer also contacted Dr. Hochheimer, who had been on Ludendorff's staff for some time. He presented the situation to him and told him that Ludendorff, in addition to his work in the past years, had now had to endure eight weeks of bitter setbacks and had fallen into a deep depression as a result. Bauer asked, in this strictly confidential conversation -he knew his boss's short-tempered nature- whether Hochheimer would like to use his influence to help improve Ludendorff's mental state. 'Even Von Hindenburg no longer has any influence over him'. [520]

Dr. Hochheimer immediately agreed and to Ludendorff's surprise the doctor reported to him the same day. 'What's the hurry?' asked an astonished Ludendorff. Dr. Hochheimer played his cards open, in a warm and calm voice. He pointed out to Ludendorff that he had given all his strength in all those years, except to his own spirituality. Ludendorff had only worked, his body and mind exhausted. He had had no relaxation, no joy, no appetite, hardly breathed, not laughed, seen nothing of nature or art. Ludendorff listened to Dr. Hochheimer's lecture and remained silent in his chair after the doctor had finished his story. Then Ludendorff nodded: 'You are right about everything, I have felt the same way for a long time, but what can I do?' A relieved Hochheimer immediately seized his opportunity. He thought Ludendorff should leave Avesnes, with its stuffy atmosphere. He had to rest his eyes, enjoy nature, relax again. Dr. Hochheimer prescribed breathing exercises, which Ludendorff, always punctual, immediately began. He moved his headquarters to Spa, walked through the rose gardens and enjoyed the view of the mountains again for the first time.

On 8 September, Hochheimer was already able to see an improvement: 'He seems happier, fresher', he noted. On 11 September he wrote: 'Today, after deep breathing exercises, he literally fell asleep under my hands. I open doors for him to worlds he has never known. When I tell him about my children, he himself seems like a child telling you a story about India. I avoid any conversation about military matters. I am interested in Ludendorff only as a human being, I want to see nothing of his other side, that of a great commander'. Three days later, on 14 September 1918, he stated that he was working on the rebirth of Ludendorff, who was now 'lonely, and married to his work'. [521]

Dr. Hochheimer's approach was successful, his staff noticed. General von Kuhl remarked that Ludendorff was 'much calmer and friendlier on the telephone', and Hochheimer noted that for the first time in years, Ludendorff had slept for six consecutive hours. Von Hindenburg, meanwhile, had taken care of business and had even travelled to the front. Like a quiet oak tree he let things pass, and Ludendorff found the way back to himself. Colonel Wilhelm Heye, commander of operations, had always respected his chief Ludendorff; now he felt the warmth of man in Ludendorff. [522]

On 29 September, an important meeting took place in which the imminent downfall was the focus. There were two parties working together: the OHL, represented by Ludendorff and Von Hindenburg, and Foreign Affairs, represented by Admiral Paul von Hintze. The Admiral was - perhaps not coincedentally - a man of the fleet, who also realised that the German submarines had not been able to stop the American military, and despite successes had not brought the British to their knees. Both sides were convinced of the need for an armistice. The restless home front was also on the agenda. Von Hintze had come up with the idea that a 'revolution from above' was in this case far preferable to an unstoppable revolution from the streets. But this revolution from 'above' required sacrifices. The idea was that a broad national government should be formed as soon as possible, so that it could operate with the greatest possible political unity. In order to achieve this, the current Chancellor of the Exchequer, Graf von Hertling, had to resign. Hertling, who had succeeded Georg Michaelis, who in turn had succeeded Bethmann-Hollweg, was the next 'civilian' victim of the conflict; also called 'der Kanzlersterben'. Von Hertling was seen as the 'war chancellor' and there was a need for new blood. Von Hertling felt the urge and initially refused to come to hotel Brittannique in Spa, until the OHL, via Detlof von Winterfeldt, made it clear to him that Admiral Von Hintze was not alone, but that similar noises had been made known to the OHL. Here once again the influence of the Ludendorff-Von Hindenburg duo became apparent. Chancellor Hertling left Berlin at once and Ludendorff, Von Hindenburg, Von Hintze and Von Hertling met each other at Spa.

But before Hertling could sit down, the decision had already been made in Hotel Brittannique. There were several rounds of talks that day. First of all, there was a meeting between Ludendorff, Von Hindenburg and Hintze, during which Ludendorff made the military presentation and concluded that an immediate armistice was inevitable. These words from Ludendorff's mouth nailed even the professional pessimist Von Hintze to the ground. In the end, the developments had gone so fast that even Ludendorff and Von Hindenburg did not quite see eye to eye. Von Hindenburg thought that perhaps the area around the coal mines of Longwy could be kept for Germany. Ludendorff, however, thought that the time for demands was over. Von Hertling, who arrived late that day, was confronted with a fait accompli. There was nothing left for him but to offer his resignation, which was accepted immediately. [523]

With Von Hertling's departure, the new "bourgeois government" was one step closer. The liberals and social democrats were warming up in the wings to participate in the new political upheavals that were necessary. But first the OHL had to inform the military. It had been a public secret for some time that the OHL was heading for an armistice, but the moment Ludendorff actually proclaimed it was impressive. Ludendorff looked grim as he delivered the news. Albrecht von Thaer, a staffer, was impressed. 'He is a truly magnificent German hero', he said. Ludendorff reminded him of Siegfried, who received Hagen's deadly spear in the back. Von Thaer did not know then how proverbial and visionary these sentences were. [524]

Chapter 11

Exile in Sweden by 'Nacht und Nebel'

While the end of Ludendorff's military career was in sight, two forces were fighting for precedence in Germany: on the one hand, those who wanted to carry out the necessary revolutions within the framework of the established parties, and on the other hand, those who mobilised the streets and wanted to revolutionise Germany. The first group was plagued by a problem of legitimacy and faced the difficult task of keeping the ranks closed for as long as necessary. The political leadership, a new government under Prince Max von Baden, tried to form a black-red coalition and sought a way out of the conflict. One starting point was the lifeline thrown out by US President Wilson in his 14-point programme in January 1918. This plan consisted of eight compulsory conditions and six discussion conditions, and with its ban on secret agreements it had a certain idealistic basis. Berlin did wonder whether the army could be kept in the field long enough to work out the plan. The front faltered, more so in politics and in the OHL than in the field, noted the historian Michael Freund.[525]

At the beginning of October, Ludendorff's thoughts and conversations were dominated by the coming armistice. Ludendorff still used the term 'pause' which made it clear that as far as the OHL was concerned, the armistice had to be used primarily to strengthen the German negotiating position in order to achieve a better peace. On 7 October, during consultations at the large headquarters in Spa, he suggested that Germany could once again, as in 1916-1917, proceed to a radical reduction of the front. It was in itself a very good military plan, and Ludendorff showed that he was no longer insisting on gaining ground. He argued that a retreat behind the River Maas would shorten the German front from approximately 400 kilometres to 245 kilometres. This would make more soldiers available per kilometre of front line. This would be a luxury, for on 9

October, during consultations in Berlin, Ludendorff declared that he was systematically 70,000 men short (that was still a cautious estimate), for which there was no replacement.[526]

On 17 October 1918, they met again, with politicians and soldiers and in the presence of the Reich Chancellor. Once again, all possibilities were discussed. The problem was that the peace initiatives towards the American president Wilson had not led to the desired results. Wilson, probably under British and French pressure, increased the demands on Germany. The Germans considered whether they could gain time, without the front collapsing. The question was, however, where to get the men to achieve this. One of the plans on the table was the evacuation of the occupied eastern areas, whereby especially the evacuation of the Ukraine would free up large numbers of German soldiers. Ludendorff felt ambivalent about this. On the one hand, he desperately wanted the troops and it became clear that if he had the means, he would to continue the fight; however, on the other hand, he believed that Germany could not do without the raw materials that Ukraine provided for the already impoverished German war economy. If the decision was to be made, Ludendorff stated that it had to be made quickly and ruthlessly.

Quite unexpectedly, the Minister of Defence, Heinrich Scheüg, came up with a remarkable proposal. It was possible to make a one-off injection of troops from the homeland to the front. Scheüg claimed that 637,000 men could be freed up in one go if the 1901 peergroup was brought to the front early. However, as a result of this, they would get 100,000 men instead of 190,000 men as reinforcements for six months.[527] Ludendorff was perplexed. For years he had asked for reinforcements and now they were suddenly available. This news made him 'Hoffnungsfreudig' again. 'With such reserves we would not have had the present crisis in the West', he thought. [528]

Philipp Scheidemann, who represented the political factor in the conversation, was more reserved. According to him, the home front would not react positively to a new injection of blood at the front. Many furloughed soldiers already brought negative reports from the home front. In addition, more soldiers was no solution to the 'Kartoffelfrage' - the ongoing hunger on the home front - which caused war fatigue to spread. Besides, how would things work without the oil from Ukraine? Despite these objections, Ludendorff returned to Spa somewhat optimistic.

Everything focused on the question of how realistic Minister Scheüg's proposal was (it was questionable). Apart from the fact that the need for the proposed emergency mobilisation was the result of extended positive reporting by the OHL itself, the 'Scheüg Plan' evoked comparisons with other desperate statements, such as those made by the industrialist Carl Duisberg, who believed that a further rationalisation of the economy (10% increase in production) would free up 700,000 men for the front.[529] A nice plan, but in view of the raw material problems and shortages, and new plans to evacuate the raw material supplier Ukraine, not very realistic. Often, such reasoning was a short-term solution. The company also had to keep running, and Scheidemann was aware of this. In doing so, they balanced between plans to push ahead and meet Wilson's demands. One of them was to stop the submarine war immediately. Ludendorff was strongly opposed to this, but nevertheless, as a result of the meeting at 17 October, it was brought to an end. Scheidemann had given Ludendorff a hard time: 'on the one hand you wanted to stop the fight immediately, on the other hand you want to continue the fight now'. Ludendorff referred to Scheüg's news, but politicians remained hesitant, especially in view of the home front. And understandably so, for had it not been Ludendorff himself who believed that the home front was 'the greatest problem' for his soldiers?

Yet, talk of these tactical and strategic matters obscured the fact that the real decisions were actually already being made at the political level. With Hertling's departure, the trend towards political reform had been set. Germany was now moulding itself so as to be able to move forward, as it were, and people were coming forward in Germany's name to do what needed to be done. The upheaval was bound to cost heads. Hertling had been the first, but not the last. A power struggle was underway, in which the Kaiser hoped that if he sacrificed key subordinates, he might be able to stay in power. Some in the OHL may have thought they could outlive the Emperor, but the politicians concluded that neither could be spared.

Ludendorff had expressed a very negative opinion on the Wilsonian demand for an end to the submarine war on 17 October 1918, and believed that Germany should fight to the last man for its honour if the enemy demanded the impossible.[530] However, on 23 October, a new letter arrived from President Wilson, in which he stated unequivocally that there would be no future between the Entente and Germany as long as the monarchy and the military ruling the roost sat on the plush. This was unacceptable to the OHL. A proclamation signed by Von Hindenburg went out to the army stating that this was actually a request for unconditional surrender and that this was unacceptable; the soldiers would continue to fight.[531] The result was a storm of protest in the German Reichstag. The gap between the politicians and the OHL became substantial. On 25 October 1918, discussions took place between the politicians and the pair of generals. The Emperor was on the fence and did not know what to do, but for the time being mainly supported the generals. As time went on, it became clear that the politicians were leaning towards an agreement on the Wilson plan. In reply to General von Winterfeld and Von Haeften, Ludendorff let slip: 'There is no hope. Germany is lost'.[532] At 08.00 a.m. on 26 October, Ludendorff sat behind his desk at the General Staff office in Berlin and wrote his letter of resignation. Around 09.00 a.m., Von Hindenburg entered the room. He tried to convince Ludendorff not to do it and they were still discussing when they were summoned to report to Kaiser Wilhelm II in Bellevue Palace.

Should Ludendorff's letter of resignation have been a political weapon, it had already lost its effect upon arrival. The atmosphere was completely different from the day before. The Emperor received the military coolly. 'The politicians demanded a victim,' said von Hindenburg later, and Ludendorff felt that the Kaiser was 'very different from yesterday'.[533] Wilhelm II addressed Ludendorff on the proclamation they had issued. This clearly did not correspond to Wilhelm's intentions. Ludendorff then threw in his last weapon. 'I get the impression that I no longer enjoy His Majesty's trust and therefore humbly request that I be relieved of my duties'. The emperor immediately agreed. Ludendorff clicked his heels, saluted, turned and left the room. Field Marshal von Hindenburg then also offered his resignation, but the Kaiser refused. Von Hindenburg, the Kaiser believed, was a symbol of unity for the German people.

Ludendorff, after years of inexhaustible efforts, was suddenly a 'free man' when he entered the street in front of Bellevue. The relationship with the Emperor, which Bernhard Wien characterised as 'cordial mutual antipathy', had come to an abrupt end.[534] Yet this was a strange situation for Ludendorff, and he went to his home in Kürfurstenstrasse. His wife Margarethe was very surprised when Ludendorff's car was at the door again at 11 o'clock. 'I felt a strange depression', she wrote. Pale as death, Ludendorff walked in and sat down resignedly in a chair by the fireplace. 'The Emperor has let me down. I have been dismissed', he muttered, looking ahead seemingly without emotion. A few hours later, staff member Wilhelm Breucker reported to his former superior. He found Ludendorff leafing through a detective book. Ludendorff told him what he had experienced this morning. 'They needed a scapegoat', he said. He also spoke bitterly about Von Hindenburg, by whom he felt betrayed. 'You'll see, in a few days the Emperor himself will fall too'.

Ludendorff showed himself to be a visionary here. Von Hindenburg, the unyielding oak tree, had meanwhile returned to the headquarters at the front. He too was moved by the events of the day and would try to reach out to his increasingly unreasonable former colleague Ludendorff several more times, without success. 'I entered our common headquarters', said Von Hindenburg, 'and it felt as if I was standing in front of the grave of a good friend'.[535]

Between November 1918 and the spring of 1919, the revolution took hold in Germany. In practice, two forces were fighting against each other: the forces that wanted to shape the revolution from 'above' (and thus in fact wanted to regulate events) and the forces that believed that power lay in the streets and wanted to bring the Marxist doctrine of salvation to Germany in a Leninist way. What both camps had in common was that a way back was no longer possible. Friedrich Ebert, leader of the Social Democrats, had made it clear to General Max von Baden that the revolution from above was only possible if the Empire was sacrificed. Of course, this was a very bitter pill for the more conservative forces, as well as for the OHL. However, these two parties needed each other to contain the rapidly growing unrest of the revolution from the streets, before it would take hold of all of Germany.

Indeed, the 'konsequenten Linken' increasingly stirred. The most radical forces of the USPD, the Spartakists under Karl Liebknecht and Rosa Luxemburg, brought, as the Marxist historian Wolfgang Ruge put it, a 'storm wind' over Germany, in which 'the crowns fell by the dozen'.[536] The warships Thüringen, Helgoland, Seydlitz, Von der Tann and others had fallen into the hands of mutinous sailors on 4 November 1918. Workers and soldiers councils were founded in Stuttgart, Hannover, Cologne, Strasbourg, and there were demonstrations in Hamburg, Braunschweig, Halle, Leipzig and strikes in Berlin. On 8 November, the revolution broke out in Karlsruhe, Essen, Breslau, Köningsberg.[537] On 7 and 8 November 1918, the unrest also spread to Bavaria, where Kurt Eisner seized power in Munich and proclaimed the 'soziale Republik', and at the same time, in order to emphasise the revolutionary character of the 'new era', immediately declared war on the Vatican, as well as secret diplomatic channels to France, in order to break Bavaria away from Germany.[538]

These developments were at odds with the 'Ruf nach parlamentarisierung', as discussed in Spa in the presence of Ludendorff at the time. 'The bourgeoisie is confused, eingeschüchtert and helpless', said the journalist Theodor Wolf.[539] However helplessly conservative-Völkisch Germany watched these developments, for the communists they were a logical outcome of their social vision. The revolution of November 1918, Wolfgang Ruge believed, was not a coincidence but a 'legitimate event'. This event was fuelled by the 'historical obsolescence' of capitalism.[540]

For Ludendorff, a period of deep humiliation had begun. The press did not hold back, even in the neutral countries. Everything that had built up in anti-German sentiment was now released, also in the Netherlands. The Berlin correspondent of the *NRC* wrote: 'Ludendorff gone! The new government has shown strength by getting rid of the man who, for two years, has been more powerful than anything or anyone else in the German Reich. [...] It is not an inviting job to write about him now. One cannot be but one-sided. Only a historian will one be able to appreciate him. We, as intimate spectators, have too often feared his influence, we have seen too much annoyance about him around us [...] for us spectators it was at first an interesting, but gradually also frightening and even an irritable spectacle as Ludendorff's political influence spread'. The correspondent was only slightly more positive about his military prowess: 'This, however, may perhaps be said: Had a man like Ludendorff been provided with all the resources of the Entente, he would probably not have lost the war'.[541]

Another newspaper reported that retreating soldiers felt slighted by the Kaiser, the Crown Prince and Ludendorff, while Von Hindenburg was somewhat spared. *Het Centrum* cynically wrote: 'Ludendorff will have been very happy to go; now that he would have to stand among bourgeois men, for whom he had such unlimited contempt'.[542] *Het Volk* wrote: 'It is certain that with the dismissal of Ludendorff, not only a high-ranking military man steps down, but with him, the embodiment of militarism as a ruling class or caste in the German state disappears. As the person who, together with the actual commander, Marshal Hindenburg, not only directed the war operations but also the entire war effort, Ludendorff was considered to be the most influential person in Germany, to whose advice the Kaiser listened, according to whose will the Chancellor and the Government acted and cherished'.[543] On 7 November 1918, *Het Volk* added that 'militarism had been defeated', and that a 'new era' would begin.[544] The French *Petit Parisien* saw in Ludendorff's resignation mainly a victory for Foch's strategy, as well as a political manoeuvre.[545]

After his dismissal, Ludendorff sat silently at his desk for days. His wife tried to comfort him, but nothing seemed to help. She had proudly been wife to war hero Ludendorff and now, in his hour of need, where Ludendorff was the subject of enmity and invective, she stood beside her husband. The Raden Republic was not harmless to Ludendorff. 'There is no longer a protective roof for his head in Germany', Margarethe Ludendorff wrote in her memoirs. 'He is not sure of his life'. Friends of the general also urged him to flee Germany now that the situation had become so dangerous. Ludendorff hesitated. Margarethe thought that an escape would be out of character for her husband, but she decided, as so often in their marriage, to remain silent. Eventually Ludendorff gave in and decided to leave Germany. He left at 'Nacht und Nebel', with a beard and blue glasses on, so as not to be recognised.

At first, Ludendorff left for the Potsdam area, where his brother, an astronomer, lived. Then he went to Wilhelm Breucker, a comrade from the army. But there too, Spartakists managed to find him and the host was also threatened. Ludendorff had to move on again. There was contact with the Ministry of Defence (General Scheuch), but he said he could not do anything and, after consultation with Ebert and Geheimrat Trautmann, indicated that the best thing for Ludendorff to do was to go abroad. For this purpose, a Finnish nationality was created under the name Ernst Lindström.[546] Ludendorff was deeply offended that the Ministry of Defence let him down like this. Later, in an angry mood, he said that he 'would not hesitate for a moment to have Ebert hung from the highest tree' and that it was 'a great mistake that they did not kill him immediately'. It was, of course, also a bizarre situation that the man of the dictatorship, Ludendorff, who had led offensives in which a million soldiers operated, was now hunted like a wild animal in Germany and could not be kept safe.

From Breucker, the jump abroad was prepared. The first destination was to be Copenhagen, an idea of Captain Fischer, an acquaintance of Breucker's, who was associated with the Red Cross in the Danish capital. Ludendorff was given a lift in the car of the Finnish ambassador. He was taken to Stettin station, where the disguised Ludendorff, accompanied by Fischer and Breucker, travelled on by train to Copenhagen, after which the journey continued by boat. 'I feel like a Reichstag delegate who has not been re-elected', Ludendorff mused with gallows humour. [547]

On board the ship, despite his disguise, Ludendorff was recognised by a naval officer who reported his famous guest to his captain. The news spread like wildfire, and Ludendorff became the subject of prying eyes, much to his own displeasure. In the German Embassy in Copenhagen it was decided that it would be best for Ludendorff to continue his journey to Sweden. The naval attaché of the Copenhagen embassy had good contacts in Sweden and Ludendorff travelled to Malmö, Sweden's third largest city. But once again things did not go as planned. The couple that had to receive Ludendorff unexpectedly split up and Ludendorff could no longer stay. However, friends - Mr and Mrs Ohlsen -[548] made the Hässleholmsgard estate near Hässleholm, 80 kilometres north-east of Malmö, available for him and here Ludendorff enjoyed hospitality for two and a half months. [549]

In his memoirs, Ludendorff looked back on this difficult time. He called the day of his dismissal the 'bitterest hours of his life'.[550] 'I never saw the Emperor again', he wrote. After his dismissal, he travelled back to Oberst von Haeften and some of his other loyal collaborators, where he made his prediction about the fall of the empire. On 26 October, he made the last arduous journey to Spa. He collected his personal belongings and said goodbye to his staff. On 27, he was at the OHL for the last time. 'It bothered me', he wrote.[551] 'I have only followed the path of duty', he thought, looking back, and this moment was the 'end of an enormous responsibility that few people bear in their lives', he stated, not without a sense of drama. In the evening, he left Spa and re-entered Germany near Aachen. He thought back to the historic days near Liège, which had been so profound in his personal history.[552] In his memoirs, he denounced the 'Umsturzgedanke', which then took hold of Germany. The Raden Republic was a 'planned underground struggle' prepared against Germany. He saw 'scenes that had not been thought possible since 1806' (Prussian defeat against Napoleon at Jena).[553] He watched the army marching homewards behind the Rhine with trepidation. 'A dark future lies ahead of us, only the deeds of the men of Scapa Flow give us light,' he wrote in his *Kriegserinnerungen*.[554]

'Everything is a bad dream for me', Ludendorff wrote from Copenhagen to his wife who had stayed behind in Germany. 'I don't know whether I did the right thing in leaving, because its not sustainable in the long run'. On the other hand, he pointed to the developments that had forced him to leave Germany: 'In a few days Liebknecht will be at the helm and the social revolution will begin'. He was also worried about his contact with Margarethe. 'My dear wife, it was a bitter feeling in my heart to have to leave you alone. It hurt me most that shortly before my departure I was still angry with you. We shall meet again, Herzensweib, and then I shall be different to you. I love you, and my heart is sad. I beg you, go away from where you are now, I am so restless, knowing that you are there'.[555]

Again and again Ludendorff begged Margarethe to come to him. Circumstances made her leave on 22 December 1918. Meanwhile, the situation had become unbearable for Margarethe too. In the beginning, she had held her head high, despite all the setbacks. For years she had been the acclaimed wife of the popular and powerful general. Now there were hostilities and invective. Spartakists also threatened to take her hostage and the landlady did her best to hide Margarethe Ludendorff. However, the biggest problem came from her own circle, from the officers' wives who also lived in the boarding house. Women with whom she had shared her life for years, and who had profited from her special position, now turned against her and demanded that she leave the boarding house because she would endanger everyone. In the end the landlady gave in and Margarethe was thrown out.

Margarethe Ludendorff was determined to resist, but in barely ten minutes she was out of the house. 'God, protect me from my friends', she noted in her memoirs.[556] 'I was full of anger and disappointment and for the rest of my life I would be restrained in my love for people'.[557] Fortunately, friends were willing to take in the wife of the 'most hated man in Germany', as Margarethe Ludendorff herself described it. It was the sculptor Manzel and his wife who offered Margarethe Ludendorff shelter in a secluded forest villa in Pankov-Berlin, a completely different district than where the Ludendorff boarding house was located. The Spartakists would not find Margarethe there easily. Meanwhile, the Red Revolt had broken out in Berlin and Margarethe was in serious danger. After a visit to the villa that was made available, just when Margarethe Ludendorff was putting on her fur coat, a sailor reported that the workers' battalions were already marching down Brunnenstrasse. Barricades were being built. He offered to take Margarethe carefully to a safe address. The sailor, a communist, wearing a red ribbon, from the Jannowitz-Brücke sailor's division, saw it as his duty to do this for Margarethe Ludendorff. He refused her payment on her return home. [558]

'I was anxious and scared', Margarethe noted in her memoirs as she began her journey to Sweden. It was a Germany in turmoil that she left behind. An officer, Captain Fischer, who had also accompanied Ludendorff, brought her to Stettin station. Here, the revolution mingled with the returning and transiting soldiers from the front. Everything was crowded and Margarethe Ludendorff was surrounded by what Ernst Jünger called the 'trench aristocracy', with their worn and dirty uniforms and their unwashed and exhausted bodies. Fischer had to take good care of the gear, finally sat down on it and unceremoniously placed Margarethe Ludendorff on his lap. 'It was not very comfortable', Margarethe Ludendorff thought, 'but we were lucky to have a seat'. Despite the cold, soldiers had even settled on the roof of the train, wanting to be home for Christmas after all the trench misery. This is how the train left Stettin station. In the train it almost came to an incident when a 'Rotgardist' loudly accused Ludendorff of all sorts of things. He was supposed to have enriched himself and fled abroad: 'I know, I was in the council of soldiers', he added. According to her own recollections, Margarethe Ludendorff was so seized with anger that she would have liked to attack the man. However, her companion urged her to calm down, so as not to cause any incidents and not to betray her identity. After a primitive night in Sassnitz, following a twenty-hour train journey, the journey continued by boat. On landing in Sweden, customs threatened to 'loot' her bags until the officer on duty saw the name in the passport, saluted and let Margarethe Ludendorff through. From there she continued by rail and sledge until she met Ludendorff again.

The meeting took place in a picturesque winter environment. Nevertheless, it was not a warm welcome. 'He was not able to express his joy at my arrival,' Margarethe wrote in her memoirs, although she knew that he had missed her terribly. The host did his best to please the couple. He showed them around the high rooms of his mansion, furnished with classical furniture that had been handed down from generation to generation. He proudly showed them the garden and especially the stables and horses, and demonstrated the dressage he practised himself. Ohlsen was a well-known competition hippy rider and spent hours daily with his horses. Margarethe and Erich Ludendorff took part in all the 'obligations', eating the typical Swedish stockfish and celebrating Christmas, but later that evening they both sat in silence in their room. 'Never have I known a more melancholy, sad Christmas than that year', wrote Margarethe in her memoirs. [559]

But Ludendorff would not be Ludendorff if he had not already turned to 'duty' again. He had started writing down his war memories in Sweden. He did this with enormous diligence as well, so that he wrote the monumental booklet very quickly. Some people think that he wrote it entirely from memory, but that is not true. He regularly had material sent to him from Germany, with Wilhelm Breucker once again playing a part. The book was completed in two and a half months, a remarkable achievement and not to be taken for granted. The German General Constantin von Alvensleben is known to have said that 'a Prussian general dies but leaves no memoirs'.[560] In this case, and not only for Ludendorff, several memoirs would follow, including that of von Hindenburg, although he received more help than Ludendorff.

But there was also another kind of motive behind it. Von Alvensleben made his statement after the Franco-Prussian war had been won. Now, a war had been lost, and Ludendorff struggled with the question of why and, of course, with his own role in the whole thing. Remember Margarethe Ludendorff's statement about 'the most hated man in Germany', and of course Ludendorff knew that after the debacle, people wanted his head. He wanted to report, also because new and uncertain times had dawned on Germany, in which he feared the Entente, Bolshevism in Russia, the Council Republicans in Germany and, moreover, had no confidence in the powers that were supposed to fight them.

Ludendorff's judgement was not always that sharp in those days. Walther Rathenau, for instance, sent him a nice letter on 27 October 1918, which was supposed to encourage him. In this letter, Rathenau emphasised that although his opinion on the submarine war differed from Ludendorff's, he had been one of the advocates of his coming to power at the OHL and that he was grateful to him for his commitment to Germany. A few weeks after this letter, Rathenau had a conversation with Wilhelm Breucker, in which he strongly condemned the Radenrepublikans and said that they had succeeded in shifting all the blame onto Ludendorff at the last moment. Later, Ludendorff attributed this statement to Rathenau himself, and Rathenau was outraged by this behaviour. Breucker was also unable to correct this prejudice. Ludendorff had already spoken about 'Judenfürst' Rathenau, and he had thus slowly fallen under the spell of radicalism. [561]

But we are getting ahead of ourselves, in essence, Ludendorff's *Kriegserinnerungen*, published by Ernst Siegfried Mittler & Sohn in Berlin, was a remarkably objective book. Perhaps this was because Ludendorff was the first to publish his memoirs and thus did not yet have to distance himself from others. However, he avoided a number of conflicts, such as the one with Von Falkenhayn and Von Bethmann-Hollweg, although these conflicts had been serious. Ludendorff was not (yet) concerned about the characters, but mainly about the report of the war. Perhaps the most important opinion was expressed in the epilogue, in which Ludendorff mainly lashed out at the 'blood of the brothers' in Germany. Due to the revolution, the Germans had become 'the pariah among the nations', he thought, and were 'no longer reliable as an ally'. They had become 'helots' in the service of 'foreign men' and 'foreign capital'. 'In twenty years' time, Germany will damn those forces that brought the revolution,' he prophesied.[562] At the same time, he expressed his fear for Germany in a frank letter to Wilhelm Breucker. Germany had been 'raped by the Entente', he said, and just as in antiquity, when peoples disappeared, the Entente tried 'to erase the German people from history'.[563] From Sweden, Ludendorff carried on his struggle for justice, constantly asking for support and information for his book from old faithful, such as Von Bartenwerffer, Crantz, Heye and others, including Sven Hedin, who visited him in foreign lands and took mail from him for Germany.

Ludendorff's *Kriegserinnerungen* were followed by Von Falkenhayn's memoirs. This one did expose the quarrels with Oberost. That was in 1922. Meanwhile, a cheaper popular edition of Ludendorff's *Kriegserinnerungen* was published, in which Ludendorff had deleted the most angry passages from his book. Uhle Wettler made a case for Ludendorff's *Kriegserinnerungen*. The 'violence' of Ludendorff was often placed against the 'mildness' of Bethmann-Hollweg. The truth was more nuanced, and that the other side could also 'bite' was evident from the memories that were recorded on paper.[564]

Margarethe Ludendorff could not stay long in Sweden. She had children and family in Germany and was worried. Ludendorff was also constantly in Germany in his thoughts. He wrote to his stepdaughter: 'What I miss most is the fatherland and my work for my deserted country'.[565] Ludendorff was not the only one who saw a role for himself in post-war Germany. It was the industrialist Hugo Stinnes who approached Ludendorff about his plans for the future and also immediately made him an offer. Stinnes approached Ludendorff via Breucker, whom he invited to the well-known Adlon Hotel in Berlin. Here, he told him that he considered Ludendorff to be one of the 'best people in Germany', 'clear and quick-witted', he called Ludendorff, also referring to his time in Kaunas.[566] Stinnes offered to go abroad for a few years, at his own expense and while retaining his current benefits, in order to reflect on and make contacts with foreign countries and, enriched by this view of the big world, to take on the role that awaited him in Germany, namely that of leader of the 'patriotic movement', by which Stinnes meant the reactionary section of the people.

Stinnes was one of Germany's most important industrialists along with men like Krupp, Thyssen, Haniel and Kirdorf. The journalist Maximilian Harden attributed to him coal, iron, ore, steel, blast furnaces, electricity works, cotton, zinc, half of East Prussia, a large part of southern Sweden, the port area of Emden, Bremen, Hamburg and Copenhagen, as well as hotels, estates, forests, estates and houses from the Moselle to the Mosquito. According to Stinnes' biographer Gert von Klass, Harden always exaggerated a little, but was still close to the truth at the core of his argument. Stinnes was a brilliant industrialist and until the outbreak of the First World War, he had hardly meddled in politics. The disastrous days of August 1914 had radically changed this. There were days when Stinnes spent fourteen hours on the phone safeguarding his global interests. However, apart from defending his own interests, Stinnes was also very concerned about the course of the war for Germany. One of his first actions was to use his international contacts to supply coal to the German warships *Goeben* and *Breslau*, which were operating in the Mediterranean region far from home. He spoke to fellow entrepreneurs such as Albert Vögler in Döberitz to hear their views on the future of Germany, paying particular attention to the weak raw materials situation. Furthermore, he was afraid of dualism between Bavaria and Prussia, and did not like small states. During the war, he became increasingly involved in direct war production. Thus, he became interested in the aircraft industry and worked together with Castiglioni, the son of a rabbi in Trier, who co-founded the Motor-Luftfahrzeuggesellschaft mbH in Austria in 1909, and became active in the Hanse und Brandenburgischen Flugzeugwerke A.G. in Brandenburg. In order to make all this economically successful, he worked together with Hjalmar Schacht, who would make a great career as an economist under Hitler. Admiral Von Tirpitz asked for Stinnes' help with the submarine problem and from this point of view Stinnes had his first contact with Ludendorff during the war. The latter immediately recognised Stinnes' capabilities and promised to keep professionals away from the front so that they could be employed in war production. Stinnes sought contact with Albert Ballin for his contribution to submarine production, but plans came too late. It was already 1918 and the days of November had become unavoidable. Ballin chose death; Stinnes, who watched the rapidly increasing chaos with disgust, decided to continue his path of great social engagement, which brought him into contact with Ludendorff again and led him to his proposal.[567]

Stinnes' plan was not such a bad idea and was actually the best advice Ludendorff had gotten in a long time. Stinnes realised that, despite the current criticism and delusion against Ludendorff, somewhere he still possessed his 'Ruf' as a great man, the victor of Tannenberg, the saviour of Berlin for the Russians and the man who ended the Verdun massacre. This 'Ruf' could eventually be brought back to life, enabling Ludendorff to propel the helpless country upwards again after the change of 1918. This would also give Ludendorff some time to get to grips with the scale of politics, which was no superfluous luxury. Another important motive was Stinnes' fear that Ludendorff would react to the growing army of blacksmiths who tried to damage his name. In Stinnes' view, crossing swords with them was the stupidest mistake Ludendorff could make. It would have destroyed his own 'above the parties' myth. Unfortunately, Ludendorff always set his own course, and he believed that the fatherland was now in danger. Under these circumstances, a foreign stay of several years was not an option for him.

Indeed, the tidings of doom came over Germany from all sides. In the homeland, Radencommunists and Spartakists were active, separatist movements tried to seize their chance. In the East German homeland too, dear to Ludendorff, things were rumbling on all sides. Large numbers of units fell back in western direction. Polish, Ukrainian, Baltic and Russian-Bolshevik forces tried to jump into the vacuum. The last commander of Kaunas, then part of Oberost, noted in January 1919 that 'an evil dream had come true'. There were, as he wrote, 'terrible conditions' and he was horrified that even for the military nothing seemed sacred anymore. 'One begins to be ashamed of one's uniform'. There were regiments that now stood behind the red banner. Yet, other units remained loyal to the Reich flag; especially cavalry units that had a higher blue-blood content. Bavarian ulans and 'Schill' hussars ensured that the German position remained secure. They waited for the right moment to move westwards. 'The Poles acted as if they had won the war on their own', one eyewitness said. [568]

Kaunas, Ludendorff's 'throne city' during his administrative functions there, presented a sad picture of hoarding, unrest and flaring nationalism. The Saxon Volunteer Regiment 18, commanded by Major Von Zeschau, struggled here with the so-called 'Grand Council' of forty members that had been formed and was trying to push through Spartakist ideas. In the eyes of the nationalist officers, the Council jobs were mostly filled by stage soldiers who had seen little of the front, and who now bought themselves a nice desk at state expense and had secretaries brought in from the German hinterland.[569] In April 1919, the German units withdrew from Kaunas. [570]

In February, Ludendorff had informed the German authorities that he would be returning to Germany. On 21 February 1919, he took the steamship in

Malmö. It was an historic day. Exactly on that day, Kurt Eisner was shot dead in the street in Bavaria, which would usher in a wild revolutionary era. Unaware of this, the steamship set sail for Sassnitz. The Swedish authorities had urged Ludendorff not to publicise his departure. It was feared that the Swedish ship might be harassed at sea by Entente warships, who ruled the waters. However, nothing happened and in the evening the ship from Malmö arrived on the mainland of Europe. The captain had made his personal cabin available to Ludendorff.

On board, Ludendorff could see the first effects of the turbulent days with his own eyes. 'Reds and light-skinned types', as he described it in his memoirs, populated the station. He managed to keep out of the way and, armed with his manuscript of war memories, he took the train to Berlin, spending the night in Stralfund along the way and finding in Stettin that Raden soldiers controlled the station. Old faithful, Von Pflugk-Harttung and Breucker, ensured that Ludendorff could quickly leave the dangerous terrain by means of a truck - which had been made available by the Garde Kavallerie Schützen Division. On the way, Ludendorff informed himself and heard that it looked like the Ebert/Noske government would hold out under the Spartakist violence, and that Freikorps, former soldiers from the right-wing camp, played a decisive role in this.

For Ludendorff, this experience must have been ambiguous. On the one hand, he snuck through his own country almost like a thief in the night; on the other hand, it was clear to him that there was still a small but not insignificant group of soldiers and officers who had made themselves indispensable to the new government by their strength against the Spartakists. Here, Ludendorff could play a role again, especially if he could effectively resist the growing criticism, he thought, of his performance in the war. To this end, his *Kriegserinnerungen*, which he had in his pocket, served him well, despite all Stinnes' warnings.

There were also tragic reports, such as the death of Oberstleutnant von Kübler, fallen in battle with Spartakists, and the bloody fighting in Halle. In Weimar, in relative peace under the protection of General Maercker, work was carried out to establish the new regime. 'Bavaria is still completely Bolshevik', Ludendorff thought, even after Eisner's death.[571] It was not until April that German units, under General von Oven, in cooperation with Ritter von Epp's Freikorps, were able to liberate the city. In the press, little was spoken about the deployment of the Prussian units of Von Oven, and more attention was paid to Von Epp. Ludendorff was worried by this development. The Empire seemed to almost crumble; even in the right-wing nationalist camp, small particularism seemed to offer a way out of the general malaise which had resulted from the downfall of 1918 and the collapse of the Empire. It was clear that Ludendorff saw an important role for himself in the organisation of the counter-revolution and this did not end with the suppression of the Spartakist insurgency. 'The Social Democrats have the power, and with them the Jews', he noted in his reminiscences. [572]

There were more and more signs that Ludendorff was radicalising under the shock of the defeat. Ludendorff, who for a long time had been a typical product of Prussian society, would, also under the influence of the literal loss of those areas of the empire (the province of Posen fell to Poland), become more and more open to the Völkisch answer to the rapidly spreading cultural pessimism, and eventually also be receptive to ariosophical race theories, which also formed the driving force behind National Socialism, making the cement between the old order which Ludendorff partly still represented and the rising right revolutionaries around the NSDAP possible.

Chapter 12

The Counter-Revolution

The fact that Erich Ludendorff was immediately protected after his return to Germany, by men who had served in the Garde Kavallerie Schützen division, and continued to be under their protection in the period thereafter was not without significance. This showed that immediately after the war, Ludendorff became part of the political game and found himself on the extreme reactionary right wing. Moreover, Ludendorff returned to Germany on the day that the Bavarian Council revolutionary Kurt Eisner was murdered. There was no connection between the two, at most that 'Der Reaktion im gange'. Still, it was a harbinger of many internal German tensions to come, in which Ludendorff would play a leading role. Ludendorff first moved into the house of his confidant Wilhelm Breucker in the Guentzelstrasse in Wilmersdorf, later into the Hotel Adlon and then, from early spring 1919, into the house of Mrs Newman-Hamburg in the Viktoriastrasse.

The military elite played a very important and dubious role in the initial period of the Weimar Republic. Since the proclamation of the Republic was accompanied by great political upheaval, it was of the utmost importance for the bearers of the new political course to be able to count on the support of 'das Militär'. The historian Herbert Rosinski even believes that the young republic had become completely dependent on the support of the Reichswehr (army of the Weimar Republic) for its survival, and that the politicians had so little influence that the army had become a state within the state. [573]

In fact, the situation was even worse. The Kapp-Putsch, which was soon to take hold of Germany, showed that the Weimar politicians could not rely on their military. Fortunately, the SPD politicians who had to work with them understood their trade and were shamelessly prepared to make the necessary pacts.

In doing so, the first Reich Chancellor Friedrich Ebert had to bring together unbridgeable camps.

Ebert was part of the Social Democrats, the 'Mehrheitssozialisten', who had not opposed the war. The more radical USDP of Hugo Haase had always opposed the war. Ebert was not a politician who appealed to the imagination as a person, but he was a pragmatist and a good negotiator. He immediately understood that he could only contain the radical Socialists by force; and thus save the young Weimar democracy. Only the army could help him.

Unfortunately, the German army, as even the social democratic defence minister Gustav Noske had to admit, was a reflection of society, and in confusion. One of the first actions to crush the Raden uprisings failed miserably. In consultation with Groener, Ludendorff's successor, Noske and Ebert, together with the OHL in Kassel and the new government, had decided to operate temporarily with volunteer units: the so-called 'Freikorps'. These then sprang up like mushrooms and by the summer of 1919 had grown to about 400,000 troops. This threatened to turn them into a state within the state, but for the time being Ebert managed to save the Weimar Republic with these units and the Freikorps were an equally miraculous and effective ally of the Social Democrats against the communist danger. In Bremen, Halle and in Berlin, to which Ludendorff had just returned, the Freikorps were successfully deployed. This was followed by actions in Magdeburg and Munich, where the Council revolutions were also crushed with brute force.

An important part of the pact between Ebert and Noske and 'das Militär', was the Garde Kavallerie Schützen division, the same unit that protected Ludendorff on his return and which was commanded by Waldemar Pabst von Ohaim. Pabst has been largely ignored by historians, and wrongly so. He was a very important key figure in the reactionary camp. The historian and contemporary E.O. Volkmann described Pabst, who came from Hamburg, as a man with 'a glowing face, ambitious and with an ambition for politics'.[574] Although the name suggests otherwise, Pabst's cavalry unit consisted largely of naval officers. A son of Margarethe Ludendorff also served in the unit. The navy - in particular - had reasons to react extra fiercely to the political disturbances. The naval elite understood that the revolutionary wave which Germany had entered could have dangerous consequences for them. A splintered Germany could not afford any maritime ambitions.

The Council communists in Bavaria had contacted the French authorities to seek support for separating Bavaria from the German Reich. Separatist tendencies were also noticeable in the Rhineland. A group of Rhinelanders around the lawyer Hans Adam Dorten[575] tried to separate from Germany. This resulted in the so-called Rheinische Republik in 1923. After the battle of the Aegidienberg, which was not much more than a bloody incident, the separatists made their way to France, which had also been the only country to recognise the 'republic'. Leader Dorten also fled.[576] When the other Entente powers, too, did not see any point in breaking away from the left bank of the Rhine, the danger came to an end. [577]

These disturbances strengthened the naval officers of the Kavallerie-division in their endeavours. The top brass of the navy, Emperor Wilhelm's 'favourite' armies at the time, had always been very nationalistic and generally favourable to the monarchy. While Waldemar Pabst's 'naval cavalry' took care of Erich Ludendorff's safety, the unit made a bloody drive through Germany. Everywhere they went, the revolutionaries were violently eliminated. Among the most famous victims of the counter-revolution were Rosa Luxemburg and Karl Liebknecht, as well as Eugen Levine, the leader of the Munich Council Revolt.

The cooperation between the Ebert government and the Freikorps, such as Pabst's troops, suggests a closer relationship than existed in reality. It was mainly a pact against the communists, for some of the Freikorps were so reactionary that they considered Ebert's social democrats, and his growing alliance with other forces of the political centre, almost as dangerous as the Raden revolutionaries. Initially, Ludendorff tried to reach out to his 'lost fatherland'. He did so in three ways: he wrote his military memoirs, he offered his services to the Ebert government and he tried to restore the friendship with Von Hindenburg and the military apparatus.

He put a lot of energy, but remarkably little time, into his memoirs, published by Mittler & Sohn, as we have already seen. He asked staff officer Gabriel to check the dates and such in his manuscript and then also worked on his follow-up book, about the most important orders and documents, which in fact had to underpin his *Kriegserinnerungen*. Now that he was back in Germany, writing such a book was easier for him. This book was finally published in 1920 by Mittler & Sohn under the title *Urkunden der Obersten Heeresleitung*. This book, like his war memories, received several printings.

Immediately after his return to Germany, on 26 February 1919, he had also thrown in his first ball with Ebert.

Ludendorff's goals were twofold: he wanted to serve his country and he wanted to restore his honour. He therefore presented his return as a call from conscience, which it was to some extent, although he did not mention that there was also growing opposition in Sweden, from socialist quarters, to his stay in the country, and that his return was inevitable in any case. Waldemar Pabst arranged for a group of officers of the Ehrhardt Brigade, one of the most reactionary Frei corps, commanded by Captain-Lieutenant Horst von Pflugk-Harttung (a former officer of a special unit within the Garde Kavallerie Schutzen division), to act as guards for Ludendorff's safety. Ludendorff hoped that this would be temporary, and that he could make his comeback at Defence. However, the 'Verständigung' with Ebert and politics did not materialise. 'In this hour of need, the country can use everyone who makes himself available with full devotion,' Ludendorff said in his letter to Ebert, but Berlin remained silent. [578]

Politics had other things on its mind than Ludendorff's position. In the spring and summer of 1919, the Treaty of Versailles hung like a sword of Damocles over the country's head. Some politicians believed that such a one-way agreement should not be signed, others believed that there was no way back. Four ministers, among them Scheidemann, resigned, but eventually the agreement was signed. Ludendorff never made a clear statement about what he would have done. His answer to his confidant Breucker's question on the matter was typical: 'If I had been there, I would have known'.[579] Breucker later speculated that Ludendorff would probably have signed as well, since refusal was tantamount to 'suicide'. [580]

With no response from Ebert and the Treaty of Versailles beginning a new tragic chapter in Germany's young history, Ludendorff quickly became a pivotal figure to which reactionary forces were drawn. Ludendorff was to become the focus of ridicule, debate, and revolt. Stinnes' gloomy prediction became reality in abundance and even this visionary man could not foresee that Ludendorff would become an important trailblazer for the Nazis because of his position. The rift with the Ministry of Defence quickly deepened. Ludendorff's successor Groener had repeatedly spoken very disparagingly of Ludendorff and from Sweden, Ludendorff had already ordered Breucker to counterattack and had called upon Von Hindenburg for helpn as well. The latter, however, also had to steer clear and did not intervene. Franz Uhle-Wettler has called this painfully cut-off path back to an 'official career' a tragedy. Ludendorff was full of anger and fire, also towards his former colleagues. 'Groener himself possesses all the bad qualities of which he accuses me,' he said to Breucker. 'He is a scoundrel, a red democrat and stupid'.[581]

Furthermore, Ludendorff tried to restore the contact with Von Hindenburg through General von Hahndorf. Due to his special relation with Von Hindenburg, Ludendorff had restrained himself from criticising him. When the relationship eventually did not develop positively, he regretted this and was angry with the person who had advised him; the explorer Sven Hedin. Ludendorff would later explain his behaviour by pointing out that Sven Hedin was a 'freemason'. Von Hindenburg wrote Ludendorff on the latter's birthday: 'God had brought them together, and they must not separate', 'There was much that I forgot', Ludendorff said after the comforting letter, in which Von Hindenburg showed understanding for 'the infinitely heavy' wight that had fallen on Ludendorff.

There was no unity within the military elite regarding the attitude towards the Weimar Republic. A part of the military apparatus was prepared to follow and support the new government, despite monarchist sentiments. They may not have constituted a great broadsword in Ebert's hands, but they were certainly not a revolutionary element. In addition, there was more opposition in various other circles, in which the military played an important role. This opposition was not uniform, but it was driven by and concentrated on mainly in three collecting basins:

- The Alldeutsche Verband around Heinrich Class
- the counter-revolutionaries around Wolfgang Kapp
- The Thule Society and the DAP in Bavaria

The first two were Protestant and mainly filled with professional soldiers. The 'Alldeutsche Verband' consisted above all of the somewhat older rich wilhelminian elite, in which both Class and Kapp were in direct and indirect contact with the royal houses. The Thule Society, as the most active part of the so-called 'Germanenbund', a lodge-like organisation of völkische and ariosophische forces, and the Deutsche Arbeiter Partei (DAP, predecessor of the NSDAP), founded by them in order to save the German worker from communism, were mainly concentrated in the catholic south of Germany. [582]

These forces would become the allies of the 'Kleinkrieg' which, as Stinnes had predicted, developed around Ludendorff. Ludendorff had scarcely moved into his new home in Viktoriastrasse, Wilmersdorf near Tiergarten, when he heard of the reproach made against him by Prime Minister Scheidemann. The latter thought that Ludendorff had 'gambled' with the interests of Germany. Ludendorff then demanded that Scheidemann retract these words. The latter replied indirectly, the letters were published in the press and everyone could 'enjoy' them. Journalist Theodor Wolff thought it inappropriate for everyone to vent their displeasure on Ludendorff. Ludendorff, 53 years old and in the prime of life, reacted to everything with fighting spirit. He wanted to fight, had to, and now he did so with words.

Apart from publicity debates, Ludendorff also had to answer officially. In November 1919, an 'Untersuchungsausschuss' was set up to shed light on the causes of the 1918 defeat. In practice, this investigation concealed more than it clarified. The stab-in-the-back myth was more or less officially supported here. It became clear that the truth served nobody. The myth meant that it was believed the German soldier had not been defeated at the front, but had received a stab in the back. 'Treacherous elements' on the home front were said to be responsible for this. According to the historian Hans Herzfeld, the stab-in-the-bakc myth had an 'enormously suggestive power'[583] and was to poison the political climate in Germany for a long time. The legend liberated the military from its fiasco for which they were responsible, and the Weimar politicians, who had to move on after all, and needed the military badly, were also prepared to endorse the legend. Friedrich Ebert, for example, believed that the German army 'was not defeated at the front'.

The stab-in-the-back myth would have far-reaching consequences for the political climate in the years to come. It became the spiritual fuel for the rise of National Socialism. After all, the myth of betrayal also created 'traitors' and this led to dangerous sentiments. Despite the endorsement of the legend by Weimar politicians, they too, were soon in the dock for the ultra-nationalists. The 'Erfüllungspolitik' was seen as treason.

There is controversy as to when the term 'stab-in-the-back myth' first appeared. During the above-mentioned investigation into Ludendorff and Von Hindenburg, who also had to give evidence, the latter used a slightly different word variant. Von Hindenburg spoke of a 'hinterlistige Speerwurf'.[584] Furthermore, he spoke about a British general who would think that the German army had been 'stabbed in the back by a dagger'. The 'good core of the German army was not to blame', according to Von Hindenburg. As 'proof' of the stab in the back, he pointed to the Entente's 'boundless astonishment at the sudden German collapse', thus insinuating that there was no military necessity for the German failure in 1918. Von Hindenburg ignored Ludendorff's statement of 14 August 1918, in which he stated that military victory was no longer possible, which was again confirmed by telegram on 3 October 1918.[585]

Who was the British general of whom Von Hindenburg spoke? For some time it was suspected that it was Sir Frederick Maurice. Others believed that it was not a British man at all, but a Swiss journalist from the *Neue Züricher Zeitung*, who had reported on the stab-in-the-back myth in December 1918. Others pointed to the British military attaché Sir Neil Malcolm.

Apart from the debate about the dagger shot legend and its origins, the course of the German government's investigation was a moral victory for Ludendorff. The conservatives had mobilised the streets to make it clear that the two men, Von Hindenburg and Ludendorff, were not on trial. There was a company of honour, units of the Freikorps Lüttwitz marched through the street, there were personal aides for both veterans and about three hundred students shouted: 'Wir dulden nicht dass unser grösster Mann von dummen Jungen vernommen wird'. Of course, 'greatest man' meant von Hindenburg, although Ludendorff could also count on support. Von Hindenburg and Ludendorff therefore did not enter the chamber of the session shaken. They underlined their clear conscience by emphasising that they had come voluntarily. Historian Emil Ludwig, who left a vivid description of this investigation, believes that this was just as well, because the Weimar government, in his opinion, did not have sufficient authority and moral credit to actually seize the two high officers and call them to account. Von Hindenburg emphasised this special position once more by stating that he had not wanted to come at first 'because of the bad weather'. It was clear that these were not two gentlemen who were looking back on their careers with regret and that some self-reflection had not yet taken place.

It had been thirteen months since Ludendorff and Von Hindenburg had last seen each other. Much had happened since then. Both were now standing side by side in civilian clothes. 'Everything was fine with the giant', said Ludwig about Von Hindenburg. There were flowers on their chairs in the courtroom. The intention was that a number of facts would come to light during the session, but the authorities lost control almost immediately. Von Hindenburg, who otherwise always kept silent, held a lengthy discourse on the historical role of the OHL, pointing out - not without justification - that the war had already been going on for two years when he and Ludendorff assumed military command. The war had been started by the politicians. The internal weakness of German military doctrine, where politicians and military had surrendered the fate of their country to the deterministic script of the Schlieffenplan, was not mentioned in a single word. The chairman tried several times to interrupt Von Hindenburg in his speech, but this was hardly tolerated by a murmuring audience because of the authority Von Hindenburg still exuded. After several interpellations by the chairman, who felt that Von Hindenburg was mainly making value judgements and not shedding much light on the matter, Von Hindenburg imperturbably picked up where he had left off and continued his plea. 'The U-boats that the judge wanted to talk about drifted out of the room', joked Emil Ludwig. [586]

Ludendorff's position was somewhat less comfortable. Normally, he operated under cover behind von Hindenburg's back. Now he had to defend himself publicly. The committee was also pushing him harder and his standing was vulnerable in the room. Besides, Ludendorff was a different person, more nervous, and with a high voice when he was nervous. Ludendorff reacted tauntingly to the requests for clarification. 'What are facts, what are opinions? If I am not allowed to give my opinion, I come into conflict with my conscience'. Tempers flared when the issue of the US joining the First World War was raised. According to Von Hindenburg, the US had been in cahoots with the Entente powers for a long time, and it was obvious that the US would join the conflict at some point. Two others who had to give account, Bethmann-Hollweg and the former German ambassador in the US, Count Johann Heinrich von Bernstorff, had a more nuanced view and did not subscribe to this vision. Ludendorff could not restrain himself and shouted: 'That is a bold-faced lie. The people will hear about it. It is claimed that we are guilty of everything, but the truth is that we have acted loyally through and through'. He added: 'And yes, I confess that I find Count Bernstorff distinctly unsympathetic. He misinformed the Chancellor about Wilson... and Count Bernstorff would have claimed that I did not want peace (punch on the table). These words I have never spoken... that is an insult to those responsible that I feel in my heart'.[587]

Apart from the 'Untersuchungsausschuss', there was also the foreign world that wanted to call Ludendorff and other important German officers to account. Even the Kaiser was not safe from the call for justice.[588] A list of no less than 890 names of war suspects circulated and the announcement of this on 5 February 1920 caused deep indignation in Germany.[589] There was anger and frustration. On the list, there were well-known names, such as Von Hindenburg, Tirpitz and also Erich Ludendorff. In addition to individuals, there were also indictments of bodies such as the German army and sections of it, and of troop contingents who were suspected of war crimes. The Entente indictment was as ambitious and ill-considered as the castration of the Reichswehr. The Freikorps and the politicians were driven into each other's arms and the inimitable demand provided mental fuel for all the forces opposed to the 'Erfüllungspolitik'. In the process, it fed the radical sentiments.

Ebert was realistic enough to keep his distance in the face of the extradition requests with France and Belgium, with 334 'requests', taking the crown.[590] Ebert promised the electorate that he would 'deflect' these heavy demands, and his Minister of Defence, Gustav Noske, also understood that granting the demands would cost the support of the Reichswehr.[591] The demand was eventually toned down and Ludendorff immediately announced that he would not comply. Ludendorff's homeland, East Prussia, also put up a spirited defence against the Entente requests for extradition. August Winning, a social democrat who would develop into a reactionary, threatened the Ebert government with strikes if the requests were complied with. From Gumbinnen, administrator Freiherr Magnus von Braun resisted.[592]

The extradition demands of the Entente led the circle of people around Ludendorff to the first underground activities towards the Entente, which were probably tolerated by Berlin. Waldemar Pabst and Heinz von Pflugk-Harttung (and his lesser-known brother Horst) founded an organisation with the innocent-sounding name 'Organisation Ferienkinder'. This umbrella organisation had emerged from the 'Hauptstelle zur Verteidigung Deutscher vor feindlichen Gerichten', which had met in October 1919. The aim of this organisation was to help German soldiers go into hiding in order to prevent extradition to the Entente. In fact, it was an early variant of the escape routes, such as the convent route of organisation 'Odessa' known after the Second World War.[593]

The demands of the Entente were, just like Ebert's resistance, dictated by domestic pressure. In France, the 'Ligue pour perpetuer le Souvenir des Crimes Allemands', who had set themselves the goal of keeping the German war crimes firmly in the public eye, were the most active.[594] The international judicial process that started with the Entente demands got off to a slow start and got bogged down in formalities, such as the question of what constituted a war crime. In fact, new history was being written here in the field of international law, but it made little impression on the ordinary citizen. Ludendorff was safe. So was the German emperor. The Netherlands had not been part of the warring parties and refused to extradite Wilhelm II. In addition, according to Dutch jurists, the Kaiser was accused of matters for which there was no case law before the war and for which there were even no laws. Moreover, the Netherlands had no extradition treaty with the Entente. The German emperor could settle in Huis Doorn without any worries.

In the network around Ludendorff, after the first steps such as the 'Organisation Ferienkinder', as well as the already acquired blood experience in the crushing of the Council republics, it became more and more noisy. This culminated in the Kapp-Putsch. Wolfgang Kapp, born in New York in 1858, was the son of a lawyer and returned to Germany in 1871. Kapp, like Ludendorff, belonged to the wealthy families of the eastern part of Germany. In Pilsen, then East Prussia, the Kapp family owned a 'Rittergut'. From 1891, Kapp was active in politics, and in 1906 he was appointed 'Generaldirektor der ostpreussischen Landschaft'. In 1916, the first voices of opposition were heard, and he became, in the words of the historian Werner Maser, an "incorrigible Scharfmacher".[595]

In a secret 'Denkschrift', Kapp criticised German domestic and foreign policy under the title: *Die national Kreise und der Reichskanzler*. When the first pacifist voices in German politics were heard, as a result of growing war weariness, Kapp founded, together with Alfred von Tirpitz, the 'Deutsche Vaterlandspartei' in 1917. This alliance with von Tirpitz (1849-1930), the man who had put the 'Hochseeflotte' on the political map in the wilhelminian era, had created a monstrous alliance between the conservative 'Ost-Elbian' elite and the monarchist-reactionary top of the navy. The 'Deutsche Vaterlandspartei' eventually gave rise to the 'Nationale Vereinigung'. Waldemar Pabst, Ludendorff's protector, was also one of the initiators of this organisation.

The most important military man in the field was Captain Ehrhardt. He was called 'Red Ehrhardt', not because of his socialist sympathies, that is clear, but because in naval circles he was compared to Erik the Red, a notorious Viking. General von Estorff characterised Ehrhardt as 'self-assured, ruthless in action, and spartanly simple'. Erhardt was the type of soldier with whom you could make revolutions. When Lüttwitz, at one point during the Kapp-Putsch, expressed his displeasure with many fellow generals to Ehrhardt, he simply asked if he should shoot half a dozen of them.

Ehrhardt's actions during the First World War confirmed the image of a decisive figure. As commander of the IX. torpedo boat *flotilla,* he took part in the Skagerak battle, during which his boat, the V-27, was badly damaged, forcing him to fight on from another boat. He took part in operations around the islands of Oesel, Dagoe and Moon off the Baltic coast, was active in the waters off Flanders and in September 1918, rammed his boat into British submarine 210, which sank as a result. [596]

Through the pact with Kapp and Ehrhardt, Ludendorff entered revolutionary territory. Immediately after his arrival, Ludendorff had shown some reluctance towards such putschist-ironmen. When he was approached by many veterans, he had ordered his 'adjutants', the officer Rittmeister von Treuenfeld and Breucker, to keep them away from him: 'Keep them off me', he told Breucker, 'these people will only compromise me'.[597] Ludendorff abandoned this cautious course.

The historiography of the Kapp-Putsch focuses mainly on the role of Wolfgang Kapp and Walther von Lüttwitz. However, the putsch could just as well have been called Ludendorff-Putsch, because the general did not have to be dragged along by the hair, but was a key figure from the very first moment. His confidant, Wilhelm Breucker, wrote unequivocally in his memoirs: 'The soul and the centre of the Kapp-Putsch was not Kapp but Ludendorff, who had to remain in the background at first because of the possible failure of the enterprise'.[598]

Ludendorff's role was major. First of all, he was prepared to put his historical "Ruf" to use. The victory at Tannenberg carried with it a memory of a heroic time. Secondly, Ludendorff played a full part in the planning. He was the central figure in northern Germany for the national and völkisch opposition. With Ludendorff's arrival in Berlin, the opposition became more open and above ground. With the Stinnes money and other money Ludendorff received, he financed groups with which he felt an affinity, like the Freikorps and also the early Nazis.[599]

Ludendorff's active role also fitted in with the aim of the national opposition. A military dictatorship was to be established until order was restored in the country. After that, one could start thinking about a restoration of the empire. The role of military dictator was given to Ludendorff.

Not all soldiers and military interest groups would support this dictatorship just like that. One of the most important was the 'Deutsche Reichskriegerbund Kyffhaeuser', which was primarily a welfare organisation. The 'Reichsbanner' association was loyal to the Weimar Republic and defended their Jewish front colleagues who were coming under increasing pressure and who were partly represented in the 'Reichsbund jüdischer Frontsoldaten'. Other soldiers had become communists and sympathised with the Spartakists and the Council Republics and had pinned their hopes on Moscow.[600]

The Freikorps and men like Ehrhardt and Pabst were the ones to talk to. Ludendorff spoke their language. He thought that the German officers were treated as 'a bunch of beggars' by the Weimar politicians. They had been relied upon during the Raden Republic, but now Weimar preferred to get rid of the Freikorps. 'The Reichswehrofficers now knew what to expect from the Social Democrats', he said. In an article in his periodical the *Kreuzzeitung*, Ludendorff spoke of a 'lonely army',[601] in which he referred to the plans to dissolve the Freikorps, the undermining of the power of the military courts, the fiddling with the right of honour of the German officer, the poor payment, the stop on the recruitment of new soldiers as a response to the Entente wishes in Versailles and the uncertain future and the 'lack of Manneszucht'.[602] 'The high ethic of the military is not understood', Ludendorff later commented in his reminiscences.[603] It was the track he would not leave for the rest of his life and which gave him a lifelong struggle.

This struggle would first focus on the figure of General Von Lüttwitz, the commander of the 'Reichswehrgruppenkommando I'. On 13 January 1920, the Treaty of Versailles had come into force, which meant that the Ebert government and Minister of Defence, Noske, now had to take serious steps to disarm the Freikorps, which had earlier saved the Republic from communism. Von Lüttwitz was not in favour of this. However, in the script of the 'Erfüllungspolitik', the army had to be reduced to 100,000 men by 1 April 1920. The camps were diametrically opposed. Central to this were two elite Freikorps, the Ehrhardt Naval Brigade, which was located near Berlin, and Löwenfeld in Silesia. The former was formed by naval personnel from Wilhelmshaven and was stationed at the Döberitz military training area near Berlin, the latter was composed of, among others, naval veterans of the light cruiser *Breslau* and naval personnel from Kiel.[604] Ludendorff met with Von Lüttwitz at the beginning of the escalation. The latter spoke positively about Kapp and thought that he was politically ready for the case. He believed that the putschists could count on sufficient support from the army. Von Lüttwitz had carefully reached out to the other district commanders, such as General Von Schöler and his chief General Von Lossberg in Kassel, General Watter in Münster and General Möhl in Munich.[605] Von Lüttwitz also believed that there was no need to fear the Entente. Just as the Entente had given the Freikorps in the east (the Baltic area) a free hand in the fight against communism, so were forces within the Entente, and especially the British, afraid of French irredentism on the Rhine and therefore less unfavourable to a national reveille from the German side than one would superficially suspect.[606]

Little is known about Von Lüttwitz's contacts with the Entente, but Ludendorff writes in his memoirs that they went 'via Cologne'.[607] The history of Cologne politics in the period immediately following the First World War is a study in itself. At the helm was perhaps the greatest political tightrope walker in contemporary German history: Konrad Adenauer. More talented than sympathetic, he steered his city - and not least himself - between Skila and Caribdus. He had skilfully resisted the Council Revolution in Cologne by forbidding the panicky military to fire on the demonstrators and relying on the split between Spartakists and more moderate Socialists. Indeed, this provided a balance, and he also managed to win French support against the revolutionaries. Adenauer knew that the French, with their territorial ambitions in the Rhine region, would not appeal to the internationalism of communism, but rather to the nationalism of the Rhinelanders. The French liked to evoke the memory of the Napoleonic Rhineland, when the region joined the French tricolour and was rewarded for this by becoming a tax haven.

Adenauer kept his options open. His biographer Charles Wighton has rightly observed that Adenauer went very far with his support for the 'Rheinische Republik': 'an act of dubious character, to say the least'.[608] Adenauer again chose a great-German (pro-Prussian) course at the right time, which in turn earned him British support because of fears of French Rhine expansion at the expense of Germany. Gordon A. Craig wrote in the *New York Review of Books* that Adenauer constantly changed his Rhenish positions in response to pressure.[609] In this wasp's nest of Cologne, Von Lüttwitz had apparently gained his contacts.

Lüttwitz's contacts with the Entente were not isolated. Via Pabst and the journalist Schnitzler, the Kapp group had already discussed a common denominator under which the Entente and the German reactionaries could be brought together. Apart from their anti-communism, an amalgamation of conservative forces internationally also played a role. Pabst and Schnitzler were already working on a kind of government in exile for nationalistic Russians (Whites) who had fled the revolution, and there was speculation about an amalgamation of major industrial and military interests between the Entente and Germany, with the US as the financier in the background. The aim was the restoration of prosperity in Europe, which would also benefit the US, so that there would be a good market for American products.

Negotiations were held with various people, such as the British Sir Malcolm Robertson, an experienced professional diplomat who had served in Peking, Washington, Rio de Janeiro and Madrid, among other places, and who was a High Commissioner at the Inter-Allied Rhineland High Commission, with the Chief Representative of the same commission, Colonel Ryan in Cologne (probably also Von Lüttwitz's contact person), while the industrialist Arnold Rechberg, who in turn worked with Ludendorff's colleague General Hoffmann, consulted with the French. Ludendorff is silent about this mysterious part of his life in his memoirs. Wilhelm Breucker, in his *Die Tragik Ludendorffs*, wrote a few sentences about this case. He underlined the 'cool scepticism' of Von Seeckt, the commander-in-chief of the German armed forces, about these manoeuvres, who apparently had heard something, and reported that Ludendorff soon cut his teeth on this complicated diplomacy, after fruitless negotiations with Lord Edgar Vincent d'Abernoon and others. This makes the tapped network (all people around the 'High Commission') a little more insightful, but it didn't come to any results. Neither did Rechberg and Hoffmann produce any results. Were they just castels in the sky? It does not seem so. When Von Schleicher - Von Seeckt's successor - wanted to strengthen ties with France in 1931, he made use of Arnold Rechberg's network.[610]

In spite of all negotiations, Von Lüttwitz's estimation of the Entente's position was 'dangerously optimistic',[611] Ludendorff rightly concluded in his memoirs afterwards. Von Lüttwitz' estimation of the support of 'das Militär' would turn out to be too optimistic as well. Strengthened by his optimism, Von Lüttwitz did not intend to take any notice of the order to disband the Ehrhardt and Loewenfeld unit. On 1 March 1920, Von Lüttwitz publicly pledged his honour by declaring, during a visit to the Ehrhardt Brigade in Döberitz, in front of the troops, that he would not allow the disbandment of the Freikorps. He received loud support from the men. Among those present were Adrian Dietrich Lothar von Trotha, the man who had defeated the Hereros in East Africa at the Battle of Waterberg, and the later 'Abwehr' (intelligence) chief, Admiral Wilhelm Canaris.[612] 'I waited for the developments with suspense',[613] Ludendorff noted ostentatiously 'innocently' in his memoirs. He was not himself, but anything but an outsider.

In the Viktoriastrasse, Von Lüttwitz, Pabst, Kapp, the officers Max Bauer and Hoffmann and the adventurer Trebitsch-Lincoln walked in and out. However, spies also came forward. In her memoirs, Margarethe Ludendorff who, to her annoyance, was kept out of the loop by Ludendorff (while he did confide in other women), describes how one day a young officer reported. He told a dramatic story about his fight in the 'Baltikum' against the communists. Ludendorff was moved by his story and handed him a hundred mark note at the end of their meeting. A few days later, Ludendorff received the report that the young soldier's story had been a lie from beginning to end and that it was a case of espionage. [614]

Meanwhile, negotiations between the Ministry of Defence in Berlin and Von Lüttwitz were busy. His opponents were, apart from Noske, mainly Hans von Seeckt, his political referent Kurt von Schleicher, his right-hand man Oberst Hasse and General Reinhardt, head of the 'Heeresleitung'. Von Seeckt was a difficult negotiator for Von Lüttwitz. He was known as 'the sphinx', and was keen to keep the Reichswehr out of politics. Of course, he shared Von Lüttwitz's concerns about Germany's military strength as a result of the 100,000-strong army, but Von Seeckt wanted to establish a 'Führerheer' (officer's army), which would preserve the training quality for the future as much as possible. In addition, Von Seeckt was prepared to go along with the Versailles Treaty whenever possible, as would soon become clear with the rapprochement around Rapallo (secret collaboration with the Soviet Union) and the establishment of 'Selbstschutz'-units in the east of Germany, when riots with Czech and Polish nationalists arose. As long as these units were 'bodenständig', i.e. not mobile, the Entente turned a blind eye.

On 10 March 1920, Noske's call to disarm the Freikorps followed. It was decided to remove the Ehrhardt brigade from Von Lüttwitz's command and to send him packing. This happened after Von Lüttwitz, in a personal conversation with Noske and Ebert, had demanded a kind of 'business cabinet'. Trade ministers were to replace politicians, he himself was to become Minister of Defence and the disbandment of the naval brigades was to be reversed. [615]

Politicians reacted as if bitten by a viper. Several leaders of the Kapp camp were subject to arrest warrants, and two of them, Friedrich Grabowski and Karl Schnitzler, were actually arrested. From that moment on, there was no turning back. The Ehrhardt brigade stayed behind Von Lüttwitz, left the Döberitz troop area and started the march on Berlin, which was thirty kilometres away. Wolfgang Kapp hastened to report that he had not yet finished. Von Lüttwitz shrugged his shoulders. He trusted his battalions more than politics anyway. [616]

The Kapp-Putsch was a fact. The Ebert government learned of the brigade's mobilisation on 12 March, when Von Lüttwitz's chief of staff, Generalmajor

Von Olderhausen, had Noske pulled out of the cabinet meeting to report the bad news.[617] Hectic activities followed, sometimes with miraculous scenes. When the Prussian Minister of Agriculture, Otto Braun, walked into the large library of the Reichskanzlei, he was 'greeted' by groups of officers, with Von Seeckt standing by, who looked at him with telling smiles on their faces. Braun was one of the most hated people in the reactionary camp, and even in this hour of need the military opponents of Von Lüttwitz and Kapp did not seem entirely without sympathy for the putschists.[618]

There were two solutions to the developments. Noske and General Walter Reinhardt thought that the revolutionaries should be stopped by all means, if necessary with weapons. Von Seeckt, however, was much more reserved. Not so much out of sympathy for the Ehrhardt brigade or Von Lüttwitz, but because he believed that the Reichswehr as such had to survive this conflict and should therefore keep out of politics, and certainly not shoot at other Reichswehr troops. There was also a practical military problem. The Ehrhardt brigade was by far the best army unit in the wider Berlin area and Von Seeckt did not believe that one had the means to stop the brigade even if one wanted to. The Potsdam garrison was not entirely reliable, nor was the police. Besides, Von Seeckt feared a civil war.[619]

Ebert and Noske were in a particularly difficult position. With only the support of General Reinhardt, military action against Ehrhardt's disciplined and front-running units was out of the question and a rapid fall of Berlin was feared. Moreover, a military operation with the opposite visions of Von Seeckt and Reinhardt was also very problematic. The men were of opposite natures. In a letter to his wife, Reinhardt had written that, as a Württemberger, he did not really belong in Berlin; he had 'too much heat and too little coolness in him'. Von Seeckt had plenty of coolness. Reinhardt was a man who sought a solution to the division between left and right that was dividing the country. As early as October 1918, he had concluded: 'all are to blame, left and right'.[620] Reinhardt had always looked upon Ludendorff with great respect, and his dismissal had moved him. It was 'more Schicksal than Schuld',[621] he thought, and he described Ludendorff as a 'more powerful recruit'. He would always 'think of him in grateful memory'.

Yet, that was before his transfer to Berlin. In the capital, Reinhardt found it difficult. During the First World War, he had been responsible for the France section of the staff, an important post, but he lacked weight due to the fact that he had hardly been to the front. He had only been with a Hessian regiment for three weeks, and people were a bit scornful about that. 'I am on thin ice', he wrote home, 'Nun los mit Gott'.[622] Despite his kind words about Ludendorff, he had to revise his opinion in the following months. It was clear that Ludendorff was plotting against the Weimar Republic and in doing so, Ludendorff was so unreasonable in defending himself that he made enemies; among them was General Reinhardt. Ludendorff demanded at every turn that people should all stand up for him when the press reported negatively about him, but the Reichswehr was fighting for its own survival and had other things to do than to occupy itself with Ludendorff's long toes. When Reinhardt, during a parliamentary enquiry, said a few kind words about General Beseler, who was also under pressure, but not about Ludendorff, the relationship was ruined. [623]

Loyal forces within the army feverishly sought a way to parry Ehrhardt's approaching brigade. Generals Von Olderhausen, Von Oven and Oberst Wetzell visited the brigade, without result. They also tried to replace Von Lüttiwtz with the more malleable Von Trotha, without result. So there was nothing left to do but pack their bags as quickly as possible, and the government moved to Stuttgart, and later to Dresden. At 7 a.m. the units of the Ehrhardt brigade, 5,000 strong, marched under the Brandenburgertor. The first major military uprising in German history was a fact.

On the afternoon of 11 March, Waldemar Pabst rushed past Ludendorff's house and told him that a warrant had been issued for his arrest, for Kapp's arrest, for Bauer's arrest and for that of others. Ludendorff advised him to go to the Ehrhardt brigade who could guarantee his safety. On the morning of 13th, Ludendorff had to walk only a short distance to encounter the first units of the Ehrhardt brigade at the Tiergarten at the beginning of Viktoriastrasse. Ludendorff described it as a more or less chance encounter during the morning walk, but he was in full uniform and taking a parade of the troops.[624] Wolfgang Kapp also appeared, last, and apologised for oversleeping. The revolution was characterised by amateurism and sentiment.[625] From the outset, reality moved faster than Kapp could keep up.

Initially, the putsch seemed to be developing favourably. The Weimar-politicians had made way for the Kapp-putschists. Only the 'Jewish-blooded', as Ludendorff wrote,[626] young politician Schiffer, had remained behind as a kind of negotiator between the official government and the Kapp people.

It soon became apparent that a number of naval strongholds in Germany sided with Kapp. In Wilhelmshaven, where Vice-Admiral Michelsen ruled, they pledged allegiance to the new regime. Also in Kiel, under Admiral Magnus von Levetzow, one chose for Kapp and his people. Von Levetzow's action was yet another indicator that the loyalty of some officers had been misjudged by the Weimar administration. Von Levetzow had only been in office for a short time, replacing Admiral Meurer, who had heavily criticised the 'Erfüllunsgpolitik'. With the appointment of his successor, Noske had fallen between two stools.[627]

In the land forces, the parties were divided. Germany was divided into military districts, and especially the eastern districts, numbers 1 to 3, East Prussia (General von Estorff, the former commander of Ehrhardt), Mecklenburg-Pommern (General von Lettow-Vorbeck) and Brandenburg-Schlesien (General von Huelsen) supported the putsch. Districts IV to VII, Saxony-Thuringia (General Maercker), Württemberg/Baden (General von Bergmann), Westphalia (General von Watter) and Bavaria (General von Moehl) did not support the putsch.[628]

None of this was immediately clear. The days were chaotic. Paul von Lettow-Vorbeck, for example, was called right at the beginning of the conflict by Von Lüttwitz's chief of staff, who thought that his chief was going a bit too fast. Von Lettow-Vorbeck did not hesitate and travelled by train to Berlin in order to prevent Von Lüttwitz from making mistakes. By the time he arrived, however, Kapp was already ruling Berlin and Von Lüttwitz was nominated as the new Minister of Defence. Von Lüttwitz ordered Von Lettow-Vorbeck to keep order in Mecklenburg. Von Lettow-Vorbeck then hurried back.[629]

While the revolution initially seemed to be developing favourably in Wilhelmshaven and Kiel, the opposition also quickly mobilised. In Wilhelmshaven, counter-revolutionaries gathered around the Ebert-leader Arthur Grunewald, and in Kiel, the SPD leader Gustav Radbruch stirred. In the latter place, there were open firefights and a struggle over the arms depots. Dozens of people lost their lives. The biggest windfall for the putschists was that the Reichswehr in Berlin offered no resistance. Von Seeckt and Von Schleicher simply left and decided to wait for developments. A miraculous situation.

However, dark clouds soon gathered over the Putsch. 'It soon became clear that Kapp's preparations were not good,' Ludendorff wrote, looking back, 'and he was also abandoned by several people at the last moment'.[630] A number of faithful initially presented themselves for ministerial posts, Von Wangenheim, Dr Martin Schiele, the Berlin police chief Traugott Von Jagow, Dr Gottlieb Traub. Nevertheless, the meeting in Berlin on 13 March was 'not a pleasant one'.[631] Not all military commanders joined in, since some seemed to want to wait to see what would happen. 'The position of General von Watter was not clear', Ludendorff wrote in his memoirs, 'it was particularly difficult'.[632] An apparently favourable report came from Bavaria. There, the national opposition was used to overthrow Hoffmann's Socialist government and replace it with Von Kahr. With this, the conservative forces in Bavaria pulled the strings. But this did not immediately mean recognition or support for Kapp. The recognition did not materialise, and Ludendorff was very disappointed. Later, he attributed the lack of support to the fact that, in his opinion, ultra-montane forces were at work, which saw Bavaria as part of a Catholic belt that ran through the German-speaking regions, from Stuttgart via Munich to Austria. [633]

The civil servants had largely left the ministries. As strikes were called by Ebert, the chaos accelerated. Kapp did not even have a typewriter at his disposal and had to get one from a shop. There were no typists either, so Kapp's daughter had to type out the new government's proclamations. This meant that the Germans were too late to get the weekend papers in Berlin. An important propaganda battle was thus lost for Kapp. Also, they did not know exactly what to do with the military force. Ehrhardt and his men just hung around. Kapp finally ordered them to go and get money from the state bank, because he had promised a higher reward for the Freikorps soldiers. But Ehrhardt encountered closed doors because it was Sunday. The next day he returned and showed a cheque for ten million marks with the caption 'Kapp'. The deputy director of the bank, a courageous man, however, shook his head gloomily; he did not know a 'Reichskanzler' by that name. Ehrhardt relayed the message to Kapp, who exclaimed that Ehrhardt would have to get the money by force, to which Ehrhardt replied that he was an officer and not a bank robber. [634]

That same Monday, the 'Generalstreik', which the Bauer government, in consultation with Ebert, had announced, officially began. In parts of the capital, the electricity failed and there was no water. In the government districts, emergency generators kept things running, but the strike underlined the fiasco with which people were confronted. The trade unions and civil servants had turned against the putschists, Paris announced a food blockade, and there was also much doubt and resistance among the traditional allies of the right-wing parties and within 'das Militär'.

On the night of 16-17 March, the Garde Pionier battalion began to defect to the Ebert camp. The whole situation became quicksand. Negotiator Von Bergmann was sent out to negotiate with the Ebert government, Von Lüttwitz addressed the mutinous soldiers. 'I started this cause and I will finish it', he said bravely. On 17 March, consultations took place between several officers in Berlin. While the conversation was going on, Ludendorff and press officer Trebitsch-Lincoln followed it in the room next door and - as they could hear - it did not go too friendly. 'I do not want to intervene yet', Ludendorff said to Trebitsch-Lincoln, 'the time has not yet come'. Trebitsch-Lincoln stared open-mouthed at Ludendorff. 'When will you intervene then, Excellency?'[635] Immediately afterwards Colonel Bauer threw open the door and came running in, dead tired. 'All is lost', he exclaimed, 'of the fifty commanders, only six will go with us'. 'The men, Excellency, whom you brought to the front in the war and raised to rank, are now betraying us'.

Ludendorff looked serious and stood motionless. Then he reached out to Bauer: 'Bauer, we have gained a bitter experience'. At that moment a young officer, captain lieutenant Lentsch, came running in. He saluted Ludendorff, begging him: 'Your Excellency, put yourself at the head of the troops, then the matter can still be saved'. Bauer seemed to draw hope from this sudden situation, and proposed to let the troops that were stationed on the Wilhelmsplein join him. They could surround the Chancellor's palace and stop anyone who was defeatist. 'Who leaves this building will be shot immediately', Bauer said.[636] All looked at Ludendorff now. 'He stood motionless like a statue', Trebitsch-Lincoln thought. At that moment, Count Westarp and Helfferich intervened. 'Your Excellency, for heaven's sake do not spill blood'.[637] And so it happened.

When Kapp announced his resignation to Ludendorff on 17th, the latter did not stop him.[638] Immediately afterwards he disappeared, no one knew where he went.[639] The case was lost. He fled to Sweden by plane. Ludendorff left the Reichskanzlei at the same time as Von Lüttwitz. The general took Ludendorff with him in a truck, in which he drove back to his official residence in the Generalkommando III. Armeekorps in the Hardenbergstrasse. On the way, Ludendorff was dropped off in Viktoriastrasse. They shook hands and went their separate ways. 'I was aware that an indescribable witch hunt would now break out against me,' Ludendorff wrote in his memoirs.[640] Trebitsch-Lincoln had meanwhile arrived at his own hiding place. It was evening and his hand automatically went to the light switch. Click. The light was back on, power was back on. There could not be clearer proof that the putsch was over.[641]

The Kapp-Putsch would only be the beginning of a new era. General Buat, Ludendorff's former French opponent, had foreseen this. Buat had gained some notoriety for his opinion that the German troops would attack through the Ardennes in 1914, rather than through Belgium, which later brought him criticism. This 'sin', however, did not prevent a glorious military career and he became deputy commander of the French armed forces. On 10 March 1920, when the Kapp-Putsch was just beginning to unfold, he gave his views on Erich Ludendorff via, among others, the press agency *Universal Service*. He already pointed out then that Ludendorff's patriotism had acquired 'almost mystical features', that he blamed the German defeat on 'das Militär', and mainly blamed the politicians. Buat called Ludendorff 'vindictive' and 'proud', but above all, still combative.

He saw Ludendorff as a great danger, who could bring Germany to war again. 'Everything in Ludendorff is consistent', he thought; 'he is made of a block'. And that 'bloc' was convinced that the national 'religion', patriotism, had not disappeared from Germany after 1918, but was merely 'dormant'. Politics had to breathe life into it again; the people 'were badly led'. According to Buat, Ludendorff had become a kind of 'prophet', a 'Moses' who would mobilise the German people to regain what they had lost. He characterised Ludendorff's message as a 'fatal echo'.

Buat saw it as a very real danger, which he described very graphically. There were 'signs that people were longing for Ludendorff again, people were gathering around him. Flowers were thrown at his feet, people cheered him on again'. Yet 'the gambler', as he characterised Ludendorff, would not hurry, and would bide his time. His military talent would serve him well. He was 'a good organiser, energetic and farsighted'. Buat also praised Ludendorff's specialisation of the 'inner lines'. 'We shall be hearing from him,' he predicted. Ludendorff 'Would Spur Germany to New War', was the headline of the American newspaper *Oakland Tribune*, which copied, among other things, the article by General Buat from *Universal Service*. The newspaper's ink was still wet when the Ehrhardt brigade marched to Berlin.

In December 1923, shortly after the Feldherrnhalle-Putsch, Ludendorff's second putsch in Munich, Buat died in hospital following a botched operation. His prophecy of an active Ludendorff, watching his chances from the wings, had come true. [642]

Chapter 13

The aftermath of the Kapp-Putsch

The Kapp-Putsch had burst like a bubble. The most important leaders of the counter-revolution fled in all directions. Wolfgang Kapp fled to Sweden with a hastily bought plane and an arranged pilot, Pabst to Austria, Oberst Bauer and Trebitsch-Lincoln to Hungary, Von Stephani and Ehrhardt to Munich, Magnus von Levetow took off his uniform and went into hiding in civilian clothes (but was later arrested), as did Von Trotha. Von Lüttwitz announced through the press that his health would not tolerate a stay in prison and that he had therefore fled abroad.[643] Heinrich Brüning, the later Reich Chancellor, saw Ehrhardt's soldiers marching back to Döberitz. 'I saw part of the Ehrhardt brigade marching from my office in Leipzigerstrasse on its way back from Wilhelmstrasse to Döberitz. I had never seen such first-class soldiers. They consisted of naval officers, selected non-commissioned officers and men, especially from the 'U-boats', all with the highest decorations for bravery on their chests. Like the people in the street, I averted my gaze, because the tragedy of these thoroughly patriotic men, abused by politics, was unbearable'.[644]

The historian Werner Maser estimated the damage of the Kapp-Putsch at 3,000 deaths (most of which occurred in the crushing of the new left-wing uprisings that followed the Putsch), as well as 1 billion Reichmarks.[645]

The Ludendorff household was greatly shocked. 'What failures, their words were out of proportion to their deeds', said a shocked Margarethe Ludendorff. She believed that her husband had allowed himself to be persuaded by 'their smooth talk', and she blamed him for 'not demanding any guarantees'.[646] It was incomprehensible, she concluded looking back, that 'a man as conscientious and thorough as Ludendorff took part in a case whose organisation was so rattled'.[647] Nothing remained of the 'victory atmosphere' that had reigned in the house when the Ehrhardt brigade marched into Berlin. Ludendorff never had any knowledge of people, otherwise he could not have fallen under the influence of people who plunged him into unhappiness. Even the most untrustworthy figures could get through to Ludendorff, Trebitsch-Lincoln in particular. [648]

While the Kapp-Putsch unexpectedly spread quickly in Berlin, a change of power took place in Bavaria, with the conservatives gaining a much stronger grip on power. At the centre of the counter-revolution in southern Germany - as in the north - were mostly soldiers. A central figure here was Adolf Hitler's then commander, Captain Mayer, who headed a department of political espionage. Within these departments, soldiers were trained to keep an eye on the multi-faceted political landscape of the Weimar Republic. The main interest here was in communist parties, which were feared to endanger the interests of Germany and, above all, the military. One of his agents had been Hitler, who turned out to be an orator. As a result, he was eventually discharged from service in order to secure his entry into politics. Through the DAP and the NSDAP that grew out of it, this party, and Hitler's efforts, were intended to keep the workers away from the communists and win them over to the national cause.

One of Hitler's political teachers was Dietrich Eckart. Eckart was the only teacher who openly recognised Hitler as such. *Mein Kampf* was dedicated to him. Eckart was a well-known figure on the nationalist scene in Munich. Hitler biographer John Toland called Eckart a 'coffeehouse intellectual' who divided his attention between drink and politics. Fest called him 'a primitive orator and a friend of good wine'. But Eckart was also a unifying figure in the scene, and it was not without reason that Reichswehr circles around Mayer sent him and Hitler to make contact with Kapp. Hitler's later press secretary, Franz Hanfstaengl, pointed out that Eckart belonged to the 'narrowest Vertrauensgruppe' around Hitler and that he was 'a splendid specimen' and a living witness to old Bavaria. Eckart had talents in addition to his weaknesses, and his translation of Ibsen's *Peer Gynt* enjoyed a certain notoriety. More importantly, he knew the Munich 'incrowd' and helped introduce Hitler to socially acceptable circles. His magazine *Auf gut deutsch*, which was full of anti-Semitism, was not without influence on Hitler. Through Eckart, Hitler also got to know the Balten German Alfred Rosenberg, who would later become the (controversial) chief ideologist of the National Socialist movement. Max Erwin von Scheubner-Richter, also a Balten German, also moved in these circles. 'Follow Hitler! He will dance. But it was I who determined the melody', Eckart is reported to have said on his deathbed in 1923. [649]

Hitler's chief Mayer was in good contact with the other conservative circles in Bavaria. First of all, there was the brand-new President of Upper Bavaria, von

Kahr, the police commander Poehner, the leader of the people's militias ('Einwohnerwehren') who had grouped themselves against the Communists under Forstrat Escherich and the Freikorps commander Ritter von Epp and the later SA chief Ernst Röhm. They were favourable to the Kapp-Putsch, but the Bavarian military district commander, General Mohl, as we have already seen, was very cautious. When the counter-revolution in Berlin had run fairly smoothly in military terms, but had failed to get off the ground politically, the Bavarian army remained at the ready. Things were so unclear that it was decided to send Hitler and Eckart to Berlin.

On 16 March 1920, Hitler and Eckart travelled to Berlin.[650] The Reichswehr had provided them with several forged documents, including identity papers that would show that they were representatives of the socialist USPD. These documents proved more than useful when the open World War I aircraft in which Pour-le-Merite pilot Lieutenant a.D. Ritter von Greim flew them to Berlin had to make a stopover in Jüterborg. The workers at the airport had taken control. Eckart and Hitler claimed that they were on a secret mission to Berlin, to buy paper for the USPD. They were let through.[651] When they finally arrived in Berlin, they went straight to the Reichskanzlei. There they found abandoned offices. One of the few of the putschists who was still there was Trebitsch-Lincoln. He told Hitler and Eckart that Kapp had fled and that they had better keep under cover or they would be arrested. Eckart was astonished to be addressed by a Jew of all people, who 'acted as if he was in charge'.[652] Eckart took Hitler by the arm: 'Come Adolf, we have no more business here'. [653]

Margarethe Ludendorff had instinctively sensed that Trebitsch-Lincoln was a controversial figure. This had more to do with his strange and adventurous life than with his ethnic background, although this would soon prove to be the most important blueprint for a person's future in the newly formed Germany.

Trebitsch-Lincoln was a man without principles. He was of Jewish-Hungarian descent, born 4 April 1879 in Pacz, south of Budapest. His father had gambled on the stock market and lost the family capital. From then on, Trebitsch-Lincoln's life was devoted to regaining the wealth and status he had lost. In his younger years he was suspected of theft, but tried his luck in England where he joined the Christian mission. For Benjamin Seebohm Rowntree, a wealthy liberal Quaeker, he travelled to Canada. His German wife, Margarethe Kahlor, the daughter of a German captain, he could marry as a Jew because he converted to Christianity and because she already had a one-year old child without being married. Thanks to his good appointment, he was able to enter politics and was elected to parliament. With a financial handshake, Trebitsch-Lincoln left the mission in 1910 and went into the oil business, accumulating money, but also going bankrupt twice. This cost him his political career.

This led him to offer his help to British intelligence in the First World War. He knew the German language well, and started as a translator of telegrams, but soon offered spy services as well. For this purpose he travelled to the Netherlands, and from Rotterdam he made contact with German intelligence. They gave him some harmless material and when he offered this in London to the British secret service, they were not interested, and - more importantly - they did not pay. So in 1915 he emigrated to the US, leaving his wife in debt. In the US, he then offered his services as a spy to the German embassy. In 1916, the British caught sight of him and he was brought to Britain, where he remained in prison until 1919. Shortly afterwards, Trebitsch-Lincoln resurfaced in revolutionary Berlin. There, he became friends with Max Bauer, general staff officer to Ludendorff. Bauer saw Trebitsch-Lincoln as a man with international contacts. His knowledge of the American media landscape was especially impressive, and this earned Trebitsch-Lincoln the post of foreign press officer for the Kapp-Putschists. Some Freikorps officers objected to a Jew in this position, but Bauer had protected him.

After the failed putsch, Trebitsch-Lincoln and Bauer fled to Hungary, where the Horthy regime, which had itself come to power by crushing Bela Kuhn's communist revolution, received them benevolently. They even received financial support, and Trebitsch-Lincoln was able to continue his life of luxury in Hotel Pannonia in Budapest. But now there were also voices that gave the wind to the distrust that Eckart and Hitler also harboured. Trebitsch-Lincoln feared that he could become the victim of a *Feme murder* (a right-wing revenge killing for betrayal) and in 1920 he disappeared in haste to Vienna, stealing a full suitcase of secret documents from Bauer with him. For the first time Trebitsch-Lincoln really had something to sell to secret services, as Bauer was deep in the anti-communist camp, and had contacts with Belarusian forces. After first offering his material to the French and the British, he finally went with the Czechs. They paid him a large sum of money in two instalments, after which he sent his wife to Prague. When he wanted to travel to the US, it turned out that the Czechs did not want to pay the second instalment and the US did not issue visas. He eventually arrived there with false papers, was caught, but not deported. He was allowed to travel on to China via the West Coast.

In 1923, Trebitsch-Lincoln, again under one of his many pseudonyms, this time Patrick Keelan,[654] set foot on European (Italian) soil as part of a Chinese delegation under General Wu Hung Chiang. Due to his international contacts and flair, Trebitsch-Lincoln had once again managed to penetrate the international diplomatic world. He took the plunge and contacted his former friend Max Bauer, who now lived in Austria. The latter, who had been somewhat on the sidelines, was happy to play a role again and got over the problems of the past. He even arranged for a meeting between Hugo Stinnes and Erich Ludendorff in 1923, but we are getting ahead of ourselves.[655]

Despite the frustrations of Ludendorff, Eckart and Hitler over Trebitsch-Lincoln, Hitler's visit to Berlin was nevertheless an important turning point. The trip to the Kapp Putschists literally marked Hitler's last steps under the Reichswehr umbrella. When Hitler returned to Munich on 31 March 1920, he had become a civilian. It is clear that the men of the counter-revolution in Bavaria saw Hitler as an up-and-coming man, and that contact with the North German counter-revolution was important to them. For example, Hitler's then boss Karl Mayr, a veteran of the Alpine and Turkish fronts, wrote to Kapp in Sweden that they were in the process of building the NSDAP in Bavaria into a real base, a 'Stosstrupp'. It is true that the programme was still 'incomplete', but there were 'capable young people', a Mr. Hitler for instance. About Hitler, he wrote that he had become 'a driving force and a popular speaker (Volksredner). The membership of the NSDAP in Munich was rising sharply, and now stood at 2,000 people'. In an article published in 1941, Mayr stated that Hitler was at first a 'politically unwritten leaf', was during the Raden period rather SPD-oriented (remarkably, he wrote almost nothing about the Raden Republic in Bavaria in *Mein Kampf*) and only later had sided with Reichswehr and Reaktion.[656]

At that time, Kapp himself did not yet realise that his historical role had ended. In view of the inevitable trial that was to take place against him, he was preparing to justify himself to Germany. In Kapp's eyes, the putsch had primarily been an example of the 'national act', and he hoped to rehabilitate himself. The putsch failed because the high military and civil servants did not serve the national interest. Furthermore, he was annoyed that the civilists were treated more harshly by the Weimar administration than the military, even though it had been primarily a military coup.[657]

The Kapp-Putsch brought the meeting between Ludendorff and Hitler. An important meeting, because despite the fast-growing prestige of the young Hitler, Ludendorff was the figurehead. Ludendorff represented the sentiment to past times, which was symbolised in the 'Pickelhoube' (the traditional helmet) that he would always wear, while the new era definitively appropriated the 'Stahlhelm'. Hitler and Eckart decided - since they were in Berlin anyway - to visit Ludendorff.[658] Many meetings of the right-wing camp took place in the salon of the widow of the wealthy industrialist Carl Albrecht Heckmann ('Haus Heckmann') in the Maassenstrasse. Here, the meeting between Ludendorff and

Hitler took place.⁶⁵⁹ There were probably no people for whom Hitler had more respect (and sometimes even fear) than Erich Ludendorff. Little is known about this meeting, and it seems that Ludendorff did not remember Hitler's presence at all, because he let the first meeting take place in Bavaria. Hitler was probably a bit 'eingeschütert' and Eckart did the talking. That the meeting actually took place was proven by other useful contacts Hitler made here.

Hitler met Kapitänleutnant a.D. Ernst Graf zu Reventlow, who was married to Countess Marie Gabriele Reventlow, born Graefin d'Allemont, who believed that Hitler was 'the new messiah'.⁶⁶⁰ Ernst Graf zu Reventlow was an important leader of the 'Deutschvölkische Freiheitspartei' (DVFP), which was to be merged into the NSDAP in 1927, and had contacts with the influential 'Nationalklub', where the financial elite of reactionary Germany sat.⁶⁶¹ Zu Reventlow was a politician as well as a writer, like his sister, Franziska zu Reventlow, and editor in chief of the periodical *Der Reichswarte*. Zu Reventlow was an adept of *The Protocols of the Magi of Zion*, which mentioned a Jewish world conspiracy, and over the years became an increasingly strong supporter of Hitler and the NSDAP. ⁶⁶²

Hitler also met the Freikorps leader Walter Maria Stennes, who at the time was a member of the Berlin police force and would later become SA chief until internal tensions prevented his further career in 1932. He also came into contact with Helene Bechstein, born Capito in Düsseldorf, the wife of the wealthy piano manufacturer Edwin Bechstein, who was an enthusiastic supporter of the Nazis. She shared with Hitler a great passion for the composer Richard Wagner and she was motherly to him. Her salon at Johannisstrasse 6, which was heavily damaged in a bombing raid in 1944, became a breeding ground for the 'Alldeutschen'.⁶⁶³

It is interesting to note that Ludendorff places the encounter at a much later date, namely when he has already moved to Bavaria. In his memoirs, he writes that in the spring of 1921, around the funeral of Emperor Wilhelm's wife Auguste Viktoria, sometime in April, he received a visit from a 'fresh young man', as he described Rudolf Hess, who suggested that he get acquainted with Adolf Hitler.⁶⁶⁴ Probably, as we saw, the acquaintance had already taken place earlier in 'Haus Heck'. That Ludendorff indeed had an earlier acquaintance with Hitler is also shown by a statement of Hitler's military chief, Mayr, who immediately discharged Hitler from military service after his visit to Berlin, in order to give him access to active politics 'to please Ludendorff', he added.⁶⁶⁵ So, apparently there had been contact between Ludendorff and Mayr about Hitler's future role. The 'gap' in Ludendorff's memory may also be due to his desire to keep his role in the failed coup small, just as he was ignorant of Lenin and the Russian revolution. The historian Toland added to this remark by Mayr: '(Ludendorff's) wishes were still respected in the army'. [666]

The meeting with Hitler and the Bavarian 'Reaktion' was not the only consequence of the Kapp-Putsch. There was also a legal prosecution of the putschists. But this was of little consequence. The SPD politician Paul Levi, who operated on the far left of the SPD, expressed his displeasure about this. When Kapp and Von Lüttwizt putsched, and posed a much greater danger than the Spartakists, no one thought of putting down the putsch by force. Once again it was up to the forces that had formed the republic: 'the proletariat'.[667] A total of 170 officers, non-commissioned officers and men were dismissed from the army, but of the 700 criminal offences identified, 412 had been amnestied after two years, 176 criminal cases had been dropped, seven had not yet been sufficiently developed to be prosecuted, and Traugott von Jagow, the police commander, had been sentenced to five years imprisonment for his collaboration. [668]

Strangely enough, the heaviest blows fell on the side of the Weimar Republic. Gustav Noske was increasingly criticised from within the SPD ranks, where he was accused of having put too much faith in the military, as a result of which the Kapp-Putsch had surprised the government. He had to resign, even though Ebert initially tried to save his position. 'I bid him farewell with a moved heart', Ebert wrote to his political comrade, his 'deeds would not be forgotten by the history of his homeland'.[669] Otto Gessler, associated with the Deutschen Demokratischen Partei, and former mayor of Nuremberg, became his successor.

Cynically, the Chief of the Army, Generalmajor Reinhardt, the only senior officer who had clearly supported the Republic in its hour of need, also had to resign. His solidarity with Noske was fatal to him and it was Hans von Seeckt, the exponent of the wait-and-see military, the so-called 'Attentismus', who took over his position. Reichskanzler Bauer and the Prussian Minister of the Interior, Heine, also had to step down. The Social Democrat Hermann Mueller replaced Bauer. [670]

The gracious way in which the putschists got away with it, as well as the rolling of heads within the military apparatus and politics, had everything to do with the strike weapon deployed by the republicans. In the literature, the role of the strikes in the final decline of the Kapp-Putsch has been rather exaggerated. The strike only started on Monday the 15th and on the 16th, the putsch was already over. What was much worse was the fact that the strikes were an encouragement for new communist uprisings in large parts of Germany.

In the Ruhr area, 50,000 to 60,000 men were quickly mobilised for the 'Red Army'. This led to the curious situation where the Weimar politicians simply could not afford to be principled towards the rebellious Freikorps of the Kapp-

Putsch, because the soldiers were badly needed again. The historian Robert Gerwarth was right to note that the previous restraint in arms use during the Kapp-Putsch was abandoned here. Nevertheless, the 2nd and 3rd naval brigades, Ehrhardt and Loewenfeld, were still dismantled in March 1920. On 30 March, the last parade of Ehrhardt's 2nd marine brigade took place. The brigade was ultimately unsalvageable, but, in Ehrhardt's opinion, Noske had in any case also been overthrown. The men could keep the '7 Reichsmark financial aid', which had been introduced by Von Lüttwitz, and was clearly a conciliatory gesture from Berlin, which understood that the men might still be needed. Indeed, many Erhardt soldiers were to fight with Polish nationalists on the German side during the May 1921 riots in Upper Silesia. [671]

The government now made no direct use of the old Freikorps, but of so-called 'Zeitfreiwilligen', a kind of temporary soldiers. This violated Versailles rules, and when the Weimar troops had to operate in the neutral zone on the western border as well, France occupied the cities of Frankfurt and Darmstadt. Despite these setbacks, the new pact succeeded in putting down the communist revolt. In May 1920, peace slowly returned. [672]

The concept of the 'Zeitfreiwilligen' was a clever move by Noske's successor, Otto Gessler. Together with Von Seeckt, he succeeded in reducing the dependence on the Freikorps in this way, and to keep the available places in the army for reliable officers. The soldiers were now simply hired. Gessler himself played an important role in this. He was seen as an intermediate pope but developed into a professional who lasted almost eight years in this difficult political post. Ludendorff was comforted by the fact that by appointing Gessler, his rival Groener had at least been passed over.

Erich Ludendorff was among those who were legally spared from the Kapp-Putsch. Although he had been a key figure in the revolution and had been assigned an important role after the revolution, he was only heard as a witness in the legal settlement of the Kapp-Putsch. During this hearing, on 8 July 1920, Ludendorff had difficulty exonerating himself, which was not surprising.[673] In his memoirs, Ludendorff showed himself to be very unreasonable. According to Ludendorff, the government took the sharpest action against the putschists, which was contrary to reality. Even the trials for high treason against the leaders of the putsch ended in a scandal. The most important court sessions took place in December 1921, when Ludendorff was already sitting at the table with Hitler and other extreme nationalists planning the next putsch. Only Von Jagow was thus sentenced for a longer period, and even Ludendorff had to admit that during the sessions, many Reichswehrofficers who had opposed the Kapp-Putsch at the time 'sobered up' their incriminating statements.[674] Kapp himself also returned to Germany, but he died before he could be tried.

Ludendorff escaped. Due to the lack of prosecution, Ludendorff's role in the Kapp-Putsch has never been properly investigated. Consequently, an important fact went unnoticed, even among historians: Ludendorff's visit to his old comrade Paul von Hindenburg in Hanover just before the putsch. Ludendorff writes little about it in his memoirs, but they are unreliable - as we know. The memoirs are all about small talk, and that from a man who was really worried about the smallest things, and who could seldom escape from debates and arguments. In addition, the relationship with von Hindenburg was already under pressure and the visit was not self-evident.

It seems obvious that Ludendorff had gone to Hanover just before the Kapp-Putsch to carefully sound out what Von Hindenburg's position would be in case of a military coup. Since nothing was leaked from either side, it probably happened with a lot of circumlocution. Von Hindenburg's reaction is understandable. On the one hand, he wanted to spare his sensitive friend Ludendorff, on the other hand, he was already being probed for politics and did not want to alienate himself from the Republic. Of course, he also knew better than anyone that it would not be clear how all military district commanders would behave and a wait-and-see attitude was by far the smartest thing to do.

That Ludendorff's visit was not a spontaneous impulse is also evident from the few sentences he wrote in his memoirs. He claimed that he had made the appointment on a 'passage'. He also wrote that he 'seemed to remember that there was talk of a possible Reich Presidency for Von Hindenburg in the future'.[675] A very vague description for an important fact, especially considering Ludendorff's own political ambitions. It is evident that Ludendorff pretends to be more innocent than he was.

In the aftermath of the Kapp case, there was another case that went unnoticed, both by the legal authorities and by historians. Here, too, it was a minor line, this time in the memoirs of Ludendorff's confidant Wilhelm Breucker. When the Kapp-Putsch faltered, Ludendorff is said to have made one last attempt to reach an accommodation with the Communists. Breucker does not say with whom, how or what. At first sight, this seems no more than a curious anecdote, as Breucker himself emphasized, for he spoke of a 'grotesque attempt'.[676] On the other hand, Breucker could not oversee everything, and this rumour was in line with previous events, whereby thoughts naturally turn first to Lenin and the revolutionisation of Russia. Allies of Ludendorff, people like Hugo Stinnes, also operated across a wide field, keeping in close contact with radical forces in the trade unions. Adenauer's career showed the broad field of chess that sometimes had to be played on. There were also National Bolshevik tendencies within the Freikorps, and finally, there were also approaches by the Reichswehr to Soviet Russia.

Ludendorff noted in his memoirs towards the end of the Kapp-Putsch that there were still appointments with the trade unions in his diary. However, due to the developments, it did not happen again. Ludendorff was remarkably positive about his chances in the conversations with them, which was remarkable given their totally different political leanings. It seems that Stinnes, who had good contacts with trade union leaders, played a role here. A central role was played by trade union leader and Stinnes confidant Carl Legien, as Ludendorff's memoirs show. 'I knew him from my time at the military headquarters in Kreuznach', Ludendorff wrote, and 'he had a certain confidence in me'. He added that it was known that he was 'not hostile to workers'. [677]

In socio-economic terms, Ludendorff was somewhat of an exception within Germany's military elite. Perhaps his relatively simple background played a role in this. In any case, he was always quite immune to the temptations of nobility, even though Wilhelm II often toyed with these thoughts. In his criticism of Stinnes in his memoirs, the latter's overly critical attitude towards the workers also played a role, although this did not detract from the fact that he simply worked together with a Stinnes, as well as with his thoroughly aristocratic military colleagues. It is very well possible that Ludendorff had a conspiracy against the Weimar Republic in mind, that he hoped to get out of this cooperation. It is important to underline here that most of the resistance against the Kapp-Putsch did not come from the supporters of the Republic, but from the solidified socialist and communist opposition. They were fighting not so much for the republic, or against Kapp, but for their own ends. These radicals did not need Ebert's or Noske's encouragement to go on strike, but simply saw an opportunity here for their revolutionary plans.[678] In their view, Ebert and Noske could not succeed in restoring order. So, here was a mutual interest of left and right radicals against Weimar under the motto: 'the enemy of my enemy is my friend'.

Even in those days there was speculation, from the left as well, as to whether there was cooperation between right-wing and left-wing radicals during the Kapp-Putsch. In any case, there were similarities between their methods. The left-wing magazine *Vorwärts* believed that the Russian revolution was imitated by the right. They even spoke of right-wing Bolshevism. *Vorwärts* wondered: 'Were there secret agreements? As good as the military handiwork of the right was, as bad was their political performance. Ludendorff was kicked out in *Vorwärts*. Ludendorff will never learn the political trade',[679] was the opinion. It seems as if Margarethe Ludendorff was heard here. This did not alter the fact that there were positive undertones in the left-wing reporting on the Kapp Putschists. 'Only here lies the opportunity for the left Bolsheviks',[680] was believed, looking at the activism of the right. In May 1920, a month after the putsch, *Vorwärts* reported that there was sympathy for Bolshevism among the 'Baltikum' officers. The mutual contempt for democracy was central to this. 'They all sympathise with dictatorship'.[681] In those days, people also openly spoke of left-wing and right-wing 'Kapp-putschists'. So, the gap was clearly not as wide as one would think at first glance.

Whether there was also direct contact with Soviet Russia is not clear. The problem is that such contacts, like the ones mentioned above, were so politically incorrect and purely a result of momentary pacts that it was in everyone's interest to conceal them. Ludendorff and his supporters talked to diplomats from various countries before the Kapp-Putsch, and this may have included contacts with Soviet Russia. Through the many 'White' contacts, such connections were easily made. It has been claimed that contacts with Soviet Russia were made through Trebitsch-Lincoln, but this has not been proven.[682] Hugo Stinnes demonstrated that there were no fundamental objections to working with the communists in the Ludendorff camp. It is known that only ten months after the Kapp-Putsch, he already sat down with the Soviet authorities to see what his economic empire could mean for the (re)construction of the Russian economy.[683]

A source is again to be found in Breucker. In the appendices of his book *Die Tragik Ludendorffs*, there is a very interesting passage. Here, Ludendorff reacted to an accusation against the Kapp-Putschists that, just like in 1917, they wanted to revolutionise foreign countries for their own benefit. In this case, it was about supporting the communists in Poland. This is piquant, since the Ludendorff camp apparently had an even greater hatred of an independent Greater Poland than it did of a Bolshevik Russia on its eastern border. In May 1920, a discussion arose in the national camp about a donation of 700,000 'Reichsmark' from Geheimrat Othmar Strauss to Pabst. The latter was supposed to use this money for a Bolshevisation of Poland, but in the end had used the money for the Kapp-Putsch. To Breucker, Ludendorff reported that he knew nothing about this money donation. 'It is out of the question that P.(Pabst) has used this money for the 'Nationale Vereinigung' or for the Kapp-Putsch', Ludendorff wrote in his letter of 10 May 1920.[684] In any case, Ludendorff pretended in the letter to Breucker that he thought it was an inconceivable assertion. 'I have always strongly disapproved of the combination of the right with Bolshevism',[685] he wrote. That Strauss, together with people like Rechberg and the ironmonger Otto Wolff, supported (foreign) political forces was a fact. Strauss was, among other things, associated with the financing of the Russian revolutionary Fedor

Vinberg.[686] Ludendorff's letter also contradicted Breucker's remark about Ludendorff's 'grotesque attempt' to cooperate with the communists. Ludendorff himself made a reservation in his letter of 10 May as well: 'If he (Pabst) has done it, he thinks differently from me, despite his loyalty he is also his own lord', and he added tellingly 'und soll es immer bleiben'.[687] With this, Ludendorff underlined his 'official position' as he did in his memoirs about his own part in the Kapp-Putsch: that of 'innocent' spectator. Reading the biography of Pabst by Klaus Gietinger, it seems unlikely that the communist eater Pabst wanted to support the communist revolution and Russian occupation of Poland. It was a fact that there were such noises, among others from Von Seeckt. Catholic Poland was hated by the ostelbian Protestant officers.[688]

What we also know is that the Reichswehr followed a multi-track policy and had contacts with Moscow. Here, too, there were sharp ideological differences and conflicts of interest, but there were also practical agreements of interest which offered opportunities for cooperation. In retrospect, we can judge that the more sectarian Ludendorff's actions became, the more principled his views became. This was a logical consequence of the fact that his ideas no longer needed to be tested. In this period, both the Weimar-politicians and the men around Ludendorff were still in the middle of the power politics arena and the options were being weighed up one by one.

Both Soviet Russia and Germany, both outside the League of Nations, were distrusted by the outside world and were economically and militarily curtailed as a result. Already in the winter of 1920-1921, secret meetings took place between Soviet representatives and German soldiers. On 6 May 1921, this finally led to a trade agreement and on 16 April 1922 to the Treaty of Rapallo. Officially, the latter was a trade agreement, but in the secret documents to the treaty were also all military agreements. The Soviet Union could very well use German military technology, the Germans needed raw materials and training possibilities, for those parts of the Reichswehr that did not officially exist, the so-called 'black Reichswehr'. Piquant was the fact that part of the secret negotiations that led to all this took place in Von Schleicher's private residence, but of course Von Seeckt and the new chancellor since May 1921, Joseph Wirth, knew about it. Among the visitors to von Schleicher's private residence were the revolutionary Karl Radek, whose real name was Sobelsohn and who had been on the train with Lenin, and Leonid Krassin, the chairman of the Soviet Foreign Trade Committee. The fact that this 'black' expansion of the Reichswehr also had to be financed by black money was intriguing. These financiers included (besides Thiessen and Krupp, among others) Hugo Stinnes.[689]

Another practical motive for Von Seeckt to cooperate with Moscow, which was also shared by Ludendorff, was his concern about Poland. In a 'Denkschrift' from September 1922, Von Seeckt's interference went very far in politics, when he wrote that the German ambassador in Moscow, Brockdorff-Rantzau, would not be the right man in the right place. Von Seeckt was of the opinion that German-Russian relations were so important that a real 'draufgänger' had to be in this position. Von Seeckt saw Poland as a French bastion and was afraid that in the event of a future conflict with France, the Poles would attack Germany from behind. Poland could therefore be held in check by a good relationship with Moscow. Gessler turned a blind eye to this far-reaching interference, and defended it by pointing out that Von Seeckt was still under the impressions of the Great-Polish agitation in Silesia and Lithuania. Ebert was more reticent, Wirth put little in Von Seeckt's way. [690]

Important for the political future of Ludendorff and his future ally Hitler was the fact that politics never fully got a grip on the military. The Reichswehr only accepted defence ministers who had their interests at heart. Thanks to secret funds, the Reichswehr was independent of politics to a certain extent and, finally, there was an unwritten right of veto of 'das Militar' over politics if their interests were at stake.[691] The Reichswehr was a weak link within the young republic, and proved willing to serve various lords if the price was right. Hitler would prove willing to pay that price, even with the blood of his own SA men.

It did not yet come to that, but Ludendorff took an important step. He decided to leave Berlin and to go to Bavaria, to Munich, the city that was to become 'Hauptstadt der Bewegung' (capital of movement). This period, so soon after the Kapp-Putsch, Ludendorff described in his memoirs as a transitional period. Familiarities from the past were fading even more, and not all new beginnings were yet visible. He disapproved of democracy, he said, but he was also no longer in favour of a return to the monarchy. Dictatorship was the right way to go, but Ludendorff looked for a way to win the people over to it. 'Coercion alone cannot unite a people', he believed with some realism. 'Doubt and more doubt came over me,' he wrote. [692]

He also saw his own limitations. Due to his extremely busy life before the First World War and in the years that followed, he had not had the time to study domestic politics or economic issues in depth. He wanted to make up for this in a quieter period, or so he had decided. He also questioned the roots of his own ideas, Christianity, and became more aware of his racial heritage, which he had ignored too much. 'In these days I was national',[693] he said, but he was on the verge of conversion; the völkische Ludendorff presented himself.

With this, his world view became more and more mythical, just as he would soon escalate his own role in world history. There was no better 'Umfeld' for the development of this ideology than Bavaria, where the young Hitler was preparing to storm the Berlin offices from Munich. He would proceed 'with the assurance of a sleepwalker'.[694] Ludendorff, too, would soon overcome his doubts and take up the march together: the general and the corporal; the Prussian Protestant and the Austrian Catholic, an alliance as unnatural as it was fatal. 'The people's soul has raised its voice', Ludendorff noted in his memoirs, 'but millions have not yet heard it'.[695] The racial heritage had emerged from the subconscious, he believed, and descended into consciousness.[696] This was not only the result of moving to Bavaria or meeting Adolf Hitler, but also of getting to know the woman who would later become his second wife, Dr Mathilde von Kemnitz. Ludendorff had found his 'Blavatsky' who would unveil the riddle of the world to him.

CHAPTER 14

The Völkisch movement

'I need to get out and be alone. What has the world got to do with where I am? I am a private man... but unfortunately my name has become a burden'.

Ludendorff to Breucker

In the beautiful villa suburb Prinz Ludwig Höhe near Munich, Ludendorff found his new home, now that the ground in Berlin had become too hot for him. A beautiful property was offered to him for rent by 'Geheimrat' industrialist Dr Fritz Hornschuch from Kulmbach Bavaria, and Ludendorff made use of it. From his garden he had a magnificent view of the deeply carved valley of the river Isar. Ludendorff enjoyed it, but would never quite get used to this landscape, which was strange to him. The longing for Prussian soil remained.[697]

The final move took place in August 1920. Ludendorff's thoughts were only half way through his new home. The geopolitical developments in Europe kept him in their grip. The most important ones were taking place at Germany's eastern border. While the Russian civil war started to benefit Lenin, now the Poles and the Communists were fighting as well. Especially this last development worried Ludendorff. He saw in Pilsudsky's advance eastward the long arm of Paris. French politicians would like to see Ukraine as Warsaw's 'lapdog'.[698] For a moment, it did indeed look like this when Polish troops entered Kiev. Fortunately, the communists recovered and pushed deep west, approaching the borders of the German empire. Now a new opportunity also threatened German communists, but eventually the front stabilised after French help for the Poles.

'It was at the cutting edge,' Ludendorff said in his memoirs.[699] It surprised and annoyed him that so few Germans had an eye for the major developments in the East, let alone for the geopolitical developments between Turkey and Greece, in which the influence of Kemal Pascha, Atatürk, was growing in the first mentioned country. Ludendorff still felt misunderstood, as in the days before the 'guns of August', when no one seemed to care about the 'watered-down' Schlieffen Plan.

Still, many Germans had enough of their own worries, and that also applied to Bavaria. The political climate there had become seriously radicalised since November 1918. After the murder of left-wing politician Kurt Eisner by Count Arco-Valley, who was affiliated with the right-wing Thule Society, on 21 February 1919, the region had endured the horrors of the Raden Republic and the white reaction. USPD and anarchists supported the Raden Republic, but the communists took the lead on 14 April. The socialist government moved to Bamberg and sided with the 'Reaktion', as Noske and Ebert had done. When 'Freikorps' and 'Heimwehren' came to Munich, ten hostages, all members of the Thule-Gesellschaft, were executed in the Luitpold Gymnasium. After this 'Geiselmord', the whole thing was over. 'Pardon will not happen' was the watchword for the reactionary troops of Major Von Unruh, Von Oven's chief of staff. The Gardekavallerie-Schützen-Division of Pabst and his men announced that finding weapons automatically meant the death penalty. A trail of blood was drawn through Bavaria. [700]

Hundreds were shot 'on the run'. 'Die mächtigen Generale wollen kein Verständigung', writer, revolutionary and 'Red Army captain' Ernst Toller noted in his diary, and so it was. Only through great efforts of well-known Germans, such as Heinrich Mann, could Toller be prevented from receiving the death penalty. Less fortunate were many other revolutionary leaders, such as Eugen Levine and Gustav Landauer, who paid for the Raden adventure with their lives.[701]

After the Kapp-Putsch in Northern Germany, a further political shift to the right had become apparent in Bavaria. Ludendorff had access to the most important political men in the region: Prime Minister Gustav von Kahr and police chief Ernst Pöhner. The man who took care of this was Oberst Bauer, who had reconnected with his comrades in arms after his period with Trebitsch-Lincoln in Hungary. The old Kapp camp also included Captain Ehrhardt, who had arranged accommodation in Munich for some of his old (naval) men and continued the struggle more below ground than above it. In his memoirs, Ludendorff distanced himself from Erhardt's secret operations, which reminded him too much of the 'Secret Orders', such as the Freemasons, who evaded supervision. Ludendorff considered these to be non-transparent organisations, which did not always serve the 'patriotic cause'. In the case of Ehrhardt, he thought that the captain served more and more Bavarian-Catholic affairs, by which Ludendorff insinuated Bavarian small-particularism and separatism.[702]

As of old, "das Militär" and the veterans organisations were Ludendorff's connections in the reactionary camp. This was not a homogeneous group in Bavaria. There were small-particularist forces who wanted above all to put Bavaria and the house of Wittelsbach on the map; 'Alldeutschen' who were in favour of Deutschtum, supporters of the restoration of the house of Hohenzollern, underground fighting squads of Ehrhardt and associates, and there were the Nazis, all fishing in the conservative pond. Ludendorff, who liked to think of himself as above the parties, straddled these forces, in the course of which he would increasingly align himself with the Nazis and embrace political anti-Semitism.

One of the driving forces in the military camp in Bavaria was Crown Prince Rupprecht, the son of King Ludwig III. Rupprecht had an eye for ceremony and looked like a prince. Although he was considered a 'Freigeist', Ludendorff soon realised that Rupprecht was above all working for the Wittelbach cause and for the restoration of the Bavarian monarchy. During the First World War Ludendorff had already noticed that Rupprecht was less of a Roman Catholic than his father, but that he had been disturbed by Berlin's centralism. True, Rupprecht had always been positive towards Kaiser Wilhelm II, but now that the Kaiser was in the Netherlands, he seemed to see opportunities for the House of Wittelsbach. Ludendorff, who was brought up in the Bismarckian 'Kulturkampf' of Protestantism against Catholicism, distrusted Rupprecht and emphatically mentioned his stay in the Spanish (read: Habsburg-Catholic) embassy in Brussels during the period of Bavarian revolution. In Ludendorff's mind, the image of Bavarian separatism had arisen, which, like Rhineland separatism, could be a real danger. Was Rupprecht a Roman counter-candidate for the Hohenzollerns? For Ludendorff, the possibility of a Bavarian secession from Germany was an abomination. Ludendorff turned out to be very suspicious of everything ultramontane.

How real was Ludendorff's fear of a Bavarian 'Alleingang'? First of all, let us note that already during the war things did not go well between Rupprecht and Ludendorff. Ludendorff thought that Rupprecht was 'not a military man by birth' and that he experienced the war mainly as a burden.[703] This attitude led to a pessimism which Ludendorff considered harmful for a man in Rupprecht's position. After all, the leadership had to radiate confidence. Ludendorff also distrusted the anti-Prussian sentiments in the Catholic south. Author Rudolf Schrikers, in his book *Rotmord über München (Death by Munich)*, on the occasion of the communist revolution, called not only for 'hatred of Jews' and 'hatred of communists', but also for hatred of Prussia.[704] In the Catholic South, anti-Protestantism was in some circles as salacious as anti-Semitism. Rupprecht had said he 'regretted' that Ludendorff had come to Bavaria.

The fear that Rupprecht might be a roomy alternative to the Hohenzollerns was provided by Ludendorff's experiences with other high-ranking military officers in Bavaria, such as with General Krafft von Delmensingen, who did military historical research and turned out to be an important supporter of Rupprecht. Von Delmensingen had been Rupprecht's Chief of Staff during the war and later commanded a cavalry corps and units on the Isonzo. Ludendorff had written a letter of recommendation for obtaining the *Max Joseph Order* for Krafft von Delmensingen, which in Bavaria was almost equal to an elevation to the peerage, but their relationship had never been cordial.[705] In October 1920, Ludendorff attended the annual day of officers with the Max Joseph Order in the Michael Hofkirche in Munich and he met many Bavarian officers at 'Totensonntag'. He noticed that Rupprecht had confidants among many Catholic officers. Ludendorff's distrust grew as he realised that Bavarian nationalism was a political force.

Bavarian nationalism was not limited to Rupprecht and some of the generals. The government of Eugen Ritter von Knilling and the Northern Bavarian government of von Kahr were known as conservative, but the word Bavarian could be added to them. Born in 1862 in Weissenburg, Bavaria, Gustav von Kahr did not make a very 'völkische impression' on Ludendorff. 'He was small, a busybody and not very Nordic', Ludendorff said in his memoirs. Ludendorff was outraged that he was not invited to take part in a parade of the 'Heimwehr' and this fed his growing conspiratorial thoughts.[706] Police chief Ernst Pöhner was 'tall and with energetic lines in his face', but, according to Ludendorff, was equally committed to the Wittelbach royalty. Von Knilling had followed in Von Kahr's footsteps from 12 September 1921, after the latter had resigned in protest when the 'Einwohnerwehren', similar to the Freikorps, had to be disbanded under pressure from Berlin (and the Entente).

It was not a home game for Ludendorff in Bavaria, and he believed that the driving force in the background was the 'Bayerische Volkspartei' of 'Geheimrat' Heim, where Ludendorff saw connections with the nuncio Eugenio Parcelli (later Pope Pius XII) and Cardinal Michael Faulhaber, the 'long arm of the Vatican'. This was a typical characteristic of Ludendorff. When he formed his opinion, he was consistent to the bone. In these exaggerations, he overlooked quite a few nuances. Thus, the same distrusted Pöhner provided Ludendorff with a car and driver in order to be able to respond to the fast incoming requests for performances and lectures from all over Bavaria. The 'icon' of '14-'18 had been discovered and people wanted to hear the general speak. Ludendorff had chartered his old confidant Oberleutnant von Grolmann as his driver.[707]

The other military force besides Rupprecht and his supporters that belonged to Ludendorff's 'Umfeld' were the Freikorps and 'Heimwehren', or their successor organisations. In the power vacuum created by the shrinking army (Versailles), they played a larger role in politics than desirable. The police and judiciary, as we also saw with Pöhner, often turned a blind eye. The German Judges' Association had 12,000 members, but only 400 of them belonged to the organisation for social-democratic judges. The judiciary consisted mainly of conservative imperial judges in a new era.

As a result of this policy, politics became criminalised. Both left and right disposed of political opponents. The right did this with the support of a turning away legal apparatus and invoked Noske's 'Schiesserlass' of 9 March 1919, in which Noske gave permission to resist the Raden revolutionaries by force of arms. The 'Fememurder' was born, and would reach a sad climax with the murder of Walther Rathenau, at that time Foreign Minister. Germany was rocked by a series of murders carried out by soldiers of the Gardekavallerie-Schützendivision and Freikorps Lützow. These were simple people, such as a cigar trader, who was shot because he allegedly had a weapon.[708] Infamous too was the so-called 'sailor's murder' in Berlin, December 1919. Thirty soldiers of the Volksmarinedivision were shot here on the orders of officer Otto Marloh, a confidant of Von Lüttwitz, who was later involved in the Kapp-Putsch, purely because they were suspected of left-wing ideas. The white terror in the Ruhr area that followed the unsuccessful Kapp-Putsch and crushed the uprisings was also a spectre. There were chilling examples of terror. Seven workers had to dig their own graves while singing '*Ub immer Treu und Redlichkeit*', after which they were shot.[709] 'Reichskommissar' Carl Severing, from Westphalia, reported that even suspects were dragged out of hospitals and executed summarily.[710]

Gradually, this open violence was replaced by the underground murders. Carl Mertens, active for years in extreme nationalist circles, told in the left-oriented magazine *Weltbühne* that 'whoever was suspected was already condemned'. Left-wing opponents and traitors were dealt with. Murder, incitement to suicide, staging or causing accidents were committed, according to Mertens.[711] Not only the judiciary, but also high-ranking officers were complicit in these actions. General Franz von Epp thought that the 'Fememurder' was a 'sittliches Recht'.[712] Von Epp referred to a time-honoured tradition of 'Fememurder' in Germany. In the absence of central authority, this phenomenon had existed for a long time. The oldest descriptions went back to the 13th century.[713] The phenomenon disappeared in the 18th century, to return now. The *Feme* were always dominated by secret, furtive murders. In the fifteenth century, the cult around this phenomenon led to the creation of secret societies of initiates in the *Feme secret*. So-called 'knowers' could become members of the *Feme-*'court', but had to execute a sentence themselves if necessary. The noose was the most common punishment.

An important motivation behind the 'Fememur murders' was a direct 'military interest'. The Treaty of Versailles had severely curtailed the Reichswehr and Freikorps, and reactionary soldiers who did not want to know about the 'Erfüllungspolitik' concealed weapons in secret, in order to evade the Versailles provisions. Traitors to these secret depots could not count on any understanding. Even politically ignorant women who did not speak up were ruthlessly murdered. The fate of the maid Maria Sandmeyer was shocking. She had discovered an illegal weapons stockpile at her boss' house in Holzen Castle near Wertingen. Since 7 August 1920, it was forbidden for private persons to possess weapons. She decided to report it, but it ended up with a reactionary civil servant. He reported the matter and shortly afterwards the barely 20-year-old woman was found strangled in a park in Munich. Around her neck was a plaque with the text: 'Du Schandweib hast verraten dein Vaterland, du wurdest gerichtet von der Schwarzen Hand'.[714]

An important role in the 'Fememur murders' was played by the actions of the Ordnungs Celle (O.C.), which operated under the name Consul, and which was commanded by Ludendorff's fellow Kapp-putschist Hermann Ehrhardt. The name Consul was derived from the pseudonym, Consul Eichmann (what's in a name) that he initially used. Ehrhardt's organisation was closest to the secret organisation that had existed around the 'Fememurders' in the fifteenth century. Only few people were 'knowing'. His former adjutant, Hartmund Plaas, wrote in his diary about this period 'We could never quite fathom Ehrhardt's thinking. It was always like that. One sacrifices oneself and does not know for how long or for what'.[715] After a brief period in hiding on the Lüneburger Heide, Ehrhardt had settled in Bavaria. The core of his confidants formed the 'Bund ehemaliger Ehrhardt offiziere', chaired by his former chief of staff, Alfred Hoffmann. This group had been formed on the eve of the disbandment of the 2nd and 3rd marine brigade after the failed Kapp-Putsch. This group had two specific objectives, firstly to try to keep the mutual relationship intact. There had to remain a 'reservoir' of reliable men for the national cause. Secondly, they were looking for a financial-economic existence. A handful of Ehrhardt men found shelter on estates in Pomerania, where they helped put down farm labour riots, while the majority went to Bavaria. Here, Ehrhardt set up a front organisation, the so-called 'Holz-Verwertungs-Gesellschaft mbH', at Trautenwolf Street no. 8 in Munich.

Ehrhardt thus operated in a very shadowy area. Ludendorff kept his distance, possibly for ideological reasons (Catholicism) but also possibly for political and judicial reasons. After all, Ludendorff could not afford to be associated with the 'Fememurders'. The last word has not been spoken about the truth of Ehrhartdt's flirtation with small-particularism. It cannot be ruled out, but Ehrhartt followed winding roads to his goal. On the one hand, he probably accepted Bavarian nationalist support (after all, social and financial survival was high on the Consul's list of priorities), but he also maintained contacts with the 'Prussian' Reichswehr, for whom he kept an eye on the 'turbulent' Bavaria.

Wilhelm Canaris played a prominent role in this. He had initially been arrested after the Kapp-Putsch, but covered himself up by an order from Trotha, which dropped a treason charge against him. He was transferred to the Kiel naval base, where he reunited with Ehrhardt's confidants. The cunning Canaris, who abhorred the 'Erfüllungspolitik' mainly due to monarchist sentiments, got his hands on extensive (and Versailles prohibited) arms depots, with which he started a lucrative trade. Through the Danish company Daug & Co, he supplied secret weapons far beyond the German borders (to China). Part of the proceeds were passed on to Ehrhardt. [716]

Finally, there were the Nazis. They quickly gained ground and would become an important focal point in the Völkisch camp for Ludendorff. Not in the least because many soldiers were also involved in Hitler's party. Hitler had been catapulted into politics by the military and given (political) 'freedom' immediately after the failed Kapp-Putsch. The support from military circles was understandable. They wanted a 'Regierung der Tat', feared the 'Erfüllungspolitik' and were afraid of Bavarian separatism and communism. In this sense, the soldiers who supported the NSDAP were men with a Great-German point of view, so there was a natural alliance with Ludendorff. Important names in the Nazi camp were Hauptmann Rudolf Berthold and Hauptmann Eduard Dietl, the latter, an officer born in Bad Aibling, who would become 'the hero of Narvik' during the Second World War, because of his energetic action in Norway. Later in the war he was killed in a plane crash. Dietl was prepared at a very early stage to provide 'ushers' for the many speeches the NSDAP organised in Greater Munich. This reveals a direct collaboration with the Reichswehr, even after Hitler's demise from their ranks. Dietl was at that time company commander in the 19. Bayerischen Infanterie Regiment, and confidant of Franz Ritter von Epp.[717] Dietl's political commitment also came to the fore as he worked to free Anton Graf Arco auf Valley, the murderer of Kurt Eisner. [718]

Berthold was also an important liaison between the interest groups around Ludendorff and the NSDAP. Berthold had been a pilot in World War I and was a recipient of the high award *Pour le mérite*. After the war, Berthold had emerged as Freikorps leader and commander of the notorious 'Eiserne Schar' unit. During the preparations for the Kapp-Putsch, Ludendorff's confidant Waldemar

Pabst and Berthold had also consulted one another. Berthold had offered to support Ehrhardt's unit with his men.

The political line between Hitler's teacher Dietrich Eckart and the Kapp Putschists also went back further than is generally assumed. It is not widely known that Eckart had already visited Kapp before the putsch and had given him tips for measures after the coup. For example, he advised Kapp to take the Jews in Northern Germany into 'Schutzhaft', in order to secure the revolution. These anti-Semitic measures even went too far for Kapp, but they do show how interwoven the net was between politics, völkisch and anti-Semitic thinking and 'das Militär'.[719] Eckart 'knew' Kapp as a reader of the heavily anti-Semitic and reactionary *Auf gut Deutsch* magazine, which he published. When the Kapp-Putsch failed, Eckart believed that this was due to Kapp's 'cowardly and half-hearted behaviour', referring to his reticence towards the Jews.[720]

The Nazis represented the Great-German idea in the conservative camp, thus connecting Bavaria with the right wing in Northern Germany. The position of the Nazis towards the House of Hohenzollern was also interesting, with which Ludendorff had a problematic relationship. In search of legitimacy, one of the reasons why a good relationship with Ludendorff was high on Hitler's list, the way to the blue blood was kept open as well. The musical chairs around the emperor's grandson, Louis Ferdinand, was a striking example of this.[721]

But the knee-jerk reaction to the blue blood was limited. It was assumed that the heyday of the nobility was over. Hitler's vision was strongly social-darwinian. In March 1925, he told author Adolf Bartels that Kaiser Wilhelm II had 'reacted instinctively' to the upheavals of 1918. He objected to the succession system, which allowed weak brothers to gain seats on the plush sofa.[722] Where the nobility had worshipped the 'blue blood', the new order had created the 'new nobility', a nobility of 'blood and soil', as Richard Walther Darré, Hitler's 'agrarian philosopher' described it. The horrors of the First World War had everything to do with this realisation. A 'trench aristocracy' had emerged. The Nazis linked this to ariosophy, the belief in a new, Aryan man, to the völkisch world view. The 'new guard' also included the 'Grandseigneurs', men like Hugo Stinnes, who also believed that the Wittelbachers and Hohenzollerns were dead and who gathered in their 'Herrenklubs' under a smoke of good cigars and cognac.

The nobility had their own reasons for getting involved with the Nazis. They hoped for the restoration of the monarchy. There were also similarities in their thinking. Both parties were characterised by an anti-bourgeois element and often an anti-Semitic attitude. Shulamit Volkkov spoke of an anti-Semitic code among the (German) nobility. The historian Jonathan Petropoulus pointed out that the nobility was especially disappointed in both the imperial era (Wilhelminian Germany) and the republican era, with its political turmoil. The 'tradition-bound' nobility sought a way out. Lothar Machtan spoke of a 'flight to the front'. Hitler's anti-communism also played an important role. August Wilhelm (*Auwi*), one of Kaiser Wilhelm II's sons, and Friedrich Wend Fürst zu Eulenburg-Hertefeld, the eldest son of Wilhelm II's confidant Philip Fredrick (Phili) Fürst zu Eulenburg-Hertefeld, sent out a letter to large landowners and nobility in which they expressed a pro-Nazi opinion. The message was: 'If we do not want communism, there is no choice but to join the party (the NSDAP)'.[723]

Hitler, advised by 'Putzi' Hanfstaengl, did his best to gain a foothold in wealthy circles. It was striking that he was especially popular with the female public, and not only with rich, more bourgeois descendants, such as Winifred Wagner, Helene Bechstein and Elsa Bruckmann, but also with noble ladies of important families, such as Princess Marie Adelheid zur Lippe, Princess Lucy zu Sayn-Wittgenstein, Princess Ingeborg-Alix zu Sachsen-Meiningen and others. At the end of 1934, 147 members of German royal houses were registered as NSDAP members.[724] It has been joked that the Nazis 'had no shortage of princes'.[725] Hermine von Reuss, the Kaiser's second wife, was also initially positive towards the Nazis.[726] Crown Prince Wilhelm travelled to Germany when the Feldherrnhalle-Putsch was in progress, in an attempt to represent the interests of the royal family.[727] What is significant for the Bavarian political field is the observation that the Prussian (Protestant) ostelbian nobility was much more strongly represented by the Nazis than the Bavarian (Catholic) nobility. There were many big names active within the NSDAP, from well-known families such as Arnim, Bassewitz, Bismarck, Bothmer, Bredow, Goltz, Kleist, Puttkamer, Von Schlieffen, Schweinitz, Victinghoff, Wangenheim, Wrangel, Zitzewitz and many others.[728] Typical Bavarian family names such as Arentin, Franckenstein and Leonrod were absent from the NSDAP membership list. The Prussian nobility thought Great-German and were therefore on the same line as Ludendorff. In the Night of the Long Knives, in which the SA was swept into power, many noblemen later saw their 'right'. The NSDAP chose the traditional forces, not the revolutionaries. They were wrong about that. Hitler was a balancer, balancing between revolution and reaction, and would always use the divide and rule principle.

In reality, Hitler shared Ludendorff's antipathy towards those whom Robert Ley would later refer to as "those blue-blooded swine" (statement after the Von Stauffenberg attack), but Hitler was more realistic, in as much as he did not openly offend the Church, he calmed down the anticlerical Nazi ideologue

Alfred Rosenberg, and he kicked out the faithless Artur Dinter. Hitler kept his options open. In the early years of the movement, when Hitler needed all the support he could get, he was in regular contact with Crown Prince Rupprecht. These contacts were maintained by Max Erwin von Scheubner-Richter, among others. As the NSDAP grew stronger, the distance to the monarchists increased. Kaiser Wilhelm II in Doorn later looked back on a visit by Hitler confidant Hermann Göring with such bitterness that he exclaimed: 'Burn the chair on which this man sat'.

Initial pact negotiations between the NSDAP and Rupprecht's cabinet eventually turned into open combat, leading to a legal battle between Hitler and Joseph Maria Graf Soden-Fraunhofen, a confidant and chief of cabinet of Crown Prince Rupprecht. During the Feldherrnhalle-Putsch, Rudolf Hess had this man arrested without mercy and taken hostage. He labelled him as 'a missionary of the Vatican'.

According to Ludendorff's memoirs, it was Rudolf Hess - 'a fresh, youthful man' - who made the 'first contact' between himself and Adolf Hitler.[729] Hess told Ludendorff about Hitler, the NSDAP and the party's 'striving for freedom'. Of course, in the jargon of Ludendorff and the NSDAP, freedom did not mean parliamentary democracy, but freedom from the yoke of their enemies. According to Ludendorff's memoirs, the meeting with Hess and then Hitler in Bavaria would have taken place around April 1921. However, like the uncertainty about the possible Berlin meeting between Hitler and Ludendorff, some questions remain.

From correspondence of Rudolf Hess, compiled by Wolf Rüdiger Hess and released in 1987, we know that the first contact between the Hitler camp, namely Hess and Ludendorff, already took place in September 1920, so about eight months before Ludendorff's report in his memoirs. It was then a written contact, about which a very enthusiastic Rudolf Hess reported to his family, Klara and Fritz Hess. In this letter, Hess recounted the amount of work that had been done within the party leadership to draw up a party programme. He then wrote that he had 'written to Ludendorff about the whole matter'. He continued: 'I also sent him the programme [...] to my great joy he replied to me that same day in a nice and very interesting, long letter. He expressed his warmest sympathy for the cause and he also elaborated on several points in an approving manner. Since he asked for discretion, I cannot say more. Unfortunately, he cannot go to public meetings. He asked me to report on the movement regularly'. Hess added a PS to this letter, in which he wrote: 'L. [Ludendorff] sent me two more brochures, which follow the same [purpose] and are published in Berlin. Please do not speak about it, about what I wrote to L. [Ludendorff]'. About what, 'über was', Hess wrote in his original letter in italics. The letter was dated 22 September 1920 and was sent to the family in Reicholdsgrün.[730]

This letter is an important document to understand Ludendorff's post-war role. From Hess' letter, we can read that Ludendorff officially did not (yet) want to be linked to the NSDAP. In fact, the devil would come out of the box only during the Feldherrnhalle-Putsch. That would be the moment of openly declaring one's colours. Until then, Ludendorff operated from the wings. Even to his family, Hess was reluctant to reveal anything. It is also interesting to learn that Ludendorff supported the party programme of the NSDAP ("warmest sympathy"), so that we get an important insight into the ideas that Ludendorff stood for at that time. In his memoirs, Ludendorff himself characterised his Berlin period as nationalistic and signalled the transition to the völkische phase in Bavaria.[731] Before we look at what the party programme meant in that early hour of the NSDAP, and what the völkische movement to which Ludendorff began to count himself stood for, we must address another question first: how likely is it that it took another eight months after this long and cordial letter from Ludendorff before there was a real contact with Hitler?

There had been contact before. In 1920, the Nazi Otto Strasser, who later fell out of favour, was invited by his brother Gregor Strasser to Landshut, Bavaria, to meet Ludendorff and Hitler. Gregor, a pharmacist, was active in the Freikorps (Epp/Röhm) and was thus also in contact with Ludendorff and Hitler.[732] Some nice anecdotes about the meeting have been preserved. In those days, Otto Strasser was under the influence of the upcoming communism, and had heard nothing but bad things about Hitler. Otto was already with Gregor when the guests arrived. A car drove up and Otto Strasser was waiting at the top of the stairs. Otto Strasser immediately jumped to his feet. He introduced himself with rank and service number. Ludendorff was, wrote Strasser biographer Günter Bartsch, 'vom Scheitel bis zur Sohle General'.[733] Otto Strasser felt how 'a tremendous willpower flowed from this man'.[734] In contrast, Hitler, who said little other than 'Sehr wohl Exzellenz' and 'Wie Exzellenz meinen', came across as weak. 'He has a face like thousands'.[735]

It was the 'party-less' Ludendorff who spoke about the future of the party. So, once again, we must read Ludendorff's memoirs with some caution, especially since we know that the relationship between Ludendorff and the Nazis later deteriorated. What we do know is that the meeting between Ludendorff and Hitler was well received by Ludendorff. In his memoirs, he reported that he expressed himself positively about Hitler from that moment on. He described Hitler as a man with 'compelling willpower'.[736] Ludendorff had no lack of it himself. The combination of the forces of these two men would result in the second right-wing revolution. Ludendorff also seemed to realise that he could not rely solely on the power of the gun. The Kapp-Putsch had taught him that popular support was needed, and for this, politics was required. At his meeting with the Strasser brothers in the autumn of 1920, he put it this way: 'A general needs a strategy, a political movement needs a party programme'. [737]

The 'twenty-five point programme' of the DAP/NSDAP had already come into being at the end of 1919 and was first completed around December 1919. The historian Ian Kershaw believes that the Thule Society's Anton Drexler and Hitler himself drew up the programme's points. The most important themes were: a great Germany, authoritarian leadership, colonies, anti-Semitism, abolition of 'interest slavery', protection of the middle class, curbing the freedom of the press and land reform.[738] The church and communism were not mentioned in this first version. The programme was partly a real wish-list, and partly filled with political reality. Hitler did not want to alienate the church, but he did want to win over the communists, which had also been one of the first aims of the Thule Society, and for which the DAP had been created.

Shortly afterwards, on 24 February 1920, the first test of this party programme took place. While people in Berlin were busy planning the Kapp-Putsch, Hitler gave a stirring speech in the Hofbräuhaus in Munich, which was breathlessly followed by a full house. Kershaw noted that the speech was well received, despite its specifically anti-Semitic tendencies. A scandal of 'hang the Jews' sounded through the hall that evening. Of course, the 'Erfüllungspolitik' also got its due, led by Matthias Erzberger,[739] who had taken on the thankless task of negotiating the strict provisions of the Treaty of Versailles.

Ludendorff therefore knew with whom he was dealing. The man who had mobilised the Zionists in Kaunas for the Great-German cause found himself in the waters of political anti-Semitism. It was a whimsical twist of fate that Heinrich Himmler, the later Reichsführer SS, and Rudolf Höss, the later commandant of Auschwitz, would meet for the first time in Ludendorff's house. In his book *Krieghetze und Völkermorden*, published in 1928, Ludendorff called Matthias Erzberger 'Jew, Jesuit and Freemason in one person'. At that time, Erzberger had been resting in German soil for years. On 26 August 1921, Erzberger was murdered. The trail of the murderers led to the secret organisation Consul of Hermann Ehrhardt, Ludendorff's confidant from the Kapp days.[740]

The first public expression of anti-Semitism from Hitler's side is precisely known. It was a letter from 1919, in which Hitler, by order of his military superiors, explained the meaning of Jewry for Germany. Hitler did this in no uncertain terms, 'it (Judaism) digs itself into the democracies and sucks the blood of the well-intentioned masses, it grovels before the majesty of the people, but knows only the majesty of money'. Hitler also looked ahead to the future and believed that the final goal had to be the 'Entfernung' of the Jews.[741] Ludendorff's confidant Breucker has tried to interpret Ludendorff's anti-Semitism as an evil caused by the association with Ludendorff's second wife, Dr. Mathilde von Kemnitz, whom Ludendorff met in 1923 via Gottfried Feder.[742] However, this is not correct. Although Von Kemnitz had a great influence on Ludendorff's thinking, his anti-Semitism was of an earlier date.

It is interesting to note that already in 1919, Ludendorff came into renewed contact with a man who played an equally obscure and important role in the spread of anti-Semitism in those years, namely the aristocrat Baron Müller von Hausen. During the First World War, Müller von Hausen had been attached to Ludendorff's staff in the rank of captain.[743] Under the pseudonym Gottfried zur Beek, he was the first in Germany to publish *Die Protokolle der Weisen von Zion*. He was chairman of the association 'gegen die Überhebung des Judentums E.V', which published the radical magazine *Auf Vorposten*. The association was founded in 1912 by Fritz Bley, Ernst zu Reventlow and Müller von Hausen. The foundation, according to the historian Walter Mohrmann, 'started with a lie'. A lawyer allegedly stated on Loeb's behalf that Jews wanted to destroy the Christian state. This led to the initiative of the Anti-Semitic Society. The publication of the notorious libel book *Die Protokolle* was an almost logical next step, also in light of the fact that Müller von Hausen was well known in Russian (read white) circles, for the book originated in Russia. [744]

The Protokolle were supposedly a secret report of the First Zionist Congress in Basel, Switzerland, which had been organised by Theodor Herzl. At this congress, old world conquest plans of the Jews were supposedly revived and worked out in concrete terms. However, the Russian secret service, so the myth goes, got hold of a copy of *Die Protokolle*. In 1905, *Die Protokolle* were published for the first time, as an appendix to a doomsday book *Das Grosse im Kleinen*, which, without *Die Protokolle*, had already been published in 1901. Author of this book would be the Russian writer Sergei A. Nilus from Moscow.[745] Afterwards, the book was republished three more times, in 1911, 1912 and 1917. With the Russian Revolution, the vision of this book spread internationally. However, attentive sceptics, such as Dr. J. Stanjek and the theologian Otto Friedrich, soon discovered strange things about Nilus' so-called real protocol. A former editor of the *Kreuzzeitung* (Ludendorff's newspaper!), H. Goedsche, had published a series of historical novels under the pseudonym Sir John Retcliff, in which he pretended to be a British diplomat. One of these novels was *Biarritz*, published in 1868. One of the chapters of that book dealt with a Jewish cemetery in Prague, where rabbis met in secret. Parts of the chapter *Auf dem Prager Judenfriedhof* appeared to have striking similarities with *Die Protokolle*. Prof. H. L. Strack published about it in *Jüdische Geheimgesetze,* and Friedrich in the book *Das Buch der Fälschungen.* Then a new discovery was made, building on a discovery by Stack, who believed that parts of the text of *Die Protokolle* must originally have been in French. Indeed, a correspondent of the British *The Times* discovered that parts of the dialogues appeared to come from the French-language book *Dialogue aux enfers entre Macchiavelli et Montsesquieu.* This was a satire from 1865. In that year, this book had been published anonymously, but in 1868, a second edition of the book turned up in Brussels, and this time the book did have an official author, the Parisian lawyer Maurice Joly.[746] The Russian-French connection to *Die Protokolle* was also considered to be the work of Pyotr Ivanovich Rachekovsky, head of the foreign branch of the Russian Secret Service in Paris. Ratshkovsky, who according to Bruno Naarden was a 'dangerous professional intriguer', made extensive use of 'agent provocateurs' to eliminate political enemies. He also tried to get the French and Russian authorities to see eye to eye on their security interests.

The nascent anti-Semitism became an important part of the völkisch Ludendorff's thinking. New insights, which Ludendorff developed from and after the Kapp days and looking back on the consequences of November 1918, he eventually interpreted as the beginning of his völkisch thinking. Ludendorff's newspaper, the *Kreuzzeitung,* published many articles which referred to the discoveries from *Die Protokolle*. The *Deutsche Tageszeitung* also subscribed to the conspiracy idea. In his later publishing activities, Ludendorff would often refer to the ideas of Müller von Hausen and *Die Protokolle*.[747]

Here, Ludendorff followed in the footsteps of other thinkers who stood at the cradle of völkisch ideas, such as Paul Bötticher, better known as Paul de Lagarde, and Julius Langbehn. The völkisch ideas, which were rooted in the romanticism of the 19th century, and could also be explained in part by the late German unification, the lack of historical roots and (rapid) social changes (urbanisation, emancipation) as well as a complex geopolitical situation (many borders) and political inexperience, derailed in the Third Reich into the 'Blut und Boden' ideology. Some historians still separate völkische thought from ariosophy, i.e. the specific idea that the Aryan - as a kind of "light man" - had a special guiding role to play in the world, such as with the Austrian mystic, anti-Semite and *Ostara-publisher* Jörg Lanz von Liebenfels or Alfred Rosenberg. Ludendorff's ideas would always remain a mixture of his traditional Prussian-nationalist thinking, his new völkische insights and his at times very fierce anti-Semitism with ariosophical characteristics. In an appendix to the brochure *Die wahrheit über Ludendorffs Kampf, eine Zusammenfassende Darstellung* by Hans Kurth, which was published by his later-founded "Ludendorffs Volkswarte Verlag" and sold tens of thousands of copies, Ludendorff outlined his "Kampfziele". They form a nice introduction to the völkische Ludendorff:

1. Resilience
2. Freedom (not democracy but freedom from being enslaved by neighbouring countries)
3. Grossdeutschland
4. Strong state
5. Strong leader
6. Responsible leaders
7. Power to the regions
8. Jews and other 'foreign races' cannot be German citizens
9. Obedience
10. Organic view of the people
11. Man and woman equal but different
12. Family as a cornerstone
13. Homeland is irreplaceable
14. Racial consciousness, blood consciousness
15. German case law
16. Economy by fair standards [748]

To this list he added two more points, which clearly arose from his later contact with Dr Mathilde von Kemnitz, the so-called 'Deutsches Gotterkennen', and the resulting influence on German cultural development. We will come to these matters later.

While the ideas matured he was in secret contact with the NSDAP, and even helped to give direction, Ludendorff spent his (public) time with a seemingly endless row of meetings of war veterans, often interspersed with massive youth gatherings. In a victory parade of flags, regimental numbers and mirrored helmets, they tried to close the gap between the immense German efforts and the disappointment and disbelief about the defeat.

Ludendorff was aware of his special historical position in this matter. He represented the German successes, whereby Tannenberg was of course written in capital letters. At the invitation of Freiherr von Gayl, Ludendorff travelled to East Prussia in August 1921. Von Gayl was a former employee of Oberost. Ludendorff received the reception of a statesman. Thousands passed by as he took part in the parade. A torchlight procession passed through the streets of Königsberg. In Kaunas too, at that time the heart of Oberost, Ludendorff was festively welcomed. In front of the memorial of General von York, known from the Napoleonic Wars, he took part in the troop parades. Ludendorff reported extensively on this in his memoirs, partly to show that 'there were still good Germans'.[749] For, of course, Ludendorff's position was under discussion, and he had lost face in the final days of 1918 and because of the Kapp-Putsch. On the other hand, there was a deep division in society, and for many Ludendorff represented the threatened völkische Germany. The University of Kaunas awarded Ludendorff an honorary doctorate; it was his fourth. The universities of Breslau, Freiburg and Konigsberg preceded the University of Kaunas.[750] The certificate referred to 'the master of field arts', the 'liberator', who had 'wiped our East Prussian mother earth clean of plundering and scorching Russian hordes'. Immediately afterwards, other large-scale commemorative events took place in Frankfurt am Oder. Here, too, Ludendorff was applauded. The local commander told him that Ludendorff was applauded as much as the Kaiser at the time.[751] Ludendorff was a 'Retter und Racher' of 'our people'.[752] Precisely in these days, just before the murder of Erzberger (26.08.1921), from which Ludendorff would distance himself in his memoirs[753] Ludendorff's position within the völkisch camp swelled to unprecedented proportions. From our later knowledge, we tend to follow mainly the NSDAP and Hitler in this period, but it was Ludendorff who was the most important figure on the right between 1919 and 1923.

One day before Erzberger's murder, the *Berliner Lokalanzeiger* wrote: 'And then Ludendorff arrived. Holiest of men's faithfulness bubbled over to the languor. The many who filled the bazaars felt that a man stood before us like a rock in this feminine era'.[754] The historian Borst believes that Ludendorff's position was subject to change in this period. For a part of the German people, the decisive role that Ludendorff played within the German supreme command became increasingly clear. The memoirs of Obert Bauer, as we saw at the time an officer on Von Hindenburg's and Ludendorff's staff, also contributed to this. Bauer was very critical of Von Hindenburg's role. For Bauer, it was clear that it was actually Ludendorff who was the linchpin of the German supreme command. Von Hindenburg was so upset by these revelations in *Der grosse Krieg in Feld und Heimat* that he summoned Ludendorff and asked for support. In his memoirs, Ludendorff, who himself could not stand criticism, dismissed von Hindenburg's request as something childish and thought that others could do better. Bauer's publication stood in a growing awareness that Ludendorff had been the driving force behind the German war machine. In retrospect, one could say that Von Hindenburg was the 'beloved' general and Ludendorff the 'tüchtiger' general.[755] Or, as Maximilian Harden wrote, Ludendorff was 'without doubt' the 'most powerful figure that Germany had produced in the First World War'.[756] War theorist Delbruck, basing himself partly on Bauer, believed that Ludendorff had been the 'real general'. [757]

The trip to East Prussia stirred up a lot in Ludendorff. In his memoirs, he expressed his disgust for the Polish corridor that divided German territory in two. 'How different everything had become',[758] he mused.

Back in Munich that autumn, Ludendorff put the finishing touches to his third book, *Kriegführung und Politik*, published by Mittler & Sohn. It was Ludendorff's first political book. In this book, we see the völkische Ludendorff with ariosophical characteristics as well. In addition to an exposition of Germany's geopolitics, strategic thinkers and decisions, Ludendorff also pointed out the new dangers for Germany. Looking back on the First World War, he explicitly pointed to the Jewish elite as the enemies of the German people, who, together with France and Great Britain, had conspired against Germany. Hereafter, Ludendorff endlessly repeated the notion of 'überstaatlich'. With this, he referred to the fact that the influence of the Jewish community was not limited to one country, but was 'active behind the scenes in many countries with different political systems'. Ludendorff considered the 'Jewish' interest in World War I to be twofold: there were economic interests and there was a political interest, namely the establishment of the Jewish state of Palestine. In addition, according to Ludendorff, 'the Jews' pursued 'dominion over the people'. According to him, they were 'very driven', a character trait that had been strengthened 'through inbreeding'. In order to achieve their goals, they made use of deception, such as the slogan *freedom, equality, brotherhood*, which, in Ludendorff's view, was only intended to erode the resilience of peoples - and especially the German people, whom Ludendorff saw as particularly vulnerable.

Ludendorff also regarded new concepts that appeared in the political and social spheres, such as pacifism and internationalism, as examples of the 'alien Jewish influence'. Ludendorff regarded pacifism as unmanly, and internationalism as a destruction of the völkische. He also indirectly referred to his belief *in Die Protokolle* by pointing to a statement by Walther Rathenau of 25 December 1919 in the *Neuer Freien Presse*, in which he claimed that 300 men controlled the economy on the continent and that they all knew each other.[759] In fact, one could see Rathenau's statement in the light of the 'Herrenklubs' to which Ludendorff himself was (indirectly) connected. However, Ludendorff chose a *Protokolle* interpretation. In a side sentence, he then confessed that Jewish sacrifices had also been made in the First World War: 'das Juden auch für Deutschland blutete, sei bekannt'.[760]

This subclause was important because Ludendorff herewith distanced himself at least from the scandalous investigation that had been started in 1916 because of the rumours that Jews would hide themselves from active duty. The facts showed that about 100,000 Jews had served in the German army (out of a Jewish population of about 620,000 in 1914) and that about 12% of them had died. The number of Jewish conscripts for the war had also been high, especially in university towns such as Göttingen (27%), Königsberg (26%) and Munich (25%). More than 35.4% of Jewish front-line soldiers received some form of military recognition, in the form of rank or distinction. Thus, German Jews conformed to the 'normal' picture during the war. [761]

Chapter 15

The murder of Walther Rathenau and a rehabilitation at the Wannsee

24 June 1922 was a rainy day in Berlin. It was to be a day that contemporaries would never forget. On that day, the German Foreign Minister Walther Rathenau was murdered. At an S-corner on the Königsallee, not far from his home, Rathenau's car, sitting openly in the back seat, was overtaken by another car from which automatic weapons opened fire. A hand grenade was thrown as well. The car of Rathenau and his driver came to a stop at the pavement, while the perpetrators sped away. Bystanders took Rathenau to his home, where he died shortly afterwards. Helene Kaiser, the nurse who immediately arrived and who happened to witness the incident, could not save him. Five shots had entered the body and shattered the spinal columns and the lower jaw. The next day, Sunday 25 June, 'he lay in the same place in the open coffin,' wrote Harry Graf Kessler, 'the head bent back a little to the right, with a very placid expression, and yet an immeasurable tragedy in the deeply furrowed, dead, wounded face, over which a fine handkerchief was spread on the lower shattered half, only the grey, short-cropped, tangled moustache peeping out above it'.[762]

The Rathenau murder was not an isolated case. As we have already seen, 'Femicide' had become a common weapon for the right wing to deal with opponents. Matthias Erzberger, former Minister of Finance, and Prime Minister Philipp Scheidemann (eighteen days earlier, on 4 June 1922, but the attempt failed) had already been victims of attacks. Maximilian Harden, a publicist, would be severely injured in an attack a few days after Rathenau.

The murder of Rathenau had an enormous impact. This was because so many typical interwar issues were hidden in this one life. Yet, there was also shock internationally.[763] Harry Graf Kessler thought that since the assassination of Abraham Lincoln there had not been such a commotion after the murder of a statesman.⁷⁶⁴ Rathenau was not only a politician, he was also a writer, a publicist, a futurist in some respects, an anti-Zionist, an entrepreneur linked to the AEG group, which his father Emil Rathenau (one of the founders of German industry) built up from an old iron foundry in north Berlin, and he was Jewish and German.⁷⁶⁵ The latter would remain a constant schism in his life, more so for the outside world than for himself. As was often the case, Jewish identity became an issue, precisely because the outside world constantly mentioned it. During the First World War, as we have already seen, there was even a check on whether the young Jewish men were at the front, and of course such embarrassments had not escaped Rathenau, who had even served in the Gardekurrassiers before the war, an elite unit with a strong 'Hochdeutsch' content.

Rathenau was a man of emancipation and integration, and via the above-mentioned Harden and his magazine *Die Zukunft*, he wrote his *Höre Israel*, in which he called on German Jews to 'Anartung' the German culture. Rathenau's goal was undeniably the restoration of Germany, but the road to achieving it split German ranks. Rathenau fell somewhat between two stools, not only because of his ethnic background, but also because of his equally intriguing and complicated world of thought. Rathenau abhorred the 'primitive communist ideal of equality', but on the other hand he also had an aversion to the 'liberal overestimation of economic freedom'.⁷⁶⁶ In a time when almost every form of organised thought was militant, this was a not harmless intermediate position. It is important to emphasise here that Rathenau had been an opponent of the way in which Germany had withdrawn from the war. He was of the opinion that the course of events had created a bad starting position for the future of Germany. In October 1918, he published about this in the *Vossische Zeitung*.⁷⁶⁷ Later, he became a close friend of the then Finance Minister, Wirth, the later Chancellor of the Exchequer, and he shared this concern with him. He also stepped up behind the scenes to assist the Foreign Minister, Dr Simons, until he himself had to take the helm. The concerns of German foreign policy, and they were not small, focused on Walther Rathenau, who unintentionally became the symbol of a 'Jewish' ethnicity and culture in Germany.

As a result of the defeat of 1918, the dagger strike legend, the völkische and ariosophische thoughts that were strongly on the rise, as well as radicalisation also on the left and an unloved centre (the 'Erfüllungspolitik'), there was hardly any stable ground. In addition, Rathenau was an artist rather than an industrialist (his own business ventures often went wrong), and he also had his dreams and visions, in which he saw a future for Germany that was in many ways different from what the reactionaries saw. Rathenau was quite critical of the Prussian 'Junkerstaat', to which many Germans accused him of 'Jewish arrogance'. He believed that Germans were practical-minded and hard workers, but not actually intellectuals, and that was exactly what Rathenau thought Germany needed. This attitude was also what Rathenau radiated when he made his appearance in the administrative offices of the Weimar Republic. Tall, slender, almost African in appearance - according to Harry Graf Kessler - he thus symbolised 'the new era', which many people saw as threatening. Rathenau's criticism was not limited to the German civil servant, but he also openly attacked the House of Hohenzollern and Kaiser Wilhelm II in his publications (*Der Kaiser, Eine Betrachtung*),[768] and boasted of his international influence, thus not only becoming a symbol of the new era, but also, for the wilful or gullible misunderstander, the incarnation of *The Protocols of the Sages of Zion*. As we saw, he had written in the Christmas issue of the *Neue Freie Presse* in 1909 that three hundred men, who all knew each other, controlled the economic fortunes of the European continent. He himself was one of these three hundred.[769] A famous and, for many, infamous statement by Rathenau was that 'if the Kaiser and his paladins were to ride victoriously through the Branderburg Gate, world history would have lost its meaning'. Of course, this statement was not friendly to the Kaiser, but the anger from the reactionary camp was partly hypocritical, for the Kaiser was finished for most, both on the left and the right. Ludendorff, too, never had any concrete plan to bring back the Kaiser, should his renewed dictatorship have taken effect after the Kapp-Putsch or the Feldherrnhalle-Putsch.

The case focused on the ethnic background coupled with Rathenau's progressive views, which became an increasing thorn in the side of the reactionaries. Jakob Wasserman said about Jewishness in the Weimar Republic: 'Die Juden, die Deutschen, diese Trennung der Begriffe wollte mir nicht in dem Sinn, nicht aus dem Sinn'.[770] This separation, as Wasserman indicated, led to a hate campaign: 'Dem Rathenau, dem Walther, blueht auch kein hohes Alter', or 'Knallt ab den Walther Rathenau die gtverdammte Judensau'.[771] It was complicated by doubts on the German side about one's own 'ethnicity'. 'The definition of Deutschtum is even more complicated than that of Judaism,' stated Rathenau biographer Peter Berglar rightly.[772] Erich Ludendorff and Mathilde von Kemnitz even needed a 'religion of their own' in order to arrive at a conclusive concept. In a certain sense, they were the most consistent - and therefore also the most sectarian - representatives of the Deutschtum defined from a völkisch point of view. In that dialectical worldview, völkisch automatically stood in opposition to Judaism. The politics of those days were also seen through that ethnic lens. Reactionaries feared that the Treaty of Rapallo would be a kind of extradition of Germany to Jewish-Bolshevik Russia, whereas it was precisely the reactionary Reichswehr that benefited from Rapallo. People closed their eyes on the right and saw everything too clearly on the left. The words of pamphleteer Rathenau were weighed on a silver platter. The *Mitteldeutschen Presse* published an open letter in which conspiracy theories about Rathenau were unfolded. Rathenau was said not to serve German interests, but those of Jewish freemason circles.[773] Others believed that he served international capital, while still others saw in him a kind of Trotsky, a left-wing revolutionary.[774]

Rathenau was aware of the danger he was in. A month before his death, he told banker Max Warburg, the 'uncrowned king of Hamburg', that he constantly received threatening letters. Warburg, a member of a distinguished Jewish family, knew what Rathenau was talking about. For the same reason, Warburg had refrained from becoming the head of the German negotiators at Versailles.[775] Chancellor Wirth even warned Rathenau personally about the imminent danger, after he had been tipped off by a catholic clergyman who thought he had indications of an imminent attack. Rathenau stood 'pale and immobile' in front of Wirth after this announcement. However, Wirth also saw that despite this, he did not reach Rathenau, 'his eyes were fixed as on a distant land'.[776] Then Rathenau, 'with inner calm', let it be known that he did not want any surveillance. 'Dear friend, it is nothing. Who would harm me?'[777] Yet, these words seemed to be aimed more at reassuring Wirth than at convincing him. Rathenau suffered from the (verbal) aggression towards him. He enjoyed travelling abroad on a regular basis, to his beloved Genoa for example, where he knew every street corner and had helped build the tram in his younger years. He had met privately with a number of fierce opponents in an attempt to take the sharpest edges off the debate. Unfortunately, as soon as they were back in the full light of day, the streets had to be mobilised and the drums beaten. Antisemitic tendencies were then suddenly again politically cashable and therefore almost ineradicable. One of the reasons that anti-Semitism had become such an important part of politics in the Weimar era was the fact that the stab-in-the-back myth and the ideas of a so-called Jewish world conspiracy were directly linked by many reactionaries.[778] 'A statesman must also be prepared for martyrdom,' Rathenau sighed in conclusion.[779] The 'Rufmord' did not remain without consequences.

The German judiciary was under enormous pressure to solve the case. It had also become clear to the German public that the series of murders could hardly be the work of an individual, and that there was a pattern to these political settlements. The chief of police in Hamburg warned Max Warburg that there were indications that he, too, was being targeted. He went into hiding. Thanks to a talkative high school student from a reactionary family, the police eventually tracked down a whole network of young men who had one thing in common: a veneration of the Kapp-Putsch veteran Hermann Ehrhart and a connection - direct or indirect - to his underground organisation, 'Consul'. Apparently, 'Consul' did not hesitate to use teenagers to do the dirty work, the 'Fememurders'. The assassins and their accomplices were as young as they were unscrupulous and easy to turn against Rathenau who, as Harry Graf Kessler described it, was seen as a kind of 'arch traitor'.[780] The two main men in the direct assassination plot were Erwin Kern and Hermann Fischer, but as the historians Uwe Lohalm and Martin Ulmer state, there were many helpers and knowers.[781] After the murder, they fled from Berlin, but observers in the town of Lenzen on the Elbe River spotted the two in the Hotel Zur Sonne. Despite prompt police action, the two managed to escape and then tried to get away by bicycle. However, the courts launched an unprecedented manhunt and in mid-July the two were finally spotted at Saaleck Castle near Halle, whose owner, Hans Wilhelm Stein, was not present. Surrounded by police, the two men called out to passers-by to greet Captain Ehrhardt, 'er lebe hoch, hoch, hoch', it sounded from the roof of the castle. Eventually, after a firefight, both men died, partly from police bullets, partly from suicide.[782]

The historian Borst characterised the Völkisch action against Rathenau as 'Kesseltreiben'. Ludendorff was also responsible for the 'Rufmord' on Rathenau: as a leader and symbol of the Völkisch camp, but also in concrete terms. Ludendorff's most important public stand against Rathenau took place during the 'Untersuchungsausschuss', in which Ludendorff and Von Hindenburg had to answer for the First World War in November 1919. Here, Ludendorff referred to Rathenau's statement that the war would have lost its meaning if the Kaiser would have driven through the Brandenburg Gate. In other words, Ludendorff interpreted, with little feeling for Rathenau's symbolism, 'that there were currents that did not want us (the General Staff) to win'.[783] As we have already seen, the 'Untersuchungsausschuss' was an important symbolic moment for the right-wing camp. All those who were sceptical about the 'Erfüllungspolitik' looked with disdain on the open disciplining of Germany's former military leaders. The street was even so mobilised that Von Hindenburg and Ludendorff could leave the matter behind with their heads held high. The hatred had been sown, however, and Rathenau would increasingly become the target of it.

Ludendorff's interpretation of Rathenau's words was one-sided and one-dimensional. Ludendorff did not like Rathenau's delicacy. It was Rathenau who had published in *Zukunft* that he considered Ludendorff to be a war engineer, a great general and an organiser of the state, a terminology that would not have been out of place in the Ludendorff publishing house.[784] Rathenau also shared Ludendorff's disgust about the Versailles Treaty, which he called a 'scientific murder'.[785] Still, the image of the Jewish intellectual Rathenau apparently stood in Ludendorff's way. In doing so, Rathenau's criticism of the Kaiser, which was more of a resignation with the Kaiser's departure than the pursuit of his fall, pointed to an open nerve in the right-wing camp, for what were they doing in the direction of Doorn, where Kaiser Wilhelm II had withdrawn? In Ludendorff's memoirs, the Kaiser hardly plays a role, and if he played a role at all, it was to legitimise his own plans.

There is another interesting, almost Freudian, distortion of a Rathenau quotation. This quotation is found here and there in literature, but Ludendorff's confidant Wilhelm Breucker explained the background. During the time that Ludendorff was in Sweden, Breucker was also in regular contact with Walther Rathenau. Rathenau, according to Breucker, was one of the first to express his regret about the dismissal of Ludendorff in the final phase of the First World War. Rathenau, Breucker believed, condemned the men of the November Revolution who revered von Hindenburg but descended on Erich Ludendorff. 'They succeeded in placing all the blame on Ludendorff at the last moment'.[786] Breucker passed this quote on to Ludendorff, but was surprised to see that Ludendorff changed the quote in his writings to: 'At the last moment, we succeeded in putting all the blame on Ludendorff'.[787] Breucker pointed out this mistake to Ludendorff, but he refused to correct it: 'An author must never correct himself'.[788] Since then, this erroneous quotation has constantly appeared in publications of the House of Ludendorff and a new myth was born. The separation between Ludendorff and Rathenau was a fact. And this while these men had much in common, trivial matters, such as the fact that they both lived in the Viktoriastrasse in Berlin, and the fact that in addition to the 'Diktatur Ludendorff' at the beginning of the war, there was also a 'Diktatur Rathenau'.[789]

The relationship between Ludendorff and Rathenau was based on a complicated history, which we have already touched upon briefly elsewhere in the book. Initially, there was great admiration on Rathenau's part for Ludendorff. This had to do with Rathenau's view of Prussia and the Germans, which was not entirely without Jewish self-hatred.[790] He referred to the Prussians as 'daredevils'. After his meeting with Ludendorff in Kaunas in 1915, Rathenau saw in Ludendorff the man who could either bring victory to Germany, or at least win an honourable peace. Rathenau, who clearly pointed at Ludendorff and not at von Hindenburg, had an eye for the reality of the power relations within Oberost. His vision wasa foreshadowing, for in 1916, Ludendorff would indeed become Germany's most powerful officer with Von Hindenburg. 'From that day on', said Rathenau after his visit to Oberost in 1915, 'I joined those who did everything in their power to pave the way for him to the highest army command'.[791]

In September 1916, Rathenau urged the employment of hundreds of thousands of Belgians in the German war industry. In doing so, he showed that he was one of the most radical supporters of the war economy plans of the 'Hindenburg Programme'. His biographer Harry Graf Kessler characterised this step by Rathenau as 'being a great mistake' in the First World War, and believed that Rathenau later regretted it. In the spring of 1917, during a meeting in Berlin, things went wrong between Rathenau and Ludendorff. Rathenau had calculated the plans for the unrestricted submarine war and believed that Germany should not do so. That was typical of Rathenau. Peter Berglar has pointed out how often the word 'lawfulness' appears in Rathenau's work.[792] Rathenau had an enormous need for structures, and applied the laws and the resulting 'Mechanik',[793] another of Rathenau's favourite words, also to matters of the mind and character. 'In our life everything was law; so were the things given, so is the course bestimmt'.[794] Ludendorff, however, ignored the coldly presented facts and pointed out to Rathenau that he trusted his 'inner feeling'. 'I dare to set my calculations against your feelings,' Rathenau mused, but Ludendorff was adamant. 'I respect that,' Ludendorff said, 'but you will have to admit that I have to follow my feelings'.[795] 'I gave up on tying with him',[796] was Rathenau's opinion, but he nevertheless voiced his dissatisfaction with the course of events in various places, including the elitist 'Mittwochsgesellschaft', where he believed that 'a leap over a precipice would only be successful if 'it were 100% successful'.[797] With this, Rathenau had put his finger exactly on the sore spot. The only problem was that the submarine map within German strategy was constantly being played on the basis of a variety of plans, never solely on the basis of maritime calculations.

Ehrhardt's involvement in the murder of Rathenau does not speak in Ludendorff's favour either. As we have already seen in the memoirs of Ludendorff's first wife, Ludendorff was still in contact with Ehrhardt in these days, something that he himself contradicted in his memories. There were good reasons for Ludendorff to keep certain contacts hidden; we recall his 'accidental' morning walk in Berlin when Ehrhardt's soldiers marched in, his request to Rudolf Hess to keep his sympathy for the emerging Hitler movement quiet and the fact that the killers of Rosa Luxemburg and Karl Liebknecht were his immediate bodyguards on his return from Sweden. Was there also a direct connection between the order for the murder of Rathenau and Ludendorff?

This question is difficult to answer. The main reason is that 'Consul' or 'C' or also 'O.C'. (internally one still spoke of the marine brigade or 'E') as well as the person Ehrhardt, were difficult to deal with because the judiciary was blind in the right eye. We remember the handling of the Kapp Putschists and how they found shelter elsewhere in the Reich, even after a failed coup. Martin Sabrow spoke of a 'repressed conspiracy'.[798] Justice simply would not have it. While the men in the field were quickly convicted (until October 1922), it took until October 1924 for the trial of 'Consul' and thus of Ehrhardt to start (his lumber club paid the lawyers' fees). Here, the judiciary made grateful use of technical reasons to avoid probing too deeply into the sensitive national underbelly. The main defence was that 'Consul', in fact founded in the same year as it was, had already gone under. The men who had murdered Rathenau had done so out of a sense of congeniality, but not at the behest of 'Consul'. Even demonstrable 'Consul' activities in the 'present' were dismissed with such technical evidence, despite the fact that it eventually became clear that Ehrhardt had only cosmetically faded into the background and that his confidants Karl Tilessen and Hartmut Plaas were in charge of a very much alive and very dangerous organisation, 'Consul'.[799]

Just as Ludendorff escaped prosecution after the Kapp-Putsch, so too was Ehrhardt above the law. As a result, the judicial records do not tell much about how directly the two men were connected to the Rathenau murder. In any case, the 'Rufmord' was certainly a consequence of Ludendorff's far-reaching accusations in November 1919, against his plea to the German nation. His remarks on Rathenau reached many newspapers, such as the *Münchener Neueste Nachrichten, Deutsche Zeitung, Vorwärts, Reichswart, Kreuzzeitung, Heimatland* and others.[800] The writer Ernst von Salomon wrote in *Die Geächteten* that one of the Rathenau murderers indeed invoked Ludendorff's statement[801] and also Harry Graf Kessler wrote that it was in 'Ludendorff's spirit'.[802] Writer/journalist Kurt Tucholsky blamed what he called the 'Ludendorff parties', and said that at thousands of 'Stammtischen', the murder was applauded with 'Prost Blume'. He also criticised the democratic press, which had been asleep instead of alerting the people to the danger. Furthermore, he denounced the 'fistful' of lies about Rathenau: 'Was der Junker versaut, muss der Jude Auffressen'.[803] Tucholsky had been a harsh critic before. In April 1922, in the article *Kadett Ludendorff in Welt am Sonntag,* he had broken a lance for Ludendorff's critic Delbrueck, and had called Ludendorff a mediocre general and especially a small man, who had left the coach when it got stuck in the mud, and then blamed everyone else. He also compared Ludendorff's undemocratic view that politics should serve the military in wartime with the fire brigade, which believed that one should not interfere with the fire in order not to stop it getting wet.[804]

Ehrhardt's part in the murder was further supported by the fact that not only the two murderers could be linked to Ehrhardt, but also the driver of the car from which the attack on Rathenau was made, Ernst Werner Techow. A pattern was visible, names were mentioned, names of new potential victims, among them Ebert, Wirth, Max Warburg, Theodor Wolff and Richard Lipinksi, all 'November men'. The sources were soley Ehrhardt men, such as Herbert Lauch, foreman from Saxony and Schmidt-Halbschuh. The man who had targeted Philipp Scheidemann, Hans Hustert, also confessed to a series of actions. In his famous book *Fragebogen,* Salomon also mentions the names of Walther Schuecking, Oskar Wassermann and even Alexander Helphand ('Parvus').[805]

The figure of Parvus, who had had a hand in Lenin's journey from Switzerland to Russia, makes the step small to a conspiracy idea in 'Consul' that the Weimar Republic was part of a Jewish-left conspiracy against Germany. A witness who was interrogated about the murderer Kern, reported that he wanted to kill twelve Jews who belonged to the group of 300 who ruled the world behind the scenes.[806] Moreover, Salomon reports in *Fragebogen* about twelve men who planned to destroy the German empire, by playing it off against arch-enemy France and handing it over to the communists. The thinking of the Ehrhardt group was as much influenced as Ludendorff's thinking by *Die Protokolle der Weisen von Sion,* in which an alleged Jewish world conspiracy was revealed. Ludendorff had contributed to the spreading of the ideas of this libel and had openly expressed his belief in its authenticity. It is important to emphasise again that Ludendorff knew Gottfried zur Beek, the 'first bringer' of *Die Protokolle* in Germany, personally. The latter also referred to Rathenau's book *Der Kaiser* as 'proof' of the 'undermining role' of the Jews in Germany and worldwide. The last questions surrounding Erhardt's role in the murder of Rathenau were answered the man himself on 16 July 1933. On the occasion of the eleventh anniversary of the attack, Ehrhardt explained his role in it. He praised the murderers, but he also stated that the system (the Republic) had responded to the 'Consul's' actions with more vigour than expected. Weimar's resilience had been underestimated. [807]

Incidentally, in the legal aftermath of the 'attack-month' of June, the name Ludendorff was also mentioned in connection with the failed attempt on Philipp Scheidemann. The local leader of the right-wing national 'Schutz und Trutzbund' in Zwickau, who had connections with 'Consul' and Ehrhardt through the right-wing lodge 'Herold', had heard of Scheidemann's murder plans and could not reconcile this with his conscience. Furthermore, the regretful man said that in Bavaria alone, 500,000 men were ready to enter the power vacuum that the attacks would cause, mentioning Ludendorff as the central figure. The units that provided the men were 'Freikorps Oberland', 'Herold', 'Stahlhelm' and the NSDAP and other völkische organisations. [808]

Another curious link between the murder of Rathenau and Ludendorff was the fact that a man who played a major role in Ludendorff's political agitation was one of the last to see Rathenau alive: Hugo Stinnes; one of the few men in the Weimar era who could sit at any table. On 23 June, the day before the assassination, Rathenau had been invited to the US Embassy by Envoy Houghton for a dinner around a member of the Restoration Commission. Rathenau got into a debate about the German coal position and at one point suggested that the expert, Hugo Stinnes, be called in. He called him, and Stinnes appeared at 10pm. However, after a businesslike contribution on his part, Rathenau and Stinnes got into a fierce debate, with Stinnes attacking Rathenau's politics. It came on an already difficult day for Rathenau, as earlier he had clashed with the right-wing banker and politician Karl Hellfrich, who was a fierce opponent of the 'Erfüllungspolitik' and firmly believed in the daggerhead legend.[809] The debate went on so long that both men continued their showdown in Berlin's Hotel Esplanade until 4am.

Hours later, Rathenau was murdered. What was Stinnes role? This is even more obscure than Ludendorff's. There was probably no direct involvement, although the agitation between Stinnes and Rathenau went back further, given the fact that Stinnes was much less cooperative with the Entente than Rathenau, which the former certainly blamed on the latter. However, it was more than likely that Rathenau was at the table with the man who had co-financed his murderers, just as Stinnes had pots on the fire everywhere. Given the fact that Stinnes just as easily sat at the table with the Soviet government as with the Völkisch camp, we should not be surprised. The fact remains that Stinnes' heart was on the 'right', but that everyday economic practice had no political colour.

It was inevitable that Ludendorff's name would also fall in the wake of Rathenau's murder. The 'Fememurder' to which Rathenau fell prey was too much in line with Ludendorff's performance up to that point to keep him out of the spotlight entirely. His historical contacts with Ehrhardt, and current contacts according to his ex-wife. It is even very likely that the Ehrhardt brigade was also partly financed via Ludendorff (and the latter via Stinnes), although the distance that arose between Ehrhardt and Ludendorff in the course of time is not improbable. If there was a common thread in Ludendorff's life, it was the ever-recurring schism; against Ehrhardt bdue to his too lenient attitude towards the ultramontane and lodge-like character of his organisation. Yet, the pot is calling the kettle black here, since Ludendorff's own performance was anything but transparent, and his memoirs unreliable. In addition, he had contributed to the 'Rufmord'.

It is interesting what Ludendorff wrote about the Rathenau murder in his memoirs. On 24th, the University of Munich celebrated its 450th anniversary, and the rector magnificus, Erich von Drygalski, head of the geographical department, gave a festive speech. Many prominent people were invited, including Erich Ludendorff. Among those present was Crown Prince Rupprecht, with whom Ludendorff was at odds. Rupprecht suddenly received a telegram, informing him of the murder of Rathenau in Berlin. He bent down to Ludendorff and showed the message in a way that meant to say 'oh, but you already know that'. Of course Ludendorff reacted angrily and ignorantly, which he also wrote in his memoirs 'Nun, ich wusste nichts davon'.[810] Ludendorff then gave his analysis of the attack. According to him, it was a stupidly timed attack, which only played into the hands of the Catholic camp, as well as the Communists. He was protective of the murderers, Fischer and Kern. He spoke of a 'tragic end' for both men at Saaleck Castle. The republic reacted furiously, and wanted 'reparation'. There was a large demonstration, which Ludendorff explained entirely from his *Protokolle von Zion vision*. The demonstration, he said, took place on 18 July 1922, 18.07.1922. This added up to the number 30, which Ludendorff considered a 'Jaweh-number', a mystical number, which Jewish interest groups who believed in cabbalistic mysticism used to influence reality by means of metaphysics. Rathenau, Ludendorff said, was a 'servant' who had done 'so much for Jewish rule'.[811]

These were very far-reaching accusations that, despite Ludendorff's denial that he knew anything about the 'Fememurder' of Rathenau, do outline his relationship with the Jewish statesman. And that bad relationship had existed for some time. The fact that Ludendorff did not even mention Rathenau in his military memoirs, which Ludendorff wrote immediately after the First World War, is remarkable, not only because of their direct contacts, but also because of Rathenau's undeniable influence in the field of German raw materials policy. In addition, they had been each other's allies in the controversial issue of the employment of Belgian workers. It must be that Ludendorff did not want to remember his relationship with Rathenau, who, until late in the war, had sufficient authority to command an audience with the ever too busy Ludendorff and who also openly dared to disagree. If we add to this the fact that, before Ludendorff, there had never been a military leader who interfered so directly in the war economy, the absence of Rathenau is an important clue. Only in 1934 did Ludendorff reluctantly admit in *Am heiligen Quell deutscher Kraft,* of December that year, that he had been in correspondence with Walther Rathenau during the war. 'Blushing with shame', Ludendorff added.[812]

As a result of the Rathenau assassination, there followed new legislation to protect the Republic, which Ludendorff complained about in his memoirs, but the reality was that once again the top of the revolutionary reactionaries escaped, led by Ludendorff. As a result, the fire of counter-revolution smouldered on.

We remember the statement of the person who regretted the attack on Philipp Scheidemann. He thought that the reactionary camp around Ludendorff was ready. The numbers he quoted, 500,000 in Bavaria alone, seem exaggerated. But it is just how you count, in the equally militant and over-structured political and social life, you could get hefty numbers if you simply added up members. However, it was not a direct army, nor a well-oiled power structure, where Ludendorff only had to snap his fingers. In part, he was indeed the symbolic figure, but on the other hand, he had real power. Not for nothing did the NSDAP compete for his hand, and not only them, shortly after the Rathenau assassination, while society's sigh of indignation did not go unnoticed by Ludendorff, there came a call for contact from Berlin. Through Hugo Stinnes - again - the highest military leadership, Von Seeckt, sought contact with the 'fallen' general. 'Fallen' yes, he had been interrogated, but apparently not without influence for Berlin either. And Ludendorff came, because the fatherland called and his ego was stroked. Although he had pushed von Seeckt aside during the Kapp days, and von Seeckt wanted to receive him, while on the other hand he had gladly watched him leave to southern Bavaria.

What was going on? It was pure 'Real Politik'. The French boot from the West was the cause of the renewed handshake between the völkisch-ariosophical forces and the national-conservative forces in the service of 'Erfüllungspolitik'. For it was with this 'Erfüllung' that things went wrong. Not for nothing had Rathenau discussed with Stinnes the coal supplies that Germany had to deliver to the Entente shortly before. Germany's obligations to the Entente were not going well. The reason was that the German economy suffered from the enormous reparations, and especially inflation was a problem. The house of 'Erfüllungspolitik' built up by Wirth and Rathenau began to totter, and eventually Wirth had to step down. Ebert now put forward Wilhelm Cuno, a man who was more to the right than the progressive Wirth, and this also changed the tone with which Germany approached the Entente. The British seemed to be more understanding of Germany's position, the French on the other hand, through Henri Poincaré, took a hard and formal line. Things started to get tense and finally resulted in the fact that on 11 January 1923, five French divisions and one Belgian division entered the Ruhr area and occupied cities like Dortmund, Gelsenkirchen, Offenburg, Emmerich and Wesel. The immediate cause was the failure of Germany to deliver telegraph poles to France. Although there was no wood in the Ruhr area, there was coal. The government in Berlin panicked, the Ruhr area was of great strategic importance from a geopolitical point of view, and there was a fear of long-term occupation and even annexation, quite apart from French support for any resurgent separatism. The General Staff, too, realised that the French constituted a more than great danger so deep into the Empire. In addition, the coal barons feared for their empire. Old hands closed; Stinnes invited Ludendorff to Berlin. Old sores became subordinate to the new situation. All national hands had to be united to avert the French danger. Wilhelm Cuno, of the HAPAG concern, understood this as well as a Stinnes and a Von Seeckt, who had let Ebert dangle as much as he had turned his back on Ludendorff.

The 'safehouse' where these secret negotiations took place was owned by one of Hugo Stinnes' most important confidants, Friedrich Minoux. Minoux had initially obstructed Stinnes' work from government sources, whereupon Stinnes finally hired the man. This proved to be a golden move. Minoux turned out to be a brilliant manager who reorganised large parts of the Stinnes group and thereby returned it to economic health. He turned out to be such an economic prodigy that the Weimar Republic asked him for advice on the inflation problem. In practice, Minoux was largely in charge of the Berlin branch of the Stinnes group.[813] As if the secret meeting between Von Seeckt and Ludendorff, in which eventually Cuno also took part, was not miraculous enough, history had another sinister surprise up its sleeve. The representative building on the Grote Wannsee was the same building where, in January 1942, the so-called Wannsee Conference was held, the place where it was decided to destroy European Jewry. Ludendorff, the successful and passionate disseminator of *Die Protokolle*, had been dead for five years by then. For Ludendorff, it was not unknown territory. If he had to be in Berlin, he could use the villa. There had even been secret consultations before, with Heinrich Brüning as confidant of minister Adam Stegerwald, concerning wage agreements between the social partners, the so-called 'Essener-Programm'. Ludendorff had made a good impression at that time (1920), 'modest but with unprecedented energy, and a brain that worked like a machine'. '*I am always at your disposal*,' he said, '*if you think you need my advice.*" [814]

That moment had now arrived. The topic of conversation was the Ruhr occupation by the French. Ludendorff also felt very strongly about this; in his memoirs, he spoke of a 'rape of the German people'.[815] Coincidentally, Ludendorff had been in the region one day before the invasion at a veterans' meeting and was now very concerned about Germany's defencelessness. He understood why Berlin needed him now. The 'Ordnungszelle Bayern' was called upon, he thought, in 'Consul' jargon. According to Ludendorff, the French troops' entry into the Ruhr area was based on a strategic plan. 1923 was in Ludendorff's occult reality a so-called 'Jaweh-year'[816, 817], and that indicated far-reaching plans.[818] According to Ludendorff, Poincaré had already referred to this on 26 June 1922 by openly declaring that the 'left bank of the Rhine would remain occupied'.[819]

Ludendorff argued to Von Seeckt that passive resistance alone was not enough. There had to be a structured and centrally led reaction, Berlin and Von Seeckt had to take the reins. Ludendorff said it somewhat reluctantly, probably because in his memoirs he wrote 'that he had little faith in this man (Von Seeckt) and the strength of the government, but there was no better'.[820] He did feel, as apparently Berlin and Stinnes did, that there should be unity now that the French threat had become so serious. Ludendorff pointed to the fact that many national organisations in Bavaria had worked better together since the French invasion and that they were partly under the umbrella leadership of Commander Oberleutnant Hermann Kriebel, an old acquaintance of Ludendorff.[821] The units now fell under the so-called 'Arbeitsgemeinschaft der Vaterländischen Kampfverbände', which was founded by the later SA leader Ernst Röhm.[822] At the end of the conversation, Ludendorff was critical of Von Seeckt, from whom he had received no clarity. Nevertheless, Ludendorff promised that he would do his best to get the employable units from Bavaria at the very least behind the Reichswehrleiding.[823]

The meeting between Von Seeckt and Ludendorff could have been a new turning point somewhere. But it was not. Ludendorff's invitation emphasised his position within the national camp as an opposition leader rather than allowing him to return to the more moderate conservative camp. It is speculation whether Stinnes might have hoped for this. The fact is that Stinnes wanted to protect Ludendorff from new Kapp-like plans. 'If that is your way, then we go our separate ways', he had said.[824] In any case, Ludendorff did strive for more cooperation between the national organisations, although his own agenda also played a role in this, of course. For the Bavarian national clubs, Ludendorff was a bridge to the North German reactionaries. While there was a lot of plotting under the pretext of the French threat, the tightrope walker Stinnes was already working for his coal interests in the Rhineland. He had major interests in French territory, where 60% of his coal production came from. In addition, his impressive and barely surveyable economic empire was undergoing a major efficiency drive, with his Rheinelbe-Union, the Deutsch-Luxemburgischen Bergwerks-und-Hütten-Aktionsgesellschaft (Deutsch-Lux), the Gelsenkircher Bergwerks Aktiengesellschaft (GBAG), Siemens-Schuckert Konzern together forming Siemens-Rheinelbe-Schuckert Union (SRSU).[825] His man in the Rhineland was Konrad Adenauer, whom his biographer Charles Wighton described as Stinnes' 'shadow'.[826] In the Ruhr, according to Wighton, Stinnes was the 'leader recognised by all'.[827] The 'König der Ruhr', as his biographer Gaston Raphael called him, had even initiated a kind of private 'Wiedergutmachung' programme through Senator Marquis de Lubersac, which was questioned both in Germany and France itself. This enabled Stinnes to continue to supply the French industry on such a scale that French competitors complained. Under the guise of Wiedergutmachung, Stinnes was permitted to supply without certain export taxes, which also increased French demand for his supplies. For Stinnes, it was a way of safeguarding both his German and French interests and he presented it as 'good will', in the spirit of Rathenau's October 1921 rapprochement, the so-called 'Wiesbadener Abkommen'.[828] He used Adenauer, outside Berlin, as an intermediary to get into direct contact with the French minister Poincaré. Adenauer, with his pro-French sympathies,[829] was a convenient vehicle for this. He, who was originally from Cologne, occupied by the British, where he was mayor, had more freedom of action, yet neither Adenauer nor Stinnes could turn the wheel of history.

His wonderful life, in which we saw Ludendorff's life intersect several times, came to an abrupt end on 10 April 1924. Stinnes died at the age of 55 following gall bladder surgery. His left-wing opponents from the *Rote Fahne* wrote at the time:

He has everything on the belt
Automobiles, Wharfs, Kohlenhandel
Grand hotels, Parteien, Minister
Alles schluckt er, alles frisst er
From raw materials to newspapers, everything is under his leadership.[830]

The newspaper from the above libel poem contained another nice example of Stinnes' operation. In the summer of 1920, Stinnes bought the *Deutsche Allgemeine Zeitung*. Until then the newspaper had shown itself to be friendly to the government. That changed radically. The former editor-in-chief, Dr Rudolf Kaufmann, was replaced by Stinnes man Hans Humann, according to the American politician Morgenthau a man of 'influence', apparently referring to his former contacts with Kaiser Wilhelm II. As well as being the former editor-in-chief of the *Berliner Morgenpost,* Humann was also a former naval attaché in the Ottoman Empire and the genius behind the transfer of the hunted German warships the *Breslau* and the *Goeben* to the Turkish navy in 1914.[831] Under Humann, the newspaper turned so sharply to the right that the government issued admonishment after admonishment. The newspaper would violate the media code with the fledgling republic. It was clear that Stinnes was dealing with a principle here. He vented his feelings through the newspaper. But not much later, the *Deutsche Allegmeine Zeitung* was suddenly sold to... the state.[832]

But back to the manoeuvre of Von Seeckt and the government of Wilhelm Cuno, for it was not without risk. In fact, the audience and the request for support also legitimised the conservative revolutionaries. Now the drums were being beaten and the situation in the media was being whipped up into warlike spheres. How long could the men be kept in the barracks? Crisis, wrote the historian Ian Kershaw, was the oxygen that drove Hitler.[833] French politics and Berlin's struggles were grist to the NSDAP's mill. Not only Berlin reached out to the paramilitaries, but Von Lossow, the highest military commander in Bavaria, was sensitive to Röhms argument that the paramilitaries were a necessary patriotic front against the French threat and/or leftist insurgency. It seemed that the Kapp days had returned. Hitler even believed that the SA had been trained to such an extent (by Ehrhardt officers) that they could take on the French. On 26 February 1923, during a meeting in northern Germany, Ludendorff showed that his conversation had not been without influence. He asked the various right-wing paramilitary units to make themselves available to Von Seeckt's command. All but one agreed, including Hitler.[834]

Yet the drumbeat was also partly decorum. Although all nationalist forces were gathered and kept on standby, the 'black' Reichswehr and the Freikorps were of course not a real match for the French army. According to the memoirs of Heinrich Brüning, who as a Prussian delegate (Breslau) and leader of the 'Zentrumpartei' followed the case in the Rhineland closely and was also present at the discussion, Ludendorff showed himself to be much more realistic and cautious behind closed doors. Ludendorff pointed out to the politicians that it was precisely the Treaty of Versailles that protected Germany. After all, that was internationally recognised, while the French military trump card did put pressure on Germany, it isolated Paris at the same time. 'People are out of their minds', Ludendorff said of the hot-blooded, 'now the Treaty of Versailles is the only protection we have'.[835] He therefore warned against 'nationalistic sentiments'. In his conversation with Chancellor Cuno, Ludendorff strongly urged 'every instinctive patriotism, to resist'. [836]

In March 1923, Hitler was invited by Von Seeckt, who wanted to form as broad a front as possible. Here too, as with the earlier visit of Ludendorff, Von Seeckt showed himself to be a sphinx and did not let go. Hitler later complained about this to his Bavarian colleague Von Lossow, who remarked whether it wasn't time for Bavaria to go its own way, whereupon Hitler flew into a rage.[837] The two great German revolutionaries, Ludendorff and Hitler, were increasingly condemned to each other.

It was a time of double agendas. Finally, there was one more: Von Seeckt. In Weimar, it almost became a catchphrase: 'Wo steht Seeckt?' The Berlin administration had not forgotten that Von Seeckt had taken a dubious stance with the Kapp-Putsch either, but that he had nevertheless been retained by the ever-skilful Ebert. According to some, however, Von Seeckt's ambition went further, or as Wolfgang Stresemann stated in the biography of his father: 'politics beckoned', and Von Seeckt was 'fascinated' by it.[838] In the autumn of 1923, some people believed that the time was ripe for a military dictatorship. Von Seeckt was 'a person of stature' and a 'first-class military man', but in the end it was his (political) indecisiveness, as in the Kapp days, that prevented him from playing a historical role. Possibly, his enormous arrogance (according to Wolfgang Stresemann, even more so with his wife), stemming from an outdated class mentality, also played an important role. Germany was spared the Von Seeckt revolution, although he later entered politics, without much success.

Chapter 16

On the eve of the Feldherrnhalle-Putsch

'You may use my name'

Erich Ludendorff facing Kurt Ludecke before leaving for Italy to meet Benito Mussolini in 1923, on the eve of the putsch

The French invasion of the Ruhr and the subsequent emergency measures taken by the German government created an extremely dangerous and unstable political climate. France now had a fistful of Ruhrs in its hands, but this did not help to solve Berlin's economic problems with regard to reparations. Inflation increased hand over hand. In September 1923, the value of one dollar had risen to 142,400,000 marks and hunger was looming. Ebert was confronted with several problems:

1) The French influence in the Rheinland and Ruhr area. The German government had decided on passive resistance, but this also cost Berlin so much (strikes) that this resistance had to be abandoned soon. The danger of Rheinland-separatism loomed. On the other hand, the idea of a 'Versackungspolitik' had also arisen within Berlin's offices, whereby in fact - since France wanted to play the boss anyway - Paris was made to pay for the problems in the area. An extremely dangerous political game.

2) The call for national reconciliation as a result of the French intervention policy and the secret talks in Wannsee between army commanders and reactionary battle groups had an unclear result. Von Seeckt could count, at least temporarily, on the support of a number of national alliances, which were also pursuing their own course. The danger of a new coup from the right remained. The danger from the right came both from the conservative-national camp, to which the National Socialists and Ludendorff belonged, and from the side of the Bavarian separatists and advocates of a Bavarian leading role within the Great-German idea.

3) The communists, too, were still a significant force and, like the reactionaries, were lurking at their chance.

4) Finally, there was the role of the army itself. The loyalty of part of the officers corps and Von Seeckt was questioned.

The Berlin government was therefore walking on eggshells. Ebert was again, as in the Kapp days, a balancing act, with Scheidemann at his side. The latter travelled under a false passport and name to the Rhineland to sound out the mood.[839] The situation was anything but encouraging. It was true that Great Britain had called the French occupation illegal and that Pope Pius XII had offered to mediate, but the French were deep in Germany and all good intentions could not put an end to this.[840] Scheidemann[841], who tried to get the nation behind a united policy by means of a broad coalition, felt that Germany was being 'choked'. The Ruhr-historian Hans Spethmann thought that people were being 'plundered'.[842] Professor Kloevekorn wrote that France's reaction to Germany was a 'dangerous reflex movement', arising from nationalism, and that they opted - also with regard to the Saarland - for the 'certainty of the bayonet'.[843] And that France was prepared to rule with its fist was proven by the so-called 'Dortmunder Bartholomäusnacht', when as a result of non-compliance with an exit ban, seven German citizens in Dortmund were shot dead by the French troops. There was great indignation, and a reference to the Huguenot murders of 1572 was heard in the press. [844]

There was no hope from abroad. British Prime Minister Stanley Baldwin was not the man who could make Poincaré see sense.[845] Relations with the Rhineland itself were also difficult. There had to be compromises. The mayor of Essen and later Minister of the Interior Karl Jarres wanted to 'invalidate' the Treaty of Versailles.[846] The nationalist Karl Helffrich thought that 'diplomatic relations with France should be broken off'.[847] Still, these were not realistic options. There was no more money for passive resistance; there had to be a new line. A meeting was planned with the most important leaders from the Rheinland and the Ruhr area.

Before it could come to that, there were rumours of a military putsch. The government was shocked. Had Von Seeckt defied the government? In the end it was (at first sight) a small revolt, under the command of Major Buchrucker, which was put down by the attentive military leadership of Küstrin, where the epicentre of the revolt was located. It seemed an incident, but was it?

The fact that the leader of 'Stahlhelm', Franz Seldte, reported to Stresemann's office saying 'that the time had come for a military dictatorship' was not very encouraging.[848] Major Bruno Ernst Buchrucker was born in 1878 and had played a role in the reactionary camp for some time. He had been commander of 1st-battalion of the Freikorps Eulenburg and had taken part in the Kapp-Putsch. In the aftermath of the Kapp-Putsch, his units had crushed a strike in the city of Cottbus with the using violence, and killing several people. This cost him his job in defence. Even after that, Buchrucker remained a player in the field. As a private individual, he was connected with work at the 'Wehrkreiskommando III' of the officer Fedor von Bock (Military District of Northern Germany), who became famous in the Second World War, and he carried out work for the 'black Reichswehr'. In addition to the legal 100,000 men, all kinds of units and weapons were kept on standby and Buchrucker played a not insignificant role in organising these cells in Northern Germany. He elaborated on the preparatory work of 'Forstrat' Georg Escherin who, after an active life in the timber trade in the German-African tropics, had worked his way up to organiser of the black Reichswehr. All in all, around 18,000 men were to be deployed in the Küstrin area. The core of the men in the 'Arbeitsgemeinschaften', built up by Buchrucker, were in part former Eherhardt men (the former brigade now bore the name 'Bund Wiking') who could not have been included in the 'Schiffsstammdivision Nordsee'. These men were deployed elsewhere, and were followed and guided through the 'Mannschaftsfürsorgstelle' in Wilhelmshaven. Overarching the whole country, the construction work was mainly in the hands of Ehrhardt's confidant Killinger and later also Kautter, and the whole thing took place with the support of the naval intelligence service 'Abwehr' (Erhardt's confidant Canaris) and pillars in the Reichswehr. Buchrucker was thus not acting on his own. Paramilitary units (5,000 men) of Ehrhardt had been assembled in Franconia and another 6,000 men around Coburg. Early intervention in Küstrin dampened the revolutionary attempt in advance.[849]

Buchrucker was sentenced to ten years for high treason, but was released in 1927.[850] Later, he joined the Strasser brothers and became head of the 'Black Guard'. After 1933, he disappeared into a concentration camp for eighteen months, but was released again and rose to the rank of colonel in the Wehrmacht.[851] He died in 1966 in Bad Godesberg.

Under this pressure, the meeting with the leaders of Rheinland and Ruhrgebiet took place on 25 October 1923. In Hagen, 23 mayors and the Berlin administration met to discuss the future. Everything was tense to the extreme. Could Berlin still count on a constitutional link with these western regions of Germany? It soon became clear that opinions were divided. Paul Moldenhauer (Duitse Volkspartei) argued for moderate federalism, Konrad Adenauer (Zentrum) revealed himself to be a separatist, Bernhard Falk (Demokraten) believed that Adenauer's option was only applicable if circumstances dictated it.[852] Stresemann opposed separatism with tooth and nail, also because he feared that after the Rhineland and the Ruhr, Bavaria would follow. He called it 'utterly impossible'.[853] Adenauer's argument in favour of separatism was that an independent Rhineland and Ruhr would internationalise the cause, taking it out of French hands. Adenauer thus presented separatism as a national interest. Stresemann considered this internationalisation an enormous risk and nobody dared to make a final separatist decision in Hagen. Ebert and Stresemann ultimately held the matter together. Later, when separatism was less opportune, Adenauer presented things as if Berlin had wanted to abandon the Rhineland and the Ruhr.[854]

A crisis had been averted for the time being. At the beginning of October, Ebert also whistled back the worst arrogance of the Reichswehr. As if there were not enough problems, Von Seeckt openly stated that he had no confidence whatsoever in Gustav Stresemann, thus of course directly frustrating Ebert's policy. 'A counter-revolutionary Reichswehr would take our breath away,' said the SPD politician Paul Levi in those days.[855] This time, Ebert intervened strongly. He called Von Seeckt and his immediate superior, Defence Minister Gessler, to him. The latter expressed his confidence in politics after all. Von Seeckt kept silent as always but would refrain from further criticism. Nevertheless, Von Seeckt had sent a signal to the radical groups that the 'Erfüllungspolitiker' could not count on the support of the Reichswehr in advance.[856]

Besides Buchrucker, the communists had also understood this. On 7 October, unrest broke out in the city of Dresden - which had a communist background. Indeed, there was something in the air from the left. In particular, the strikes and unemployment and the general social misery - which resulted from the French intervention since 11 January 1923 - were grist to the mill of the communists. According to some KPD leaders, the communists were stronger among the workers than the SPD. Within the party, there were fierce debates about the direction to take. Some referred to the spring of 1920, when revolution seemed possible. Others felt that a historic opportunity had been squandered, that the party had acted too much in the spirit of Bakunin, the founder of anarchism, and that the principles of Marxism had been thrown overboard. A point of contention, again in 1923, was how to relate to the SPD: were we going to join forces, or were we going to regard them in principle as an enemy of the class, or at least as a party that misled the workers? At the end of January, beginning of February 1923, the 8th party congress took place in Leipzig and things went very badly. In particular, front man Heinrich Brandler was given a beating by the most radical corner, but in the end 'Realpolitik' won from the hotheads. Some time later, under the watchful eye of the Kommintern, the agreement was reaffirmed and streamlined in May 1923. In practice, this meant that the German communists were more and more on the leash of Moscow. However, this did not necessarily mean evolution instead of revolution. New opportunities presented themselves, alliances that one might not have thought of at first.[857]

None other than Karl Radek played an important role in this. Radek, who had lived in Germany for a long time, had a great feeling for what was going on in the streets and saw the French occupation of the Ruhrgebiet as a definite opportunity for the communists. The hatred of France was so great, so widespread (also among workers), that a popular war against France was a way to mobilise the street. In doing so, Radek was prepared to reach out to German nationalists. Radek drew on his experiences after the 2nd party congress in 1919. Back then, voices had already called for working with nationalists to overthrow the 'Erfüllungspolitik' and revolutionise Germany. In fact, Radek proposed the same plan that Ludendorff had in 1917, by forming an unnatural alliance with Lenin to revolutionise Tsarist Russia. At the time, Radek had been in contact with leaders of these thoughts, Fritz Wolffheim and Heinrich Laufenberg, with the aim of starting a 'Nationalbolschewismus'. Lenin, however, rejected these plans in January 1920. Two years later, Radek revived these plans, and in the communist periodical *Roten Fahnen*, this idea was even openly toyed with; an ideological helping hand followed to people on the right, such as Reventlow and Arthur Moeller van den Bruck. Internally, this course was also called the 'Schlageter course' (after the national martyr in the dispute with France). Moeller van den Bruck believed that Germany's main enemy was in the West and Germany's only possible ally was in the East. He spoke of Germany and Russia as the two 'young oppressed peoples', and advocated the fight against liberalism.[858]

However, the course on the right was short-lived. Eventually, they returned to the old familiar concept. In August 1923, the street was mobilised with an anti-fascism day and the following month Reventlow wrote his last article in *Roten Fahne*.[859] Moscow had given the green light for a revolution. Recently released letters and documents published by Aufbau publishers in Germany have revealed that the revolution scenario came from Moscow, as did the financial resources. In retrospect, it is striking that by no means everything was correctly assessed. The German communist Clara Zetkin, who was in a sanatorium for health reasons, announced from Moscow that Germany was facing the same big decisions as Russia at the time.[860] Barndler, but also Trotsky, warned of the poor chances of the uprising, but they persevered. One reason was the fact that on 10 and 16 October, communists had been admitted to the Landesregierungen of Saxony and Thuringia. Through this base within the establishment, Moscow believed they could get their hands on weapons and thus arm 50 to 60,000 workers and unleash the revolution.[861] However, the Politburo's plans were thwarted. Ebert not only put an end to von Seeckt's arrogance and Buchrucker's hubris, but on 20 October he even sidelined the governments in Saxony and Thuringia. He had rightly realised that this would herald a very negative trend. The Politburo's plans to arm the workers were suddenly called into question. Moscow, however, did not want to throw in the towel and ordered strikes and revolt. But the local leaders, led by Brandler, saw how the call to strike was received by their supporters. There was little enthusiasm, especially since the Reichswehr was marching into central Germany. In the end, only in isolated cases - especially in Hamburg - did a temporary uprising occur, which was quickly suppressed. Here, under the leadership of the communist leader Ernst Thaelmann, a native of Hamburg, communists had stormed police stations and armed themselves. During the three days of unrest ('Red October') several dozen people died. When it became clear that the rebels in Hamburg were operating in total isolation, and also had few weapons, the battle was broken off. The leaders, including Thaelmann, went underground.[862] The Politburo revolution failed. Once again, the Weimar Republic passed through the eye of the needle.

Meanwhile, the morally strong groups on the right were gathering. The practical unification lay mainly with Ernst Röhm. Ludendorff stood above it as a symbolic figure (and more than that). In January 1923, the groups on the right gathered within the so-called 'Arbeitsgemeinschaft'. On 5 February, they sent a letter to the Bavarian government to reassure it. This letter showed that the 'Arbeitsgemeinschaft' started thinking more and more from its own strength. Despite the fact that there were good contacts in the police and judiciary through 'Reichsflagge', the nationalistic organisation of Hauptmann Weiss, and that the NSDAP also had useful lines of communication at its disposal, a certain power struggle was palpable. In the 'Arbeitsgemeinschaft', Röhm, a former professional officer who was a member of the NSDAP, combined the national units, including 'Reichsflagge', the NSDAP, 'Oberland' and others. Names that would all play a role in the Feldherrnhalle-Putsch of November 1923 gathered in this 'Arbeitsgemeinschaft'. 'Reichsflagge' was described by Röhm as one of the best-oiled organisations and had good connections with Ludendorff. Commander Heiss personally took Ludendorff along in his car and drove him to the various departments.[863]

'Oberland' was headed by veterinarian Dr. Friedrich Weber. In Southern Bavaria, new departments had come into being, with Ingolstadt as their centre of gravity. This branch of 'Oberland' was also known as 'Unterland'. From the NSDAP side, the SA was especially important as a nascent commando group.

Initially, the SA was commanded by Von Klintsch, but Hermann Göring had just been appointed its new commander. Röhm described him as a 'spirited officer', and a 'fresh and untroubled go-getter'.[864] Göring was held in high regard because he had been commander of the famous air force unit - Jagdgeschwader Von Richthofen - during the First World War. Göring himself had twenty-eight air victories to his name. His support of the NSDAP earned him moral credit.[865]

Ludendorff himself wrote in his memoirs that he was increasingly in contact with the 'Sturmabteilungen (SA) established by Hitler'.[866] It is interesting that Ludendorff wrote about the SA instead of the NSDAP. Ludendorff undoubtedly realised that political power lay where one had managed to mobilise 'the street'. To speak with Mao: power in those days came from the barrel of a gun, and Ludendorff travelled to the paramilitary organisations one by one, such as a visit to 'Oberland' at Hoheneck Castle in Franconia near Nuremberg, a residence of the Völkische publisher Julius F. Lehmann, where a bust of Ludendorff stood in the great hall. Lehman was a Protestant and had an aversion to Catholicism and considered Jews a threat to Germany, which he had in common with Ludendorff. In Bavaria, his anti-Catholicism had earned the publisher many threatening letters, so that he at times walked the streets armed. He was a supporter of the Los-von-Rom movement and for many years had published the radical Lutheran magazine *Die Wartburg*.[867] Lehmann believed in the coming of a 'new Luther' who would free Germany from spiritual distress. For some time he believed that this new Luther was the 'Wahl-Deutscher' Houston Stewart Chamberlain, the author of *Die Grundlagen des 19 Jahrhunderts, which* was also highly regarded by Hitler and Rosenberg. Chamberlain also influenced Lehmann's view of Judaism; he believed that Germany had to be rid of its Jewish roots. Paul de Lagarde was also one of his spiritual models. His son-in-law was Friedrich Weber, the leader of the 'Bund Oberland'. The meetings with the young people of 'Oberland' or other (paramilitary/ youth) organisations, from which Ludendorff took the defilement, were balm on Lehmann's soul. 'My husband always liked to participate in these meetings', wrote his wife Melanie Lehmann, 'the freshness of youth did him good'.[868]

Revolution was in the air and Ludendorff's star was rising. It was to be his last period in the limelight of great history. As always, he played his role diplomatically, with many cards up his sleeve. Ludendorff was consulted by all and sundry who wanted to have a pot on the fire. After all, in the event of a successful putsch by the Völkisch side, Ludendorff could suddenly transform from a 'symbolic figure' into the new strong man in Germany. In his memoirs, Ludendorff is silent about his personal ambitions and about the fact that he was more than a symbol figure. However, the many visits and diplomatic initiatives, right on the eve of the putsch, prove this. Many of these were also from abroad or of his own initiative. A centre of gravity were the 'Whites' from Russia and the Balten Germans who had sought refuge in the West after the establishment of Communism and the civil war lost by the 'Whites'. There were also more exotic contacts, such as with the Chinese, and the obviously with the rising star of Benito Mussolini and Fascism in Italy.

Today, Hitler and Mussolini are mentioned in the same breath. In the year 1923, before the putsch, Hitler was still a great unknown to Benito Mussolini. His 'March on Rome' served as an example of what was to come in Munich. The launch of a line to Rome took place via one of the most curious Nazis: Kurt Ludecke. Ludecke was a gambler, entrepreneur, playboy and idealist. At first, there was little evidence of the latter. Since the age of 19, he frequently left Germany and earned large sums of money in the casinos of France and Italy. Due to amorous adventures, he had already gotten into trouble in German military service (at liberty and not in uniform) and, having become rich in the gambling world, he lived like a playboy.

The carefree life changed when the First World War broke out. Ludecke was in Mannheim at the time for a card tournament. His French driver was interned and his American girlfriend expelled from the country. There, too, he proved too fragile for the military profession and was transferred to a psychiatric hospital. After the war, he immediately took his chances as an entrepreneur. German strategic goods were confiscated by the Entente, and Ludecke tried to secure things, such as placing ships under the Mexican flag and supplying aircraft to Argentina. During a visit to revolutionary Mexico, he happened to be on the train that also carried President Venustiano Carranza, from Mexico City to Vera Cruz. The train ran into units looking for the president and Ludecke only just managed to survive. Carranza was less fortunate. Leaving the Mexican revolution behind, Ludecke fled to North America and in the US came into contact with William J. Cameron, one of the editors of Henry Ford's anti-Semitic newspaper *Dearborn Independent*. This newspaper of the car manufacturer had just started a 91-part hate series against Jews under the title *The International Jew: the World's problem*. This was not an unimportant encounter, for the hitherto not very politically educated Ludecke encountered the same anti-Semitic propaganda that he was already familiar with from Germany, at the time whispered by a friend of his, connected to the University of Heidelberg, Prof. Alfred von Domaszewski, who had alerted Ludecke to the ideas of Arthur de Gobineau, Houston Stewart Chamberlain and Paul de Lagarde. Later, Ludecke would also play a mediating role, together with Winifred Wagner, between Ludendorff-Hitler and Henry Ford, with the latter providing financial support.

The latter - American support for Nazis - had already come to a head earlier. In January 1924, Siegfried and Winifred Wagner had travelled from Bremen to the United States to raise money for the impoverished Wagner-Festspiel in Bayreuth. With the help of music agent Jules Daiber, they hoped to raise money through a tour there. They also came into contact with Henry Ford. Shortly afterwards, there was a riot in the American press because a cheque for USD 100 had been intercepted from Winifred to... Ludendorff. Despite the not shockingly large amount, the reactions were not to be trifled with. 'American money for Nazis', was the not too friendly comment. *'Ludendorff works like a red rag,'* Winifred wrote. *'The Americans are still very hostile to Germany, and infected with pacifism'*.[869] Ford supported the völkisch camp until 1927, then he revised his opinion and had his anti-Semitic works burned in public. The compensation he paid to the Jews he maltreated is unknown to this day.[870]

Back in Germany, after a temporary stay in Estonia, where Ludecke traded with the communists, he was struck by the poverty of his once-proud homeland. Ludecke felt for the first time that he had to do something in return, but was primarily in search of the 'German soul'. Through Julius Streicher, Ludecke came into contact with Hitler and his rude, unadulterated tone immediately appealed to him. 'I found myself, my leader and my cause,' he later said.

Ludecke offered his services, and the charming Ludecke soon became a kind of party diplomat. Initially, he had been in contact with North German völkisch groups and Hitler asked him to keep in touch with them, so that he would know about the competition. Völkisch groups with a (too) strong Bavarian bias had to be watched as well, such as the 'Bund Bayern und Reich' of Dr. Otto Pittinger. Glamorous as ever, Ludecke believed that international support for Hitler's cause should not be lacking, and the 'coming man' on the right was, of course, Benito Mussolini. The way to this was not the unknown Hitler, but the widely known figure of Ludendorff.

Through Von Reventlow, Ludecke was introduced to Ludendorff. 'He was the passport to any political situation', Ludecke thought, looking back at Ludendorff's position on the eve of the putsch.[871] The meeting took place in Ludendorff's house on the Ludwighöhe. In the study, Ludecke waited for Ludendorff while he stood face to face with the famous painting of Ludendorff and Von Hindenburg, bent over the maps which he had seen endlessly in reproductions. (This was in fact a preliminary study for the painting by Professor Vogel, which still hangs in Tutzing). For a moment he nervously wondered 'what am I doing here', but then the door swung open. The great general entered the room. Tall, blue-eyed, massive and powerful, calm but alert and determined, he looked like a tower separating the world. 'After saying hello to Von Reventlow, he welcomed me in a natural and simple way. He offered us a chair, with a smile and a cigar, and put us at ease'. [872]

It is interesting to see how even a 'people person' like Ludecke could not see through Ludendorff directly. He thought that Reventlow and he were doing their best to put Hitler in a good light with Ludendorff. Both visitors apparently had no idea how far Ludendorff had already moved towards the camp of Hitler and his brown battalions. Ludendorff allowed himself to be briefly shown his (Prussian) cards when Ludecke showed his disappointment in other Völkisch leaders, such as Otto Pittinger, who did not seem serious in his support of a real stand against the Republic from Bavaria. To Ludecke's surprise, Ludendorff was enthusiastic about Pittinger's failure. Ludendorff frankly stated that there were already enough 'Bavarian Catholics' involved. Moreover, Ludendorff was enthusiastic about Ludecke's plan to make contact with Mussolini. 'You may use my name,' Ludendorff said to Kurt Ludecke, the man who had transformed from playboy to diplomat. [873]

The meeting with Mussolini came about. Ludecke travelled to Milan and through the *Popolo d'Italia* newspaper, founded by Mussolini, he came into contact with the Duce. 'I bring you greetings from General Ludendorff and Adolf Hitler', he reported immediately on his arrival.[874] It turned out to be convenient that Ludecke was allowed to use Ludendorff's name. Mussolini appeared never to have heard of Hitler. The conversation continued in French and the first lines were spun between what would later be called the Berlin-Rome axis.[875]

Ludendorff was very worried about Russia and communism. He especially feared the communist propaganda. He thought that it was used effectively and that communism was a great threat in Western Europe too. From his vision of the 'überstaatliche powers', he observed that especially in those countries where the Roman Catholic influence was strong, communism got a foothold. Implicitly, Ludendorff hinted that he saw a connection between the überstaatliche power of Rome and communism. Specifically, Ludendorff referred to Spain and Italy, noting that Mussolini was responding to the communists.[876] But in Ludendorff's eyes, the situation remained worrying. He found the 'Whites' who came to him with their counter-revolutionary plans for Russia 'remarkably optimistic'. [877]

There were important parallels between the Völkisch camp around Ludendorff and the 'Whites'. Both had lost and were 'suffering' under a new regime, and both were hiding in the political wings with paramilitary organisations.

Ludendorff was pessimistic, rightly so in retrospect, about the chances of success of the 'White resistance' against the new rulers in Moscow. Nevertheless, the 'Whites' were a significant factor. After the armies of Koltschak, Judenitsch, Denikin, Wrangel and Semyonow had been defeated by Trotsky's Red Army, the great exodus of 'Whites' from Russia had begun. In total, about one and a half to two million Russians left the country. With them also went an ideology that had striking similarities with the Ludendorff camp. The 'Whites' had their own version of the stab-in-the-back myth, in which they 'explained' the downfall of the tsarist empire. These ideas were as anti-Semitic and reactionary as Ludendorff's worldview. They also brought their pogrom mentality, the veneration of the black hundred, the tsarist contempt for democracy, the dark hatreds and prejudices expressed in *The Protocols of the Sages of Zion*. As many as half a million of the Russians settled in Germany, followed by 400,000 in France, 90,000 in Poland and in many other countries, including 3,000 in New York alone. A not insignificant part of these "Whites" tried to reorganise themselves outside Russia (Soviet Union) and prepare the counter-revolution.

These were not just wild plans, they were organised politics, including (para) military units. Thus, parts of the Wrangel army were stationed in the Balkans, eight thousand Cossacks in Yugoslavia, thousands of men were in Hungary and Greece. The tsarist fleet had entered the North-African-French port of Biserta with all its crews. There were thirty ships and 6000 officers and sailors. In Poland, with Pilsudski's approval, a Russian 'white' army of about 30,000 troops had been created. There were even units in Japan.

The effectiveness of the "Whites" was hampered by the fact that there were different currents among them. There were those who thought mainly of (Great) Slavicism and others who dreamed of Eurasia. These were ideas that also appealed ideologically to an Alfred Rosenberg, for example (although he would have had problems with the Christian character), and, from a geopolitical point of view, were compatible with the 'Kernraum-Europa' idea of geopoliticologist Karl Haushofer, although this idea, like the Great Slavic, was at odds with Hitler's racial ideas. National Bolshevik ideas were also prevalent, and some hoped for an evolution within Russia. At a later stage, groups also drew on the example of Portugal, with the Salazar regime, and among the young Russians ('Mladorossy') who gathered in Munich in 1923, fascist Italy, where Mussolini became a significant power that year, played an important role. Under the leadership of Alexander Kazem-Bek, a militant anti-communism emerged. However, this did not establish a definitive link with Germany. Hitler's 'Lebensraum' philosophy was ultimately incompatible with Kazem-Bek's ideas, and many followers ended up in the resistance. [878]

Yet, in 1923 the signals were still green. The political heart was formed by the 'Torgprom' organisation, a Russian financial organisation, which included embittered nobles and Russian big industrialists such as banker G.N. Nobel, the Russian 'Rockefeller' Stepan Lianosow, merchant Vladimir Riabuschinsky and steel magnate N.K. Denisow. Bavaria, too, soon became acquainted with the 'new' Russians. In the summer of 1921 a big anti-Soviet conference was organised in the picturesque Bad Reichenhal.[879] Among the audience were representatives of the NSDAP, including Nazi ideologist and Balten German Alfred Rosenberg. Erich Ludendorff and Oberst Bauer were present as well. [880]

Rosenberg was the son of a Balten German landowner and had studied architecture at the Moscow Academy of Polytechnics. After the Communists seized power, he had fought the Red Army in the Baltic Sea regions within units commanded by General Graf Ruediger von der Goltz. Rosenberg later moved to Munich where, through another Balten German connection, the later Nazi top official Otto von Kursel, he became[881] an associate of Hitler's teacher Dietrich Eckart, who immediately saw the 'value' of the young, heavily anti-Semitic intellectual in the struggle against Yaweh religion. Rosenberg soon became part of a network that also included Max Erwin von Scheubner-Richter, as well as Arno von Schickedanz and Iwan Poltawetz-Ostranitza, former Minister of Transport under Hetmans' pro-German temporary Ukrainian government, Paul Skoropadski. These were all contacts who belonged to Ludendorff's 'Russian connection' and played an important role in the organisation and financing of the right-wing camp in Bavaria. A piquant detail in this connection was the fact that the heavily anti-Semitic *Weltdienst*, for which Rosenberg worked, and a number of other prominent people, also from 'das Militär', such as Oberstleutnant A.D Fleischhauer from Erfurt, and the former Wrangl officer Ivan Koncevic, worked for it. This soldier was married to Elena Karcova, the niece of the author of *The Protocols of the Sages of Zion*, Sergei Nilus. Koncevic worked for *Welt-Dienst* from France. During the Bern trial in 1934, in an attempt to have The *Protocols* banned, Koncevic acted as an expert witness on the side of the defenders of the authenticity of the libel. [882]

The Russian publicist R. Sh. Ganelin characterised Rosenberg as 'ethnically German' but 'Russian by mentality'[883] and there is some truth in that. Rosenberg's biographer Ernst Piper pointed out that Rosenberg was also called the 'moral athlete'.[884] Rosenberg was strict and radical in his writing, which was full of metaphysics and metahistory, but showed more 'understanding' for the ethnic interests of the many working-class minorities in Russia than the Nazi administration did. In this sense, Rosenberg was a typical product of the Russian 'Reaktion'. In his later administrative functions in the east, this regularly brought him into conflict with the local 'bosses'.[885] In addition to traditional Russian anti-Semitism, Rosenberg's writing was also inspired by (the perversion of) Theosophy. Due to these esoteric excursions, his work was considered difficult and almost unfathomable, which sometimes earned him ridicule from his fellow party members.[886] Hitler, however, was fond of his 'Russian', he forgave him a temporary defection to a rival camp during the prison period in Landsberg am Lech that followed the Feldherrnhalle-Putsch and he honoured him with a high state literary prize when Thomas Mann won the *Nobel Prize for Literature*.

Of greater practical importance, however, was von Scheubner-Richter. This 'Balten-German' was an important pivotal figure in the right-wing political spectrum, a classmate of Otto von Kursell and a fellow student of Rosenberg and Schickedanz. His strength was that he, more than anyone else, connected the radical Russian 'Whites' with Ludendorff's völkisch camp. This was partly due to the fact that he was actually a 'Reichsdeutsche', but in the corridors he passed for a 'Balt'. His father was Saxon, his mother came from Riga, and since 1908 he had a home in Munich. But he was often in the Baltic and his contacts also made him an important financial pivot. [887]

This special position made Hitler say at his death: 'We can spare everybody but von Scheubner-Richter'. The journalist and Hitler biographer Konrad Heiden even called von Scheubner-Richter the 'Führer of the Führer', and at his funeral after his death at the Feldherrnhalle in Munich in 1923, the Protestant clergyman Kreppel said that von Scheubner-Richter was 'the most German German'.[888] An unusual position for someone born in Riga.

Von Scheubner-Richter's life was surrounded by a certain mystery. He is said to have been a Cossack leader in Persia, and to have had a mysterious period of service in Turkey, where he tried to help the persecuted Armenians.[889] His confidant Paul Leverkuehn wrote a biographical sketch about this time.[890] What was more important for his contact with Ludendorff was that Von Scheubner-Richter had been involved in all secret German attempts to destabilise the tsarist empire from within, something Ludendorff also had experience with (Lenin's trip to St. Petersburg). Von Scheubner-Richter was born in Riga, studied chemistry there, and initially served in the 7. Bayerischen Chevauleger-regiment. In January 1915, he went to Turkey for six months and then became active in the Persian-Russian border region. Here, he had been given the task to encourage Dagestan separatism, with the aim to separate the important oil fields of Baku from Russia.[891] In 1916, Von Scheubner-Richter was promoted in Munich and in the summer of 1917 he started a new special mission abroad.

He left for Sweden and established all kinds of contacts with separatist groups of various Russian-ethnic origins. Goal: destabilisation of the Tsarist Empire.

Important developments were taking place in the East: the February Revolution and the October Revolution of that year. In fact, these activities, as well as his experiences in Dagestan, were the best school for his new conspiratorial work in Bad Reichenhall. Afterwards, Von Scheubner-Richter served as press officer with the German 8th army in Riga, where he later briefly fell into communist hands, but managed to escape.

Von Scheubner-Richter, although now almost forgotten, also played an important role in the direct political game on the eve of the Feldherrnhalle-Putsch. At the end of September 1923, thus only a few weeks before the putsch, Von Scheubner-Richter dared to write a high-pitched letter to the Bavarian Prime Minister Eugen von Knilling, in which he harshly criticised him for tolerating the fact that the radical left was waging a smear campaign against the 'patriotic movement'. He added a veiled threat, pointing out that the nationalists had nothing left to do but 'self-help'. [892]

Karsten Brüggemann states in an article about Von Scheubner-Richter that Von Scheubner-Richter became Ludendorff's foreign specialist at the latest in 1922.[893] It was especially Von Scheubner-Richter's informal network of contacts that was important here. Still, from his time in the 'Ostdeutschen Heimatdienst', Von Scheubner-Richter had 'sub-units' of his 'Aufbau'-organisation at his disposal in Kaunas and Mitau (Jelgava), which were also well-known by Ludendorff. The East-European connection between Ludendorff and Von Scheubner-Richter possibly went back even further. Brüggemann states that, by order of Ludendorff and 'South-German industrialists', there had been contact in 1920 with general Petr N. Wrangl concerning the Crimea. Von Scheubner-Richter had founded the so-called 'Europa-Asien Gesellschaft' for this purpose. The interests were mainly economic. Although Wrangl later lost militarily, this so-called 'Gesellschaft' was not just a figment of his imagination. Von Scheubner-Richter travelled through Eastern Europe for six months and negotiated with Wrangl personally. Rosenberg and Schickedanz were also involved in establishing these contacts. [894]

Von Scheubner-Richter characterised the international cooperation against communism as the logical counterpart of the communist international; only this was an international of the nationalists. Brüggemann called Von Scheubner-Richter's way of taking his enemy as an example a 'pragmatic cynicism'.[895] The Red Army thwarted Ludendorff's Crimean plans, but good contacts did develop in that period with Horthy-Hungary, where there were also experiences of Bela Kun's bloody communist revolutionary days. Budapest was a gathering place for conspiratorial forces from Russia, Austria, Bavaria and other parts of Germany.

The question arises who the South German industrialists behind Ludendorff's Crimean plan were? That the Crimea also had Ludendorff's military interest was obvious. Strategically, the Crimea was the gateway to the Balkans and thus a springboard to the oil fields of Romanian Ploesti. On the other hand, it could also be a springboard eastwards to the Donetsk coal basin. The natural 'flanking' position of Crimea was militarily interesting.[896] In addition, Crimea was a naval support point, important for the Black Sea, and the area was temporarily under 'white' control.

Who the industrialists who supported the contact with Wrangl and the Crimean plans exactly were is not clear. The name of politician and industrialist Theodor von Cramer-Klett comes to mind. The fact that this man was known as an advocate and champion of the Pope may not have been as big a problem for Ludendorff in 1920 as it was in his later years. Von Cramer-Klett was a foreman in Von Scheubner-Richter's 'Aufbau' programme.[897]

Besides Rosenberg and Von Scheubner-Richter, Ludendorff's Russian network consisted of Colonel Ivan Poltawetz-Ostranitza, a notorious officer who was 'suspected' of carrying out pogroms, and General Vladimir Biskupski, who would later represent the Russian immigrants in the Third Reich.[898] Arno von Schickedanz most probably also knew Ludendorff. Von Schickedanz was a close associate of Von Scheubner-Richter and involved in the Wrangl contacts that took place in 1920 at Ludendorff's request. Von Schickedanz had served in the German cavalry as a war-volunteer. He was also in good contact with Rosenberg, at whose 'Reichministerium Ost' he would later work. His speciality was diplomacy. The relationship with Rosenberg went back to his student days, when they both joined the nationalist student union 'Rubonia', of which Von Kursell and Von Scheubner-Richter were also members.[899] In the chaotic postwar period in the Baltic region, the Baltic-German students had been the first manpower reservoir for the pro-German paramilitary units that had to resist the Red Army.[900] Schickedanz later published (anti-Semitic) pieces in the *Völkischen Beobachter* (with Rosenberg as chief editor), as well as in the *NS-Monatsheften*. In 1927, he published the anti-Semitic book *Die Juden. Eine Gegenrasse.*

There was also contact with the intended heir to the Russian throne, Grand Duke Kyrill Wladimirowitsch Romanow and his wife, Grand Princess Viktoria Melita von Sachsen-Coburg und Gotha.[901] Kyrill was officially named 'Tsar in Exile' by the 'Whites' in Paris in 1924. 'We must gather a league of men', wrote Alfred Rosenberg later in his most famous work *Der Mythus des 20. Jahrhundert*. These insights, which could be traced back to the black centenarians of tsarist times, would now be translated to the paramilitary units of the völkisch camp and later to Hitler and his brown columns.

The conspiracy was fuelled by anti-Semitism. We remember the enormous influence of *Die Protokolle* on Ludendorff, which he got to know through Gottfried zur Beek. This was preceded by a Russian trajectory. Zur Beek - pseudonym of Ludendorff's fellow officer Müller von Hausen, as we saw - received *Die Protokolle* from a number of Russians who were part of the black hundred. The trail of *Die Protokolle* from Russia to Germany went via Piotr (Peter/Petr) Nikolaevic Shabelski-Bork, Fedor Viktorovic Vinberg and Serge Tabonitskil.

Shabelski-Bork, whose real name was Nikolai Popov and who also published under the pseudonym Stary Kiribey, had an adventurous life in which, at least according to his writings, he attempted to free the tsarist family in Yekaterinburg (now Swerdlowsk). This story already mentioned *Die Protokolle*. The tsarina is said to have been in possession of an early version by Sergei Nilus, *The Great in the Small*, with *Die Protokolle* attached. She is said to have scratched a swastika in the window sill before her execution. All this was food for the anti-Semites who believed that the murder of the Tsar and his family was a 'Jewish plot'. On the walls of the room where the family was murdered there was allegedly graffiti in Hebrew. When the ground got too hot for Shabelski-Bork, he - like thousands of his compatriots - fled abroad.

In Kiev, or as other sources claim in the communist cell (the 'Crosses' prison) where he was temporarily held, he came into contact with Fedor Vinberg, who shared his anti-Semitic ideas. From Vinberg we know that in personal conversations he introduced Hitler to Russian anti-Semitism.[902] Later, Serge Taboritski was added. The trio travelled on to Berlin, where they came into contact with Ludwig Müller von Hausen, who was already active in the field of political anti-Semitism. *The Protokolle*, which he received in February 1919, immediately fell on fertile soil with him. Interesting and little known is the fact that Sergei Nilus' niece, Elena Jur'evna Karcova, played a key role in it. She had lived for years in the house of Nilus and his wife Elena Alexsandrovna Ozerova and was initiated in his writings. Given the fact that Nilus had gladly emigrated to Germany, but was detained by the Soviet authorities - he spent some time in the Lubyanka prison - his niece took care of the distribution of his writings, after which she continued to live in silence in Germany, France and later the United States, where she died in 1989, aged almost 96.[903] Von Hausen immediately started to collect more information about Nilus and received help from General Kurlov, former head of the tsarist secret service 'Okhrana' and later collaborator of the Ukrainian nationalist Skoropadsky. In his *History of the Russian Revolution*, Trotsky counted Kurlov as Rasputin's 'camarilla'.[904] After a conflict with his superiors, Kurlov ended up in Berlin after the First World War.[905] Via Kurlov, a certain lieutenant Kartsev, who had worked for German intelligence in Ukraine, also turned up. He, too, fed Von Hausen's anti-Semitic ideas. Partly due to this information, Von Hausen came to the conclusion that *Die Protokolle* were first written in Hebrew and then translated into Russian by Nilus. Von Hausen, who mastered the Russian language and was already active in the association 'Gegen die Uberhebung des Judentums E.V', immediately brought it to the German market, with all its consequences. He also published about *Die Protokolle* and related matters in the *Munich Beobachter* and later in the *Völkische Beobachter*, the newspaper of Dietrich Eckart and Alfred Rosenberg.

Die Protokolle were not the only 'poisonous' document that Von Hausen borrowed from his Russian sources[906]. Von Hausen also circulated the so-called *Zunder-document* in the German-speaking regions. This document supported the thesis of *Die Protokolle*, that after the communist revolution, Russia was under 'Jewish rule'. Earlier, from the November 1919 edition of *Prizyv*, a story had been spread that the Jew Trotsky, in charge of the Red Army, and other high Soviet officials, held 'black masses' within the Kremlin walls. In other words, devil worship. A Lithuanian communist who was said to have blabbed about this was murdered on Trotsky's orders.

Besides *Prizyv*, Vinberg, Shabelskii-Bork and Taboritski also published the periodical *Lutch Sveta*. The third issue of this magazine also included *Die Protokolle*, 'a product of fantasy and fabrication', as the historian P.J.G. Pulzer rightly said, but nevertheless falling on fertile ground. [907]

By the way, the activities of these Russian connections of Ludendorff and the völkisch were not purely paper-based. All three Russians took part in the Kapp-Putsch, which shows that the Russian patriots and the völkisch had a pact for a long time. After the Kapp-Putsch, their publications were banned. That the gentlemen were no paper tigers, was also shown by their radicalism in 'own' Russian circles. In March 1922, a 'Russian Feme' took place on the politician Milukov, who was considered a traitor. However, they accidentally murdered V. Nabokov (the father of the famous writer), who, just like Milukov, was a 'Freemason' in the eyes of the murderers and a danger to the Russian people. After the failed attempt on Milukov's life, Vinberg ran away to France, where he died in February 1927. The others were in prison until 1927.[908]

The Russian Ludendorff circle around Von Scheubner-Richter also had money at its disposal, among others through the wealthy General Biskupski, Grand Duke Kyrill. These sources are obvious, but it is likely that Von Scheubner-Richter was able to tap into other channels, some not so obvious at first glance. Indeed, Von Scheubner-Richter also made use of his 'Catholic' network, in addition to his aristocratic contacts (his wife was from the nobility). We know that Ludendorff could be remarkably pragmatic at times and very puritanical at others. The money apparently eased the pain, because among the secret donors of Von Scheubner-Richter there were also ultra-montane, Habsburg-oriented forces, among which the Spanish Royal House (as protector of the - catholic - House of Wittelsbach), the House of Wittelsbach itself (prince Rupprecht) which had in common with the tsarist regime that they had been dismissed from the throne and thus hoped to buy political influence, and last but not least the French secret service. The latter can only be understood if we recall the conspiracy around Adenauer and Rhineland separatism. France liked to strengthen Bavarian nationalism and separatism as a counterweight to Prussia. A division of Germany was to their advantage. However, the flirtation with France did not take place entirely underground. After the rapprochement of the left from Radek and the so-called 'Schlageterrede' from July 1923, which was ignored by the 'white international', French nationalists were openly reached out to. The enemy of my enemy is my friend, was apparently the motto.[909]

Of course Ludendorff - and Hitler too - thought and acted 'big-German', but balancing artist Von Scheubner-Richter had a less clear agenda. In that sense, Von Scheubner-Richter was indeed, as Hitlers stated after his death, 'irreplaceable'.[910] Paris probably saw Von Scheubner-Richter primarily as a restorer of the Bavarian monarchy, and that as a stepping stone to a Bavarian 'Alleingang'. The word cynical-pragmatism had already been dropped on Von Scheubner-Richter. In fact, his bridging function between Russian monarchists and the Völkisch camp was also divided by a kind of schism. Von Scheubner-Richter presented himself in Russian monarchist circles as 'white-national', whereas during the First World War he had pursued the collapse of the tsarist empire.

Besides the contact with the 'white international', there were also the German industrialists who sought contact with Ludendorff. Here, too, Von Scheubner-Richter often played a mediating role. They helped to finance the völkische movement. That Stinnes played a role - and Von Cramer-Klett as well - will not surprise anyone.[911] In the house of Von Scheubner-Richter, Ludendorff was also introduced to another important industrialist, Fritz Thyssen. Not entirely coincidentally, this contact came about just before the Feldherrnhalle-Putsch. Interests had to be safeguarded. Incidentally, Ludendorff knew August Thyssen, Fritz' father, who had served with him in the Füsselierregiment 39 in Düsseldorf.[912]

Since Thyssen himself later opened a booklet about his contacts with the right-wing camp: *I paid Hitler*, in cooperation with the American ghostwriter Emery Reves - in Dutch it appeared in the translation by G. Borg under the title *I financed Hitler* - he has become one of the better-known financiers of the völkisch camp. In those days, of course, such agreements took place in secret. There is only one photograph which shows Thyssen and Hitler together, and it is an interesting one because the steel foremen Dr. Albert Vögler and Dr. Borbet, both of the Vereinte Stahlwerke (Stinnes), are also on it.[913] It is fascinating to note that Thyssen, on his visit to the Völkische Camp, did not give the money to Hitler but to Ludendorff. The title *I financed Ludendorff* would not have been out of place in his memoirs. Ludendorff was 'the man' at that time, Hitler the 'up-and-coming man', as, by the way, Ludendorff also told Thyssen: 'He is the only one who understands politics'. Since Ludendorff lost political importance after 1924 and due to the later course of history, Hitler's role has become bigger and bigger.

The reason for Thyssen's support of the right-wing camp was his concern for his industrial interests. Thyssen was heir to one of the largest steel companies in Germany and belonged to the 'Ruhrbaronnen'. His extremely dominant father had pushed the company to unprecedented heights, alienating the other children, so that in 1915, aged 41, Fritz Thyssen was dismissed from the service to help the Thyssen Group cope with the growing hunger of the war economy. This is where Thyssen's political contacts began. He thus entered into a corporate tradition. In the past, the politician Erzberger had already been 'worked on' and he insisted in the Reichstag that the German Navy should no longer only use steel plates from Krupp and Stumms Dillinger Hütte, but also from Thyssen. His colleagues jeered at this proposal and suspected a personal interest. Erzberger defended himself by saying that he was only interested in more competition and thus better prices. Despite this, in December 1915, Erzberger was appointed to various supervisory posts within the Thyssen group and his allowances ultimately amounted to 100,000 Reichmarks a year. [914]

The relationship with Erzberger deteriorated when, after the start of the submarine war, the latter no longer believed in the final German victory. Erzberger's peace proposals of July 1917 caused a lasting estrangement. Thysen's aversion to the political left, which he also considered to be a threat to the company, brought him more and more to the right-wing camp. He did not take part in the general smear campaign against Erzberger, who, as we saw, was murdered with twelve pistol shots in the Black Forest in August 1921. He limited his criticism of Erzberger's views to personal letters. When the war ended and the Treaty of Versailles was signed, he became an activist. He travelled to Weimar to convince politicians not to ratify the treaty - 'Friedensdiktat'. The spartakism that followed in Germany and the Council republics brought Thyssen even more into the reactionary camp. This affected him personally when his father, August Thyssen, now 76 years old, was imprisoned by the Radencommunists and accused of conspiring against the revolution. Partly due to the mediation of Friedrich Ebert and Paul Lembke, the mayor of Mühlheim, it all ended in a hollow. However, Thyssen was shocked, and feared that Germany would slide into anarchy. Such 'kidnapping' of wealthy fellow citizens was a common occurrence in the time of the Council Republic. Hugo Stinnes' son, Edmund Stinnes, was also a victim of this. The French intervention in the Rhineland in 1923 strengthened Thyssen in his growing reactionary stance. Thyssen refused to follow French orders, and thus disappeared behind bars for some time. This was not an isolated incident, as the French ambitions were high (French heavy industry had to become competitive with German industry), but German patriotism and resistance did not make it happen.[915] Eventually the French let him go, partly because the workers threatened to go on strike. Thyssen was the man of the moment, and many believed that a role in politics lay ahead of him. 'I am an entrepreneur, I am a nationalist', he said.[916]

In Munich, Thyssen, who was accompanied by his wife Amélia, sought rapprochement with the Völkisch camp. Ludendorff visited the couple in their Munich hotel, where Thyssen presented Ludendorff with 100,000 gold marks. Ludendorff also introduced Thyssen to Hitler, but no further business resulted from this, as noted by Thyssen's biographer Hans Otto Eglau.[917] As an argument that he gave all the money to Ludendorff alone, Thyssen argued that Ludendorff aimed at a merger of the national organisations. How much money ultimately flowed to Hitler remained unclear.[918] Later, Thyssen emphasised that he supported the right mainly out of Catholic idealism, and he regretted the support for Hitler. According to Henry Ashby Turner, who also inspected the original typescripts of *I paid Hitler*, and who found out about the language problems between Thyssen and his ghostwriter, Thyssen paid 100,000 gold marks to Ludendorff and did not know whether that money also reached Hitler. It possibily could have been twice as much. Later on, new financial injections from Thyssen followed, also to Hugenberg. This can be read in the book by Henry Ashbly Turner jr., *Faschismus und Kapitalismus in Deutschland*.

Thyssen was accused of financing treason after the failed Munich coup. However, Thyssen claimed that he had only discussed the 'Ruhrkampf' with Ludendorff and offered him money for it. This claim was at odds with his behaviour. A day after the failed coup, Thyssen visited Ludendorff again.[919]

Thyssen would later continue to try to influence the right-wing political camp. In the summer of 1932, just before Hitler's rise to power, he was one of the founders of the so-called 'Dr. Hjamar Schacht Arbeitstelle', a group of investors and entrepreneurs who tried to gain influence on the Nazis.[920]

The most adventurous variant of Ludendorff's financing was the story with Tausend, which, although it took place a little later, should not be forgotten here. 'Der Tausend, der Millionen versprach', the *Heimatpost* joked later about this case. [921]

Franz Seraph Tausend was born in Krumbach in 1884. He trained as a chemist, took an early interest in occult writings and later worked in chemistry. He married a servant and devoted himself to the 'refinement' of the violin as an instrument, claiming to transform simple violins into true gems through special treatment. This theory, which was related to sound waves and rhythm, he called the *'harmonic-periodic System'*. Later, Tausend extended this to metals, making him a kind of modern alchemist. In 1922, he published *180 Elemente deren Atomgewichte und Eingliederung in das harmonisch-periodisches System*. In 1929, he had perfected his theory of metals and announced his 'secret' book *Transmutation der Elemente*, which never appeared in print. Nevertheless, Tausend had his first followers, such as Rudolf Rienhardt, a very young man who had become very rich through his marriage with a lady from the old Prussian family Von Schilbach. Rienhardt did not take any chances and had asked a specialist of I.G. Farben, Dr. Karl Ludwig Lautenschläger, to check Tausend's experiments. Lautenschläger found 'new alloys', and the money flow was opened.

This enabled Tausend to really start recruiting for his new plans. Tausend sought refuge on the political right wing. According to his biographer Franz Wegener, Tausend initially tried to interest Von Hindenburg in his practices, but he was unsuccessful. He had more success with Erich Ludendorff.[922] At first glance, this was strange, because Ludendorff was not Tausend's 'natural ally', who would have acquired his knowledge partly on the basis of 'cabbalistic studies'. Still, the idea of producing gold by chemical means would be a 'deathblow' to the gold standard abhorred by the Nazis and Völkisch forces, which, as Gottfried Feder, a Nazi economist and Ludendorff's original fellow-combatant, also claimed, was above all a 'Jewish standard'. One could flood the market with gold and thus disrupt the system. [923]

There was a wonderful love-hate symbiosis in the far right camp for this 'pure' precious metal, which metaphysically satisfied their own desire for (racial) purity. Not for nothing did Indo-Germanic racial cultist Savitri Devi Mukherji call her memoir *Gold im Schmeltztiegel*. [924]

The exact date of the meeting with Ludendorff is not entirely clear, but it must have been sometime in 1924 or 1925. It was Rienhardt who made contact with Ludendorff via a confidant of Ludendorff, Hauptmann Wilhelm Weiss.[925] Here, Tausend showed his ability by showing Ludendorff his 'trick'. He gave his word of honour that he had acted honestly and that he only had patriotic motives. We know how Ludendorff hung on the 'word of honour', but Tausend also put his money where his mouth was. After a partnership had been established, mostly from Ludendorff's circle of acquaintances, connected with the 'Berliner Nationalklub' where Stinnes had once introduced Ludendorff[926] as well as others such as the Cologne entrepreneur Alfred Mannesmann, on 14 October 1925 an agreement was signed that was financially very favourable for Ludendorff. In order to demonstrate his sincere intentions, Tausend relinquished his inventions, as well as his inventions in the future, in favour of Erich Ludendorff. It was stipulated that 75% of the proceeds from the 'gold venture' would go to Ludendorff, without him having to give account. Tausend immediately assumed that this money would be used for the 'national cause'. Tausend himself was satisfied with 5%.[927]

The resulting company, which went down in history as 'Aktion Gesellschaft 164', flourished for a short time. Ludendorff's name brought in money. With his share, Tausend bought a castle (Paschbach) in Eppau with 43 rooms, a villa in Romanstrasse 25 in Munich and a beautiful estate that had belonged to the Polish Count Leszczy-Suminsky in Saxony in 1870. Ludendorff's involvement came to an end when his life-threatening thyroid condition kicked in, from which he later underwent surgery. The loss of Ludendorff's influence, coupled with the absence of promised profits, led to the rapid collapse of 'Gesellschaft 164' in 1926.[928]

From 1929 onwards, Tausend was the focus of special attention from the judiciary, especially after it became clear that he was trying to escape to Italy. In January 1931, it finally came to a trial. Under the supervision of the head of the Bavarian Mint, Dr. Josef Koell, Tausend was allowed to show whether he was really capable of transmuting gold by chemical means. To everyone's amazement, Tausend was indeed able to produce gold, although in a very small quantity. But in the end, it was not his alchemy that was on trial, but his deception.

'The goldsmith trial of the twentieth century' caused quite a stir. Alfred Mannesheim did not turn up because he was 'too old', Freiherr von Plettenberg-Mehrum suddenly had to go abroad, and a member of the wealthy Meinhold family committed suicide because part of the family capital had gone up in smoke. Ludendorff was also nowhere to be seen in the courtroom.[929] During the trial, it became clear that many of Tausend's employees were people from Ludendorff's officer circles. Many of the depositors were also acquaintances of Ludendorff. The former, by the way, did their work for very little remuneration, as it concerned the 'national cause'. In total, 790,000 marks are said to have been deposited in the organisation, of which 315,000 marks are said to have been passed on directly and not to have been used for the benefit of the company. It is suspected that this money, in accordance with the agreement between Tausend and Ludendorff, benefited the general.

There was also a second way in which Ludendorff kept his finger in the pie. His stepson Heinz Pernet, for a fee of several hundred marks, kept an eye on things. In front of the judge, Dr. Geist, Pernet declared that he had 'got on well' with Tausend, and that he really believed 'that Tausend could do what he said'[930] Pernet stayed with Tausend until 1929, when they separated after a conflict.

So it seems that Ludendorff was at least indirectly involved with the Tausend case until that time. The question remains: what happened to the money? During the trial, it was suggested that Ludendorff used the money to settle a debt of almost 300,000 marks which the *Völkischer Kurier*, the later *Kampfblatt der nationalsozialistischen Freiheitsbewegung*, with which Ludendorff was strongly associated. In the first issue, he had written the opening article. [931]

The whole thing caused a lot of commotion and hilarity. Furthermore, there was interest in the case from abroad; partly due to the fact that the famous name of Ludendorff was connected to it.[932] Ludendorff was depicted in the press with cartoons, while he tried to make gold out of lead. Pernet was also mentioned by name, and called an alchemist. All in all, it looked like a pyramid scheme that was about to collapse. Ludendorff was one of the lucky ones and passed. When reality showed its evil face, he twitched his moustache.

At first glance, one would think that the 'gullible' Ludendorff had unintentionally ended up in a swindle. However, there are indications that suggest another scenario here. The *Munich Post linked* the trial of Tausend, which started on 19 January 1931 and resulted on 5 February 1931 in a prison sentence of three years and eight months for the 'alchemist',[933] with another swindle case, namely the one against Hans Unruh and a number of his companions, among whom his brother Willie and the 'representative' of the swindle, Reinhard Krusenbaum. Hans Unruh claimed that he could make gold from salt. A wagon load of salt would yield 2 kilograms of gold. The name of Erich Ludendorff was also mentioned in this scam. The *Munich Post* had no evidence, but indirectly there are cases against him. One of the main victims of Unruh's swindle was none other than Stinnes foreman Friedrich Minoux and his right-hand man Alfred Panofsky. These were not just acquaintances of Ludendorff, but direct conspirators from the right-wing camp. For years, Minoux had been the foreman of the Stinnes group in Berlin and, as we saw, operated from 'villa Minoux', the infamous Wannsee conference villa, part of the empire. It was in fact the address where Ludendorff, as a former Putschist, had negotiated with the top of the Weimar government about the cooperation between the Reichswehr and the Freikorps in connection with the renewed French invasion of the Rhineland. In October 1923, Minoux and Stinnes had broken up, but despite the Jewish background of his associate Panofsky of the Jacquier-Securius banking house, this had no effect on his völkisch character. Reinhold Krusenbaum managed to convince Monoux of Unruh's alchemical arts and Minoux wrote out a cheque for 50,000 gold marks. ⁹³⁴

The link Unruh-Minoux-Ludendorff was not the only one in this second fraud case. Unruh also operated within white-Russian circles. Here, too, the introduction took place via the 'national cause' to be supported. Within the white-Russian migrant circles, who were striving for a return to a Bolshevik-free Russia and a restoration of the old times, this was a sure thing. Hans Unruh's and Krusenbaum's contacts were through a typical Ludendorff network, namely the *Aufbau-Wirtschaftspolitische Vereinigung für den Osten,* which had been founded in 1921 during the already mentioned White-Russian congress in Bad Reichenhall. As we remember, Ludendorff was prominently present there, together with Alfred Rosenberg. It was the circuit in which Max Erwin von Scheubner-Richter also played an important role. On the East European side, the names of Tsar Ferdinand of Bulgaria, the Russian general Von Biskupski, members of the House of Coburg, but also German personalities, such as the Bavarian Minister of Defence Otto Freiherr Kress von Kressenstein, and the firms MAN and Mannesmann, played a major role in the Unruh case. The latter also surfaced in the Tausend case.

Ludendorff's involvement in the Tausend case is proven, and in the Unruh case very likely. It seems that Ludendorff used his 'world historical name' to collect money for the national cause. The fact that friends of the past, such as Minoux, were 'used' in this, apparently mattered less. At first sight, the Tausend case seemed to be a deal between Ludendorff and the alchemist, which 'worked out well' for the general. Yet, if we look in more detail, it seems that many more people were involved in this scandal. However, it could be kept quiet because the injured parties were almost all very wealthy, feared loss of face and did not want to openly attack the national cause. Whoever burned in the Tausend-Ludendorff case was susceptible to blackmail. Of the 60 victims, only the Meinhold family filed a complaint against Tausend. ⁹³⁵

There are a number of striking things about the fraud surrounding Tausend. Tausend had a product, Rienhardt through his marriage money and connections in the 'Nationalen Klub', where Stinnes had introduced Ludendorff, and Ludendorff was in the national camp beyond any doubt. Tausend's 'staff' consisted of eight men, 'all officers from Ludendorff's circle'.⁹³⁶ The 'production process' of the gold was thus 'controllable' in 'their own hands'. The young Rienhardt (21 years old when he met Tausend) had himself come from Freikorps circles (member of 'Stahlhelm') and, as we saw, made contact with Ludendorff via the former officer Wilhelm Weiss. Now it is a strange 'coincidence' that both Rienhardt and Weiss later made a career in right-wing publicity. Wilhelm Weiss became the publisher of the *Völkischen Kurier*, the newspaper which would profit from the funds transferred from the Tausend company. Later, in 1927, Weiss would become manager of the *Völkischer Beobachter*, the newspaper of the NSDAP, to become publisher of the *Zentral Verlag der NSDAP* in 1932. Rudolf Rienhardt rose through the ranks under Max Amann at the *Völkischen Kurier*, became 'Hauptamtsleiter' at the 'Presseamt' and built up a large publishing conglomerate in the Third Reich.

The connections between Tausend and the *Völkischen Kurier* were also underlined by the fact that one of Tausend's laboratories was located in the same building as the *Völkischen Kurier*, a country house owned by Otto Fuchs. Otto Fuchs was one of the men, like Ludendorff, behind the 'Aktiengesellschaft 164'. The role of Dr August Buckeley, a völkische politician from the Munich city council, who had also put money into the initial phase of 'Aktiengesellschaft 164' and who had drawn up the statutes, was also questionable.[937] As far as can be ascertained, he too got away with a 'surplus profit'. He would have put in 53,000 gold marks and got much more in return. Immediately afterwards, he quit politics and his profession (he was a lawyer) and left for South America.[938] Buckeley, too, can be linked to the direct circle around Ludendorff. He was the co-author of two dissertations with Gottfried Feder, the financial brain of the völkisch camp, the man who introduced Ludendorff to Mathilde von Kemnitz.[939]

It is clear that the interests of the *Völkischen Kurier* and the 'Aktiengesellschaft 164' went hand in hand. The 'Aktiengesellschaft 164' was a money generator for the national camp. The payments of money from the company to the *Völkischen Kurier* were confirmed in the lawsuit against Tausend by Fritz Küchenmeister, one of the first investors.[940] He stated that money deposited in 'Aktiengesellschaft 164' was being channelled to the 'national camp' and that they held a share in Tausend's company, which therefore took on the debt. This was not only beneficial to the national camp, but also towards the taxes. It was striking that Küchenmeister also profited from the case. His own companies in Freiberg had gone bankrupt in the crisis and one of the premises, an old spinning mill, was later sold to the Tausend company. Küchenmeister was therefore not an 'accidental' participant in the Tausend-Ludendorff conspiracy. The Mercedes-Benz convertible in which Walter Rathenau's murderers had struck turned out to be registered in the name of the manufacturer Johannes Küchenmeister, Fritz' brother, in Freiberg, Saxony. The police found an arms depot on the premises on 1 July 1922. Johannes Küchenmeister took refuge in Austria. The weapons were from the 'Consul' organisation, the well-known Ludendorff network around Hermann Ehrhardt and Manfred von Killinger.

Other names that appeared in the 'Aktiengesellschaft', namely those of Adolf Kob and Friedrich von Abendroth, were also among the members of 'Consul' or other organisations. Kob served in the 'Wikingbund' in Saxony, and later made a career in the SA Reichstag. Von Abendroth was the second chairman of the 'Bund ehemaliger Ehrhardt-Offiziere'. Herbert von Oberwurzer, also one of the investors, was an old 'Baltikumer', a member of the 'Eiseren Division'. In addition, von Oberwurzer was in close contact with Ludendorff's former employee Oberst Max Bauer, a new 'coincidence' that gives food for thought. [941]

For Ludendorff, the war had not ended in November 1918. This may explain his rather strange behaviour in the Tausend case and possibly also in Unruh. The case described above seems to be an almost military operation, to channel funds for the battle, in which neither friend nor foe was spared. The men behind the 'Fememur murders' were also the men behind Tausend's gold. Even Tausend seems in a way to have been victimised in this case. In front of the judge, he indicated that he had been more or less forced to sign the contract with Ludendorff. After all, 'you don't easily contradict a general', Tausend reasoned with some logic for those who knew Ludendorff. About Tausend's involvement in political activities, he told the court: 'I have never been interested in politics'. [942]

Just as one could speak of the Kapp-Putsch and the forthcoming Feldherrnhalle-Putsch as Ludendorffputsch numbers 1 and 2, this was not the Tausend-Ludendorff conspiracy, but the Ludendorff-Tausend conspiracy. Tausend was the magician, but Ludendorff was the general who determined the direction of march.

Finally, with regard to Tausend, there is another bizarre fact that should not go unmentioned here. Tausend did not focus his activities only on making gold. For example, he also made a miracle ointment, which could 'heal wounds instantly'. More importantly though, Tausend was also involved in insecticides and all kinds of pesticides. Rienhardt's initial investments would not only focus on the production of gold, but also on insecticides. However, anyone who says 'insecticides' in the time of the Weimar Republic and the German military restrictions imposed in the Treaty of Versailles, immediately raises the suspicion of inventing and producing chemical weapons and war gases. It is known that Fritz Haber, the man behind the German poison weapon in World War I, threw himself into insecticides after 1918 as a cover for the development of war gases. The development of the lethal prussic acid had been sorely neglected within the German army in the period 1914-1918, and this was rapidly made up for. Zyklon B, the deadly gas of the Holocaust, was one of them. The question arises: did Tausend illegally produce chemical weapons? And was that perhaps also the reason for the large military involvement and the role of Ludendorff as the personification of 'das Militär' in the whole thing?

There is no way to prove this. It is known, however, that some perpetrators of the 'Fememurders' used prussic acid as a weapon of attack, among others in the attack on Philipp Scheidemann on 4 June 1922.[943] Tausend himself ultimately paid for his alliance with the highly political right with his life. The Reichsführer-SS Heinrich Himmler was interested in Tausend's gold and robbed him of his freedom. In July 1942 he died in the Schwäbisch-Hall prison. [944]

Besides 'Ruhrbaronnen', Russian migrants and alchemists, other exotic parties also sought out Ludendorff. Everyone liked to keep things on the fire, should Ludendorff return to the plush. One of the most curious visitors on the eve of the Feldherrnhalle-Putsch was Trebitsch-Lincoln. After the unsuccessful Kapp-Putsch, where he had been press officer, he had fled abroad and ended up in China via Japan. Intriguing as he was, he returned to Europe in September 1923, as a participant in a Chinese delegation led by General Wu Hung Chiang. Trebitsch-Lincoln sought contact with his old confidants from the Kapp-Putsch days, Hugo Stinnes and especially Max Bauer, who travelled to meet the delegation in Genoa. The invitation by Trebitsch-Lincoln had come as a total surprise to Bauer. The two gentlemen had not exactly parted as friends after the Kapp-Putsch. But Bauer no longer played a major role on the world stage and seized the invitation to get back into the game. Via Bauer, and also via Von Scheubner Richter, the Chinese delegation finally reached Ludendorff in Munich.

The meeting, which Von Scheubner Richter attended, took place just before the Feldherrnhalle-Putsch, on 2 November 1923. Through the Hungarian consul, who kept an eye on Trebitsch-Lincoln because a request for his arrest was still pending in Budapest, the British consul - who was apparently also following the case - later confided that 'Ludendorff had been extremely bored'. Perhaps this was because the colourful Trebitsch-Lincoln was also wanted in Germany and had therefore stayed behind in Zurich. Nevertheless, so the Hungarian consul told us, Trebitsch-Lincoln arranged for a photo with Ludendorff's signature to be given to the Chinese in order to cover their expenses in Europe.

In Wasserstein's biography of Trebitsch-Lincoln, the visit to Ludendorff is reduced to another attempt by the schemer to fill his pockets. Still, the Chinese visit came at a strategic moment. In Italy, Mussolini had come to power after the March on Rome and the March on Berlin was in the making in Munich. In any case, Bauer took Trebitsch-Lincoln seriously. He travelled to Zurich for further talks with Trebitsch-Lincoln and the Chinese delegation. On 7 November, a day before the putsch, he wrote Ludendorff a letter in which he pointed out the German interests in China and that he was prepared to devote himself entirely to the Chinese cause. Bauer referred to his loyalty to Ludendorff, but also to the fact that he had problems with the Nazis, whom he considered 'uneducable'.[945] Ludendorff, however, had other plans and ordered Bauer back to Munich immediately, which of course had everything to do with the upcoming putsch.

In the meantime, the Chinese delegation and the visit to Ludendorff in Munich have become a forgotten anecdote. In Ludendorff's later house in Tutzing, large Chinese vases still remind one of Wu Hung Chiang's wonderful Chinese delegation. Bauer continued to play a role along the Chinese line, including through the Austrian company Knoll and the Chinese delegation. In 1927, Bauer himself would go to China as advisor to Chiang Kai-shek, where he, unfortunate enough, died of smallpox.[946]

Following this Kapp veteran, another acquaintance also turned up. Here, as often in Ludendorff's life, the trail is difficult to trace. It was Waldemar Pabst, the man with the blood of many on his hands, not least that of Karl Liebknecht and Rosa Luxemburg. Since he did not play an active role in the actual putsch, it seems that Pabst was operating more from the wings this time. Just before the putsch, Ludendorff and Pabst, as Pabst-biographer Klaus Gietinger credibly writes, would have met by chance in the streets of Munich. Coincidentally? The meeting of Bill Clinton and Gerry Adams in Dublin was no coincidence either, nor, to stay closer to home, Ludendorff's chance encounter with Ehrhardt and his brigade during the Kapp-Putsch in Berlin on a 'morning walk'. The above-mentioned meeting would have taken place in front of the building of the *Münchener Neuesten Nachrichten*, a newspaper that was very critical of the 'right'. Too obvious a place to discuss a coup. The gentlemen had thought everything through in detail.[947] Earlier that year, the *Bayerischen Kurier* had also reported openly on Pabst's support for Ludendorff's ideas, although after the failure of the putsch he tried to publish a kind of rectification through his political contact Georg Heim.[948] It cannot be ruled out that the troops of Frans Stumpf's Tirolerheimwehr, who had been co-organised and trained by Pabst, eventually had a role in the putsch and its sequel. When Hermann Göring left the square of the Felldherrnhalle wounded, the trail led directly over Garmisch to Tirol, where Pabst had him accommodated in the best hotel of Innsbrück, the Arlberger Hof.[949]

While diplomacy was boisterous behind the scenes, the political arena was no less turbulent. The Communists and Buchrucker had been resisted, Von Seeckt tamed for the moment, but the problems for the young republic were far from over. The Nazis were doing their best to throw oil on the fire in an attempt to further undermine Berlin's authority and to force the Bavarian government to make a ruthless choice for the far right camp, so that Bavaria would not only be 'Ordnungszelle', but that the march on Berlin could also take place from Munich. By means of inflammatory articles in the *Völkische Beobachter*, they succeeded in doing so. In the article 'Die Diktatur Stresemann-Von Seeckt', the *Völkische Beobachter* attacked the administration in Berlin on anti-Semitic grounds. This was enough, and Berlin decided to intervene. The publication of the Völkische *Beobachter was* prohibited. This intervention by Berlin in October 1923 came at a difficult time for Munich. The government was already caught between blue-white monarchist forces and völkisch-national socialist forces, and one would seriously undermine its own credibility and strength by allowing itself to be lectured to by Berlin. Besides, the 'red' politicians in Berlin could not count on any sympathy from the Wittelsbachers and the Great Germans.

The three men at the helm in southern Germany, Prime Minister Gustav Ritter von Kahr, General Otto von Lossow (head of Bavaria's military district: Wehrkreis VII) and Hans Ritter von Seisser (police chief) decided to ignore the order from Berlin. This was insubordination of the highest order. Berlin tried to dismiss Von Lossow because he was under the direct command of Von Seeckt, but Von Kahr kept Von Lossow on his side. An understandable decision, since it had not escaped Von Kahr's notice that new putsch plans were imminent. The Republic, in turn, did not dare to intervene as in Saxony and Thuringia, simply because it exceeded its military capabilities.

It is interesting to see how Ludendorff outlines the position of this triumvirate in his memoirs. It is clear that he did not know what he had in Von Kahr and Von Lossow. Von Kahr's position had been strengthened as a result of his passive resistance to the French Ruhr occupation. Von Kahr was in the saddle with dictatorial powers. To this end, on 25 September 1923, paragraph 48 of the constitution of the Weimar Republic had been used, making Von Kahr 'Generalstaatskommissar'. On the one hand, the principled stand of Von Kahr and Von Lossow strengthened the believe that these men chose the völkische zaak. However, Ludendorff had his doubts, though - as we have already seen - sometimes motivated by very subjective matters, such as Von Kahr's not very 'Nordic appearance'. He also feared Great Bavarian sympathies.

In March 1923, there was an open outburst between Ludendorff and the Wittelsbachers when the newspaper *Regensburgeranzeiger* published a long article about Ludendorff's anti-Bavarian and anti-Wittelsbach attitude. Ludendorff replied to this in an open letter on 20 March 1923. In this letter, he made clear that he was not an enemy of Bavaria or the Wittelsbach house, but that he had a Bismarckian Germany in mind.

In September 1923, when Ludendorff met von Hindenburg around the annual 'Deutsche Tag' in Nuremberg, he also expressed his concerns about Crown Prince Rupprecht. Von Hindenburg pointed out to his old comrade that he was convinced that Von Rupprecht only wanted the best for Germany. Ludendorff was willing to confirm this in his memoirs, but added that this probably was a different Germany than in his vision.[950] On 22 September 1923, it came to a meeting with Crown Prince Rupprecht, partly due to Von Hindenburg's mediation. According to Ludendorff, he was received 'icily', both by Marshal Graf Soden-Fraunhofen, whom he partly saw as the evil genius behind the pro-Rome line of the Crown Prince, and by the Crown Prince himself. Soon the two men were quarrelling over their First World War clashes. Opinions also differed on the acute situation. Rupprecht stood behind Von Kahr, while Ludendorff showed himself to be more in favour of Knilling. The gap between Crown Prince Rupprecht and Ludendorff could not be bridged. Disappointed, Ludendorff left the meeting, only to be confronted with the Von Kahr 'dictatorship' a few days later.

According to Ludendorff, the additional powers that Von Kahr was given served not only to steer his own course with regard to Berlin and the Ruhr crisis, but also to keep the völkisch forces in check[951] This last assertion was not entirely paranoid. Although Von Kahr was on the conservative side, he also had his own agenda. Von Kahr's power, like that of the völkisch camp, was based on old battle groups that had only with difficulty allowed themselves to be disarmed under pressure from the Entente. While the Völkischen drew on 'Oberland', 'Kriegsflagge' and the SA, Von Kahr relied on the so-called 'Einwohnerwehren'. These had initially been under the command of 'Forstrat' Georg Escherich and had arisen from anti-Communist sentiments as a result of the Council Revolution. The 'Einwohnerwehren' were a large organisation, which could be compared to the 'Stahlhelm' organisation of Franz Seldte. Like the Freikorps and the Ehrhardt brigade, the Einwohnerwehren had to be disbanded by order of Berlin, since the Entente did not tolerate these paramilitary units under the Treaty of Versailles. But here too, parts of the units went 'underground'.

Georg Escherich founded the 'Organisation Escherich', also called 'Orgesch'. Later, there was a power struggle in the top of the organisation, and 'Sanitätsrat' Otto Pittinger temporarily took over the leadership, transforming this organisation into the 'Organisation Pittinger' or 'Org.Pi', to finally be renamed the 'Bund Bayern und Reich' (BBR) in 1922. This BBR remained an important power base for Von Knilling and later Von Kahr, and a counterweight to the other paramilitaries.

Von Kahr based his power politics on the BBR, the police and the army. Through the BBR, links were maintained with 'Stahlhelm', as a counterweight to the 'völkischen'. In Bavaria 'Stahlhelm' was represented by Carl Wäninger. How diffuse everything was, is shown by the fact that the 'decline philosopher' Oswald Spengler, who had just finished his famous book *Der Untergang des Abendlandes*, was worried whether Wäninger was not too pro-Bavarian and had too little regard for the Greater German idea. As a self-appointed ambassador, Spengler shuttled through Europe on behalf of the Bismarckian concept, where he gave high priority to the restoration of the House of Hohenzollern and visited the crown prince in Wieringen, the Netherlands. From that position he also contacted financiers who could keep the Von Kahr and Wäninger 'middle camp' on course. Spengler envisaged a 'directoire', similar to the one that France had experienced after the troubled days of the French Revolution, before the new strongman (then Napoleon) would take office. Spengler summarised this in his book *Neubau des deutschen Reiches*, published in 1924. It was not an isolated thought. Karl Haushofer, who taught geopolitics in Munich and had Rudolf Hess as a student assistant, also believed that Germany was ripe for a 'Caesarentum'. The question was who should be the 'new Caesar'? In the Völkisch camp there were ideas about this, of course: Ludendorff as the man 'above the parties', Hitler as the politician. For the people of the 'centre', however, it was now a matter of installing the right 'directoire', and Spengler was thinking of Von Kahr, Von Lossow and Von Seissler. To support these forces financially, Spengler appealed to various big industrialists, including Alfred Hugenberg and - how could it be otherwise - Hugo Stinnes. Money flowed, among other things to Carl Wäninger and the BBR. [952]

Still, the Völkisch camp was not sitting idle either. During the 'Deutsche Tag' in Nuremberg on 1 and 2 September 1923, all front men and a large part of their supporters had gathered. A total of 70,000 men had marched those days. Ludendorff, together with Hitler, had led the parade of the various völkische groups, the SA, 'Reichsflagge' and 'Oberland'. Ludendorff had made a speech, in which he looked back with sentiment on the Hohenzollern, which did not please Hitler completely, but in later consultations, in which the leaders of the various groups, such as Dr. Weber ('Oberland'), Hauptmann Weiss ('Reichsflagge') participated, they came to a kind of provisional agreement. Interestingly, the political proposal came out of Ludendorff's hat. In cooperation with Gottfried Feder and Hauptmann a.d. Wilhelm Weiss, Ludendorff presented a plan in which the battle had to be fought against Marxism, pacifism, Jewry and the restoration of Germany according to the ideas of Bismarck.[953] Röhm and Von Scheubner-Richter, meanwhile, combined the various combat formations into a more effective organisation under the motto ‹Durch Kampfgemeinschaft zur Volksgemeinschaft›.[954]

Like the Viktoriastrasse in Berlin on the eve of the Kapp-Putsch, Ludendorff was again caught in the net of the counter-revolution. The aim was to form as broad a reactionary front as possible. To this end, various initiatives were to be undertaken:

- They had to close their own ranks and Hitler succeeded in doing so by putting aside the differences of opinion between his vision and that of the NSDAP and Ludendorff. Hitler had an innate distrust of everything from the old establishment, but he was much more of a politician than the tunnel-visioned Ludendorff and knew when to be principled.
- People put out their feelers to conservative forces around von Kahr. Röhm's contacts, for example, were encouraging. Through his intervention, for example, the men of 'Reichsflagge' were able to take shelter in the 'Minenwerferkaserne' of the Reichswehr in Nuremberg during the demonstrations on 1 and 2 September 1923. It seemed that the army, or at least parts of the army stationed in Bavaria, could go along with the counter-revolution.
- They stuck out their feelers to the Wittelbach camp, if only as an occasional ally, appealing to anti-republican sentiments.
- Von Kahr and the 'directoire' were worked on in direct talks, but there was reason for distrust. After Von Kahr had been given licence to act, he had to follow through in Hitler's eyes. Von Kahr, however, felt that he had to be 51% sure of his success before he would 'deploy the Bavarian fists to clean up the Berlin pigsty'. Hitler wondered what kind of general that was.[955]

And finally, they built up their own strengths as best they could.

Ludendorff played an important role in several facets. Hitler was more inclined to compromise than Ludendorff. Ludendorff's visit to Crown Prince Rupprecht was made possible by Von Hindenburg's intervention, but also initiated by Hitler and Von Scheubner-Richter. 'We cannot turn *against* him', Hitler thought, 'so why not *with* him?' During his visit to Crown Prince Rupprecht, Ludendorff advocated a direct meeting between the Wittelbachers and Hitler. It came to negotiations about the how and where of the conversation. Hitler wanted to meet on neutral territory, but this failed at Soden-Fraunhofen and Crown Prince Rupprecht. Certain protocols apparently had to be observed. Or maybe the Wittelbach camp simply won time, because they were working overtime there too. It was in this period that a leader of the 'Alldeutsche Verband', Justizrat Class, pleaded for a Wittelsbach empire. This was, of course, completely at odds with the plans within the völkisch camp, which were not homogeneous either. Electorally, Hitler did not like the strong anti-apapism and anti-Catholicism of Ludendorff.

Above all, they had to rely on their own strength. The *Völkische Beobachter* indicated that it was 'five minutes to twelve' and they acted accordingly. In response to the possible counter-forces, the SA, under the leadership of Hermann Göring, was expanded as much as possible. The SA-Munich alone, led by Leutnant zur See Klintsch, grew from 400 men to almost 2000. Former Freikorps leader Freiherr Oberleutnant A.D. Rossbach, who had just been released from prison, was ordered to set up a bicycle section of the SA, Rittmeister A.D. Fürst Karl von Wrede, who had been closest to Paris in 1914 with his ulan patrol, set up an equestrian section. Horse trader Christian Weber looked after the SA's 'Autostaffel'.[956]

The events followed each other in rapid succession. The NSDAP held a meeting in Bayreuth, the city of Richard Wagner, and Hitler entered his 'sanctuary', Wahnfriedhof, and visited the grave of the composer he greatly revered. He also met the now very elderly and blind anti-Semitic philosopher and 'Wahl-Alldeutsche' Houston Stewart Chamberlain. He gave Hitler his blessing. In a letter dated 7 October 1923, Chamberlain was very positive about Hitler and reported that he had been able to sleep well for the first time in a long time. 'May God protect you', Chamberlain wrote to Hitler, who was 'childishly happy'.[957]

Belief in one's own abilities increased, despite the fact that Buchrucker had failed at the beginning of October. The meeting with Bayreuth and Winifred Wagner, the visit to the composer's grave and the visit to the already weak Houston Stewart Chamberlain later gained a certain weight in the historiography. Hitler also appealed to it later, during his closing speech at the Bürgerbräukeller trial. It had become clear to Hitler that his ambitions were 'a thousand times higher' than 'a mere ministerial post' and that he felt it his 'duty to come forward' as the 'destroyer of Marxism'. [958]

It would not be the only time that Chamberlain crossed paths with the Völkisch leaders. After the putsch, in April 1924, there was another opportunity. Chamberlain, due to his weak constitution, could not receive many visitors, and of course Ludendorff, as the most important man on the right, took precedence. His arrival at Bayreuth had been a minor sensation for the Wagnerians. 'We feel energised and inspired today. A true nobleman - who, in fact, is descended from a king, Eric XIV of Sweden - big, friendly, straightforward and very mannered and a bit unapproachable'.[959] Seven-year-old Wieland had received Ludendorff with flowers, and Winifred Wagner had accompanied Ludendorff to Cosima Wagner and Chamberlain. 'We walked on in silence. I looked at him from the side; he was deep in thought. The sky showed a blood-red sun, a sign from the Gods, for this last hero... 4000 people had stood shoulder to shoulder'. Winifred pointed out to Ludendorff the enthusiasm with which he had been received. 'Yes', he said; sometimes they shout 'Heil', other times 'crucify him'.[960] Chamberlain considered it a great honour that Ludendorff spent half an hour with him. 'What a man that he visited me for half an hour', he later thought. In Chamberlain's eyes Ludendorff was a 'Siegfried' and Hitler his 'Parcival'. Later Chamberlain expressed his views to Hitler about the general. 'Hitler, I congratulate you on your friend Ludendorff. Judging by your friendship you have risen to the highest human level imaginable'.[961] In the evening at dinner, probably the evening of 26 to 27 April 1924, Ludendorff expressed himself on the Jewish question and showed himself 'uncompromising' [962]

Chapter 17

'We are marching!' The Bürgerbräukeller-Putsch

Although Munich had been in turmoil for weeks, and there were whispers of revolutionary plans, the putsch of 8 November 1923 still came unexpectedly; even for Hitler and Ludendorff. Initially, the 11th of the 11th was planned as 'the big day'. The night before, a large paramilitary exercise was planned on the Fröttmaningerheide near Munich, and then the next day the Bavarian capital was to be taken by surprise. However, it became clear that Von Kahr would give a speech in the Bürgerbräukeller in the city, at which Von Lossow, Seisser and other leaders would also be present. Ludendorff and Hitler were afraid that Von Kahr would definitively determine the marching direction in Bavaria, especially in light of Von Knilling's resignation on 25 September 1923. An independent Bavaria was to be feared and a renewed occupation of the throne by the Wittelsbachers were the worst case scenario.[963]

The general picture of what happened on that 8 November has been recorded in many a historical work. The meeting started at 8.15 p.m. in the Bürgerbräukeller. Hitler and his entourage were supposed to storm the stage, but the crowds at the entrance to the hall were so great that Hitler had to clear them first, with the cooperation of the police. Eyewitnesses reported that Hitler, dressed in his best suit with the iron cross on, was extremely nervous, had consumed alcohol and appeared somewhat feral. As a machine gun was wheeled into the room, Hitler took one last dramatic sip, threw his beer mug to the floor in shards and, with his pistol drawn, moved forward, followed by his SA. There was great commotion in the hall, people stood up, chairs fell over. In an attempt to restore order, he jumped on a table and shot into the ceiling. 'The national revolution has broken out,' he shouted. 'The hall is surrounded by 600 heavily armed men. No one is allowed to leave the hall. If you do not calm down immediately, I will set up a machine gun in the gallery. The Bavarian government and the national government have been deposed and a temporary Reich government is being formed. The barracks of the Reichswehr and police are occupied, Reichswehr and police are already marching together under the swastika flag'.[964] He then called on Von Kahr, Von Lossow and Seisser to follow him to a side room at the 'barse command tone'[965].

A nervous Hitler made it clear to the three gentlemen, while constantly waving his gun, that if they resisted, no one would survive the evening. At the same time he apologised, because this was the only way to push through the changes and get the new people in the right seats. Pöhner was to be the new Bavarian Prime Minister, Von Kahr Landesverweser, Seiser head of police, Hitler himself would be head of the new Reich government and Ludendorff would be head of the armed forces. There was not much choice for the secluded gentlemen; Hitler made it clear that they had to accept their new posts. 'Whoever does not accept his place has no right to continue to exist,' Hitler reported plaintively. 'If things go wrong I have four bullets, three for my associates if they leave me and the last bullet for me'. Then he theatrically put his pistol to his temple: 'If I am not a victor by tomorrow afternoon, I am a dead man'. [966]

To Hitler's horror, there was actually not much reaction to his action. Kahr in particular was not intimidated and simply said that 'to die or not to die was meaningless to him'.[967] Seisser believed that Hitler had broken his word of honour. Von Lossow pointed out the opposition that this plan would meet. Not only would Von Seeckt have the Reichswehrt troops march southwards, but foreign countries would not accept the Hitler Putsch. Especially from the French and Czech sides, resistance could be expected. [968]

A dangerous impasse had arisen. However, it was Lossow who offered him a way out. 'How does Ludendorff stand on the matter?' he asked. To this Hitler could immediately reassure him: 'Ludendorff is willing to participate and will be here soon'. Then he left the triumvirate to Pöhner, Friedrich Weber and Hermann Kriebel, with the order to keep talking to them, while he himself returned to the hall. His first appearance, as the noted historian Karl Alexander von Müller described it, had not been too successful. Hitler had had something clownish, something waiter-like. He was a 'presumptuous young man, without credentials' and it seemed impossible that he would be able to impress the understatedly dignified audience.[969] Yet shortly afterwards, Alexander von Müller witnessed a turnaround in the audience. Hitler mirrored to them that Von Kahr and Von Lossow had gone along with the plan. 'There will be a national government tomorrow or we will be dead', Hitler thought, placing the whole action in the light of a self-sacrifice for the country.[970] Hitler's power of persuasion completely changed the mood in the room.[971]

Hitler's two card was Erich Ludendorff. Weber, Kriebel and Pöhner had meanwhile succeeded in relaxing the atmosphere. Only Von Kahr was still openly obstructive, but Von Lossow and Seisser seemed more unsteady. Ulrich Graf, on guard, had hidden his revolver from view. After his successful speech in which Karl Alexander von Müller described Hitler as a 'possessed fanatic, a brilliant showman and a political Mephisto'[972] Hitler came back in excitedly. Just before, he had taken Hess and Göring aside for a moment and given them a paper he had in his inside pocket. On it was a list of names of people who were in the room and who represented key positions and should be arrested. Göring offered Hess additional SA men for the job and immediately suggested adding two more names: police president Karl Mantel and Graf Soden-Fraunhofen, Crown Prince Rupprecht's chief of cabinet.[973] Hitler turned to von Kahr and the rest of the triumvirate: 'Have you heard the enthusiasm? Your Excellency, Mr von Kahr, you will be embraced as a saviour and carried on hands, received with jubilation and people will kneel down before you'.[974] Von Kahr seemed unimpressed and openly wondered whether the police were not in a position to put a stop to it.

In the meantime, Max Erwin von Scheubner Richter had gone to collect Ludendorff by car, and suddenly there were clicks of the heels in the corridor and rude orders to clear the way. The door flew open and Ludendorff 'straight and proud as ever'[975] entered. Ludendorff was in civilian clothes and 'looked like a pensioner who was going to walk his dog'.[976] He did not give Hitler the time of day - angry that he had been passed over as dictator of Germany - but immediately addressed the three. 'Gentlemen, this surprises me as much as it surprises you', were his opening sentences. He quickly came to the point: 'But the step has been taken; it is about the fatherland and the great national and völkisch cause. I assume that you will follow the road that has already been trodden with us to the end'. [977]

Ludendorff's arrival dramatically changed the atmosphere.[978] The practical fears of von Lossow, who already feared that Thomas Masaryk would allow his Czech troops to march through the Bömischewald into the Bavarian 'Wald' were brushed aside by Ludendorff with iron logic. The Czechs were only 'slaves' and Ludendorff did not fear von Seeckt's reaction or that of Berlin. In case the latter decided to have his Thuringian division, which was closest to Bavaria, attack, the Ehrhardt brigade stood in between. Ludendorff believed Reichswehr would not fire on Reichswehr. The mantra of the Kapp-Putsch was repeated here.

After some more talking, while Hess was in the hall finishing his arrests, Ludendorff asked Von Lossow what his decision was. Ludendorff spoke in a commanding officer's tone. A short pause followed. Then Von Lossow jumped up and, with tears in his eyes, he stood before Ludendorff: 'Your Excellency, your wish is my command'. He stood there 'like a recruit for a Feldwebel'.[979] 'I will organise the army the way you want it', he added. 'Na Lossow, jetzt machen wir's', replied a radiant Ludendorff.[980] A handshake confirmed everything. Seisser followed and shook hands with both of them. Now Ludendorff turned to von Kahr, who was still struggling. Straight across the room, followed by Von Lossow and Seisser, he ran to him. 'You should have been patient for another eight to ten days,' Von Kahr objected, referring to his own revolutionary plans. 'What can be done in eight days can be done now,' Ludendorff replied. Moreover, Pöhner added, the names of von Kahr and Ludendorff were so influential, and Hitler's rhetorical talents so strong, that success was inevitable.[981] Under so much pressure, von Kahr sought another way out. 'I cannot cooperate because I am a monarchist'. Pöhner replied that this had always been their mutual agreement and said that with this action they were not standing *behind* the King but *for* the King. Hitler also agreed and presented the Wittelsbacher as a victim of November 1918. Von Kahr had found the way out that he needed. He was prepared to assume the position of stadholder of the king instead of regent over the entire country. 'I shall never forget this', Hitler said, and shook hands with von Kahr. The fact that von Kahr, albeit via a strange Bavarian sidestep, supported the Great German Revolution was an important achievement. The name of von Kahr could now be trumpeted. 'The fatherland will see you as one of the greatest men', Hitler said.

A public reconciliation followed in the hall. As they came out of the side room, Hitler smiled at the clique of most loyal supporters, Amann, Scheubner-Richter, Rosenberg, Streicher, Feder, Göring and Berchtold, who stood in the shadows of the wings while von Kahr was worked towards the stage with slight urgency. They entered the hall 'slowly and with dignity'.[982] The stage was too small for everyone, but Ludendorff stood in the middle, with von Kahr to his left and Hitler to his right. The hall was 'broken' with enthusiasm. The protagonists shook hands. When a frozen Von Kahr spoke, Hitler demonstratively held his hand. To some eyewitnesses it almost gave the impression that Hitler was trying to hypnotise Von Kahr. A new era seemed to have dawned for a moment, but no one knew the facts. Hitler, on the other hand, was again up in arms: 'I want to fulfil now what I promised myself five years ago as a blind soldier in the hospital: not to rest until the November criminals are on the ground'.[983] Ludendorff also made a contribution. The historian Dornberg wrote: 'Now it was Ludendorff's turn. With his massive head, a face as if chiselled from stone, he looked as if everything was about life and death'. And so was his speech. Ludendorff emphasised that he was surprised by the events, but he immediately drew the consequences. 'It is all about the whole thing'. For a German man, Ludendorff stressed, who lived through this historic hour, there was no turning back. He had to support the cause not only with reason, but also 'with his whole German heart'. 'If we do this with a good conscience, we will receive God's blessing,' he thought.[984] 'He stood there like a candlestick, from head to foot as a general, sending his army to certain death', said Dornberg.[985] 'Long live the Bavarian government Kahr-Pöhner, *hoch hoch hoch*,' he sounded, followed by *'Es lebe die Deutsche Nationalregierung! Hoch, hoch, hoch!'*, followed by a deafening 'Heil Hitler'.

While Hitler roused his audience, the arrested prime minister, Von Knilling, was taken by SA units, led by Rudolf Hess, to the splendid home of the right-wing Cologne publisher, Julius Lehmann, and detained. The putsch seemed to be developing well. But there were also setbacks. Units of 'Oberland' were locked up in the pioneer barracks in Munich, and Hitler himself went there to mediate. Thus the 'revolution' (Hitler) left the Bürgerbräukeller and left it in the hands of 'tradition' (Ludendorff). Between the triumvirate and Ludendorff, a conversation about military strategy had developed for some time, during which Kriebel had offered to serve as Ludendorff's chief of staff for the time being.[986] When Scheubner-Richter left the room briefly to call his wife with the good news that everything had gone without bloodshed but that he would not be coming home tonight, Ludendorff turned to Von Kahr, Von Lossow and Seisser. He saw that Von Kahr was very tired, and Von Lossow and Seisser were silent. Ludendorff: 'It's time to go to your departments, and get the armed forces behind this'. To von Lossow he said: 'I suppose you want to rest. I will go to the military district command[987] and expect you there'. [988]

The three men were surprised by this gesture of Ludendorff. Von Scheubner-Richter, who returned at that moment, was shocked, took Ludendorff aside and whispered to him that this could not be allowed. One would lose all grip on the three men. Ludendorff saw it differently; these were three officers and they had given their word of honour. They had to do their duty and they could only do it from behind their desks. Von Kahr did not wait a moment, took Seisser's car, who as a result had to stay longest in the Bürgerbräukeller until his car with driver had returned, and disappeared into the night. Von Lossow, with his adjutant Hans von Hösslin, also left. And so the place of the revolution was suddenly empty again, except for some drinking and sausage-eating SA men and the girls of the service, who collected the empty beer mugs and put the chairs back in their place.

When Hitler returned in his trench coat, revolver between his belt, he did not seem to panic immediately that the triumvirate had disappeared, as if the consequences had not yet dawned on him. The later press chief Ernst - Putzi - Hanfstaengl, who had been present at the whole putsch with foreign journalists, had his reservations. 'I have read enough history books to understand that you must not let your predecessors, convinced by force, just walk away'.[989] Outside, in a windy shower, between snow and rain, four hundred young cadets gathered under the command of ironmaster Rossbach. Ludendorff and Hitler inspected the troops, during which Ludendorff constantly had to hold on to his hat to prevent it from blowing away. Then Ludendorff left for the headquarters of the military district in Schönfeldstrasse. Accompanied by Kriebel, Weber and his stepson Pernet, Hitler and Ludendorff parted company for the time being.[990] Shortly before, they had clashed over Ludendorff's decision to let Von Kahr, Von Lossow and Seisser go. Ludendorff insisted on the weight of the word of honour for a German officer. According to Joachim Fest, this was where 'bourgeois Germany' with its 'points d'honneur' clashed with the revolutionary ideas of the young Hitler and the new era.[991] The revolution thus lost important momentum.

The historian Ernst Nolte judged, looking back, that the revolution had had a chance of succeeding (although he expected the Entente to intervene in the event of a successful march on Berlin), but that the above-mentioned issue was an ugly one.[992] Barely free and safe, Von Lossow and Von Kahr began to distance themselves from the coup, and countermeasures were taken. Von Kahr issued a statement making it clear that he did not support the putsch. Meanwhile, the population was urged to take to the streets the next day (9 November). When the time came, doubts returned. The general mood in the city was not against Ludendorff and Hitler. The swastika flag was flying at the city hall and in many streets as well. But Hitler looked forward to the coming confrontation with the old authority. Surrounded by loyalists such as Dr. Weber, Göring, Kriebel, and Graf Von Scheubner-Richter, Ludendorff weighed the options until he made up his mind: 'Wir marschieren!'

'We left convinced that this was our end, come what may,' Hitler later recalled.[993] At the bridge over the Isar, the Munich police had closed the road, but the imposing Hermann Göring spoke threateningly to the police, bluffing that hostages would be shot if they were stopped here. The police hesitated, the crowd pressed on, and the officers allowed themselves to be pushed aside, disarmed, spat at and earcilled.[994] The march proceeded rather unstructured through the centre of the city, with Hitler - arm in arm with Von Scheubner-Richter - showing little leadership. In a fatalistic moment, he had even handed over the leadership of the party to Julius Streicher, who showed himself to be much more manly, and who, on the Mariënplein, in front of the town hall, had animatedly addressed a large crowd. While people began to sing '*O Deutschland hoch in*

Ehren', the long procession approached Odeon Square. Here, the police had again formed a chain.

What exactly happened next cannot be reconstructed. Was there shooting from Ludendorffs-Hitler's column? Had the police fired first? In any case, the fact is that shots were fired for a minute and thus the putsch, at the foot of the Feldherrnhalle, disintegrated. Max Erwin von Scheubner-Richter was one of the first to be (fatally) hit. Hitler was dragged to the ground by him. At the last moment someone had shouted 'don't shoot, Excellency Ludendorff is with us', but that was to no avail. While everyone else went to ground or took refuge, the solitary figure of Erich Ludendorff, in civilian form, walked on imperturbably towards the police chain. The officers finally separated and the general 'broke through' the cordon. According to Fest, Ludendorff 'trembled with rage'. Fest characterised Ludendorff's performance as 'steifes Heldentum'.[995] His enemies were more critical. The politician Wilhelm Hoegner wrote: 'Here, Ludendorff's great plan went down. When the first shot was fired, the police opened deadly fire in the direction of the procession, and immediately dozens of people lay on the ground. Although they fired back immediately, the procession broke up and fled in all directions (...) among them Scheubner-Richter, Ludendorff's secretary (...) Ludendorff, however, the stormer of Liège, the master of the art of war in the Great War, was shamelessly captured. He was beside himself with indignation, insulted the officers of the police, and swore never to wear a German uniform again'.[996]

In spite of Ludendorff's 'holding out', the revolt at Feldherrnhalle had definitively stalled. The procession that had consisted of several thousand people had dissolved. The putschists sought refuge. A number of them, besides Ludendorff, were arrested immediately - Brückner, Frick, Drexler and Dr. Weber. Others, like Ernst Röhm, were arrested later or gave themselves up, like Rudolf Hess, who had fled to the house of his teacher Prof. Karl Haushofer. Hitler fled to Uffing am Staffelsee, where his confidant Ernst Hanfstaengl lived, and where he - having been wounded in the arm - was nursed. Two days later he was arrested and transferred to the prison in the fortress Landsberg am Lech.

Just as quickly as the Kapp-Putsch, this putsch from the right had also failed. In his description of the putsch, Joachim Fest wrote that the details of the preparations will probably never be fully revealed. Who took the initiative? The historiography points to Hitler. Most sources also agree that Ludendorff himself, who was suddenly introduced via Scheubner-Richter, would have been surprised by the developments: 'Ludendorff was visibly angry about Hitler's secrecy', wrote Fest.[997] Walter Görlitz and Herbert A. Quint wrote that Ludendorff 'was completely surprised'.[998] According to Hitler-biographer Charles Bracelen Flood,

Ludendorff 'was not informed' and was 'warned by a telephone call from the Bürgerbräukeller, after which he was picked up by car'. As proof that Ludendorff indeed knew nothing, Flood pointed to the fact that Ludendorff was in civilian clothes.[999] Ian Kershaw has remarkably little to say about Ludendorff's role and simply mentions him as one of the speakers after the deliberation with Von Kahr, Von Lossow and Seisser and that he (Ludendorff) reported with 'pale face and great seriousness' that 'he himself was surprised about the sudden developments'.[1000] Others, such as Manfred Weissbecker and Kurt Pätzold, simply mention Ludendorff without asking what his precise role in the whole was.[1001] As with the Kapp-Putsch, there is not too much discernment among historians; Hitler is the trail that is followed.

However, bearing in mind Ludendorff's role in the Kapp-Putsch, here too it is important to take a closer look. A number of things speak for the official version of a surprised Ludendorff:

- Ludendorff was not there from the start
- Ludendorff expressed his anger and surprise at the state of affairs
- Ludendorff was in civil clothes
 And finally:
-Ludendorff would get off lightly in the judicial follow-up to this case.

But these points are also open to criticism. In his memoir *Meine Lebens Erinnerungen, 1919-1925*, Ludendorff is very clear on a number of issues. Without further ado, he acknowledges that he was the man who decided that there had to be a 'march'.[1002] He described the putsch as an almost logical necessity to cut off Von Kahr, who according to Ludendorff in his memoirs was 'surrounded by freemasons and Jesuits'. [1003]

Ludendorff's role becomes even more suspicious when we look at what his wife Margarethe Ludendorff wrote in her memoirs. After the failure of the Kapp-Putsch in Berlin, where she was critical of her husband's role and his poor people skills, she followed Ludendorff's rise and fall in the political arena with suspicion. Ludendorff in turn excluded his wife. According to Margarethe Ludendorff, in the months before the putsch Ludendorff's house had become 'the centre', the 'political centre of the National Socialists'.[1004] It was a place of comings and goings, with daily meetings taking place. His wifes further claims that Ludendorff tried to keep this a secret from the neighbourhood, and that he did so masterfully. He pruned the roses and did all the gardening himself, 'as if he were the most virtuous man in the world, who never thought of revolution'.[1005]

Unfortunately, Ludendorff's excluded wife could not report on the content of the discussions since she was too proud to ask,[1006] but as a general conclusion about the period immediately preceding the Feldherrnhalle-Putsch she stated: 'I could see that the stone had been thrown into the pond and that bigger and bigger circles were forming'. She also referred to the fact that the name Hitler was more and more on everyone's lips. [1007]

Moreover, Ludendorff's wife wrote about the day of the putsch. In the afternoon, she suddenly saw that their servant, Kurt Neubauer, was in uniform and in a hurry. When she asked why, he called out to her: 'Meeting in the Bürgerbräukeller (...) have been called in to help guard the hall (...) have to catch the train'.[1008] A little later, just before the next train left, she saw her son Heinz coming down the stairs in uniform. He too was going to the meeting. According to Ludendorff's wife this in itself was not strange, but the fact that he was in uniform was. This was not usual for him.[1009]

Margarethe also wrote interesting things about Ludendorff himself in her memoirs, which are forgotten by historians. Ludendorff sat in his study. Normally he sat at his desk and worked, but now she heard him pacing around restlessly. Around 9 p.m. he reported to Margarethe: 'I still have to go to town. A car will pick me up in a minute. I am needed at a national meeting'.[1010]

This information calls Ludendorff's prior knowledge into question. As with the Kapp-Putsch, Ludendorff wanted to conceal his role. Similarly, Ludendorff was not present then either, when Ehrhardt's troops from Döberitz started the march, but when they arrived in Berlin he was there in full uniform. The press blamed him, partly because the aforementioned did not help the credibility of a 'surprised' Ludendorff. In Munich 1923, Ludendorff therefore marched in wearing civilian clothes. Furthermore, the matter-of-course manner with which Ludendorff accepted Scheubner-Richter's request to come to the Bürgerbräukeller is remarkable. As Ludendorff himself writes in his memoirs, Von Scheubner-Richter first explained the state of affairs to him and then asked him if he could come and get him. Ludendorff: 'It was only natural that I should comply with Mr Hitler's request and come straight to the Bürgerbräukeller'. One may wonder how 'self-evident' this was, since Von Scheubner-Richter had already explained the state of affairs and Ludendorff thus went to a 'coup' for the second time. The ease with which he accepted course of events is also not very credible. He was greeted by Hitler in the Bürgerbräukeller, led to the room with the hostages and declared his loyalty to the putschists there, 'seized by the greatness of the moment'.[1011]

What also speaks against Ludendorff was the fact that his stepson, Heinz Pernett, not only left, as Margarethe wrote, in 'full uniform', but also that he subsequently reported in Munich in the Schellingstrasse, where all the leaders of the putsch met that afternoon. Among them were Hermann Göring, 'Stosstrupp-Hitler' leader Josef Berchtold, 'Jungsturm' chief Adolf Lenk, Hermann Kriebel, Friedrich Weber, Max Erwin von Scheubner-Richter and so Heinz Pernet, representing the Freikorps Rossbach.[1012]

Pernet's task was to win the cadets of the 'Infanterieschule' on Blutenburgstrasse for the putsch. This unit indeed offered opportunities for the putsch. The soldiers were not subject to Von Lossow and they consisted mainly of young, non-commissioned officers, who had been promoted in the trenches. They were trained in the cadet school and were politically close to the putschists. The meeting in the Schellingstrasse must have taken place at the end of the morning, because somewhere between noon and 1 p.m. that same day, Pernet had arrived by car at one of the confidants within the 'Infanterieschule', Robert Wagner, a good acquaintance of Hitler's, who would later make an obscure career in the NSDAP. As Gauleiter of Baden, he prided himself on being the 'first Jew-free Gau' of the Third Reich, and in Alsace he built up a reputation as the 'Butcher of Alsace', which would earn him a death sentence at the Strassbourg court in 1946.[1013] Wagner was then brought before the Freikorps leader and Koerland veteran Gerhard Rossbach, who initiated him into the secret that was to take place that evening; the putsch and the coming national government, with the names of Hitler and Ludendorff already being dropped. Rossbach told him that the intention was for the cadets to become the personal storm troopers of 'Excellency Ludendorff'. Wagner was full of enthusiasm, and promised his support. Rossbach was a born leader with great authority among his men. As a very young officer - born in 1893, from Kehrberg-Pommern - he had made a name for himself at the front. After the First World War, the 'Rossbachers', recognisable by an armband with a white 'R' and two stripes through it, were to be found at all the fires; the liberation of Culmsee from the Poles (now Chelmza, famous for its sugar factory), at Danzig, at Tuchelerheide and Annaberg. In October 1919 it went on a speed march - 'einer Gespenstercolonne gleich' - over a distance of 500 kilometres to the Baltic region, fighting against communism.[1014]

In retrospect, we can legitimately ask how credible it is that Ludendorff's stepson Heinz Pernet was surprised by the putsch and that his stepfather Ludendorff knew nothing about it. Released archive documents underline this picture. The representative of the Reichstag in Munich, Haniel, already concluded: 'I know, from the highest military circles, that in the afternoon of 8 November Ludendorff had already 'ordered' the non-commissioned officers of the Infantry School for that night, through his stepson. From these and other facts it is clear that he knew about the Hitler Putsch. The cadets of the Infantry School were persuaded by Ludendorff's great prestige to join the cause'.[1015]

We can conclude that Ludendorff knew about the Feldherrnhalle-Putsch, but he succeeded in deceiving contemporaries and historians. Ludendorff not only knew, he was also one of the most important spiritual fathers of the putsch. The aureole of 'being above the parties' was maintained to the outside world. When Scheubner-Richter's car, with Michael Ried at the wheel, drove at great speed into Heilmannstrasse, Ludwigshöhe, it was Pernet who got out together with Scheubner-Richter to pick up 'an impatient Ludendorff'. Pernet helped his stepfather into his heavy coat and pressed his hat into his hand. [1016]

Ludendorff's 'being angry' and 'being surprised' must therefore be seen in the light of his role. Many other confidants only knew what would happen on the day itself. Ernst Hanfstangl, for example, heard from Hitler on the morning of the day itself, in the office of the *Völkische Beobachter*. That was before the meeting in the party office on Schellingstrasse. Alfred Rosenberg, one of the party ideologues, also heard it there for the first time. Hermann Göring and Gregor Strasser were still being tracked down at the time.[1017] The 'Hour U' had been chosen by Hitler. Hitler was the practical implementer, the revolutionary, Ludendorff was to be the national reconciler. The fact that Hitler would determine the 'momentum' was also in line with Ludendorff's earlier strategy during the Kapp-Putsch. Whether Ludendorff possibly was somewhat disappointed because he actually had to serve under Hitler does not seem to have played a role. From Rossbach's words, it seems obvious that Ludendorff was aware of the fact that his position would involve the leadership of the Reichswehr, which would be logical given his military background. Moreover, Hitler's remarks to the Strasser brothers in the autumn of 1920 suggest that Ludendorff assigned himself a military role and Hitler a political role. The lesson of the Kapp-Putsch was that popular support was necessary and that is where Hitler came in. It is also interesting that in the autumn of 1920, the Strasser brothers made a difference between the political leader (of the NSDAP), i.e. Hitler, and the 'Führer', Erich Ludendorff.

The putsch had taken its toll on the Ludendorff household. Margarethe Ludendorff - who had to read about the night in the Bürgerbräukeller in the newspaper - had received a telegram mentioning a warrant for the arrest of Ludendorff and Hitler. 'I clung to the back of the chair', she wrote in her memoirs. 'This blow came totally unexpected'. Suddenly son Heinz Pernet appeared. Exhausted, he dropped into a chair. Margarethe begged him to tell what was going on, and she told her about the arrest warrant. Then he broke down. 'He no longer had to pretend to be stronger than he was, and he cried desperately'.[1018] Kurt Neubauer, their servant, had been killed at the Feldherrnhalle. Then General Hildebrandt called for Pernet. 'You are aware that Ludendorff was also killed?' he inquired. Heinz Pernet confirmed this, but added that he had 'not yet dared to tell mother'. Margarthe Ludendorff heard these words and collapsed. She sat silently in a room filled with people, all full of questions and full of dismay. Towards evening, news came that Ludendorff was still alive, and in the evening, after long police interrogations, he arrived home. Nobody had dared to hold the father of the putsch. Despite this fact, Ludendorff was deeply affected; 'his disappointment was boundless'.[1019]

Chapter 18

'There are few Germans behind me anymore'

On 26 February 1924, the trial of the putschists began. It started lucky for the defendants, although the indictment itself - high treason and the death of four policemen - gave no reason for optimism. The defendants, including Ludendorff and Hitler, could in theory receive the death penalty. Theory, because the trial was held in Munich, Bavaria, and not in Leipzig, which would have been possible and where it, would have been a trial of the German authorities. Now, it was a Bavarian affair. To the outside world, however, which was mainly Berlin, a serious face was put on it. The Bavarian Minister of Justice, Dr Grüner, declared to Berlin's special envoy, Haniel, that the putschists would be dealt with firmly. About Ludendorff, he stated that he had been temporarily put in 'Schutzhaft' and that Ludendorff had to abide by a ban on writing. Hitler was forbidden to talk to his lawyer without a witness, something that was normally allowed.

They were goodies to keep Berlin out of the courtroom. As an argument, another treason case was brought up, the Fuchs-Machhaus case, in which the editor of the *Münchener Neuesten Nachrichten*, George Fuchs and the former editor Hugo Machhaus of the *Völkischen Beobachter* had been involved.[1020] During the Saar crisis, these had been in contact with the French officer Augustin Xavier Richert for a Bavarian-French anti-communist collaboration. Within the national circles there was soon resistance against this 'Alleingang', and only the 'Blücherbund' and 'Bund Wiking' showed interest. Thanks to the attentiveness of former Hitler commander Karl Mayr and later SA boss Ernst Röhm, this action could be prevented. This treason trial also took place in Munich and formed the basis for the trial of the participants of the Feldherrnhalle-Putsch in Bavaria.

The president of the court, Georg Neithardt, was known as a law enthusiast. He had earlier, as a deputy director of the court, handled the case against Eisner murderer Anton Graf Arco Valley. Later, Neithardt would rise to the position of president of the 'Oberlandesgericht', which he would hold until his retirement in 1937. The Bavarian 'nomenklatura' had little reason to put Ludendorff and Hitler under fire. They simply had too much butter on their heads. The Bavarian separatists, and crown prince Rupprecht, also tried to close the case quickly. Too much light on their own actions was not to their advantage.[1021] Nobody wanted to face the truth. Not least the Reichswehr, which was deeply entwined in the various militias. Here, too, high heads would eventually roll, but not too soon on the putsch itself, so as not to give Ludendorff wind in the sails.

Hitler appeared in court in civil clothes, but with the iron cross on his chest. The court allowed him to make speeches that lasted for hours. Witnesses for the relief of the accused were given easy access, more critical voices often did not make it to court. The historian Richard J. Evans stated in his standard work on the Third Reich that incriminating material against Erich Ludendorff was withheld.[1022] 'As expected, Ludendorff was acquitted'.[1023] Hitler got five years for high treason.

In practice, Hitler was able to continue some of his political work from the prison; a spacious cell with facilities. The state of emergency had ended after the trial, so the NSDAP and the *Völkische Beobachter* could be revived. For Hitler, the time came to give shape to his political theory (*Mein Kampf*) in prison and to try to maintain his authority outside prison. Ludendorff, who had been acquitted, was in a certain sense a rival to Hitler in this. Still, the putsch and the trial had given Hitler martyr status. He had become a well-known man nationally and internationally. The court was so influenced by right-wing thinking that the judge defended the lenient sentence for high treason by stating that Hitler had acted in 'patriotic spirit', and that he had been driven by 'noble motives'.[1024] The judge's verdict sounded almost like a warm recommendation.

Ludendorff, on the other hand, did not possess the same rhetorical qualities as Hitler. In addition, his unclear position, half behind and half in front of the scenes, did not only arouse sympathy. Foreign correspondent Carl Christian Bry, who was in Bavaria during the putsch, gave some apt characterisations of Ludendorff in those days that were not very flattering. According to Bry, Ludendorff had 'failed again at a decisive moment in history'.[1025] He also thought that Ludendorff was one of the 'most damaged' main characters of the Feldherrnhalle-Putsch.[1026] He already concluded this on 10 November 1923. On 13 November, Bry thought that 'even Ludendorff's fiercest supporters now thought soberly of him'. Bry blamed Ludendorff for the casualties as well. A decent lieutenant would have taken responsibility, Bry thought, and 'shot himself in the head'. Ludendorff, on the other hand, 'hid behind a civilian cloak, with a heavy floppy hat'.[1027] For others, even if they were somewhat disappointed in Ludendorff, he nevertheless remained a man of great symbolic significance. Ernst Jünger once described this feeling in *Das Deutsche Blatt*: 'For us front soldiers of the Great War, the name Ludendorff will always have a special sound. This sound is metallic and hard, an embodiment of the will to power that also belongs to war (...) Whenever we hear the name Ludendorff, we will think of the grey army waltzing forward into the West'. Jünger was mild about Ludendorff's failures too: 'We therefore take him as a person, without reservation, and we venerate in him the nature of the warrior who consciously sets out to achieve his goal, who sometimes misses, but in the end will persevere'.[1028]

Applause had sounded in the courtroom when Ludendorff had been acquitted, but Ludendorff did not have much reason to rejoice. In his defence speech, he had spoken in favour of a Bismarckian Germany and a defence against the ultramontane. It was a message that could be less appealing than Hitler's. Moreover, the political landscape on the Völkisch wing was now fragmented. The elections of April 1924 in Bavaria had to save the Völkischen, while they were under judicial attack and had been deprived of their leadership, which caused the right wing camp to split up again like a divisive swamp.

Ludendorff tried to manoeuvre himself back into the most favourable position, the one above the parties. This would give him time again to follow developments, and to act at the right moment. However, this was more difficult than ever. After all, with the putsch of 1923, Ludendorff had come out of his shell, and the way back was difficult.

Three tracks in the life of Ludendorff were now important to follow. Firstly, the continuation of his active political life, especially his contacts and relations with Hitler and the NSDAP. In addition, as we shall see in the next chapter, there would be a major change in his private life: the break with his wife Margarethe and his new love, Dr Mathilde von Kemnitz. Finally, there was his eternal love, that of the armed forces, which increasingly focused on a smaller and smaller group of loyalists in, among others, the 'Tannenbergerbund'.

Around the second echelon, in which Anton Drexler, Gregor Strasser, Ernst Pöhner, Julius Streicher and later the anti-Semitic writer Artur Dinter played a role, the völkisch camp tried to regain a foothold. The 'Grossdeutsche Volksgemeinschaft' (GVG), became the first attempt to continue the underground NSDAP.[1029] Hitler had put Alfred Rosenberg in charge. He was faced with a difficult task. Besides the GVG, new parties emerged, such as a resurrected DAP in Nuremberg, a 'Liste Streicher', and the Völkische Block, founded in Bamberg on 6 January 1924, which had emerged from the NSDAP's right-wing counterpart, the 'Deutschvölkischen Freiheitspartei' (DVFP), founded in 1920 and partly composed of former NSDAP members from northern Germany. This party subsequently merged into the Nationalsozialistischen Freiheitspartei (NSFP).

Ludendorff's search for a Völkisch bloc that was as large and broadly based as possible was supported by an old acquaintance of his, Gregor Strasser. Strasser's SA organisation was still quite intact and under firm leadership, and Strasser was a realist. He was tall, broad, and an impressive man who exuded authority. He was also a good orator. Together with Ludendorff and Albrecht von Graefe, the leader of the DVFP-Völkische Block (later NSFP), they were soon seen as the triumvirate. The initiative, Ludendorff writes in his memoirs, came from his side. He saw it as an answer to the rudderlessness in the völkische camp, and he found that the cooperation of Strasser-Graefe and himself resulted in a fruitful course, at least for a while. [1030]

Although the GVG and the 'Völkische Block' saw both Ludendorff and Hitler as their leaders, Hitler viewed the situation with distrust. The already shaky position of Rosenberg, more a theoretician than a doer, was not strengthened when Hitler tried to steer the political process from prison. When Hitler saw the limitations of this too, he decided to stay out of direct politics completely, until his release.

Elections followed in Bavaria on 6 April 1924, where the völkisch camp won 23 seats (over half a million votes), the Reichstag elections - 4 May 1924 - also went reasonably for the völkisch camp, considering the blows they had received in November 1923. Ludendorff called the 32 seats that the bloc won in the Reichstag a 'complete success'. Ten of these were taken by National Socialists. The communists also did well. They won mainly against the Social Democrats. The Republic had suffered a defeat. [1031]

In the previous weeks, Ludendorff had been travelling from meeting to meeting in order to win seats for the Völkisch camp, and he himself was also up for election. In Rosenheim, Bamberg, Kulmbach, Bayreuth and other places he appeared as a speaker. In the latter, he was a guest of Cosima Wagner and Houston Stewart Chamberlain, who increasingly saw him as a 'German man' and less as a general. Ludendorff did not mention this without pride.[1032] The politician in the field became more and more voluminous.

Ludendorff followed the results of the elections in the Bürgerbräukeller in Munich closely. The old stage of the revolution now became the setting for the parliamentary conquest of Germany. For Ludendorff, the result was a shock for 'Rome and the Jews'.[1033] On the other hand, he did make an immediate comment. The beginning of the parliamentary career was the start of 'an agony'.[1034]

The unruly Ludendorff, who was not a bridge builder and was uncompromising and principled, was by definition totally unsuited to the meandering political game, where the backroom and handshakes were part of the decision-making process.

The best result was achieved in Graefe's home bastion, Mecklenburg, with 20.8% of the votes. This effectively sealed Graefe's political fate, for Hitler saw in him - and also in Ludendorff - a growing rival. Yet, for the time being, he would be in charge, which was also a logical decision for Ludendorff, as Graefe was 'an important parliamentarian' who understood the language of political business. Frick became the second man. [1035]

Graefe was a former hussar officer whose family had been raised to the nobility by Tsar Alexander and owned a knightly estate in Goldebee. His mother was said to have Danish noble blood in her veins. Even before the First World War, Graefe was a member of the German parliament. When the 'Konservative Partei' in Germany was defeated in 1918, Graefe joined the 'Deutschnationale Volkspartei' (DNV). Within this party Graefe soon belonged to the so-called 'völkische wing' (together with Reinhard Wulle and Wilhelm Henning) and in 1922, after a party day in Görlitz, he split off from the DVFP, which later became the 'Völkische Block'. Already before the putsch, the NSDAP and Graefe, who had participated in the march to the Feldherrnhalle, had become closer. [1036] The consequences of the putsch brought Graefe his historic opportunity.

'Officers are usually bad politicians', wrote the NSDAP historian Billung in his book *Rund um Hitler*, published in 1931, with some justification. He was referring to Graefe,[1037] but could just as well have mentioned Ludendorff. According to Billung, Graefe should have played the role of 'intermediate pope', and should have stepped back when Hitler was released from Landsberg prison at the end of 1924. Instead, Graefe entered the struggle for power.[1038] Graefe belonged to the nobility, the 'caste' that Hitler both admired and whose recognition he craved, but at the same time despised. The later propaganda minister Joseph Goebbels characterised Graefe as 'a born aristocrat, somewhat decadent. I see him as a thoroughbred'.[1039] Elsewhere, Goebbels reported that Graefe made a 'great impression' on him[1040]. However, there were already tensions with Graefe before the 1923 putsch. Since the NSDAP in Northern Germany was under scrutiny, they had to rely on Graefe's help. Still, this help also led to interference in strategic decisions. For instance, Graefe, supported by Ernst Graf zu Reventlow, believed that the putsch should not rely on Von Lossow or other Bavarian schemers, but on none other than Von Seeckt.[1041] Hitler ignored this advice.

Although Hitler's own plans ultimately failed, his objection to von Seeckt was understandable. Von Seeckt never made a decision when it mattered.[1042]

The fact that his name was mentioned at all showed once more the utter unaccountability of Von Seeckt. 'The army is behind me', he said, but who was Von Seeckt behind? The historian and Hitler-biographer H.B. Gisevius certainly has a point when he states that the unrest on the right was partly possible because of the attitude of Von Seeckt, who, by politically manoeuvring his own key position, bore an important responsibility for the political instability.[1043] It is also interesting to see how Oxford's John W. Wheeler-Bennet described Von Seeckt in his standard work *The Nemesis of Power, The German Army in Politics*: 'his genius lay not in creating great armies, but in creating a military microcosm, complete with himself in every detail, ready for unbridled expansion at the given moment'.[1044] Others could only guess at that moment.

Already during Hitler's imprisonment, Ludendorff had found himself in an awkward intermediate position. Hitler tried to encourage the fusion of the different camps, under the supremacy of the NSDAP of course. Graefe resisted, Ludendorff was caught between the two parties, who each tried to get him on their side. In a letter from Hitler to NS-'Ortgruppenleiter' Ludolf Haase from Göttingen, Ludendorff's awkward position becomes clear. This letter was written somewhere in June 1924.[1045] It also made clear that Ludendorff tried to bring the parties together again.[1046] We know that in this period, Ludendorff travelled three times to the prison in Landsberg, to visit Hitler. Twice with Alfred Rosenberg, and once with Gottfried Feder.[1047] Only Hitler's lawyer and Ernst Röhm visited Hitler more often.[1048] On 15 and 17 August 1924, Ludendorff and Feder tried to effect the merger during a large political manifestation in Weimar. The supporters of the fusion seemed to have the wind in their sails, not least, according to the historian Ernst Piper, biographer of Alfred Rosenberg, because of the 'great impression made by Ludendorff', which 'caused many participants to come'.[1049]

In retrospect, this performance was also one of Ludendorff's first public appearances, in which the new ideas he had gained through his future wife, Dr Mathilde von Kemnitz, were made public. Impressed by her work *Das Weib und seine Bestimmung*, Ludendorff argued for a greater role for women in the politics of the Völkische movement. This was not an easy subject within the conservative camp. Furthermore, Ludendorff pleaded to raise the issue of religion in Weimar, which was not an easy topic either. In Ludendorff's eyes, the German-Volcian soul was at odds with religion, echoing Mathilde von Kemnitz's book *Triumpf des Unsterblichkeitswillen*. This would be the beginning of more than just criticism of Catholicism. Ludendorff and his second wife were to develop a 'deutscher Gottglaube', a 'faith' in line with German nature. The change of course did not go unnoticed: 'Ludendorff is steering towards a 'Kulturkampf','[1050] was the opinion of his opponents, and of an increasing number of 'supporters' as well.

Ludendorff stayed in Weimar with Admiral Von Leventow, former right-hand man of Admiral Scheer, and went combatively to the Weimar theatre, where in 1919, parliamentarianism in Germany had begun. 'Not in honour of Illuminati and Freemasons',[1051] Ludendorff stated in his memoirs. The unification of the völkisch camp was the idea, but without Hitler's centrifugal force it did not work.

The meeting was also the last time that Ludendorff could take political decisions on such a scale. It was Ludendorff who determined the division of positions, such as the appointment of Von Reventlow and Wille as the political leaders of Prussia. He did this, as he himself stated, in consultation with Graefe and Gregor Strasser, but *he* did it.[1052] On Sunday, 17 August, Ludendorff took part in a parade of 'Frontbanne' at the airport near Weimar, after which he left again for Berlin for his work in the Reichstag. He did not yet realise that an era had ended that day.

The break came in early 1925, shortly after Hitler's release. Graefe, supported by Ludendorff, together with Von Reventlow and other supporters (re) founded the DVFP and left the NSFP. It is a fact that Ludendorff had a meeting shortly after the release of Hitler (and Kriebel) on 20 December 1924. Ludendorff reported in his memoirs that this was disappointing. Ludendorff namely directly urged Hitler to step up the fight against Rome. Hitler was evasive. It is clear that so many principles were in Hitler's way electorally. On the other hand, he did not want to alienate himself (yet) from the historical figure of Ludendorff. What followed was a period of hesitation on Hitler's part, in which no direct decisions were taken. 'Hitler was silent', Ludendorff wrote, 'there was no clear decision'.[1053] A meeting in January 1925 could not clear the air,[1054] and Graefe grabbed the pen in the *Völkischen Kurier* on 18 February and opened the attack on Hitler.[1055] It was about power on the right and the game was soon played very hard. Initially, the door was left ajar to Hitler, but he would have to back down. Hitler was said to be 'not a real politician',[1056] but a messenger, a 'Trommler'[1057] and was still welcome in that position. That is why people no longer recognised Hitler's leadership. Hitler's critics also believed that he had made a bargain with the Bavarian nationalists, and had made a pact with the Catholics.[1058]

The battle plan with which Ludendorff, Graefe and Strasser went to war was of a dubious level and content. There were the obvious points, such as veterans' pensions, tax cuts, protests against bureaucracy and the like, but they also spoke of 'capitalist-Jewish polyps' and the 'Jewish-capitalist international', and usurers were referred to as 'gold hyenas'.[1059] There was also great anger about the so-called Dawes Plan, named after Charles G. Dawes, in which the reparations of

Germany were arranged. This came into effect in September 1924 and proved to be a heavy burden on the German treasury. [1060]

Hitler was in a complicated dilemma with regard to Graefe, Ludendorff and Strasser. The later dictator was, of course, often seen and portrayed as a very decisive person, but in reality he could also hesitate for a long time when it came to important decisions. Militarily, this would later play tricks on him, like during the summer battle of Kursk in 1943. Such matters also played a political role. Hitler was in a transitional phase. Sebastian Haffner felt that Hitler had an immature personality. There was no maturing of character and personality.[1061] But he had discovered his political talent and his oratorical skills. Kurt Tucholsky initially thought of Hitler: 'The man does not exist at all, he is just the noise he causes'. Yet, that was not true. Hitler may have been one-dimensional, but in that role - the role of politician who slowly grew into Führer - he did develop. Hitler had always looked up to the Graefes and Ludendorffs of his world, as a man of humble origins. Still, now that he was working with them he also saw his own opportunities. According to Haffner, he was losing respect for them.[1062] It took a remarkably long time before he really dropped Graefe, for example, and for Ludendorff there always remained a basis of respect, but Hitler did slowly distance himself. He realised more and more that his own course could bring him success, that Graefe lacked charisma and that Ludendorff, above all, was a man of the past. Or, as the Bavarian politician Wilhelm Hoegner wrote: 'Ludendorff never was able to overcome the black day (the Feldherrnhalle-Putsch), he became a tragicomic figure'.[1063]

His hesitation to break away may also have been caused by the fact that deep in his heart he saw in Ludendorff the more principled man, the man who put his money where his mouth was. In fact, Ludendorff was in many respects more national-socialist than Hitler himself, who needed leeway and avoided painful themes. However, the choice was ultimately made for Hitler. Thereupon he resumed and the new course was set. Looking back, 1924 was the year of ideas - the writing of *Mein Kampf*, and the period from 1925-1929 the disciplining of the right-wing camp, until it became a well-oiled machine for Hitler. [1064]

On 27 February 1925, the NSDAP was re-established and the final phase of the internal struggle began, which continued until 1928 and ultimately dealt the final blow to Graefe's political career. After Graefe, supported by Von Reventlow, launched a frontal attack on Hitler in the press - *Munich Augsburger Abendzeitung*, among others - Hitler sought revenge. The SA gangs quickly found the bazaars of Graefe and Von Reventlow and went on a rampage. In the *Völkischer Beobachter* of 17 March 1926, Hitler announced that he had had 'donkey's patience' with the obstructionists, who even tried to portray him as some kind of friend of the Jews. In an open letter, Hitler instead opted for a full-blown rampage, because Graefe and Von Reventlow had 'poisoned the völkische soul'.[1065] 'Bravo', wrote Goebbels after the publication of the letter, and Von Reventlow was so shocked that he spontaneously defected to the NSDAP-camp.[1066] This was followed by lawsuits and scandals in the press, but Graefe's political influence declined noticeably. Even the re-establishment of a party, the 'Völkischen Kampfblock' with the old comrade Reinhold Wulle, could not change this. Graefe died on 18 April 1933.

By that time, Ludendorff had long since detached himself from Graefe. In his open letter in the *Völkischen Beobachter* of 17 March 1926, Hitler already spoke conciliatory of Ludendorff, who would have been used by the Graefe camp. He emphasised that Ludendorff now belonged to the enemies of Graefe.[1067]

Despite all these efforts, the political period was a time of transition for Ludendorff. The work did not suit him. Ludendorff himself wrote in his memoirs that he 'detested the political game to the depths of his soul'. The long speeches were a torment to him, and he was enormously annoyed by what he called the party press, which wrote politicians' mouths off. It was one big 'theatre play' for Ludendorff. In addition, his parliamentary period was overshadowed by the internal destabilisation. He regretted the tensions that grew between Graefe and Hitler, but saw no chance of bridging them. How irreconcilable everything was is shown by the fact that he himself eventually broke with both camps.[1068]

The way there was one of many disappointments for Ludendorff. A fraternisation of the völkisch movement failed to materialise, and as soon as the NSDAP could go above ground again, Hitler pulled the strings. The armed units had to conform to the ranks of the SA, which Hitler brought under the authority of the NSDAP. Parts followed, some remained independent, others dissolved into nothingness. Ernst Röhm temporarily left for South America in protest. Some relatively large organisations, such as 'Stahlhelm', could not be reconciled. Ludendorff's relations with the Reichswehr crumbled even further. The relations with Von Hindenburg were already cooled down, but would get worser and worser around the tenth anniversary of the battle of Tannenberg.

For Ludendorff, the visit to the old battlefield was an emotional reunion. The festivities, which were organised by former pioneer General Kahns, gave Ludendorff the opportunity to return to old places, such as the village of Tannenberg, Neidenburg, Hohenstein and, of course, the cemetery at Waplitz, where the soldiers of the 41st infantry division had found their last resting place.[1069]

Ludendorff arrived in a sombre state of mind. His parliamentary performance had not been very happy up to that point, and his aversion to parliamentarianism had been used by his opponents to put him in the dock together with the communists, who were just as agitated. In his memoirs, Ludendorff cites the *Forchheimerzeitung* as an example, which indeed gave him a harsh beating, and in fact called him a friend of the communists. 'Erich und Iwam, beide auf dem Divan'.[1070]

Ludendorff spoke of a smear campaign.[1071] Indeed, we know from recently released archives that Ludendorff was closely watched by the Republic. Von Lossow, for instance, was kept in office for the time being, in order to prevent a loss of prestige in favour of Ludendorff, whereas Von Lossow indicated to Ludendorff that he would rather fade away as a wallflower.[1072] It was also indicated that there was a danger that Ludendorff would use the Tannenberg commemorations to put himself back on the map. This was prevented by giving him little space in the press. The speeches of Von Hindenburg and Von Seeckt were heard. Ludendorff's words remained out of sight for the general public. It was literally stated: 'The Minister of Defence reports that in the province of East Prussia various commemorative celebrations are being organised [...] General von Seeckt has decided that the Reichswehr and he will only cooperate in this if only von Hindenburg, and not Ludendorff, appears'.[1073]

The old companion of Ludendorff, Wilhelm Breucker, described the break with Von Hindenburg. In fact, the beginning of the break came on 26 October 1918, Ludendorff's farewell from the big headquarters. Ludendorff had never fully forgiven von Hindenburg for staying. In the following years, publications about the battle of Tannenberg followed, with the necessary discussions. Von Hindenburg wisely kept his mouth shut, but Ludendorff reacted to every haggling of his position as if stung by a hornet. A visit by Von Hindenburg to his old comrade was so laden with emotion that Von Hindenburg had to cancel at the last moment. Ludendorff then felt that his 'domestic honour' had been violated.[1074] 'Ludendorff was foaming with rage, he felt humiliated to the bone', wrote Margarethe Ludendorff. 'I rarely saw him like that'.[1075] Ludendorff wrote to Von Hindenburg that he was looking forward to the day when Von Hindenburg would 'dare to visit him without shame'.[1076] That Ludendorff had discredited himself and those around him did not cocur with him.

At the commemoration of Tannenberg, Von Hindenburg tried to reach out: 'How happy I am to see you', he said to Ludendorff. 'I will never forget who you once were to me'. Ludendorff would not be Ludendorff if he did not immediately see this as an imputation. Apparently, the Ludendorff of today was no longer the same as he was then.[1077] Von Hindenburg's helping hand failed to reach him. Von Hindenburg then deployed General von Cramon and later Wilhelm Breucker to glue the matter together after all.[1078] This was a hopeless task. In his memoirs, Breucker included the report that he later presented to

Von Hindenburg. It was quite a laundry list of points. It was clear that Ludendorff felt aggrieved with regard to Crown Prince Rupprecht, who, after all, was also an enemy of the Republic, but was politely visited by Von Hindenburg. The fact that Ludendorff aligned himself with the monarch was, to say the least, non-conformist and unrealistic at that time. Ludendorff also intertwined his ever radicalising ideas in his point of view. The Tannenberg commemoration would be politically exploited. All this had forced Ludendorff to literally keep his distance from the other generals at Tannenberg and not to take a seat in Von Hindenburg's car.

Photographs have been preserved of this commemoration. Ludendorff looks as impressive as he is unyielding, with flapping cape and rigid face. Here, Ludendorff showed that he was media-conscious. Amid the 'Stimmungsarchitektur' of the immense *Tannenberg National Monument*, later renamed *Reichsehrenmal Tannenberg*, he personified the uncompromising Deutschtum. The memorial was to become a place of pilgrimage for national-minded Germans, and a place of duty for soldiers in training and on leave. It was also to be the resting place of Von Hindenburg, who was buried there on 7 August 1934. According to Dieter Bartetzko, the memorial looked like a cross between *Stonehenge* and *Castel del Monte*.[1079] The GDR historian Wolfgang Ruge was less enthusiastic and thought it was a 'bombastic, fortress-like building of dark red brick'. The towers were 'Wehrtürme', and on inauguration days black, white and red flags flew over the 'Monstrum'.[1080]

Von Hindenburg thanked Breucker for his efforts and wrote to him that he had meant well after all, and that he had had 'tears in his eyes' when he greeted Ludendorff with the words Ludendorff had misinterpreted.[1081]

The sudden death of Friedrich Ebert on 28 February 1925 would indirectly deal the death blow to Ludendorff's political career. The Reichstag elections at the beginning of the year were followed by political chaos. Wilhelm Marx did not succeed in forming a cabinet and new elections had to be called. These elections, on 7 December 1924, did not go so well for the radical parties. The more moderate parties, the Social Democrats and Zentrum, who in fact carried the Republic, recovered from the defeat in May 1924. The wind suddenly seemed to be out of the sails of the Völkische Bloc and the Communists. According to the historian Hagen Schulze, a kind of habituation to the republic began to develop; a republic that had once started 'without republicans'. People were looking for a way out. The death of Ebert from an appendicitis that had been neglected for too long, one day after the re-founding of the NSDAP, brought about a significant change.

The call for a new Reich President initially brought new national divisions. Each party had its own candidate, the 'Zentrum' put forward Wilhelm Marx, the SPD Otto Braun, the Right Dr Karl Jarres and many other candidates followed. 'They were relatively unknown politicians, scientists, and a general,' noted the historian/journalist Emil Ludwig, 'and this general was Ludendorff'.[1082] The results of the presidential elections were not satisfactory and above all not convincing; the right wing had some eight million votes, the left wing ten million, with a turnout of 69% of those entitled to vote.[1083] And so a second round followed. In the end, they chose a somewhat artificial way out, to a man who stood above the parties ... the ever immensely popular Paul von Hindenburg. Even Wilhelm Marx, during his campaign, had constantly praised von Hindenburg and his military past.[1084] Von Hindenburg was an icon that could not be ignored.

For Ludendorff this was undoubtedly a double blow. It involved his old boss. In addition, Ludendorff had run for the presidency on behalf of the völkische kamp/NSDAP as Jarres' opponent. Dr. Karl Jarres, the big man on the right, had made a name for himself in the Rheinland crisis, and as 'Aussenvertreter der Zentralstelle Rhein-Ruhr' of the Reich government was mentioned in the same breath with the 'Versackungs'-strategy (having the Entente pay the state costs in the Rheinland), and was for some time minister of internal affairs and mayor (of Duisburg). Hitler, Ludendorff and the Völkischen considered Jarres as 'too moderate'. The press in those days characterised Jarres as a Bismarckian.[1085]

The anti-Jarres plan had emerged from a visit by Hitler to Ludendorff. It would be their last pact for a long time. They had talked until after midnight, and then Ludendorff had reported back to his wife and her daughter. 'I have just had a thorough consultation with Hitler,' he told them, 'and we must do what we can to prevent the election of Dr Jarres. Something must be done, that is clear. We have come to the conclusion that I too must stand as a candidate. Hitler is convinced that we must take this risk. If we do not manage to get enough votes, it will at least help to disrupt unity and prevent Jarres from winning the election'.[1086] For Margarethe Ludendorff and her daughter this was a great shock. 'We jumped up startled', she wrote in her memoirs. 'What a terrible plan'. Margarethe asked the justified question why Hitler did not put himself up as a candidate, or as she put it even more sharply, why he did not 'make this sacrifice' himself.

Ludendorff thought for a moment and then considered that although Hitler had a fairly solid base in southern Germany, Ludendorff's Prussian ancestry could help in northern Germany, where Hitler would fall short. 'The East Prussians and Silesians are still grateful to me from the war', Ludendorff thought.[1087] 'I kept silent', wrote Margarethe, 'I knew that every further word would be in vain'.[1088] Ludendorff's new political move came as no surprise to others either.

Earlier that year, Rudolf Hess had already noted in his diary that Ludendorff had a 'hard head'.[1089]

The result was devastating for Ludendorff, with 1.1% of the votes. Even in East Prussia and Silesia, people had turned their backs on him after two failed coups and endless fratricidal battles. 'The splintering of the right-wing camp had succeeded', Margarethe Ludendorff wrote, looking back, 'neither Jarres nor Braun got what they wanted, but Ludendorff's defeat was a high degree of disgrace'.[1090] She denounced the fact that her husband had acceded to Hitler's request. Once again the general had done the hard work for others and received a slap in the neck in gratitude. As was to be expected, the anger (from the lack of unity in the right-wing camp) was not directed against Hitler or the National Socialists, but against Ludendorff. People now openly called him 'a querulous person who was causing trouble everywhere'.[1091]

This new calling came as a question of conscience for Von Hindenburg. He asked for three days' consideration when he was offered the position. But after six years of misery, the symbolic figure of Von Hindenburg, 77 years old and untainted by politics, was a breath of fresh air. 'He was the egg of Columbus', wrote Emil Ludwig. Others, like Stresemann, feared an angry reaction from abroad. Von Hindenburg, together with Ludendorff and the Kaiser, had been the face of Wilhelmine Germany. Harry Graf Kessler visited Stresemann during these days and wrote in his diary that Stresemann was 'desperate'.[1092] However, he did not dare to oppose the grey eminence openly.

After the death of his wife, Von Hindenburg lived alone in his 'too big to be around' house in Hanover, which was known as the most boring city in Germany. Although it meant a break with his past - a military man did not interfere in politics - the will of the people also played a role. It also gave his life a new purpose and vocation. Von Hindenburg answered the deep longing of the people for an anchor of recognition in the turbulent times. And had he not already been in a similar position for a short time, after the Kaiser's flight to the Netherlands in November 1918? A circle closed, Von Hindenburg made the next step in his long, extraordinary career. He was and remained a military man, and duty called. He endured the elections as he endured everything else; he did what he always did, he went to bed on time, and the next morning heard from his son that he had won the elections.[1093]

At the inauguration, the communists angrily left parliament, but Von Hindenburg took the oath. The text of the oath, Harry Graf Kessler noted, was written in cow letters on his cheat sheet,[1094] because Von Hindenburg's eyesight had become poor over the years. Nevertheless, the words followed stumblingly, and he accidentally addressed the Social Democrat Paul Löbe as 'Herr Reichspräsident'.[1095] Von Hindenburg would often be uncertain in his new office. In thick notebooks, which he personally burned when they were full, he made cheat sheets with names and functions. He relied heavily on Dr Otto Meissner, the President's Chief of Bureau. They had a relationship that British historian John W. Wheeler-Bennet compared to the 'Von Hindenburg-Ludendorff marriage'.[1096]

Nevertheless, the swearing-in was a fact and the beginning of a more stable era. Ludendorff was in Berlin that day and attended the inauguration. He saw his old comrade take office. 'I did not visit the Reichstag any more,' he wrote, 'nor did I take part in any votes later.'[1097]

Ludendorff did not recover from this political setback. 'What the results of the elections tell us,' Rudolf Hess wrote in a letter to his partner Ilse Pröhl, 'Is that we are not even a fraction anymore [...] whether dear L. (Ludendorff) will draw conclusions from this is the question. As far as I know him, he will blame God and the whole world, only not himself'.[1098] In his memoirs, Ludendorff is brief about it. He did try to defend his candidacy. Personal motives 'naturally' played no role. A fist had to be made against the 'Erfüllungspolitik'. He knew in advance that he had no chance, he wrote in his memoirs, but the higher goal simply took its toll.[1099] 'Between 280,000 and 290,000 people voted for me',[1100] wrote Ludendorff, who kept silent about the percentages. In the polling booth, the voters had chosen effective politicians. Ludendorff felt himself ignored by the press, and where he was mentioned, the tone was more than critical. Even by his own völkisch camp, he was criticised. 'There are only a few Germans left who support me', he concluded.[1101]

Indeed, a moment in history had passed for Germany. Even the radical NSDAP had reflected after the failed putsch and chosen the parliamentary path. Revolution was no longer an option. In 1925, Germany recovered a little. In addition to the not unimportant symbolic effect of Von Hindenburg, this was also the work of Gustav Stresemann, who translated the slowly returning domestic peace into better relations with the rest of Europe. A better understanding with France was crucial in this respect and, in the Treaty of Locarno, Germany recognised and accepted the provisions of the Treaty of Versailles as far as the borders in the West were concerned. This also muffled radical voices on the French side. Although Stresemann still had a secret agenda, never lost sight of possible cooperation with Austria and remained cautious towards the young Poland, he still managed to use his 'navigational skills'[1102] to manoeuvre Germany out of its isolation, so that it was admitted to the League of Nations in 1926. Economically and financially, Germany was also doing better. A period of prosperity that would last until 1929.

The lost election was the watershed moment. Old-timers, such as Graefe and Graf zu Reventlow, dropped Ludendorff. According to Margarethe Ludendorff, the 'splintering policy' which Ludendorff had envisaged with his nomination had succeeded even better than the general had predicted. Not only had the Jarres camp been weakened, but the schism between Ludendorff and the NSDAP was a fact. 'Without any visible reason, Ludendorff felt compelled to announce in writing that he was breaking off all ties with Hitler', wrote Margarethe.[1103]

Ludendorff described it briefly as follows: 'We talked businesslike, and went our separate ways'.[1104] Later it has been suggested, among others by Peter Longerich, that Hitler, by putting Ludendorff forward as a candidate, elegantly eliminated him politically.[1105] Although Hitler would have shown remarkable political skill, and of course saw Ludendorff as a competitor, this seems to be a misrepresentation. The NSDAP had really just risen from its ashes. Under Ludendorff, it had still received two million votes in May, and the change from Ludendorff as 'fighter for the fatherland' to 'ewig gestrigen' had crept past almost invisibly, as had the revolutionary fatigue that had settled in the country. By the end of 1925, the NSDAP was a party of barely 27,000 members, and with rising prosperity, its prospects were mainly cause for modesty. We also saw from Hitler's behaviour towards Graefe that he could act rather cautiously when it came to such decisions. It is important to point out here that Ludendorff was already so openly anti-clerical before the 1923 putsch that even American newspapers ran headlines: *Ludendorff is in open war with the Pope.*[1106] In this sense, one could also say that Hitler had angelic patience with Ludendorff. In addition, the unexpected death of Ebert left Hitler little room or time for a political trap. Yet, the fact that he followed his political instinct and - to quote Margarethe Ludendorff - let Ludendorff 'pull the rug out from under the fire' was a politically wise move for his own position; intended, or unintended. The side effect was, of course, that Ludendorff turned his back on politics with bitterness. Hitler, too, was at peace: 'I would like this name (Ludendorff) to disappear from the movement, it is a hindrance to winning the workers' favour'.[1107] Misunderstood and humiliated, Ludendorff took a fast, narrow and sectarian path. This made Hitler, more than before, the man on the far right. Ludendorff, who had played the central role in the völkisch camp from his return from Sweden, had thrown himself off the throne.

Chapter 19

No Man's land

'Compared to the Tannenbergerbund, Alfred Rosenberg is just a choirboy'.

Friedrich Muckermann in his memoirs *Im Kampf zwischen zwei Epochen. Lebenserinnerungen.*

If you gave Ludendorff advice, he always gave the same answer: 'I'm going my way'. With these words, Margarethe Ludendorff ended her memoirs, *Als ich Ludendorff's Frau war*. After his failed political and revolutionary career, Ludendorff was indeed facing a new beginning. Dr Mathilde von Kemnitz played a special role in this.

Mathilde von Kemnitz was introduced to Ludendorff by Gottfried Feder. In the hagiographic work *Mathilde Ludendorff ihr Werk und Wirken*, Erich Ludendorff writes that the meeting took place in October 1923 - thus just before the putsch.[1108] Feder was his advisor on economic issues. The Würzburgerer was an engineer by trade, but had founded the 'Deutschen Kampfbund zur Brechung der Zinsknechtschaft' immediately after the First World War. This body particularly opposed the stock exchange and share system and the 'Hochfinanz' - against which Ludendorff, as a publisher, would also turn - which he considered responsible for the economic chaos and inflation that plagued Germany. It goes without saying that he mainly blamed this on the Jews and capitalism. Feder initially had the wind in his sails, but as Hitler came closer to power, he was forced to bend the knee to big business, which Feder criticised so much. At the insistence of other economic leaders in the party, such as Hjamar Schacht and Walther Funk, Feder therefore lost influence over the years.[1109]

According to Ludendorff, Mathilde von Kemnitz immediately drew his attention to the religious question, which was still unclear within the Völkisch movement.[1110] Ludendorff immediately saw the importance of this and soon, as we have already seen, to the astonishment of many, Ludendorff's appeal for religion and the role of women in the Völkisch movement resounded at a meeting of the Völkisch bloc in Weimar in August 1924. Mathilde herself had also spoken at that meeting, at the proposal of Ludendorff and Gottfried Feder, and had spoken about the *Allmacht der reinen Idee*.[1111]

Von Kemnitz's role would lead to much discussion. Ludendorff had 'stumbled upon Mrs. Dr. Mathilde von Kemnitz',[1112] his old comrade Breuckner wrote, rather uncharmingly. According to Breuckner, Ludendorff was very impressed by her knowledge and read her books. A friendship developed, and from this friendship, love, and finally a divorce from his wife Margarethe, followed by a marriage to Mathilde von Kemnitz. The love was experienced by both 'as a very great happiness', but the roles were not fairly distributed, according to Breuckner. 'Frau Mathilde Ludendorff controlled her husband and made him obedient as no man has ever been obedient', he wrote in his book *Die Tragik Ludendorffs*. It is clear that Breuckner believed that part of the tragedy of Ludendorff's life lay in the influence of Mathilde von Kemnitz. Guided by his wife, the general now took up the fight against the 'überstaatlichen Mächte', and he was mistaken in thinking that it had been these forces that had snatched the victory of 1914-1918 from his hands, and had brought 'salvation and damnation to the German people'.[1113] It was not without pain that he wrote: 'The tragedy for Ludendorff was that he did not realise how much he was making a fool of himself and how tragic it was for us, his old friends, to see the general go down this road of destruction'. The satirical magazine *Simplizissimus* published a caricature of a grim-looking Ludendorff, Breuckner reported, with the 'apt caption': 'So-die Freimaurer hätte ich nun vernichtet, jetzt kommen die Radfahrer dran'.[1114]

The moment of meeting between Dr. von Kemnitz and Erich Ludendorff was significant. Just as Hitler had known his philosophical phase in Landsberg am Lech, and had recorded his roadmap for the future with startling honesty in *Mein Kampf*, the meeting with Von Kemnitz also meant the elaboration of a series of already existing but partly still loose ideas for Ludendorff. Already in 1919, Ludendorff had read *The Protocols of the Sages of Zion* and anti-Semitic thoughts were already alive in him, which fed the 'stab-in-the-back myth'. His suspicion of Rome and Catholicism were also already present. In addition, he struggled with 'secret orders', such as the Freemasons, of whom he was very suspicious. Under the influence of Mathilde von Kemnitz, these thoughts would become more streamlined and be placed in a meta-historical perspective.

For Ludendorff, it was already clear that the First World War had awakened the völkische consciousness of the German people, and that this was further strengthened by the post-war 'agony'. Threatened by revolution, inflation and Erfüllungspolitik, the German people's will to live was undermined. For this will to live was 'the hereditary instinct' of the German people, as Ludendorff believed, and 'the soul of German man was in danger'. As luck would have it, the war and the traumatic events that followed had transformed the people's will from something unconscious to something conscious.[1115] This was the 'mission' of what was soon to be called 'House Ludendorff'.

In an earlier publication I called Mathilde von Kemnitz a 'kind of German Madame Blavatsky'.[1116] Although this comparison, like any personal comparison, is flawed in many areas, and Mathilde also fought Theosophy, there are striking similarities. Both women had extraordinarily strong personalities and were particularly militant. Moreover, they were very feminist for their time, intelligent, and spokespersons and figureheads of an alternative religious movement. In addition, they both had a passion for writing.

Mathilde von Kemnitz was born as Mathilde Friederike Karoline Spiess in Wiesbaden on 4 October 1877. She was the fourth of eight children, three of whom died in infancy. Her father was the theologian Professor Bernhard Spiess, who was born in Herborn in 1845. Her mother was Johanna Spiess, born Peipers, from Geilenkirchen (1852). Bernhard Spiess had studied in Tübingen and Erlangen, theology, philosophy and languages and later taught theology and Hebrew.[1117] It is striking that Mathilde von Kemnitz's father had also, albeit in a much more modest way, come into conflict with the existing religious consensus.

In a translation of Michael Servet's *Restitutio Christianismi*, from 1553, he showed himself to be a little too liberal in his preface, which had to be dropped.[1118] This was Servetus' work, in which fundamental criticism of Christianity was expressed. Servetus particularly attacked the Holy Trinity. Notable in this was his criticism of Jesus Christ, whom he did not regard as the Son of God, but as a perfect human being, and he also turned against the baptism of children (original sin). Both these points would also be underlined by Mathilde von Kemnitz. Servetus, born in Toulouse, but mostly working from France, was on the run as a result of his writings. Eventually, he was recognised and tried in Geneva. When Calvin visited him in prison, and tried to change his mind, but failed, he demanded the cruellest punishment; and this Servetus got. He was burned at the stake alive, with the *Restitutio Christianismi* at his feet. Given the fact that there was no professional executioner in the city, Servetus died a gruesome and slow death, which resulted in criticism at Calvin. Today, Servetus - apart from a series of street names mainly in Spain and a few in France - is mainly commemorated by the so-called Unitarian Christians, who like Servetus do not recognise the Trinity. Their leaders Theophilus Lindsey and Joseph Priestly got a foothold in the US.[1119] The fact that Father Spiess did not entirely agree with the Church was also evident from an earlier career change, when he gave up a church service in Kronberg to teach at the grammar school in Wiesbaden.[1120]

The family lived in modest circumstances, given the fact that they also had to support family members financially. Mathilde von Kemnitz grew up with siblings, Auguste (Gustel), Karoline (Lina), Friedrich (Fritz) and Friederike (Frieda). In order to make financial ends meet, they kept boarders. Initially, they were English students who wanted to brush up their German, later also Germans who had lessons in Wiesbaden. Here, Mathilde met her future husband, anatomist Gustav Adolf von Kemnitz from Münsterberg. He lived with the family for three years and married Mathilde in October 1904, after a blossoming love in 1900/1901 in Freiburg, where both studied. Mathilde studied medicine at the Albert-Ludwig University. They also had a long letter relationship while Gustav von Kemnitz lived in London, where Mathilde also visited him. For both families the marriage came more or less as a surprise. The von Kemnitz family opposed the marriage because a rich American suitor was also involved. Mathilde only informed her parents at the very last moment.[1121] The tensions within the Spiess family were short-lived and the couple settled in Berlin, where Mathilde's youngest sister studied at the conservatoire. Mathilde continued her medical studies here. As the years passed, the passion disappeared from the marriage. Gustav had fallen in love with another woman and confessed this to Mathilde, who magnanimously gave her husband free rein. Mathilde von Kemnitz believed in voluntariness as a prerequisite for true love.[1122]

Gustav Adolf von Kemnitz lived a dangerous life. His love of climbing had almost cost him his life once. He had fallen thirty metres, only to end up hanging from a protruding point by his coat. Six months later, in 1917, he went skiing with two friends to Rosan. First they snowed in, in a mountain hut, then one friend went back down into the valley, while Von Kemnitz went skiing with the other, whom Mathilde referred to as G. in her memoirs, despite the danger of avalanches. Then a fatal accident occurred. Mathilde vom Kemnitz looked back fondly on Gustav in her memories: 'He was the happiness of my youth and the father of my children.[1123] Tears had given way to a peaceful friendship'.[1124]

However, the winter lasted long that year in Garmisch, as we read in Mathilde's memories. Even when the fruit trees were in blossom, there was still plenty of snow on the mountains. The bodies had not yet been recovered. Mathilde spent a lot of money, and finally they were found.

'Was your husband wearing a brown coat?' one of the salvagers asked.

'No, blue,' said Mathilde.

'Then this is G'.'

Those were sad days, as it turned out that both had most likely lived for some time in the position in which they were found.[1125]

Mathilde von Kemnitz received her doctorate in Munich in 1913. During her studies she was strongly influenced by the lectures of the biologist Weismann, who pointed out the life force of cells, and that this was almost inexhaustible in a single cell. Death occurred primarily when cells multiplied. This created a basis in Mathilde's thinking that would later also be found in her view of religion and her own interpretation of religion; the 'Deutsche Gotterkenntnis'. For Mathilde von Kemnitz, Weismann's theory showed that there were divine forces in creation.

After her studies and doctorate - *Astenian Infantilismus* was her dissertation - she initially worked as an assistant physician to the well-known psychiatrist Emil Kraepelin. This increased her interest in psychiatry, especially the phenomenon of hysteria. She came to the conclusion that hysteria was less common where 'a people' showed more self-control and had a strong will. [1126]

In 1915, she took over 'Kainzenbad', an 'Offiziersgenesungsheim' and sanatorium in Garmisch-Partenkirchen. She also developed an interest in the human fascination for occultism. The reason for this was a swindle in which a well-known professor, Schrenck-Notizt, had become the victim. His 'medium' was found to be an impostor, and the danger of occultism was exposed.[1127] She looked at the human inclination towards occultism from her interest in hysteria and neurosis and never drew half conclusions. The soul of man was in danger, for the neuroses that many people suffered were, according to Von Kemnitz, connected with the fact that the 'individuality' was denied or ignored. One had lost the relationship with one's 'private heritage'. Von Kemnitz saw examples of this in her sanatorium, where officers with war traumas lay. She also saw it in 'wrong' treatments that had no eye for the 'private heritage', such as Sigmund Freud's psychoanalysis, of which Mathilde was a great opponent. According to her, this scientist focused entirely on sexual neurosis, whereas in her view, within the 'Northern race', that only concerned 5% of cases.[1128]

Women, too, were victims of neuroses arising from social injustices. The subordinate role of women, also dictated by the church, and the consequent lack of opportunities to develop, resulted in pathologies.[1129] As a doctor, Von Kemnitz not only sought treatment and comfort, she was also guided by the 'will to truth'. The human being was caught in a spectrum of forces, originating from occultism and order-dressing, through which delusion, superstition, paralysis of will and anxiety neuroses gained influence on the people. 'Suggestivbehandlung' was used from an early age to train children. Von Kemnitz saw as one of the evil forces behind this the forces that realised the power of all this. She pointed to the lodges, orders and the church. [1130]

Against these - in her eyes destructive - forces she placed the 'Deutscher Gotterkenntnis', also called 'Deutscher Gottglaube'. The uniqueness and the vulnerability of mankind was the fact that he was the only one in creation to realise that life was finite. While the rest of nature accepted this fact, it presented man with an enormous problem. In his primal memory, man still had in mind the immortality of the first cell and longed for that state of being. The Church and the orders made full use of this fear. Yet, if man would succeed in living again in equilibrium with his own primal consciousness, in harmony with the soul, then the stage of the *Triumph of the Unsterblichkeitwillens* could occur, as was the title of her most important work. As an example of such a feeling, she quoted the mountaineer who, sitting on top of the mountain, looking out over the world, felt this triumph.

This feeling of triumph should be pursued and experienced by man, if he would listen to his own soul. The system of 'reward and punishment', as in the church dogmas, would have to be abandoned for this purpose. In addition, in Von Kemnitz's view, dogmas were an obstacle to genius, through which the divine could also be expressed. The 'Moral Theologians' in fact stood in the way of man's upward development; anyone who really wanted to undergo *'Sein wollen wie Gott'* had to listen to the 'Sittengesetz' that was still dormant in us and place himself in the service of the natural order, the tribe and the people.[1131] Von Kemnitz was in fact arguing for the 'call of the blood', because the 'God in one's own soul' was 'damaged' when mixed with 'foreign blood'.[1132] Here, Von Kemnitz's social Darwinism touched upon the racial doctrine of those years. Von Kemnitz herself underlined the differences with Darwin. Darwin opposed the divine, Von Kemnitz put the divine back where it 'belonged': in the soul of man.

This meta-biological and meta-historical view of the 'German man' had new aspects, especially when it came to its explanation of the neuroses and the 'primal memory' of 'immortality', but it also partly fitted in well with the romantic view that already existed of the German national character, as it also existed in the völkische movement - and with Ludendorff. In the second half of the nineteenth century, authors such as Paul Böttischer, better known as Paul de Lagarde and Julius Langbehn had already written about the vulnerability of Germany, and especially of the German people.

In his *Deutsche Schriften*, published in 1878, De Lagarde believed that the German Empire may have had a physical unity, but that it lacked spiritual unity. The völkische thought had sprung from Romanticism and was characterised by a penchant for the irrational and the emotional. Völkisch people felt mystically connected to their land and the ancient generations who had always lived there. They assumed that one was 'born into' a country and a people and that each people had a 'Volksgeist'. In the Völkische publications, much attention was therefore paid to the rhythm of the seasons, depicted as a cyclical, biological development. The aim was to create perfect relations between man and nature.[1133] The Austrian Guido von List spoke of the necessary return of the 'Armanenschaft', the Aryan-Germanic man.[1134]

Hitler's great example, Richard Wagner, advocated 'das reinmenschliche', the ideal of the 'aesthetic man', living in harmony with nature. Lagarde wrote that this bond had to be 'restored'. History had to become the binding element of a people, not the economy or class consciousness, which gave both capitalism and communism a sweeping blow. In Lagarde's work, the Jews already played a negative role. He thought they were a 'fremdkörper', a 'rootless' people, who did not know the völkische anchoring to the ground, and imposed themselves on other peoples.[1135]

Langbehn, like Mathilde, went back to the earliest forms of life and 'recalled' the 'Adamidealmensch' man as he was once 'meant to be'. This 'Originalmensch' had been damaged in the course of time. He saw the real problem, like Von Kemnitz, but without any 'biology' to back it up, in the 'soul attitude' of the German people. He called upon Germany's spiritual elite to change course. His book *Rembrandt als Erzieher*, in which he depicted the painter, working with his organic colours, as a 'nature man', became widely known. The fact that this man lived outside German territory should have been taken as a big warning. With the introduction of Rembrandt as an 'example' the 'Germanic' card had in fact been drawn.[1136]

Christianity had also been tinkered with earlier from the völkische field. The claim by an Antwerp physician at the time of the Eighty Years' War - that Adam would have spoken a kind of 'Germanic dialect' - was eagerly picked up.[1137] Houston Stewart Chamberlain claimed that there had been an Aryan primitive Christianity, which over time had been perverted into Judeo-Christian doctrine.[1138] Dr Georg Traue claimed that Jesus Christ was the son of a Roman soldier, and in so doing fiddled with his 'Jewish identity'. Alfred Rosenberg also claimed Jesus for 'the Aryans'. In the course of the 20th century, a series of 'Aryan variants' of the Jesus story emerged. Ludendorff considered the 'Germanisation' of Jesus a dangerous development. According to him, this allowed Christianity to penetrate deeper into the German people's soul 'undercover'. Ludendorff got into a debate with Dr. Eicke and Herbert Lauch of the 'Politischer Arbeitsgemeinschaft der Nationalverbandes Deutscher Offiziere', who considered the 'Germanic variant' a good solution to help 'close the gap' German-Christian and to reduce the Jewish element.[1139]

According to the French researcher Leon Poliakov, Germany struggled more than other countries with descent theories.[1140] This had to do with - to stay in Von Kemnitz jargon - the 'neurosis' in which the German nation found itself with regard to its history. The German state was young, and large parts of the history that people liked to reflect - such as Charlemagne or Clovis - were largely outside their own twentieth-century territory. In short, 'Germanic' history had a different territory than German history. This was also partly the spiritual root of Hitler's later lebensraum philosophy, which the geopoliticologist Karl Haushofer provided with 'scientific' arguments. At the heart of his argument was the assertion that Germany would perish if the territorial status quo was maintained. Von Kemnitz was in fact in the same role with regard to the peace of mind of the völkisch movement. Where Arianism also assumed a kind of mysterious pneuma - a divine spark in the Aryan - Von Kemnitz tried to do so through her cell theory interpretation of Weismann's ideas.

The blood and soil theories and the anti-Semitism of the Nazis came on top of this. If Von Kemnitz had been consistent, she should have realised that these theories were also full of (Christian) 'neuroses', but they were embraced. The most important exponents of this were Dietrich Eckart, to whom Hitler dedicated *Mein Kampf*, Alfred Rosenberg - party-ideologist and author of the theosophically racially tinged book *Der Mythus des 20.Jahrhunderts*, inspired by Houston Stewart Chamberlain, the 'Wahldeutsche' whom Ludendorff also knew, Julius Streicher and Arthur Dinter, the spokespersons of perverse anti-Semitism, von Haussen, the *protocol disseminator*, the Wagner family, the economic anti-Semite Gottfried Feder; all belonged to Ludendorff's circle.

This made Erich Ludendorff the perfect vehicle for Von Kemnitz to get her ideas across. For women at the time, this was also the most effective way of gaining influence. All this does not alter the fact that the love that bloomed between Ludendorff and Mathilde von Kemnitz was genuine. It should also be pointed out that von Kemnitz had also made many a 'feminist' attempt on her own initiative to promote her ideas. In 1920, for instance, she organised the so-called 'Frauenkonzil' in Munich and contributed to the establishment of the 'Weltbund nationaler Frauen'. She had also shown that she could hold her own during the Raden Republic period in Garmisch, where she had been one of the driving forces behind the counter-revolution.

Ludendorff received Von Kemnitz and Gottfried Feder at the Ludwighöhe, and was immediately impressed by Von Kemnitz. Her theories, of course, also connected directly with an inner need (neurosis) of Ludendorff, namely the fact that the German army had collapsed in 1918 with all its social and political consequences. For Ludendorff, it was an attractive option not to blame the failure of the army command and of politics - for which he bore a heavy responsibility - but to blame the 'sickness' of the German soul. Von Kemnitz's theory fitted in well with Ludendorff's pre-existing thoughts, which could be briefly summarised as the 'stab-in-the-back myth'. The cause of the collapse in November 1918 lay in Germany's 'sick soul', and whoever wanted to reveal the 'key to world history',[1141] as Ludendorff literally called it, had to unveil the forces behind this 'sickness'.[1142]

For the unveiling of these forces, a 'Rasse-erwachen', a racial awakening, was necessary, for 'Jews' played in Ludendorff's and Von Kemnitz's eyes 'a leading part' in the 'subversive forces'. They concluded that not only November 1918 was the work of the 'überstaatliche' powers, but that the failure of the 1923 putsch was also due to this. The government in Berlin had been under the influence of Jews, Freemasons, Marxists, and Bavarian separatists (including the Wittelbachers) had hidden among the putschists.[1143]

The 'perfect conspiracy' had been created. From Ludendorff's own words, we know that Von Kemnitz referred him to the stories she had heard from a German clergyman about the Bolshevik murders of the Volga-Germans. It was 'mainly Jews' who played a leading part in this. Pamphlets had been discovered in Hebrew in which the Russian Revolution was celebrated as a Jewish success. At the same time - in line with *The Protocols of the Sages of Zion* - the final Jewish victory was predicted. 'She recognised the Jewish danger', Ludendorff thought[1144] and soon Ludendorff believed in the terminology of Von Kemnitz, in 'the agony of the nations'.[1145] Gottfried Feder pointed Ludendorff to Mathilde von Kemnitz's main work, *Triumph des Unsterblichkeitwillens*, the first edition of which appeared in 1921.

Quite soon thereafter, von Kemnitz's ideas began to influence Ludendorff's political actions. For the elections of 7 December 1924, Ludendorff also had to reflect on the role of women in the völkische movement and for this purpose took note of Von Kemnitz's work *Das Weib und seine Bestimmung*, from 1917.[1146] When Ludendorff's political life finally came to an end, he saw a new future for himself along the strict lines of his new insights.

After the failed elections, and his collapsing authority thereafter - Ludendorff spoke of his 'liquidation'[1147] - he also broke with his last friends in 'das Militär'. At the Tannenberg commemoration it had already become a difficult union, as we saw, and Ludendorff's constant agitation against the house of Wittelsbach had also seriously disturbed his relations with many officer corpses, especially those of Bavarian or Catholic origin. Ludendorff's quarrel with Prince Rupprecht went back to the war, and now, in the aftermath of the putsch trial, Ludendorff's explanation of Rupprecht's role had been added. Lawyers and legal experts - a libel action was pending - were busy. Ludendorff was as ruthless as ever, regardless of who he faced. Mediation attempts were made. Prince Ruppre-

The way the 'House of Ludendorff' saw the world, propagandistic caricatures in which 'überstaatlichen' divide the world up

Nazism also got a beating

cht sent Graf Törring-Jettenbach to Ludendorff, who in turn brought General Hildebrandt into the field. Meanwhile, Ludendorff had an excuse for every failure. When the parties could not reach an agreement, the 'culprits' were quickly found; Graf Törring-Jettenbach was 'very Catholic', and Ludendorff discovered that General Hildebrandt was connected to freemasonry. In reality, Ludendorff overplayed his hand. The election results had made it clear that Ludendorff's star was waning, and he could count on more and more opposition. The officers' unions turned away from him, and even the Völkisch officers had their reservations. What did not help either was that Ludendorff thwarted the negotiations with open letters in the *Völkische Kurier*. As a result of all this, there was another farewell. 'Auf das Leben für das Vaterland kommt es an', Ludendorff merely concluded. [1148]

After the unsuccessful political career, which was completely at odds with Ludendorff's sectarian character, there followed a new attempt to rise above the parties, a position he actually aspired to most, in order to be asked for higher office. For this purpose, the 'Tannenbergbund' was founded. Here, Ludendorff turned to the oldest loyalists he had left, veterans and their supporters, and then only to those who had remained most loyal to him. The name 'Tannenbergbund', linked to the historical battle with which his name was connected, already indicated Ludendorff's personal attachment. The historian Wolfgang Ruge rightly called the choice of name 'infamous'.[1149] It was a new attempt by Ludendorff to link the success of Tannenberg to his own person.

The union was founded on 5 September 1925 in Regensburg by his childhood friend, East Prussian General A.D. Friedrich Bronsart von Schellendorf from Brunshaupten in Mecklenburg who had been associated with the Turkish army command in the First World War, and Konstantin Hierl, a former staff officer from the First World War, a fellow putschist around the Feldherrnhalle, who had lost his rank in the army as a result. Later, he would make a career for himself in the Reichs Arbeitsdienst of the Third Reich. The patron of the union was Ludendorff, who was in fact the central figure. As 'Schirmherr', he drew up the guidelines, Von Bronsart became 'Bundesführer', while Hierl was to be one of the 'Landesleiter' (Süddeutschland). The organisation was as follows: the union divided the country into 'Landesverbänden', which were in turn divided into 'Gauen', 'Ortsgruppen' and finally 'Zellen'. Most supporters came from parts of the Freikorps 'Rossbach' and 'Oberland', the 'Deutschvölkischer Offiziersbund' (Generalmajor a.D. J. von Aechter), 'Altreichsflagge' (Oberleutnant a.D. W. Liebel), Frontkriegerbund, Bund Frankenland, Frontbann Nürnberg, Frontbann Ostsee (Hugo Alletter), Frontbann

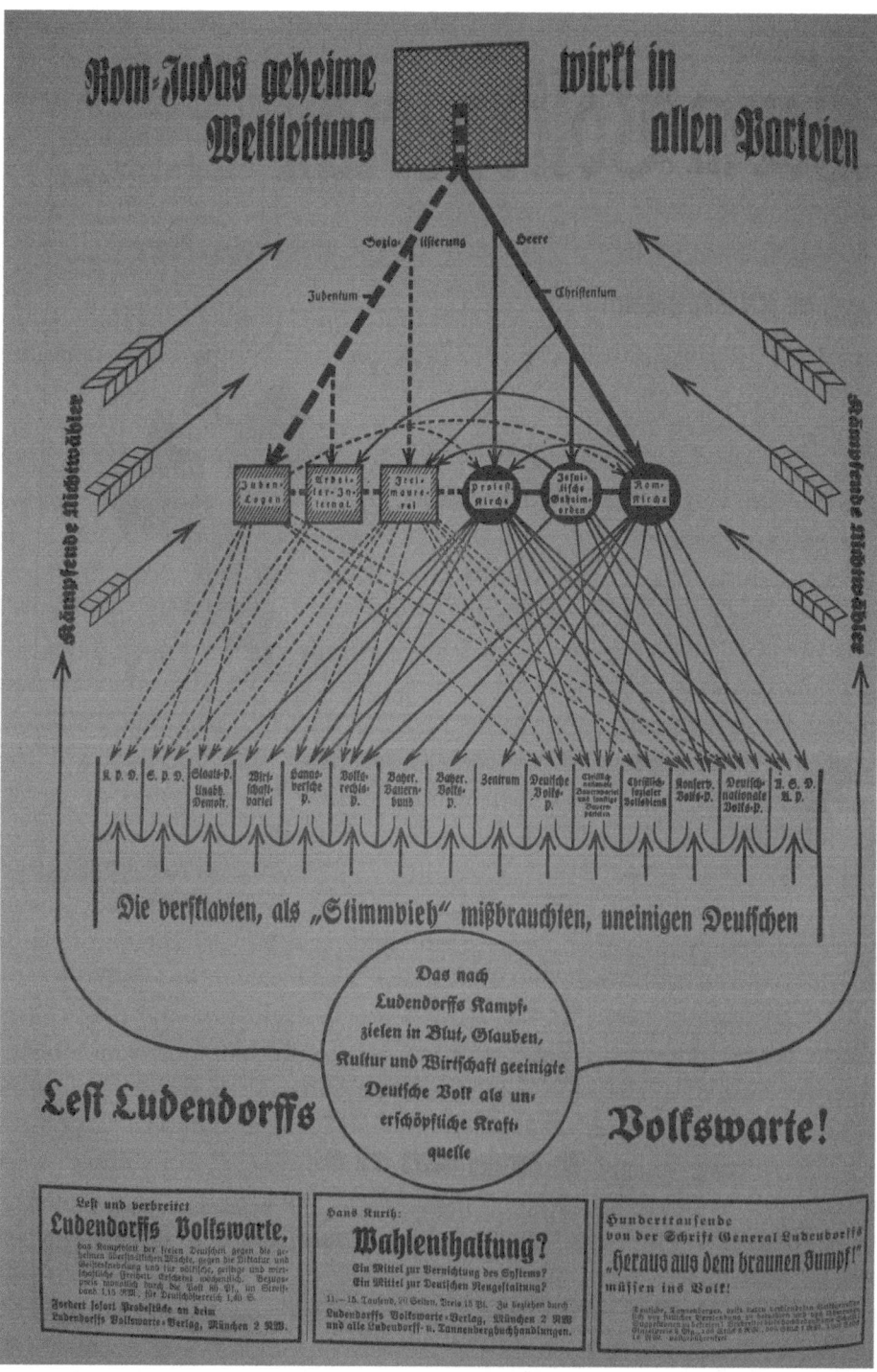

The ultimate world conspiracy, ruled from 'the cube'. From *Ludendorff's Volkswarte*

Sachsen, Verband Hindenburg, Wehrwolf (Studienrat Kloppe) and other small groups. [1150]

The tone of the union was entirely Ludendorffian, although Bronsart von Schellendorff uttered these words at the founding meeting of the union:

'In the name of the Tannenberg co-conqueror and leader of the German liberation struggle, I call on the non-partisan front soldiers and youth organisations that are committed to the Völkische ideology and strive for German renewal to work together in the Tannenberg League. We want to be free. And we want to be able to carry freedom on proud German shoulders. Under our patron Ludendorff we do not want to forget the lesson of the two times Tannenberg[1151] and we want to create lasting values from this in our common endeavour. No fate will bestow on us what we have not already acquired through hard work'.[1152]

As always with Ludendorff, the struggle was central. But here lay the problem. The front had expanded, partly due to the new insights Ludendorff had gained through Mathilde von Kemnitz, to an almost endless list of enemies: The Weimar parliamentary system, the Entente, communists, Jews, freemasons, the Catholic Church and its representatives (Jesuits), the house of Wittelsbach, the NSDAP and more moderate völkisch and nationalistic groups. It was a battle that could not be won. In fact, it was a break with civil society and broadly drawn boundaries to both the left and the right. In short, the union had a sectarian character right from the start and would suffer the fate of every sectarian movement: purging and splitting up. The union was also characterised by fierce polemics in newspapers, and where necessary, it was fought out in court. While the world was portrayed as a conspiracy, people themselves were quick to take offence. An example of this was the lawsuit filed by Bronsart von Schellenberg against the Protestant theologian Claus August Elfers, who had called the teachings of the Tannenbergers 'new paganism'. [1153]

For supporters with opportunistic motives, the road with Ludendorff would ultimately prove to be a dead end, so that those members would choose to take their chances elsewhere. Ludendorff saw such 'betrayal' only as a confirmation of his already existing ideas; a constant pacting of the outside world against him. We have already referred to Hierl's later career in the NSDAP, as well as the running off of editors of his new mouthpiece, the völkische krant *Deutsche Wochenschau*, Major a.D. Hans Weberstedt and Oberstleutnant a.D. Georg Ahlemann from the union.[1154] Ludendorff's age and health problems also did not work in his favour, and in addition, his enemies did not sit still, resulting in a written guerrilla without end. It became Ludendorff's fate that he wanted to be above the parties (Stinnes' advice) but in practice always found himself at the centre of the debate.

After the Concordat with Rome Ludendorff considered Hitler a traitor

The challenges were met. After all, it was about the 'Aufklärung' of the country. By means of various periodicals, such as the - in May 1929 founded - *Ludendorffs Volkswarte* under the management of Hauptmann a.D. Helmuth Pfeifer and editorial management by the Breslauer Hans Kurth and later Karl von Unruh and Erich Biermann (1930 and 1931), *Am heiligen Quell* (later renamed in *Monatschrift des deutschsvolks e. V.*, 1933 banned and 1937 republished as *Bund für Gotterkenntniss Ludendorff e.V.*), as well as many other periodicals, leaflets, pamphlets, stickers, lectures and readings, and via *Ludendorffs-Lichtbildstätte* even visual material, the message had to be spread. Women's sub-sections were set up, a medical department, Ludendorff bookshops (several dozen), a 'Tannenbergbundesheim' in Rehau, built by the 'Deutsch-völkischen Sport und Wanderverein Rehau' in 1926,[1155] and many thousands of people attended the nationwide lectures organised by the league. Under the title *Was Ludendorff will*, people were summoned to attend the lectures. This sometimes involved large numbers, 6,000, 7,000 visitors in Berlin, Hamburg or Stuttgart, where Ludendorff and his wife spoke personally, but also many smaller gatherings in the provinces, where - besides the Ludendorff couple - other central figures visited the union, such as Dr. Erich Rosikat, Oberst. Erich Rosikat, Oberst a.d. Goetze, Hans Ludwig Schulze, Carl Kressel, H. Adam, Dr. Seeger, J. Marquardt, D. Gerstenberg, F.H. Hoffmann, H. Stössl, to name only a few. Among them were two Austrians, Dr Weisspeiner from Graz and G. Gräf from Vienna.[1156]

There are no longer any sources that can clarify the size of the union. A positive publication for Ludendorff and the union mentions 30,000 members, but this cannot be verified.[1157] The magazine *Ludendorffs Volkswarte*, which was affiliated with the Union, and which jumped in the gap of the *Deutsche Wochenschau*, would have had a circulation of 61,000 by the end of 1932 and 90,000 when it was banned in 1933, with peaks of up to 110,000 for special issues.[1158]

Ludendorff's direct involvement with the union was initially limited. This was mainly for private reasons. The marriage between Margarethe and Erich Ludendorff had failed. Ludendorff himself indicated the period autumn 1925 spring 1926 as the turning point. 'With a divorce', he reported, 'everyone looks for the question of guilt'. In reality, according to Ludendorff, it was not so much a question of guilt but of an 'inner separation' of the two former lovers. A 'not-unforgiven-krankheit' also played a role. Ludendorff described here rather opaquely what in the corridors was quickly referred to as an 'addiction'. 'The reader will understand that I will elaborate on this as little as possible'. For although the marriage had fizzled out, the divorce still cost 'a lot of nerves', as Ludendorff noted.[1159] Miraculously, it was Mathilde von Kemnitz who assisted Margarethe

'The Germanic people settled with Rome, Hitler restored the ties'
Drawings from *Ludendorff's Volkswarte*

Caricature of the relationship between Christianity and Nazism according to Ludendorff

as a doctor in the last phase of the marriage. According to Hartmuth Mahlberg, who had some kind words for Margarethe Ludendorff in his otherwise hagiographic memoir, Margarethe 'used heavy sedatives'. Attempts to withdraw failed, according to Mahlberg.[1160] After her divorce Margarethe moved to Kiel, where her daughter Margot lived, and where she remained until her death.[1161]

Margarethe did not leave the stage without a final pause. In 1929, Drei Masken Verlag in Munich published her memoirs, *Als ich Ludendorffs Frau war*, compiled by Walther Ziersch, but the slightly amateurish tone of the book shows that little editing had taken place and that Margarethe was speaking personally here. In its simplicity, it became a moving book and, like Wilhelm Breucker's memoirs, an insight into the general's life, even though she had no knowledge of major politics. Ludendorff was not pleased to learn that this book was reported abroad. 'Ex-Wife of War Lord stirs with new book', was the headline of *The Charleston Daily*.[1162] An English translation by Raglan Somerset followed, and publication followed in 1930.

Even where there was criticism of Margarethe's book, this criticism was not flattering to him, for example, from Kurt Tucholsky in *Die Karikatur Preussens*. Tucholsky directly ridiculed Margarethe Ludendorff's naivety and ignorance. He called her 'gullible', and a 'typical representative of her caste'. Although she was a 'not unsympathetic presence', she spoke like 'a cancer patient, who lists all the symptoms of the disease and thinks of it as anything but lethal'. Finally, shaking his head, he said: 'This woman has lived in her world without any sense and has remained so', only to conclude: 'That was them? Did that rule Germany? And that still rules in part today. Du lieber Gott'. 'A shameful book', were his last words in *Die Weltbühne*. Ludendorff also got a slap in the face. This hit him all the harder, because Tucholsky attacked him by defending him: 'The attacks on Ludendorff are slowly becoming a cowardly act. After all, there is nothing left'.[1163]

Ludendorff reacted to Margarethe's book in the *Deutsche Wochenschau*. He stated that it violated the good habit of silence between divorced people. As an explanation, he mentioned his wife's addiction to morphine. She is said to have started using this drug before the First World War. He called the book a 'sentimental fantasy', in which a 'happy marriage' was depicted, while that was 'objectively a false picture'. In reality it had been an unhappy marriage, with a hate-filled 'Morphistin'.[1164]

The marriage to Mathilde von Kemnitz took place in Tutzing, south of Munich, a small town on the shores of the Starnbergersee, where Mathilde lived in a characteristic villa. Ludendorff characterised the wedding day on 14 September 1926 as the most important day of his post-war period, if not of his entire

Hitler balancing between brown shirts and Vatican

Historical 'positioning' Ludendorff in relation to Frederick the Great from the point of view of the propaganda of the House of Ludendorff

life. 'Marriage gave my life a new content,' he confided in his memoirs. 'A new world opened up for me'. He was frank about his happiness: 'I have found a rich happiness in this marriage'.[1165] His memoirs include a photograph of the wedding day. The fresh couple, with Ludendorff in full uniform and with Pickelhaube, Mathilde with a bunch of flowers which she holds somewhat defeated and looking down at the ground, still seem somewhat uncomfortable, as if they already feel the weight of the coming sectarian battle. Their paths would not be parted again.

Chapter 20

The paper front:
The publications of the Ludendorff House

The most important collaboration between Erich Ludendorff and Mathilde undoubtedly took place on the paper front. Through their own publishing house, enormous quantities of books, pamphlets and brochures were to be published in order to spread the new ideas. The focus was on books about theology, the Bible, the 'Catholic Action', the 'danger of the Jesuits', Judaism linked to all kinds of conspiracy theories, Ludendorff's debates with Nazis and other apologists, and the fight against occultism. The role of women was also given a special place. In this chapter, we will first consider the publicity surrounding Ludendorff himself.

Initially, Ludendorff worked through existing publishers. We already mentioned his first work, *Meine Kriegserinnerungen* (1920), partly written in Sweden, *Urkunden der Obersten Heeresleitung* (1920) and *Kriegführung und Politik* (1921). These books were published by Mittler & Sohn and achieved large print runs. It were his war memories that attracted most attention. Three years after its publication, there were already eight printings with a print run of 170,000 copies. In addition, there were also abridged versions, the so-called 'Volksausgabe', of which about 40,000 copies were sold. Parts of the books were also published in smaller booklets, preceding or supporting the larger books, such as *Ueber Unbotmässigkeit im Kriege, Dirne Kriegsgeschichte, vor dem Gericht des Weltkrieges, Das Marne Drama,* and *der Fall Moltke-Hentsch* as well as editions by others which were affiliated with Ludendorff's publishing company, such as *Ludendorff's Handstreich auf Lüttich* and *Die Schlacht von Tannenberg* by generalleutnant Ritter von Wenninger.[1166]

In these pamphlet-like books, the tone changed from military historical work to polemic. Two military themes were central, the 1918 defeat and Ludendorff's defence that he had not suffered a nervous breakdown, as well as the battle of

Tannenberg. This last battle had assumed mythical proportions. Although Ludendorff himself was responsible for this, he tried to put it into perspective by pointing out in *Dirne Kriegsgeschichte* that the German army had collected even more victories between '14 and '18. The aim of Ludendorff's publication was to 'correct' the untruths about Tannenberg. He believed that historical truth had been 'raped', whereas it was supposed to be 'the people's teacher'.[1167] What followed was an ugly mud-fight over who should get the most credit and praise. Here, too, Ludendorff was unable to rise above the discussion. Among his opponents in this debate were, painfully enough, many of his former colleagues, as well as a series of authors and publicists, such as the prolific writer Werner Beumelburg, Professor Elze, author of a book on Tannenberg, and 'the Professor-strategist' - as Ludendorff disparagingly called him - Dr Hans Delbruck. The crumbling of his role at Tannenberg or anywhere else in the war was, for Ludendorff, a chilling of the historiography, which became 'Dirne'. It is striking how often Ludendorff uses the word 'ungeheuer' in his writings. In his eyes, almost all criticism was unacceptable and he fought this with the same energy as he had studied Von Schlieffen's stage policy at the time.[1168]

In addition to these writings, Ludendorff wrote in this period regularly for various newspapers, such as the *Deutschen Zeitung, Kreuzzeitung, Tag, Berliner Lokalanzeiger* and the specialist journal *Militärwochenblatt*. After the Kapp-Putsch, he moved to Bavaria, and his journalistic production shifted to the newspapers *Heimatland* and *Völkischer Beobachter*.

The reactions to *Meine Kriegserinnerungen* were not bad, even from people who could not be counted among Ludendorff's admirers. To start with two important publicity opponents, Hans Delbruck and Walter Schotte, the former said: 'Powerful style, drags the reader along. Short sentences, stroke by stroke. Despite the details, not tiresome'.[1169] Schotte went even further in the *Preussischen Jahrbücher*, saying that while reading he was reminded of Julius Caesar's *Bellum Gallicum*, although he added 'without wanting to make a comparison', which he of course implicitly did.[1170] 'He writes like a victorious general. When one sees what this man has accomplished, one understands the tone of the text'. There was a catch in this last sentence of course, the tone did not please publicists like Delbruck and Schotte, but friend and foe agreed that Ludendorff had written an extraordinary book. Gert Borst, who researched Ludendorff's publicity activities, judges in his book with some justification that Ludendorff had 'a certain publicity talent'.

On the conservative side, Ludendorff's war memories were praised. The *Kreuzzeitung* of 8 April 1920, thought that this book would 'awaken the German people again', that it was written in a 'noble form', with 'unsurpassed language', and that it was a 'political bible' for the 'coming generations'.[1171] Reviewer Von Bissing of the newspaper *Deutschlands Erneuerung* spoke of a 'classic book', 'good for children', and full of 'German spirit'. These reviews echoed the veneration of the figurehead that Ludendorff was to many, along with Von Hindenburg. Typical for the veneration of Ludendorff in certain circles was the text by Alfred Falb, in the *Deutsche Zeitung* 21 September 1919:

Ludendorff

Wer trug - wie Du! - des Krieges grösste Burden
Auf Haupt und Schultern - ohne Ruh und Ras?
And the Völker und der Welt
Ein unerschuttert treuer - grosser Held!
Wer schirmte so wie Du das Deutsche Reich -
Ein Atlas und ein Herakles zugleich...
Wer sah wie Du sich nah dem letzten Ziel,
Als eignes Volk ihm in den Rüken fiel!
Das Volk-? Nein, ein erbarmlicher arger Wicht.
In Hohlen treib sein Werk er, scheu dem Licht
Und wob aus Scheelsucht, Blindheit, Habgier, Neid
Der Lüge und Verleumdung Nessuskleid!
Dass Dich die Lasterglut der ganzen Welt
Verderben sollt' - Du letzter grosser hero!
Der wie aus Vorziet Tagen zu uns spricht...
Wer war Soldat - und achtete Dich nicht?!
Wer sah in wilddurchwogter schwerer Schlacht
Der Feinde ungeheuere Wucht und Macht
Und fühlte nicht - in jeden feuersturm:
Der Ludendorff ist unser Schild und Schwert!
Wer hat - wie Du in Deinem Feldherrnhaupt
An Sieg und an - das deutsche Volk geglaubt - ?!!
Dein name wird - ob Welten auch verwehn! -
Ein heller Stern am dunklen Himmel stehn -
Und alle Seelen, deren Lieb erblich
Im schweren kämpfe - Feldherrn grüssen Dich!
Die Seelen, deren Ringen gross und klar
Wie Deins - und doch - zuletzt! - vergeblich war....[1172]

Ludendorff's later works became more and more politically charged and thus more pamphlets than military historical reference works.

Weltkrieg droht auf Deutschem Boden should be seen in this light. This book from 1931 is largely in the light of his metahistorical view of history, in which the 'überstaatsliche' powers play an important role. Interesting is his assertion that, in the face of a world of enemies, the German army had victory in sight, but that 'the unrecognisable enemy could still reap the harvest for the Entente'.[1173] This was the ultimate stab-in-the-back myth. In this book, Ludendorff described the German people, but also peoples in general, as 'naive' and 'ill-informed' about the real influence of the 'überstaatsliche' powers.[1174] In addition, Ludendorff also dwelt on other, more geopolitical, problems with which the German security was struggling. Due to its location in Europe, Germany had to deal with 'vertical alliances' (in the north-south direction: e.g. Germany-Austria-Hungary) while Germany's enemies had 'horizontal alliances' (e.g. France-Russia) that were advantageous for encircling Germany. German geopolitics was partly shaped by Spenglerian doom. Germany was not only sandwiched between powers, the encirclement was military and mental; Russian byzantinism on the one side and the Western world on the other.[1175]

German scientists and soldiers tried to provide the answer to the dilemma of the many borders. Albrecht Penck and Wilhelm Volz tried to protect Deutschtum with an emphasis on language, Heinrich Schnee and Arthur Dix saw more in colonies, Friedrich Burgdorfer pointed out the importance of demography, Ewald Banse sought, partly in agreement with Ludendorff, in the 'soul' of the German people, Adolf Grawbrowsky, loyal to the 'Erfüllungspolitik', thought that border treaties had to secure Germany, Karl Haushofer and Sir Alfred Mackinder saw more in the creation of the 'Heartland Europe', or 'Kernraum Europa', partly inspired by their spiritual predecessors, the German Friedrich Ratzel and the Swede Rudolf Kjellén. The ideas of Mackinder and Haushofer had certain similarities with those of Ludendorff. Both scientists, who were influential in their time, started from deterministic thoughts. They assumed a 'Sehnsucht' to the continental empire, whereby a final battle (a variant of Ludendorff's *Entscheidungsschlacht*) between Germany and Russia would be the ultimate (logical) consequence. Mackinder considered the chances of the Soviet Union as the best.

The clash between the two nations arose not only from the permanent revolution preached by Trotsky, but also from the historical dominance of the 'Grossrussians', who had been following their own directions since time immemorial; the Mediterranean programme (Crimea, Dardanelles), the Atlantic programme (towards the West - read: Germany), the Asian programme (Pacific) and the Indian programme (Transcaucasus). In the *Zeitschrift für Geopolitik,* which was formed after the First World War around Karl Haushofer and Kurt Vowinckel,

Otto Muck pointed out the problem of conflicts with neighbouring countries, which had been recurring for centuries. With regard to the East, in *Der Sinn der fünftausend Jahren Kampf im Osten,* he pointed to a highly deterministic interpretation of history. The history between east and west was thus depicted in a relentless wave of attack and defence, with Alexander the Great, the Teutons and Napoleon as 'western' and partly 'German' representatives versus Huns, Mongols and Tatars as 'eastern' ones.[1176] Oskar Ritter von Niedermayer, connected to the 'Sonderstab R' (Russia) of defence/foreign affairs and involved in the preparations for the Treaty of Rapallo (the secret German-Russian military cooperation to circumvent the requirements of the Treaty of Versailles) believed that the whole of Russian history was a sequence of 'Kolonisations- und Siedlungsgeschichte'. Von Niedermayer spoke of a 'Wandertrieb'.[1177]

In *Weltkrieg droht auf Deutschem Boden*, Ludendorff expressed his fear for a future offensive of Russia and Turkey against Germany. This joint military force of 6.2 million men (of which 5 million Russians) would be unstoppable. According to Ludendorff, this danger was real. Walther Rathenau, whom, as a Jew, he distrusted very much, is said to have mocked the future downfall of Germany in the Swiss press. 'Whoever visits Germany in twenty years time will find half stone ruins with dilapidated people', said Rathenau, drawing a comparison with Thebes and Babylon and other biblical cities that had disappeared from the face of the earth.[1178]

Furthermore, the geopoliticians highlighted Ludendorff's problem with Germany's central location in Central Europe, noting that Germany was a typical 'transit country'.[1179] The historian Michael Stürmer said that the German national state 'went against historical and geographical logic'.[1180] In addition to the structure of the alliances (vertical versus horizontal), the vulnerability was emphasised by the unfortunate river positions as well. Germany had to deal with 'Parallelschaltung', rivers that cut through the country from north to south and were partly (like the Rhine) border rivers that could not be used optimally. This is in contrast to, for example, Russia and the 'Zentralraum' around it, with 'spreading' rivers.[1181] The 'devil's belt' that encircled Germany in the east was also reinforced by pan-Slavist cooperation; the *Zeitschrift für Geopolitik* spoke of an 'Absperrung des Deutschtums vom Osten'.[1182] In line with the ideas of Friedrich Ratzel in his *Politische Geografie* (1899), which were then only more radically elaborated by his successors, Ludendorff saw the world darwinistically (with states as living organisms) moving around in the carousel of 'Auflösung' and 'Neubildung'.[1183] According to Ratzel, it was characteristic that the states grew larger and larger over the course of time. This idea later became the model for the 'Lebensraum' philosophy, which found its way to Hitler via Rudolf Hess and his professor Karl Haushofer.

What Ludendorff wrote in his last military work, *Der Totale Krieg*, is interesting. Somehow, it was the final symphony of his long road. He immediately declared himself to be an 'enemy of all theories'. Pragmatism thus prevailed in Ludendorff's military thinking. It also provided explanations, above all for Ludendorff's actions at the end of the First World War, during the spring offensives of 1918. Ludendorff changed his firing directions several times when it was convenient. He subordinated theory, or strategy, to tactics. With the latter, however, he was very thorough. Tactical conditions for his offensives were worked out in detail and implemented with great punctuality by the German army; for example, in the performance of the German artillery in the spring of 1918, or the introduction of the shock troops, a revolutionary concept that would later be developed into a special feature of the elite units of the Waffen-SS, Hitler's 'political soldiers', as the historian Bernd Wegner described them, by the officer Felix Steiner.[1184]

One could say that with his *Der Totale Krieg*, Ludendorff said goodbye to Schlieffen thinking. However, in Ludendorff's view there was no difference between his anti-theoretical thinking and the Schlieffenplan. He simply reduced the Schlieffenplan to a core idea, namely the concept of destruction (the all-decisive battle) to which all other military thinking and working was subordinate. In a similar way, he also dealt with Von Clausewitz's thinking. He recognised his thesis that waging war was politics done differently, but then brought it directly to the point of the decisive battle, a matter that Von Clausewitz 'had seen correctly'.[1185]

For Ludendorff, the concept of total war implied that - according to Von Clausewitz's thinking - sovereign, people and field lords (the miraculous trinity) had to be on one line. The people had become more and more involved in the war through technological developments, such as the war economy and possible (food and raw material) shortages, new weapons, such as air bombardments, as well as the effect of propaganda, and the rise of, for example, the radio.[1186] According to Ludendorff, it was of the utmost importance in this 'total war' to maintain the 'seelische geschlossenheit'.[1187] Looking back on the First World War, Ludendorff thought that this necessary unity initially was threatened by the social-democrats. These lost ground after some time, only to gain strength again at the end of the war. Ludendorff spoke of a socialist revolution in Germany.[1188]

This revolution of the country also affected the army. Kaiser Wilhelm II's request to flee to the Netherlands was not for nothing prompted by the military leadership, Ludendorff thought. He drew a comparison with the uprising against the tsarist empire in March 1917, in which officers of the tsarist army

Book covers of Ludendorff's publishing house in which various conspiracy theories are propagated

Attacks on the Catholic Church and the Jesuits

were also involved. Actually, Ludendorff accused the German General Staff of treason, or at least treason to the House of Hohenzollern.

The 'unity of the German soul' was therefore lacking, and Ludendorff also had an explanation for this, pointing to the essentially already corrupt German soul due to Christian-Jewish influence. 'Unfortunately, the Christian peoples no longer had their own religion', he wrote, looking up in admiration to Japan, which still had an 'Arteigene' religious experience.[1189] This adoration of the Japanese soul was also a feature of other (strategic) thinkers, such as the stimulator of the 'Lebensraum' concept Karl Haushofer, the Asia expert Alexander von Falkenhausen, and the Reichsführer-SS Heinrich Himmler himself, who in his SS periodical *Schwarze Korps* praised Japanese (samurai) history through writings by Heinz Corazza.[1190]

The influence of religion and originally non-Germanic cultures on the events of the war was also highlighted by other authors. What the Leipzig historian Professor Karl Lamprecht wrote about this in his book *Krieg und Kultur (War and Culture),* which was published at the outbreak of the war in 1914, is interesting. He, too, stated that the popular mentality was important and was formed by what he called the 'pre-cultures'. Here, he pointed out that the Christian and Jewish influence - of which he saw the Romans as the bringers - was seen as much stronger in France (Gaul) and in Great Britain than in Germany, where it was more or less confined to the Rhine region. Somewhere, this instinctive boundary remained in Ludendorff's thinking as well. The borders of the Roman Empire partly corresponded to the borders between the Catholic west of Germany and the Lutheran east and north. The relatively limited Judeo-Christian influence on Germany, according to Lamprecht, was the basis of the difference between Western European culture and the Central European thinking of the Germans. Moreover, Lamprecht had an eye for the role of the USA, about which he wrote a book in 1906 under the title *Americana.*[1191]

Besides these works, Ludendorff also wrote his 'normal' autobiography, in three volumes, *Meine Lebenserinnerungen,* with the significant subtitle *Vom Feldherrn zum Weltrevolutionär und Wegbereiter Deutscher Volksschöpfung.* The three volumes cover his life chronologically, from 1919 to 1925, from 1926 to 1933 and from 1934 to the year of his death in 1937. As fluently as his military memoirs are written, the discourse in the works is jerky. The more Ludendorff's life went from political schism to schism, the more his discourse lengthened, and small details became big issues. His meta-political and conspiracy theory-like thoughts also formed the common thread, mixed with a remarkable vanity and fighting spirit. The memoirs, therefore, actually served to report on his work as a 'world revolutionary'. In a way, this was similar to the memoirs of Dr Mathilde von Kemnitz, who needed no less than six volumes to describe her life. Of course, the volumes, which were given the overarching title *Statt Heiligenschein oder Hexenzeichen Mein Leben*, contain interesting biographical data, such as her role in the Raden period or her studies, but they are also underpinned by the same introverted world view that we find in Ludendorff's memoirs too. Furthermore, it is an account of how she arrived at her world of ideas, with the main title *Triumph des Unsterblichkeitwillens*, and the series *Der Seele Wirken und Gestalten, Der Seele Ursprung und Wesen*.

With regard to metahistory, the (re)interpretation of ancient and even early history, as well as religious debates, the view of Ludendorff's second wife played a very important role for the writing and publishing activities of what we can call the 'House of Ludendorff'.

The work of Dr Mathilde von Kemnitz was dominated by philosophy and religion, especially a philosophy *of* religion. She even went so far as to say that culture was the same as the way in which a people experienced its God.[1192] In *Deutscher Gottglaube,* she briefly outlined the core of her ideas. From the very first pages, Von Kemnitz raged against Christianity, which she usually referred to as 'Jaweh-glauben'. For her, racial theories and religious practice went hand in hand. Or, as Ludendorff described it in the periodical *Am Heiligen Quell Deutscher Kraft*: Christian doctrine with its universal goals had awakened the racial consciousness of Germans. 'We are not Christian, not universal, we are German'.[1193]

Mathilde von Kemnitz's philosophy, which she spoke of in numerous publications, was characterised by the widely held view of doom in Völkisch circles. Whereas Völkisch thinkers such as Paul de la Garde and Julius Langbehn were of the opinion that the German Reich had taken a wrong turn since the unification of 1870, Von Kemnitz went much further back, to the advent of Christianity. Religion was a concept that was actually 'alien' to the Germans'as a 'species'. Religion, according to Von Kemnitz, was characterised by the bond with God, but 'we Germans do not know this bond at all'. According to the philosophy, 'the Germans' did have a perception of God ('Gotterleben') and a wisdom of God ('Gottweisheit'), and from this a belief in God was born. The understanding of God was actually already anchored in man. She pointed out that this anchoring was different for each type of human being (race) and that here the specific characteristics of the peoples were expressed. Von Kemnitz spoke of a 'racial character':[1194] the purer the blood, the stronger the character. Racially pure peoples were therefore characterised by great steadfastness and determination. Von Kemnitz argued in her book *Deutscher Gottglauben* that those who voluntarily

Ludendorff's Volkswarte makes propaganda for Mathilde Ludendorff's religious 'Krischna' ideas

'converted' to another religion during their adult lives were usually 'racially inferior'.¹¹⁹⁵ 'The Christian missionaries knew all about this,' she added.¹¹⁹⁶ As an example, she cited coloureds and Chinese who had been converted to Christianity and who, in her opinion, clearly bore these characteristics. Imposing a different faith or having it imposed led to hypocrisy. People tried to please the missionary, but they partly lacked the right qualities to conform to the new religion. All this led to a lack of freedom and a racial 'Entartung'. ¹¹⁹⁷

According to Von Kemnitz, Germany was also in an extremely dangerous situation in this respect. There, too, the influence between race and religion had been loosened by the power of Christianity. 'It had been wrong for 1100 years,' (since Charlemagne), said Von Kemnitz. Formerly Germans were 'fit, high-minded, powerful and healthy in body and soul', but then the ancestors became systematic victims of the 'sword killings'. They were murdered by the thousands and their original religious practice was presented as the work of the devil.¹¹⁹⁸ The 'Noble People' were reduced to the status of 'Unmoral'.¹¹⁹⁹ The Yahweh faith had the nations of the earth in the grip of the 'Mitgartschlange' and the 'faithful' and 'innocent' Germans were at their mercy.

However, the First World War was seen by the House of Ludendorff as a major turning point. Due to these events, the German blood had been revived and was ready to break Jaweh's power. It was the German people who, according to Von Kemnitz, would play a leading role in the fight against the 'annihilating powers'. People had come to realise that the myth of the chosen Jewish people was a fairy tale. How is it possible, thought Von Kemnitz, that God revealed himself to the Jews only after 298,000 years, when the human race had already existed for 300,000 years, to point out their special position?¹²⁰⁰ Von Kemnitz therefore saw embracing the Judeo-Christian faith as a 'shadow faith'. She defined the art of religion in terms such as 'light faith'.¹²⁰¹

At its core, Von Kemnitz's philosophy consists of a gnostic basis. Alongside the classical and Judeo-Christian heritage, Von Kemnitz placed the 'deutscher Gottglaube'. Characteristic of the gnosis is that the experience of being, in which intuition and irrationality play an important role, is considered more important than 'merely' believing. In gnosis, man still has the 'divine spark' within him and tries to develop it. It is a mode of thinking that can strongly determine consciousness. Divine self-realisation must come from the so-called 'pneuma', the divine substance that still lives in man. Von Kemnitz insisted on the specifically German character of religious experience. It is, to quote the Gnostics, 'the consciousness of a divine descent'. Von Kemnitz considered the bloodline to be of great importance, as well as racial purity. This is a typical point of gnosis, which is always characterised by dualism, morality and good and evil thinking.

Am heiligen Quell Deutscher Kraft

Ludendorffs Halbmonatsschrift

Inhalt dieser Folge:
- Sittliche Freiheit und sittlicher Zwang. Von Dr. M. Ludendorff . . 177
- Der Staat Platons in völkischer Betrachtung. Von W. v. Josch . 181
- Die bedeutende Schrift des toten Feldherrn. Von Dr. M. Ludendorff 185
- Die Heiligsprechung des Weltkriegspapstes – ein Symbol. Von Walter Löhde 188
- Auf „absolute Wahrheit" kommt es nicht an? Von W. v. Josch . 194
- Deutschlands Partner in Fernost. Von Hermann Rehwaldt . . 197
- Die Augendiagnose. Von Professor Dr. Groenouw 202

Die Hand der überstaatlichen Mächte – Judas Marsch zur Macht – in USA. – Hintergründe der Friedensbotschaft – Schöne Seelen finden sich – Aus anderen Blättern – Umschau – Auch ein Pfingstwunder! – „Weder Jungfrau noch Geist" – Roman „Das Priestererbe" – Kunstdruckbeilage: Die Enthüllung der Büste des Feldherrn im Zeughaus am 21.5.1939 – Das Gastmahl des Plato – Japanischer Schintokult.

Postverlagsort München / Einzelpreis 40 Pfg. zuzügl. ortsüblicher Zustellgebühr

Folge 5   2.6.1939   Zehntes Jahr

The magazine *Am heiligen Quell Deutscher kraft*

Here, the blood-pure German is diametrically opposed to the foreign-blooded (Jewish) Yahweh worshipper. It is not difficult to see these camps in the light of the later Nuremberg Race Laws.

In *Ein Leben der Freiheit,* Von Kemnitz looked back on her youth, in which she first became aware of the pneuma and her dissident beliefs. 'Is not the search for truth, the divine in ourselves?'[1202] I turned away from the imperfect conception of God,' she said, 'and the recognition of good and evil began. It was the rejection of the imperfect. In the soul I experienced something pure, deep and holy (...) the young person was freed from the delusion of heaven and hell.'[1203] Von Kemnitz continued to support these ideas later in life. In his book *Vom Wahren Leben, Philosphische Essays (*1972, reprinted in 2002), Von Kemnitz argued that 'Gotterkentniss' provided freedom and guaranteed the personal uniqueness of religious life as a response to the many 'uprooted people' and those who followed the 'fear-filled sacrifices' of the church.[1204]

In view of Von Kemnitz's field of activity and interest, and Ludendorff's need for explanations and legitimation of his own actions, publishing practices were strongly dominated by the 'all-embracing alternative' and the conspiracy. This was also part of the image of the times. The Dutch historian Jan Romein called the early twentieth century a 'time of change' and Max Weber spoke of 'spiritual escape routes'.[1205] The crumbling of Christianity had caused a resurrection of Gnosis. Within this resurrection, there were theories (mostly) without the racial exponent, as in the ideas of Pierre Teilhard de Chardin, Rudolf Steiner and Friedrich Rittelmeyer; in others, the racial aspect played a very important role, including spiritual teachers of Hitler, such as *Ostara publisher* Jörg Lanz von Liebenfels, who reinterpreted *the Bible* in a racial way, or in Theosophy, of Helena Petrovna Blavatsky, who believed that root races played a decisive role in history. Such ideas were perverted by Alfred Rosenberg in his *Der Mythus des 20. Jahrhunderts* and other writings.[1206] The idea that there was a special 'German variant' of religion was not new either. Interesting here is the parallel with Houston Stewart Chamberlain, author of the *Grundlage des Neunzehnten Jahrhunderts* (a title that inspired Rosenberg), in which he presented 'true Christianity' as a 'German Christianity'. He went on to warn that the 'Jewish era' had now dawned, and that one did not even need to read *The Protocols* to understand their 'world conquest plans', but could refer back to the biblical *Deuteronomy.*[1207] Moreover, the debate about the correct interpretation of Christianity involved the discussion about whether Jesus was Jewish or not. In any case, there was agreement on one thing: the 'alien element' in Von Kemnitz's view, as well as in that of Chamberlain, Rosenberg,

Eckart, Von Liebenfels and many other völkisch and ariosophische thinkers, was the Jew. [1208]

Indeed, the figure of Jesus Christ has been the subject of much debate to this day. Mathilde von Kemnitz had her own vision of Jesus of Nazareth as well, drawing on the work of Artur Drews, among others. For her, the discussion was not so much about whether Jesus was Jewish or not, but rather about whether Jesus had existed at all. In her book *Erlösung von Jesu Christo*, which appeared in Ludendorff's Volkswarte-Verlag, she writes that Christian indologists had covered the true origin of Jesus (and the image of Jesus) all along with the cloak of love. The so-called Bible texts were in part of much older origin, and according to Von Kemnitz, stemmed from the spiritual legacy of Krishna and Buddha. These texts had been available for a long time, that of Krishna already some 4,000 years before Christ and that of Buddha some 600 years before Christ.[1209] Von Kemnitz therefore spoke of a 'Völkerbetrug'. She also pointed to the large number of contradictions in the Biblical texts. Jesus of Nazareth is the only religious founder of whom it can be proven that he did not adhere to his own teachings.[1210] Von Kemnitz did not participate in the ariosophising of the figure of Jesus Christ. To her, that was a betrayal of her 'own' religion, for Jesus could not be an Aryan.[1211] In the struggle against one's own religion, other religions got a beating too, or were dismissed as 'Okkultlehre'. In part, this was a reaction to the slow penetration of Eastern ideas into the West, which was reflected in the first important works in this field in Germany, such as *Buddhistischen Katechismus* by Friedrich Zimmermann from 1888[1212], or the work of Karl Eugen Neumann, who translated important Buddhist texts at the end of the First World War.[1213]

The anti-clerical attitude of the Ludendorffs ultimately led to direct attacks on the core of Christianity: the *Bible*. In the pamphlet *Das grosse entsetzen, Die Bibel nicht Gottes Wort* that Erich Ludendorff and Mathilde von Kemnitz wrote together (1936), they dismissed the *Bible* as a credible source of faith. The core of their argument was that the *Bible* was seen as the direct revelation of God too much by the (well-)believers, who believed that they were taking in one of the oldest worldly wisdom. Again, however, the Ludendorffs argued that the so-called *Old Testament* was actually only a 'young' book. The 'Jewish religion', they wrote, was 'one of the youngest religions on earth'.[1214] To prove their theses, the Ludendorffs brought forward the theses of dissident theologians, such as Friedrich Thudichum, author of the two-volume work *Kirkliche Fälschungen*, or the Englishman Stewart Ross, author of *God's Book*, translated into German under the title *Jehowahs gesammelte Werke*. These books were, according to the

Ludendorffs, 'hushed up' in the media, and Ross had died in poor conditions in London in 1906. Nevertheless, Erich Ludendorff and Mathilde von Kemnitz believed that the criticism of the *Bible* was justified. The main arguments were that 1) the time frame was wrong, 2) linguistically it was an 'impossible work' with 800,000 language disputes alone, so that it was endlessly open to interpretation and that 3) the *Bible* was in reality nothing more than the reflection of the oral tradition of Jewish Rabbis who had collected these texts between 450 BC and 100 AD. [1215]

Additionally, *The New Testament* took a beating and was considered 'manufactured'. Here, they relied, among others, on the theologian Johannes Leipoldt, who believed that it was 'made up'. The Ludendorffs immediately underlined the 'curious and questioning history' of the writing. In the same year, Kurt Fuegner, in *Die Wahrheiten der Bibel - die einzige Regel und Richtschnur des Glaubens*, published by Ludendorff-Verlag, reiterated the theses of *Das grosse Entsetzen*.

There were fierce reactions. In *Ludendorff und die heilige Schrift, Antwort auf die Schrift 'Das grosse Entsetzen-Die Bibel nicht Gottes Wort'*, Dr Karl Pieper, a theologian from Paderborn, took up the gauntlet. The counter-pamphlet, which appeared in a huge edition (at least 125,000 copies), was published by none other than the Archdiocese of Munich. The introduction to this pamphlet also says something about the position Ludendorff still held. Pieper almost apologised for having to take on Erich Ludendorff. He called Ludendorff 'the bearer of a name that is highly revered in this country, and an exceptional man of rank and file'.[1216] After this apology, Pieper stated that he now had to 'get to the point'.

It was mainly the Ludendorffs' sources that were critically examined. According to Pieper, Stewart Ross - pseudonym Saladin - was not such an unknown as the Ludendorffs would have their readers believe. He pointed out that none other than the controversial Ernst Haeckel, in his book *Die Weltraetsel*, had extensively referred to Ross' image of Jesus and Christianity. For the religious, Haeckel's work was highly questionable material. In 1899, the book *Die Welträtsel* by the then 65-year-old zoologist Haeckel was published. Inspired by the German biologist Emil du Bois Reymond, who had earlier spoken of seven world riddles, Haeckel had unfolded his world vision, the so-called monism. The core of his argument was that there was no separation at all between the heavenly and the earthly; or to put it more clearly, there was only matter. Haeckel was a very outspoken man, and was sometimes characterised as 'one of the most remarkable men of the nineteenth century'. Still, he was a great admirer of Darwin and the theory of evolution, and was also outspokenly critical of the Pope and the Vatican. This led him to cite Ross in his work, but, Pieper argued, even for an 'anti-Christian' like Haeckel, Ross was not credible in the long run.

Pieper stated that in the 5th edition of *Die Welträtsel*, the chapter on Ross' theory had been removed. 'For shame', said Pieper.[1217] A further slip of the tongue was that the German edition of Ross' (Saladin) book, *Jehovas gesammelte Werke*, was brought by a certain W. Thunderstruck. Pieper revealed his real name: the Jew Schaumburg. The criticism of Ross' book was an important part of the criticism of the Ludendorffs. It had used 'inferior sources'.[1218] The work was 'not its own study'.[1219] The German edition of *Jehovas gesammelte Werke* did not even contain a place and year of publication, although the university library of Gottingen noted 1897 as the year of publication of the work. He further insisted that Ludendorff constantly misquoted the title of Ross' book: it was not *God's Book* but *God and his Book*.

Piper's anger towards Ludendorff's writing, as well as towards Ross and Haeckel, was mainly due to the fact that, starting with Ross, the existing image of Jesus had been compromised. It was Ross who had Jesus descend from a Roman father - a certain Pandera (a theory later embraced by Mussolini)[1220] - and thereby brought Jewish descent into question. Other völkisch thinkers and ariosophers elaborated on this, such as Artur Dinter who in *Die Sünde wider die Liebe* believed that although Jesus was born in the Jewish country, he was racially an Aryan. It compared Jesus' historical origins with the position of the Jews in Germany: although they had German citizenship, they remained Jews.[1221] Prof. Loofs of the University of Halle judged this to be 'an outrageous piece of writing' when he read back to Haeckel the theory put forward by Ross.[1222] Pieper was also very negative about the other important source of the Ludendorffs. The verdict on Thudichum's book *Kirchliche Fälschungen* 'could not be other than scathing'.[1223]

In *Abgeblitz, Antworten auf Theologengestammel*, compiled by Erich Ludendorff in the year 1936, Ludendorff again replied to the countermoves. The booklet was published with a bright orange waistband over an illustration by Lenie Richter, Von Kemnitz's sister, with the text: *Die christlichen Angriffe auf die Schrift 'Das grossen Entsetzen-die Bibel nicht Gottes Wort' sind hier zurückgewiesen!* This less than one hundred-page document - a pamphlet - demonstrated once again the widening gap between the 'world revolutionary' Ludendorff and church authority. Walter Loehde, one of Ludendorff's comrades-in-arms who would regularly write for the Ludendorffs, wrote this volume together with the general.

Interestingly, it is through this writing that we know what Erich Ludendorff thought of Haeckel. Ludendorff's opinion was very positive; the 'successful scholar', he believed, 'had opened the eyes of the astonished people' and given them a 'natural story of creation'. Ludendorff brushed aside the weaknesses of monism. Haeckel had not been able to free himself from materialism, but, he mildly stated, it would be too easy to hold the rest of his ideas hostage by this mistake. In Ludendorff's opinion, Haeckel's ideas had made an important contribution to confronting certain absurdities in the Church's dogmas. That Haeckel had been successful and that his message had reached a large audience, was obvious to Ludendorff. The circulation of his work alone - 400,000 copies in 1936 and translations in 25 countries - spoke volumes.[1224]

The Ludendorffs' religious views brought with them an interest in early and pre-Christian history. They saw the origin of the conflict between 'deutscher Gottglauben' and the Yaweh religion as far in the past. Carolus Magnus, Charlemagne, played a central role in this. In the series *Schriftenreihe, laufender Schriftenbezug 12, Heft 2,* a book by Heinrich Weichelt at Ludendorff Verlag is dedicated to this matter. In '*4500', Eine geschichtswissenschaftliche Untersuchung über die Ereignisse zu Verden an der Aller im Jahre 782*, Charlemagne's Christianisation of the Saxons is the focus. The battle against Widukind, the Saxon rebel leader, lasted for years and was bloody. Near the town of Verden on the River Aller, 4,500 Saxons were finally beheaded on Charlemagne's orders. For Erich and Mathilde Ludendorff, this was 'proof' of Christian aggression and they saw the Saxons in this case as the 'real Germans'. Therefore, Charlemagne should not be called 'the Great' but the 'Sachsenschlachter'.

This historical figure would remain part of the debate. The Dutch National Socialist-inspired historian F.J. Los wrote the book *Karel de Frank-De Groote?*, of which the title already made clear where the author stood. He believed that Charlemagne had 'strange features' in his face, and that the massacres he ordered were an 'Assyrian method' and 'characteristic of the all-embracing and race-destroying character of Asiatic despots'. The views of Ludendorff-Verlag and Los later came under pressure as the National Socialists sought to frame Charlemagne's success as 'Germanic/Aryan'.[1225]

Ludendorff-Verlag denounced even more 'Assyrian practices'. In *Rom mordet, mordet Seelen, Menschen, Völker,* A.W. Rose dwelt on the history of the 'Allemannen', who, according to the author, were regarded as 'cattle' by Christianity.[1226] Kurt H. Holscher wrote the book *Der Todeskampf der Stedinger* in memory of the 700th commemoration of the death of 5000 free farmers in Stedinger on 27 May 1234. Here, too, it was the long arm of Rome that was held responsible for the death of 'free Germans'. The church at Sutherbroke, built in 1299, was said to have been placed right on the mass grave of the 'German' peasants. The brochure ended with the words in dialect: 'Lewer dod as Slav!' Professor Winter also published the brochure *De Stedinge*, about 'Rome's rape of the freedom struggle'.

In *Geplanter Ketzermord im Jahre 1866 aus neuer Jesuitenspiegel*, by Karl Conrad Ludwig Maurer, a Protestant clergyman, the 'blood trail' that Ludendorff and Von Kemnitz thought they saw was extended to the nineteenth century. The war in 1866 against the Catholic Habsburg Empire was to be used by the ultra-montane side as an occasion to massacre Protestants. However, things turned out differently: at Königgratz, the Austro-Hungarian troops were crushed by the Prussians. Thus, in Ludendorff's eyes, they escaped. 'Il mondo casa' - 'The world is falling', Cardinal Antonelli, the Pope's personal secretary, is said to have exclaimed when the news of the Austro-Hungarian defeat at Königgratz reached the Vatican.[1227] 'Only the revolution can help us', the papal nuncio in Stuttgart thought, looking back on the conflict.[1228] Ludendorff saw the November Days of 1918 as a consequence.

The pope was constantly being beaten by the 'House of Ludendorff', both Pius X and his predecessor Benedict XV. According to Ludendorff, the pope had been a staunch enemy of Germany during the war. Rome, from the point of view of 'Catholic action', waged a permanent battle, culminating in the 'entry' of the US into the war. According to Ludendorff, President Wilson, a Freemason, had ended up in the war through pressure from Rome, Jesuits, Jews, Freemasons and big business (billionaire Morgan).[1229] They were also eager to point out scandals from the past, dubious money speculations by Pope and Jesuits at the Morgan bank, but also more piquant matters, like sex scandals. Hans Hagen-Konigshorst, writing for Ludendorff's magazine *Am heiligen Quell deutscher kraft*, reported about it in volume 9 of August 1937. The case was leaked at the time by a flood of what we nowadays would call 'hatemail', addressed to 'Mon vieux cochon' (my old boar). This referred to homosexual excesses in the part of the Vatican where, in the past, the controversial Borgia had raged. [1230]

The suppression of women by the church was another (historical) concern of the Ludendorffs versus Rome. In *Die Frau, Die Sklavin der Priester* by Ilse Wentzel from 1939, and *Christliche Grausamkeit an Deutschen Frauen*, consisting of two articles by Mathilde von Kemnitz and W. v.d. Cammer from 1934, the perception of women from the 'Deutscher Gotterkenntnis' is contrasted with the views from Rome. According to the authors, women played a secondary role in church morals, but in the Nordic tradition, they were the guardians of 'Seele, Sitte und Sein'. The Ludendorffs also denounced the persecution of witches by the church authorities. Mathilde von Kemnitz Ludendorff thought that the way the church used hell in its dogmas would lead to trauma and neurosis. Furthermore, the House of Ludendorff regretted that some Germans, such as the 'solitary poet and thinker Friedrich Nietzsche', had an eye for the Church's damaging vision, but that the latter 'had understood nothing' of the profound religious thinking of the Germanic people and of the role of women, 'das Weib', about which Nietzsche was disparaging.[1231]

A not insignificant part of the publicity activities of Ludendorff and his second wife as well as of his publishing activities was directed against the ultramontane and the 'Katholische Aktion'. In his Bavarian years, we already saw the struggle against Bavarian nationalism, represented by the church, separatist movements, and Crown Prince Rupprecht and the Wittelbach dynasty. Protestantism, which was the Prussian Ludendorff's 'house religion', was viewed more leniently, although this branch of Christianity was not yet a 'deutscher Gottglaube' either. In the book *Ein Priester ruf: 'Los von Rom und Christo'*,[1232] written by the Catholic renegade Franz Griese, who had emigrated to Argentina, the tradition and arguments of the Church are once again critically examined. The title, which clearly refers to the anti-Pope *Los-von-Rom policy*, already pursued under Bismarck, further indicates the tradition that was to be highlighted here.

In another work by Ludendorff's publishing house, *Katholische Aktion im Angriff auf Deutschland*, written by Dr Ludwig F. Gengler, a statement by Freiherr von Buss is quoted from 1851: 'With a network of Catholic associations, the old Protestant community in Prussia is surrounded from the east and the west and strengthened by innumerable monasteries, so that Protestantism will be suppressed'.[1233] As in all Schlieffen thinking, a Darwinian all-or-nothing thinking had grown in political thought. In his pamphlet, which appeared in 1937, the author warned against the so-called 'Catholic Action'. This was the slogan under which Rome would pursue its monopoly over the world. The 'actio catholica' was a 'Dauermobilisierung' that concealed the politics of Pope Benedict XV. Of course, the hatred of the Deutschtum was enormous in this endeavour. Here again, the First World War played an important role. Gengler tried to expose the true nature of the war by drawing attention to the secret ultramontane script surrounding this conflict. The Pope had let it slip to the 'Jewish author' Emil Ludwig - as Gengler called him - that it was 'Luther who had lost the war'.[1234] The Pope's critical statements after the sinking of the passenger ship *Lusitania* by the German submarine fleet were also heavily criticised.[1235] In a letter to Cardinal Amette in Paris, the Pope himself is said to have given his blessing to the Treaty of Versailles, which was humiliating for Germany.[1236]

For Gegler it was clear that the 'actio catholica' was in full swing and was recruiting 'vassal states', which initially included Ireland, Poland and Lithuania, but increasingly also France, Italy, Germany, the Netherlands and Switzerland. Some countries became the separate subject of books and brochures of Ludendorff's publishing company, such as: *Österreich, die Europaische Kolonie des Va-*

Erich Ludendorff

British cartoon of unknown hand about Ludendorff's influence on Hitler

tikans by Ritter Georg, *Nie wieder Habsburg!* by Kuntz Iring, and *Der Weg zur Jesuitendiktatur in Österreich 1918-1935* by B. Dietrich and H. Janow, *Rom, Polen und die Ukraine*.[1237] One of the most secret weapons of the Church - and the world government - was Esperanto: the new world language. Its only purpose was to promote common plans. The author pointed out that it was a Jew, Zamenhof, who had invented this language.[1238] Esperanto was hidden behind 'Welt-Caritas', but that was only a cover, according to Gengler. The hard core of the 'Katholische Aktion' could be considered a secret society, according to Gengler. Not for nothing, he thought, were members of this organisation forbidden to be members of the NSDAP. [1239]

In connection with Ludendorff's vision of a 'secret world government', Gengler also touched upon the relationship of the Roman Church with other interest groups, such as communism. For this, he relied on statements by the Vatican prelate Dr Viktor Bede, who believed that faith and communism had many similarities. Both pursued an 'improvement of the world', both were 'moral powers'.[1240] Moreover, in the periodical *Am heiligen Quell deutscher Kraft*, the fate between the House of Ludendorff and the Nazis with regard to religion was occasionally emphasised. In volume 6, 1934, a publication by Fritz Kaiser in the magazine *Hakenkreuzbanner* (Mannheim, 13 May 1934) received remarkable attention because Kaiser warned that confessional forces were trying to bring back the 'Kulturkampf' in Germany. Kaiser listed fourteen reasons why this was undesirable from the NSDAP's point of view, the first of which, 'Jeder Deutsche kann nach seiner Fassung selig werden', made it immediately clear what the author thought. As long as Rome exists, there will be 'Kulturkampf', *Am heilgen Quell Deutscher Kraft* judged. [1241]

The position of Stalin was not always very clear to the House of Ludendorff. In *Am heiligen Quell deutscher Kraft*, the contacts between the (Jewish) freemasonry and Stalin were emphasised, for instance in France, where Henri Barbusse, freemason and communist, was presented as a key figure.[1242] When Stalin carried out his purges in the second half of the 1930s, it was noted that Jews were also the victims, and that the 'Jewish world government' had called on Jews to leave the Soviet Union via Italian radio stations. How could this be reconciled with the Ludendorffs' idea that Russia was a 'Jewish stronghold' in 1917? For J. Strunk in *Am heiligen Quell Deutscher Kraft*, one could not conclude from this that überstaatliche powers were losing influence or ground here. The sacrifice of the Jesuit secret service leader (Tscheka) Yagoda was only cosmetic. Russia, according to Strunk, was more and more in the grip of the oriental priestly castes, harking back to Byzantine roots. Here, the work - *Der heilige Teufel* - by René Fülöp-Miller, about the Siberian miracle healer Rasputin was recalled, because he too would have warned against this oriental überstaatliche mysticism.[1243] Fülöp-Miller, by the way, was an author whose themes had more in common with the House of Ludendorff. In his intriguing study on the Jesuits, he mentions the closing of ranks between Freemasons and the Black Pope of the Jesuits during a meeting in Germany at Aachen in the summer of 1928. The reason for the meeting was a shared knowledge of sacred geometry.[1244]

In the vision of the Ludendorff couple, the 'world conquest plans' of Catholicism were part of a much larger 'internationalism' which ultimately concealed the hand of Judah. Other Völkische and ariosophische thinkers, such as E. Freiherr von Engelhardt, a protocol believer connected to the anti-Semitic 'Institut der Judenfrage', had already pointed this out when he emphasised that Theodor Herzl and Ascher Ginsberg (Achad Ha'am) were both Jews and Freemasons, members of Bnei Brith and Bnei Moische respectively.[1245] That historically there were also complicated relations between Freemasonry and Judaism was not a theme for House Ludendorff.[1246] Partly due to the insights of Mathilde von Kemnitz, Ludendorff's suspicions were transformed into a conclusive system. Ludendorff was so convinced of his rightness that he printed the super conspiracy in a diagram in his memoirs.[1247] As always, once Ludendorff had chosen, he was a man without doubt. At the top of the überstaatliche powers stood the so-called (secret) world government, at the bottom the 'voting public'. In this model, the political parties and social organisations, such as trade unions and religious communities, were led by inaccessible and unfathomable secret organisations, which reported directly to the world government. These organisations included Jewish secret organisations, internationalist workers' organisations, freemasons, the Protestant Church, secret Jesuit orders, and the Catholic Church.[1248]

This again fitted into the atmosphere of *The Protocols of the Wise Men of Zion* and into the views of contemporaries. Ludendorff's fear of universalism, a world order, as outlined above, was equivalent to the criticism that Chamberlain and Rosenberg had of it.[1249] In their view, universalism meant the destruction of individuality, and thus of the blood-bound 'Gotterkenntnis'. Internationalism was an aspiration that united what Ludendorff saw as destructive forces, for in this way national identity could be snapped up and, to take Christianity as an example, the 'Holy Spirit' rather than the 'Holy Blood' could be given a place as a binding factor in society.

In Ludendorff's view, the various power centres of the secret world government sometimes merged. An example was the cooperation between the Vatican and the Kremlin. This was a continuation of the 'katholische Aktion', the political work from the power interests of the Vatican. In Russia, they had worked for a long time - according to J. Strunk, author of *Vatican and Kremlin*, which appeared in 1934[1250] - to eliminate the schism between church and state. In 1581, the Jesuit Antonio Possevino had crossed the border at Dubrowna with a secret mission. The goal was the 'Jesuitisation of Russia'. According to Strunk, heavy means were used, and when Ivan IV, in 1584, was not prepared to cooperate, he was murdered by the Jesuits. It was comparable to the 'attack on Pope Clement XIV', who, in 1773, had banned the Jesuit order and paid for it with his life, as claimed by Strunk.[1251] The commonality of the überstaatliche powers was to be found in two things. In the first place, both the internationalist 'katholische Aktion' and the Jesuits operating within it, and the internationalist communist revolutionaries, were interested in breaking through the national element. Secondly, as put forth by Strunk, both organisations were Jewish Internationals.[1252] W. von der Cammer, who published in *Am heiligen Quell Deutscher Kraft*, added that it had been the Jewish lodge 'Bnai Brit' that pointed out that the three most important manifestos in world history - the Mosaic Law, the Sermon on the Mount and Marx's Communist Manifesto - were 'Jewish'. Believers and communists invoked Clement of Alexandria who believed that 'from the point of view of nature, private property was an injustice'. Ownership was seen as theft. This view, according to Von der Cammer, served the pursuit of 'Jewish world domination'.[1253]

Here, we see an example of what regularly occurred in Ludendorff literature. The 'pillars' of the secret world government regularly intermingled, and like a kind of staccato, the accusations against Jews, Jesuits, Freemasons constantly resounded, the first category often appearing as the ultimate 'Drahtzieher'. In one of his articles, Erich Ludendorff stated that whether it was Fascism, Bolshevism, Rome, Moscow, Gross-Orient or France, they all wanted the destruction of nations.[1254]

The conspiracy theory of the Ludendorffs is a variant of other models by contemporaries such as List, Von Liebenfels, Dinter, Heackel, Rosenberg and others.

It is interesting to see what W. Marr, who was also a reader at the time, wrote about this, as early as 1879 in *Der Sieg des Judenthums über das Germanenthum, vom nicht confessionellen Standpunkt betrachtet*. According to Marr, whose book was reprinted many times, history should be seen as a battle between conquerors and subjects. Normally, the conquerors forced their ideas on the conquered or assimilated with them. The latter happened, for example, in the Tatar campaigns against China, or the Lombards in Italy. With the Jews in Europe, things were very different. They did not come as conquerors but as internees. Thanks to the Romans, the Jews arrived in Europe and, thanks to the ghettos, they retained their individuality. As Marr stated, this led to a 'Kulturkampf' that lasted for 1800 years and was finally won by the Jews. Germany, Marr argued, had become 'the new Palestine',[1255] and, he believed, 'the Jews would elevate Germany to world power'.[1256] The vehicle that had brought the Jews to their powerful positions had been social democracy, according to Marr, one of the 'pillars' in Ludendorff's 'exposure' of the world conspiracy.[1257] Marr's last words were: 'Finis Germaniae',[1258] about which, incidentally, he did not act childishly. In his organicist world view - in which states were seen as living beings that rose and fell - this was a 'natural fact', a 'natural selection', in which 'Germanism' in Germany, just like the Lombards once did in Italy, lost out.[1259] Marr's ideas were in line with the then influential thoughts of the Swedish geopolitician Rudolf Kjellén, author of, among others, *Der Staat als Lebensform*.[1260]

Others fought the 'world government' that presented itself, such as the Nationalrat Dr. Franz Wichtl, author of the book *Weltfreimaurerei, Weltrevolution, Weltrepublik, Eine Untersuchung über Ursprung und Endziele des Weltkrieges*, who died in 1921 and was often quoted by Ludendorff.[1261] This book, which was printed and sold in huge numbers, was published in 1923 by J. F. Lehmanns Verlag in Munich, a well-known sympathiser of the brown movement which would play a not unimportant role in the Hitler-Ludendorff putsch of 1923. Wichtl was, as Ernst Berg wrote in his preface, an important collector of 'voices of his time', who pointed out the danger of Freemasonry. B. Segel, an important advocate against *Die Protokolle*, mentioned Wichtl by name as one of the most important exponents of work influenced by *Die Protokolle*.[1262] At that time, the introduction stated, there were already 40,000 critical works on the role of Freemasonry, but it was still a shadowy piece of history. Almost simultaneously with Wichtl's book, the works of Karl Heises, *Entente Freimaurerei und Weltkrieg*, Alfred Rosenberg's *Das Verbrechen der Freimaurerei* and Dr. Josef Hofer's *Freimaurerei, Neuheidentum und Umsturtz*, all emphasising the Jewish role in Freemasonry, were published. Ludendorff's conspiracy scheme was in line with this. Within the fund of House Ludendorff, this was emphasized by Hermann Rehwaldt, in *Die Kriegshetzer von Heute*.[1263] Freemasonry was considered to be partly 'the uncircumcised Jews' and, like the Jesuits, a secret organisation in the service of the world government.

Wichtl was of special interest to Ludendorff because he too saw the First World War and the collapse of the German Empire as a fault line in history. Initially, according to Wichtl, Freemasonry had not been entirely anti-German (Prussian). Some German princes and emperors had also been members of Freemasonry. According to Wichtl, at a certain moment in the 'Grosslogen', there was a power struggle in Germany, in which the dividing line was pro-Jewish (western) or pro-Prussian. Wichtl believed that the majority of Freemasons at that time were still Prussian patriots, but by means of 'cunning' the four Western-oriented lodges, which were also situated in West Germany and were aimed at the French lodge 'Grand Orient', succeeded in silencing the Prussian lodges (three of them) by voting per lodge instead of per head. The four (in fact smaller) 'Western' lodges won the argument. The 'Jewishisation' of German society (and of Europe) that had been going on since the French Revolution in 1798 (its leaders were Jewish according to Wichtl - just as the Russian Revolution was Jewish in Völkisch eyes) was the result.

In his memoirs, Ludendorff constantly makes a clear distinction between his 'knowing' period and his 'not knowing' period, with phrases such as 'at that time I had no insight', and so on. Yet, it was through publishing that he eventually fought the 'überstaatliche Powers' and their 'secret organisations'.

Ludendorff's personal and direct attack on freemasonry, *Vernichtung der Freimaurerei durch Enthüllung ihrer Geheimnisse*, which appeared in 1927 and nine years later already had a circulation of more than 170,000 copies, showed that Ludendorff had mastered the conspiracy theories. The title referred to his other 'revealing' work on the Jesuits. Ludendorff's struggle was the start of yet another endless debate and fight. Graf Reventlow, not very afraid of political incorrectness himself, believed that Ludendorff had 'stung himself into a hornets' nest'.[1264] Ludendorff claimed that Freemasonry was not a secret, but a secret. It was the means to the establishment of a secret esoteric Jewish empire. In this sense, he dismissed the various lodges, as well as related organisations such as the Odd-Fellows, as an organisation, or at least a movement with a purpose.

Furthermore, Ludendorff immediately drew parallels between Freemasonry and World War I. In two speeches, held in 1926 for the 'Deutschvölkischen Offiziersbund' in Munich, which were published in the *Völkischen Herolds* and later collected in the booklet *Die Revolution von Oben*, published by Karl Rohm Verlag in Lorch, Württemberg (with bold headline: Aufsehen erregende Enthüllungen), the Versailles Peace was presented as a conspiracy between German democrats and the American president Wilson.[1265] The Rosicrucians were also given a run for their money. This is where German Nording (probably a pseudonym, given the very 'Nordic' name) took up the gauntlet in the book *Geheimnisse vom Rosenkreuz*, published by Ludendorffs Verlag in 1938, thus after Ludendorff's death.[1266] 'There is only one Freemasonry', Ludendorff thought in spite of the different organisations.[1267] This freemasonry, and this is where the 'deutsche Gotterkentniss' came into play, was completely determined by 'Jewish thinking' and was 'unworthy' of the German people.[1268] The Jewish influence, Ludendorff thought, in line with Wichtl, was so strong in Freemasonry in Germany that it had to be considered as lost for Germany.[1269]

Besides exposing such structures, and pointing out the influence of the 80,000 German freemasons (in comparison: according to Ludendorff, there were three million freemasons in the US at that time), Ludendorff also tried to expose the secret rituals of the freemasons. In lawsuits that followed Ludendorff's publications, he seems to have succeeded reasonably well. In the introduction of the 1936 edition (circulation 169-173,000) of *Vernichtung der Freimaurerei*, several German freemasons are quoted as saying this under oath.[1270] Ludendorff's 'revelations' included his remarks on Jewish mysticism, the Kabbalah, which he called a 'sinister superstition'.[1271] He elaborated on the meaning of the Star of David, the Seal of Solomon, the meaning of geometry and numbers and all other mystical matters. Ludendorff believed in the existence of so-called Jaweh years, which had special meaning for the Jews, and that 1914, the year the First World War broke out, had been such a year. A new 'dangerous' year for the non-Jews would be 1941, Ludendorff predicted. Remarkably, it was not 'world Jewry' that dealt Germany its death blow in 1941, but Hitler himself when he voluntarily opened a second front with Operation 'Barbarossa' (the attack on the Soviet Union) with all the consequences that this entailed. 1923, the year of the Feldherrnhalle-Putsch was a Jaweh-year as well, according to Ludendorff. [1272]

The House of Ludendorff argued that freemasonry also played a role in a number of historical 'murders', at least it was claimed here that they were freemason-related murder cases, namely in the books *Der ungesuehnte Frevel an Luther, Lessing. Mozart und Schiller* and the book *Mozarts Leben und gewaltsamer Tod*. The basic idea behind this was, of course, that the 'German genius' had to give way to the 'stab-in-the-back' of freemasonry, because it feared influence or the loss of secrets. This discussion continues to this day, particularly around Mozart. Was *Die Zauberflöte*, the most popular opera ever, actually the unravelling of a secret initiation, and the uncovering of alchemical symbols? In any case, the piece evoked strong reactions from the very beginning, also from Mozart's biographers, such as Otto Jahn. There was strong criticism, calling it a 'nonsensical or foolish' product, suggesting that Mozart apparently needed money. Mozart recounted the mysteries of Isis.[1273] Initially, Mozart had named the opera *Egyptian Secrets*, but later chose the name *Die Zauberflöte*. As revenge for the betrayal of the initiation, the main character was tormented by the Queen of the Night. According to Mathilde von Kemnitz, this also applied to Mozart himself, who had to pay for his frankness with his death. Among other things, a picture of Mozart's coffin with only a little dog behind it, Masonic symbolism for traitors, was given as evidence. In this way, House Ludendorff played on already old myths and legends.[1274] Yet, real riddles surrounding Mozart's death remain. Recent research into the supposed skull and bones of Mozart, who died in 1791 at the age of 35, has revealed that the bones have different DNA material. 'The dead man has taken his secret to the grave,' pathologist Walther Parsons ruled.[1275] Ludendorff saw overlaps between Judaism and Freemasonry not only on the Christian and/or communist side, but also on the capitalist side. In the booklet *Der Kampf zwischen Juda und Japan, Japan als Vorkämpfer freier Volkswirtschaft*,[1276] and the undated pamphlet *Der Raubzug gegen Japan! Wann endlich wehren sich die Völker?*[1277] by corvette captain off-duty Alfred Stoss[1278] Gottfried Feders' 'völkische' economic anti-western views resounded.

Buddhism, as an 'occult doctrine', and its priestly caste on 'the roof of the world', referring to Blavatsky's followers and Theosophy, were also criticised. Ludendorff stated that Buddhism was the oldest religion in the world, and a great source of inspiration for Christianity: Christ as Krishna, as it were. Ludendorff drew a comparison with Freemasonry, which had been influenced by Ancient Egypt.[1279]

In *Am heiligen Quell Deutscher Kraft*, for example, they also took up the battle axe with Rudolf Steiner's Anthroposophy. At the beginning of the 1990s, the anthroposophical *Flensburgerhefte* believed that the Ludendorffs were among the fiercest opponents of anthroposophy.[1280] According to Robert Schneider, a lawyer writing for the Ludendorff House, Steiner had a negative influence on Moltke. Under Steiner's influence, the German military commander had lost his 'soul force'. Moreover, Steiner is supposed to have maintained contacts with spies on the general staff, mentioning Oberstleutnant Joachim. Steiner's aim would be a lodge-like influence in Germany, through the so-called Memphis system and the Misriam system, consisting of 90 and 95 degrees.[1281]

Ludendorff was also inclined to attribute the failures of the early days of the war to occult influences on Moltke. In his brochure *Das Marne Drama,* he listed the alleged influences. It was especially Moltke's wife who was the key to the alleged 'occult' contacts. Moltke was under the influence of his wife, who, as a nurse, also moved to Koblenz and Luxembourg, where the German general staff was located. This made her an influence on Moltke during the decisive days. Besides the above-mentioned Rudolf Steiner - who followed Moltke to Koblenz - (others claim that Steiner was not in Koblenz but in Ehrenbreitstein, however, according to Ludendorff, this did not matter for the truth), the medium Lisbeth Seidler also played a role. She had already predicted war to the Moltkes in Potsdam. She also travelled 'disguised' as a nurse with Mrs Moltke. In Jewish circles, Ludendorff claimed, this case was known as the 'Heeressybille' and Seidler was praised for her silence. Indeed, in certain theosophical circles, the influence of Moltke was invoked, which only made Ludendorff more suspicious. For example, the Jewish philosopher Fritz Mauthner claimed in his book *Der Atheismus und seine Geschichte im Abendlande* that Moltke was a friend and representative of the Theosophists. [1282]

Besides the Moltke case, the case of Oberleutnant Hentsch also played a role. At the time, it was rumoured that Hentsch, on his own authority, would have ordered the retreat of the German units at the river Marne. This concerned the German 1st and 2nd army. Ludendorff defended Hentsch and stated that he had acted on Moltke's orders and only carried out his orders. In *Das Marne Drama*, Ludendorff returned to this point, which, knowing Ludendorff's character, was already a remarkable step. Nevertheless, Ludendorff stated that 'the Hentsch case' was not as clear-cut as the Moltke case. The main evidence against Hentsch was rather thin. His father was said to have been a freemason and a military man. Frits Hentsch was an overseer of German fortifications and for a time during his career, he was responsible for the technical running of the fortresses near Berlin. Ludendorff suspected, on the basis of these scarce data, that Hentsch's Masonic sympathies had played a role in the historic days around 8 and 9 September 1914. [1283]

As we can see from the Steiner, Seidler, and Hentsch case, the 'mindset' was very important. Since Ludendorff considered Freemasonry and Theosophy/Anthropophy to be very important and hostile, every possible link was immediately seen as evidence. His own memoirs contain another interesting example. One day on the Eastern Front there was almost a train accident. Due to a switch malfunction, a train bore into a stationary carriage, where shortly before, the Von Hindenburg-Ludendorff command train had been parked. Of course, for Ludendorff this was not a point failure or human error, but an attack. In the course of time, the truth within the House of Ludendorff moulded itself. The development of this debate was entirely along these lines after 1933, when the Nazis seized power. In January 1933, Lisbeth Seidler died and she and her relationship to Moltke were suddenly in the spotlight again. The House of Ludendorff immediately took advantage of this by writing about this case in, among others, *Ludendorff's Volkswarte*. Still, after Hitler's seizure of power, a different 'publicistic' wind blew through Germany and the brown censors stopped several Ludendorff publications. The House of Ludendorff immediately pointed to occult forces within German politics as the cause for silencing the truth behind the Marne drama. That Hitler simply preferred to leave the education of the people to men like Goebbels, apparently did not occur to House Ludendorff. [1284]

Although initially, both in political practice and in the publications of House Ludendorff, there was a rapprochement with Hitler and the NSDAP, Ludendorff's conspiracy theory eventually spread to the offices of the brown movement. Here, too, it was mainly the question of faith that caused the split. After the failed putsch of 1923 and the later activities of the 'Tannenbergbund', the relationship between the Nazis and House Ludendorff had already deteriorated. For a man like Hitler, who was in part also a Realpolitiker, the anticlerical thinking of House Ludendorff constituted an electoral problem. Ludendorff translated this directly into a merger between the ultramontane and the Hitler movement.

In 1931, Ludendorffs Volkswarteverlag published the booklet *Nationalsozilismus und katholische Kirche, Meine Schriftwechsel mit der Gauleitung Rheinland und der Reichsparteileitung der NSDAP sowie mit der Kanzlei Adolf Hitlers*. The author was the former 'Kreisleiter' Heinsberg (Rheinland) of the NSDAP Dr. Armin Roth. Roth wrote his battle text out of concern and anger about the rapprochement between Rome and the NSDAP. According to Roth, it had become clear that Hitler was 'in direct dependence' on the church, and Rome, in line with Ludendorff, was anti-German. Roth presented a bird's eye view of the anti-German measures, for example, Pope Benedict XV is said to have informed French Cardinal Amette in October 1919 that he supported the Versailles Treaty, which was difficult for Germany. In 1922, the German Cardinal in Rome, Faulhaber, with whom many Völkischen, including Ludendorff, were constantly at odds, had described the Germans as 'arrogant' and that they now hoped for 'God's mercy' after the failed war. The sociologist Professor Franz Back had the papal newspaper *Osservatore Romano* note that 'nationalism was a curse', and the Catholic priest Moenius believed that it was Catholicism that could 'break the back' of nationalism. At the canonisation of Peter Canisius in May 1925 in Rome, Martin Luther was branded an anti-Semite and Munich clergyman Dr Ehard Schlund openly opposed the 'Neuheidentum'. [1285]

The attack on Luther was painful, because several Ludendorff-adepts saw the general as following in Luther's footsteps, taking his opposition to Rome, of course, as the guiding principle. In a book written by Hermann Andress and published by the Verlag Deutsche Revolution in Düsseldorf, Germany was confronted with the choice: Priesterherrschaft oder Deutscher Gottglaube. The main title of the work was *Luther, Friedrich der Grosse, Ludendorff*, with an increasing number of exclamation marks each time. 'Germany', Andress mused immediately at the front of his book, 'why do you forget the eternal sources of your strength', and he expressed his fear of the 'Jewish demoedsleer'.[1286] In an article called *Das Schreckgespenst von Halle*, Mathilde Ludendorff von Kemnitz said that a wax figure of Luther in a church in Halle had been deformed on purpose in order to alienate Luther from his supporters. Luther was not depicted wearing the famous beret, but was bare-headed and bald. His head had also been changed into an egg shape. Moreover, he stood in a dark corner and even the *Bible* in his hands was closed. In Cold War terms, one could speak of a Fidel Castro without a beard and cigar. In short, Luther was no longer Luther. Protest calls even appeared in periodicals of the House of Ludendorff.[1287]

Over the years, Ludendorff placed Hitler on the same level as the 'Erfüllungspolitiker'. 'The NSDAP', he said in 1931, was 'the same as the dictatorship Bruning'. Ludendorff referred to a text by Hitler in the *Illustrierten Beobachter*, in which Hitler indeed advocated the choice of Germany for national-socialism (as an alternative to the threat of communism), but at the same time ordered Germany to fulfil its 'kaufmaennischen Verpflichtungen'. Ludendorff particularly fell over this last point. In his eyes, the 'Tributzahlungen' were treason. The fact that Hitler, on his way to power, had to take into account national and especially also foreign powers and obligations, was a form of 'Realpolitik' which Ludendorff apparently did not understand.[1288]

The deepest break with Hitler came when the 'Reichskonkordat' came into being on 20 July 1933. It was, among others, the same Dr. Armin Roth who opposed this in a publication of the House of Ludendorff. In *Das Reichskonkordat vom 20.Juli 1933*, he saw a deep knee-jerk reaction of the Hitler regime towards Rome. A concordat, he believed, was a testimony to 'inner conviction' and was linked to the 'dogmas of the Church'. He pointed to previous research on 'concordats' in history, and to the statement by the Jesuit professor Deluca who believed that the concordat was there to 'subject heretics to the Pope'. Germany had become such a 'heretic'.[1289] The concordat was thus seen by the House of Ludendorff as the decisive influence that ultramontane Rome would have on the Brown movement and Hitler.

This was in stark contrast to how the Concordat was generally received. The historian Guenter Lewy believes that the Concordat was seen as a great diplomatic victory for Hitler, not for Rome.[1290] It is true that Hitler's negotiator, Von Papen, gave the Church some guarantees - besides financial ones, especially the matters concerning education were of great importance - but Hitler had lost his 'internal enemy'. The *Völkischer Beobachter* thought that with this step, the Vatican had recognised National Socialism. 'The provocative agitation by the church against National Socialism is now condemned by the church itself'.[1291] The House of Ludendorff had difficulty in recognising the success of Hitler's policy. It followed the coming to power of the Nazis with 'the greatest anxiety', as he described it in his memoirs.[1292] Moreover, he feared publicity restrictions, which indeed came. Ludendorff's publicity zeal turned not only against the NSDAP but also against other Völkisch 'allies', whom he now accused of treason. He considered the 'Alldeutsche Verband' and 'Stahlhelm' to be organisations which were ruled by freemasons and Jews. Stahlhelm's chairman Franz Seldte got a beating. When he laid a wreath at an Italian war memorial in 1931, Ludendorff immediately suspected him of having a secret catholic agenda. Seldte's friendship with Mussolini, to which Ludendorff also referred to Hitler, was also part of Ludendorff's vendetta with the 'Catholic Action'. Ludendorff saw Mussolini as a profiteer of two internationals: Catholicism and socialism/communism.

Seldte also openly turned against Ludendorff, whom he accused of being 'a sick spirit'. Seldte thought that one should keep Ludendorff's ideas about freemasons, Jews and 'überstaatliche powers' far away from 'Stahlhelm'. [1293]

Over the course of years, hundreds of publications would appear, mostly in brochure/pamphlet form. From the mid-thirties, these were partly streamlined in the series, mentioned before: *Die Erste Schriftenreihe*, between October 1934 and March 1935, *Die zweite Schriftenreihe*, between April 1935 and September 1935, with authors such as Ludwig Engel, Kunz Iring, Kurt Fügner, Walther Löhde, Hermann Rehwaldt, Arnim Roth, W. Wendt, Generalleutnant Ritter von Wenninger and Mathilde Ludendorff, followed by the series *laufender Schriftenbezug*. [1294]

Besides the many book and brochure publications, there were also periodicals of the 'House of Ludendorff'. Initially, these were grouped around a veteran's organisation, the 'Tannenberg-Bund', named after the famous battle. The 'Plichtorgan', as the historian Borst called the periodical, was the newspaper *Ludendorffs Volkswarte*. The editorial office of *Ludendorffs Volkswarte* was located in Karlstrasse 10/II in Munich. The newspaper was published weekly on Sunday, and could be bought for 25 pfennig. In it, well-known Ludendorff focal points reappeared with clock-like efficiency. Regular features between 1929 and 1932 were: 'Das schaffende Volk', 'Das Wehrhafte Volk', 'Die Sippe', and 'Die Rast'.[1295] It was the formula of blood, faith, law, culture and economy. As a periodical, linked to the *Volkswarte,* there was also *Am Heiligen Quell deutscher Kraft*, which the Ludendorffs themselves characterised as a 'Monatschrift (later bi-weekly) des Deutschvolks'.[1296] The *Quell* had a very broad orientation, and covered many themes, such as bible study, biology, education, history, art, literature, philosophy, folklore and other subjects.

Volkswarte was primarily a political battle organ. Borst calculated that some 36.5% of the articles in the *Volkswarte* were about politics. To this were added 19.3% of pieces that concentrated on the 'überstaatliche' powers.[1297] *Ludendorff's Volkswarte* started with a circulation of 26.000 copies, initially dropped to 21.000 (still in its foundation year of 1929) but in 1932, according to Ludendorff's own statement, it reached a circulation of 61.000[1298] copies, which rose to 90.000 when it was banned by the Nazis in 1933.[1299] In 1932, the *Quell* started as an independent magazine, and in addition to this, the *Tannenberg-Jahrweiser* appeared from 1931 onwards. It is difficult to follow the trail of these publications, which have almost disappeared from the face of the earth. In any case, it is clear that the *Tannenberger-Jahrweiser* changed its name several times, although Lenie Richter's illustration of a protective knight watching over his wife and child remained. At least from the end of the 1930s, the *Tannenberg-Jahrweiser* was called *Tannenberg-Jahrbuch* and from 1940 *Deutsche Rast*. Louise Raab was the editor from 1935 onwards, then Mathilde Ludendorff von Kemnitz' son Hanno von Kemnitz. In these yearbooks, old heroic deeds, such as the Stedinger battles, were retold, with the emphasis on their resistance to Rome.[1300]

In addition to these yearbooks, Ludendorff's publishing house also issued the so-called *Deutsche Kampfkalender*, in which national celebrities such as Bismarck, Scharnhorst, Ruckert and Frederick the Great were placed next to Erich and Mathilde Ludendorff. This self-praise appeared in the Tannenberg annals as well. Hans Hugo Brinkmann's *Bildnis Ludendorffs* is an example. In his poem, commissioned by Schiller - 'Von den Parteien Gunst und Hass verwirrt, schwankt sein Charakterbild in der Geschichte' - Ludendorff's struggle against 'Juda und Rom' is dramatised.[1301] Moreover, there was an eye for historically important dates, such as the murder of the tsarist family by the communists. Additionally, there were illustrations at the end of the 1930s that referred to National Socialism, with photographs of the 'Hitlerjugend' being preferred.[1302] The publisher also offered photo and song books. Needless to say that apart from a picture of Luther - who was apparently above suspicion in the religious field - the pictures were all about Ludendorff (and his wife), with titles such as: *General Ludendorff spricht*, *General Ludendorff in Uniform* etc. The songs were national in character and composed by Fritz Hugo Hoffmann.[1303]

In addition to all these publications and periodicals, there was an ongoing debate about the person of the general himself over the years as well. In a series of books, booklets and pamphlets, both friend and foe took a stand. The most famous debate was with Hans Delbruck, who criticised Ludendorff in the *Prussian annals* and, together with Tirpitz, was considered the gravedigger of Wilhelminian Germany. The discussion went back to 1919 when Ludendorff's memoirs appeared, which Delbruck described as 'Ludendorffs Selbstporträt'. This was not the only 'Federkrieg' which was waged. Wolfgang Förster wrote *Hans Delbruck ein porträtmaler?* which was published by Mittler & Sohn. Other titles were *Die Wahrheit über Ludendorffs Kampf* (Hans Kurth), *Ludendorffs Kampf für Dich* (Hans Schneider), *Ludendorffs gerader Weg* (Walther Loehde),*Ludendorff Lebt!* (Helmuth Blume) *General Ludendorff Sein Weg und Wille* (Guenther Weidauer), *Der völkische Ludendorff* (Adolf Viktor von Koerber), *Ludendorff eine Erledigung!* (Dr.Martin Lezius), *das ist Ludendorff* (Wilhelm Crone), *Der Feldherr Ludendorff im Unglück* (Wolfgang Foerster), *Der Feldherr Ludendorff* (Oberstlt. a.D.. Theobald von Schaefer), *Ludendorff, der ewige Recke* by Alfred Stoss and of course the two early Ludendorff biographies by K.Tschuppik, *Ludendorff, die Tragödie des Fachmanns* and Wilhelm Breuckers *Die Tragik Ludendorffs*. The titles often already indicated whether one took a stand for or against the House of Ludendorff.

In spite of the enormous publicity activities of the Ludendorff House, the combination of vanity and sectarianism caused an ever-increasing schism within the Ludendorff ranks.[1304] The actual following became smaller and smaller and with it, the interest in the work and the writing Ludendorffs decreased. The political developments did the rest. After the failure of the Feldherrnhalle-Putsch, Ludendorff's influence continued to decline rapidly. The increasing influence of Dr. Mathilde von Kemnitz, who was regarded as sectarian, strengthened this, so that even fellow fighters from the very beginning, such as Wilhelm Breucker, eventually dropped out. Ludendorff and von Kemnitz had no choice, it was 'Der gerade Weg',[1305] that they had chosen, and criticism could only lead to schism. Or, as Von Kemnitz once put it when some of her listeners angrily walked out: 'At last we are among ourselves'.[1306-1308] After the offices of the publishing house fell victim to the Allied bomb carpet and Ludendorff was brought back into the collective memory of the German nation via a state funeral in 1937 by Hitler, who limited his role to that of a general in '14-'18, the echoes of the House of Ludendorff hardly penetrated further than the walls of their last bastion in the small town of Tutzing, crouched on the Starnberg lake.

Even the attempt to immortalise Ludendorff literarily did not succeed. The famous writer Arnold Zweig portrayed Erich Ludendorff as Generalquartiermeister Schieffenzahn in his novel *Der Streit um den Sergeanten Grischa*. The novel dealt with the Russian prisoners unjustly put to death within the Oberost area where Ludendorff ruled at the time. It was about the struggle of people to maintain their dignity and humanity under the pressure of the all-consuming war machine that Schieffenzahn symbolised.

Chapter 21

Ludwig Beck and Ludendorff's last chance at a return to the political arena

While Ludendorff fought his rearguard action against the world, Hitler strengthened his position.

Although Hitler's path to power was followed and commented on in the periodicals of House Ludendorff, real political influence was not involved. Moreover, Ludendorff's aversion to practical politics ran deep. The fact that between 1919 and 1932, twenty-six new governments took office, will also have contributed to this. Yet, in 1934, Ludendorff's chances were not over yet. The military apparatus, of all things, was to lend a final hand.

Still, Ludendorff's life consisted of more than politics alone. 'A greater harmony was not conceivable', Ludendorff wrote about his marriage to Mathilde. Indeed, life seemed to smile on Ludendorff again. Ludendorff and Mathilde went on their honeymoon, first to Tyrol and later to Mathilde's mother in Wiesbaden. Unfortunately, during the mountain hikes in Tyrol Ludendorff had become short of breath and suffered from dizziness. If he kept calm, he would feel better, but something was wrong. In Wiesbaden, he witnessed French soldiers marching through the streets. Although they behaved correctly, Ludendorff was concerned. After visiting Mrs Spiess, Mathilde's mother, whom Ludendorff characterised as a 'quiet German woman', they went back to Ludwigshöhe, where Mathilde's twin sons moved into the large house. [1309]

In the meantime, X-rays of Ludendorff's neck and throat had been taken and it was clear that the windpipe was becoming obstructed by a tumour on the thyroid gland. The doctor in charge, Professor Sauerbruch, was reluctant to operate on this man, who was no longer very popular, but still world-famous. Ludendorff himself, however, wanted to go under the knife immediately. In the end, a way out was found: Mathilde Ludendorff took responsibility for the operation which was planned for the end of 1926. The operation ended well, but the nerves in the neck had been numbed, and swallowing was extremely painful for Ludendorff. There was also a very dangerous complication in the form of a streptococcal infection. Ludendorff was in mortal danger for some time, but eventually recovered. 'The Jewish newspapers were already celebrating my death', Ludendorff wrote in his memoirs, and Mathilde was called in the evening by the *Vossische Zeitung* to ask whether it was true that the general was dying. [1310]

Ludendorff recovered, and he was able to leave the clinic after a fortnight. Some time of rest followed at the Ludwigshöhe in Munich. They spent the Christmas holidays there, during which Mathilde's daughter also visited. After that, the hatchet was taken up again as firmly as before. 'The battle is over', [1311] Ludendorff noted in his memoirs when the year 1927 dawned. Lectures and publications followed in quick succession.

Within the Tannenbergbund offices and the publishing house, Ludendorff followed his hobbyhorses with an iron line. It became an ever-deeper groove which he pursued with increasing consistency and loneliness. The battle that followed shifted from enemy image to enemy image, with the paper front playing an increasingly important role. Ludendorff was very excited when, in 1927, he received 'important' secret sources from a masonic sympathiser. Mathilde and a family member immediately started transcribing them, because the material could not stay at home for too long. At last, Ludendorff had 'the weapon' he wanted. He had been encouraged to uncover the riddle of Freemasonry, but had also been warned that this would be dangerous. Still, Ludendorff persevered, and the documents of 'brother' Hieber, the man who provided him with the material, could be revealed in Ludendorff's book *Vernichtung der Freimaurerei durch Enthüllung ihrer Geheimnisse*. The 'salomon seal' of silence was thus broken, he assumed. Sometimes, various conspiracy theories went hand in hand, entirely in accordance with Ludendorff's idea of a secret world government, which, with a sense of cabal, he also called the 'Judenkubus'. In order to give it some punch, *Ludendorffs Volkswarte* published the outline, including the 'cube' of the secret world government, on 24 August 1930 over the full width of the front page of the newspaper.[1312] Thus, the *Volkswarte* believed that Mussolini in practice prevented the distribution in Italy of *The Protocols of the Sages of Sion*, which had been translated by Dr. Giovanni Preziosi and published by the publishing house *Societa Editrice Mezzogiorno*. Mussolini would have let *The Protocols* 'slip through his fingers', and would have put the translator in 'a madhouse'. According to the *Volkswarte*, this showed how Mussolini 'conspired with Jews and Rome'.[1313]

Such articles with 'double denouement' were no exception in the *Volkswarte*. In the same issue, under the heading *Jude und Jesuit bei der Arbeit*, there was an article on Catholic scholars, Professor Schemann, author of *Die Rasse in der Geisteswissenschaft*, and theologian Wittig, who had become 'victims' of the alleged 'pact' described above and thus fell prey to the 'Knebelung System'. Due to their criticism of 'Juda' or 'Rom', they lost their jobs.[1314]

It was a busy and active life, but ultimately on the sidelines and sectarian. However, anyone who takes the trouble to look at Ludendorff's *Volkswarte*, published weekly on Sundays, will be surprised at how much was organised, especially around the 'Tannenbergbund'. In an issue from February 1930, for instance, there were some fifteen meetings in Hamburg that month alone. As always, everything was neatly divided according to district in the city, so that there were meetings of the Gruppe Hamburg Nord-West, at the Eppendorferweg, Gruppe Hamburg-Osten, at the Freiligrathstraat 13, Gruppe Hamburg-Beddel, at E. Rabe in the Beddel-Siè. Rabe at 39 Beddel-Sieldeich, Gruppe Hamburg-Nord-Ost, where a 'Judenfilm' was shown on 27 February in Hamburg Street, and a 'Freimaurerfilm' on 24 March in Schur Restaurant, Gruppe Hamburg Innenstadt met at 19 Stadthausbrücke and so on. They were 'camaraderie evenings', and sometimes lectures were organised.[1315] In the same period, for example, Friedrich Hasselbacher, a man who had made a name for himself with 'revelations' about Freemasonry in the First World War, travelled through the Gau Hannover-Ost; 18 February Dergenthin-Westpriegnitz, 19 February Lenzen, 20 February Wittenberge, 22 February Polz, 23 February Lanz, 24 February Dribow, 25 February Waddenweitz, 26 February Steine. One may therefore conclude that the plots were firmly drummed in.

Hasselbacher's work and lectures were an addition to the stab-in-the-back myth. *Ludendorffers* like Dr. Wilfried Meynig relied on his revelations.[1316] Even in Liège during the war, the city of Ludendorff's military success, Hasselbacher saw all kinds of influences of freemasonry, which were after all 'überstaatlich', and simply took up residence in the local lodge of the Belgian freemasonry. Of course, Hasselbacher suspected evil intentions behind the Loge *Zum eisernen Kreuz*.[1317] Hasselbach's 'revelations' about the field lodge in Kaunas, *Deutsche Wacht an der Memel*, must also have put Ludendorff to sleep. Hasselbach called Kaunas, where Ludendorff resided for a long time as 'viceroy', a 'masonic paradise', where 'Master of chair' Generaloberst dr. Alwin Baudler ruled.[1318] Following this, the *Volkswarte* published a large article by Hellmuth Pfeifer about the field lodges that 'conspired' with the Entente, and came to the conclusion that the war could not be won militarily and that only internal destabilisation would help. A typical product again of the stab-in-the-back myth.[1319]

Meanwhile, history did not stand still. Hitler was unstoppable and on his way to absolute power in Germany. In 1933, the Reichstag fire raged on 27 February. Hitler seized power through the Reichstagbrandverordnung. Between Hitler and the dictatorship stood three more 'institutions': the SA under Ernst Röhm, who had political ambitions, the 'icon' Paul von Hindenburg, and finally the army. In 1934, two of the three 'opponents' fell away. The SA was 'decapitated' in the Night of the Long Knives, 30 June 1934, during which Röhm and a whole series of other opponents of Hitler were liquidated. Paul von Hindenburg died on 2 August 1934. With this, another cornerstone of the old Wilhelmine era had fallen away. The army stood 'alone'. The murder of Kurt von Schleicher, former chancellor and high-ranking military officer, who was highly critical of Hitler,[1320] was a vague sign that the Nazis were also prepared to take action against 'das Militär'. With hindsight, we know that it would take until 1938 before the Blomberg-Fritsch affair would put the army out of action, and through generals such as Alfred Jodl and Wilhelm Keitel a new course would be set, obedient to Hitler. However, in the mid-thirties, that race was not yet over. In this transitional phase, a special opportunity presented itself for Erich Ludendorff.

The army was in a difficult position due to the impetuous advance of Hitler and the NSDAP. The Prussian tradition was threatened by the new state. The army had a two-pillar strategy in mind, in which the army could exist more or less next to the state - as the balancing artiste Von Seeckt understood it - but with the fall of Von Hindenburg and the internal opposition within the NSDAP (the SA), the NSDAP was more powerful than ever.

On Von Hindenburg's deathbed, a discussion had already begun within parts of the German officer corps about how to proceed. The central question was not only Hitler, but also the party, and some even wondered whether Hitler would be strong enough to be Chancellor and Reich President at the same time.[1321] In any case, the influence of the NSDAP on 'das Militär' was growing. This could be measured by the anti-Semitism that, more than before, reared its head in the ranks of the army. In army publications, the myth of the slight 'blood sacrifice' made by the Jews in 1914-1918 once again loomed large. Counter-arguments, such as those of Hauptmann Dr Leo Löwenstein, who quantified the Jewish losses, were ignored. [1322]

The army went along with the Nazi Aryan Paragraph, introduced on 7 April 1933, which no longer allowed Jews to work in the state service. Within a year, on 28 April 1934, the Minister of Defence, Werner von Blomberg, decided to lift the tacit military resistance to this. It did not have major personnel consequences - about 70 Jewish soldiers lost their jobs - but it was a major step in principle.[1323] The army was no longer autonomous in its own personnel policy.

Blomberg's indulgence was prompted by the tensions surrounding the SA at the time. Hitler was showing his 'loyalty' to the traditional armed forces (Reichswehr) over the revolutionary armed forces (the SA), and the Reichswehr in turn was showing loyalty to 'the nation' with which the NSDAP had been increasingly identified since 1933. It was also significant that the swastika - a party insignia - was added to the uniform. Blomberg wrote an article in the *Völkischer Beobachter* in which he highlighted the fusion of army and state.[1324]

In 1935, the 'Wehrgesetz' followed. It became clear that the army would once again develop into an organisation of millions. The Reichswehr merged into the Wehrmacht. Nazi Germany's geopolitical and military ambitions took their first tentative shape. Germany was less and less concerned with the restrictive international agreements. For many generals, such as Blomberg, Werner Freiherr Von Fritsch and the Chief of the General Staff of the Army Ludwig Beck, this posed a dangerous risk. It was not so much feared that Hitler and the Party would bring Germany into conflict, but rather that this would happen before the army was ready for it. That Hitler was indeed prepared to take great risks would become clear in 1936, when he reoccupied the Rheinland, with a relatively weak army. The military reforms themselves were also very drastic, and were sometimes accompanied by measures that did not please the traditional military, such as the constant breaking up of existing units in order to use elements of them for the hasty construction of new units.[1325] This hasty development, more in width than in depth, would remain a lasting weakness in the otherwise excellently disciplined German army.

A recent study of the life of General Ludwig Beck shows that he played an important role in the search for the right answer to this development, which was further strengthened by the fact that the number of Nazis within 'das Militär' was growing rapidly. In 1933, General Reichenau was one of the few open Nazis within the ranks of the army, but a few years later there were hundreds.[1326] Beck looked for a way to restore the pillar structure. Earlier, he had warned Von Schleicher through his confidant Arno Moysischewitz about Hitler's long arm, but the latter underestimated the danger.[1327] Now a symbol figure was needed, who represented the memory of the Wilhelmine era. After von Hindenburg's death this could only be one person, his right hand man within the old OHL and Oberost: Erich Ludendorff.

In the winter of 1934-1935, a rapprochement was sought. The moment was propitious for Beck, because Ludendorff was, as usual, involved in trench warfare again. The general had followed the events of 1933 and subsequent developments with care. Before 1933, it had already become clear that the radical anticlerical ideas of the Tannenbergbund were difficult to reconcile with the

NSDAP. Ludendorff attributed Hitler's rise to power to a pact between occult forces, in which he especially pointed to Hugenberg, and Roman Catholic forces. In fact, according to Ludendorff, a dissident branch of the völkische movement was active, which was inspired by the 'new Buddhist'. By this, Ludendorff meant the Thule Society as a part of the Germanic League, which from the beginning, founded by the fierce anti-Semite Theodor Fritsch and continued by Von Sebottendorf and Dietrich Eckart, had exerted its influence and was active in various national interest groups and parties. Ludendorff referred to von Sebottendorf's banned book, *Bevor Hitler kam*, in which he had also read that the 'Egyptian' Rudolf Hess belonged to them.[1328] 'I decided to continue the line that I had followed with my wife until then and to remain silent rather than change course'.[1329]

Ludendorff's distrust was strengthened when the Reichstag went up in flames. The extent to which he had become anchored in his own 'doctrine' was shown by the fact that he examined the date, 27.02.1933, and twice arrived at the number 27; a number that was 'holy' to all occultists, and not only to the cabalists.[1330] He did not believe that the communists were behind it.[1331] When parliament met on 5 March, Ludendorff already predicted that this would be the last session of his *Ludendorffs Volkswarte*. He was also worried about the army. He was convinced that soon generals would be replaced by National Socialists. Furthermore, he criticised the increasing police violence and waves of arrests.[1332] Yet, the greatest excitement came from a case that touched Ludendorff personally: the Elze affair.

Professor Walter Elze was connected to the Berlin Humboldt University and occupied himself with the First World War, in which he clearly appreciated the role of Von Hindenburg more than the role of Ludendorff. Especially painful was the fact that Enze elaborated on a fragment in Von Hindenburg's memoirs, *Aus meinem Leben*, in which was written that Ludendorff would have had a breakdown on the night of 26 August 1914. Ludendorff was devilish, and answered in letter and book to the allegations, constantly coming up with 'improved editions' of his 'open letters', such as in *Dirne Kriegsgeschichte* or in *Tannenberg, geschichtliche Wahrheit über die Schlacht*. In these, he indicated that the consternation on his part stemmed from the fact that he heard around that time that the German High Command had moved units from the Western Front, where the decision against France was to be made, to the Eastern Front, against Schlieffen thinking.[1333]

Ludendorff felt that his good name had been tarnished once again and it went hard against hard. The Ministry of Defence did not want an open mud-slinging match that would also affect the Von Hindenburg icon and tried to settle the matter with discretion. However, this role did not suit Ludendorff and he chose for openness by sending Hitler a telegram. Ludendorff's lonely struggle was an opportunity for Beck. If he could reach out and help Ludendorff, he might be able to win him back to Prussian tradition.

Since Ludendorff had also sent a telegram to the Ministry of Defence, one could react. Beck decided, together with one of Ludendorff's confidants, General a.D. Georg Wetzell, to visit Ludendorff in Tutzing on 6 January 1934. When Hitler got wind of the imminent visit, the musical chairs began to circle around Ludendorff. Hitler wanted Ludendorff to be given a letter of his own. The visit was not easy. Of course Ludendorff was honoured with the 'high visit', but he kept insisting on the Elze case and threatened with legal action.[1334] The Ministry of Defence was uncomfortable with this. On the one hand, Beck wanted to bring Ludendorff in, but on the other hand, one could not just demolish the good name and prestige of Von Hindenburg, because that was a valuable legacy and legitimisation of 'das Militär'. For Beck, the visit to Tutzing was the beginning of a long journey, during which he practised remarkable patience.

According to his biographer, Klaus-Jürgen Müller, Beck was involved with 'the case' of Ludendorff on an almost daily basis. Despite Ludendorff's failure during the elections, Beck, who was not uncritical of Ludendorff otherwise, believed that there was still an 'enormous admiration' for the general's 'Gesamtleistung'.[1335] Through Major a.D. Holtzmann, a confidant of Ludendorff in Berlin, Beck kept in touch with Ludendorff. From this contact, it became clear that Beck wanted much more than just a reconciliation between Ludendorff and the army. That this became clear to Ludendorff was, as stated by Müller, shown by the reaction Ludendorff gave towards Holtzmann. Ludendorff spoke of a changed climate towards his person since the death of Von Hindenburg.[1336]

A charm offensive was launched. Ludendorff's 70th birthday offered opportunities for military honours, and to commemorate the spring offensive of 1918, Ludendorff could still be promoted to marshal. Both Beck and Von Fritsch approached Ludendorff about this.[1337] Ludendorff declined: 'I have become a general by myself'.[1338] Beck travelled again to Tutzing on 22 February. However, Ludendorff remained obstinate. He distrusted the matter. Without clear insight into the aim and purpose of the conversation, Ludendorff refused. Beck got no further than Munich after intervention by Holtzmann.[1339] Ludendorff also invoked his new insights as a 'world revolutionary', which he said were 'too unfamiliar' to Beck, but weighed particularly heavily on him. 'I am following a path in life worthy of me and giving the Germans the opportunity in times of need to rely on me as their last reserve of trust',[1340] he announced. The bar was therefore set high. Beck did not allow himself to be swayed, but went to Tutzing, without being able to get through to Ludendorff. Ludendorff gave him his book *Mein militärischer Werdegang*, with his signature in it, as a sign of respect and a message: 'The leaders of the army must not limit themselves to the military field alone, they must make the strength of the people available to the army already in peacetime'.[1341] Beck's biographer Müller said that these were words to Beck's heart, for he would quote them several times later.[1342]

According to a statement by Mathilde Ludendorff, a far-reaching conversation between the two men finally took place in Tutzing. Here, the 'problem' of Hitler and the NSDAP was openly discussed. As Ludendorff's second wife states, the army had wrongly failed to intervene in 1934 (Night of the Long Knives) and had thus missed an important opportunity. Beck agreed, making it clear that a new opportunity should not be wasted.[1343]

Then, the preparations for Ludendorff's 70th birthday on 9 April 1935 began. Von Fritsch, Blomberg and Beck were all involved. Via Holtzmann, close contact was maintained with Ludendorff, who kept an iron grip on the 'party' from his residence at Starnbergersee. There was to be a guard of honour, and fifteen Luftwaffe planes, double-deckers, passed over Tutzing.[1344] It was made clear that the two 'H's (Von Hindenburg and Hitler) were not to be mentioned in the speech of honour.[1345] Beck personally delivered the radio address. The anniversary was of course part of 'high politics'. In this sense, Beck had a real connection with Ludendorff's view that the military field was more than the issue of 'das Militär' itself. Historically, however, there was a deep knee-jerk reaction to the facts. According to Beck's speech, 'by dismissing Ludendorff in 1918, we went down the road of capitulation'.[1346] So many generals had signed up that Breucker had to hold off a little on Ludendorff's behalf. Ludendorff pointed out that his birthday was a private affair after all, and that he had such a rift with many of his colleagues that he did not think a reunion would be useful.[1347] Hitler, too, is said to have tried to come, but was held off.[1348]

It was clear that after the failure to intervene in 1934, the military saw Ludendorff as a last resort. General Graf von der Schulenburg expressed to Holtzmann that 'Ludendorff was the only one who could still save the situation'.[1349] As Beck stated: 'a sigh of relief went through the German people when the name Ludendorff was mentioned openly again'.[1350] But Ludendorff would not let himself be charmed. He thought that Von Fritsch and Blomberg tried to use him 'for their own ends'.[1351] Ludendorff had learned from the Kapp-Putsch, the Feldherrnhalle-Putsch and his political career. Each time, he felt he had done the dirty work for others, and when things went wrong, people had sheltered behind his back. Beck continued his attempts, through Holtzmann, in April and May 1935. He played a dangerous game, letting Holtzmann know that 'in the circumstances one would have to reckon with a military dictatorship'.[1352] Furthermore, Beck devoted himself to Ludendorff supporters who had problems within the military apparatus, he listened to his ideas about the 'Deutscher Gottglaube' and 'überstaatlichen' Powers, and he even suggested to Ludendorff that he teach these theories within Defence.[1353] To Holtzmann, Beck also admitted his reservations about the Jesuits, although he saw the Freemasons as more of a 'bowling club'.[1354]

Blomberg and Von Fritsch were not as persistent as Beck and dropped out. Beck continued to keep them informed of his contacts, without involving them further. In the end Blomberg was even irritated by Beck's persistence and called Holtzmann - who apparently was easier to correct than Beck - to account.[1355] Joachim Fest pointed out that Blomberg had no clear world view, which he characterised as a 'lack of character'. By this he meant that Blomberg had manifested himself ideologically from anthroposophist to almost communist (after a visit to Moscow) and practically everything in between. He also harboured a degree of admiration for Hitler. Typical of his 'Führer' perception was the fact that he seriously claimed to have been cured of a cold because he had shaken hands with Hitler.[1356]

Ludendorff had his thoughts about Blomberg as well. He called him a 'cautious officer', who 'did not want to be dragged into the mire of politics'. And if he stood for anything at all, Ludendorff saw him mainly as a 'Hitler loyalist'.[1357] In November, General von Reichenau and General Fedor von Bock travelled to Tutzing at Beck's instigation. Now that the minister - Blomberg - no longer participated, other means had to be used. At the end of November, Beck informed Holtzmann that he was very impressed by the general's latest fruit of the pen, *Totalen Krieg*.[1358] On 3 December, he informed Holtzmann once again how much the army wanted to use Ludendorf's vision to develop and informed him the next day that he wanted to leave for Tutzing. That Beck was buttering him up was shown by his later lecture for 'Die Mittwochsgesellschaft'. On 17 June 1942, during the 1026th meeting of this intimate circle, Beck spoke on the theme *Die Lehre vom totalen Krieg* (*eine kritische Auseinandersetzung*).[1359] Holtzmann reported to Ludendorff that Beck wanted to discuss important matters which could not be put down on paper. It was so secretive that Holtzmann himself could not quite indicate what it was about. This initiative went against the 'Blomberg ban'.[1360]

Just before Christmas 1935 Beck's visit to Tutzing took place. This conversation was followed by another between Holtzmann and Beck on Boxing Day. Beck emphasised that the 'contacts between the army and Ludendorff should continue, and on no account should they be broken off'. Beck fought for what

Ban on *Ludendorffs Volkswarte*

he could. Should the great goal not succeed - Ludendorff as von Hindenburg's direct deputy - then at least the best possible surrogate had to remain: 'uniformed generals had to visit Ludendorff regularly', thought Beck, who clearly wanted to suggest unity to the outside world.[1361] Ludendorff's unruly attitude also placed Holtzmann in an uncomfortable position. He insisted on several occasions to receive Beck back in Tutzing, highlighting that the army was the only effective counterforce in the country.[1362]

On 11 February 1936, Beck did it one last time. He had got Von Fritsch on his side again for a final assault on the stronghold at Starnbergersee. The conversation took place, but Von Fritsch had little 'Fingerspitzengefühl' for the sensitivities of Ludendorff. According to the German historian Walter Görlitz, Von Fritsch looked like a robust soldier, but was in fact a very sensitive man. He was conservative-Christian by birth, and 'politically not much smarter than the other soldiers'.[1363] At a certain point, Von Fritsch asked Ludendorff if he could not temporarily stop his worldly struggle, in order to come closer to each other. Ludendorff reacted as if stung by a wasp. For Ludendorff it was clear. Von Fritsch had understood nothing of his ideas and his books. These were 'nur-Soldaten', with whom he could not work. Poor Holtzmann was bombarded from Tutzing with recommendations and especially rejections towards 'das Militär'. On 21 February 1936, Ludendorff concluded to Holtzmann that the soldiers were 'Christian reactionaries', and that was the end of it. 'Schluss mit jenen Leuten', said Ludendorff at the end of April. [1364]

With this, Ludendorff had in fact missed his most serious chance since November 1918 to return to executive power. During the Kapp-Putsch and at the Feldherrnhalle, his supporters had been, at best, (disengaged) parts of 'das Militär', coupled with opportunists, dreamers and adventurers. Now Ludendorff could have made his comeback with cover from Blomberg, Von Fritsch and Beck, coupled with a large-scale rehabilitation of his person and his ideas. Still, Ludendorff as a counterweight to the radicals, since his own way with Mathilde, the House Ludendorff, and the Tannenbergbund was a wishful thinking. 'He was the only one for whom (Hitler) still had respect,' Beck thought looking back in 1938, when Nazi Germany was already heading for World War II.[1365]

Thus, Ludendorff had once again become a plaything on the greatest stage, but this time he let the leading role pass him by. However, the events had not left him cold. On the eve of the Night of the Long Knives in the summer of 1934, Ludendorff and Mathilde had just returned from their mountain hut in Klais, where they regularly stayed. This time they had been there from mid-May to mid-June. Back in Tutzing, the mail suddenly stopped. Normally, Ludendorff received mail twice a day. Due to his political activities and publicity, there was always a lot of mail. The 28th passed without mail, the 29th followed, stil no mail. Mathilde smelled danger, and Ludendorff decided to call the post office. When he did not receive a clear answer, he immediately turned to the heavy artillery and decided to call the leader of the Sicherheitspolizei, Heinrich Himmler, an old acquaintance from his putsch days. He also had his confidant in the Beck case, Major Holtzmann, find out what was going on.

Finally, the mail arrived the evening of 30th. People groped in the dark until the news of the Night of the Long Knives arrived: Hitler had settled with Röhm and the SA. There had been talk of a coup and the name of the French ambassador, François Poncet, had been mentioned. The list of people who had been murdered grew by the day. 'With horror, my wife and I turned away from the events', Ludendorff wrote in his memoirs.[1366] Ludendorff was, rightly, sceptical about the official statements. He did not believe that Röhm had actually planned a coup. Ludendorff had kept Röhm at arm's length after learning of his homosexuality. *Ludendorff's Volkswarte* openly wrote about Ernst Röhm's 'Knabenliebe',[1367] but did not consider him a traitor. 'All men had sworn allegiance to Hitler,' he said of those executed. The word of honour - especially that of a soldier - was still important to Ludendorff, even after the Feldherrnhalle-Putsch.[1368] The vulnerability of his own position becomes clear when we look at the list of victims. Hitler, as we have already seen, had no qualms about disposing of a high-ranking soldier like Von Schleicher.

In February 1933, in *Ludendorff's Volkswarte*, Ludendorff already pointed to the far-reaching political influence of the SA within the 'new' Germany. Under the revealing title, *Die SA wartet und erwartet*, he sketched a picture of an SA that increasingly penetrated German society, the civil service, the army and the police. For example, it was alarming, and typical of the growing influence, that SA units held shooting drills on an army training ground. Ludendorff's concern was justified; the boundaries between state and politics were fading. On the other hand, the SA and the Ehrhardt revolutionaries operated no differently in Ludendorff's day.[1369] That the Night of the Long Knives had been in the air for some time is also clear from Joseph Goebbels' diary. On 29 June, the day Ludendorff was without mail, he wrote: 'The situation is getting worse. The Führer must act. Otherwise 'die Reaktion' will grow over our heads. [...] We have many enemies [...] the people expect us to act. [...] how much longer? This morning a telephone call from the Führer [...] 'Es geht los' in the name of God. Anything is better than this terrible waiting. Ich bin bereit.'[1370]

In a conversation shortly after the Night of the Long Knives with Von Fritsch, Ludendorff pointed out the danger of Hitler. 'Hitler does not remain loyal to anyone, he will betray you too within a few years', he said prophetically.[1371] Mathilde pointed out to Von Fritsch 'the blood that now adheres to the uniform of the Wehrmacht, as long as it is under Hitler'.[1372] Ludendorff supported this, and told Von Fritsch that this event should give enough room to act against Hitler. As we know, nothing happened, at least not by the army itself, which, via Beck, knocked on Ludendorff's door, who pointed out to them (with some justification), that it was their own duty. Hartmuth Mahlberg, who wrote an uncritical memoir about Ludendorff, concluded that this made the general one of the first resistance fighters against Hitler, and that this special merit was not sufficiently recognised. Certainly, Ludendorff had become an opponent of Hitler, but mainly because he found Hitler too moderate in many respects.[1373]

The death of Von Hindenburg, on 2 August 1934, was a lesser shock for Ludendorff. He called him 'one of the worst characters that ever lived'. As an example of his 'indecency', he shared the insantce with the Emperor: 'He spoke of his love for the Empire, but he advised the Emperor to travel to the Netherlands'.[1374] The case with Professor Elze about the Battle of Tannenberg and Ludendorff's unremitting anger about the 'betrayal' of 26 October 1918 would not let go of Ludendorff until his death. He also blamed Hindenburg for the 'pact' with Hitler. In his book *Im Angesicht des Galgens*, Hans Frank wrote that on 30 January 1933 (Hitler became Reichskanzler), Ludendorff wrote von Hindenburg a hard letter: 'Sie haben durch die Ernennung Hitlers zum Reichskanzler einem der grössten Demagogen aller Zeiten unser heiliges Deutsches Vaterland ausgeliefert. Ich prophezeie Ihnen feierlich, dass dieser unselige Mann unser Reich in den Abgrund stützen , unsere Nation in unfässliches Elend bringen wird, und kommende Geschlechter werden Sie verfluchen in Ihrem Grabe, dass Sie das getan haben.' I give this quote here verbatim and untranslated, because this telegram became a discussion document itself.

Thus, the original source was Hans Frank, and the letter was afterwards repeatedly quoted in other works, also within the Ludendorff House, such as volume III of Ludendorff's *Meine Lebenserinnerungen von 1933-1937*, which was published in the 1950s.[1375] Later, the existence of the telegram was questioned by historians Fritz Tobias and Lothar Gruchmann in 1990 and 1999.[1376] The problem is that the document has not surfaced in the archives. However, much argues for the historical authenticity of the document. Many other telegrams and letters from Ludendorff have been preserved (partly in the Moscow archives), and although they may not have been as strongly formulated as the above-mentioned letter, they too are an indictment of the political upheavals and their consequences for the House of Ludendorff.[1377] The German historian Ingo Balding pointed out that Frank at that time worked for the Bavarian justice system - with which Ludendorff frequently came into contact - and was well informed.[1378] Finally, it is important to note that the House of Ludendorff, certainly in the post-war justification of its own actions, benefited from Ludendorff's 'angry letter', but that this could not be said of Hans Frank. This also argues for the authenticity.

With regard to the 'Deutscher Gottglaube', there were also clashes. In spite of frequent letters from Ludendorff - and also from Von Unruh -[1379] to Von Hindenburg, to take action against the maltreatment of Tannenbergers, nothing happened. Von Hindenburg tacitly allowed it. Confidants reported to Ludendorff that Von Hindenburg was positive about the ban against Ludendorff's organisations, such as the youth organisations 'Deutschvolk'. 'My religion is no less deep and serious than yours,' Ludendorff wrote to Von Hindenburg on 12 July 1933.[1380] Von Hindenburg also ignored Ludendorff in this matter, which was understandable given the sometimes harsh tone: 'I have long ago torn up your autographed photograph, which you gave me in Kaunas', Ludendorff wrote on 4 December 1933.[1381] Von Hindenburg, on the other hand, seems to have spared his photograph of Ludendorff. According to his biographer Wolfgang Ruge, Von Hindenburg showed his 'magnanimity' by keeping the photograph of Ludendorff 'at the door of his bedroom'.[1382]

Ludendorff did not match up to the greater political talent of Von Hindenburg. Von Hindenburg's biographer Pyta wrote that although Ludendorff had a point when criticising Hindenburg's stylised version of the Battle of Tannenberg, he as a 'nur-Soldat', lost out to Hindenburg's historical-political strategy. Von Hindenburg's veneration was enormous. *Ludendorffs Volkswarte* mocked - with some justification - the vision of the hereditary expert Professor Robert Sommer, who believed that von Hindenburgs was so brilliant a strategist that he probably had to descend from the equally brilliant mathematician Karl Friedrich Hindenburg.[1383] Hindenburg had managed to be seen in the line of the famous von Schlieffen, and to act as his worthy successor at Tannenberg.[1384] Ludendorff's street-fighter mentality - Pyta spoke of a 'manic obsession' - did his business no favours either.[1385]

There was a small riot at the death of von Hindenburg. We know from Alfred Rosenberg's diary that Hitler 'spoke beautifully' at the funeral ceremony on 8 August 1934. Alfred Rosenberg, who knew his stuff and was in close contact with Ludendorff, listened tensely to whether Hitler would mention Ludendorff's name. Hitler was in a difficult position. Ludendorff's name had become politically charged, especially in Von Hindenburg circles. However, Hitler knew his trade and spoke of 'the great helper' of Von Hindenburg. Ludendorff had been mentioned, but his name had not been mentioned. Later, at the table in the Reichskanzlei, Ludendorff was the subject of discussion. It turned out that the general had refused to hang his flag at half mast for Von Hindenburg. Initially, people had thought that this was a misunderstanding and had pointed it out to him. However, he firmly rejected the flag. Hitler then told about the difficult ceremony around the Tannenberg memorial, and the tensions between Von Hindenburg and Ludendorff. He thus knew the background, but was nevertheless baffled by the event, and brought it up several times. Hitler called Ludendorff's behaviour a 'lack of discipline, for the whole nation'- these were almost the same words with which Ludendorff had been expelled from the Moltke Staff so many years earlier. 'He should never have done this', Hitler said repeatedly, adding: 'He cannot escape his fate anyway, if he dies we will add him to the heroes of the nation'. The cause was also clear to Hitler. It was due to Mathilde Ludendorff's 'Drüsenoperation', which had 'thrown the general off balance'. 'Despite everything, I feel sorry for Ludendorff,' Rosenberg wrote in his diary. 'He was the driving force and brain behind the German resistance' (an interesting admission by a Hitler worshipper); 'Hindenburg was more the symbol of bourgeois sentimentality, although I do not do him justice. But Ludendorff stood in his shadow; he was deprived of public fame. Von Hindenburg made peace with the political centre, Ludendorff became an open opponent of Germany's enemies. That he turned from a soldier into a thinker was his fate. Because he felt insecure in this field, and did not dare to ask for men's advice, he fell prey to the half-soft philosopher (Mathilde) whose nonsense, chivalrous as he was, he defended to the end'. Rosenberg concluded in the line of Hitler: 'When Ludendorff dies, he must lie by his side (Von Hindenburg) just like the quarrelling emperors in Speyer Cathedral. The line of the fate of the people is stronger than the individual obstinacy of those who think they can escape it'.[1386]

It would not be the only time that frustration over the conduct of Ludendorff, or the House of Ludendorff, was attributed to the (negative) influence of Mathilde. In the unpublished typescript of attorney Rüdiger Graf von der Goltz[1387] there is a remarkable anecdote: Von der Goltz was in Stettin when an old acquaintance invited him to a 'secret meeting'. He was invited to meet an 'old general' to whom he was 'indebted'. He had to comply with formal dress codes. Von der Goltz, who had been involved in the trials surrounding the 'Fememurders', did not feel up to it and declined the honour. Not much later, he was at a meeting where Ludendorff and Mathilde were to speak and it dawned on him who the general had been. Ludendorff spoke about the Great War, and it would have been a 'nice evening' if Ludendorff had left it at that. He had spoken sternly, but it was not a scolding. It remained businesslike. Von der Goltz and his wife took Ludendorff's political speeches that followed for granted, even though they could not follow him very well. But then Mathilde Ludendorff entered the rostrum. She put both her arms to her sides, showed her elbows and looked defiantly into the audience. Her first words stayed with Von der Goltz: 'You may be glad that you had the opportunity to hear the general speak in person today. The others will have to make do with what the newspapers write about it. And what this will be, we already know in advance, considering that one of these gentlemen (she pointed to the journalists in the front row) was drawing dolls during the general's speech. Yes, I mean you'. The journalist from the *Ostseezeitung* got up and left the room with his colleagues. 'So', Mathilde Ludendorff shouted triumphantly through the hall, 'now we are finally among ourselves'. Von der Goltz felt sorry for Ludendorff when he walked past afterwards. [1388]

It was the same wording that Rosenberg used. Ludendorff was, as in 1920 and 1923, still 'above the law', even though he made himself impossible. Mathilde Ludendorff was the perfect scapegoat for all the frustrations that Ludendorff and the House of Ludendorff evoked and they did little to avoid this fate.

Chapter 22

A grave in Tutzing

Hitler's rise to absolute power and the polarisation that ensued meant that Ludendorff's political activities were increasingly under threat. After the Night of the Long Knives, Ludendorff even felt physically threatened. Hitler showed himself ruthless towards his enemies, even when they were old allies. They were conscripted, murdered, 'kaltgestellt' or were 'lucky' to die in time. The latter happened, for example, to Dietrich Eckart. Hitler did him the wonderful honour of dedicating *Mein Kampf* to him. This was possible because Eckart died already at Christmas 1923. A 'living soul' could of course never have been Hitler's 'teacher'. Another man who provided Hitler's mental ammunition, geopoliticologist Karl Haushofer, ended up in the Dachau concentration camp and his son was murdered by the Gestapo. Ernst Hanfstaengl fled abroad. Theologian Bernhard Stempfle, who had corrected *Mein Kampf* but later criticised the book in a review, was deported to the Dachau concentration camp and later found dead in a forest near Harlaching. Jörg Lanz von Liebenfels was banned from writing. Von Kahr was taken to Dachau in the aftermath of The Night of the Long Knives. 'Now he can work honestly,' Alfred Rosenberg noted cynically in his diary. But it did not happen, he was mistreated and almost immediately murdered. Von Lossow fled to Turkey, Pöhner died in a car accident near Feldkirchen in April 1924. Von Seeckt left for China, where Max Bauer had also gone, and Kriebel also reported to the Kuomintang (Chinese National People's Party) as a military advisor. After Bauer's death, he took over his position. On his return to Germany, he advocated German friendship and cooperation with China rather than Japan, to which he incurred the enmity of other Nazis. 'Two men should be shot immediately,' Kriebel said, 'Goebbels and Von Ribbentrop. Kriebel remained an NSDAP member and ended up as ambassador. Anton Drexler became an insignificant party member, Frans Seldte of 'Stahlhelm', chose to join the NSDAP, Schleisser was temporarily imprisoned in Dachau, Graefe died 'in time' (1933), Gregor Strasser was also murdered in the aftermath of the Night of the Long Knives, Otto Strasser emigrated abroad in 1933. Arthur Dinter, like Ludendorff a fervent Catholic, was 'kaltgestellt' in 1928. The monarchist Soden-Fraunhof only survived because Rudolf Hess protected him.[1389] This list could easily have been a lot longer.

The periodicals of the Ludendorff House suffered from the polarisation and growing power of the state. Already in January 1932, *Ludendorff's Volkswarte* was banned for the first time. Under the title *Bekämpfung politischer Ausschreitungen*, the magazine was banned from 6 January 1932 for some time. On 20 December 1931, Ludendorff had a pamphlet distributed which was the size of the cover page, in which the decision of the Munich police was announced.[1390] The start of the fourth year of publication of *Ludendorff's Volkswarte* was therefore not under a favourable star, but on 10 January it could be published after all. However, the number of black censorship bars in the magazine increased quickly. This concerned, for example, sentences on Von Hindenburg in the article *Zum Jahreswechsel*, written by Ludendorff himself.[1391]

Open hostilities between the *Ludendorffers* and their political opponents increased rapidly, especially from 1933 onwards. In the town of Neu Mittenwalde, for example, pastor Steinhäufer sent an open letter against the 'heretical' *Ludendorffers*. The small, but according to the *Volkswarte*, loyal group of followers was oppressed. In Wels, a police action took place against the Tannenberger. In February 1933, incidents also occurred in the communities of Loose, Pommern, and Tilsit. Church authorities, National Socialists and even the eldest son of Crown Prince Wilhelm acted against the Tannenbergers. 'The House of Hohenzollern is falling deeper and deeper,' concluded the *Volkswarte*. The *Nationalsozialistische Beamtenzeitung* stepped up the pressure by writing on 5 February that year that: 'Whoever understands the spirit of the House of Ludendorff today can only be seen as abnormal'.[1392] In Gross-Heide Angela, Ratzeburg and Wesselburen there were direct confrontations with the SA. A lecture by teacher and Ludendorffer Bluhm-Friedrichsholm, *Soll Deutschland das Schwert der katholische Kirche werden?* was disrupted by SA men. 'We know no freedom, no tolerance, we know only violence and brutality,' the teacher complained. In Raztebug, beer mugs flew through the hall when Mrs Wentzels' lecture, *Die Deutsche Gotterkenntnis als Weg der Freiheit*, was interrupted. In Wesselburen, beatings took place under the watchful eye of the deputy mayor K. Herwig, a National Socialist. A lecture by a certain Michaelis about freemasonry was cancelled.[1393] The page *Vor'm Volksgericht* in *Ludendorff's Volkswarte* was banned on 5 March 1933 by order of the Berlin police.[1394] This was followed by the banning of meetings, e.g. in East Prussia.

The House of Ludendorff took up arms and wrote an open letter, which was published in *Ludendorff's Volkswarte* on 19 March 1933, and addressed to the Minister of the Interior, Wilhelm Frick, Vice-Chancellor (here addressed as Reichskommissar of Prussia) Franz von Papen, Minister of Culture, Bernhard Rust and the Police President of Berlin, Magnus von Levetzow. In the letter, entitled *Aufklärung der Regierung über den Tannenbergbund*, it was pointed out that the *Ludendorffers'* 'battle aims', formulated in 1927, were 'German'. Furthermore, they defended themselves on the thorny issue of criticism of religion, and the alternative vision of Mathilde Ludendorff, formulated in her book *Deutscher Gottglaube*,[1395] which in 86 pages expressed the essence of thinking. According to the open letter, 'anyone with enough Nordic blood should be grateful to the author'.[1396] Moreover, enclosed was an introductory work by Hans *Kurth, Die Weltdeutung Dr. Mathilde Ludendorffs. Eine Einführung in die Werke der Philosophin*, which had a circulation of 27,000 in 1934,[1397] as well as the better known book by Gottfried Feder, *Der Deutsche Staat auf nationaler und sozialere Grundlage*, in which Mathilde Ludendorff was used as a source, and of which Hitler wrote the introduction.

Reich President Von Hindenburg received a letter as well,[1398] after Ludendorff bookshops were attacked in Dresden, Magdeburg, Essen, Elberfeld, Düsseldorf and Gotha. In Düsseldorf, for example, about 20 uniformed SA men armed with rifles were involved. In another city, SA men forced their way into a Ludendorff bookshop, seized *Vor'm Volksgericht*, and 'rebuilt' the entire shop. The insurance company refused to pay for the damage.[1399] An economic pamphlet, *Der Bauer stirbt, mit ihm das Volk*, was also banned in March. In it, the Ludendorffs opposed the collectivisation of agriculture. In general, the *Ludendorffs* were very critical of economic policy, where the accusing finger was pointed at the 'freemason' Hjalmar Schacht.[1400]

Ludendorff's Volkswarte would not survive the year 1933, just as the Tannenbergbund was eliminated. Ludendorff related it all directly to the Concordat (20.07.1933) which had been concluded with the Pope. On the eve of this, Ludendorff had already observed intensified attacks. In *Ludendorff's Volkswarte*, Fritz Sauckel was quoted, at the time the 'Gauleiter' of Thuringia and later responsible for the 'Arbeitseinsatz', who openly pleaded for 'more intolerance'. There was supposed to be 'impatience' in society, the 'national revolution' had to be carried out. At the end of July, *Ludendorff's Volkswarte* had to close its doors. The immediate cause was the fact that the Italian Minister of Aviation, Balbo, had been called 'a Jew'.[1401] The deeper cause was the relentless criticism of the New Order by the House of Ludendorff. For Ludendorff, it was somehow a relief, he wrote in his memoirs.[1402] After all, one could not compromise in order to avoid collaboration. Closing the doors of *Volkswarte* meant that one could stick to one's own principles. 'I am treated the same way as the communists and marxists', Ludendorff complained to Breucker.[1403]

This was close to Ludendorff's heart. A letter he wrote to his own editors in Munich in 1932 showed how seriously he took his periodicals. After a complaint by Ludendorff-author Rehwaldt that corrections were not properly carried out, he told the editors: 'My magazine is not a newspaper, but a document of world historical importance'. He hoped that the editors would 'take this to heart', and that in the future the cooperation would be 'harmonious'.[1404]

In response to the closing of *Volkswarte*, it was decided to issue *Am heiligen Quell*, the other monthly periodical, now fortnightly. *Am heiligen Quell* was less dangerous than Ludendorff's *Volkswarte*. *Volkswarte* constantly played on political topicality, and thus was in the hottest part of the struggle. *Am heiligen Quell* was more cultural and could therefore continue to exist for the time being. The *Tannenberg-Jahrweiser* (later called *Tannenberg-Jahrbuch*, and from 1940 *Deutsche Rast*) also continued to exist. However, there was a return in the form of a book by Dr. Armin Roth, *Das Reichskonkordat vom 20 Juli 1933*, which appeared in the same year, and which in fact was an elaboration of his *Nationalsozialismus und Katholische Kirche*, published in 1931. *Mein Schriftwechsel mit der Gauleitung Rheinland und der Reichsparteileitung der NSDAP sowie mit der Kanzlei Adolf Hitlers*. It was interesting to see that the struggle between the NSDAP and House Ludendorff was a kind of internal tribal struggle, which was no less fierce. In fact, Roth wondered why the NSDAP did not act harder against (catholic) enemies of the people, by which he meant, among others, Cardinal Faulhaber and other critics.[1405] Roth was both a Tannenberg sympathiser (possibly also a member) and a member of the NSDAP. The answer he received from the NSDAP was interesting. In principle, Ludendorff was right in many things, they reluctantly admitted, but propagandistically it was all wrong. Upon further insistence, the administration of Dr. Robert Ley (Gauleiter Rheinland, later leader of the 'Deutsche Arbeitsfront' - DAF) informed him that the NSDAP did not interfere in the choice of religion of individual party members, and that Dr. Roth was free to leave the party if he wanted to.[1406]

It was the tone that made the music, and Ludendorff and his Tannenbergers were seen as a danger, although Hitler and the Nazis could never entirely free themselves from an admiration for 'der ewige Recke' from Tutzing. Mathilde was often seen as the evil genius. Hitler, who was good at imitating people - above all the publisher (Eher-Verlag) Max Amann - was also notorious for his imitation of Mathilde Ludendorff; 'in doing so, he peeled off all the skins, the priests, the esotericism, the science, the eroticism, until only a biting onion remained'.[1407] As a result, the relation Ludendorff and the NSDAP muddled along. Ludendorff wrote endless rows of open and personal letters to the party leadership and to the state, which often went unanswered, only to suddenly send a polite letter to Ludendorff after all. Usually, these letters were about mistreatment of Tannenbergers or their property. Sometimes they were more direct confrontations. On 27 November 1936, Goebbels gave a speech to the 'Reichskulturkammer'. In it he criticised Mathilde Ludendorff's book *Der ungesühnte Frevel an Luther, Lessing, Mozart und Schiller*. The Nazis did not like how the House of Ludendorff characterised 'national heroes' as victims (and sometimes as perpetrators, such as Goethe). On the contrary, the Nazis needed 'precursors', and 'tradition'. Ambivalently, this was the reason why Goebbels pushed aside Mathilde Ludendorff's book, but then also wrote an apologetic letter to Ludendorff on 12 December 1936.[1408] For Ludendorff belonged to 'tradition', as an 'icon' of Wilhelmine Germany. They could neither get along with nor go without each other.

Again, just as Beck operated, the tension was used to strengthen the ties. Goebbels hinted via Von Treuenfeld that a personal meeting between Hitler and Ludendorff could take the pain out of the air.[1409] In his diaries, Goebbels had usually expressed himself kindly about Ludendorff. Even about his painful electoral defeat against Von Hindenburg, in which he embellished the result (400,000 votes, almost half more than in reality) and indicated to be 'satisfied'.[1410]

Ludendorff was just as stubborn towards Hitler as he was towards Beck. He was only prepared to enter into dialogue under certain conditions. Here again the word 'honour' was central. Ludendorff made it clear that he must not appear to have 'crawled to the Cross'. He insisted that 'any appearance that he was acting out of fear must be avoided'. He was more than clear about himself and his wife: 'Hands off me, my wife and the publishing business'. It was striking that Ludendorff no longer fought for the reestablishment of *Ludendorff's Volkswarte*, the 'Tannenbergbund' and 'Deutschvolk'. In the meantime, four years had passed, there had been the necessary internal tensions, and Ludendorff probably simply lacked the strength to bring these time-consuming organisations back to life. In addition, many executives had left in the meantime. He did insist that the former Tannenbergers should be left alone by the Gestapo and that their membership should not be an obstacle in society.

He was stricter towards some opponents. He demanded that the books by Walter Elze, *Tannenberg*, Fritz Hartung, *Hindenburg* and Von Beumelburg, *Sperrfeuer um Deutschland*, be removed from libraries. Furthermore, he demanded that the ban on books by the Ludendorff publishing house be lifted. From the Ministry of Propaganda, he demanded that the image of the hesitant Ludendorff at Tannenberg no longer be supported. Finally, he demanded that the 'Deutsche Gotterkenntniss (Ludendorff)' be given the same rights and status as other religions in Germany.[1411]

After a long period of back and forth, the meeting with Hitler finally came about. This took place on 30 March 1937 in the Wehrkreiskommando of the army in Munich. This meeting immediately brought a double recognition for Ludendorff. Politically, because the Führer received him, and by the fact that it took place within 'das Militär'. It was also a success for Hitler; he succeeded in doing what Beck had not succeeded in doing; reaching out to Ludendorff. Speculation about Hitler's motives will continue. Of course, there were arguments for closing the front with Ludendorff, but they were not very important anymore. It looks more as if Hitler had kept his respect for Ludendorff and had a personal need to 'close the book' as well. Hitler immediately went for reconciliation and told Ludendorff that it had only been a 'war on paper', to which the unyielding Ludendorff immediately replied that there was also 'immortal paper'. Moreover, he warned that there must not be another war. Ludendorff thought that initially the German army could go far, 'from Cairo to India', but eventually Germany would perish. Hitler denied that he had war plans, upon which Ludendorff stated that he 'did not believe that'.[1412]

It came to a hand and Ludendorff got what he wanted. In their own periodicals this was celebrated on 9 April 1937. It was made clear that the restrictions of the regime against the House of Ludendorff had been lifted and that everything had arisen from a series of misunderstandings. The 'Deutscher Gottglauben' was given the same rights as other religions in Germany. Ludendorff was prepared to acknowledge that Hitler had put an end to the disgraceful influence of the 'Diktat' of Versailles. The new army and the old-timers were back on the same page, just like the comrades in arms of the putsch of that time, 9 November 1923. Ludendorff concluded that his struggle for a 'total völkische staat' had become 'more effective' with this new pact.[1413]

According to his wife, a burden fell from his shoulders after this, although the skirmishes continued to a certain extent. Accusations - partly anonymous - against Ludendorff and his supporters continued to circulate. Some seemed to have been translated from a foreign language into German, and Ludendorff suspected the long arm of Rome. Thus, there would have been the call of communists (Komintern) to infiltrate into Ludendorff's organisations in order to oppose Hitler. In addition, Ludendorff would have criticised Franco's troops in the Spanish Civil War. Ludendorff denied this. He reacted with a bombardment of letters, among others to the Reichskanzlei (Dr. Lammers) and Hitler's former bodyguard Ulrich Graf. The skirmishes did not alter the fact that the 'Deutscher Volkskirche' of another right-wing opponent, Arthur Dinter, was banned by the Reichsführer SS Himmler, while Ludendorff was allowed to continue.[1414]

For a long time, Ludendorff had worried about what to do next after his death. Now the way was clear. On 19 June 1937, the 'Bund für Deutsche Gotterkenntniss (Ludendorff) e.V.' was officially registered.[1415] Hitler was also satisfied, although he told Blomberg that 'it had been hard going again'.[1416] Ludendorff's birthday was celebrated in a big way. Like his 70th birthday, an honorary company was assigned, also because it was 55 years ago that Ludendorff had entered military service. Ludendorff, however, rejected this, believing that it could wait until his 60th anniversary. Nevertheless, Blomberg spoke on his birthday.

Escaping the crowds, they moved back to the house in the mountains, where they stayed until June. Ludendorff and his wife went for long walks and swam in the mountain lakes. Mathilde spoke of a 'deep harmony of our happiness'.[1417] Trips followed, including to Tyrol, and Mathilde met her sister Frieda Stahl. He wrote to Wilhelm Breucker about his time in the mountains. 'We stay here at 1,000 metres at our mountain hut and march happily through the world from there. Today five hours and fifty minutes without rest. Then another hour in the afternoon. My old bones have not let me down yet. The air and nature are wonderful'. He then went on to talk about his meeting with Hitler: 'The meeting of 30 March has made many things easier for me. In my life I have seen many come and go, now many come again, others leave. That is how it goes. They have kept the same attitude'.[1418]

Shortly after returning to Tutzing, just before Mathilde's birthday, things went wrong. Ludendorff became seriously ill and there was bleeding. On 4 November of that year, an operation for liver cancer followed. The operation could not save the general's life and an eleven-week sick bed was the result. During this time, Hitler again visited Ludendorff in hospital. According to Breucker, Ludendorff would have warned Hitler again about war plans. Hitler apparently left the hospital. When someone made the remark that Ludendorff would soon be out of the picture, Hitler abruptly turned around and snapped at him: 'Ludendorff saw it sharper than all of us'.[1419]

According to Mathilde Ludendorff, Ludendorff was lucid on his deathbed and faced the approaching end with appropriate calm. Mathilde thought that death apparently had to know what kind of special man was lying on his deathbed, because the feared prolonged pain did not occur. Ludendorff died on 20 December 1937, in the first floor corner room of a Catholic hospital in Munich, the Josephinum Krankenhaus. Although there was a crucifix hanging on the wall, Ludendorff remained faithful to his wife's religious interpretation. 'He died a heathen,' Breucker said. The nurse later said that she had 'never seen anyone bear his suffering and die so bravely'.[1420] Ludendorff was, as Mathilde described it, 'returned to the German earth'.[1421] When I inquired, via email, whether anything in the hospital still reminded of the patient Ludendorff, a Dr. med. Reinhard Aigner of the Verwaltungsdirektion, replied that he did not want to bring back painful memories.[1422]

The major newspapers, friend and foe alike, looked back on the life of Erich Ludendorff. The focus was entirely on the period 1914-1918. *Le Journal* and *Petit Parisien* considered that 'our greatest and most feared opponent has died' and that Ludendorff 'had undoubtedly been one of the best generals of World War I'. *The Daily Telegraph* stated that he was 'Germany's best soldier, and creator of operations'. The *Evening Standard* called him a 'master of strategy' and the *Wiener Zeitung* even a 'genius', which was confirmed by the Swedish *Aftonbladet*. The Poles were more cautious and the *Gazeta Polska* called him 'interesting'. The German general Von Einem placed Ludendorff in the same league as Moltke and Schlieffen. [1423]

For Hitler, now was the time to cash in on his reaching out with a grand state funeral, in which he and many generals participated. It was a harmonious union of past and present, of the military and the political; the unity Hitler needed for his coming plans. Mathilde Ludendorff had to accept this. Ludendorff did prevent that his remains - like those of Paul von Hindenburg - were buried in the monument at Tannenberg. The final resting place was Tutzing, where his 'Germanic' grave still lies today. In front of the lion statues of the Feldherrnhalle, the coffin was laid out, officers alongside and medals on display. The weather was misty and cold. Mathilde Ludendorff, her daughter and two sons and stepson, who gave the Hitler salute, stood behind the coffin, with Hitler between them. After the ceremony at the Feldherrnhalle, Ludendorff's coffin was transported from Munich to the village at the Starnbergersee on the mount of a cannon. Hitler was annoyed by this, but accepted the wish.[1424] Even after death, the general was not contradicted.

Die Woche devoted almost its entire magazine issue (5 January 1938) to the death of Ludendorff. One of the authors who wrote about it was Major Von Wedel, of the Ministry of Defence. Here the peace, at least for the outside world, was definitively signed. Von Wedel stated that Ludendorff sometimes interfered too much in politics, but that this was not motivated by personal interests, but only to intervene in the face of the complete failure of politics.[1425]

A whole series of places, streets and squares were named after Ludendorff, such as Ludendorff-Platz in Tilsit, the Ludendorff-Bank in Dresden, the Ludendorff Barracks in Fulda, the Ludendorff Bridge over the Rhine near Remagen (which turned out to be of strategic importance during the war), the Ludendorff Barracks in Stahnsdorf and the General-Ludendorff-Strasse in Magdeburg. The latter street was close to the monument for Stahlhelm, his opponent Seldte.

At Ludendorff's funeral, Blomberg confided in Hitler that he wanted to marry a bourgeois woman. He got this permission, but it would be the stepping stone to his downfall. In January 1938, he resigned. As did General Von Fritsch, who was soon sent packing in a staged scandal for alleged homosexuality. As commander of an artillery regiment, he sought death on the Polish battlefield in Warsaw 1939. General Beck resigned from the army in 1938 in the wake of the Blomberg-Fritsch affair and was murdered in the aftermath of the Von Stauffenberg attack.

Hitler now felt powerful enough to break the last resistance within 'das Militär'. The Anschluss with Austria and the occupation of Czechoslovakia were imminent, as a prelude to the Blitzkrieg against Poland, which would start the Second World War. Hitler broke his word to Ludendorff and unleashed the war, which would indeed take him far, but also meant the downfall of the Third Reich.

Chapter 23

House no. 2 on Mühlfeldstrasse

Time seems to have stood still when you drive into Tutzing, although a McDonald's along the main road says otherwise. Not far from Ludendorff's house is one of the most beautiful terraces I have ever sat on. The Starnberg Lake presents itself there like a postcard. It is warm, and in the shade of a parasol I enjoy the view that Erich Ludendorff and his wife Mathilde had every day from their backyard. You really wonder how the couple could have spent their lives so conflicted among so many lovely things. Wooden jetties and small boats dominate the waterfront. Across the lake, a larger boat pulls from side to side. The boat moves so slowly that it looks like a photograph.

House number 2 on Mühlfeldstrasse cannot be overlooked. It is unmistakably the villa of Mathilde von Kemnitz, built in 1922, which Ludendorff would later move into and which was renovated in 1932. Flower boxes hang from the balcony, but otherwise it looks quiet. At the entrance to the white wall above a large white two on a blue board the name Ludendorff is written in gothic letters. Above the doorway is a copper plaque with Ludendorff's effigy. I ring the bell, but nothing happens. Prior to my visit, I had a correspondance with members of the still existing 'Bund für Deutsche Gotterkenntnis e.V.', but rather impulsively, on a summer's day, I got into the car and drove to Tutzing. In the local bookshop, I first enquired. A woman of around fifty years of age, who lives in the area, runs the shop. She has heard of Ludendorff, but knows very little about him. There are no books about Ludendorff. Not by the 'Bund für Deutsche Gotterkenntnis e.V' either. But there is interest, and a conversation ensues. History has linked Ludendorff with Tutzing, but the love is no longer mutual.

Suddenly, the back door of house no. 2 on Mühlfeldstrasse opens. An elderly lady, Frau Barbara Korte, announces herself on the other side of the fence door, but does not show herself. I introduce myself as a historian from Holland who would like to get to know the residents, and the house of the Ludendorff couple. But distrust is heard in the voice on the other side. To this day, 'the union' is under the watchful eye of the German Verfassungschutz. I cannot get any further. Then I hold a book over the fence, with a picture of the Ludendorff couple on the terrace at the back of the house, where a relief is incorporated in the wall. This arouses curiosity. The woman wants to see the picture and opens the door. I do not want to miss the opportunity and go straight into the garden with the book under my arm. 'Oh, that's it,' she immediately says and walks ahead of me. Indeed, the relief is still clearly visible. A table with a red-and-white chequered cloth stands beneath it and flower pots flank the whole. I immediately recognise the place from the many photos that were taken here, especially around Ludendorff's 70th birthday. It was one of his last moments of glory in Tutzing, where, after being vilified, he suddenly found himself once again at the centre of attention. The garden doors were open and I was allowed to walk in.

Mühlfelstrasse 2 is like a museum where time has stood still. Large paintings (the storming of Liège) hang on the walls. The desks seem untouched. The Chinese vases of the Trebitsch-Lincoln delegation are still there and boxes full of rolls of photos, mainly of nature, are still in the house. A very old lady comes down the stairs and introduces herself as the last secretary of Mathilde Ludendorff, who died on 12 May 1966. Mathilde Ludendorff always remained loyal to her business. In 1949, she had to answer to the court and her own religious interpretation was banned in 1961. The *Ludendorffers* themselves do not speak of 'faith', because that would be too 'religiously charged', but of 'Erkenntnisphilosophie'.[1426] In 1960, the well-known magazine *Der Spiegel* opened a frontal attack on Mathilde as the 'great-grandmother of German anti-Semitism'. Nevertheless, the ban on the 'Gotterkenntnis' was lifted again in 1977. Apparently, the Verfassungschutz, which continued to count the *Ludendorffers* among the right-wing camp, had come to the conclusion that it posed little danger. Procedural errors also played a role in the prohibition. The *Ludendorffers* continued their publicity work - among others via the magazine *Mensch und Mass* - and published via the publishing company *Hohe Warte* in Pähl, which was led by Mathilde's son-in-law, Franz Karg von Bebenburg. The son-in-law died in 2003, and rests not far from Ludendorff's grave.

My meeting with Mathilde Ludendorff's secretary, who is well into her nineties, turns into a fiasco. The woman, Annemarie Kruse, is stone deaf and answers questions that I did not ask. For substantive questions, I am referred to Hans Binder, gymnasium 'Oberstudienrat' in Lindau am Bodensee, who speaks on behalf of the *Ludendorffers*, although, entirely in line with tradition, new schisms have occurred. Recently, especially the group around 'Studiengruppe

Naturalismus' (around Dr. Ingo Bading) seems to have made itself heard. The 'Bund für Gotterkenntnis (BfG)' seems to group itself around the pharmacist Gudrun Klink. The babylonian confusion of tongues in the Ludendorffs' house is somewhere symbolic for any sectarian organisation. Where principles become dogmas, reason is lost. In Kirchmöser near Brandenburg, an alternative Ludendorff archive has been built up, because the old guard keeps 'Tutzing' shut.

When I visit the cemetery in Tutzing for Ludendorff's grave, the question of dogma lingers. It is freudian to explain how Erich Ludendorff, in the second half of his life, became so fixated on the question of guilt for the defeat. The sacrifice of Germany and its fusion with Moltke and Schlieffen was simply too great to explain the 'ordinary' defeat. There had to be another explanation. With Ludendorff's death, not only one of the most important military leaders of the First World War was buried, but also the biggest advocate of the stab-in-the-back myth. The resentment that arose from this myth was fuel and humus for the coming National Socialism and Hitler. The Führer of the Third Reich was catapulted into politics by 'das Militär', and his first militia and the street fighters of the SA were trained by officers from the Black Reichswehr and the Freikorps. The blood of unsympathetic people like Liebknecht, Luxemburg and Rathenau stuck to their hands.

The National Socialists ultimately turned against Ludendorff. He represented the old days, and a new, even more vulgar nationalism had emerged. More brutal than before, and not even respecting the old-timers. Ironically, it was Hitler who ultimately shielded Ludendorff. He still had one foot in the old days and could not deny his respect for the general. It is my conviction that Hitler sought peace of mind with regard to Ludendorff, as Ludendorff did in 1937. Of course both with their own thoughts; Ludendorff the survival of his movement, the safety of his wife and followers and his historical status. Hitler wanted to be part of the historical canon, sought legitimacy and history, but also admired the unprecedented straightforward course Ludendorff uncompromisingly followed. This was the course that Hitler would take as well in December 1941, when he declared war on the USA; and the Wannsee Conference as part of the war against the Jews, without any hesitation. Until then, Hitler had been vacillating, to some degree, between his - sometimes remarkable - pragmatism and his deeply morbid convictions. Ludendorff had warned Hitler about a new war, but let him get away with it, regarding the Jews. The evil of *The Protocols of the Wise Men of Zion* had nestled in him, and would not leave him. Both the war and the Holocaust followed his death. The resentment of '14-'18 brought about a new, even more terrible war.

The grave is impressive and I have been there several times. It is at the very back of the cemetery. A large copper plate on the ground states the names Erich and Mathilde Ludendorff and the years underneath. Around the grave lie many relatives, such as Frieda Stahl (born Spiess) and Franz Bebenburg. A bust of Ludendorff with a broadsword towers above the grave. The eternal battle.

Notes:

1	This was mainly the 3rd Belgian division. Franz Uhle Wettler, *Ludendorff in seiner Zeit*, p.109/Jules Brabers/Rob Lemmens, *Luik, augustus 1914. Zoektocht naar een vergeten slag*, p.27
2	Rian van Meeteren, De slag om Luik, 4-16 augustus 1914 In: Leo Dorrestijn/Henk van der Linden/Perry Pierik/Robert Jan de Vogel (ed.), *De Grote Oorlog. Kroniek 1914-1918. Volume 32*, p.251
3	Erich Ludendorff, *Meine Kriegserinnerun-gen*, p.27
4	Ibid., p.27
5	Ibid., p.28
6	Sophie de Schaepdrijver, *De groote oorlog. Het koningkrijk België tijdens de Eerste Wereldoorlog*, p.70
7	Ibid., p.70
8	A photo of this study appears in Erich Ludendorff, *Mein militärischer Werdegang. Blätter der Erinnerung an unser stolzes Heer*
9	Manfred Nebelin, *Ludendorff. Diktator im Ersten Weltkrieg*, p. 29
10	'The autocrat'; a name Ludendorff would live up to in '14-'18
11	Ibid., p.30
12	Ludendorff, *Meine Miltärische Werdegang*, p.5
13	Nebelin, p.30, 31
14	*Meine mi-ltärische Werde-gang*, p.4, 5
15	Ibid., p.8
16	Ibid., p.12
17	Ibid., p.24, 25
18	Ibid., p.33
19	Z.R.Dittrich, *De opkomst van het moderne Duitsland*, Band I, p.5
20	Ludendorff, *Meine Militärische Werdegang*, p.39, 40
21	Ibid., p.5
22	Ibid., p.46
23	Ibid., p.48
24	Ibid., p.48-9
25	Ibid., p.50
26	Ratti, the later Pius XI

27	Ibid., p.50
28	Ibid., p.66
29	Ibid., p.55-6
30	Ibid., p.63
31	Ibid., p.66
32	Ibid., p.86-7
33	Herbert Rosinski, *Die deutsche Armee. Vom Triumph zur Niederlage*, p.83-103
34	Barry Leach, *De Duitse generale staf*, p.15
35	*Meine militärischer Werdegang*, p.87
36	E.Bircher/W.Bode., *Schlieffen. Mann und Idee*, p.51-57
37	Nebelin, p.72
38	*Meine militärischer Werdegang*, p.94
39	Ibid., p.100 and Annex 7
40	*Schlieffen. Mann und Idee*, p.59
41	*Meine Militärischer Werdegang*, p.102
42	Karl Tschuppik, *Ludendorff. Die Tragödie des Fachmanns*, p.41, 426, 427
43	Hartmuth Mahlberg, *Erich Ludendorff. Zum Gedenken an seinen 100.Geburtstag*, p.46, 47
44	Eberthard Jäckel, *Das Deutsche Jahrhundert. Eine historische Bilanz (The German Century)*, p.79, 80
45	Graf zu Reventlow, *Der Weg zum neuen Deutschland*, p.338, 347, 350, 365, 378/Emil Ludwig, *Wilhelm II*
46	Karl Tschuppik, *Ludendorff, the Tragödie des Fachmanns*, p.44
47	*Meine militärischer Werdegang*, p.101
48	*Ludendorff, Die Tragödie des Fachmanns*, p.11
49	Erich Ludendorff, *Meine Kriegserinnerungen*, p.31
50	*Marine Cannon Battery* No. 3 'Erdmann-Wesener'
51	*Meine Kriegserinnerungen*, p.31 For a detailed account of the effects of heavy artillery on the fortifications see: Clayton Donnell, *Breaking the Fortress Line 1914* and the *Denkschrift über Ergebnisse der Beschiessung der Festungen Lüttich, Namur, Antwerpen und Maubeuge, sowie des Forts Manonviller im Jahre 1914*, Brussels 1915, compiled by the General des Ingenieurskorps beim General-Gouvernement in Belgien. (germandocsinrussia.com 16347)
52	'Luftkreuzer' No. 6
53	*Der Völkerkrieg* p. 88/Sophie de Schaepdrijver, *De groote oorlog*, p. 70/Brabers/Lemmens, *Liège August 1914*, p.117
54	*Der Völkerkrieg*, p.90
55	H.P.Geerke/G.A.Brands, *The War*, p.176, 177
56	Ibid., p.88
57	*Der Völkerkrieg*, p.89
58	Der Völkerkrieg, p.89
59	John Horne/Alan Kramer, *Deutsche Kriegsgreuel 1914. Die umstrittene Wahrheit*, p.636-7
60	Bernhard Wien, *Weichensteller und Totengräber. Ludendorff, Von Hindenburg und Hitler 1914-1937*, p.28
61	*Kriegserinnerungen*, p.31
62	*Soldatenschicksale des 20.Jahrhunderts als Geschichtsquelle. Band I* (hg.) Dermot Bradley: *Hermann Balck, General der Panzergruppe a.D. Ordnung im Chaos. Erinnerungen*

1893-1948, p.16-7
63   *Kriegserinnerungen*, p.32, *Schlachten des Weltkrieges Band 19 Tannenberg*, p.18-9
64   *Kriegserinnerungen*, p.36
65   Wolf J.Bütow, *Hindenburg, Heerführer und Ersatzkaiser* p.67-84/Hindenburg, *Aus meinem Leben*, p.74
66   John W.Wheeler-Bennett, *Der Hölzerne Titan, Paul von Hindenburg*, p.34
67   Bütow, p.83-4
68   Here the German edition used: J.W.Wheerler-Bennett, *Der Hölzerne Titan, Paul von Hindenburg*, p.33
69   Barbara W.Tuchman, *The Guns of August. August 1914*, p.304-5
70   Max Hoffmann, *Der Krieg der versäumten Gelegenheiten*, p.24
71   Von Francois, *Hindenburgs Sieg bei Tannenberg*, p.71
72   Tuchman, p.307, for an overview of Von Francois's forces see *Reichsarchiv* band 19, p.258-9
73   Tuchman, p.307
74   Hoffmann, p.26
75   Ibid., p.26
76   Theo Schwarzmüller, *Zwischen Kaiser und 'Führer'. Generalfeldmarschall August von Mackensen. Eine politische Biographie*, p.92, 93
77   Hoffmann, p.27
78   The Reichsarchiv band 19 comes to 9,000 man losses, p.95-6, which is confirmed by Mackensen-biographer Schwarzmüller, p.106. Keegan mentions a number of 8,000 lost lives, p.159, Barbara W. Tuchman, Venohr as well as Ludendorff and Hindenburg did not mention loss figures around Gumbinnen
79   Tuchman, p.310
80   Schwarzmüller, p.106
81   Reichsarchiv, p.17
82   Hoffmannn, p.22
83   Ibid., p.28
84   Ibid., p.26, 27
85   Ibid., p.34
86   Ibid., p.34
87   Tuchman, p.303
88   Venohr, p.27, The Reichsarchiv speaks of 1428 Russian artillery pieces, p.263
89   Reichsarchiv, p.95, 96
90   Ibid., p.33
91   Ibid., p.34
92   Ibid., p.35, 36
93   Ibid., p. 38, 39
94   Ibid., p.42, 43
95   Ibid., p.45
96   Ibid., p.45
97   Ibid., p.46
98   Ibid., p. 48
99   For overview I. Army Corps see Reichsarchiv p.259
100 Venohr, *Ludendorff. Legende und Wirklichkeit* p.36
101 Ibid., p.36
102 H. Rewaldt, *Tannenberg*, p.42

103	Venohr p.36, 37
104	Reichsarchiv p.50-53
105	Venohr, p.37
106	Ibid., p.37
107	Reichsarchiv, p.53
108	Ibid., p.58
109	Ibid., p. 64
110	Ibid., p.59, 60
111	Ibid., p. 60
112	Ibid., p.69
113	Ibid., p. 77
114	Ibid., p.78
115	Ibid., p.83
116	Ibid., p.97
117	Ibid., p. 114
118	Ibid., p.117
119	Albert Benary, *Die Schlacht bei Tannenberg*, p.51, 52
120	Ibid., p.134
121	Ibid., p.56
122	Reichsarchiv, p.141-144
123	Ibid., p.183
124	Ibid., p.182
125	Ibid., p.182
126	Ibid., p.188
127	Ibid., p.188
128	Ibid., p.196, 198
129	Ibid., p.202
130	Ibid., p.204
131	Ibid., p.205
132	Ibid., p.217, 218
133	Ibid., p.205
134	Ibid., p.211-213
135	Hoffmann, p.35, 40
136	Benary, p.83
137	Ibid., p.86, 87
138	Von François, *Hindenburgs Sieg bei Tannenberg*, p.59
139	Ibid., p.60, 61
140	Reichsarchiv, p.240-1, Tuchman speaks of between 300 and 500 artillery pieces, p.343, Baer speaks in *Der Völkerkrieg* of 93,000 prisoners of war and at least 500 artillery pieces, as well as 150,000 killed Russian soldiers. These last figures are certainly an overestimate, Baer, zweiter Band p.53. Rewaldt holds 92.000 men as prisoners of war and 50.000 Russian killed, p.83
141	Reichsarchiv, p.241
142	Ibid., p.242
143	Reichsarchiv, p.243
144	Von Francois, *Hindenburgs Sieg bei Tannenberg. Das Cannae des Weltkrieges in Bild und Wort*, p.3, more modern historical works still speak of a Cannae as well, see for example Michael Freund, *Deutsche Geschichte von den Anfangen bis zur Gegenwart*, p.620.

145	Tuchman, p.344
146	Von Francois, title page
147	Benary, p. 94
148	Karl-Heinz Janssen, *Tannenberg-ein deutsches Verhängnis* (*Die Zeit* no.39 16 September 1977 p.60)
149	H. Rewaldt, p.84, 85
150	Tuchman p.344
151	Karl-Heinz Janssen, p.60
152	Karl-Heinz Janssen, p.60
153	Franz Uhle-Wettler, p.140
154	Tschuppik, p.32
155	Tschuppik p.27, 28
156	Robert Asprey, *The German High Command at War: Hindenburg and Ludendorff Conduct World War I*. p.91
157	Emil Ludwig, *Hindenburg, Legende und Wirklichkeit*, p.68
158	Venohr, p.44-46
159	Wheeler-Bennett, p.46
160	Rudolf van Werth, *Tannenberg. Wie Hindenburg die Russen schlug*, p.272, 273
161	Tuchman p.342, 343/Joachim von Kuerenberg, *Russlands Weg nach Tannenberg* p.242-244/Wheeler-Bennet p.44
162	Tuchman, p.345
163	Wheeler-Bennett, p.39, 40
164	Von Kuerenberg, p.90
165	Ibid., p.91
166	Ibid., p.91
167	Tuchman, p.302
168	Reichsarchiv, p.237
169	Wheeler-Bennett, p.35
170	Hoffmann, p.33
171	Goodspeed, p.88-9
172	Norman Stone, *The Eastern Front 1914-1917*
173	S.D. Sasonoff, *Sechs schwere Jahre*, p. 273
174	Stone, p.17-21
175	Tuchman, p.344
176	Ludendorff, *Kriegserinnerungen*, p.44
177	Hindenburg, p.90-1
178	Alexander Watson, *Ring of Steel. Germany and Austria-Hungary at War 1914-1918*, p.168-171
179	Hindenburg, p.91
180	Ludendorff, *Kriegserinnerungen*, p.45
181	Ibid., p.45
182	Ibid., p.45-47
183	Ibid., p.47, 48
184	Venohr, p.54, 55
185	Von Kuerenberg, p.251, 252
186	Venohr, p.55
187	Hoffmann, p.48
188	Asprey, p.88

189	Venohr, p.59
190	Kriegserinnerungen, p.49, Venohr, p.59
191	Max Hoffmann, p.46
192	*Kriegserinnerungen*, p.49
193	Ibid., p.50
194	Ludendorff, *Kriegserinnerungen*, p.50, 51
195	Wolfgang Foerster, *Mackensen, Briefe und Aufzeichnungen*, p.66
196	Hindenburg, p.97
197	Baer, *zweiter Band* p.58, Stone, p.68, Goodspeed, p.101, Ludendorff, p.51. The press of those days reported about the losses around the battle of the Masurian Lakes several times, but here it relied on press reports by Von Stein (Koblenz) and Von Hindenburg. The *Frankfurter Zeitung*, for example, reported 10,000 Russian prisoners of war on 12 September 1914 and corrected this to 20 or 30,000 on 13 September. The own losses were said to be 'comparatively small'. In: *Der Grosse Krieg. Eine Chronik von Tag zu Tag. Urkunden, Depeschen und Berichte der Frankfurter Zeitung* (1914). Michael Freund thinks that Von Rennenkampf had 40.000 dead to mourn. *Deutsche Geschichte, von den Anfängen bis zur Gegenwart*, p.620
198	Goodspeed, p.101
199	Stone, p.69
200	Foerster, p.67
201	Franz Uhle-Wettler, p.148
202	Ludendorff, *Kriegserinnerungen*, p.51
203	John Keegan, *The First World War*, p.163
204	*Der Völkerkrieg*, zweiter Band, p.45
205	Gerhard Schulze-Pfaelzer, *Hindenburg. Drie Zeitalter deutscher Nation*, p.100
206	*Kriegserinnerungen*, p.53
207	Manfried Rauchensteiner, *Der Tod des Doppeladlers. Österreich-Ungarn und der Erste Weltkrieg*, p.104
208	Ibid., p.105
209	Ibid., p.104
210	Goodspeed, p.102
211	Rauchensteiner, p.135
212	Ibid., p.134
213	Ibid., p.136
214	Goodspeed, p.103
215	Ibid., p.103
216	Ibid., p.103
217	Ibid., p.104
218	Goodspeed, p.105, Rauchensteiner, p.163, Hoffmann p.53
219	Goodspeed, p.105, Hoffmann, p.53
220	Goodspeed, p.105
221	Goodspeed, p.105
222	Ibid., p.224, 225
223	Rauchensteiner, p.163, C.H.Baer, p.225
224	Hoffmann, p.53
225	Goodspeed, p.106
226	Ibid., p.107
227	C.H. Baer, p.226-229

228	Goodspeed, p.107, 108, Hoffmann, p.55
229	Hoffmann, p.55
230	Ibid., p.57
231	C.H. Baer, p.215-217
232	Ibid., p.217, 218
233	Ludendorff, p.68
234	Schwarzmüller, p.97
235	*Kriegserinnerungen*, p.69
236	Ibid., p.69
237	Rauchensteiner, p.166
238	Ibid., p.168
239	Hoffmann, p.63
240	Venohr, p.90
241	Schwarzmüller. p.97
242	Erich von Falkenhayn, *Die Oberste Heeresleitung 1914-1916*
243	Ibid., p.9
244	Ibid., p.23
245	Ibid., p.16
246	Venohr, p.88, 89
247	*Kriegserinnerungen*, p.74
248	Ibid., p.75
249	Ibid., p. 76
250	Ibid., p.78
251	Venohr, p.97
252	Hoffmann, p.76
253	Foerster., p.90
254	Ibid., p.90, 91
255	Ibid., p.96
256	*Kriegserinnerungen*, p.83
257	Foerster., p.108
258	Ibid., p.108
259	Hoffmann, p.81
260	Foerster., p. 106-108
261	Paul Lindenberg (hg.), *Hindenburg Denkmal für das Deutsche Volk,* p.183
262	Generalstabes des Feldheeres (hg.), Der grosse Krieg in Einzeldarstellungen. Heft 20 *Die Winterschlacht in Masuren*. Unter Benützung amtlichen Materials bearbeitet von Redern, Hauptmann der Reserve damals Kompagnie-Führer im Infanterie-Regiment Graf Barfuss (4.Westfäl.) Nr.17, p.10
263	Ibid., p.16-7
264	Ibid., p.18, 19
265	Ibid., p. 18
266	Ibid., p.23
267	Ibid., p.24-5
268	Winter Battle p.33/ *Hindenburg Denkmal für das Deutsche Volk* p. 51
269	Winter Battle, p.35-37
270	Ibid., p.41
271	Ibid., p. 44
272	Goodspeed mentions the number 200, p.128

273	Winter Battle p. 43-51/Hindenburg Memorial, p.210
274	Venohr, p.111
275	Venohr, p.111
276	Vehnor, p.111
277	Tschuppik, p.65
278	Venohr, p.111
279	Goodspeed, p.127
280	Perry Pierik, *De pendel des Doods*. Five times rokade. 'Oberost' and the war on the Eastern Front between August 1914 and February 1915. In: Henk van der Linden/ Perry Pierik, *Het dramatische jaar 1914*.
281	Goodspeed, p.124, 125
282	Venohr, p.108
283	Bütow, p.105
284	Ibid., p.104
285	Uhle-Wetter, p.174
286	Foerster., p.138
287	Foerster., p.134-137
288	Uhle-Wetttler, p.180
289	Venohr, p.124-126
290	Foerster, p.141, 142
291	Schwarzmüller, p.107
292	Reichsarchiv Gorlice, p.68
293	Ibid., p.42, 44, 196, 197
294	Asprey, p.183-185
295	Goodspeed, p.133
296	Reichsarchiv Gorlice, p.200-202
297	Schwarzmüller, p.108
298	Schwarzmüller, p.108, 109
299	Hoffmann, p.105
300	Max Hoffmann, p.108
301	Schwarzmüller
302	Hoffmann, p.112
303	Uhle-Wettler, p.182
304	Max Hoffmann, p.114
305	Uhle-Wettler, p.180
306	Goodspeed, p.135, Ludendorff mentions the figure of 80,000 in his memoirs, p.119
307	Goodspeed, p.136
308	*Kriegserinnerungen,* p.121
309	Goodspeed, p.136
310	Baer, p.203, 204
311	Schwarzmüller, p.109
312	Uhle-Wettler, p.179
313	Hans Frentz, *Hindenburg und Ludendorff,* p.123, 124
314	Uhle-Wettler, p.188
315	Ibid., p.188
316	Frentz, p.125, 126
317	Generaloberst von Einem, *Erinnerungen eines Soldaten 1853-1933,* p.185, 186
318	Dr. med.et Phil.gerh.Venzmer.,Körpergestalt und Seelenanlage. Ein Ueberblick über

die biologische Verwandschaft zwischen Körperreform und Wesenskern des Menschen.

319 Ernst Sikorski, *Der Feldherr als Organisator*, In: *Das Vermächtnis des Feldherrn Erich Ludendorff*
320 Goodspeed, p.138
321 Ibid., p.139
322 *Der Feldherr als Organisator*, p.772-775
323 *Der grosse Krieg*, p.4966, 4968
324 Detlef Brennecke, *Sven Hedin*. Rorobildmonographien p.82, 83
325 Frentz, p.132
326 Sikorski, p.774
327 Jonas Kreppel, *Der Weltkrieg und die Judenfrage*, p.16
328 W.Bruce Lincoln, In *War's dark Shadow. The Russians before the Great War*, p.396, 397
329 Goodspeed, p.138
330 *Kriegserinnerungen*, p.161
331 Stazhas, p.13
332 Ibid., p.21
333 Ibid., p.15
334 Ibid., p.14
335 Goodspeed, p.144
336 *Kriegserinnerungen*, p.164
337 Norman Stone, p.212
338 Geoffrey Jukes, Carpathian Disaster. *Death of an Army*, p.120
339 Jukes, p.118
340 Rauchensteiner, p.348, 349
341 Rauchensteiner, p.356, Asprey uses even higher loss figures
342 Asprey, p.237-239
343 *Veltzés Internationaler Armee Almanach*, p.314
344 *Meine Kriegserinneringen*, p.183
345 *Der grosse Krieg*, p.5018, 5019
346 Ibid., p.5018
347 Nebelin, p.221
348 Goodspeed, p.151
349 Pyta, p.225
350 Goodspeed, p.151
351 Wolfram Pyta, p.224
352 Tschuppik p.95
353 Ibid., p.97
354 Ibid., p.97
355 Ibid., p.98
356 Ibid., p.99
357 Herzfeld, p.101
358 *Meine Kriegserinneringen*, p.191
359 Herzfeld, p.102
360 *Meine Kriegserinneringen*, p.191
361 Nebelin, p.227
362 Goodspeed, p.166. Von Lossberg was attached to the 1st German army.
363 Ibid., p.166

364	Venohr, p.162
365	Ibid., Venohr, p.165
366	Uhle-Wettler, p.213
367	Goodspeed, p.168
368	Uhle-Wettler, p.220, 221
369	Rainer Karlsch/Raymond G.Stokes, *Faktor Oel. Die Mineralwirtschaft in Deutschland 1859-1974*, p.111
370	Erwin Rommel, *Infanterie greift an*, p.131
371	Nebelin, p.221
372	See for example the memoir of Hermann Balck, *Ordnung im Chaos*, p.76
373	Bütow, p.129
374	Schwarzmüller, p.139
375	Stone, p.276, 277/Rauchensteiner, p.416
376	Schwarzmüller, p.139
377	Rommel fought against Romania within the framework of the 11th Bavarian division, which had been brought in from the Vosges. He fought at the Vulkan and Skurduk Pass, among other places. *Infanterie greifft an*, p.119, 132, 138
378	Stone, p.280
379	Ibid., p.280
380	Madol, H.R., *Ferdinand von Bulgarien. Der Traum von Byzanz*, p.224, 225
381	Anthony Bruce, *An illustrated Companion to the First World War*, p.180-181
382	JH. Buitenhuis, *Artillerie en gas. The artillerie-inzet tijdens de gevechten tussen april en december 1916 en de grote gasaanval van de Duitsers op fort Souville in juni 1916* in: H.Andriessen/Martin Ros/Perry Pierik, *De Grote Oorlog. Kroniek 114-1918 part 1*, p.62-64
383	Bruce, p.181
384	Hoffmann
385	Heinz Guderian, *Achtung Panzer! The Development of Armoured Forces their Tactics and operational Potential*, p.57-80
386	Chris Ellis/Peter Chamberlain, *The Great Tanks*, p.21/Bruce p.372
387	Oppelland, p.63
388	For the remarkable career of Albert Ballin see: Leo Sievers, *Der Mann, der den Krieg verhindern wollte*. In: *Juden in Deutschland (15)* in *Stern*
389	Walter Hubatsch, p.122
390	Bruce, p.367, 368
391	Erich Czech-Jochberg, Die Verantwortlichen im Weltkrieg, p.95
392	Ibid., p.97
393	Von Einem, p.157-161
394	Oppelland, p.95
395	Fritz Fischer, *Theobald von Bethmann Hollweg, der rätselhafte Kanzler*, in: Fritz Fischer, *Hitler war kein Betriebsunfall*, p.136
396	Ibid., p.144
397	Ibid., p.147
398	Eberhard von Vietsch was the first to call him that.
399	John Lee., *The Warlords. Hindenburg and Ludendorff*, p.119
400	Prinz Max von Baden, *Erinnerungen und Dokumente*, p.53
401	Ferguson p.247-250/ Aris Gaaff, *Financiering van de Eerste Wereldoorlog. Vier jaar vechten op krediet*.

402 *Ludendorffs Monopole*, p.54
403 Ibid., p.44
404 Ibid., p.16
405 Ibid., p.51
406 Ferguson, p.253
407 Ferdinand Otto Miksche, *Vom Kriegsbild*, p.116-117
408 Aris Gaaff, p.116, 117
409 Jaap Hofman, *De oorlog op het thuisfront*, in: Hans Andriessen, Martin Ros, Perry Pierik (ed.), *De Grote Oorlog, kroniek 1914-1918*, p.368
410 *Ludendorff's Monopole*, p.41
411 Kessler, p.254
412 He boasted in a Swiss newspaper that he was one of the 300 most important men in the world
413 Kessler, p.255
414 *Ludendorff's Monopole*, p.41, 42
415 Franz Uhle-Wettler, p.274
416 Ibid., p.275
417 The first case is often read in the literature, a.o. Uhle-Wettler, p.275, the mention of the Jews, in Hellmüth Weber p.50, is much more unknown
418 Liddell Hart, *History of the First World War*, p.400, 401
419 Maarten van Rossem, *De Verenigde Staten in de twintigste eeuw*, p.43
420 *Meine Kriegserinnerungen 1914-1918*, p.363, 364
421 Ibid., p.320, 321
422 Ibid., p.306, 307
423 Robin Neillands, *The Great War Generals on the Western Front 1914-1918*
424 *Meine Kriegserinnerungen*, p.394-396
425 *Meine Kriegserinnerungen*, p.394, 395/ Gerhard Hirschfeld/Gerd Krumreich/Irina Renz, *Enzyklopädie Erster Weltkrieg*, p.403, 404
426 For the role of General Cardona see Miro Simčič, *Die Schlachten am Isonzo. 888 Tage Krieg im Karst in Fotos, Karten und Berichten*.
427 *Meine Kriegserinnerungen*, p.400/ Simčič, p.204
428 Ibid., p.327
429 Ibid., p.327
430 Wien, p.95
431 Elisabeth Heresch, *Geheimakte Parvus. Die gekaufte Revolution*, p.65/Introduction to Z.A.B.Zeman (ed.), *Germany and the Revolution in Russia 1915-1918. Documents from the Archives of the German Foreign Ministry*.
432 Gerhard Schiesser/Jochen Trauptmann, *Russian Roulette. Das deutsche Geld und die Oktoberrevolution*, p.63
433 Heresch, p.159-161
434 Heresch, p.228, 229/The Canadian historian D.J.Goodspeed simply stated that Parvus was in 'German service'. Goodspeed, p.169-171
435 In practice, one spoke of the 'Diktatur Ludendorff'.
436 *Meine Kriegserinnerungen*, p.287, 288
437 Ibid., p.289-296
438 Heresch, p.330/Maximilian Terhalle, *Otto Schmidt (1888-1971) Gegner Hitlers und Intimus Hugenbergs*, p.28
439 Heresch, p.331

440 John W. Wheeler-Bennett, *Brest-Litowsk, The Forgotten Peace,* March 1918. p.37, Gerhard Schiesser/Jochen Trauptmann, p.60. Historian Werner Maser has pointed out the role of Friedrich Ebert with regard to Parvus' influence; Werner Maser, *Hindenburg, eine politische Biographie,* p.150, 151

441 Nebelin, p.311; Historian Helen Rappaport emphasised in her book *Conspirator* that Ludendorff was responsible for the transport, p. 285

442 Nebelin, p.311

443 Nebelin, p.311

444 Schiesser/Trauptmann, p.136,137/Wien called Ludendorff 'no innocent bystander', p.96

445 Schiesser/Trauptmann p.134-137, 141, Wheeler-Bennett, p.36, 37; Robert Service, *Spies & Commissars. Bolshevik Russia and the West,* chapter 1; Goodspeed, p.170; Ivanov is cited in Michael Pearson, *The Sealed Train,* p.81

446 Wolfram Pyta, Hindenburg. *Herrschaft zwischen Hohenzollern und Hitler*

447 Uhle-Wettler, p.30

448 Wolfgang Venohr, *Ludendorff, Legende und Wirklichkeit,* Martin Lüders, *Der Soldat und das Reich, Paul von Hindenburg* (1961); William J. Astore/Dennis E, Showalter, *Hindenburg, Icon of German Militarism;* Wolfgang Ruge, *Hindenburg;* Gerhard Schultze Pfaelzer, *Hindenburg,* (Leipzig 1930); Gerhard Hirschfeld/Gerd Krumeich/Irina Renz, *Enzyklopädie Erster Weltkrieg,* p.676/ Werner Hahlweg, *Lenins Rückkehr nach Russland 1917* In: *Studien zur Geschichte Osteuropas,* p.3

449 For the 'battle plan' Parvus, see appendix book Elisabeth Heresch. For German psychological warfare at the front see Alexander Watson, *Ring of Steel* p.463. The role of Parvus is left relatively small in the book by Will Brownell and Denis Drace-Brownell, *The First Nazi. Erich Ludendorff The Man who made Hitler possible.* According to the authors, Parvus was approached by the Germans, but it was the other way round.

450 Helmut Altrichter, *Russia 1917. Ein Land auf der Suche nach sich selbst.*

451 John W. Wheeler-Bennet, p.16

452 Robert V. Daniels, *A Documentary History of Communism.* Volume 2. *Communism and the World,* p.24/ Ruth Fischer, *Stalin and German Communism. A Study in the Origins of the State Party,* chapter 2

453 Venohr, p.230

454 Venhor, p.241, Hirschfeld/Krumeich/Renz, p.552

455 Venohr, chapter *Kritik der Führung*

456 Goodspeed, p.193, 194

457 Uhle-Wettler, p.325

458 Martin Middlebrook, *The Kaiser's Battle,* p.21

459 Middlebrook, p.21

460 Hoffmann, p.205

461 Parkinson, *Tormented Warrior,* p.146, 147

462 Ibid., p.47

463 Hoffmann p.222

464 Ludendorff, *Kriegführung und Politik,* p.208

465 Goodspeed, p.195

466 Watson, p.518

467 Keegan, p.424

468 Ibid., p.424, 425

469 Aspery, p.383

470	Ibid., p.386
471	Keegan, p.429
472	Ibid., p.434, 435/Venohr, p.347
473	Ibid., 435
474	*Meine Kriegserinnerungen*, p. 482
475	Werner Maser, Hindenburg, p.167
476	These were only the uninjured prisoners of war according to Ludendorff's memoirs, p.483, Hindenburg-biographer Werner Maser also uses the figure of 90,000
477	Ludendorff, *Meine Kriegserinnerungen*, p.488
478	Liddell Hart, p.514
479	Ibid., p.514
480	*Meine Kriegserinnerungen*, p.489
481	Ibid., p.490
482	Ibid., p.491-493
483	Ibid., p.493
484	Ibid., p.493
485	Venohr, p.350, 351
486	Venohr, p.350, 351/Goodspeed, p.200
487	Goodspeed, p.203
488	*Meine Kriegserinnerungen*, p.514-518
489	Gerhard Foerster/Nikolaus Paulus, *Abriss der Geschichte der Panzerwaffe*, p.44
490	For production numbers see Gerhard Foerster/Nikolaus Paulus, *Abriss der Geschichte der Panzer Waffe*. The British planned to produce a total of 6684 heavy tanks by mid-1919, some of which were produced in France at the Chateauvoux factory near Paris. The French, with American support, planned production of about 8 to 10,000 tanks.
491	Goodspeed, p.204
492	Keegan, p.439
493	Goodspeed, p.203
494	Goodspeed, p.204
495	Goodspeed, p.204
496	Venohr, p.351
497	Venohr, p.351
498	Reichsarchiv, *Die Katastrofe des 8.August 1918*, p.12
499	Foerster/Paulus, p.46
500	Reichsarchiv, *Die Katastrofe des 8.August 1918*, p.13
501	Ibid., p.27
502	Ibid., p.26
503S	F. Wise, *1918 Defining Victory. The Black day of the german Army. Australians and Canadians at Amiens, August 1918*
504	see map Reichsarchiv, the 24th division belonged to the German 18th army, which operated south of the 2nd army
505	Reichsarchiv, p.79
506	Ibid., p.79
507	Reichsarchiv p.197/For the losses of the Entente see: *1918: Defining Victory* (various contributions seminar)
508	Goodspeed, p.205
509	Ibid., p.205
510	Ibid., Goodspeed, p.205

511 Keegan. The American corps were the I. and IV. corps p.440,441
512 Hellmut Andics, *Der Untergang der Donau-Monarchie. Oesterreich-Ungarn von der Jahrhundertwende bis zum November 1918* p.203
513 Ibid., p.263, 264
514 Ibid., p.264, 265
515 Ibid., p.268
516 Hans Roger Madol, *Ferdinand von Bulgarien*, p.228,229
517 Andics, p.292
518 Goodspeed, p.209
519 Wolfgang Foerster, *Der Feldherr Ludendorff im Ungelueck. Eine Studie ber seine seelische Haltung in der Endphase des Ersten Weltkrieges.*
520 Parkinson, *Tormented Warrior*, p.176
521 Ibid., p.177-8
522 Ibid., p.178
523 Martin Kitchen, p.255-6
524 Ibid, p.256
525 Freund, *Deutsche Geschichte von den Anfaengen bis zur Gegenwart*, p.659
526 Hans Andriessen, *De ineenstorting van het Duitse Keizerrijk* in: Hans Andriessen/ Martin Ros/ Perry Pierik (ed.), *De Grote Oorlog, Kroniek 1914-1918. Essays over de Eerste Wereld Oorlog*, p.25
527 Ibid., p.27
528 Ibid., p.27
529 Manfred Weissbecker, *Macht und Ohnmacht der Weimarer Republik*, p.11
530 Parkinson, p.181
531 Ibid., p.181, 182
532 Ibid., p.182
533 Ibid., p.182
534 Wien, *Weichensteller und Totengräber*, p.81
535 Ibid., p.183
536 Wolfgang Ruge, *Weimar Republik auf Zeit. Kleine Bibliothek nr.179*. This book was originally published in the GDR
537 Werner Maser, *Der Sturm auf die Republik. Frühgeschichte der NSDAP*
538 Hennig Köhler, *Beziehungen des französischen Geheimdienstes zu deutschen Linksradikalen 1917/1918* in: *Veröffentlichungen der historischen Kommission zu Berlin band 37.* Dietrich Kurze (hg.), *Aus Theorie und Praxis der Geschichtswissenschaft. Festschrift für Hans Herzfeld zum 80. Geburtstag*
539 Wolfgang Ruge, p.22
540 Ibid
541 Rubriek: *De Oorlog*, In: The NRC 01.11.1918; the article under the headline *Ludendorff* was dated 27 October
542 Algemeen Overzicht De Oorlog In: *Het Centrum* 28.10.1918
543 De oorlog, Ludendorff neemt ontslag, In: *Het Volk* 28.10.1918
544 Het militarisme verslagen, In: *Het Volk* 07.11.1918
545 De Franse pers over het aftreden van Ludendorff, In: NRC 29.10.1918
546 Breucker p.78, 79
547 Ibid., p.78, 79
548 Sometimes you see other spellings, such as Oolsen. We stick to Breucker's spelling, because he was the closest to the case.

549   *Als ich Ludendorffs Frau war*, p.208-210/Uhle-Wettler, p.377-8
550   *Meine Kriegserinnerungen*, p.617
551   Ibid., p.617
552   Ibid., p.617
553   Ibid., p.619
554   Ibid., p.621
555   Margarethe Ludendorff, p.211-2
556   Ibid., p.216
557   Ibid., p.217
558   Ibid., p.220
559   Ibid., p.240
560   Uhle Wettler, p.378
561   Ibid., p.376-7
562   *Meine Kriegserinnerungen*, p.621-2
563   Breucker, p.165, Letter from 1918 (December; date unknown)
564   Uhle-Wettler, p.379, 380
565   Ibid., p.381
566   Breucker, p.80-1
567   Gert von Klass, *Hugo Stinnes*, p.11, 12,67, 176-179, 185, 189
568   Salomon, *Das Buch vom deutschen Freikorpskämpfer*, p.129
569   Ibid., p.136-7
570   Ibid., p.137-142
571   Ludendorff, Lebenserinnerungen, part 1919-1935, p.47
572   Ibid., p.48
573   Herbert Rosinski, *Die deutsche Armee*, p.153
574   Volkmann, *Revolution über Deutschland*, p.322, 323
575   For a brief history see Dr.Herbert Michaels/Dr.Ernst Schraepler (hg)., *Ursachen und Folgen vom deutschen Zusammenbruch 1918-1945 bis zur staatlichen Neuordnung Deutschlands in der Gegenwart. Eine Urkunden und Dokumentensammlung zur Zeitgeschichte*. Dritter Band, p.152, 153.
576   Elmar Scheuren/Christoph Trapp, *Separatistsen im Siebengebirge. Die Rheinische Republik des Jahres 1923 und die 'Schlacht' bei Aegidienberg Königswinter*: Siebengebirgsmuseum der Stadt Königswinter. See also: Perry Pierik, *Het geluid van vreemde laarzen. Het Rheinland in roerige dagen tussen de nederlaag van 1918 en de Vrede van Versailles* (unpublished: archive author)/Die *Deutschen in Frankreich 1987-1873-Die Franzosen in Deutschland, 1918-? Nach englischen Augenzeugen* in: *Süddeutsche Monatshefte April 1922*. Important völkische 'protests' against the separatist politics were published by Nationalverlag in Berlin, including the titles: F.Walther Ilges, *Die geplante Aufteilung Deutschland, Hochverrat von Zentrum und Bayerischer Volkspartei 1918-1923*, Berlin: Walter Bacmeisters Nationalverlag 1933 and F.Walther Ilges and Dr.Hermann Schmid, *Hochverrat des Zentrums am Rhein. Neue Urkunden über die wahren Führer der Separatisten*.
577   An interesting American analysis of the French action can be found in Henry T. Allen, *Mein Rheinland Tagebuch*
578   Breucker, p.93
579   Ibid., p.94
580   Ibid., p.94, 95
581   Ibid., p.172

582	On the political role of the 'Germanenbund' see Perry Pierik (ed.) *Thule en het Derde Rijk. De genesis van nationaal-socialisme.*
583	Hans Herzfeld, *Die Weimarer Republik*, p.54
584	Maser, p.188/For Ludendorff's role in the stab-in-the-back myth see Will Brownell/ Denise Drace-Brownell, *The First Nazi. Erich Ludendorff, The Man who made Hitler possible*, p.182
585	Herzfeld, p.50-97, recently there was a reprint of the book *The Stab in the back*, published in 1988, in which the different scenarios around the emergence of the myth are examined: George S.Vascik/Mark R.Sadler (ed.), *The Stab in the Back Myth and the Fall of the Weimar Republic. A History in Documents and Visual Sources.*
586	Ludwig, *Hindenburg. Legende und Wirklichkeit*, p.196
587	Ibid., p.197
588	Nigel J. Ashton/ Duco Hellema, *Hanging the Kaiser: Anglo-Dutch Relations and the Fate of Wilhelm II 1918-20* in: *Diplomacy & Statecraft vol 11 No.2 July 2000*
589	Gerd Frankel, *Die Leipziger Prozesse*, p.41
590	Hankel, p.42
591	Ibid., p.44-5
592	Ibid., p.45
593	Ibid., p.42-3
594	Ibid., p.46
595	Werner Maser, *Friedrich Ebert, Der erste deutsche Reichspräsident*, p.276
596	Günther Bardey, *Die Brigade Ehrhardt. Vom Kampf der 2.Marine-Brigade ' Wilhelmshaven' 1919-1921, Teil I und Teil II*, p.364-366
597	Breucker, p.94
598	Ibid., p.97
599	Dieter Fricke/Manfred Weissbecker/Siegfried Schmidt (et al.). (Hg.), *Geschichte der bürgerlichen und kleinbürgerlichen Parteien und Verbände. Lexikon zur Parteiengeschichte Band 3*, p.467-8
600	Christian Saehrendt, *Der Stellungskrieg der Denkmäler. Kriegerdenkmäler im Berlin der Zwischenkriegszeit 1919-1939*
601	*Meine Lebenserinnerungen*, p.95
602	Ibid., p.94
603	Ibid., p.94
604	Heinz Höhne, *Admiraal Wilhelm Canaris, Nieuwe visie op de loopbaan het hoofd van het Duitse Abwehr. Het einde van een verzetsmythe*, p.48
605	*Meine Lebenserinnerungen*, p.107
606	Ibid., p.107
607	Ibid., p.107
608	Charles Wighton, *Adenauer. Democratisch Dictator. Een kritische biografie* p.27/Peter Berglag, *Konrad Adenauer. Konkursverwalter oder Erneuerer der Nation.*
609	Gordon A.Craig, *Founding Father* in: *New York Review of Books November 1 2001*, p.19
610	Friedrich-Karl von Plehwe, p.139
611	*Meine Lebenserinnerungen*, p.107
612	Kees M. Paling. *Galgemaal voor Pruisen. De mestvaalt van de geschiedenis. Het opmerkelijke levensverhaal van Paul von Lettow-Vorbeck, Pruisisch generaal, guerrillero en putchist*, p.124
613	*Meine Lebenserinnerungen*, p.108
614	*Als ich Ludendorff's Frau war*, p.274, 275

615 Hohhne, p.55
616 Hans-Ulrich Thamer, Verführung und Gewalt. Germany 1933-1945. In: *Die Deutsche und Ihre Nation*, p.214. The Freikorps claimed that they had taken an oath on the flag, but that they had not been told which flag. See: Hannsjoachim W. Koch, *Der deutsche Bürgerkrieg. Eine Geschichte der deutschen und österreichischen Freikorps 1918-1923*, p. 58,59
617 Ibid., p.214
618 Ibid., p.214
619 Friedrich-Karl von Plehwe, *Reichskanzler Kurt von Schleicher. Weimars letzte Chance gegen Hitler*, p.43, 44
620 Fritz Ernst, *Aus dem Nachlass des Generals Walther Reinhardt*, p.4
621 Ibid., p.5
622 Ibid., p.11
623 Ibid., p.11/ William Mulligan, *The Creation of the Modern German Army. General Walther Reinhardt and the Weimar Republic 1914-1930*
624 *Meine Lebenserinnerungen*, p.108, 110-1. Strikingly enough, Robert G.L.Waite states that Ludendorff was in civilian cloths, *Vanquard of Nazism. The Freekorps Movement in Postwar Germany 1918-1933*, p.141.
625 Thamer, p.214, 215
626 *Meine Lebenserinnerungen*, p.111
627 Gerhard E. Gruendler, *Deutsche Admirale putschen nicht?*, see website Gerhard E.Gruendler, previously published in *Stern* 12/1970
628 For the position of the different districts see Günther Bardey, part 1 p.122
629 Paling, p.125, 126
630 *Meine Lebenserinnerungen*, p.111
631 Ibid., p.111
632 Ibid., p.111
633 Ibid., p.111-113
634 Thamer, p.215, 216
635 J.T.Trebitsch-Lincoln, *De grootste avonturier der twintigste eeuw. Mijn leven naar waarheid geschetst*, p.151
636 Ibid., p.152
637 Ibid., p.153
638 *Meine Lebenserinnerungen*, p.113
639 Trebitsch Lincoln, p.153
640 *Meine Lebenserinnerungen*, p.114
641 Trebitsch-Lincoln, p.153
642 General Buat, *Ludendorff Would Spur Germany to New War, French General Asserts*: In: *Oakland Tribune*, Sunday Morning 21.03.1920 (the heading of the article reads: Paris, March 10)/For further info on Buat see a.o. *Who's Who in day's News: General Buat*: In: *The Cpaital Times* 30.11.1921/Operation *Fatal to General Staff Chief*, In: *Bridgeport Telegram*, 31.12.1923
643 For information on Von Luttwitz see: Erwin Koennemann, *Kapps Vorbereitungen auf einen Prozess, der nie stattfand. Dokumente aus seinem Nachlass*. In: *Zeitschrift für Geschichtswissenschaft Heft 7*, p.699
644 Heinrich Brünning, *Memoirs 1918-1934*, p.66
645 Maser, *Friedrich Ebert, Der erste deutsche Reichspresident*, p.276
646 *Als ich Ludendorffs Frau war*, p.275

647 Ibid., p.276
648 Ibid., p.276
649 For an overview of how the different historians thought about Eckart, see: Perry Pierik *Hitlers Lebensraum*, p. 120,121 and *De geopolitiek van het Derde Rijk*, ch 3.
650 A.Joachimsthaler, *Korrektur einer Biographie. Adolf Hitler 1908 - 1920*, p.63
651 Walter Görlitz/Herbert A.Quint, *Adolf Hitler, Eine Biographie*, p.142
652 Toland, *Adolf Hitler. Het einde van een mythe*, p.116-7
653 Ibid., p.117. Another of his pseudonyms was Trautwein. The Lincoln in his surname was also added deliberately. See *New York Times*, Bernard Wasserstein, *On the Trail of Trebitsch-Lincoln*, April 2006
655 Trebitsch-Lincoln was also in contact with the German secret service later in the Second World War and had to set up a radio station for them in Tibet. In October 1943, he died during an operation in a hospital in Shanghai. Shortly before his death, he seemed less fascinated by Buddhism, which had taken hold of him for some years, and speculated about a solution to Zionism, believing that a new Tel Aviv might arise in China. Frank Westenfelder, *Trebitsch-Lincoln. Der grosste Abenteurer des XX.Jahrhunderts*/ Wasserstein/ Eliezer Segal, *The Treacherous Mr. Trebisch. From The Sources*, 2004 (?)
656 Letter to Kapp is printed in Ian Kershaw, vol. 1, p.154/Thomas Weber has shed new light on Karl Mayr's role in Thomas Weber, *Wie Adolf Hitler zum Nazi wurde. Vom unpolitischen Soldaten zum Autor von 'Mein Kampf'*.
657 On the details of Kapp's justification see Könnemann
658 Toland, p.117
659 Görlitz/Quint, /Joachimsthaler, p.63
660 Görlitz/Quint, p.143
661 Dieter Fricke/Manfred Weissbecker/Siegfried Schmidt e.a. (hg.), band III p.399/Joachimsthaler called Von Reventlow a 'prominent author', p.63
662 Werner Braeuniger, *Hitlers Kontrahenten in der NSDAP 1921-1945*, p.309
663 A.Joachimsthaler, *Hitlers Liste. Ein Dokument personlicher Beziehungen* München: Herbig 2003, p.63-4/Toland, p.117
664 *Mein Lebenserienerungen*, p.159-161/For the meeting controversy see Bernhard Wien, p.265, who pointed out that Hans Frank's memoirs indicated the year 1920.
665 Toland, p.103
666 Ibid., p.103
667 Charlotte Beradt, *Paul Levi, Ein demokratischer Sozialist in der Weimarer Republik*, p.38
668 Arthur Rosenberg, *Geschichte der Weimarer Republik*, p.110
669 Ibid., p.111
670 Ibid., p.98-9
671 Gunther Bardey, *Die Brigade Ehrhardt part II*, p.122-126/ Robert Gerwarth, *The Vanquished. Why the first Wolrd War failed to end, 1917-1923*, p.166-7
672 Von Plehwe, *Reichskanzler Kurt von Schleicher. Weimars letzte Chance gegen Hitler*, p.48-9
673 Koennemann, p.700
674 *Meine Lebenserinnerungen*, p.116
675 Ibid., p.108-9
676 Breucker, p.97
677 Ibid., p.114/For the role of the 'Arbeiterführer' see Karlludwig Rintelen, Arbeiterführ-

er und Reichsleitung vor und bei Inszenierung des ersten Weltkrieges. In: *Beitrage zur Geschichte der Arbeiterbewegung 199*, p.723-735

678 Ernst H.Posse, *Die politischen Kampfbunde Deutschlands. Quellentexte zur Konservativen Revolution*. Die Nationalrevolutionare: Band 3, p.19
679 K-U., Merz, *Das Schreckbild. Deutschland und der Bolschewismus 1917 bis 1921*, p.188
680 Ibid., p.188
681 Ibid., p.189
682 There are no good sources for this. Wolfgang Eggert mentions this in his very controversial work *Israels Geheim Vatikan, als Vollstrecker Biblischer Prophetie*
683 Renata Bournazel, *Rapallo: Ein Französisches Trauma*, p.71
684 Breucker, p.180
685 Ibid., p.180
686 Johannes Baur, *Die deutsche Kolonie in München 1900-1945. Deutsch-Russische Beziehungen in 20 Jahrhundert*, p.217
687 Breucker, p.180
688 Klaus Gietinger, *Der Konterrevolutionär. Waldemar pabst-eine deutsche Karrier*, p.205/ For the difficult Polish-German relations see a.o. Marek Kornat, *Poland zwischen Hitler und Stalin. Studien zur polnischen Aussenpolitik in der Zwischenkriegszeit.*
689 Plehwe, p.63-4, H.Toorenvliet, Reichswehr and Red Army between the World Wars. In: *Spiegel Historial*, 9th year, volume no.2 February 1974, p.75
690 Plehwe, p.66/For the Franco-Polish relationship of honour see also Perry Pierik, *Vanaf vandaag wordt er teruggeschoten. Spionage, geheime diplomatie, oorlogseconomie en andere facetten van de Poolse veldtocht van 1939*
691 Arthur Rosenberg, *Geschichte der Weimarer Republik*, p.103
692 *Meine Lebenserinnerungen*, p.117
693 Ibid., p.119
694 John Toland
695 *Meine Lebenserinnerungen*, p.119
696 Ibid., p.119
697 Ibid., p.126
698 Ibid., p.132
699 Ibid., p.133
700 Perry Pierik, *Thule en het Derde Rijk. De genesis van het nationaal-socialisme,* including the translation of *Bevor Hitler kam* by Rudolf von Sebottendorff, and his account of the Radical Age
701 Margreet den Buurman, *Heinrich Mann, het goede in eens mens, biograpfie*, p.113 - 135
702 *Meine Lebenserinnerungen*, p.139
703 Ibid., p.141
704 Rudolf Schricker, *Rotmord über München*, p.91
705 *Lebenserinnerungen*, p.147
706 Ibid., p.138
707 Ibid., p.155
708 Hannover, p.35-44
709 Ibid., p.88
710 Ibid., p.88
711 Ibid., p.152
712 Ibid., p.153
713 Ulrike Claudia Hofmann, *"Verräter verfallen der Feme!". Femeморden in Bayern in den*

	zwanziger Jahren, p.15
714	Hoffmann, p.51
715	Martin Sabrow, *Die verdrängte Verschwörung. Der Rathenau-Mord und die deutsche Gegenrevolution,* p.45
716	With a generous hand he provided the OC with money, says Heinz Höhne in his biography of Canaris. Heinz Höhne, *Admiraal Wilhelm Canaris. Nieuwe visie op de loopbaan van het hoofd van de Duitse Anbwehr. Het einde van een verzetsmythe,* p.56-7/ According to Bernhard Wien, Canaris was a 'Ludendorff worshipper'. It seems more likely that Canaris considered Ludendorff to be a good representative of imperial Germany, p.412
717	Hans-Günter Richardi, *Hitler und seiner Hintermänner, neue Fakten zur Frühgeschichte der NSDAP,* p.133
718	Ibid., p.133
719	Ibid., p.144-146
720	Ibid., p.146
721	Pierik/Pors, *De verlaten monarch, Kijzer Wilhelm II in Nederland,* p.138-9. Ernst Hanfstaengl, Hitler's German-American press secretary, introduced Louis Ferdinand to Hitler in 1933.
722	Hans Severus Ziegler, *Wer war Hitler? Beiträge zur Hitler-Forschung,* p.166-169
723	Jonathan Petropoulos, *Royals and the Reich. The Princes von Hessen in Nazi Germany,* p.373/Lothar Machtan, *Der Kaisersohn bei Hitler.* Hoffmann und Campe, p.212
724	At last, according to Petropulus, 270 members of German royal houses would become members of the NSDAP. Petropulus, p.100, 371/Stephan Malinowski, *Vom König zum Führer. Deutscher Adel und Nationalsozialismus,* p.597
725	Nikolaus von Preradovich formulated the contribution of the nobility to the Nazi party in this way in 1981.
726	Pierik/Pors, p.145
727	Ibid., p.146
728	Malinowski, p.573
729	*Meine Lebenserinnerungen,* p.161
730	Wolf Rüdiger Hess (hg.), *Rudolf Hess. Briefe 1908-1933* Munich/Wien: Langen Müller 1987, p.265
731	*Mein Lebenserinnerungen*
732	Douglas Reed, *Nemesis? Het leven van Otto Strasser,* p.73/Günter Bartsch, *Zwischen drei Stühlen. Otto Strasser. Eine Biografie,* p.24
733	Bartsch, p.25
734	Ibid., p.25
735	Ibid., p.25
736	*Meine Lebenserinnerungen,* p.161
737	Bartsch, p.26
738	Ian Khersaw, *Hitler, Hubris 1889-1936,* p.145
739	Ibid., p.145, 146
740	Sabrow, ch. 4
741	Norman Cohn, *Die Protokolle der Weissen von Zion. Der Mythus von der jüdischen Weltverschwörun,* ch. 1.
742	Gert Borst rightly distances himself from this, *Die Ludendorff-Bewegung 1919-1961. Eine Analyse monologer Kommunikationsformen in der sozialen Zeitkommunikation.* Augsburg: Dissertationsdruck, p.29, although anti-Semitic views were not foreign

743 Walter Mohrmann, p.120
744 Walter Mohrmann, Antisemitismus, p.120
745 Few facts are known about Nilus, and even fewer are certain. There are various reports about his profession, and even about the spelling of his name. There are also different versions as to how Nilus would have got hold of *The Protocols*. For an inventory of the views on Nilus, see: Michael Hagemeister, *Sergei Nilus und die Protokolle der Weisen von Zion* In: Wolfgang Benz (hg.), *Jahrbuch für Antisemitismus Forschung 5*, p.127-147
746 Segel, p.20-1/Norman Cohn, *Die Protokolle der Weisen von Zion. Der Mythos von der jüdischen Welt-Verschwörung*, 1969, p.83-89
747 Segel, p.17
748 Hans Kurth, *Die Wahrheiten über Ludendorffs Kampf. Eine zusammenhangengende Darstellung*, p.44-47
749 *Meine Lebenserinnerungen*, part I, p.165
750 Ibid., p.165
751 Ibid., p.167
752 Ibid., p.165
753 Ibid., p.139
754 Ibid., p.169
755 Chest, p.86
756 Ibid., p.87
757 Ibid., p.87
758 *Meine Lebenserinnerungen*, p.162
759 Ludendorff, *Krieg und Politik*, p.51
760 *Kriegführung und Politik*, p.51, about the role of Jews in World War I see a.o. Perry Pierik, Een joodse dubbeldekker met een swastika in: Hans Andriessen/ Martin Ros, Perry Pierik, *De Grote Oorlog, Kroniek 1914-1918*, p.25-46
761 Rolf Vogel, *Ein Stück von uns. 1813-1976, Deutsche Juden in deutschen Armeen*, p.141-146; Jacob Segall, *Die deutschen Juden als Soldaten im Kriege 1914-1918, Eine statistische Studie.*
762 H. Graf Kessler, *Walther Rathenau, zijn leven en zijn werk*, p.389
763 For various reactions, also in Jewish circles, see: Dieter Dowe/Michael Schneider, Historisches Forschungszentrum der Friedrich Ebert-Stiftung, Reihe: Politik-und Gesellschaftsgeschichte, Band 62: Cornelia Hecht, *Deutsche Juden und Antisemitismus in der Weimarer Republik.*
764 Kessler, p.391
765 See a.o. Koos Vorrink, *Walther Rathenau*, H.W.von der Dunk, Walther Rathenau 1867-1922. Leven tussen aanpassing en kritiek, In: *Tijdschrift voor Geschiedenis* vol. 3.
766 P.J.Bouwman, *Jaures, Wilson, Rathenau*, p.159
767 Ibid., p.164
768 Walther Rathenau, *Der Kaiser. Eine Betrachtung*
769 Kessler, p.129, later Rathenau confirmed this theory once more in a letter to Frank Wedekind
770 Perry Pierik/Henk Pors, *De verlaten monarch*, p.43

771	Kessler, p.377
772	Peter Berglar, *Walther Rathenau, Seine Zeit, Sein Werk, Seine Persönlichkeit*, p.296,-7
773	Sabrow, p.30
774	Ibid., p.30-1
775	Dr Melchior had gone in his place. Max Warburg feared anti-Semitic reactions if a Jewish man would be at the head of this historically sensitive German delegation. Furthermore, he feared a confrontation with his brother Paul Warburg, who was on the side of the Entente. This would give the impression of an 'überstaatliche' position, to use Ludendorff's words. On Max Warburg see: David Farrer, *The Warburgs*, p.76
776	Kessler, p.374
777	Ibid., p.375
778	Walter Mohrmann pointed this out in: Walter Mohrmann, *Antisemitismus. Ideologie und Geschichte im Kaiserreich und in der Weimarer Republik*, p.88-9
779	Sabrow, p.32
780	Kessler, p.376
781	Uwe Lohalm/Martin Ulmer, *Alfred Roth und der Deutschvölkische Schutz- und Trutz-Bund. Schrittmacher' für das Dritte Reich*, p. 5 In: Daniel Schmidt/Michael Sturm/Livi Massimiliano (hg.), *Wegbereiter des Nationalsozialismus. Personen, Organisationen und Netzwerken der extremen Rechten zwischen 1918 und 1933*.
782	Sabrow, p.123-129
783	Borst, p.105
784	*Zukunft* 01.07.1922 used here Borst, p.104
785	Berglar, p.148
786	Breucker, p.114
787	Ibid., p.114
788	Ibid., p.114
789	This is how economic competitors labelled his raw material policy for the Kriegswirtschaftsgesellschaften, Breucker p.114, Bouwman, p. 155.
790	Udo Leuschner called it 'self-abasement': Udo leuschner, *Walther Rathenau, Ein Dissident seiner Klasse, seiner Rasse und seines Geschlechts* in: http://www.udo-leuschner.de/liberalismus/liberalismus4.htm
791	Kessler, p.255
792	Peter Berglar, p.237
793	Ibid., p.241
794	Von der Dunk, p.353
795	Kessler, p.257
796	Ibid., p.257
797	Ibid., p.257
798	*Die verdraengte Verschwörung*, book title of the same name
799	Sabrow, p.211-214
800	For exact publication dates see Borst p. 106
801	Borst, p.107
802	Kessler p.378
803	Kurt Tucholsky, *Das Opfer einer Republik* in: *Glossen und Essays. Gesammelte Schriften 1907-1935*
804	Kurt Tucholsky, *Cadett Ludendorff*
805	Sabrow, p.212
806	Sabrow, p.212

807 Sabrow, p.215
808 Ibid., p.216
809 Benz/Graml, *Biographisches Lexikon zur Weimarer Republik* p.134-5
810 *Meine Lebenserinnerungen*, p.209
811 *Meine Lebenserinnerungen*, p.209
812 Bouwman, p.161
813 *Biographie Friedrich Minoux 1877-1945*, www.dhm.de/lemo/biografie/biografie-friedrich-minoux.html
814 Heinrich Brüning, p.72
815 *Meine Lebenserinnerungen*, p.218
816 Just like 1933, by the way, which was supposed to be 'important' especially for Freemasonry.
817 Es geht aufwärts, In: *Ludendorffs Volkswarte* 15.01.1933
818 *Meine Lebenserinnerungen*, p.217
819 Ibid., p.211
820 Ibid., p.220
821 Ibid., p.219, 220
822 Ian Kershaw, *Hitler, Hubris 1889-1936*, p.193
823 *Meine Lebenserinnerungen*, p.220
824 Graf zu Reventlow, *Der Weg zum neuen deutschland Der Wiederaufstieg des deutschen Volkes Zentralstelle für den deutschen Freiheitskampf*. Journalist Maximillian Harden thought that Stinnes and Ludendorff worked together until the end, but this was not the case. Maximillian Harden, *Köpfe. Porträts, Briefe und Dokumente*, p.154
825 Bodo Harenberg, *Chronik des Ruhrgebiets*, p.349
826 Wighton, *Adenauer. Democratisch Dictator. Een kritische biografie*, p.39
827 Ibid., p.39
828 Harenberg, p.349
829 Wighton, p.39: These sympathies were a convenient sideline later in the relationship between Adenauer and De Gaulle.
830 Harrenberg, p.363
831 The share of naval officers in key positions in the right-wing camp remains striking. Several naval officers would also play a leading role in the Ludendorff movement. See Perry Pierik, Landverraders en steunpilaren in blauw, in: Hans Andriessen/Perry Pierik (ed.), *De Grote oorlog. Chronicle 1914-1918* part 15, p.174-186
832 Kurt Koszyk, *Deutsche Presse 1914-1945*, p.145
833 Khersaw, p.200
834 Ibid., p.195
835 Brüning, p.93
836 Ibid., p.93
837 Khersaw, p.195
838 W.Stresemann, *Mein Vater Gustav Stresemann*, p.239
839 Ibid., p.220
840 Ibid., p.233
841 Ibid., p.226
842 Hans Spethmann, *Das Ruhrgebiet im Wechselspiel von Land und Leute, Wirtschaft, Technik und Politik. Dritter Band*, p.695
843 Kloevekorn, prof.dr.(hg.), *Das Saargebiet. Seine Struktur, seine Probleme*, p.549
844 Harenberg, p.354

845	Stresemann called him a 'weak politician', p.235
846	Ibid., p.236
847	Ibid., p.236
848	Ibid., p.245
849	For the Buchrucker revolt see; Richard Schapke, *Hakenkreuz am Stahlhelm. Kapitaen Ehrhardt und seine Brigade* taken from: www.die-kommenden.net/dk/zeitgeschichte/erhardt.html/; Johannes Huerter, Sehepuntke; review Bernhard Sauer, *Schwarze Reichswehr und Feme morde*, www.sehepunkte.de/ Thorsten Stegemann, *Vorbereitung auf den Nationalsozialismus, Die Schwarze Reichswehr als mentalitätsgeschichte* www.heise.de.
850	Douglas Reed talks about 1928, *Nemesis? Het leven van Otto Strasser*. p.166
851	Reed, p.166
852	Ibid., p.253-255
853	W.Stresemann, p.255
854	Ibid., p.255-260
855	Charlotte Beradt, p.72
856	W.Stresemann, p.273
857	*Deutscher Oktober* Ibid., p.23-25
858	Stern, p.297, 298
859	Ibid., p.26
860	Gilbert Badia, *Clara Zetkin. Eine neue Biographie*, p.224, Luise Dornemann, *Clara Zetkin, Leben und Wirken*, p.494-5
861	*Deutscher Oktober*, p.27
862	The investigators of the Stadtteilkollektiv speak of eighty-eight dead, however, Ruediger Michael notes a somewhat lower figure: Stadtteilkollektiv Rotes Winterhunde (hg.), *Der Hamburger Aufstand 1923. Verlauf-Mythos-Lehren*, Hamburg: Rote Winterhuder Texte 4/ Ruediger Michael, *Weimar unter Druck* in *Y.on Line, Magazin der Bundeswehr part 3* in: www.rhein-main.net. Thaelmann's underground operation was only temporary, in May 1924 he took his seat in the 'Reichstag'. See: Guenter Hortzschansky, *Ernst Thaelmann*, Leipzig: VEB Bibliographisches Institut, p. 40. The Communists also attributed Thaelmann's failure to their own internal dissension: see *Grundriss der Geschichte der deutschen Arbeiter Bewegung*, p.132, 133, See also Gilbert Badia, who believes that after the failure, 'a scapegoat had to be found, and that one of the persons designated was Brandler, p.224
863	Ludendorff, *Meine Lebenserinnerungen 1919-1925*, p.201-2
864	Röhm, *Geschichte eines Hochverräters*, p.173
865	For Göring see a.o. Werner Maser, *Hermann Göring. Een politieke carière*, / Leonard Mosley, *Göring*, /Eitel Lange, *Der Reichsmarschall im Kriege*
866	*Meine Lebenserinnerungen 1919-1925*, p.201
867	Between 1902 and 1908, illness forced him to give up this magazine
868	Anne-Marie Greijen, *Opportunisme of ideologie? Over de rol van de uitgeverswereld in München bij het opkomen van het nationaal-socialisme*, unpublished doctoral thesis Political History of Utrecht University supervised by Dr.Mr.F.W. Lantink, 20 January 2006. Weber later divorced Mathilde Lehmann, the eldest daughter of the publisher, and remarried Maria Necker: Svantje Insenhöfer, *Dr.Friedrich Weber. Reichstierärzteführer von 1934 bis 1945. Inaugural-Dissertation*, p.55-57
869	Hamann, *Winifred Wagner. A Life at the Heart of Hitler's Bayreuth*, p.78
870	Ibid., p.83

871	Flood, p.293
872	Ibid., p.294: 'He seemed a tower that defies the world'.
873	Ibid., p.294
874	Ibid., p.295
875	Ibid., p.295/296
876	*Meine Lebenserinnerungen 1919-1925*, p.202-3
877	Ibid., p.203
878	Denis Jdanoff, *'Russische Faschisten'. Der nationalsozialistische Fluegel der russischen Emigration im Dritten Reich*, Digitale Osteuropa-Bibliothek: Geschichte 3, p.18-23
879	Some sources speak of the last week of May, others of June 1921
880	James/Suzanne Pool, *Wie financierde Hitler?*, p.56, 57
881	o.a. at the *Volksdeutschen Mittelstelle* - VoMi- an organisation that watched over the interests of the 'Volksdeutschen', see Pierik, *Karl Haushofer*, p.76-7
882	Hagemeister, p.137-8
883	R.SH.Ganelin, In: recepter.livejournal.com
884	Erst Piper, *Alfred Rosenberg, Hitlers chefideologe*, p.391
885	Pierik, *Hitlers Lebensraum*, see. o.a. chapter 3 *Reich and Romantik*, in which Rosenberg points out the 87 nationalities of Russia, /Pierik, *Het onbekende rijk. Minder bekende feiten over het Oostfront*, p.55, /Molau, chapter 8/Piper chapter 10, and Martin Cüpers, *Wegbereiter der Shoa. Die Waffen-SS, der Kommandostab Reichsführer SS und die Judenvernichtung 1939-1945*.
886	See for example the memoirs of Gauleiter Rudolf Jordan, *Erlebt und Erlitten*
887	It must be noted, however, that the historian Wolfgang Zdral depicts the flow of money from Ludendorff to Scheubner-Richter rather than the other way round. On the other hand, Zdral does not pay much attention to the Russian connections, and the flow of money remains foggy. See: Wolfgang Zdral, *Der finanzierte Aufstieg des Adolf H.*, chapter 2. Von Scheubner-Richter had an eye for political power as well as for its financing, which was also expressed in his own political mantel organisation, the 'Gesellschaft Aufbau-Wirtschaftpolitische Vereinigung für den Osten', as well as in his publishing company, the 'Wirtschaftspolitische Aufbau-Korrespondenz' (WAK), which originated from an earlier organisation in 1919, the 'Ostdeutschen Heimatdienst', Garleff, p.141 footnote 61.
888	Konrad Heiden, p.122-3
889	Brüggemann points out that his sympathy for the Armenians did not stem from a genuine interest in them, but from the fact that as a Christian, he felt that Europe could not remain silent in the face of genocide. It was later claimed that through the fate of the Armenians, Von Scheubner-Richter indirectly initiated Hitler's 'Final Solution' to the Jewish question. Brüggemann relegates this to the realm of fables. Brüggemann, p.124-5
890	The title of this book was *Posten auf ewiger Wache. Aus dem abenteuerreichen Leben des Max Erwin von Scheubner-Richter*, Essen 1938
891	Ibid., p.125
892	Garleff, *Deutschbalten, Weimarer Republik und Drittes Reich. Band 1*, p.119
893	Ibid., p.119
894	Ibid., p.141
895	Brüggemann, p.127
896	During the Second World War, the Crimea was interpreted in this way by the German military as well. According to Oberst Paul, when German troops reached Taganrog on

19 October 1941, the Red Army decided to make Sebastopol a 'permanent' fortress. See: Obert Paul, Kurze Darstellung der sowjetrussischen Kämpfe auf der Krim und um Sewastopol vom Oktober bis Juli 1942 In: *Militär-wissenschaftlicher Rundschau, 1942, 2.Heft.*

897 Cramer-Klett is mentioned by Pool, p.56; for the relation with 'Aufbau' see Brüggemann, p.29
898 Michael Kellog, *The Russian Roots of Nazism. White Emigres and the Making of National Socialism.*
899 Rubonia, founded in Riga in 1875. There was also a branch of this organisation in Munich.
900 For the special role of the student associations see Harald Loennecker, '...*Boden für die Idee Adolf Hitlers auf kulturellem Felde gewinnen'. Der 'Kampfbund für deutsche Kultur' und die deutsche Akademikerschaft.* In: Dateiabruf unter www.burschenschaft.de / Ueber *Burschen in den Freikorps im Baltikum 1918-1920* In: https://www.nadir.org/nadir/periodika/anarcho_randalia/br_6/br6la5.htm.
901 Her official name in Russia was Grand Duchess Victoria Fyodorowna
902 Kellog, p.2
903 Hagemeister, p.137
904 Trotsky, Chapter 5
905 Rene Fueloep-Miller, *Der Heilige Teufel. Rasputin und die Frauen*, p.68-71
906 The triumvirate started the magazine *Prizyv:* 'The Call'.
907 P.J.G.Pulzer, *The Rise of political anti-semitism in Germany and Austria*, p.316-7
908 Shabelsky-Bork died in Argentina in 1952. For biographical data on Ludendorff's Russian connections see: Andre Ivanov in www.rusk.re
909 Brüggemann, p.129
910 *Die Rubonia in München 1918-1923.* In: www.nadir.org/periodioka/anarcho-randalia/br7/rubonia-1918.htm (01.01.2008)
911 A contact that, according to Brüggemann, went via Von Scheubner-Richter as well
912 Eglau, p.86
913 Photo from: Fritz Thyssen, *Ik financierde Hitler*
914 Hans Otto Eglau, *Fritz Thuyssen, Hitler Göner und Geisler*, p.80-1
915 Peter Hüttenberger/Hans Georg Molitor (hg.), *Französen und Deutsche am Rhein 1789-1918-1945*, p.163
916 Thomas Rother, *Die Thyssens, Tragödie der Stahlbarone*, p.95-6
917 Eglau, p.87
918 Thyssen once claimed that most of the money had gone to Hitler and the NSDAP, p.87
919 Eglau, p.88
920 Turner, *Faschismus und Kapitalismus in Deutschland*, p.103
921 Heimatpost Issue 16, no. 21, 24.05.1964, quoted from Franz Wegener, *Der Alchemist Franz Tausend. Alchemie und Nationalsozialismus*
922 F. Wegener, *Der Alchemist Franz Tausend. Alchemie und Nationalsozialismus*, p.43
923 Witness statement of Rudolf Rienhardt, during the trial in January 1931, Wegener, p.76
924 Savitri Devi Mukherji, *Gold im Schmeltztiegel, Erlebnisse im Nachkriegsdeutschland, Kritik, Die Stimme des Volkes*, No. 60
925 Wegener, p.82-3
926 This was Rudolf Rienhardt

927 Wegener, pp.40-44
928 Ibid., p.44-46
929 Ibid., p.49-50
930 Ibid., p.59
931 Ibid., p.80-1
932 See e.g. *Pharos Tribune*, 10.10.1929, *The Salt Lake Tribune, Visionaries still dreams of making gold, experimenter stays in jail*, 17.11.1929, *The Capital Times, official paper of the State of Wisconsion, Alchemist makes gold out of lead; scientist stunned*, 10.10.1929/ *The Viudette Messenger valparasio*, Indiana, *Test of Mint fail break claim of lead made gold*. (discussing 'field marshal' Ludendoff), 10.10.1929, *The Lethbridge Herald, German tinker real ponzi*, 21.03.1929, also discussing the Alfred Mannesman case. The newspaper claimed that a total of $1,750,000 had been raised by Tausend. *The San Antonio Light, Gold produced from lead in test: germans not so sure they were not hoodwinked by alchemist*, 10.10.1929 and *The Decatur Review, Alchemist makes Gold for Police. Still Skeptical that there is no fraud*, 10.10.1929.
933 Wegener, p.66
934 Ibid., p.92
935 Ibid., p.51
936 Ibid., p.44
937 Ibid., p.56
938 Ibid., p.43
939 *Der kommende Steuerstreik and Die soziale Bau-und Wirtschaftsbank*
940 Wegener, p.81
941 Ibid., p.103-106
942 Ibid., p.108
943 Ibid., p.112
944 Ibid., p.117
945 Wasserstein, p.208
946 Ibid., p.211
947 Klaus Gietinger, *Der Konter Revolutionär*, p.249
948 Ibid., p.251
949 Ibid., p.249, 250
950 *Meine Lebenserinnerungen*, p.243
951 Ibid., p.245
952 Boterman, p.251
953 Walter Görlitz/Herbert A.Quint, *Adolf Hitler, eine Biographie*, p.190-1
954 Ibid., p.190
955 Ibid., p.197
956 Ibid., p.192
957 Ibid., p.194, Brigitte Hamann, *Winifred Wagner, A Life at the Heart of Hitlers Bayreuth*, p.58-9
958 Allan Bullock, *Hitler, Leven en ondergang van een tiran*, p.74
959 Hamann, p.91
960 Ibid., p.91
961 Ibid., p.91
962 Ibid., p.91
963 W.L.Shirer, *The Rise and Fall of the Third Reich. A History of Nazi Germany*, p.67
964 Fest, *Hitler, a biografie*, p. 261

965	Ibid., p.261
966	Ibid., p.262
967	Ibid., p.262
968	Dornberg, *Der Hitlerputsch. Munich, 8 und 9 November 1923*, p.106
969	Fest., p.262
970	Ibid., p.263
971	Ibid., p.263
972	Dornberg, p.114
973	Ibid., p.115
974	Ibid., p.115
975	Ibid., p.115
976	Ibid., p.115
977	Ibid., p.115
978	Ibid., p.115
979	Ibid., p.119
980	Ibid., p.119
981	Ibid., p.119
982	Ibid., p.122
983	Fest, p.264
984	Dornberg, p.123
985	Ibid., p.123
986	Ibid., p.126
987	Wehrkreiskommando
988	Ibid., p.150
989	Ibid., p.151
990	Ibid., p.154
991	Fest, p.265
992	Hitler was much more popular than Kapp, he thought, Ernst Nolte, *Der europäische Bürgerkrieg 1917-1945. Nationalsozialismus und Bolschewismus*, p.33
993	Fest, p.268
994	Ibid., p.268
995	Ibid., p.273
996	Wilhelm Hoegner, *Die Verratene Republik. Deutsche Geschichte 1919-1933*, p.188
997	Fest, p.263
998	Görlitz/Quint, p.204
999	Flood, p.494
1000	Khersaw, p.207
1001	Pätzold, p.95
1002	Meine Lebenserinnerungen, p.259
1003	Ibid., p.255, 256
1004	*Als ich Ludendorffs Frau war*, p.293.
1005	Ibid., p.293
1006	Ibid., p.295
1007	Ibid., p.293-4
1008	Ibid., p.296
1009	Ibid., p.296
1010	Ibid., p.296-7
1011	Ibid., p.256

1012 Dornberger, p.32
1013 He was mentioned as a leading Nazi in the *Taschenwörternbuch des National Sozialismus* published in 1934 by Hans Wagner: Hans Wagner, *Taschenwörterbuch des nationalsozialismus A bis Z*
1014 Dornberger p.32, 33/L.Greil., *In memoriam Freikorpsführer Gerhard Rossbach* in: Damerau,H.(hg.).,*Deutsches Soldaten Jahrbuch 1968, 16. deutscher Soldatenkalender*, p.110, 111, Kurt Oskar Bark, *Rossbachs Marsch ins Baltikum* In: Ernst von Salomon (hg.)., *Das Buch vom deutschen Freikorpskämpfer*, here used facsimile edition 2001, p.202-203.
1015 R43 I/ 2218 Bl 319 No 256 *Der Vertreter der Reichsregierung an die Reichskanzlei 14 November 1923*
1016 Dornberg, p.103-4
1017 Ibid., p.27/Easy hour-by-hour overview can also be found here: Hubert Beckers, *Adolf Hitler Tag für Tag. Eine Chronologie mit Literaturangaben. Band 1 1889-1938*
1018 *Als ich Ludendorffs Frau war*, p.299, 300
1019 Ibid., p.302
1020 R 43 I/2264 Bl 340-342: [1159] No 277: *Der Vertreter der Reichsregierung in München aan die Reichskanzlei. Munich, November 21, 1923*
1021 Görlitz/Quint, p.218
1022 Richard J. Evens, *Das Dritte Reich, Aufstieg*, p.284
1023 Ibid., p.285
1024 Ibid., p.285
1025 Martin Gregor-Dellin (hg.), *Carl Christian Bry, Der Hitler-Putsch. Berichte und Kommentare eines Deutschland-Korrespondenten (1922-1924) für das 'Argentinische Tag- und Wochenblatt'*, p.155
1026 Ibid., p.157
1027 Ibid., p.158
1028 Berggötz, S.O., (hg.), Ernst Jünger, Politische Publizistik 1919-1933, p.44-5
1029 Ernst Piper, p.98, Görlitz/Quint, p.227
1030 *Meine Lebenserinnerungen*, p.335
1031 Ibid., p.335, Helmut Heiber, *Die Republik von Weimar*, p.155
1032 *Meine Lebenserinnerungen*, p.334
1033 Ibid., p.335
1034 Ibid., p.335
1035 Ibid., p.335
1036 Billung, *Rund um Hitler*, p.142
1037 Ibid., p.142
1038 Ibid., p.142-144
1039 Werner Bräuninger, Hitlers Kontrahenten in der NSDAP 1921-1945, p.38
1040 Ibid., p.38
1041 Ibid., p.40
1042 Gisevius, *Adolf Hitler*, p.71
1043 Gisevius spoke a.o. of the fateful role of the Reichswehr, p.68
1044 John W.Wheeler-Bennet, *The Nemesis of Power. The German Army in Politics 1918-1945*, p.83
1045 It was an answer from Hitler to a letter dated 14 June 1924, Bräuninger, p.41
1046 Bräuninger, p.41, 42
1047 Piper, p.102

1048	Piper, p.102
1049	Piper, p.108
1050	*Meine Lebenserinnerungen*, p.271
1051	Ibid., p.349
1052	Ibid., p.351
1053	Ibid., P.396-7
1054	Ibid., p.397
1055	Ibid., p.397
1056	Bräuninger, p.43
1057	Ibid., p.430
1058	Ibid., p.430, Piper, p.122
1059	*Meine Lebenserinnerungen*, p.370-374
1060	Ibid., p.373
1061	Sebastian Haffner, *Kanttekeningen bij Hitler*, p.12
1062	Ibid., p.23
1063	Wilhelm Hoegner, *Die verratene Republik. Deutsche Geschichte 1919-1933*, p.188
1064	See also Ian Khersaw, *Hitler 1889-1936 Hubris*, p.259
1065	Bräuninger, p.56
1066	Ibid., p.58
1067	Ibid., p.56
1068	*Meine Lebenserinnerungen*, p.335-6, Peter Ross Range speaks in his book of 'the tipping year 1924'. I would like to refer to the tipping point as being somewhat later, at the break between Ludendorff and Hitler. After this, the 'Alleingang' of Hitler began.
1069	Ibid., p.359
1070	Ibid., p.358
1071	Ibid., p.358
1072	Document R 43 I 2264 BL 358-363: Der Chef des Truppenamts an Staatssekretär Bracht, 14 January 1924, on the fate of Von Lossow
1073	*Meine Lebenserinnerungen*, p. 363, For citation see: Ausserhalb der Tagesordnung: Feier in Ostpreussen 17 July 1924, Edition: Die Kabinette Marx I,II Band 2: Dokumente nr 253 Ministerbesprechung von 17 Juli 1924
1074	Breucker, p.116
1075	Ibid., p.339
1076	Ibid., p.340
1077	Breucker, p.116
1078	Ibid., p.117
1079	Dieter Bartetzko, *Illusionen in Stein. Stimmungsarchitektur im deutschen Faschismus. Ihre Vorgeschichte in Theater-und-Film-Bauten*, p.82-3
1080	Wolfgang Ruge, *Hindenburg*, p.243
1081	Breucker, p.126
1082	Emil Ludwig, *Hindenburg. Legende und Wirklichkeit*, p.198
1083	Ibid., p.199
1084	Anna von der Goltz, *Hindenburg. Power, Myth and the Rise of the Nazis*, p.94
1085	Hagen Schulze, p.331/ One of Jarres' speeches of those days was also entitled *Zurück zur Bismarck* in: *Stralsunder Tageblatt* 24.jahrgang 24.03.1925: *Jarres hat das Wort*.
1086	*Als ich Ludendorffs Frau war*, p.331-2
1087	Ibid., p.332
1088	Ibid., p.333

1089	Letter from Rudolf Hess of 21.10.1924 to Ilse Pröhl, Wolf Rüdiger Hess (hg.), *Rudolf Hess, Briefe 1908-1933*, p.354
1090	*Als ich Ludendorffs Frau war*, p.333
1091	Ibid., p.333
1092	Harry Graf Kessler, *Tagebücher 1918-1937*, p.435, note of 19 April 1925
1093	Pytra, p.476
1094	Ibid., p.441
1095	Ibid., p.441. Löbe was Reichtags president
1096	Wolfgang Ruge, p.227
1097	*Meine Lebenserinnerungen*, p.23
1098	Rudolf Hess in a letter dated 11.12.1924 to Ilse Pröhl in: *Rudolf Hess, Briefe*, p.357
1099	*Meine Lebenserinnerungen*, p.406, 407
1100	Ibid., p.407
1101	Ibid., p.407
1102	A term from Wolfram Pyta, p.461
1103	*Als ich Ludendorffs Frau war*, p.334
1104	*Meine Lebenserinnerungen*, p.408
1105	Peter Longerich, *Goebbels Biografie*, p.12
1106	Karl H. Wiegand, Ludendorff is in open War with the Pope In: *The Davenport Democrat and Leader*, 20 September 1923
1107	Hitler quoted in a letter from Rudolf Hess to Ilse Pröhl, date 11.12.1924, In: *Rudolf Hess Briefe*, p.357
1108	Erich Ludendorff, Als Lebens-und Kampfgefährtin, In: General Ludendorff (hg.), *Mathilde Ludendorff. Ihr Werk und Wirken*, p.39
1109	Robert Wistrich, *Wer war wer im Dritten Reich? Ein biographisches Lexikon*, p.88-9
1110	*Meine Lebenserinnerungen*, p.252
1111	*Mathilde Ludendorff, Ihr Werk und Wirken*, p.43
1112	Breucker, p.158
1113	Ibid., p.158
1114	Ibid., p.158
1115	*Mathilde Ludendorff, Ihr Werk und Wirken*, p.39, 40
1116	Perry Pierik, *Hitlers Lebensraum*, ch. 3
1117	Frank Schnoor, *Mathilde Ludendorff und das Christentum. Eine Radikale völkischen position in der Zeit der Weimarer Republik und des NS-Staates*, p.13
1118	Schoor, p.13
1119	The first church was established in Boston in 1785
1120	Ibid., p.13
1121	Ibid., p.15
1122	Mathilde von Kemnitz, *Erkenntnis-Erlösung*, p.5
1123	Mathilde Ludendorff (Dr. von Kemnitz), *Durch Forschen und Schicksal zum Sinn des Lebens, II. Teil von Statt Heiligenschein oder Hexenzeichen, mein Leben*, p.288-9
1124	Ibid., p.289
1125	Ibid., p.290
1126	Ibid., p.74
1127	Ibid., p.75
1128	Ibid., p.79
1129	Ibid., p.79-81
1130	Ibid., p.81-84, See also Hermann Rehwaldt, *Das schleichende Gift. Der Okkultismus*,

seine Lehre, Weltanschauung und Bekämpfung. 7.8.und 9.Heft der 1.Schriftenreihe, Ludendorffs Verlag

1131 *Mathilde Ludendorff, Ihr Werk und Wirken.* p.206-208
1132 *Deutscher Gottglaube,* p.28-9
1133 *Hitlers Lebensraum,* p.94-5
1134 Ibid., p.130
1135 For Paul de Lagarde see a.o. Ludwig Schemann, *Paul de Lagarde. Ein Lebens und Erinnerungsbild.*
1136 For Langbehn's life, see among others: Benedikt Momme Nissen, *Der Rembrandtdeutsche, Julius Langbehn.*
1137 *Hitlers Lebensraum,* p.101
1138 Ibid., p.101
1139 Jesus Germanicus? In: *Ludendorffs Volkswarte* 15.01.1933
1140 *Hitlers Lebensraum,* p.101, 102
1141 *Mathilde Ludendorff, Ihr werk und Wirken,* p.40
1142 Ibid., p.39,40
1143 Ibid., p.39-69
1144 Ibid., p.41
1145 Ibid., p.40
1146 Ibid., p.44
1147 *Meine Lebenserinnerungen,* p.399
1148 Ibid., p.413
1149 Wolfgang Ruge, p.219
1150 *Ein Kampf für Freiheit und Frieden. Ludendorffs Tannenbergbund 1925-1933,* p.17-8
1151 Refering the earlier battle of Tannenberg lost by 'the Germans' in 1410
1152 *Ein Kampf für Freiheit und Frieden,* p.19
1153 It never came to a trial because the union was dissolved before the trial, due to pressure from the Nazis. For details on Elfers and this case see: *Biographisch-Bibliographisches Kirchenlexikon Band XXX,* Gunther Schendel on Claus August Elfers. See also internet: www.kirchenlexikon.de
1154 *Ein Kampf für Freiheit und Frieden,* p.21
1155 Ibid., p.25
1156 Ibid., p.23
1157 Ibid., p.25
1158 Ibid., p.25
1159 *Meine Lebenserinnerungen,* p.38-39
1160 Ibid., p.49/Hartmuth Mahlberg, p.263
1161 Mahlberg, p.263
1162 Milton Bronner, Ex-Wife of War Lord stirs with new book, in: *The Charleston Daily,* 7 July 1929
1163 Die Karikatur Preussens in: Kurt Tucholsky, *Gesammelte Werke Band* 7
1164 Mahlberg, p.264
1165 *Meine Lebenserinnerungen,* p.49
1166 Erich Ludendorff, *Ueber Unbotmässigkeit im Kriege,* Munich: Ludendorffs Verlag 1935/Erich Ludendorff, *'Dirne Kriegsgeschichte. Vor dem Gericht des Weltkrieges. Zum Feldzug in Süd-Polen Anfang Oktober 1914,* München: Ludendorffs Verlag/ Erich Ludendorff, *Das Marne Drama. Der Fall Moltke-Hentsch,* München: Ludendorffs Verlag 1934/Werner Kybitz, *Ludendorffs Handstreich auf Lüttich,* München: Ludendorffs

Verlag 1939/ Von Wenninger, *Die Schlacht von Tannenberg, 1.2.u.3.Heft der 2.Schriftenreihe*, München: Ludendorffs Verlag 1935. Generalleutnant Ritter von Wenninger died on 08.09.1917

1167 *Dirne' Kriegsgeschichte*, p.1-2
1168 *Dirne' Kriegsgeschichte*, p.1-7
1169 Chest, p.80
1170 Ibid., p.80
1171 Ibid., p.81-2
1172 Ibid., p.86-7
1173 Erich Ludendorff, *Weltkrieg droht auf deutschem Boden*, p.3
1174 Ibid., p.3
1175 Men spoke of a 'devil's belt', and Rudolf Kjellén spoke of a 'geographische Einklemmung' and 'konzentrische Druck'. Werner Beumelburg described it even more plastically: *Sperrfeuer um Deutschland*. Rudolf Kjellén, *Die politische Probleme des Weltkrieges*, p.24-5/Werner Beumelburg, *Sperrfeuer um Deutschland*.
1176 Otto Muck, Der Sinn von fünftausend Jahren Kampf im Osten In: *Zeitschrift für Geopolitik*, Heft 10 Oktober.
1177 Oskar von Niedermayer, Wachstum und Wanderung in russischen Volkskörper, *Zeitschrift für Geopolitik*, Heft 6 1933, p.334-348
1178 *World War Droht auf deutschem Boden*, p.82
1179 See also Z.R.Dittrich, *De opkomst van het moderne Duitsland, deel 1, Dromen, worstelingen, tegenslagen1806-1862*
1180 Michael Stürmer, *Ein Nationalstaat gegen Geschichte und Geographie: das Deutsche Dilemma*
1181 Perry Pierik, *Karl Haushofer en het nationaal-socialisme. Tijd, werk en invloed*, p.115
1182 Karl Haushofer, Fromme Wünsche, Die slawische Idee der Absperrung des Deutschtums vom Osten in: *Zeitschrift für Geopolitik* Heft 6, 1933 p.330-333
1183 Friedrich Ratzel, *Politische Geographie*, Munich: R.Oldenbourg 1897, p. 4-19/Pierik, p.85
1184 For Steiner's ideas and life course see: Felix Steiner, *Die Armee der Geächteten*, Felix Steiner, *Die Freiwilligen, idee und Opfergang*, Paul Hausser, *Waffen-SS im Einsatz*, Bernd Wegner, *Hitlers politische Soldaten: Die Waffen-SS 1933-1945, Leitbild, Struktur und Funktion einer nationalsozialistischen Elite*, Felix West, *In de brandhaarden van het front. De Waffen-SS, opbouw, strijd en ondergang*.
1185 Ratzel, p.3
1186 Ibid., p.15
1187 Ibid., p.12
1188 Ibid., p.12
1189 Ibid., p.17
1190 *Karl Haushofer en het nationaal-socialisme*, ch. 4.7, Heinz Corazza, *Die Samurai. Ritter des Reiches in Ehre und Treue*
1191 Karl Lamprecht, *Krieg und Kultur*, p.9
1192 Mathilde Ludendorff, *Der Seele Wirken und Gestalten, Band III: Das Gottlied der Völker. Eine Philosphie der Kulturen*, ch. 1
1193 Erich Ludendorff, Die Stimme des Bluts in *Am heiligen Quell Deutscher kraft*, Folge 24 20.03.1937, p.937
1194 *Deutscher Gottglauben*, p.5
1195 Ibid., p.6

1196   Ibid., p.6
1197   Ibid., p.6
1198   Ibid., p.7
1199   Ibid., p.7
1200   Ibid., p.55-6, other works on 'Deutscher Gotterkenntniss' are a.o. E.Meyer-Dampen, *Deutsche Gotterkenntnis als Grundlage wehrhaften Deutschen Lebens*, München: Ludendorffs verlag 1934, I.,Wentzel, *Das geistige Ringen zwischen Christentum und Deutscher Gotterkenntnis,*, Munich: Ludendorffs Verlag 1936, H.G.von Waldow, *Ludendorffs Kampf gegen die Knechtung des deutschen Volkes durch Priesterherrschaft*, Munich: Ludendorffs Volkswarte Verlag, Hermann Andress, *Luther!!!, Friedrich der Grosse!!!, Ludendorff!!!* , *Priesterherrschaft oder Deutscher Gottglaube?* Dusseldorf, Verlag deutsche Revolution 1935
1201   'Schachtreligion' and 'Lichtreligion', see: Mathilde von Kemnitz Ludendorff, *Der Seele Wirken und Gestalten Band II Die Volksseele und ihre Machtgestallter, Eine Philosophie der Geschichte*, p.379
1202   Mathilde von Kemnitz, *Ein Leben der Freiheit, Zu ihrem 100. Geburtstag am 4. im Gilbhart 1977* zusammengestellt von Günther Duda, p.27
1203   Ibid., p.27, see also: Erich Ludendorff, Statt okkulter Priesterherrschaft-Gotterkenntnis. Mathilde Ludendorff im Werk und Wirken. In: *Am heiligen Quell deutscher Kraft*, Folge 13 5.10.1937 p.498-505, Richard Hoyer, Frau Dr. Mathilde Ludendorff als Rednerin in: *Am heiligen Quell Deutscher Kraft* Folge 13 5.10.1937, p.505-508
1204   Mathilde Ludendorff, *Vom Wahren Leben, Philosophische Essays*, p.38-41, see also Mathilde Ludendorff, *Hohewege und Abgründe, zwei Einführungsvorträge in Deutsche Gotterkenntnis gehalten auf der Tagung in Tutzing vom 2.-5. Erntings 1937*
1205   J.W. de Groot, *'Arische Gnosis'*, p.5, 28
1206   Alfred Rosenberg, *Der Mythus des 20.Jahrhunderts. Eine Wertung des seelisch geistigen Gestalten Kämpfe unserer Zeit*, Alfred Rosenberg, *Blut und Ehre. Ein Kampf für deutsche Wiedergeburt*, chapter *Weltanschauung und Kultur*, chapter *Blut, Boden, Kultur*
1207   De Groot, p.44/Perry Pierik/Henk Pors, *De verlaten monarch. Keizer Wilhelm II in Nederland*, p.35
1208   De Groot, p.45
1209   *Erlösung von Jesu Christo*, p.21
1210   Ibid., p.23
1211   Mathilde Ludendorff von Kemnitz, *Der Seele Wirken und Gestalten, Band II Die Volksseele und Ihre Machtgestalter, eine Philosophie der Geschichte*, p.385-388
1212   Written under the pseudonym Subhadra Bhikshu
1213   Michael M. Leria, Buddhas Wanderung von Ost nach West, In: *Börsenblatt für den Deutschen Buchhandel*, 8 März 1996, Nr.20 p. 124-128
1214   E. u. M. Ludendorff, *Das grosse Entsetzen, Die Bibel nicht Gottes Wort!* , p.3
1215   Ibid., p.11
1216   K.Pieper, *Ludendorff und die heilige Schrift, Antwort auf die Schrift 'Das grosse Entsetzen-Die Bibel nicht Gottes Wort'*, p.2
1217   Ibid., p.4
1218   Ibid., p.2
1219   Ibid., p.2
1220   In 1938, Mussolini showed Hitler a portrait of Jesus and pointed out the 'specifically Roman facial features' of Jesus, Pierik, *Hitlers Lebensraum*, p.101
1221   Artur Dinter, *Die Sünde wider die Liebe*, p.93

1222 Pieper., p.4
1223 Ibid., p.5
1224 Erich Ludendorff, *Abgeblitz, Antworten auf Theologengestammel*, p.8
1225 Perry Pierik, *Frans J. Los, In de ban van de 'nordische' geschiedschrijving. Karel de Grote in de ogen van het nationaal-socialisme* in: Perry Pierik/Martin Ros (ed.), *Vierde Bulletin van de Tweede Wereldoorlog*, p.371-381, other 'Saxon literature' from Ludendorffs Verlag is the work of Dr. Robert Lust, *Die Franken und das Christentum*, Munich: Ludendorffs Verlag 1936
1226 A.W.Rose, *Rome Mordet, mordet Seelen, Menschen, Völker*, Munich: Ludendorffs Verlag 1935
1227 Karl Conrad Ludwig Maurer, *Geplanter Ketzermord im Jahre 1866 aus neuer Jesuitenspiegel*, p.25 in honour of Ludendorff
1228 Ibid., p.25
1229 Erich Ludendorff, Der römische Pabst, Deutschlands Feind im Weltkriege. Eine Erinnerung an 1917, In: *Am heiligen Quell Deutscher kraft*, Folge 7, p.257-262/ see also: Erich Ludendorff, Das enthüllte Papsttum, In: *Am heiligen Quell Deutscher kraft*, Folge 6 20.6.1937 p.217-221, Mathilde Ludendorff, Fehlbare Wörte des unfehlbaren Papstes, In: Am heiligen *Quell Deutscher kraft*, Folge 2 20.4.1937, p.53-62
1230 Hans Hagen-Königshorst, Orgien am papstlichen Hof! In: *Am heiligen Quell Deutscher kraft* Folge 9 5.8.1937 p.362-364
1231 Dr.Mathilde von Kemnitz/W.v.d.Cammer, Christliche Grausamkeit an Deutschen Frauen. 2. Aufsätze. München: Ludendorffs verlag 1934/ Ilse Wentzel, *Die Frau, Die Sklavin, der Priester*, München: Ludendorffs Verlag 1939, Mathilde von Kemnitz Ludendorff, Rom im starken Vormarsch In: *Am heiligen Quell Deutscher kraft* Folge 15, 1934, Die Stellung der Frau in Heidentum und Christentum (Beleuchtet an dem Schicksal der Hexen) In: *Am heiligen Quell deutscher Kraft* Folge 6 1934
1232 Franz Griese, *Ein Priester ruft: 'Los von Rom'*, Munich: Ludendorffs Volkswarte Verlag 1932
1233 Motto book Gengler: *Dr.Ludwig F.Gengler, Katholische Aktion im Angriff auf Deutschland. Die Luge von 'rein religiösen' Werbefeldzug*, Munich: Ludendorff Verlag 1937
1234 Ibid., p.4
1235 Ibid., p.4
1236 Ibid., p.4
1237 Ritter Georg, *Oesterreich, Die europäische Kolonie des Vatikans*, München: Ludendorffs Verlag/Kuntz Iring, *Nie wieder Habsburg!Die Habsburger in der Geschichte der Deutschen* and B.Dietrich, *Der Weg zur Jesuitendiktatur in Oesterreich 1918-1935* in one volume: *Nie wieder Habsburg!*, Munich: Ludendorffs Verlag 1936, H.Janow, *Rom, Poland, die Ukraine*, Munich: Ludendorffs Verlag 1939
1238 Gengler, p.12
1239 Ibid., p.26
1240 Ibid., p.31
1241 Amt für kulturellen Frieden In: *Am heiligen Quell deutscher kraft*, Folge 6 1934, p.235-6
1242 Erich Ludendorff, Abrüstung und Sicherheit, In: *Am heiligen Quell deutscher kraft*, Folge 6 1934, p.201-204
1243 J.Strunk, Was will Stalin? In: *Am heiligen Quell Deutscher kraft*, Folge 8 20.7.1937 p.302-307

1244 Rene Fueloep-Miller, *Macht en geheimen der jezuïeten*, p. 310-313. The combination of Jesuit and Freemasonry is a little described subject in the literature. A kind of open plea for cooperation appeared by T.(Tohotom)Nagy, *Jesuiten und Freimaurer*, Wien: Wilhelm Frick Verlag 1969 which originally appeared in Spanish, in Buenos Aires.

1245 E.Freiherr von Engelhardt, *Weltmachtpläne. Zur Entstehung der sogenannten zionistischen Protokolle. Neue Zusammenhänge zwischen Judentum und Freimaurerei [1036]* Here used Archiv Edition, *Reihe Hintergrundanalysen-Band* 35, Vioel, 2000, p.12-15

1246 For the Dutch language area see Ab Caransa, *Vrijmetselaarij en jodendom. De wereld een tempel*, Hilversum 2001

1247 *Meine Lebenserinnerungen*, p.313

1248 Ibid., see diagram p.313

1249 Andreas Molau, *Alfred Rosenberg, der Ideologe des Nationalsozialismus. Eine politische Biografie*, p.97. P. J. Verstraete, *Houston Stewart Chamberlain*, Hfst. 9

1250 J.Strunk, *Vatikan und Kreml*, Munich: Ludendorffs Verlag 1934

1251 Ibid., p.17

1252 Ibid., p.17

1253 W.von der Cammer, Die kommunistischen Agitation im Christentum, In: *Am heiligen Quell Deutscher kraft*, Folge 14, 20.10.1934, p.533-4

1254 Erich Ludendorff, Heraus aus der Weltkrise in: *Ludendorffs Volkswarte*, 04.01.1931

1255 W. Marr, *Sieg des Judenthums über das Germanenthum, vom nicht confessionellen Standpunkt betrachtet*, p.11

1256 Ibid., p.29

1257 Ibid., p.32

1258 Ibid., p.48

1259 Ibid., p.11, 25, 29, 32

1260 *Karl Haushofer en het nationaal-socialisme. Tijd, werk en invloed*, p.86-7

1261 Dr.Fr.Wichtl, *Weltfreimauerei, Weltrevolution, Weltrepublik, Eine Untersuchung über Ursprung und Endziele des Weltkrieges*, Munich: J.F.Lehmanss Verlag 1923

1262 B.Segel, *Welt-krieg, Welt-Revolution, Welt-Verschwörung, Welt-Oberregierung*, p.11

1263 Hermann Rehwaldt, *Die Kriegshetzer von Heute*, Ludendorffs Verlag Munich 1938

1264 Erich Ludendorff, *Vernichtung der Freimaurerei durch Enthüllung ihrer Geheimnisse*, p.9

1265 Erich Ludendorff, *Die Revolution von Oben. Das Kriegsende und die Vorgänge beim Waffenstilstand*, Lorch:Karl Rohm Verlag, 1926

1266 German Nording, *Geheimnisse vom Rosenkreuz*, Munich: Ludendorffs Verlag 1938, kindly supplied by AMORC, Grossloge Baden-Baden

1267 Ibid., p.5

1268 Ibid., p.5

1269 Ibid., p.6

1270 Ibid., introduction, p.3-12

1271 Ibid., p.45

1272 *Auf dem Weg zur Feldherrnhalle*

1273 Isis often turns up in grail literature, see for instance in Graham Hanock/Robert Bauval, *De talisman. De zoektocht naar het eeuwenoude complot van geheime genootschappen*, Baarn: Tirion 2004/Jan Smulders, *De ware Graal en zijn valse hoeders*, Soesterberg: Aspekt 2005

1274 Herbert van Erkelens, Het geheim van *Die Zauberflöte* in: *HN* 12 June 1999, p.22-25/ Marcel S.Zwitser, Die Zauberflöte by Mozart. Mysteriespel of sprookjesopera? In:

Luister May 2006, p.8-71/Mathilde Ludendorff, *Mozarts Leben und gewaltsamer Tod*, illustration on p.189

1275 Kasper Jansen, Raadsel rond Mozart toch niet opgelost in: *NRC-Handelsblad* 9 January 2006

1276 Alfred Stoss, *Der Kampf zwischen Juda und Japan. Japan als Vorkämpfer freier Volkswirtschaft*. Munich: Ludendorffs Verlag 1934

1277 Alfred Stoss, *Der Raubzug gegen Japan! Wannn endlich wehren sich die Völker?*, Munich: Ludendorffs Volkswarte Verlag z.j.

1278 Stoss may have been a temporary commander on submarine U-8 between 1 September 1914 and 4 March 1915

1279 Erich Ludendorff, Mysterien-und sonstige Politik. (Die Hand der überstaatlichen Mächte) in: *Am heiligen Quell deutscher kraft*, Folge 24 20.3.1937, p.944-950

1280 *Flensburgerhefte Sonderheft* No. 8 p.53

1281 Robert Schneider, Der zehnjahriger Kampf des Feldherrn gegen den Freimaurerbund In: *Am heiligen Quell deutscher kraft*, Folge 9, 5.8.1937 p.341-347

1282 Das Marne Drama p.4

1283 Ibid., p.8, 9

1284 The revived discussion around the Marne drama after Seidler's death is described in: Arfst Wagner, Anthroposophen in der Zeit des nationalsozialismus (Teil III), In: *Flensburger Hefte*, Anthroposophie im Gespräch. Anthroposophen in der Zeit des deutschen Faschismus-Zur Verschwörungsthese, Sonderheft Nr. 8 1991 p.55

1285 All examples from Dr. Armin Roth, *Nationalsozialismus und katholische Kirche, Meine Schriftwechsel mit der Gauleitung Rheinland und der Reichsparteileitung der NSDAP sowie mit der Kanzlei Adolf Hitlers*, p.6-8, for the Ludendorffs criticism on Faulhaber see also; Dr. Ludwig Engel, *Der Jesuitismus eine Staatsgefahr*, 9.Heft der 2.Schriftenreihe, p.11

1286 Hermann Andress, *Luther!, Friedrich der Grosse!! Ludendorf!!! Priesterherrschaft oder Deutscher Gottglaube*, Düsseldorf Verlag deutsche Revolution 1935. For the debate on Luther and national socialism see also: Berthold Rubin, Die Realitäten der deutschen und jüdischen Geschichte: Im Spiegel des Streites um die Umdichtung der Lutherbibel In: *Kirche*, 1 September 1978

1287 Mathilde Ludendorff, Das Schreckgespenst in Halle in *Ludendorffs Volkswarte* 04.01.1931

1288 Erich Ludendorff, Was wollen die Nationalsozialisten? In: *Ludendorffs Volkswarte 22 February 1931* Folge 8 3.Jahrgang

1289 Armin Roth, *Das Reichskonkordat vom 20.Juli 1933*, p.4

1290 Guenter Lewy, *De Rooms-Katolieken kerk en Nazi-Duitsland*, p.84

1291 Ibid., p.121

1292 *Meine Lebenserinneringen 1929-1933*, p.341

1293 Herr Seldtes Selbstkennzeichung In: *Ludendorffs Volkswarte* 22.2.1931

1294 Borst, p.235, 236, the titles of the series: Kurt Iring, *Not und Kampf deutscher Bauern. (Bauernkriege)*, 4 und 5. Heft der 2.Schriftenreihe, Ludendorffs. Kurt Füger, *Im 'Geist von Potsdam' wider den fremden Geist*, 4.Heft der 1.Schriftenreihe, Ludendorffs Verlag: Walther Löhde, *Schiller. Eine Deutscher Revolutionär*, 10.Heft der 1.Schriftenreihe,/ Mathilde Ludendorff., *Ist das Leben sinnlose Schinderei?* , 5.Heft der 1.Schriftenreihe, /Mathilde Ludendorff, *Verschüttete Volksseele. Nach Berichten aus Südwestafrika,*/ Arnim Roth., *Weltanschauung und Wirtschaft*, 6.Heft der 1.Schriftenreihe,/ W.Wendt, *Die irreführende Denkart der Abergläubigen und ihre falsche Institution*, 3.Heft der

1.Schriftenreihe,/ Generalleutnant Ritter von Wenninger., *Die Schlacht von Tannenberg*, 1.2.und 3.Heft.

1295   Chest, p.162
1296   Ibid., p.168
1297   Ibid., p.165
1298   *Meine Lebeserinnerungen*, p.383
1299   Borst, p.208
1300   Kurt Heimart Holscher, *Ein Gott-nahes Volk*, in: Luise Raab (hg.), *Tannenberg-Jahrweiser*, Munich: Ludendorffs Verlag 1935, p.41-44, see also the poem by Lotte Huwe on the following page, *Schon-Isa vom Stedingerland*
1301   Hans Hugo Brinkmann, *Das Bildnis Ludendorffs* in: Hanno von Kemnitz, *Tannenbergjahrbuch 1939*, Munich: Ludendorffs Verlag 1939, p. 20
1302   *Deutsche Kampfkalender*, Munich: Ludendorffs Verlag 1937 and 1938
1303   An overview of this can be found in Herbert Frank, *Freiheit*, Ludendorffs Verlag: Munich 1934
1304   An example of vanity was the series *Die Rothe Reihe*, consisting of 'Feldherrnwörte', consisting solely of Ludendorff quotations. Several volumes appeared, see for example: Erich Ludendorff, *Worte Erich Ludendorffs über Wehrhaftigkeit, Soldaten und Feldherrntum*, Die Rote Reihe Band 2, Munich: Ludendorffs Verlag 1938
1305   Title pamphlet by Walther Loehde
1306-8 *Mit anderen Augen. Jahrbuch der Sonntags-Zeitung 1920-1929*, p.126, 127
1309   *Meine Lebenserinnerungen*, p.51, 52
1310   Ibid., p.52
1311   Ibid., p.53
1312   *Ludendorffs Volkswarte* 24 August 1930: Die geheime Weltregierung wirkt in allem Parteien
1313   Die Geheimnisvollen Protokolle der Weisen von Zion im Faschistenstaate, In: *Ludendorffs Volkswarte* 23.0.1930
1314   Jude und Jesuit bei der Arbeit, *Ludendorffs Volkswarte* 23.02.1930
1315   Onder kop Tannenbergbund, Landesverband Nord In: *Ludendorffs Volkswarte* 23.02.1930
1316   Meynig claimed, relying on Hasselbach, that there were direct links between Jesuitism and Freemasonry; Wilfried Meynig, *Christliche Wissenschaft*, ch. 2
1317   Hasselbacher, F. (hg.), Hochverrat der Feldlogen im Weltkrieg (1935)/The mention of his lectures in the *Volkswarte* is in the newspaper of 23.02.1930
1318   Ibid., p.56
1319   Hellmuth Pfeifer, Verunglimpfungen des feldgrauen Ehrenkleides In: *Ludendorffs Volkswarte* 03.08.1930
1320   Friedrich-Karl Plehwe, *Reichskanzler Kurt von Schleicher. Weimars letzte Chance gegen Hitler*, p.328
1321   General a.d. Graf von der Schulenburg expressed himself this way, see; Klaus - Jürgen Müller, *Generaloberst Ludwig Beck*, Eine Biographie, p.157
1322   Wolfram Wette, *Die Wehrmacht. Feindbilder, Vernichtungskrieg, Legenden*, p.81
1323   Ibid., p.77
1324   Ibid., p.75/Walter Görlitz, *Der Deutsche Generalstab*, p.237
1325   Gordon A. Graig, *The Politics of the Prussian Army 1640-1945*, Oxford University Press 1955, p.485
1326   He was also called 'Parteigeneral', Walter Görlitz, p.233

1327 Von Schleicher declined General Eugen Ott's offer to stay in Japan for a longer time in February 1934, see Plehwe chapter 24
1328 *Meine Erinneringen*, p.15-19
1329 Ibid., p.19
1330 Ibid., p.22
1331 He later drew a parallel with the London fire at the Cristal Palace in December 1936, in which he saw the hand of Freemasons. Ibid., p.22
1332 Ibid., p.20, 27
1333 Erich Ludendorff *Tannenberg, geschichtliche Wahrheit über die Schlacht*, p.108, 109
1334 K.J.Müller, *Generaloberst Ludwig beck. Eine Biographie*, p.155
1335 Ibid., p.156-7
1336 Ibid., p.158
1337 *Meine Lebenserinnerungen*, p.130
1338 Ibid., p.130
1339 Müller, p.152
1340 Ibid., p.159
1341 Ibid., p.160
1342 Ibid., p.160
1343 Ibid., p. 160
1344 This was recorded by photographer Richard Woersching
1345 Ibid., p.160
1346 Ibid., p.161
1347 Letter to Breucker on 1 March 1935, in Breucker p.197
1348 Ludendorff would see this as propaganda for Hitler, letter from Hans Binder to author 9 September 2006
1349 Müller, p.162
1350 Ibid., p.162
1351 Ibid., p.162
1352 Ibid., p.163
1353 Ibid., p.164
1354 Ibid., p.164
1355 Ibid., p.166
1356 Joachim Fest, *Hitler, a biografie*. Vol 2, p.85, see also Kirstin A.Schafer, *Werner von Blomberg, Hitlers erster Feldmarschall. Eine Biographie*. Schoningh: Paderborn 2006
1357 Erich Ludendorff, Die SA wartet und erwartet, In: *Ludendorffs Volkswarte* 12.2.1933
1358 Müller, p.167
1359 Klaus Scholder, *Die Mittwochsgesellschaft*, p. 292-2940
1360 Müller, p.167
1361 Ibid., p.167
1362 Ibid., p.168
1363 Görlit , *Der Deutsche Generalstab*, p.233
1364 Müller, p.168
1365 General Heinz Gaedcke wondered in his memoirs why the German generals had not carried out a putsch against Hitler in 1938. The answer to this question undoubtedly lies in the fact that preparations with Ludendorff had come to nothing. Gerhard Brugmann (hg.), Heinz Gaedcke, *Wege eines Soldaten*, p.327
1366 *Meine Lebenserinnerungen*, p.89
1367 *Ludendorffs Volkswarte* 22.01.1933

1368 *Meine Lebenserinnerungen*, p.89
1369 Erich Ludendorff, Die SA wartet und erwartet, *Ludendorffs Volkswarte* 12.02.1933
1370 Diary note Joseph Goebbels, 29 June 1934 In; Ralf Georg Reuth (hg.), *Joseph Goebbels Tagebücher* Band 2 1930-1934, p.841-2
1371 *Meine Lebenserinnerungen*, p. 91
1372 Ibid., p.91
1373 Mahlberg, p.123 et seq.
1374 *Meine Lebenserinnerungen*, p.2
1375 In this book it is a part of the appendix, Anhang 2
1376 Fritz Tobias, Ludendorff, Hindenburg and Hitler. Das Phantasieprodukt des Ludendorffs-Briefes. In: Uwe Backes/ Eckhard Jesse/ Rainer Zitelmann (hg.), *Die Schatten der Vergangenheit. Impulse zur Historisierung des Nationalsozialismus*, p.559-562/Lothar Gruchmann, Ludendorffs 'prophetischer' Brief an Hindenburg vom Januar/Februar 1933. Eine Legende. In: *Vierteljahrshefte für Zeitgeschichte* 47 (1999) p.319-342. It is strange that Wolfram Pyta, Anna von der Goltz, and other 'recent' Hindenburg biographers like William J.Astore and Denis E.Showalter, say nothing about this.
1377 See for example the letters printed in Henrik Eberle (hg.), *Briefe an Hitler. Ein Volk schreibt seinem Führer. Unbekannte Dokumente aus Moskauer Archiven - zum ersten mal veröffentlicht*, p.57 et seq.
1378 Brief Ingo Balding to author 30 January 2010
1379 For example on 28 September 1933, *Meine Lebenserinnerungen*, p.248, 249
1380 *Meine Lebenserinnerungen*, p.234
1381 Ibid., p.252
1382 Wolfgang Ruge, *Hindenburg*, p.219
1383 Die mathematische Erbmasse Hindenburgs, In: *Ludendorffs Volkswarte* 08.01.1933
1384 Pytra, p.529
1385 Pytra, p.529
1386 Hans-Günther Seraphim (Hg.), *Das politische Tagebuch Alfred Rosenbergs*, DTV-Dokumente, p.54-5
1387 Not to be confused with Gustav Adolf Joachim Graf von der Goltz, the General
1388 Rüdiger von der Goltz, Lebenserinnerungen. Kleine Erwerbung 653 *Archiv Koblenz*, p.171 - p.184 of the typescript-
1389 See a.o. Brauninger p.98 et seq.
1390 *Ludendorffs Volkswarte* 20 December 1933: Ludendorffs Volkswarte verboten, Polizeidirektion München nr VIc925/31
1391 Erich Ludendorff, Zum Jahreswechsel In: *Ludendorffs Volkswarte*, 10.01.1932
1392 Aus unserem kampf. In: *Ludendorffs Volkswarte*, 19.02.1933
1393 Aus unserem Kampf, In *Ludendorffs Volkswarte*, 05.03.1933
1394 Regulation, 6036/33
1395 Mathilde Ludendorff, *Deutscher Gottglaube*, Ludendorffs Verlag; Munich 1934
1396 Aufklärung der Regierung über den Tannenbergbund In: *Ludendorffs Volkswarte*, 19.03.1933
1397 Hans Kurth, *Die Weltdeutung Dr.Mathilde Ludendorffs. Eine Einführung in die Werke der Philosophin*, Ludendorffs Verlag, Munich 1934
1398 Erich Ludendorff, Auss unserem Kampf. Terrorakte gegen unsere Buchhandlungen. 'Der Kampf gilt dem Marxismus'. In: *Ludendorffs Volkswarte*, 19.03.1933
1399 Tannenberg-Buchhandlung eine Gefahr für Ordnung und Sicherheit, In: *Ludendorffs Volkswarte*, 26.03.1933

1400   See also: Erich Ludendorff, Schluss mit Wirtschaftskrise, In *Ludendorffs Volkswarte*, 08.01.1933/ 'Ländliche Kollektivwirtschaft in Deutschland', Ludendorffs Volkswarte, 05.03.1933/ Politik und Wirtschaft im Kabinett Hitler-Von Papen-Hugenberg, In: *Ludendorffs Volkswarte*, 19.02.02.1933/ Freimaurer Schacht will 'mobilisieren', In: *Ludendorffs Volkswarte*, 12.02.1933/ Erich Ludendorff, Bauerschaft im Verderben, In: *Ludendorffs Volkswarte*, 05.02.1933/ Gedanken zur heutigen Deutschen Landwirtschaft In: *Ludendorffs Volkswarte*, 22.01.1933

1401   *Meine Lebenserinnerungen*, p.49

1402   Ibid., p.49, 50

1403   Letter to Breucker 14 November 1933, in Breucker, p.195

1404   Letter of 3 February 1932, copy in possession of author, original in private archive

1405   Arnim Roth, *Nationalsozialismus und Katholische Kirche. Mein Schriftwechsel mit der Gauleitung Rheinland und der Reichsparteileitung der NSDAP sowie mit der Kanzlei Adolf Hitlers*, p.2-9

1406   Ibid., p.25

1407   Volker Ullrich, *Adolf Hitler, Die Jahre des Aufstiegs*, p.413

1408   *Meine Lebenserinnerungen*, p.145

1409   Ibid., p.145

1410   Ralf Georg Reuth, *Joseph Goebbels Tagebücher Band I 1924-1929*, p.171

1411   *Meine Lebenserinnerungen*, p.148-165

1412   Uhle-Wettler, p.418

1413   Erich Meinecke (hg.), *Erich und Mathilde Ludendorff. Die machtvolle Religosität des Deutschen Volkes vor 1945*, p.228

1414   *Studiengruppe Naturalimsus*. 30-01-2013 Blog Archiv

1415   Ibid, Blog 30-01-2013

1416   Uhle-Wettler, p.418

1417   Mathilde Ludendorff. *Freiheitskampf wider eine Welt von Feinden an der Seite des Feldherrn Ludendoff*, p.285-6

1418   Breucker, p.198

1419   Hugo Beer, *Moskaus As im Kampf der Geheimdienste: die Rolle Martin Bormans in der deutschen Führungsspitze* (1984), p.72.

1420   Uhle-Wettler, p.419, Breucker, p.161-2

1421   *Freiheitskampf wider eine Welt von Feinden an der Seite des Feldherrn Ludendoff*, p.292-296

1422   Letter Dr.med. Reinhard Aigner to the author 11.03.2016

1423   Hartmut Mahlberg, p.190-193

1424   Uhle-Wettler, p.419

1425   Major von Wedel, Der Feldherr Ludendorff. In: *Die Woche* 5 Januar 1938

1426   Letter Ingo Henn to the author 19.04.2016

Literature

-Aleff, E. (Hg.)., *Das Dritte Reich*. Hanover: Fackelträgerverlag 1970

-Allen, H. T., *Mein Rheinland Tagebuch*. Berlin: Verlag von Reimar Hobbing 1923

-Altrichter, H., *Russia 1917. Ein Land auf der Suche nach sich selbst*. Paderborn: Schöningh 1997

-Andics, H., *Der Untergang der Donau-Monarchie. Österreich-Ungarn von der Jahrhundertwende bis zum November 1918. Neue Österreichische Geschichte in 4 Bänden, Band 2*. Wien-Munich: MTV-Molden-Taschenbuch-Verlag 1976

-Andress, H., *Luther!, Friedrich der Grosse!!, Ludendorff!!!, Priesterherrschaft oder Deutscher Gottglaube?* Düsseldorf: Verlag 'Deutsche Revolution' 1935

-Andriessen, J. H. J., *Een andere waarheid. Een nieuwe visie op het ontstaan van de Eerste Wereldoorlog 1914-1918*. Soesterberg: Aspekt 1999

-Asprey, R., *The German High Command at War: Hindenburg and Ludendorff Conduct World War I*. William Morrow & Company 1991

-Astor, W.J., & Showalter, D. E., *Hindenburg. Icon of German Militarism*. Washington D.C.: Potomac Books 2005

-Baden, Prinz M.von, *Erinnerungen und Dokumente*. Berlin und Leipzig: Deutsche Verlags Anstalt 1927

-Badia, G., *Clara Zetkin. Eine neue Biographie*. Berlin: Dietz, 1994

-Baer, C. H., *Der Völkerkrieg. Eine Chronik der Ereignisse seit dem 1.Juli 1914* (28 volumes). Stuttgart: Verlag von Julius Hoffmann 1914-1922

-Balck, H., *Ordnung im Chaos. Erinnerungen 1893-1948*. Osnabrück: Biblio Verlag 1981

-Bartetzko, D., *Illusionen in Stein. Stimmungsarchitektur im deutschen Faschismus. Ihre Vorgeschichte in Theater-und-Film-Bauten.* Reinbek bei Hamburg: Rowohlt 1985

-Bartsch, G., *Zwischen drei Stühlen. Otto Strasser.Eine Biographie.* Koblenz: Verlag Siegfried Bublies 1990

-Baur, J., *Die deutsche Kolonie in München 1900-1945. Deutsch-russische Beziehungen in 20. Jahrhundert.* Wiesbaden: Harrassowitz Verlag 1998

-Bauert-Keetman, I., *Deutsche Industriepioniere.* Tübingen: Rainer Wunderlich Verlag 1966

-Bayerlein, B. H., Broue, P., & Ferro, M., et al. (Hg.), *Archive des Kommunismus-Pfade des XX. Jahrhunderts, Band 3* and in: Bayerlein, B. H., Babicenko, L. G., & Firsov, F. I. et al., *Deutscher Oktober 1923. Ein Revolutionsplan und sein Scheitern.* Berlin: Aufbau Verlag 2003

-Beck, K., & Berlin, J. B. (Hg.), *Stefan Zweig, Briefe 1932-1942.* Frankfurt am Main: S.Fischer 2005

-Beckers, H., *Adolf Hitler Tag für Tag. Eine Chronologie mit Literaturangaben. Band 1 1889-1938.* Voorschoten: Selbstverlag 2006

-Beckh, R., *Der Islam und seine Bedeutung im Plane der überstaatlichen Mächte.* Munich: Ludendorffs Verlag 1937

-Beer, H., *Moskaus im Kampf der Geheimdienste: die Rolle Martin Bormans in der deutschen Führungsspitze.* Pähl: Verlag Hohe Warte, 1984

-Benary, A., *Die Schlacht bei Tannenberg.* Leipzig: Franz Schneider Verlag 1933

-Ben-Itto, H., *Anatomie van een vervalsing. De Protocollen van de Wijzen van Sion.* Soesterberg: Aspekt 2000

-Benz, W., & Graml, H., *Biographisches Lexikon zur Weimarer Republik.* Munich: Verlag C.H.Beck 1988

-Beradt, C., *Paul Levi. Ein demokratischer Sozialist in der Weimarer Republik.* Frankfurt am Main: Europäische Verlagsanstalt 1969

-Berggötz, S. O. (Hg.), *Ernst Jünger, Politische Publizistik 1919-1933.* Stuttgart: Klett-Cotta z.j.

-Berglar, P., *Walther Rathenau, Seine Zeit, sein Werk, seine Persönlichkeit.* Bremen: Schünemann Universitatsverlag 1970

-Berglar, P., *Konrad Adenauer. Konkursverwalter oder Erneuerer der Nation.* Göttingen: Muusterschmidt 1975

-Bergsträsser, L., *Geschichte der politischen Parteien in Deutschland.* Munich: Isar verlag 1952

-Beumelburg, W., *Sperrfeuer um Deutschland.* Oldenburg: Gerhard Stalling 1929

-Billung, R., *Rund um Hitler.* Munich: Bernhard Funck Verlag 1931

-Bircher, E., & Bode, W., *Schlieffen. Mann und Idee.* Zürich: Verlag Albert Nauck 1937

-Borst, G., *Die Ludendorff-Bewegung 1919-1961. Eine Analyse monologer Kommunikationsformen in der sozialen Zeitkommunikation.* Augsburg: Dissertationsdruck Werner Blasaditsch 1969

-Boterman, F., *Oswald Spengler. Der Untergang des Abendlandes. Cultural pessimist, political activist.* Assen and Maastricht: Van Gorcum 1992

-Bournazel, R., *Rapallo: Ein Französisches Trauma.* Köln: Markus Verlag 1976

-Bouwman, Dr. P. J., *Jaurès, Wilson, Rathenau.* Amsterdam: H.J.Paris 1936

-Brabers, J., & Lemmens, R., *Luik, augustus 1914. Zoektocht naar een vergeten slag.* Soesterberg: Aspekt 2009

-Bracher, K. D., *Wendezeiten der Geschichte. Historisch-politische Essays 1987-1992.* Stuttgart 1992 [Munich: Taschenbuchausgabe 1995].

-Bräuninger, W., *Hitlers Kontrahenten in der NSDAP 1921-1945.* Munich: Herbig Verlagsbuchhandlung 2004

-Brennecke, D., *Sven Hedin. Mit Selbstzeugnissen und Bilddokumenten. Rororo bildmonographien.* Reinbek bei Hamburg: Rowohlt 1986

-Breucker, W., *Die Tragik Ludendorffs. Eine kritische Studie auf Grund persönlicher Erinnerungen an den General und seine Zeit.* Stollhamm (Oldb): Helmut Rauschenbusch Verlag 1953

-Brownell,W./ Drace-Brownell, D., *The First Nazi. Erich Ludendorff, The Man who made Hitler possible.* Berkeley: Counterpoint (2016)

-Bruce, A., *An Illustrated Companion to the First World War.* London: Michael Joseph 1989

-Brugmann, G. (Hg.), *Heinz Gaedcke, Wege eines Soldaten.* Books On Demand Gmbh 2005

-Brüning, H., *Memoirs 1918-1934.* Stuttgart: Deutsche Verlags-Anstalt 1970

-Bry, C. C., *Der Hitler-Putsch. Berichte und Kommentare eines Deutschland-Korrespondenten (1922-1924) für das 'Argentinische Tag- und Wochenblatt'.* Nordlingen: Franz Greno Verlag 1987

-Buetow, W. J., *Hindenburg, Heerführer und Ersatzkaiser.* Bergisch Gladbach: Bastei und Lübbe Verlag 1984

-Bullock, A., *Hitler. Leven en ondergang van een tiran.* Utrecht: A.W.Bruna en zoon 1952

-Buurman, M. den, *Heinrich Mann, Het goede in een mens, een biografie.* Soesterberg: Aspekt 2014

-Bijlsma, F., *Raoul Wallenberg. Biografie onder redachtie van Perry Pierik en Martin Ros.* Soesterberg: Aspekt 2006

-Cahill, E., *Freemasonry and the anti-christian Movement.* Dublin: M.H.Gill and Son, LTD. 1930

-Caransa, A., *Vrijmetselarij en jodendom. De wereld een tempel.* Hilversum: Lost 2001

-Carlebach, E., *Hitler war kein Betriebsunfall. Hinter den Kulissen der Weimar Republik: Die programmierte Diktatur.* Bonn: Pahl-Rugenstein Verlag Nachfolger 1996

-Cherep-Spiridovich, A, Count., *The Secret World Government or 'The Hidden Hand'. The Unrevealed in* History. Chicago 1925. Used here: photomechanical reprint Escondio: The Book Tree 2000

-Cohn, N., *Die Protokolle der Weisen von Zion. Der Mythus von der jüdischen Weltverschwörung.* Köln, Berlin: Kiepenheuer und Witsch 1969

-Corazza, H., *Die Samurai. Ritter des Reiches in Ehre und Treue.* Berlin-Munich: Zentralverlag der NSDAP, Franz Eher Verlag 1937

-Cornwell, J., *Hitler's Paus. De verborgen geschiedenis van Pius XII.* Amsterdam-Antwerp: Balans/Van Halewyck 1999

-Craig, G. A., *The Politics of the Prussian Army 1640-1945.* Oxford: Oxford University Press 1955

-Cüppers, M., *Wegbereiter der Shoa. Die Waffen-SS, der Kommandostab Reichsführer SS und die Judenvernichtung 1939-1945.* Darmstadt: Wissenschaftliche Buchgesellschaft 2011

-Czech-Jochberg, E., *Die Verantwortlichen im Weltkrieg.* Leipzig: Verlag von R. F. Koehler 1932

-Daniels, R. V., *A Documentary History of Communism. Volume 2. Communism and the World.* London: Vermont Books, Publishers 1987

-Deschner, K., *Mit Gott und dem Führer. Die Politik der Päpste zur Zeit des Nationalsozialismus.* Cologne: Kiepenheuer und Witsch 1988

-Devi Mukherji, S., *Gold im Schmeltztiegel. Erlebnisse im Nachkriegsdeutschland, Kritik. Die Stimme des Volkes, Nr.60.* Padua 1982

-Deutsche *Kampfkalender.* Munich: Ludendorffs Verlag 1937 and 1938

-Dinter, A., *Die Sünde wider das Blut.* Leipzig: Im Wolfverlag 1919

-Dinter, A., *Die Sünde wider den Geist.* Leipzig: Verlag Matthes und Thost 1921

-Dinter, A., *Die Sünde wider die Liebe.* Leipzig: Matthes und Thost, 1922

-Dittrich, Z. R., *De opkomst van het moderne Duitsland. Dromen, Wostelingen, Tegenslagen 1806-1862.* Groningen-Djakarta: J. B. Wolters 1956

-Dittrich, Z. R., Naarden, B., & Renner, H. (ed.), *Knoeien met het verleden. Dertien beroemde gevallen van geschiedvervalsing.* Het Spectrum: Utrecht 1984

-Donnel, C., *Breaking the Fortress Line 1914.* South Yorkshire: Pen & Sword 2013

-Dornberg, J., *Der Hitlerputsch. Munich, 8 und 9 November 1923.* Frankfurt am Main: Ullstein 1989

-Dornemann, L., *Clara Zetkin, Leben und Wirken.* Berlin: Dietz Verlag 1974

-Dowe, D., & Schneider, M., Historisches Forschungszentrum der Friedrich Ebert-Stiftung, *Reihe: Politik-und Gesellschaftsgeschichte, Band 62:* Hecht, Cornelia., *Deutsche Juden und Antisemitismus in der Weimarer Republik.* Bonn: Dietz Verlag 2006

-Eberle, H. (Hg.), *Briefe an Hitler. Ein Volk schreibt seinem Führer. Unbekannte Dokumente aus Moskauer Archiven - zum ersten mal veröffentlicht.* Bergisch Gladbach: Gustav Lübbe Verlag 2007

-Eglau, H. O., *Fritz Thyssen. Hitlers Gönner und Geisel.* Berlin: Siedler Verlag 2003

-Einem, Generaloberst von, *Erinnerungen eines Soldaten 1853-1933.* Leipzig: Koehler 1933

-Ein *Kampf für Freiheit und Frieden. Ludendorffs Tannenbergbund 1925-1933.* Pähl: Verlag Hohe Warte 1997

-Eitner, H-J., *Hitler. Das Psychogramm.* Munich: Ullstein 1994

-Ellis, C., & Chamberlian, P., *The Great Tanks.* London-New York: Hamlyn 1975

-Engel, L., *Der Jesuitismus eine Staatsgefahr. 9. der 2.Schriftenreihe.* Munich: Ludendorffs Verlag 1935

-Engelhardt, E. Freiherr von, *Weltmachtpläne. Zur Entstehung der sogenannten zionistischen Protokolle. Neue Zusammenhänge zwischen judentum und Freimaurerei.* Used here: *Archiv Edition, Reihe Hintergrundanalysen-Band 35.* Viöl 2000

-Erler, G. H. J., *Der Einfluss überstaatlicher Mächte auf die Kriegs- und Völkerbundpolitik Woodrow Wilsons. Institut für ganzheitliche Forschung, Materialien zur Geschichtsforschung Heft .* Verlag für ganzheitliche Forschung [1938] 1996

-Ernst, F., *Aus dem Nachlass des Generals Walther Reinhardt.* Stuttgart:Kohlhammer 1958

-Falkenhayn, E. von, *Die Oberste Heeresleitung 1914-1916 in ihren wichtigsten Entschliessungen.* Berlin: Ernst Siegfried Mittler und Sohn 1920

-Farrer, D., *The Warburgs.* London: Michael Joseph 1974

-Fehst, H., *Bolschewismus und Judentum. Die führende Rolle jüdischer Kader bei der Entwicklung, Durchsetzung und Herrschaft des Bolschewismus.* Bremen: facsimili Archiv Edition 2002

-Ferguson, N., *Der Falsche Krieg. Der Erste Weltkrieg und das 20. Jahrhunderts.* Stuttgart [1998] 1999

-Fest, J., *Hitler, een biografie. Deel 1 en 2.* Baarn: Torenboeken [1975] 1989

-Fischer, R., *Stalin and German Communism. A Study in the origins of the State Party.* New Brunswick - London: Transition Books 1982

-Flood, C. B., *Hitler. The Path to power.* Boston: Houghton Mifflin Company 1989

-Foerster, W., *Der Feldherr Ludendorff im Unglück. Eine Studie über seine seelische Haltung in der Endphase des Ersten Weltkrieges.* Wiesbaden: Limes Verlag 1952

-Förster, G., & Paulus, N., *Abriss der Geschichte der Panzerwaffe.* Berlin: Militärverlag der DDR 1976

-Ford, H., *Der Internationale Jude. Ein Weltproblem. Das erste amerikanische Buch über die Judenfrage.* Leipzig: Hammer Verlag (Th.Fritsch) 1922

-Francois, H. von, *Hindenburgs Sieg bei Tannenberg. Das Cannae des Weltkrieges in Bild und Wort.* Berlin: Kribe-Verlag z.j.

-Frank, H., *Freiheit.* Munich: Ludendorffs Verlag 1934

-Fredrickson, G. M., *Rassism. Eine historische Abriss.* Hamburg: Hamburger Edition, [2002] 2004

-Frentz, H., *Hindenburg und Ludendorff und ihr Weg durch das Deutsche Schicksal.* Berlin: Morawe & Scheffelt Verlag 1937

-Freund, M., *Deutsche Geschichte von den Anfängen bis zur Gegenwart.* Leipzig: Wilhelm Goldmann [1975] 1981

-Fricke, D., Weissbecker, M., & Schmidt, S., (et al.). (Hg.), *Geschichte der bürgerlichen und kleinbürgerlichen Parteien und Verbände. Lexikon zur Parteiengeschichte Band 3.* Leipzig: VEB Bibliographisches Institut Leipzig 1985

-Fritsch, T., *Handbuch der Judenfrage. Die wichtigsten Tatsachen zur Beurteilung des jüdischen Volkes.* Leipzig: Hammer Verlag 1933

-Fügner, K., *Die Wahrheiten der Bibel - Die einzige Regel und Richtschnur des Glaubens*. Munich: Ludendorffs Verlag 1936

-Fügner, K., *Im 'Geist von Potsdam' wider den fremden Geist, 4.Heft der 1.Schriftenreihe*. Munich: Ludendorffs Verlag 1934

-Fülöp-Miller, R., *Macht en geheimen der jezuïeten*. Amsterdam: Allert de Lange z.j.

-Fülop-Miller, R., *Der Heilige Teufel. Rasputin und die Frauen*. Berlin-Wien: Paul Zsolnay Verlag 1927

-Gaaff, A., *Financiering van de Eerste Wereldoorlog. Vier jaar vechten op krediet*. Soesterberg: Aspekt 2014

-Garleff, M. (Hg.), *Deutschbalten, Weimarer Republik und Drittes Reich. Band 1*. Köln-Weimar-Wien: Bohlau-Verlag 2001

-Geerke, H. P., & Brands, G. A., *De oorlog. Deel 1 en 2*. Amsterdam: Meulenhoff 1915

-Generalstabes des Feldheeres (Hg.), *Der grosse Krieg in Einzeldarstellungen. 20.Heft Die Winterschlacht in Masuren. Unter Benützung amtlichen Materials bearbeitet von Redern, Hauptmann der reserve damals Kompagnie-Führer im Infanterie-Regiment Graf Barfuss (4.Westfäl.) Nr.17* Oldenburg: Stalling 1918

-Gengler, L. F., *Katholische Aktion im Angriff auf Deutschland. Die Lüge vom 'rein religiösen' Werbefeldzug*. Munich: Ludendorff verlag 1937

-Georg, R., *Österreich, die europäische Kolonie des Vatikans*. Munich: Ludendorffs Verlag z.j.

-Gerwarth, R., *The Vanquished. Why the First Wolrd War failed to end, 1917-1923*. London: Allen Lane 2016

-Gietinger, K., *Der Konterrevolutionär. Waldemar Pabst-Eine deutsche Karriere*. Hamburg: Nautius Verlag 2009

-Gisevius, H. B., *Adolf Hitler*. De Bilt: De Fontein [1963] 1973

-Goltz, A. von der, *Hindenburg. Power, Myth and the Rise of the Nazis*. Oxford-New York: Oxford University Press 2009

-Goodspeed, D. J., *Ludendorff. Soldat, Diktator, Revolutionär*. Gütersloh: Bertelsmann 1966

-Görlitz, W., *Der Deutsche Generalstab. Geschichte und Gestalt*. Frankfurt am Main: Verlag der Frankfurter Hefte 1953

-Görlitz, W., & Quint, H. A., *Adolf Hitler, Eine Biographie*. Stuttgart: Steingrüben Verlag 1952.

-Gregor-Dellin, M. (Hg.), *Carl Christian Bry, Der Hitler-Putsch. Berichte und Kommentare eines*

Deutschland-Korrespondenten (1922-1924) für das 'Argentinische Tag- und Wochenblatt'. Nördlingen: Greno 1987

-Griese, F., *Ein Priester ruft: 'Los von Rom'.* Munich: Ludendorffs Volkswarte Verlag 1932

-Grimm, F., *Frankreich am Rhein. Rheinlandbesetzung und Separatismus im Lichte der historischen französischen Rheinpolitik.* in: Archiv edition Verlag für ganzheitliche Forschung. Facsimile reissue of the 1931 edition

-Groot, J.W.de., *'Arische' Gnosis* (unpublished)

-*(Der) Grosse Krieg. Eine Chronik von Tag zu Tag. Urkunden, Depeschen und Berichte der Frankfurter Zeitung.* Frankfurt am Main: Verlag der Frankfurter Societäts-Druckerei 1914 - 1919.

-*Grundriss der Geschichte der deutschen Arbeiterbewegung.* Berlin: Dietz Verlag 1963

-Guderian, H., *Achtung Panzer! The Development of Armoured Forces their Tactics and operational Potential.* London: Arms & Armour Press [1937] 1996

-Haeckel, E., *De wereldraadselen.* in: *De groote denkers der eeuwen.* General Library of Philosophy: *Ernst Hackel and his Monism.* Amsterdam: Van Holkema & Warendorf z.j.

-Haffner, S., *Kanttekeningen bij Hitler.* Amsterdam: H.J.W.Becht Amsterdam 1978

-Hahlweg, Werner, *Lenin's Rückkehr nach Russland 1917.* in: *Studien zur Geschichte Osteuropas.* Leiden: E. J. Brill 1957

-Hamann, B., *Winifred Wagner. A Life at the Heart of Hitler's Bayreuth.* Orlando-London: Harcourt Inc 2005

-Hankel, G., *Die Leipziger Prozesse. Deutsche Kriegsverbrechen und ihre strafrechtliche Verfolgung nach dem Ersten Weltkrieg.* Hamburg: Hamburger Edition HIS Verlag 2003

-Hannover, H., & Hannover-Drück, E., *Politische Justiz 1918-1933.* Frankfurt am Main: Fischer Verlag 1966.

-Harden, M., *Köpfe. Porträts, Briefe und Dokumente.* Hamburg: Rütten-Loeningverlag 1963

-Harenberg, B., *Chronik des Ruhrgebiets.* Dortmund: Chronik-Verlag 1987

-Hass, H., *Sitte und Kultur im Nachkriegsdeutschland.* Hamburg: Hanseatische Verlagsanstalt 1932

-Hasselbacher, F. (Hg.), *Hochverrat der Feldlogen im Weltkrieg.* Magdeburg: Nordland Verlag 1935

-Hausner, G., *Die Vernichtung der Juden. Das grösste Verbrechen der Geschichte.* Munich: Kindler, 1979

-Hausser, P., *Waffen-SS im Einsatz*. Preussisch Oldendorf: Verlag K.W.Schutz 1953

-Heiber, H., *Die Republik von Weimar. Dtv-Weltgeschichte des 20.Jahrhunderts Band 3*. Munich: dtv 1977

-Heresch, E., *Geheimakte Parvus. Die gekaufte Revolution*. Munich: Langen Müller Verlag 2000

-Herr, F., *Der Glaube des Adolf Hitler. Anatomie einer politischen Religiosität*. Munich: Bechtle Verlag 1963

-Herzfeld, H., *Die Weimarer Republik*. Frankfurt am Main: Ullstein 1966

-Hess, R.W. (Hg.), *Rudolf Hess. Briefe 1908-1933*. Munich-Wien: Langen Müller 1987

-Hindenburg, P. von., *Aus meinem Leben*. Leipzig: S. Hirzel Verlag 1927

-Hirschfeld, G., Krumeich,G., & Renz, I., *Enzyklopädie Erster Weltkrieg*. Paderborn: NZZ Verlag 2004

-Hoegner, W., *Die verratene Republik. Deutsche Geschichte 1919-1933*. Munich: Ullstein 1989

-Hoffmann, M., *Der Krieg der versäumten Gelegenheiten*. Munich: Verlag für Kulturpolitik 1923

-Hoffmann, M., *Tannenberg wie es wirklich war*. Berlin: Verlag für Kulturpolitik 1926

-Hofmann, U.C., *Verräter verfallen der Feme! Fememorden in Bayern in den zwanziger Jahren*. Weimar-Wien: Böhlauverlag 2000

-Höhne, H., *Admiraal Wilhelm Canaris, Nieuwe visie op de loopbaan van het hoofd van de Duiste Abwehr. Het einde van een verzetsmythe*. Amsterdam: uitgeverij Amsterdam boek 1978

-Holscher, K. H., *Der Todeskampf der Stedinger. Zur 700. Wiederkehr des Tages der Ermordung von 5000 freien Deutschen Bauern am 27.5.1234*. Munich: Ludendorff Verlag 1934

-Horne, J., & Kramer, A., *Deutsche Kriegsgreuel 1914. Die umstrittene Wahrheit*. Hamburg: Hamburgeredition 2004

-Hortzschansky, G., *Ernst Thaelmann*. Leipzig: VEB Bibliographisches Institut 1976

-Hubricht, E., *Buchweiser für das völkisch-religiöse Schrifttum und dessen Grenzgebiete*. Freiberg i.Sa.: Th. E.Hubricht Verlag: used here: *Toppenstedter Reihe, Sammlung bibliographischer Hilfsmittel zur Erforschung der Konservativen Revoltution und des nationalsozialismus nr. 5*. Toppenstedt: Uwe Berg Verlag 1983

-Hüttenberger, P., & Molitor, H.G. (Hg.), *Franzosen und Deutsche am Rhein 1789-1918-1945*. Essen: Klartext 1989

-Ilges, F. W., *Die geplante Aufteilung Deutschland, Hochverrat von Zentrum und Bayerischer Volkspartei 1918-1923.* Berlin: Walter Bacmeisters Nationalverlag 1933.

-Ilges, F. W, & Schmid, H. G., *Hochverrat des Zentrums am Rhein. Neue Urkunden über die wahren Führer der Separatisten.* Berlin: Walther Bacmeisters Nationalverlag 1934.

-Insenhöfer, S., *Dr.Friedrich Weber. Reichstierärtzeführer von 1934 bis 1945. Inaugural-Dissertation* Hannover: MV-Wissenschaft 2008.

-Iring, K., *Not und Kampf deutscher Bauern. (Bauernkriege), 4. und 5.heft der 2.Schriftenreihe.* Munich: Ludendorffs Verlag Munich 1935

-Iring, K., *Nie wieder Habsburg! Die Habsburger in der Geschichte der Deutschen;* and B.Dietrich, *Der Weg zur Jesuitendiktatur in Osterreich 1918-1935* in:*Nie wieder Habsburg!* Munich: Ludendorffs verlag 1936.

-Jäckel, E., *Das Deutsche Jahrhundert.* Stuttgart: Deutsche Verlags-Anstalt 1996

-Janow, H., *Rom, Poland, Ukraine.* Munich: Ludendorffs Verlag 1939

Jansen, H., *Diagnose van racisme en antisemitisme in Europa.* The Hague: Sdu 1994

-Jdanoff, D., *'Russische Faschisten'. Der nationalsozialistische Flügel der Russischen Emigration im Dritten Reich.* Virtuelle Fachbibliothek Osteuropa: Geschichte 3 2003

-Joachimsthaler, A., *Korrektur einer Biographie. Adolf Hitler 1908 - 1920* Munich: Herbig 1989

-Joachimsthaler, A., *Hitlers Liste. Ein Dokument personlicher Beziehungen* München: Herbig 2003

-Jukes, G., *Carpathian Disaster. Death of an Army.* New York: Ballantine 1971

-Karlsch, R., & Stokes, R.G., *Faktor Öl. Die Mineralölwirtschaft in Deutschland 1859-1974.* Munich: Verlag C.H.Beck 2003

-Kautsky, K., *Hoe de oorlog ontstond.* Soesterberg: Aspekt 2001

-Keegan, J., *The First World War.* Hutchinson: Vintage 1998

-Kemnitz, H.von. (Hg.), *Tannenberg-Jahrbuch 1939.* Munich: Ludendorffs Verlag 1939

-Kemnitz, H.von. (Hg.), *Deutsche Rast.* Munich: Ludendorffs Verlag 1940

-Kershaw, I., *Hitler 1889-1936, Hubris.* London: Penguin Books 1998

-Kessler, H.Graf., *Walther Rathenau, zijn leven en zijn werk.* Arnhem: Van Loghum Slaterus 1929

-Kessler, H. Graf., *Tagebücher 1918-1937*. Frankfurt am Main: Insel-Verlag 1961

-Kitchen, M., *The Silent Dictatorship The Politics of the german High Command under Hindenburg and Ludendorff, 1916-1918*. London: Croom Helm 1976

-Kjellén, R., *Die politische Probleme des Weltkrieges*. Leipzig-Berlin: B.G.Teubner 1918

-Klass, G. von, *Hugo Stinnes*. Tübingen: Rainer Wunderlich Publishing House 1958

-Kloevekorn, Prof. Dr. (Hg.), *Das Saargebiet. Seine Struktur, seine Probleme*. Saarbrücken: Gebr. Hofer A.G. Verlag 1929

-Koch, H. W. , *Der deutsche Bürgerkrieg. Eine Geschichte der deutschen und österreichischen Freikorps 1918-1923*. Berlin/Frankfurt am main Ullstein 1978

-Koch, P., *Konrad Adenauer. Die Biographie*. Düsseldorf: Albatros 2004

-Kochan, L. (ed.), *The Jews in Soviet Russia since 1917*. Institute for Jewish Affairs, Oxford: Oxford University Press 1978

-Könnemann, E., & Krusch,H-J., *Aktionseinheit contra Kapp-Putsch. Der Kapp-Putsch im Marz 1920 und der Kampf der deutschen Arbeiterklasse sowie anderer Werktätiger gegen die Errichtung der Militärdiktatur und für demokratische Verhältnisse*. Berlin: Dietz verlag 1972.

-Kornat, M., *Poland zwischen Hitler und Stalin. Studien zur polnischen Aussenpolitik in der Zwischenkriegszeit*. Berlin-Brandenburg: be.bra Verlag 2012

-Koszyk, K., *Deutsche Presse 1914-1945*. Berlin: Colloquium Verlag 1972

-Krummacher, F. A., & Wucher, A. (Hg.), *Die Weimarer Republik. Ihre Geschichte in Texten, Bildern und Dokumenten*. Munich: Kurt Desch Verlag 1965

-Kurth, H., *Die Wahrheit über Ludendorffs Kampf. Eine zusammenhängende Darstellung*. Munich: Ludendorffs Volkswarte Verlag 1932

-Kurth, H., *Die Weltdeutung Dr.Mathilde Ludendorffs. Eine Einführung in die Werke der Philosophin*. Munich: Ludendorffs Verlag 1934

-Kybitz, W., *Ludendorffs Handstreich auf Lüttich*. Munich: Ludendorffs Verlag 1939

-Lamprecht, K., *Krieg und Kultur*. Leipzig: S. Hirzel Verlag 1914

-Landowsky, J., *Rakowsky Protokoll. Über die Vernehmung des Sowjetbotschafters Kristjan Jurjewitsch Rakowskij durch den Beamten der GPU Gabriel G.Kuzmin am 26.Januar 1938 in Moskau*. Bremen: Faksimile-Verlag 1987

-Lange, E., *Der Reichsmarschall im Kriege*, Stuttgart: Curt E.Schwab 1950

-Larsson, G., *Waarheid of bedrog? DE protocollen van de wijzen van Zion.* Stichting voor Bijbelstudie en Onderzoek ter Jaruzalem. Nijkerk: AMI 1996

-Leach, B., *De Duitse generale staf.* Amsterdam - Antwerp: Standaard uitgeverij 1979

-Lee, J., *The Warlords. Hindenburg and Ludendorff.* London: Orion Books 2005

-Leider, S., *Widersprüche überall. Wilhelm II in psychiatrischen Beurteilungen nach 1918* in: *Der letzte Kaiser. Wilhelm II im Exil.* Munich: Bertelsmann Lexikon Verlag 1991

-Lemm, R., *De kruisgang van het christendom.* Soesterberg: Aspekt 2000

-Lewy, G., *De Rooms Katholieke kerk en Nazi-Duitsland.* Amsterdam: Polak & Van Gennep, 1964

-Liddell Hart, B., *History of the First World War.* London: Cassell [1970] 1973

-Lincoln, W. B., *In War's Dark Shadow. The Russians before the Great War.* Oxford: Oxford university press 1983

-Linden, H.van der/Pierik,P., *Het dramatische jaar 1914,* Soesterberg: Aspekt 2014

-Lindenberg, C., *Rudolf Steiner.* Baarn: Tirion 1992

-Lindenberg, P. (Hg.), *Hindenburg Denkmal für das Deutsche Volk.* Berlin: Vaterländischer Verlag Weller 1925

-Löhde, W., *Schiller. Eine Deutscher Revolutionär. 10.Heft der 1.Schriftenreihe.* Munich: Ludendorffs Verlag 1935

-Longerich, P., *Goebbels. Biografie.* Amsterdam: Bezige Bij 2010

-Ludendorff, E'., *Dirne Kriegsgeschichte. Vor dem Gericht des Weltkrieges. Zum Feldzug in Süd-Polen Anfang Oktober 1914.* Munich: Ludendorffs Verlag z.j.

-Ludendorff, E., *Meine Kriegserinnerungen 1914-1918.* Berlin: E. S. Mittler Verlag 1920

-Ludendorff, E., *Urkunden der Obersten Heeresleitung.* Berlin: E. S. Mittler & Sohn 1920

-Ludendorff, E., *Kriegführung und Politik.* Berlin: Mittler & Sohn 1921

-Ludendorff, E., *Die Revolution von Oben. Das Kriegsende und die Vorgänge beim Waffenstillstand.* Lorch: Karl Rohm Verlag, 1926

-Ludendorff, E., *Vernichtung der Freimaurerei durch Enthüllung ihrer Geheimnisse.* Munich: Ludendorffs Verlag [1927] 1936

-Ludendorff, E., *Kriegshetze und Völkermorden in den letzten 150 Jahren.* Munich: Ludendorffs Verlag [1928] 1936

-Ludendorff, E., *Das Marne Drama. Der Fall Moltke-Hentsch*. Munich: Ludendorffs Verlag 1934

-Ludendorff, E., *Mein militärischer Werdegang. Blätter der Erinnerung an unser stolzes Heer*. Munich: Ludendorffs Verlag 1935

-Ludendorff, E., *Über Unbotmässigkeit im Kriege*. Munich: Ludendorffs Verlag 1935

-Ludendorff, E. (Hg.), *Abgeblitz, Antworten auf Theologengestammel*. Munich: Ludendorffs Verlag 1936

-Ludendorff, E., *Der Totale Krieg*. Munich: Ludendorffs Verlag 1936

-Ludendorff, E. (Hg.), *Mathilde Ludendorff. Ihr Werk und Wirken*. Munich: Ludendorffs Verlag 1937

-Ludendorff, E., *Auf dem Weg zur Feldherrnhalle*. Munich: Ludendorffs Verlag 1937

-Ludendorff, E., *Worte Erich Ludendorffs über Wehrhaftigkeit, Soldaten und Feldherrntum. Die Rote Reihe Band* 2. Munich: Ludendorffs Verlag 1938

-Ludendorff, E., *Meine Lebenserinnerungen 1919-1925, Vom Feldherrn zum Weltrevolutionar und Wegbereiter. Deutscher Volksschöpfung Band 1*. Munich: Ludendorffs Verlag 1941

-Ludendorff, E., *Meine Lebenserinnerungen 1933-1937, Vom Feldherrn zum Weltrevolutionar und Wegbereiter Deutscher Volksschöpfung Band 3*. Pähl: Hohe Warte 1955

-Ludendorff, E., *Meine Lebenserinnerungen 1926-1933, Vom Feldherrn zum Weltrevolutionar und Wegbereiter Deutscher Volksschöpfung Band 2*. Pähl: Hohe Warte 1987

-Ludendorff, E., *Tannenberg. Geschichtliche Wahrheit über die Schlacht*. Munich: Ludendorffs Verlag [1939] 1998

-Ludendorff, E., & Ludendorff-von Kemnitz, M., *Das Geheimnis der Jesuitenmacht und ihr Ende*. Munich: Ludendorffs Volkswarte Verlag 1929

-Ludendorff, E., & Ludendorff-von Kemnitz, M., *Das grosse Entsetzen. Die Bibel nicht Gottes Wort*. Munich: Ludendorffs Verlag 1936

-Ludendorff, M., *Als ich Ludendorff's Frau war*. Munich: Drei Masken Verlag 1929

-Ludendorff-von Kemnitz, M., *Erlösung von Jesu Christo*. Munich: Ludendorffs Volkswarte Verlag 1933

-Ludendorff-von Kemnitz, M., *Der Seele Wirken und Gestalten. Band 2: Die Volksseele und ihre machtgestalter. Eine Philosophie der Geschichte*. Munich: Ludendorffs Verlag 1934

-Ludendorff-von Kemnitz, M., *Deutscher Gottglaube*. Munich: Ludendorffs Verlag 1934

-Ludendorff-von Kemnitz, M., *Ist das Leben sinnlose Schinderei? 5.Heft der 1.Schriftenreihe*. Munich: Ludendorffs Verlag 1934

-Ludendorff-von Kemnitz, M., *Verschüttete Volksseele. Nach berichten aus Südwestafrika*. Munich: Ludendorffs Verlag 1934

-Ludendorff-von Kemnitz, M., *Der Seele Wirken und Gestalten. Band 3: Das Gottlied der Völker. Eine Philosophie der Kulturen*. Munich: Ludendorffs verlag 1936

-Ludendorff-von Kemnitz, M., *Der ungesühnte Frevel an Luther, Lessing, Mozart und Schiller. Ein Beitrag zur Deutschen Kulturgeschichte*. Munich: Ludendorffs Verlag 1936

-Ludendorff - von Kemnitz, M., *Die Volksseele und ihre Machtsgestalter*. Munich: Ludendorff Verlag 1936

-Ludendorff-von Kemnitz, M., *Mozarts Leben und gewaltsamer Tod*. Munich: Ludendorffs Verlag 1936

-Ludendorff-von Kemnitz, M., *Statt Heiligenschein oder Hexenzeichen. Mein Leben. Teil II: Durch Forschen und Schicksal zum Sinn des lebens*. Munich: Ludendorffs Verlag 1936

-Ludendorff-von Kemnitz, M., *Höhenwege und Abgründe, zwei Einführungsvorträge* in: *Deutsche Gotterkenntnis gehalten auf der Tagung in Tutzing vom 2.-5. Erntings 1937*. Munich: Ludendorff Verlag 1937

-Ludendorff-von Kemnitz, M., *Statt Heiligenschein oder Hexenzeichen. Mein Leben. Teil VI: Freiheitskampf wider eine Welt von Feinden an der Seite des Feldherrn Ludendorff. Die Jahre von 1929-1933*. Pähl: Franz von Bebenburg 1968

-Ludendorff-von Kemnitz, M., *Statt Heiligenschein oder Hexenzeichen. Mein Leben. Teil I: Kindheit und Jugend*. Pähl: Verlag Hohe Warte 1974

-Ludendorff-von Kemnitz, M., *Statt Heiligenschein oder Hexenzeichen. Mein Leben. Teil III: Erkenntniss - Erlösung*. Pähl: Verlag Hohe Warte 1980

-Ludendorff-von Kemnitz, M., *Ein Leben der Freiheit, Zu ihrem 100. Geburtstag am 4. im Gilbhart 1977* zusammengestellt von Gunther Duda. Pähl: Verlag Hohe Warte 1977

-Ludendorff-von Kemnitz, M., *Vom Wahren Leben, Philosophische Essays*. Pähl: Hohe Warte 2002

-Ludendorff-von Kemnitz, M., & Cammer, W. v. d., *Christliche Grausamkeit an Deutschen Frauen. 2. Aufsätze*. Munich: Ludendorffs verlag 1934

-Ludwig, E., *Wilhelm II*. Berlin: Rowohlt 1926

-Ludwig, E., *Hindenburg. Legende und Wirklichkeit*. Hamburg: Rütten et Loening 1962

-Lust, R., *Die Franken und das Christentum*. Munich: Ludendorffs Verlag 1936

-Machtan, L., *Der Kaisersohn bei Hitler*. Hamburg: Hoffmann und Campe 2006

-Madol, H.R., *Ferdinand von Bulgarien. Der Traum von Byzanz*. Berlin: Universitas 1931

-Mahlberg, H., *Erich Ludendorff. Zum gedenken an seinen 100. Geburtstag*. Hanover: Hans Pfeiffer 1965

-Malinowski, S., *Vom König zum Führer. Deutscher Adel und Nationalsozialismus*. Frankfurt am Main: Fischer Verlag, 2004

-Margolina, S., *Das Ende der Lügen. Russland und die Juden im 20.Jahrhundert*. Berlin: Siedler Verlag 1992

-Marr, W., *Der Sieg des Judenthums über das Germanenthum. Vom nicht confessionellen Standpunkt aus betrachtet*. Bern: Rudolph Costenoble, 1879.

-Maser, W., *Der Sturm auf die Republik. Frühgeschichte der NSDAP.* Düsseldorff - Frankfurt am Main: Ullstein [1979] 1980

-Maser, W., *Hitler. Legende, mythe, werkelijkheid*. Amsterdam: Arbeiderspers 1985

-Maser, W., *Hindenburg. Eine politische Biographie*. Berlin: Werner Moewig Verlag [1989] 1990

-Maser, W., *Friedrich Ebert. Der erste deutsche Reichspräsident*. Frankfurt: Ullstein1990

-Maser, W., *Hermann Göring. Een politieke carrière*. Soesterberg: Aspekt 2002

-Matthiessens, W., *Israels Geheimplan der Völkervernichtung. Unbekannte Geheimnisse der Bibel*. Munich: Ludendorffs Verlag, 1938

-Maurer, K. C. L., *Geplanter Ketzermord im Jahre 1866. Aus: Neuer Jesuitenspiegel*. Munich: Ludendorffs Volkswarte Verlag 1932

-Merz, K-U., *Das Schreckbild. Deutschland und der Bolschewismus 1917 bis 1921*. Berlin-Frankfurt am Main: Propyläen-Verlag 1995

-Meyer-Dampen, E., *Deutsche Gotterkenntnis als Grundlage wehrhaften deutschen Lebens*. Munich: Ludendorffs verlag 1934

-Meynig, W., *Christliche Wissenschaft*. Munich: Ludendorff Verlag 1938

-Michaelis, Dr. H., & Schraepler, Dr. E., (Hg), *Ursachen und Folgen vom deutschen Zusammenbruch 1918-1945 bis zur staatlichen Neuordnung Deutschlands in der Gegenwart. Eine Urkunden und Dokumentensammlung zur Zeitgeschichte. Band 3*. Berlin: Dokumenten-Verlag Dr.Herbert Wendler & Co.

-Miksche, F.O., *Vom Kriegsbild*. Stuttgart: Seewald 1976

-Mit anderen Augen. *Jahrbuch der Sonntags-Zeitung 1920-1929*. Stuttgart: Verlag der Sonntags-Zeitung 1929

-Mohrmann, W., *Antisemitismus. Ideologie und Geschichte im Kaiserreich und in der Weimarer Republik*. Berlin: Deutscher Verlag der Wissenschaften 1972

-Molau, A., *Alfred Rosenberg, der Ideologe des nationalsozialismus. Eine politische Biografie*, Koblenz: Verlag Siegfried Bublies, 1993

-Mosley, L., *Göring*. Bergisch Gladbach: Bastei Lübbe 1977

-Müller, K-J., *Generaloberst Ludwig beck. Eine Biographie*. Paderborn: Ferdinand Schöningh 20008 [2009].

-Mulligan, W., *The Creation of the Modern German Army. General Walther Reinhardt and the Weimar Republic 1914-1930*. New York-Oxford: Berghahn Books 2005

-Mumm, R., *Der christlich-soziale Gedanke. Bericht über eine Lebensarbeit in schwerer Zeit*. Berlin: Mittler & Sohn 1933

-Nagy, T., *Jesuiten und Freimaurer*. Wien: Wilhelm Frick Verlag 1969

-Nebelin, M., *Ludendorff. Diktator im Ersten Weltkrieg*. Munich: Siedler verlag 2010

-Neillands, R., *The Great War Generals on the western front 1914-1918*. London: Magpie Books 2004

-Nissen, B.M., *Der Rembrandtdeutsche, Julius Langbehn*. Freiburg im Breisgau: Herder 1927

-Nolte, E., *Der europäische Bürgerkrieg 1917-1945. Nationalsozialismus und Bolschewismus*. Frankfurt am Main: Propyläen Verlag 1987

-Nording, G., *Geheimnisse vom Rosenkreuz*, Munich: Ludendorffs Verlag 1938

-Oppelland, T., *Reichstag und Aussenpolitik im Ersten Weltkrieg. Die deutschen Parteien und die Politik der USA 1914-1918* in: Kommission für Geschichte des Parlamentarismus und der politischen Parteien (Hg.), Beiträge zur Geschichte des Parlamentarismus und der politischen Parteien. Band 103. Düsseldorf: Droste Verlag 1995

-Oslo, A., *Die Freimaurer*. Düsseldorf: Albatros 2002

-Otto, H., & Schmiedel, K., *Der Erste Weltkrieg. Dokumente. Schriften des militärgeschichtlichen Institutes der DDR. Kleine Militärgeschichte, Kriege*. Berlin: Militärverlag der DDR [1977] 1983

-Paling, K. M., *Galgemaal voor de Pruisen. De mestvaalt van de geschiendenis. Het opmerkelijke levensverhaal van Paul von Lettow-Vorbeck, Pruisisch generaal, guerrillero en putchist*. The Hague: BZZToH 1995

-Parkinson, R., *Tormented Warrior. Ludendorff and the Surpreme Command*. London: Hodder & Stoughton 1978

-Pearson, M., *The Sealed Train*. London: Macmillan 1975

-Petropoulos, J., *Royals and the Reich. The Princes von Hesse in Nazi Germany*. Oxford-New York: Oxford University Press 2006

-Pieper, K., *Ludendorff und die heilige Schrift, Antwort auf die Schrift 'Das grosse Entsetzen-Die Bibel nicht Gottes Wort'*. Munich: hrsg. vom Erzb. Ordinariat München z.j.

-Pierik, P., *Hitlers Lebensraum. De geestelijke wortels van de veroveringsveldtocht naar het oosten*. Soesterberg: Aspekt 1999

-*Erich Ludendorff and the Defence of the Eastern German Border in 1914*. Soesterberg: Aspekt 2003

-Pierik, P., *Karl Haushoferen het nationaal-socialisme. Tijd, werk en invloed*. Soesterberg: Aspekt 2006

-Pierik, P., *Thule en het Derde Rijk. De genesis van het national-socialisme*. Soesterberg: Aspekt 2013

-Pierik, P., *Het onbekende Reich. Minder bekende feiten van het oostfront*. Soesterberg: Aspekt 2014

-Pierik, P., *Vanaf vandaag wordt teruggeschoten. Spoinage, geheime diplomatie, oorlogseconomie en andere facetten van de Poolse veldtocht van 1939*. Soesterberg: Aspekt 2016

-Pierik, P., & Pors, H., *De verlaten monarch. Keizer Wilhelm II in Nederland*. Soesterberg: Aspekt 1999

-Piper, E., *Alfred Rosenberg, Hitlers Chefideologe*. Munich: Karl Blessing Verlag 2005

-Plehwe, F-K. von, *Reichskanzler Kurt von Schleicher. Weimars letzte Chance gegen Hitler*. Munich: Bechtle 1983

-Poliakov, L., *De arische mythe*. Amsterdam: De Arbeiderspers, 1979

-Pool, J., & Pool, S., *Wie financieerde Hitler? Nieuwe en onthullende feiten over de geheime geldschieters van het Derde Rijk*. Amsterdam: Elsevier 1979

-Pors, H., *De prins van Wieringen. De internering van kroonprins Wilhelm op Wieringen (1918-23) en zijn verdere levensloop*. Soesterberg: Aspekt 2000

-Posse, E. H., *Die politischen Kampfbünde Deutschlands. Quellentexte zur Konservativen Revolution. Die Nationalrevolutionare: Band 3*. Toppenstedt: Uwe Berg Verlag (facsimile of the 1931 edition) 2004

-Pulzer, P. J. G., *The Rise of political anti-Semitism in Germany and Austria.* London-Sydney: John Wiley & Sons 1964

-Pyta, W., *Hindenburg. Herrschaft zwischen Hohenzollern und Hitler.* Munich: Siedler 2007

-Raab, L. (Hg.), *Tannenberg-Jahrweiser 1935.* Munich: Ludendorffs Verlag 1935

-Range, P.R., *Het kanteljaar van Hitler. 1924.* Amsterdam: Atlas/Contact 2016

-Rappaport, H., *Conspirator. Lenin in Exile.* New York: Basic Books 2010

-Rathenau, W., *Der Kaiser. Eine Betrachtung.* Berlin: Fischer Verlag 1919

-Ratzel, F., *Politische Geographie.* Munich: R.Oldenbourg 1897

-Rauchensteiner, M., *Der Tod des Doppeladlers. Österreich-Ungarn und der Erste Weltkrieg.* Wien: Styria 1993

-Reed, D., *Nemesis? Het leven van Otto Strasser.* Batavia: Koll & Co 1940

-Rehwaldt, H., *Das schleichende Gift. Der Okkultismus, seine Lehre, Weltanschauung und Bekämpfung. 7.8.und 9.Heft der 1.Schriftenreihe.* Munich: Ludendorffs Verlag 1935

-Rehwaldt, H., *Die Kriegshetzer von heute.* Munich: Ludendorffs Verlag 1938

-Rehwaldt, H., *Tannenberg.* Lengerich: Bischof & Klein Verlag 1935

-Reichsarchiv. (Hg.), *Battles of the World War Band 3 Antwerp 1914.* Berlin: Stalling Verlag 1925

-Reichsarchiv. (*Schlachten des Weltkrieges Band 19 Tannenberg.* Berlin: Stalling Verlag 1927

-Reichsarchiv. (*Schlachten des Weltkrieges Band 30 Gorlice.* Berlin: Stalling Verlag 1930

-Reichsarchiv. (Hg.), *Schlachten des Weltkrieges Band 36 Die Katastrophe des 8.Augustus 1918.* Berlin: Stalling Verlag 1930

-Repgen, K. (Hg.), *Veröffentlichungen der Kommission für Zeitgeschichte. Reihe A, Band 15: Friedrich Muckermann, Im Kampf zwischen zwei Epochen. Lebenserinnerungen.* Mainz: Matthias Grünewald Verlag z.j.

-Reuth, R. G. (Hg.), *Joseph Goebbels Tagebücher Band 1 1924-1929.* Munich: Piper Verlag 2000

-Reuth, R. G. (Hg.), *Joseph Goebbels Tagebücher. Band 2 1930-1934.* Munich: Piper Verlag 2000

-Reventlow, Ernst Graf zu., *Der Weg zum neuen deutschland Der Wiederaufstieg des deutschen Volkes.* Essen: Central institution for the German Freedom Campaign 1931

-Reventlow, Ernst Graf zu., *Von Potsdam nach Doorn.* Berlin: Klieber Verlag 1940

-Richardi, H-G., *Hitler und seine Hintermänner. Neue Fakten zur Frühgeschichte der NSDAP.* Munich: Süddeutscher Verlag 1991

-Riegel, P., & Rinsum, W. van., *Deutscher Literaturgeschichte. Band 10, Drittes Reich und Exil 1933-1945.* Munich: DTV 2000

-Röhm, E., *Geschichte eines Hochverräters.* Munich: Franz Eher Verlag 1934

-Rommel, E., *Infanterie greift an.* Potsdam: Voggenreiter Verlag 1942

-Rose, A. W., *Rome Mordet, mordet Seelen, Menschen, Völker.* Munich: Ludendorffs Verlag 1935

-Rosenberg, A., *Die Protokolle der Weisen von Zion und die jüdische Weltpolitik.* Munich: Deutscher Volks verlag, Dr. Boepple 1923

-Rosenberg, A., *An die Dunkelmänner unserer Zeit, eine Antwort auf die Angriffer gegen den Mythus des 20. Jahrhunderts.* Munich: Hoheneichen Verlag 1935

-Rosenberg, A., *Blut und Ehre. Ein Kampf für deutsche Wiedergeburt.* Munich: FranzEher Verlag 1935

-Rosenberg, A., *Der Mythus des 20. Jahrhunderts. Eine Wertung des seelisch-geistigen Gestalten Kampfe unserer Zeit.* Munich: Hoheneichen - Verlag 1934

-Rosenberg, A., *Protestantische Kompilger. Der Verrat an Luther und der Mythus des 20. Jahrhunderts.* Munich: Hoheneichen Verlag 1937

-Rosenberg, A., *Geschichte der Weimarer Republik,* Frankfurt am Main: Europäische Verlagsanstalt [1961] 1971

-Rosinski, H., *Die Deutsche Armee. Vom Triumph zur Niederlage.* Munich: Heyne [1966] 1977

-Roth, A., *Nationalsozialismus und katholische Kirche, Meine Schriftwechsel mit der Gauleitung Rheinland und der Reichsparteileitung der NSDAP sowie mit der kanzlei Adolf Hitlers.* Munich: Ludendorffs Volkswarte Verlag 1931

-Roth, A., *Das Reichskonkordat vom 20. Juli 1933 unter besonderer Berücksichtigung seiner historischen Vorgänger in 800 Jahren Deutscher Geschichte.* Munich: Ludendorffs Verlag 1933.

-Roth, A., *Weltanschauung und Wirtschaft. 6. Heft der 1. Schriftenreihe.* Munich: Ludendorffs Verlag 1934

-Rother, T., *Die Krupps. Through five generations of Stahl.* Frankfurt am main: Bastei Lübbe [2001] 2006

-Rother, T., *Die Thyssens. Tragödie der Stahlbarone.* Frankfurt am Main: Bastei Lübbe [2003] 2005

-Ruge, W., *Hindenburg. Porträt eines Militaristen*. Berlin: VEB Deutscher Verlag der Wissenschaften 1977

-Ruge, W., *Weimar Republik auf Zeit. Kleine Bibliothek nr. 179*. Cologne: Pahl-Rugenstein 1980

-Rühle, J., *Literatur und Revolution. Die Schriftsteller und der Kommunismus*. Frankfurt am Main-Wien-Zurich: Büchergilde Gutenberg 1960

-Sabrow, M, *Die verdrängte Verschwörung. Der Rathenau-Mord und die deutsche Gegenrevolution*. Frankfurt am Main: Fischer verlag 1999

-Saehrendt, C., *Der Stellungskrieg der Denkmäler. Kriegerdenkmäler im Berlin der Zwischenkriegszeit 1919-1939*. Bonn: Dietz 2004

-Salomon, E. von. (Hg.), *Das Buch vom deutschen Freikorpskämpfer*. Viöl: Archiv, used here: facsimile edition of 1938, 2001

-Sasonoff, S. D., *Sechs schwere Jahre*. Berlin: Verlag für Kulturpolitik 1927

-Schaefer, K. A., *Werner von Blomberg, Hitlers erster Feldmarschall. Eine Biographie*. Paderborn: Schöningh 2006

-Schaepdrijver, S. de., *De grote oorlog. Het koningrijk België tijdens de Eerste Wereldoorlog*. Amsterdam: Atlas 1997

-Schemann, L., *Paul de Lagarde. Ein Lebens und Erinnerungsbild*. Leipzig und Hartenstein: Erich Matthes Verlagsbuchhandlung 1919

-Scheuren, E., & Trapp, C., *Separatisten im Siebengebirge. Die Rheinische Republik des jahres 1923 und die 'Schlacht' bei Aegidienberg*. Königswinter: Siebengebirgsmuseum der Stadt Königswinter 1994.

-Schiesser, G., & Trauptmann, J., *Russian Roulette. Das deutsche Geld und die Oktoberrevolution*. Berlin: Verlag Das Neue Berlin 1998

-Schnoor, F., *Mathilde Ludendorff und das Christentum. Eine Radikale völkischen Position in der Zeit der Weimarer Republik und des NS-Staates*. Egelsbach: Dr.Hänsel-Hohenhausen A.G. 2001

-Schoeps, J. H., & Schlör, J., *Antisemitismus. Vorurteile und Mythen*. Munich-Zurich: Piper Verlag 1995

-Scholder, K., *Die Mittwochs-Gesellschaft. Protokolle aus dem geistigen Deutschland 1932 bis 1944*. Zürich: Buchlub Ex Libris 1984

-Schreiner, H., *Der National-Sozialismus vor der Gottesfrage. Illusion oder Evangelium!* Berlin: Wichern Verlag 1931

-Schricker, R., *Rotmord über München*. Munich: Zeitgeschichte Verlag 1934

-Schulze, H., *Weimar. Deutschland 1917-1933. Die Deutschen und ihre Nation.* Berlin: Severin und Siedler 1982

-Schulze-Pfaelzer, G., *Hindenburg. Drie Zeitalter deutscher Nation.* Leipzig-Zürich: Grethlein & Co 1930

-Schumann, H., *Kriege der Milliardäre. Transaktionen des Hauses Morgan. Laufendes Schriftenbezug 9, 2.Heft.* Munich: Ludendorffs Verlag 1939

-Schwarzmüller, T., *Zwischen Kaiser und 'Fuhrer'. Generalfeldmarschall August von Mackensen. Eine politische Biographie.* Paderborn-Munich: Ferdinand Schöningh Verlag 1995

-Segall, J., *Die deutschen Juden als Soldaten im Kriege 1914-1918, Eine statistische Studie.* Berlin: Philo Verlag 1922

-Segel, B., *Welt-Krieg, Welt-Revolution, Welt-Verschwörung, Welt-Oberregierung.* Berlin: Philo Verlag 1926

-Seraphim, H-G. (Hg.), *Das politische Tagebuch Alfred Rosenbergs.* DTV-Dokumente. Munich: DTV 1956

-Service, R., *Spies & Commissars. Bolshevik Russia and the west.* London: Macmillan 2011

-Shirer, W.L., *The Rise and Fall of the Third Reich. A History of Nazi Germany* Book Club Associates 1973

-Simčič, M., *Die Schlachten am Isonzo. 888 Tage Krieg im Karst in Fotos, Karten und Berichten.* Graz-Stuttgart: Leopold Stocker Verlag 2003

-Snethlage, J. L., *Democratie en dictatuur.* Arnhem: Van Loghum Slaterus 1933

-Sppethmann, H., *Das Ruhrgebiet im Wechselspiel von Land und Leute, Wirtschaft, Technik und Politik. Band 3.* Berlin: Verlag für Sozialpolitik Paul Schmidt 1938
-Steffens, M., *Freimaurer in Deutschland. Bilanz eines Vierteljahrtausends*, Frankfurt: Bauhütten-Verlag 1966

-Steiner, F., *Die Freiwilligen, Idee und Opfergang.* Rosenheim: Deutsche Verlagsgesellschaft 1992

-Steiner, F., *Die Armee der Geachteten.* Rosenheim: Deutsche Verlagsgesellschaft 1993

-Stern, F., *Kulturpessimismus als politische Gefahr. Eine Analyse nationaler Ideologie in Deutschland.* Bern-Stuttgart: Scherz 1963

-Stone, N., *The Eastern Front 1914-1917.* London: Hodder & Stoughton 1975

-Stoss, A., *Der Raubzug gegen Japan! Wann endlich wehren sich die Völker?* Munich: Ludendorffs Volkswarte Verlag 1932

-Stoss, A., *Der Kampf zwischen Juda und Japan. Japan als Vorkämpfer freier Volkswirtschaft*. Munich: Ludendorffs Verlag, 1934

-Strauss, W., *Unternehmen Barbarossa und der russische Historikerstreit*. Munich: Herbig 1998

-Strazhas, A., *Deutsche Ostpolitik im Ersten Weltkrieg. Der Fall Ober Ost 1915-1917* in: Hoesch, Edgar (Hg.), *Veröffentlichungen des Osteuropa-Institutes München, Reihe: Geschichte*. Wiesbaden: Harrassowitz 1993

-Stresemann, W., *Mein Vater Gustav Stresemann*. Munich: Herbig 1979

-Strunk, J., *Vatikan und Kreml*. Munich: Ludendorffs Verlag 1934

-Terhalle, M., *Otto Schmidt (1888-1971) Gegner Hitlers und Intimus Hugenbergs*. Bonn: Universität 2006

-Thyssen, F., *Ik financierde Hitler*. Amsterdam: Novel, book and art dealer H.Nelissen 1957

-Toland, J., *Adolf Hitler. Het einde van een mythe*. Utrecht: A.W.Bruna & Son 1983

-Tolstoy, N., *Stalin's Secret War*. London: Pan books 1981

-Trebitsch-Lincoln, J. T., *De grootste avonturier der twintigste eeuw. Mijn leven naar waarheid geschetst*. Zutphen: W.J.Thieme 1932

-Tschuppik, K., *Ludendorff. Die Tragödie des Fachmanns*. Wien-Leipzig: Verlag Hans Epstein 1931

-Tuchman, B. W., *The Guns of August. August 1914*. London: Hurst and Blackett [1962] 1965

-Turner jr., H. A., *Faschismus und Kapitalismus in Deutschland*. Göttingen: Vandenhoeck-Rupprecht 1972

-Uhle-Wettler, F., *Erich Ludendorff in seiner Zeit. Soldat, Stratege, Revolutionar. Eine Neubewertung*. Berg: Verlagsgesellschaft Berg [1995] 1996

-Ullrich, V., *Adolf Hitler. Die Jahre des Aufstiegs*. Frankfurt am Main: S. Fischer Verlag 2013

-Vaksberg, A., *Stalin against the Jews*. New York: Random House 1994

-Vascik, G.S./Sadler, M.R., *The Stab in the Back Myth and the Fall of the Weimar Republic*. Bloomsbury: London [1988] 2016

-Venner, D., *Ein deutscher Heldenkampf. Die Geschichte der Freikorps 1918-1923. Söldner ohne Sold*. Kiel: Arndt verlag 1989.

-Venohr, W., *Ludendorff. Legende und Wirklichkeit*. Frankfurt am main: Ullstein 1993

-Venzmer. G., *Körpergestalt und Seelenanlage. Ein Überblick über die biologische Verwandschaft zwischen Körperform und Wesenskern des Menschen.* Stuttgart: Kosmos, Gesellschaft der Naturfreunde Franckh'sche Verlagshandlung 1930

-Vermaat, E., *Heinrich Himmler en de cultus van dood.* Soesterberg: Aspekt 2010

-Verstraete, P. J., *Houston Stewart Chamberlain rassenideoloog en wegbreider van het nationaal-socialisme.* Soesterberg: Aspekt 2016

-Vogel, R., *Ein Stück von uns. 1813-1976, Deutsche Juden in deutschen Armeen.* Mainz: Von Hase & Koehler Verlag 1977

-Volkmann, E. O., *Revolution über Deutschland.* Oldenburg: Gerhard Stalling 1930

-Vorrink, K., *Walther Rathenau.* Amsterdam: Workers' Press 1936

-Wagner, H., *Taschenwörterbuch des Nationalsozialismus A bis Z.* Leipzig: Quelle & Meyer 1934

-Waite, R. G. L., *Vanquard of Nazism. The Free Corps Movement in Postwar Germany 1918-1933.* New York: The Northon Library 1952

-Waldow, H. G. von., *Ludendorffs Kampf gegen die Knechtung des deutschen Volkes durch Priesterherrschaft.* Munich: Ludendorffs Volkswarte Verlag 1931

-Walser Smith, H. (ed.), *Protestants, Catholics and Jews in Germany 1800-1914.* Oxford, New York: Berg 2001

-Watson, A., *Ring of Steel. Germany and Austria-Hungary at War 1914-1918.* London: Bloomsbury 2014

-Weber, T., *Wie Adolf Hitler zum Nazi wurde. Vom unpolitischen Soldaten zum Autor von 'MeinKkampf'.* Propyläen: Berlin 2016

-Wegener, F., *Der Alchemist Franz Tausend. Alchemie und Nationalsozialismus.* Gladbach: KFVR 2006

-Wegner, B., *Hitlers politische Soldaten: Die Waffen-SS 1933-1945,. Leitbild, Struktur und Funktion einer nationalsozialistischen Elite.* Paderborn-Munich-Wien: Ferdinand Schöningh 1997

-Wehler, H-U., *Politik in der Geschichte. Essays.* Göttingen-München: Vandenhoeck & Ruprecht 1998

-Weichelt, H., *"4500", Eine geschichtswissenschaftliche Untersuchung über die Ereignisse zu Verden an der Aller im Jahre 782. In Schriftenreihe, laufender Schriftenbezug 12, 2.Heft.* Munich: Ludendorff Verlag 1940

-Weissbecker, M., *Macht und Ohnmacht der Weimarer Republik.* Berlin: Haufe 1990

-Wendt, W., *Die irreführende Denkart der Abergläubigen und ihre falsche Instuition. 3.Heft der 1.Schriftenreihe.* Ludendorffs Verlag : Munich 1934

-Wenninger, *Generalleutnant Ritter Von, Die Schlacht von Tannenberg. 1.2.u.3.Heft der 2.Schriftenreihe.* Munich: Ludendorffs Verlag 1935

-Wentzel, I., *Das geistige Ringen zwischen Christentum und Deutscher Gotterkenntnis.* Munich: Ludendorffs Verlag 1936.

-Wentzel, I., *Die Frau, Die Sklavin, der Priester.* Munich: Ludendorffs Verlag 1939

- West, F., *In the Fires of the Front. The Waffen-SS, construction, struggle and downfall,* Soesterberg: Aspekt 2016

-Wette, W., *Die Wehrmacht. Feindbilder, Vernichtungskrieg, Legenden.* Frankfurt am Main: Fischer Taschenbuch Verlag 2005

-Wheeler-Bennet, J. W., *The Nemesis of Power. The German Army in Politics 1918-1945.* London: Macmillan & Co Ltd 1954

-Wheeler-Bennet, J. W., *Brest-Litovsk. The Forgotten Peace. March 1918.* London: Collins 1966

-Wheeler-Bennett, J. W., *Der Hölzerne Titan, Paul von Hindenburg.* Tübingen: Wunderlich 1969

-Werth, R. van., *Tannenberg. Wie Hindenburg die Russen schlug.* Berlin: Ullstein 1934

-Wichtl, Fr., *Weltfreimaurerei, Weltrevolution Weltrepublik. Eine Untersuchung über Ursprung und Endziele des Weltkrieges.* Munich: J.F.Lehmanns Verlag 1923

-Wien, B., *Weichensteller und Totengräber. Ludendorff, Von Hindenburg und Hitler 1914-1937.* Norderstedt: BoD 2014

-Wighton, C., *Adenauer. Democratic Dictator. A critical biography.* Amsterdam: H.J.W.Becht 1964

-Wildt, M. (Hg.), *Nachrichtendienst, politische Elite und Mordeinheit. Der Sicherheitsdienst des Reichsführer SS.* Hamburg: Hamburgeredition 2003

-Wistrich, R., *Wer war wer im Dritten Reich? Ein biographisches Lexikon. Anhänger, Mitläufer, Gegner aus Politik, Wirtschaft und Militär, Kunst und Wissenschaft.* Frankfurt am Main: Fischer Taschenbuch Verlag 1987

-Witt, P-C., *Friedrich Ebert.* Bonn: Dietz 1992

-Woltersdorf, H. W., *Die Ideologie der neuen Weltordnung. Rakowski und die Protokolle der Weisen von Zion.* Remagen: Selbstverlag 1992

-Zarnow, G., (pseudonym Karl Ewald Moritz), *Gefesselte Justiz. Politische Bilder aus deutscher Gegenwart. Recht und Willkur im politischen Parteistaat*. Munich: J.F.Lehmanns Verlag 1930

-Zdral, W., *Der finanzierte Aufstieg des Adolf*. Wien: H. Ueberreuter 2002

-Zeman, Z. A. B.(ed.), *Germany and the Revolution in Russia 1915-1918. Documents from the Archives of the German Foreign Ministry*. London-Oxford: Oxford University Press 1958

Articles:

-Alchemist makes gold for police. Still skeptical that there is no fraud. In: *The Decatur Review* (10.10.1929)

-Alchemist makes gold out of lead; scientist stunned. In: *The Capital Times, Official Paper of the State of Wisconsion* (10.10.1929)

-Algemeen Overzicht De Oorlog. In: *The Centre* (28.10.1918)

-Amt für kulturellen Frieden. In: *Am Heiligen Quell Deutscher Kraft, Folge 6* (1934)

-Andriessen, H., De ineenstorting van het Duitse Keizerrijk in 1918. In: Andriessen, H., Ros, M., & Pierik, P. (Ed.), *De Grote Oorlog, Kroniek 1914-1918 Essays over de Eerste Wereldoorlog. Deel 1*. Soesterberg: Aspekt Publishers (2002)

-Ashton, N. J., & Hellema, D., Hanging the Kaiser: Anglo-Dutch Relations and the Fate of Wilhelm II 1918-20. In: *Diplomacy & Statecraft, Vol 11 (2)* (July 2000)

-Augstein,R., Sünder ohne Reue. In: *Der Spiegel 13* (1998)

-Aus unserem Kampf. Hetze gegen die Tannenbergbund. In: *Ludendorffs Volkswarte* (19.02.1933)

-Aus unserem Kampf. In: *Ludendorffs Volkswarte* (05.03.1933)

-Aufklärung der Regierung über den Tannenbergbund. In: *Ludendorffs Volkswarte* (19.03.1933)

-Bardey, G., Die Brigade Ehrhardt. Vom Kampf der 2.Marine-Brigade 'Wilhelmshaven' 1919-1921, Teil I und Teil II. In: *Deutsches Soldatenjahrbuch (DSJB)*. Munich: Schild-Verlag (1988)

-Bolwijn, M., Rol van Pius XII tijdens de oorlog blijft onhelder. In: *De Volkskrant* (10 August 1991)

-Brinkmann, H. H., Das Bildnis Ludendorffs. In: Hanno von Kemnitz, *Tannenbergjahrbuch 1939*. Munich: Ludendorffs Verlag (1939)

-Buat, E. A. L., Ludendorff Would Spur Germany to New War, French General Asserts. In: *Oakland Tribune, Sunday Morning* (21.03.1920)

-Buitenhuis, J. H., Artillerie en gas. De artillerie-inzet tijdens de gevechten tussen april en december 1916 en de grote gasaanval van de Duisers op fort Souville in juni 1916. In: Andriessen, H., Ros, M., & Pierik, P. (Ed.), *De Grote Oorlog, Kroniek 1914-1918 Essays over de Eerste Wereldoorlog. Deel 1.* Soesterberg: Aspekt Publishers (2002)

-Bronner, M., Ex-Wife of War Lord stirs with new book. In: *The Charleston Daily* (7 July 1929)

-Cammer, W. von der, Die kommunistischen Agitation im Christentum. In: *Am Heiligen Quell Deutscher Kraft, Folge 14* (20.10.1934)

-Craig, G. A., Founding Father. In: *New York Review of Books* (01.11.2001)

-Crijnen, T., Confusion about status Vatican confession. In: *Trouw* (27.05.1994)

-De Franse pers over het aftreden van Ludendorff. In: *NRC* (29.10.1918)

-De oorlog. In: *NRC* (01.11.1918)

-De oorlog, Ludendorff neemt ontslag. In: *Het Volk* (28.10.1918)

-Die deutschen in Frankreich (1871-1873) nach deutschen u.franz.Urkunden.die Franzosen in Deutschland (1918-?) nach englischen Augenzeugen. In: *Süddeutsche Monatshefte* (April 1922)

-Die geheime Weltregierung wirkt in alle Parteien. In: *Ludendorffs Volkswarte* (24.08.1930)

-Die Geheimnisvollen Protokolle der Weisen von Zion im Faschistenstaate. In: *Ludendorffs Volkswarte* (23.02.1930)

-Die mathematische Erbmasse Hindenburgs. In: *Ludendorffs Volkswarte* (08.01.1933)

-Die Stellung der Frau in Heidentum und Christentum (Beleuchtet an dem Schicksal der Hexen). In: *Am Heiligen Quell Deutscher Kraft, Folge 6* (1934)

-Dunk, H. W. von der, Walther Rathenau 1867-1922. Leven tussen aanpassing en kritiek. In: *Tijdschrift voor Geschiedenis* (3) (1967)

-Dunk, H. W. von der, Lapid: mislukte poging Pius XII te rehabiliteren. In: *Nieuw Rotterdamse Courant* (11.03.1967)

-Erb,R., Der 'Ritualmord'. In: Schoeps, J. H., & Schlor, J., *Antisemitismus. Vorurteile und Mythen.* Munich-Zurich: Piper (1995)

-Erkelens, H. van, Het geheim van Die Zauberflote. In: *HN* (12.06.1999)

-Fischer, F., Theobald von Bethmann Hollweg. Der Rätselhafte Kanzler. In: *Fritz Fischer, Hitler war kein Betriebsunfall.* Munich (1992). Previously published in: Sternburg, W. von (Hrsg.), *Die deutschen Kanzler von Bismarck bis Schmidt.* Königstein im Taunus: Athenäum Verlag (1985)

-Freimaurer Schacht will 'mobilisieren'. In: *Ludendorffs Volkswarte* (12.02.1933)

-Gruendler, G. E., Deutsche Admirale putschen nicht? In: *Stern* (12.1970)

-Gedanken zur heutigen Deutschen Landwirtschaft. In: *Ludendorffs Volkswarte* (22.01.1933)

-German tinker real ponzi. In: *The Lethbridge Herald* (21.03.1929)

-Gold produced from lead. In test: Germans not so sure they were not hoodwinked by alchemist. In: *The San Antonio Light* (10.10.1929)

-Greil., L., In memoriam Freikorpsführer Gerhard Rossbach. In: Damerau, H. (Hg.), *Deutsches Soldatenjahrbuch (DSJB) 1968 - 16. deutscher Soldatenkalender*. Munich: Schild-Verlag (1968)

-Gruchmann, L., Ludendorff's 'prophetischer' Brief an Hindenburg vom Januar/Februar 1933. Eine Legende. In: *Vierteljahrshefte für Zeitgeschichte 47* (1999)

-Hagemeister, M., Sergei Nilus und die Protokolle der Weisen von Zion. In: Benz, W. (Hg.), *Jahrbuch für Antisemitismusforschung 5*. Frankfurt-New York: Campus Verlag (1992)

-Hagen-Konigshorst, H., Orgien am papstlichen Hof! In: *Am Heiligen Quell Deutscher Kraft Folge 9* (05.08.1937)

-Haushofer, K., Fromme Wünsche, Die slawische Idee der Absperrung des Deutschtums vom Osten. In: *Zeitschrift für Geopolitik Heft 6* (1933)

-Heering, A., Huidige Paus is de aangewezen man voor schulderkenning. In:*De Gelderlander* (27.05.1994)

-Heering, A., & Bouwmans, J., Vatican: Document over antisemitisme 'niet goedgekeurd'. In: *De Gelderlander* (27.05.1994)

-Herr Seldtes Selbstkennzeichung. In: *Ludendorffs Volkswarte* (22.2.1931)

-Het militarisme verslagen. In: *Het Volk* (07.11.1918)

-Hofman, J., De oorlog aan het thuis front. In: Andriessen, H., Ros, M., & Pierik, P. (Ed.), *De Grote Oorlog, 1914-1918 Essays over de Eerste Wereldoorlog. Deel 1*. Soesterberg: Aspekt Publishers (2002)

-Holscher, K. H., *Ein Gott-nahes Volk*. In: Raab, L. (Hg.), *Tannenberg-Jahrweiser*. Munich: Ludendorffs Verlag (1935)

-Hoyer, R., Frau Dr. Mathilde Ludendorff als Rednerin. In: *Am Heiligen Quell Deutscher Kraft Folge 13*.

-Huwe, L., Schon-Isa vom Stedingerland. In: Raab, L. (Hg.), *Tannenberg-Jahrweiser*. Munich: Ludendorffs Verlag (1935)

-Jansen, K., Raadsel rond Mozart toch niet opgelost. In: *NRC* (09.01.2006)

-Janssen, K-H., Tannenberg -ein deutsches Verhängnis. In: *Die Zeit* (39) (16.09.1977)

-Jarres hat das Wort. In: *Stralsunder Tageblatt, Jahrgang 24* (24.03.1925)

-Jesus Germanicus? In: *Ludendorffs Volkswarte* (15.01.1933)

-Jude und Jesuit bei der Arbeit. In: *Ludendorffs Volkswarte* (23.02.1930)

-Kimmerling, B., Die neuen Israelis: Vielfältige Kulturen ohne Multikulturalismus? In: *Babylon. Beiträge zur jüdischen Gegenwart, Heft 20*. Frankfurt am Main: Verlag Neue Kritik (2002)

-Klijn, E., Voor Paus stond lijfsbehoud voorop. In: *De Volkskrant* (29-11-1997)

-Koennemann, E., Kapps Vorbereitungen auf einem Prozess, der nie stantfand. Dokumente aus seinem Nachlass. In: *Zeitschrift für Geschichtswissenschaft Heft 7* (1995)

-Köhler, H., Beziehungen des französischen Geheimdienstes zu deutschen Linksradikalen 1917-1918. In: *Veröffentlichungen der historischen Kommission zu Berlin band 37*. Kurze, D. (Hg.)., *Aus theorie und Praxis der Geschichtswissenschsaft. Festschrift für Hans Herzfeld zum 80. Geburtstag*. Berlin-New York: De Gruyter (1982)

-'Ländliche Kollektivwirtschaft in Deutschland'. In: *Ludendorffs Volkswarte* (05.03.1933)

-Leria, M. M., Buddhas Wanderung von Ost nach West. In: *Börsenblatt für den Deutschen Buchhandel* (08.03.1996)

-Lohalm,U./Ulmer,M., Alfred Roth und der Deutschvölkische Schutz- und Trutz-Bund. Schrittmacher' für das Dritte Reich. In: Daniel Schmidt/Michael Sturm/Livi Massimiliano (hg.).,*Schriftenreihe des Instituts für Stadtgeschichte. Beiträge bd. 19, Wegbereiter des Nationalsozialismus. Personen, Organisationen und Netzwerken der extremen Rechten zwischen 1918 und 1933*. Essen: Klartext (2015)

-Ludendorff, E., Heraus aus der Weltkrise. In: *Ludendorffs Volkswarte* (04.01.1931)

-Ludendorff, E., Was wollen die Nationalsozialisten? In: *Ludendorffs Volkswarte* (22.02.1931)

-Ludendorff, E., Zum Jahreswechsel. In: *Ludendorffs Volkswarte* (10.01.1932)

-Ludendorff, E., Schluss mit Wirtschaftskrise. In: *Ludendorffs Volkswarte* (08.01.1933)

-Ludendorff, E., Es geht aufwärts. In: *Ludendorffs Volkswarte* (15.01.1933)

-Ludendorff, E., Bauerschaft im Verderben. In: *Ludendorffs Volkswarte* (05.02.1933)

-Ludendorff, E., Die SA wartet und erwartet. In: *Ludendorffs Volkswarte* (12.2.1933)

-Ludendorff, E., Aus unserem Kampf. Terrorakte gegen unsere Buchhandlungen. 'Der Kampf gilt dem Marxismus'. In: *Ludendorffs Volkswarte* (19.03.1933)

-Ludendorff, E., Abrüstung und Sicherheit. In: *Am Heiligen Quell Deutscher Kraft, Folge 6* (1934)

-Ludendorff,E., Die Stimme des Bluts. In: *Am Heiligen Quell Deutscher Kraft, Folge 24* (20.03.1937)

-Ludendorff, E., Mysterien -und sonstige Politik. (The hand of the überstaatlichen Mächte). In: *Am Heiligen Quell Deutscher kraft, Folge 24* (20.03.1937)

-Ludendorff, E., Das enthullte Papsttum. In: *Am Heiligen Quell Deutscher kraft, Folge 6* (20.06.1937)

-Ludendorff, E., Der römische Pabst, Deutschlands Feind im Weltkriege. Eine Erinnerung an 1917. In: *Am Heiligen Quell Deutscher kraft, Folge 7* (05.07.1937)

-Ludendorff, E., Statt okkulter Priesterherrschaft-Gotterkenntnis. Mathilde Ludendorff im Werk und Wirken. In: *Am Heiligen Quell Deutscher Kraft, Folge 13* (05.10.1937)

-Ludendorff-von Kemnitz, M., Das Schreckgespenst in Halle. In: *Ludendorffs Volkswarte* (04.01.1931)

-Ludendorff-von Kemnitz, M., Rom im starken Vormarsch. In: *Am Heiligen Quell Deutscher kraft, Folge 15* (05.11.1934)

-Ludendorff-von Kemnitz, M., Fehlbare Worte des unfehlbaren Papstes. In: *Am Heiligen Quell Deutscher kraft, Folge 2* (20.04.1937)

-Ludendorffs Volkswarte verboten. In: *Ludendorffs Volkswarte 20 December 1933: Polizeidirektion München nr VIc925/31* (1933)

-Meeteren, R. van., De slag om Luik, 4-16 augustus 1914. In: Dorrestijn, L., Linden, H van der, Pierik, P., & Vogel, R-J de. (Ed.), *De Grote Oorlog. Kroniek 1914-1918. Essays over de Eerste Wereldoorlog. Deel 32.* Soesterberg: Aspekt Publishers (2016)

-Muck, O., Der Sinn von fünftausend Jahren Kampf im Osten. In: *Zeitschrift für Geopolitik XIX, Jahrgang 1942, Heft 10* (10-1942)

-Niedermayer, O. von, Wachstum und Wanderung in russischen Volkskörper. In: *Zeitschrift für Geopolitik, Jahrgang 1933, Heft 6* (1933)

-Nolte, E., Revolution und Reaktion. Exempel einer verdrängten Dialektik. In: *Frankfurter Allgemeine Zeitung nr.293* (17.12.1977)

-Operation Fatal to General Staff Chief. In: *Bridgeport Telegram* (31.12.1923)

-Paul., Kurze Darstellung der sowjetrussischen Kämpfe auf der Krim und um Sewastopol vom Oktober bis Juli 1942. In: *Militär-wissenschaftlicher Rundschau, Heft 2.*

-Peters, S., Het Vaticaan en de Holocaust. In: *Historisch Nieuwsblad.* (05.1988)

-Pfeifer, H., Verunglimpfungen des feldgrauen Ehrenkleides. In: *Ludendorffs Volkswarte* (03.08.1930)

-Pierik, P., Een joodse dubbeldekker met swastika. In: Andriessen, H., Ros, M., & Pierik, P., *De Grote Oorlog. Kroniek 1914-1918. Essays over de Eerste Wereldoorlog. Deel 3.* Soesterberg: Aspekt Publishers (2003)

-Pierik, P., Landverraders en steunpilaren in blauw. In: Andriessen, H., & Pierik, P. (Ed.), *De Grote Oorlog. Kroniek 1914-1918. Essays over de Eerste Wereldoorlog. Deel 15.* Soesterberg: Aspekt Publishers 2007

-Pierik, P., Frans J. Los, In de ban van de 'nordische' geschiedschrijving. Karel de Grote in de ogen van sociaal-nationalisme. In: Pierik., & Ros, M. (Ed.), *Vierde Bulletin van de Tweede Wereldoorlog.* Soesterberg: Aspekt Publishers (2002)

-Politik und Wirtschaft im Kabinett Hitler-Von Papen-Hugenberg. In: *Ludendorffs Volkswarte* (19.02.1933)

-Reichel, P., Freiheit verspielt und verraten. Die Weimarer Republik zwischen Revolution und Gegenrevolution. In: *Die Zeit, No 42* (13.10.1989)

-Repgen, K., Das Reichskonkordat bot einen gewissen Schutz. Mehr Dokumentation als Darstellung: Gerhard Besier über die kirchen in den Jahren 1934 bis 1937. In: *Frankfurter Allgemeine Zeitung 11* (35). (02-2002)

-Rintelen, K. L., Arbeiterführer und Reichsleitung vor und bei Inszenierung des Ersten Weltkrieges. In: *Beitrage zur Geschichte der Arbeiterbewegung, nr.6* (1999)

-Rubin, B., Die Realitäten der deutschen und judischen Geschichte: Im Spiegel des Streites um die Umdichtung der Lutherbibel. In: *Kirche* (01.09.1978)

-Schaik, T. H. M. van., De moed tot broedershap. In: *Roodkoper* (04-1998)

-Schendel, G., On Claus August Elfers. In: *Biographisch-Bibliographisches Kirchenlexikon Band XXX.* Nordhausen: Traugott Bautz (2010)

-Schneider, R., Der zehnjariger Kampf des Feldherrn gegen den Freimaurerbund. In: *Am Heiligen Quell Deutscher Kraft, Folge 9* (05.08.1937)

-Schotanus, G., Als Christenen zijn wij schuldig aan de Holocaust. In: *Christians for Israel.* (06.2001)

-Schütz, H. J., Hoffen nach Auschwitz. In: *Börsenblatt für den Deutschen Buchhandel, No.20* (08.03.1996)

-Segal, E., The Treacherous Mr. Trebisch. In: *The Sources* (2004)

-Sievers, L., Der Mann, der den Krieg verhindern wollte. Series: Juden in Deutschland (15). In: *Stern (1976)*

-Sikorski, E., Der Feldherr als Organisator. In: *Das Vermächtnis des Feldherrn Erich Ludendorff.* Munich: Ludendorffs Verlag (1937)

-Spilker, A., Rechtsextremes Engagement und völkisch-antisemitische Politikvorstellungen um Mathilde Ludendorff (1877-1966) und die Frauengruppen im Tannenbergerbund. In: *Schriftenreihe des Instituts für Stadtgeschichte. Beiträge bd. 19, Wegbereiter des Nationalsozialismus. Personen, Organisationen und Netzwerken der extremen Rechten zwischen 1918 und 1933*. Essen: Klartext (2015)

-Spoor, A., 'Rode Graaf' Harry Kessler opnieuw in de belangstelling. In: *Leidsch Dagblad* (14-06-1962)

-Stadtteilkollektiv Rotes Winterhude (Hg.), Der Hamburger Aufstand 1923. Verlauf-Mythos-Lehren. In: *Rote Winterhuder Texte 5*. Hamburg : Verein zur Förderung Antifaschistischer Kultur und Kommunikation (2003)

-Strunk, J., Was will Stalin? In: *Am Heiligen Quell Deutscher Kraft, Folge 8* (20.07.1937)

-Stürmer, M., Ein Nationalstaat gegen Geschichte und Geographie: Das Deutsche Dilemma. In: Schöllgen, G. (Hg.), *Flucht in den Krieg? Die Aussenpolitik des kaiserlichen Deutschland*. Darmstadt: Wissenschaftliche Buchgesellschaft (1991)

-Tannenberg-Buchhandlung eine Gefahr für Ordnung und Sicherheit. In: *Ludendorffs Volkswarte* (26.03.1933)

-Test of mint fail break claim of lead made gold. In: *The Vidette Messenger*. Valparasio, Indiana (10.10.1929)

-Tobias, F., Ludendorff, Hindenburg und Hitler. Das Phantasieprodukt des Ludendorffs-Briefes. In: Backes, U., Jesse, E., & Zitelmann, R. (Hg.), *Die Schatten der Vergangenheit. Impulse zur Historisierung des Nationalsozialismus*. Frankfurt am Main-Berlin: Propyläen Verlag (1990)

-Toorenvliet, H., Reichswehr en het Rode Leger tussen de wereldoorlogen. In: *Spiegel Historiael, 9ᵈᵉ jaargang, nr.2*. (02-1974)

-Treue, W., Figuren der Zeitgeschichte. In: *Deutsches Allgemeines Sonntagblatt no.42* (20.10.1968)

-Tucholsky, K., Das Opfer einer Republik. In: *Glossen und Essays. Gesammelte Schriften 1907-1935*. Reinbek: Rowohlt Verlag (1960)

-Tucholsky, K., Cadett Ludendorff. In: *Glossen und Essays. Gesammelte Schriften 1907-1935*. Reinbek: Rowohlt Verlag (1960)

-Tucholsky, K., Die Karikatur Preussens. In: Tucholsky, K., *Gesammelte Werke Band 7 1929*. Reinbek: Rowohlt Verlag (1969)

-U moet weten. In: *Trouw, jaargang 1, nr.8* (20.06.1943)

-Vaticaan boos op onderzoekers. In: de *Volkskrant* (08.08.2001)

-Vaticaan plande actie tegen Hitler. In: *Katholiek Nieuwsblad* (05.08.2005)

-Visionaries still dreams of making gold, experimenter stays in jail. In: *The Salt Lake Tribune* (17.11.1929)

-Vollnhals, C., 'Endlösung der religiösen Frage. Die grosse Abrechnung sollte nach dem Krieg erfolgen: Religionspolitik des Sicherheitsdienstes der SS. In: *Frankfurter Allgemeine Zeitung no. 35* (11.02.2002)

-Wagner, A., Anthroposophen in der Zeit des nationalsozialismus (Teil III). In: *Flensburger Hefte, Anthroposophie im Gespräch. Anthroposophen in der Zeit des deutschen Faschismus-Zur Verschwörungsthese, Sonderheft Nr. 8*. Flensburg: Flensburgerhefte Verlag (1991)

-Wasserstein, B., On the Trail of Trebitsch-Lincoln. In: *New York Times* (04.2006)

-Westenfelder, F., Trebitsch-Lincoln. In: *'Der grösste Abenteurer des XX.Jahrhunderts'*. Leipzig: Amalthea(1931)

-Who's Who in Day's News: General Buat. In: *The Capital Times* (30.11.1921)

-Wiegand, K. H., Ludendorff is in open War with the Pope. In: *The Davenport Democrat and Leader* (20.09.1923)

-Wilhelm, H-H., Die 'nationalkonservativen Eliten' und das Schreckgespenst vom Jüdischen Bolschewismus. In: *Zeitschrift für Geschichtswissenschaft 43* (1995)

-Wise, S. F., The Black Day of the German Army. Australians and Canadians at Amiens, august 1918. In: *1918 Defining Victory*. Australia: Department of Defence, Army History Unit (1999)

-Ziegler, H. S., Wer war Hitler? In: *Beiträge zur Hitler-Forschung*. Tübingen: Verlag der Deutschen Hochschullehrer-Zeitung, Grabert Verlag (1970)

-Zimmermann, M., 'Die aussichtslose Republik' -Zukunftsperspektiven der deutschen Juden vor 1933. In: *Menora, Jahrbuch für deutsch-jüdische Geschichte*. Munich-Zurich: Piper Verlag (1990)

-Zürcher, E-J., Het Britse leger onderdrukte Irakese opstand met gifgas. In: *Historisch Nieuwsblad* (04.2003)

-Swiss, M. S., Mozart's Die Zauberflöte. Mysteriespel of sprookjesopera? In: *Luister* (05.2006)

Archive documents:

-Ausserhalb *der Tagesordnung: Feier in Ostpreussen 17 July 1924.* In: *Die Kabinette Marx I/II, Band 2: Dokumente nr 253 Ministerbesprechung von 17 Juli 1924.* Edition: *Akten der Reichskanzlei. Weimarer Republik.* Munich: Historische Kommission bei der Bayerischen Akademie der Wissenschaften und Berlin: Bundesarchiv

-*Geeherter Herren!* Letter Ludendorff 03.02.1932 to the editorial board Ludendorff periodical. (1932) Private archive

-Goltz, Rüdiger Graf von der, *Lebenserinnerungen. Kleine Erwerbung 653.* Koblenz, Bundesarchiv

-Pierik, P., *Het geluid van vreemde laarzen. De Rheinland in roerige dagen tussen de nederlaag van 1918 en de vrede van Versailles.* Private archive Pierik

-*R43 I/ 2218, Bl 338-342: nr 256: Der Vertreter der Reichsregierung an die Reichskanzlei 14 November 1923.* In: *Die Kabinette Stresemann I/II, Band 2.* Edition: *Akten der Reichskanzlei. Weimar Republic.* Munich: Historische Kommission bei der Bayerischen Akademie der Wissenschaften und Berlin: Bundesarchiv

-R43 *I/ 2264, Bl 340-342: [1159] no 277: Der Vertreter der Reichsregierung in München an die Reichskanzlei (21.11.1923).* In: *Die Kabinette Stresemann I/II, Band 2.* Edition: *Akten der Reichskanzlei. Weimar Republic.* Munich: Historische Kommission bei der Bayerischen Akademie der Wissenschaften und Berlin: Bundesarchiv

-*R43 I/ 2264, Bl 358-363: Nr. 60: Der Chef des Truppenamts an Staatssekretär Bracht.* Munich (14.01.1924). In: *Die Kabinette Marx I/II, Band 1.* Edition: *Akten der Reichskanzlei. Weimarer Republik.* Munich: Historische Kommission bei der Bayerischen Akademie der Wissenschaften und Berlin: Bundesarchiv

Digital resources:

-Bailer, von., Denkschrift über Ergebnisse der Beschiessung der Festungen Lüttich, Namur, Antwerpen und Maubeuge, sowie des Forts Manonviller im Jahre 1914. Brussels: Buchdruckerei des General-Gouvernements in Belgien (1915). Accessed at: http://www.germandocsinrussia.org/de/nodes/1-russisch-deutsches-projekt-zur-digitalisierung-deutscher-dokumente-in-den-archiven-der-russischen-foderation

-Biographie Friedrich Minoux 1877-1945. Accessed from: https://www.dhm.de/lemo/biografie/biografie-friedrich-minoux.html

-Die Rubonia in Munich 1918-1923. Accessed at: https://www.nadir.org/nadir/periodika/anarcho_randalia/br_7/rubonia_1918.htm

-Ganelin, R. SH. Accessed from: http://recepter.livejournal.com/

-Gruendler, G.E., Deutsche Admirale putschen nicht? Consulted via: website Gerhard E.Gruendler, previously published in: *Stern* 12/1970

-Huerter, J., Sehepunkte, Bernard Sauer, Schwarze Reichswehr und Feme morde. Accessed from: http://www.sehepunkte.de/2006/11/9365.html

-Leuschner,U., Walther Rathenau, Ein Dissident seiner Klasse, seiner Rasse und seines Geschlechts. Accessed from: http://www.udo-leuschner.de/liberalismus/liberalismus4.htm

-Loennecker, H., '...Boden für die Idee Adolf Hitlers auf kulturellem Felde gewinnen'. Der 'Kampfbund für deutsche Kultur' und die deutsche Akademikerschaft. Frankfurt am Main (2003) Consulted via: http://www.burschenschaftsgeschichte.de/pdf/loennecker_kampfbund.pdf

-Michael, R., Weimar unter Druck. In: Y.on Line, Magazin der Bundeswehr vol. 3. Consulted via : www.rhein-main.net

-Mreijen, A-M., Opportunisme or ideologie? Over de rol van de uitgeverswereld in Müchen bij de opkomst van het nationaal-socialisme. *Ongepubliceerde doctoraalscriptie politieke geschiedenis van de Universiteit Utrecht onder begeleiding van Dr. Mr. F. W. Lantink.* (20.01.2006) Accessed from: http://dspace.library.uu.nl/bitstream/handle/1874/8437/Scriptieversie20-1-06.doc?sequence=1 .pdf
-Schapke, R., Hakenkreuz am Stahlhelm. Kapitän Ehrhardt und seine Brigade. Accessed from: www.die-kommenden.net/dk/zeitgeschichte/erhardt.html)

-Schendel, G., On Claus August Elfers. In: *Biographisch-Bibliographisches Kirchenlexikon Band XXX, Gunther Schendel.* Consulted at: http://www.kirchenlexikon.de/

-Sluszkiewicz, A., An Index of German-Polish and Polish-German names of the localities in Poland and Russia. Consulted via: http://www.atsnotes.com/other/gerpol.html

-Stegemann, T., Vorbereitung auf den Nationalsozialismus, Die Schwarze Reichswehr als Mentalitätsgeschichte. Accessed at: http://www.heise.de/tp/artikel/20/20995/1.html

-Über Burschen in den Freikorps im Baltikum 1918-1920. Accessed at: https://www.nadir.org/nadir/periodika/anarcho_randalia/br_6/br6la5.htm